Y0-EIB-728

Other Kaplan Books for College-Bound Students

College Admissions and Financial Aid

Guide to the Best Colleges in the U.S.

High School 411

Kaplan/*Newsweek* College Catalog

Parent's Guide to College Admissions

Scholarships

What to Study: 101 Fields in a Flash

You Can Afford College

Yale Daily News Guide to Succeeding in College

Test Preparation

AP Biology

SAT

SAT II: Biology E\M

SAT II: Chemistry

SAT II: Mathematics

SAT II: Writing

SAT Math Workbook

SAT or ACT? Test Your Best

SAT Verbal Workbook

ACT*
2001

BY THE STAFF OF KAPLAN EDUCATIONAL CENTERS

Simon & Schuster

NEW YORK · LONDON · SINGAPORE · SYDNEY · TORONTO

*ACT is a registered trademark of ACT Inc., which neither sponsors nor endorses this product.

Kaplan Books
Published by Simon & Schuster
1230 Avenue of the Americas
New York, New York 10020

Contributing Editor: Trent Anderson
Project Editor: Donna Ratajczak
Cover Design: Cheung Tai
Interior Page Production: Joseph Budenholzer
Production Editor: Maude Spekes
Desktop Publishing Manager: Michael Shevlin
Managing Editor: Dave Chipps
Executive Editor: Del Franz

Special thanks to: Amparo Graf, Grace Begany, Kiernan McGuire, Michael Palmer, Sara Pearl, Jobim Rose, and David Stuart.

Manufactured in the United States of America
Published Simultaneously in Canada

July 2000

10 9 8 7 6 5 4 3 2

ISBN 0-684-87332-X
ISSN 1093-3387

Table of Contents

Preface vii

How to Use This Book ix

ACT Emergency Plan xi

A Special Note for International Students xiii

SECTION I: ACT Basics

1. Introduction to the ACT 3

2. The Four Subject Tests: A Preview 11

3. Taking Control: The Top Ten Strategies 25

SECTION II: Skill-Building Workouts

4. English Workout 1: When in Doubt, Take It Out 43

5. Math Workout 1: The End Justifies the Means 53

6. Reading Workout 1: Know Where You're Going 71

7. Science Workout 1: Look for Patterns 83

8. English Workout 2: Make It Make Sense 99

9. Math Workout 2: Shake It Up! 115

10. Reading Workout 2: Look It Up! 125

11. Science Workout 2: Always Know Your Direction 135

12. English Workout 3: Trust Your Ear—Make It All Match 147

13. Math Workout 3: Figuring It Out 159

14. Reading Workout 3: Arts and Sciences 173

15. Science Workout 3: Keep Your Viewpoints Straight 187

SECTION III: Ready, Set, Go

16. Strategic Summaries 201

17. Last-Minute Tips 213

SECTION IV: Practice Tests

Practice Test 1 219

Practice Test 1—Answers and Explanations 273

Practice Test 2 317

Compute Your Score 371

Practice Test 2—Answers and Explanations 375

SECTION V: Appendixes

A. English Review for the ACT 419

B. Math Glossary 429

C. 100 Key Math Concepts for the ACT 443

SECTION VI: CDROM User's Guide

Higher Score on the ACT 465

Foreword

The ACT is an opportunity, not a barrier. In fact, you should be grateful that you have to take it. Really. Because a strong ACT score is one credential that doesn't depend on things you can't control. It doesn't depend on how good or bad your high school is. It doesn't depend on how many academic luminaries you know, or how rich and famous your family is, or whether any of your teachers are gullible enough to swear in a letter of recommendation that you're the greatest scientific mind since Isaac Newton. No, your ACT score depends only on you.

Granted, the ACT is a tough exam. It's probably one of the toughest exams you'll ever take. But you should be grateful for that too. Really. If the ACT were easy, everyone would do well. A good score wouldn't mean much. But because it's such a bear of a test, the ACT can be your single best opportunity to show what you can do, to prove to colleges that you are the candidate of choice—for admission, for advanced placement, for scholarships.

It's important, though, that you take the test in the right spirit. Don't be timid in the face of the ACT. Don't let it bully you. You've got to take control of the test. Our mission in this book is to show you exactly how to do that.

It helps to think of the ACT challenge as a contest—not only between you and the test, but also between you and that other person trying to get your spot in college. The ACT, after all, is meant to provide a way for all college applicants to compete on an even playing field. How do you compete successfully in a fair academic fight? You train—harder and smarter than the next guy. First, you learn whatever knowledge and skills you need to know. But then, just as important, you learn how to show what you know, in ways that the test is designed to reward. You learn how to be a savvy test taker.

And that's where Kaplan comes in. We've been helping students prepare for college entrance exams for decades, and one thing we've learned is that great standardized test takers are made, not born. We believe that anybody, given the right kind of training, can earn a strong ACT score. Why? Because ACT test taking is a learnable art. True, the ACT is designed to measure a complex set of skills, knowledge, habits, and intellectual powers that add up to a good college prep background. But it can't help measuring something else at the same time—namely, how well you take the ACT. That's why you need more than the typical academic training you get in high school. You need focused, test-smart preparation, designed specifically for success on the ACT.

This book represents just that kind of preparation. By using it conscientiously, you'll learn everything you need to know to earn your "personal best" ACT score. You'll gain the familiarity with the test necessary for optimum performance, but you'll also develop the kind of test mastery that gives you confidence, self-assurance, and that certain special way of handling your No. 2 pencils.

At Kaplan, we've been helping students take control of the test-taking experience—and raising their scores—for over 60 years. Our founder, Stanley Kaplan himself, was the inventor of test prep in the United States. We know what it takes. So start putting aside some choice study time in your schedule, and let us help you boost your score.

How to Use This Book

Ideally, you should take a couple of months to work through this book and CD ROM package, though it's certainly possible to work through in far less time. Here's how to go about training with it, assuming you have at least a month. If you have less than a month to prepare, read the Emergency Plan section that follows this one.

1. Read the user's guide at the back of the book to learn to use the *Higher Score on the ACT* CD-ROM for your training.

2. Read the section of this book entitled **ACT Basics** to get a handle on the test, its format, and the basic Kaplan strategies for approaching the test.

3. Go on to the **Skill-Building Workouts**. These will prepare you in a more focused way for each type of ACT question, and teach you all sorts of test-taking strategies and techniques. If you find that you're weak in one of the knowledge-based areas (if, for instance, your geometry principles are a little rusty) refer to the **Appendixes** at the back of the book.

4. When you've finished the Workouts, review what you've learned by going over the **Strategic Summaries**.

5. Take **Practice Test 1** *under strictly timed conditions*.

6. Go over the **Explanations for Practice Test 1**. Find out where you need help and then review the appropriate Workouts.

7. Take **Practice Test 2** under testlike conditions.

8. Go over the **Explanations for Practice Test 2**.

9. Read the **Last-Minute Tips** and review the **Strategic Summaries** once more before taking your actual ACT.

10. Give yourself a day of rest right before the real exam.

If you have time, do just two or three Workouts a week, and let it sink in slowly. Don't hesitate to take some time off from the ACT when you need to. Nobody can take this stuff day in and day out for weeks at a time without a break.

This book contains two complete practice tests written by our staff of Kaplan ACT gurus to provide you with real testlike practice. We have included explanations for this test, so you can better understand your mistakes (and your successes) and use that information to shore up your weak points before test day.

For additional practice, you should consider ordering sample practice tests from ACT. They are called "Form 9652A" and "Form 9954D." If you want to use these real past exams for additional practice, obtain these tests as quickly as possible. One of the tests is included in the ACT registration materials. To order any official ACT materials, including copies of the booklets called *Registering for the ACT Assessment* and *Preparing for the ACT Assessment*, you should write or call: ACT Registration Department, P.O. Box 414, Iowa City, IA 52243-0414; (319) 337-1270. This is also the place to register for the ACT if you can't do it through your high school. (You can also register or order material online at www.act.org.)

ACT Emergency Plan

Maybe you have only two or three weeks. Or even less. Don't freak! This book has been designed to work for students in your situation, too. If you go through a Workout or two every day, you can finish this book in a couple of weeks. If you have very limited time to prepare for the ACT (less than two weeks), we suggest you do the following:

1. Take a slow, deep breath. Check out the **CD-ROM User's Guide** to find out how to use the *Higher Score on the ACT* software.

2. Read the section of this book entitled **ACT Basics.**

3. Skip to the **Strategic Summaries** and go over them thoroughly.

4. Take **Practice Tests 1** and **2** under timed conditions.

5. Review your results, with special attention to the questions you missed. Then read the **Last-Minute Tips.**

Give yourself the day before the test off.

If you have more time, read as many of the Workouts as you can, especially in areas you know will give you trouble. The English and Math subtests require specific knowledge of the rules of grammar and mathematics. If you have trouble with English or Math because you just don't know the material being tested, we suggest you use the Appendixes.

Scattered throughout the book you'll find sidebars which spotlight some very important test-prep information. Sidebars also highlight key points, fun facts, and real-world stories.

ACT EMERGENCY FAQS

Q: It's two days before the ACT and I'm clueless. What should I do?

A: First of all, don't panic. If you only have a day or two to prepare for the test, then you don't have time to prepare thoroughly. But that doesn't mean you should just give up. There's still a lot you can do to improve your potential score. First and foremost, you should become familiar with the test.

Read the section called **ACT Basics**. And if you don't do anything else, take one of the full-length **Practice Tests** at the back of this book under reasonably testlike conditions. When you finish the practice test, check your answers and look at the explanations to the questions you didn't get right.

Q: Math is my weak spot. What can I do to get better at math in a big hurry?

A: Review the **Math Glossary** and the **100 Key Math Concepts for the ACT.** Then do as many of the **Math Workouts** as you have time for. If you don't have time to do the Workouts, just read the sidebars in those chapters. They contain really helpful facts and tips.

Q: I'm great at Math, but terrible at English. How can I improve my English score right away?

A: Go straight to the **Appendix** and read through the **English Review.** Then do as many of the **English Workouts** as you have time for. If you don't have time to do the Workouts, just read the sidebars in those chapters. The strategies can help boost your score. Remember the words "when in doubt, leave it out." This strategy will get you far in a pinch.

Q: I'm not very good at Science in school. How can I improve my Science Reasoning score right now?

A: Fortunately, the Science Reasoning section of your ACT tests your ability to think critically and interpret data, and not your ability to memorize specific scientific facts and theories. Cutting through the jargon and not being intimidated by this section is the first, best step to a higher science reasoning score.

Q: I read very slowly. How can I boost my Reading score quickly?

A: Remember that ACT Reading is all about getting the gist of the passage, and not focusing on the details. Focus on the first third of the passage, paraphrase, and skim past any confusing details so you can get to the questions quickly. You don't get any points for reading the passage: All your points on the reading section will come from answering the questions. Get the gist of the passage, and skim the details, and you'll have extra time to handle the questions. For more ACT Reading tips, check out the **Reading Workouts.**

Q: The ACT is tomorrow. Should I stay up all night studying geometry formulas?

A: The best thing to do right now is to try to stay calm. Read the **Last-Minute Tips** chapter to find out the best way to survive the next couple of days. And get a good night's sleep.

Q: What's the most important thing I can do to get ready for the ACT?

A. Relax, stay calm, and know the basics of the test. Remember there is no penalty for wrong answers on the ACT. Take good guesses and manage your time so that you leave no questions unanswered. Focus on your strengths rather than your weaknesses, since that's where you'll earn the bulk of your points. Stay confident, and don't cram. The key to getting your best score possible is showing up on Test Day well rested, well fed, and confident.

Q. So it's a good idea to panic, right? RIGHT?

A. No! No matter how prepared you are for the ACT, stress will hurt your performance, and it's really no fun. Stay confident, and don't cram. So . . . breathe. Stay calm and remember, it's just a test.

A Special Note for
International Students

If you are an international student considering attending an American university, you are not alone. Approximately 500,000 international students pursued academic degrees at the undergraduate, graduate, or professional school level at U.S. universities during the 1998–1999 academic year, according to the Institute of International Education's Open Doors report. Almost 50 percent of these students were studying for a bachelor's or first university degree. This number of international students pursuing higher education in the United States is expected to continue to grow. Business, management, engineering, and the physical and life sciences are particularly popular majors for students coming to the United States from other countries.

If you are not a U.S. citizen and you are interested in attending college or university in the United States, here is what you'll need to get started.

- If English is not your first language, you'll probably need to take the TOEFL (Test of English as a Foreign Language) or provide some other evidence that you are proficient in English. Colleges and universities in the United States will differ on what they consider to be an acceptable TOEFL score. A minimum TOEFL score of 213 (550 on the paper-based TOEFL) or better is often required by more prestigious and competitive institutions. Because American undergraduate programs require all students to take a certain number of general education courses, all students—even math and computer science students—need to be able to communicate well in spoken and written English.

- You may also need to take the ACT or the SAT. Many undergraduate institutions in the United States require the ACT or SAT and the TOEFL of international students.

- There are over 2,700 accredited colleges and universities in the United States, so selecting the correct undergraduate school can be a confusing task for anyone. You will need to get help from a good advisor or at least a good college guide that gives you detailed information on the different schools available. Since admission to many undergraduate programs is quite competitive, you may want to select three or four colleges and complete applications for each school.

- You should begin the application process at least a year in advance. An increasing number of schools accept applications year round. In any case, find out the application deadlines and plan accordingly. Although September (the fall semester) is the traditional time to begin university study in the United States, you can begin your studies at many schools in January (the spring semester).

• In addition, you will need to obtain an I-20 Certificate of Eligibility from the school you plan to attend if you intend to apply for an F-1 Student Visa to study in the United States.

KAPLAN INTERNATIONAL PROGRAMS *

If you need more help with the complex process of university admissions, assistance preparing for the SAT, ACT, or TOEFL, or help building your English language skills in general, you may be interested in Kaplan's programs for international students.

Kaplan International Programs were designed to help students and professionals from outside the United States meet their educational and career goals. At locations throughout the United States, international students take advantage of Kaplan's programs to help them improve their academic and conversational English skills, raise their scores on the TOEFL, SAT, ACT, and other standardized exams, and gain admission to the schools of their choice. Our staff and instructors give international students the individualized attention they need to succeed. Here is a brief description of some of Kaplan's programs for international students:

General Intensive English

Kaplan's General Intensive English classes are designed to help you improve your skills in all areas of English and to increase your fluency in spoken and written English. Classes are available for beginning to advanced students, and the average class size is 12 students.

English for TOEFL and University Preparation

This course provides you with the skills you need to improve your TOEFL score and succeed in an American university or graduate program. It includes advanced reading, writing, listening, grammar and conversational English, plus university admissions counseling. You will also receive training for the TOEFL using Kaplan's exclusive computer-based practice materials.

ACT Test Preparation Course

The ACT is an important admission criterion for many American colleges and universities. A high score can help you stand out from other applicants. This course includes the skills you need to succeed on each section of the ACT, as well as access to Kaplan's exclusive practice materials.

Other Kaplan Programs

Since 1938, more than 3 million students have come to Kaplan to advance their studies, prepare for entry to American universities, and further their careers. In addition to the above programs, Kaplan offers courses to prepare for the SAT, GMAT, GRE, MCAT, DAT, USMLE, NCLEX, and other standardized exams at locations throughout the United States.

Applying to Kaplan International Programs

To get more information, or to apply for admission to any of Kaplan's programs for international students and professionals, contact us at:

Kaplan International Programs
888 Seventh Avenue, New York, NY 10106 USA
Telephone: (212) 492-5990
Fax: (212) 957-1654
E-mail: world@kaplan.com
Web: www.studyusa.kaplan.com

* Kaplan is authorized under federal law to enroll nonimmigrant alien students. Kaplan is authorized to issue Form IAP-66 needed for a J-1 (Exchange Visitor) visa. Kaplan is accredited by ACCET (Accrediting Council for Continuing Education and Training). Test names are registered trademarks of their respective owners.

ACT
Basics

Introduction to the ACT

Highlights

- Three keys to ACT success

- What the ACT is all about

- ACT FAQs

Before you plunge into studying for the ACT, let's take a step back and look at the big picture. What's the ACT all about? How can I prepare for it? How's it scored? This chapter will answer these questions and more.

THE BIG THREE

There are three basic commandments for achieving ACT success. Following any of these by itself will improve your score. Following all three together will make you nothing less than awesome.

1. Thou Shalt Learn the Test

The ACT is very predictable. You'd think the test makers would get bored after a while, but they don't. The same kinds of questions, testing the same skills and concepts, appear every time the ACT is given.

Because the test specifications rarely change, you should know in advance what to expect on every section. Just a little familiarity can make an enormous difference on the ACT. Here are a few ways in which learning the test will boost your score:

Emergency Plan

If you have two weeks or fewer to prep for the ACT, don't panic. The first thing you should do is become familiar with the test. This chapter is the place to start.

- **You'll learn the directions.** Why waste valuable time reading directions when you can have them down pat beforehand? You need every second during the test to answer questions and get points.

- **You'll learn the difficulty range of questions.** It's a fact that a typical ACT test taker gets only about half the questions right. Knowing this will stop you from panicking when you hit an impossible science passage or trigonometry question. Relax! You can skip many tough questions on the ACT and still get a great score! And once you know that the questions aren't arranged in order of difficulty, you'll know that just beyond that awful question will be one, two, or even three easy questions that you can score on with no sweat at all.

- **You'll learn how to get extra points by guessing.** Unlike some other standardized tests, the ACT has no wrong-answer penalty. Knowing that simple fact can boost your score significantly. If you can't answer a question, guess.

We'll help you get a better understanding of the ACT in the chapter following this one, entitled "The Four Subject Tests: A Preview."

2. Thou Shalt Learn the Strategies

The ACT isn't a normal exam. Most normal exams test your memory. The ACT isn't like that. The ACT tests problem-solving skills rather than memory, and it does so in a standardized-test format. That makes the test highly vulnerable to test-smart strategies and techniques.

Most students miss a lot of ACT questions for no good reason. They see a tough-looking question, say to themselves, "Uh-oh, I don't remember how to do that," and then they start to gnaw on their No. 2 pencils.

But many ACT questions can be answered without perfect knowledge of the material being tested. Often, all you need to do to succeed on the ACT is to think strategically and creatively. We call this kind of strategic, creative frame of mind "The ACT Mindset."

How do you put yourself into the ACT Mindset? You continually ask yourself questions like: "What does this mean? How can I put this into a form I can understand and use? How can I do this faster?" Once you develop some savvy test-taking skills, you'll find yourself capable of working out problems that at first reading might have scared you half to death! In fact, we'll show you how you can sometimes get right answers when you don't even understand the question or the passage it's attached to!

There are many, many specific strategies you can use to boost your score. For instance, here are just a couple of things you'll learn:

- **You'll learn the peculiarities of the ACT format.** The ACT is a multiple-choice test. The correct answer is always right there in front of you. We'll show you how to develop specific tactics for each question type to maximize the chances of selecting the correct answer. The wrong answers are often predictable. For example, in English the shortest answer is the correct answer with surprising frequency. Strange, but true. Knowing statistical information like this can give you an important edge.

KAPLAN

- **You'll learn a plan of attack for each subject test.** We'll show you some really useful ways of attacking each subject test. You'll learn how to do "question triage"—deciding which questions to do now and which to save for later. You'll learn a strategic method for each subject test designed to get you points quickly and systematically. You'll learn gridding techniques to avoid any answer-sheet disasters.

- **You'll learn "unofficial" ways of getting right answers fast.** On the ACT, nobody cares how you decide which choice to select. The only thing that matters is picking the right answer. That's different from the way it works on most high school tests, where you get credit for showing that you've done the questions the "right" way (that is, the way you were taught to do them by Mrs. Crabapple in high school). We'll show you how to find creative shortcuts to the correct answers—"unofficial" methods that will save you precious time and net you extra points.

The basic test-smart techniques and strategies for the whole test are covered in the chapter called "Taking Control: The Top Ten Strategies." General strategies for each subject test, plus specific hints, techniques, and strategies for individual question types, are found in the Skill-Building Workouts. These are then summarized in the Strategic Summaries.

3. Thou Shalt Learn the Material Tested

The ACT is designed to test skills and concepts learned in high school and needed for college. Familiarity with the test, coupled with smart test-taking strategies, will take you only so far. For your best score you need to sharpen up the skills and knowledge that the ACT rewards. Sometimes, in other words, you've just got to eat your spinach.

The good news is that most of the content of the ACT is pretty basic. You've probably already learned most of what the ACT expects you to know. But you may need help remembering. That's partly what this book is for—to remind you of the knowledge you already have and to build and refine the specific skills you've developed in high school. Here's just a few of the things we'll "remind" you of:

- **You'll learn how to read graphs and tables.** Many Science Reasoning questions rely on your ability to use data presented in the form of graphs and tables. Yes, you learned how to do that stuff in school. But let us remind you. (We'll teach you how to read graphs and tables in Science Reasoning Workout 1.)

- **You'll learn how to do trigonometry problems.** Do you remember exactly what a cotangent is? A cosine? We didn't think so. But there are four trig problems on every ACT. We'll remind you how to do them. (You can learn about trigonometry problems in the Math Appendix, items 96–100.)

- **You'll learn the difference between** *lie* **and** *lay.* Is it "I lay down on the couch" or "I lie down on the couch"? You may want to lie down yourself if you encounter such issues on the ACT. But don't fret. We'll remind you of the common grammar traps the test lays for you (or is it *lies* for you???). (For a discussion of this conundrum, see Classic Grammar Error #9 in English Workout 3.)

Specifics like those mentioned above comprise what we call the ACT "knowledge base." The components of this knowledge base are reviewed along the way throughout this book. The two appendices then summarize this information for the two sections of the ACT that explicitly test knowledge: English and Math.

In sum, then, follow these three commandments:

1. Thou shalt learn the test.
2. Thou shalt learn the strategies.
3. Thou shalt learn the material tested.

If you do, you'll find yourself just where you should be on test day: in full command of your ACT test-taking experience. Count on it.

WHAT IS THE ACT?

It was Attila the Hun who first coined this epigram: Knowing the enemy is the first step in conquering the enemy. Attila, of course, was talking about waging wars on the steppes of Central Asia, but his advice also works for taking standardized tests in central Illinois. In fact, that's probably why Attila got a Composite Score of 30 on the ACT.

Well, to be honest, we haven't fact-checked Attila the Hun's ACT score, but the point remains valid. To succeed on the ACT, you've got to know the ACT.

But is the ACT really your enemy? Only in a manner of speaking. The test is more like an adversary in a game of chess. If you know your adversary's entire repertoire of moves and clever stratagems, you're going to find it that much easier to beat him or her. Myths about the ACT are common. Even high school teachers and guidance counselors sometimes give out inaccurate information (we know you're shocked to hear this). To earn your best score, you need to know how the ACT is really put together.

So, before anything, take some time and get to know this so-called adversary. Let's start with the basics. The ACT is a three-hour exam (two hours and fifty-five minutes, to be precise) taken by high school juniors and seniors for admission to college. Contrary to the myths you may have heard, the ACT is not an IQ test. It's a test of problem-solving skills—which means that you can improve your performance by preparing for it.

Speaking of myths, you may have heard that the ACT is really the only thing colleges look at when deciding whether to admit you. Untrue. Most admissions officers say the ACT is only one of several factors they take into consideration.

But let's be realistic about ACT scores. Here's this neat and easy way of comparing all students numerically, no matter what their academic backgrounds and no matter how much grade inflation exists at their high schools. You know the admissions people are going to take a serious look at your test scores.

The ACT consists of four subject tests: English, Math, Reading, and Science Reasoning. All four subject tests are primarily designed to test skills rather than knowledge, though some knowledge is required—particularly in English, for which a familiarity with grammar and writing mechanics is important, and in Math, for which you need to know the basic math concepts taught in a regular high school curriculum.

Overview of the ACT

- The ACT is about three hours long.
- There will be a short break between the second and third subtests.
- The ACT consists of a total of 215 scored questions.
- The exam is comprised of four subject tests:

  English . . . .(45 minutes, 75 questions)

  Math . . . .(60 minutes, 60 questions)

  Reading . . . .(35 minutes, 40 questions)

  Science Reasoning . . .(35 minutes, 40 questions)

ACT FAQS

Here are some quick answers to the questions students ask most frequently about the ACT.

How Is the ACT Scored?

No, your ACT score is not merely the sum total of questions you got correct. That would be too simple. Instead, what the test makers do is add up all of your correct answers to get what they call a "raw score." Then they put that raw score into a very large computer, which proceeds to shake, rattle, smoke, and wheeze before spitting out an official score at the other end. That score—which has been put through what they call a scoring formula—is your "scaled score."

ACT scaled scores range from 1 to 36. Nearly half of all test takers score within a much narrower range: 17–23. Tests at different dates vary slightly, but the following data is typical.

* Percentage of ACT takers scoring at or below given score

What's a Good ACT Score?

Most ACT test takers score between 17 and 23. A score below 17 will seriously limit your choice of colleges. But any ACT score above 23 will become an asset in your quest for admission to a competitive college.

A Little Goes a Long Way

Just a few questions right or wrong on the ACT can make a big difference. Answering only five extra questions correctly on each subject test can move you from the bottom of the applicant pool into the middle, or from the middle up to the top.

The score data includes two very strong scores: 26 and 31. Either score would impress almost any college admissions officer. A 26 would put you in the top 10 percent of the students who take the exam, and a 31 would put you in the top 1 percent. Even a 31 requires getting only about 90 percent of the questions right. The best student in your high school will probably get at least a dozen questions wrong. There are questions that even your smartest teachers would get wrong.

ACT Approximate Percentile Rank*	Composite Score	Percentage of Questions Correct
99%	31	90%
90%	26	75%
76%	23	63%
54%	20	53%
28%	17	43%

Notice that to earn a score of 20 (the national average), you need to answer only about 53 percent of the questions correctly. On most tests, getting only a bit more than half the questions right would be terrible. Not so on the ACT. Getting about half of the ACT questions correct and earning a score of 20 won't earn you a lifetime membership in the Academy of Arts and Sciences, maybe, but it's nothing to be ashamed of. But on the ACT, answering just 75 percent of the questions correctly earns you a score of about 26, putting you in the top ten percent of ACT takers.

If you earn a score of 23, you'll be in about the 76th percentile. That means that 76 percent of the test takers did as well as, or worse than, you did—in other words, that only 24 percent did better than you. It means you're in the "top quarter" of the people who take the ACT. That's a good score. But notice that to earn this score, you need only about 63 percent of the questions correct. On most tests, a score of 63 is probably a D or an F. But on the ACT, it's about a B+.

How Many ACT Scores Will You Get?

The "ACT scaled score" we've talked about so far is technically called the "Composite Score." It's the really important one. But when you take the ACT, you actually receive twelve (count 'em, twelve) different scores: the Composite Score, four subject scores, and seven subscores. Though the subject scores can play a role in decisions at some schools, the seven subscores usually aren't important for most people, so feel free to ignore the chart below if you don't feel like looking at it.

Here's the full battery of ACT scores (1–36) you'll receive. Few people (except your parents, maybe) will care about anything except your Composite Score for college admissions, though some schools use subscores for course placement.

English Score (1–36)   Usage/Mechanics subscore (1–18); Rhetorical Skills subscore (1–18)

Math Score (1–36)   Prealgebra/Elementary Algebra subscore (1–18); Algebra/Coordinate Geometry subscore (1–18); Plane Geometry/Trigonometry subscore (1–18)

Reading Score (1–36)   Social Sciences/Sciences subscore (1–18); Arts/Literature subscore (1–18)

Science Score (1–36)   There are no subscores in Science.

How Do Colleges Use Your ACT Score?

The most important score for most test takers is the Composite Score (which is an average of the four subject scores). This is the score used by most colleges and universities in the admissions process, and the one that you'll want to mention casually at parties during your freshman year of college. The four subject scores and seven subscores may be used for advanced placement or occasionally for scholarships, but are primarily used by college advisors to help students select majors and first-year courses.

Although many schools deny that they use benchmark scores as cutoffs, we're not sure we really believe them. Big Ten universities and colleges with similarly competitive admissions generally decline to accept students with Composite Scores below 22 or 23. For less competitive schools, the benchmark score may be lower than that; for some very selective schools, the cutoff may be higher.

To be fair, no school uses the ACT as an absolute bar to admission, no matter how low it is. But for most applicants, a low ACT score is decisive. As a rule, only students whose backgrounds are extremely unusual or who have overcome enormous disadvantages are accepted if their ACT scores are below the benchmark. It also sometimes helps if you can convince your parents to donate a gymnasium to the school you're aiming for.

Should You Guess on the ACT?

The short answer? Yes! The long answer? Yes, of course!

As we saw, ACT scores are based on the number of correct answers only. This means that questions left blank and questions answered incorrectly simply don't count. Unlike some other standardized tests, the ACT has no "wrong-answer penalty." That's why you should always take a guess on every ACT question you can't answer, even if you don't have time to read it. Though the questions vary enormously in difficulty, harder questions are worth exactly the same as easier ones, so it pays to guess on the really hard questions and spend your time breezing through the really easy ones. We'll show you just how to do this in the chapter called "Taking Control: The Top Ten Strategies."

Important Strategy

By the end of each subject test, you should have answered every question, even if you had to take a random guess on some. A lucky guess will raise your score, and an unlucky guess will leave you no worse off. There's no penalty for a wrong answer. None. Zippo.

Crucially Important Point

When you sign up for the ACT, you can choose colleges to receive your score. Unless time is of the essence, don't do it, even though the first three score reports are sent for free. Wait until you get your score, then send it out (for a small additional fee) if you're happy. If you hate your score, you can take the test again and send only the new, improved score.

Can You Retake the Test?

You can take the ACT as many times as you like. You can then select whichever test score you prefer to be sent to colleges when you apply. However, you cannot take advantage of this option if, at the time you register for the test, you designate certain colleges to receive your scores. Thus it is crucial that you not designate any colleges at the time you register for the test. You can (for a small additional fee) have ACT scores sent to colleges at any time you desire after the scores are reported.

Unless you don't have enough money for that small extra fee or if you're taking the ACT under the wire and you need your scores to reach the schools your applying to ASAP, give yourself the freedom to retake the test. What this means, of course, is that even if you blow the ACT once, you can give yourself another chance without the schools of your choice knowing about it. The ACT is one of the few areas of your academic life in which you get a second chance.

2

The Four Subject Tests: A Preview

Highlights

- The directions

- How the tests are organized

Okay, you've seen how the ACT is set up. But to really know your adversary, you've got to know something about the four ACT subject tests (which, by the way, always appear in the following order):

- English
- Mathematics
- Reading
- Science Reasoning

As we'll see, the questions in every subject test vary widely in difficulty. Some are so easy that most elementary school students could answer them. Others would give even Einstein a little trouble. But, again: The questions are not arranged in order of difficulty. That's different from some other tests, in which easier questions come first. **Skipping past hard questions is very important, since otherwise you may never reach easy ones toward the end of the exam.**

Here's a preview of the types of questions you'll encounter on the four subject tests. We'll keep them toward the easy end of the difficulty scale here, as you're just becoming familiar with the test. Later, in the Skill-Building Workouts, we'll be less kind.

Emergency Plan

If you have two weeks or fewer to prep for the ACT, you should spend time getting familiar with the test. Be sure to read this chapter.

ENGLISH

Reality Check: The English test is 45 minutes long and includes 75 questions. That works out to about 30 seconds per question, but in practice you should spend less time on easier questions and more on harder questions. The test is divided into five passages, each with about 15 questions.

Don't Get Bogged Down

ACT questions are not arranged in order of ascending difficulty. Theoretically, the first question you see could be the hardest on the test. Who needs that kind of aggravation? Not you. Skip past the tough questions and spend your first minutes on the test piling up some easy points.

Students nearly always get more questions correct in English than in any other section. That tends to make students think that English is a lot easier than the rest of the ACT. But, alas, it's not that simple. Because most students do well, the test makers have much higher expectations for English than for other parts of the test. They know that it's generally easier to get English questions right than, say, Science Reasoning questions. They've got a whole department of little statistician elves who keep track of things like this. That's why, to earn an average English subscore (a 20, say), you have to get almost two-thirds of the questions right, while on the rest of the test you need to get only about half right.

The Directions

The English directions are a good illustration of why you have a big advantage if you know the directions beforehand. The English directions are long and complicated. Here's what they'll look like, but take our advice. Don't even bother reading them. We'll show you exactly how to do what you need to do:

Directions: In the following five passages, certain words and phrases have been underlined and numbered. You will find alternatives for each underlined portion in the right-hand column. Select the one that best expresses the idea, that makes the statement acceptable in standard written English, or that is phrased most consistently with the style and tone of the entire passage. If you feel that the original version is best, select "NO CHANGE." You will also find questions asking about a section of the passage or about the entire passage.

For these questions decide which choice gives the most appropriate response to the given question. For each question in the test, select the best choice and fill in the corresponding space on the answer folder. You may wish to read each passage through before you begin to answer the questions associated with it. Most answers cannot be determined without reading several sentences around the phrases in question. Make sure to read far enough ahead each time you choose an alternative.

The Format

To put the directions more concisely, let's say that almost all of the English questions follow a standard format. A word, phrase, or sentence in a passage is underlined. You're given four options: to leave the underlined portion alone ("NO CHANGE," which is always the first choice), or to replace it with one of three alternatives (the ones proposed in the other three choices).

EXAMPLE

... Pike's Peak in Southwest Colorado is

named <u>before Zebulon Pike, an early</u>
            37
<u>explorer.</u> He traveled through the
    37
area, exploring ...

37. **A.** NO CHANGE
    B. before Zebulon Pike
        became an explorer,
    C. after Zebulon Pike,
        when,
    D. after Zebulon Pike.

The best answer for number 37 above is D. The other choices all have various problems—grammatical, stylistic, logical. They make the passage look and sound like it was written by your baby brother. Only D makes the sentence sensible and correct. That's why it's the answer.

Notice that a single question can test several different kinds of writing errors. We find that about a third of the questions on the English section test your ability to write concisely (we call them Economy Questions), about another third test for logic and sense (Sense Questions) and that only the remaining third test hard-and-fast rules of grammar (Technicality Questions). There's a lot of overlap between these question types, so don't worry too much about categories. We provide them mostly to give you an idea of the kind of errors you'll be expected to correct.

To Omit or Not to Omit

Some standard-format English questions offer, as one of the alternatives, the chance to completely omit the underlined portion, usually as the last of the four choices.

EXAMPLE

Later, Pike fell while valiantly defending
America in the War of 1812.

<u>It goes without saying that this took</u>
                40
<u>place after he discovered Pike's Peak.</u>
                40
He actually died near York (now called
Toronto)...

40. **F.** NO CHANGE
    G. Clearly, this must have occurred
        subsequent to his discovering
        Pike's Peak.
    H. This was after he found Pike's
        Peak.
    J. OMIT the underlined portion.

In this case, J is correct. The idea really does "go without saying." For that reason, it shouldn't be said. On recent ACTs, when OMIT has occurred as an answer choice, it's been correct more than half of the time (As you can see, the ACT makers aren't the only ones with a department of little statistician elves ...). This doesn't mean you should always select "OMIT," however, since it's also been wrong almost half of the time.

Nonstandard Format Questions

Some ACT English questions—usually about ten per exam—don't follow this standard format. These items pose a question and offer four possible responses. In many cases, the responses are either "yes" or "no," with an explanation. Pay attention to the reasoning. Question 40 could have appeared in a nonstandard format as follows:

EXAMPLE

. . . Later, Pike fell while valiantly defending America in the War of 1812. ⟨40⟩ He actually died near York (now called Toronto) . . .

40. Suppose the author considered adding the following sentence at this point: "It goes without saying that this occurred after he discovered Pike's Peak." Given the overall purpose of the passage, would this sentence be appropriate?

   F. No, because the sentence adds nothing to the meaning of the passage.

   G. No, because the passage is not concerned with Pike's achievements.

   H. Yes, because otherwise the sequence of events would be unclear.

   J. Yes; though the sentence is not needed, the author recognizes this fact by using the phrase *it goes without saying.*

The correct answer for this question is F. Though G correctly indicates that the sentence doesn't belong in the passage, it offers a pretty inappropriate reason. The passage is concerned with Pike's achievements. Choices H and J are wrong because they recommend including a sentence that is clearly redundant.

Many of the nonstandard questions occur at the end of a passage. Some ask about the meaning, purpose, or tone of individual paragraphs or of the passage as a whole. Others ask you to evaluate the passage. And still others ask you to determine the proper order of words, sentences, or paragraphs that have been scrambled in the passage.

We think you'll like the English subject test. It can actually be fun, which is probably why the test makers put it first. We'll cover strategies for all of the English question types in the English Workouts.

MATHEMATICS

Reality Check: The Math test is 60 minutes long and includes 60 questions. That works out to one minute per question, but you'll want to spend less time on easy questions and more on the tough ones.

The Format

All of the math questions have the same, basic multiple-choice format. They ask a question and offer five possible choices (unlike questions on the other three subject tests, which have only four choices each). Why the math test has five choices while the other test have only four is one of those mysteries that only the ACT makers understand.

The questions cover a full range of math topics, from prealgebra and elementary algebra through intermediate algebra, coordinate geometry, plane geometry, and even trigonometry. We'll tell you the exact number of questions in each area later, in Math Workout 1. If you have specific weaknesses in any of these areas, the Math Appendix at the end of this book will help.

Although the math questions, like those in other sections, aren't ordered in terms of difficulty, questions drawn from elementary school or junior high tend to come earlier in the section, while those from high school math curricula tend to come later. But this doesn't mean that the easy questions come first and the hardest ones come later. We've found that high school subjects tend to be fresher in most student's minds than things they were taught years ago, so you may actually find the later questions easier. (Do *you* remember the math you learned in seventh grade?)

The Directions

Here's what the Math directions will look like:

Directions: Solve each of the following problems, select the correct answer, and then fill in the corresponding space on your answer sheet.

Don't linger over problems that are too time-consuming. Do as many as you can, then come back to the others in the time you have remaining.

Note: Unless otherwise noted, all of the following should be assumed:

1. Illustrative figures are *not* necessarily drawn to scale.
2. All geometric figures lie in a plane.
3. The term *line* indicates a straight line.
4. The term *average* indicates arithmetic mean.

Again, when it comes to directions on the ACT, the golden rule is: *Don't read them on Test Day!* You'll already know what they say by the time you take the test.

The math directions don't really tell you much anyway. Of the four special notes at the end of the math directions, #2, #3, and #4 almost go without saying. Note #1—that figures are *not* necessarily drawn to scale—seems pretty scary, but in fact the vast majority of ACT figures *are* drawn to scale, a fact that, as we'll see, has significant implications for how to guess on geometry questions.

Reading and Drawing Diagrams

We find that about a third of the Math questions either give you a diagram or describe a situation that should be diagrammed. For these questions, the diagrams are crucial.

EXAMPLE

1. The figure below contains five congruent triangles. The longest side of each triangle is 4 meters long. What is the area of the whole figure?

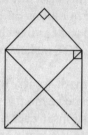

    A. 12.5 square meters
    B. 15 square meters
    C. 20 square meters
    D. 30 square meters
    E. Cannot be determined from the given information

The key to this question is to let the diagram tell you what you need to know—that each triangle represents one-quarter of the area of the square, and that the sides of the *square* are 4 meters (you can figure this out because the top side of the square is the hypotenuse—or longest side—of the triangle that makes the "roof"). Since the area of a square can be found by squaring the side, the area of the square is 16 square meters. Thus, each triangle has an area one-fourth as much—4 square meters. Since the whole figure consists of *five* triangles, each with area 4, the total area is 5 × 4 = 20. The answer is C.

> **HINT:** *In ACT math questions, the answer choice "cannot be determined" is rare. When it does appear, it's usually wrong. "Cannot be determined" is almost always wrong in a question that comes with a diagram or for which you can draw one.*

How to Get That Story

We find that about another third of the math questions are story problems like the following:

EXAMPLE

2. Evan drove halfway home at 20 miles per hour, then speeded up and drove the rest of the way at 30 miles per hour. What was his average speed for the entire trip?
    F. 20 miles per hour
    G. 22 miles per hour
    H. 24 miles per hour
    J. 25 miles per hour
    K. 28 miles per hour

A good way to comprehend—and resolve—a story problem like this is to think of a real situation just like the one in the story. For example, what if Evan had 120 miles to drive? (You should pick a distance that's easily divisible by both rates). He would go 60 miles at 30 mph, then 60 miles at 20 mph. How long would it take? Well, 60 miles at 30 mph is 2 hours; 60 miles at 20 mph is 3 hours. That's a total of 120 miles in 5 hours; 120 divided by 5 gives an average speed of 24 mph. The correct answer is thus H. (Note: We'll show you alternative ways to answer questions like this later on.)

Getting the Concept

Finally, we find that about a third of the questions directly ask you to demonstrate your knowledge of specific math concepts.

EXAMPLE

3. If angles A and B are supplementary, and the measure of
    angle A is 57°, what is the measure, in degrees, of angle B?
    A. 33
    B. 43
    C. 47
    D. 123
    E. 147

This question simply requires that you know the concept of "supplementary angles." Two angles are *supplementary* when they form a straight line—in other words, when they add up to 180°. Thus, question 3 boils down to this: What number, added to 57, makes 180? The answer is D.

These three types of math questions, of course, will be discussed more fully in the Math Workouts.

READING

Reality Check: The Reading test is 35 minutes long and includes 40 questions. The test contains four passages, each of which is followed by 10 questions. When you factor in the amount of time you'll initially spend on the passages, this works out to about 30 seconds per question—again, more for the tough ones, less for the easy ones.

The Format

There are four categories of reading passages: Social Studies, Natural Sciences, Humanities, and Prose Fiction. You'll get one passage in each category. The passages are about 1,000 words long and are written at about the same difficulty level as college textbooks and readings.

The Social Studies, Natural Sciences, and Humanities passages are usually well-organized essays. Each has a very specific theme. Questions expect you to recognize this theme, to comprehend specific facts contained in the passage, and to understand the structure of the essay. Prose Fiction passages require you to understand the thoughts, feelings, and motivations of fictional characters, even when these are not explicitly stated in the passage (we'll have a special section on Prose Fiction passages in Reading Workout 3).

After each passage, you'll find ten questions. There are really only three different categories of Reading question:

- Specific Detail Questions
- Inference Questions
- Big Picture Questions

The Directions

Here's what the Reading directions will look like:

> **Directions:** This test contains four passages, each followed by several questions. After reading a passage, select the best answer to each question and fill in the corresponding oval on your answer sheet. You are allowed to refer to the passages while answering the questions.

Nothing stupefying here. But nothing very substantive either. We'll be a little more specific and strategic than the test makers when we suggest a plan of attack in the three Reading Workouts.

Nailing Down the Details

Specific Detail Questions ask about things stated explicitly in the passage. The challenge with these questions is, first, finding the proper place in the passage where the answer can be found (sometimes you'll be given a line reference, sometimes not), and second, being able to match up what you see in the passage with the correct answer, which will probably be worded differently. Many wrong choices will be designed to trip you up by including details from other parts of the passage, or by using the same wording as the passage while distorting the meaning:

EXAMPLE

When we say "Bach" we almost always refer to Johann Sebastian Bach (1685–1750), but in fact the name "Bach" belongs to a whole family of Baroque German musicians . . .

(*7 paragraphs and 950 words omitted*)

The works of Johann Christian Bach, J. S. Bach's son, clearly prefigure the rich musical developments that followed the Baroque period. Thus, it is both surprising and unfortunate that the rest of J. S. Bach's family isn't more well known.

6. According to the author, J. S. Bach is the best-known:
   F. German Baroque musician.
   G. member of a musical family.
   H. organist in German history.
   J. composer of Lutheran hymns.

7. Johann Christian Bach was:
   A. born earlier than Johann Sebastian Bach.
   B. a composer of the "Romantic" school of music.
   C. a composer whose works are transitional in style.
   D. well known during his own lifetime.

The correct answer for question 6 is G. Both the first and last sentences in the passage refer to J. S. Bach as the most famous member of a whole family of musicians. You might think J. S. Bach is the best-known "German Baroque musician" (choice F), but that's not what the passage says, so it's wrong.

The correct answer for question 7 is C. At the end of the passage the author says that Johann Christian's work "prefigure[d]" the music that followed the Baroque. Thus, it must have had some Baroque characteristics and some new aspects. In other words, it was transitional.

Making an Inference

We find that most Reading passages also include a large number of Inference Questions, which require you to make an inference from the passage (to "read between the lines"). They differ somewhat from Specific Detail Questions. For one thing, students usually consider them harder. Here's an example of each:

EXAMPLE

. . . though schizophrenia and multiple personality disorder (M.P.D.) may be related, and are often confused by laymen, the two terms have radically different meanings . . .

32. Which of the following best expresses the relationship between schizophrenia and multiple personality disorder?
- **F.** They are two terms that describe essentially the same phenomenon.
- **G.** The two disorders have nothing in common.
- **H.** Though the two have some similarities, they are fundamentally different.
- **J.** The two are not exactly alike, but are very close.

33. Suppose that a patient has been diagnosed with schizophrenia. Based on the passage, which of the following is least likely?
- **A.** The patient's doctors immediately assume that the patient also suffers from M.P.D.
- **B.** The patient is a layman.
- **C.** The patient denies that he has M.P.D.
- **D.** The patient has several separate personalities.

Note the differences between Specific Detail and Inference Questions: Question 32, a Specific Detail Question, requires that you understand the explicitly stated idea that schizophrenia and M.P.D. have some connection, but are not the same. That's what choice H says. Question 33, on the other hand, requires you to apply the idea that the two disorders are different. If they are, it's highly unlikely that doctors would simply assume that a patient suffering from one disorder must suffer from the other. Therefore, choice A is least likely—and therefore correct. The other choices may or may not be true, and nothing in the passage leads us to think one way or the other about them. Question 33 is what we'd call a garden-variety Inference Question.

Getting the Big Picture

Although the majority of Reading questions are Specific Detail and Inference Questions, the Reading subtest also includes another type of question that we call Big Picture Questions. Some Big Picture Questions ask about the passage as a whole, requiring you to find the theme, tone, or structure of the passage. Others ask you to evaluate the writing. Here's a typical Big Picture Question that might have appeared with the Bach family passage we talked about earlier:

EXAMPLE

9. The author's main point in the passage is to:
   A. show that many of the lesser-known members of the Bach family also influenced music history.
   B. argue that J. C. Bach was actually a greater composer than his father, J. S. Bach.
   C. demonstrate that musical talent always runs in families.
   D. dispute the claim that the Bach family was the best-known family of German Baroque musicians.

In order to answer this kind of question, you've got to have a good sense of the Big Picture—of the shape and flow of the whole passage. Of course, we printed only a few selected lines from the passage, but that should have been enough to lead you to A as the answer. The first line definitely indicates that the subject of the passage is going to be the entire Bach family, with a focus on the ones who aren't as well known as the big cheese, J. S. himself.

We'll discuss strategies for all passage- and question-types in the Reading Workouts.

SCIENCE REASONING

Reality Check: The Science Reasoning test is 35 minutes long and includes 40 questions. The test contains seven passages, each with 5 to 7 questions. Factoring in the amount of time you'll initially spend on the passage, that will give you something over 30 seconds for each question.

No, you don't have to be a scientist to succeed on the ACT Science Reasoning test. You don't have to know the atomic number of cadmium or the preferred mating habits of the monarch butterfly. All that's required is common sense (though a knowledge of standard scientific processes and procedures sure does help). You'll be given passages containing various kinds of scientific information—drawn from the fields of biology, chemistry, physics, geology, astronomy, and meteorology—which you'll have to understand and use as a basis for inferences.

The Format

On most Science Reasoning subtests, there are six passages that present scientific data, often based on specific experiments. Also, there's usually one passage in which two scientists state opposing views on the same issue. Each passage will generate between five and seven questions. A warning: Some passages will be very difficult to understand, but they'll usually make up for that fact by having many easy questions attached to them. The test makers do show some mercy once in a while.

The Directions

Here's what the Science Reasoning directions will look like:

> **Directions:** Each of the following seven passages is followed by several questions. After reading each passage, decide on the best answer to each question and fill in the corresponding oval on your answer sheet. You are allowed to refer to the passages while answering the questions.

Sounds a lot like the set of directions for Reading, doesn't it? Not much substance here, either. But don't worry. We'll show you the best *strategic* way to attack the Science Reasoning subject test in the three Science Workouts.

Analyzing Data

About a third of the questions in the Science subtest require you to read data from graphs or tables. In easier questions, you need only report the information. In harder questions, you may need to draw inferences or note patterns in the data. For example:

EXAMPLE

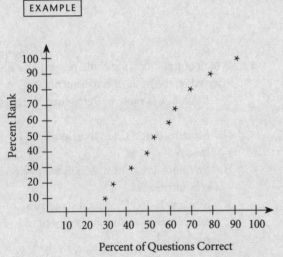

Percent of Questions Correct

1. A test taker who scores in approximately the 40th percentile has correctly answered about what fraction of the questions?

   A. $\frac{9}{10}$
   B. $\frac{2}{3}$
   C. $\frac{1}{2}$
   D. $\frac{1}{5}$

2. Which of the following best describes the relationship between percentile rank and percent of questions correct?

   F. As percentile rank increases, percent of correct questions also increases.
   G. Percentile rank is inversely proportional to the percent of correct questions.
   H. As percentile rank increases, the percent of correct questions decreases.
   J. As percentile rank decreases, percent of correct questions usually, but not always, also decreases.

The correct answer to question 1 is C. The point for the 40th percentile is slightly above the fifty percent point on the horizontal axis (percent correct). Fifty percent is the same as $\frac{1}{2}$. Note that this question involves a little simple arithmetic (translating a percent into a fraction)—not uncommon for Science Reasoning questions.

In question 2, the correct answer is F. The points that are higher on the graph (higher percentile) are always farther to the right (higher percentage of correct questions). Note that answers G and H say essentially the same thing (we'll discuss direct and inverse proportionality in Science Workout 1), and thus are wrong for the same reason: they get the relationship backwards. J is wrong because it says that the percent of correct questions does not always decrease as percentile rank decreases.

Conducting Experiments

Other Science questions require that you understand the way experiments are designed and what they prove. For example, part of a passage might describe an experiment as follows:

EXAMPLE

Experiment 1

A scientist adds one drop of nitric acid to Beakers A, B, and C. Each Beaker contains water from a different stream. The water in Beaker A came from Stream A, that in Beaker B came from Stream B, and that in Beaker C came from Stream C. Precipitates form in Beakers B and C, but not in Beaker A.

12. Which of the following could properly be inferred on the basis of Experiment 1?
    F. Stream A is more polluted than Streams B and C.
    G. Streams B and C are more polluted than A.
    H. Stream A contains material that neutralizes nitric acid.
    J. Streams B and C contain some substance that reacts in the presence of nitric acid.

The correct answer for question 12 is J. Since a precipitate forms when nitric acid is added to Beakers B and C, which contain water from Streams B and C, something in these streams must be involved. However, we don't know that it is pollution, so answers F and G are unwarranted. We also don't know exactly *why* no precipitate formed in Beaker A, so H is also an unwarranted conclusion. Scientists *hate* unwarranted conclusions.

The Principle of the Thing

The remaining Science questions require you either to logically apply a principle, or to identify ways of defending or attacking a principle. Often, the question will involve two scientists stating opposing views on the same subject. But this is not always the case. For example, a passage might describe a theory of the process whereby most "V-shaped" valleys are typically formed on Earth—by water erosion through soft rock. Then the following questions might be asked:

EXAMPLE

16. Which of the following is most likely to be a V-shaped valley?
    F. A valley formed by glaciers
    G. A river valley which is cut into very hard basalt
    H. A valley formed by wind erosion
    J. A river valley in a region of soft shale rocks

17. Which of the following discoveries would most weaken
    the theory of V-shaped valley formation given in the passage?
    A. Certain parts of many valleys formed by
        water that are U-shaped
    B. A group of V-shaped valleys almost certainly
        formed by wind erosion
    C. A group of U-shaped valleys formed by water
        erosion in hard rock
    D. A group of valleys on Mars that appear to be
        V-shaped but that are not near any running water

In question 16, the correct answer is J, since this is consistent with the passage as described. The correct answer in question 17 is B. Finding V-shaped valleys not formed by water erosion would tend to weaken the theory that they are formed this way. The other answers do not offer evidence about V-shaped valleys on Earth, and thus are irrelevant to a theory about them.

We'll be showing you strategies for each kind of Science Reasoning question in the three Science Workouts.

3

Taking Control:
The Top Ten Strategies

Highlights

- The ACT Mindset

- Ten tips for mastering the ACT

Now that you've got some idea of the kind of adversary you face in the ACT, it's time to start developing strategies for dealing with this adversary. In other words, you've got to start developing your ACT Mindset.

THE ACT MINDSET

The ACT, as we've just seen, isn't a normal test. A normal test requires that you rely almost exclusively on your memory. On a normal test, you'd see questions like this:

The "golden spike," which joined the Union Pacific and Central Pacific Railroads, was driven in Ogden, Utah, in May 1869. Who was President of the United States at the time?

To answer this question, you have to resort to memory dredging. Either you know the answer is Ulysses S. Grant or else you don't. No matter how hard you think, you'll never be able to answer this question if you can't remember your history.

Emergency Plan

This chapter will help you to take control of the ACT. You should read this chapter even if you have two weeks or fewer to prep.

KAPLAN   25

But the ACT doesn't test your long-term memory. The answer to every ACT question can be found in the test. Theoretically, if you read carefully and understand the words and concepts the test uses, you can get almost any ACT question right. Notice the difference between the regular-test question above and the ACT-type question below:

EXAMPLE

1. What is the product of n and m^2, where n is an odd number and m is an even number?
   A. An odd number
   B. A multiple of four
   C. A noninteger
   D. An irrational number
   E. The square of an integer

Aside from the obvious difference (this question has answer choices, while the other one does not), there's another difference: The ACT question mostly tests your ability to understand a situation rather than your ability to passively remember a fact. Nobody expects you to know off the top of your head what the product of an odd number and the square of an even number is. But the ACT test makers do expect you to be able to roll up your sleeves and figure it out (as we'll do below).

How to Develop the Act Mindset

Most students take the ACT with the same mindset that they use for normal tests. Their brains are on "memory mode." Students often panic and give up because they can't seem to remember enough. But you don't need to remember a ton of picky little rules for the ACT. Don't give up on an ACT question just because your memory fails.

On the ACT, if you understand what a question is really asking on the test, you can almost always answer it. For instance, take the math problem above. You might have been thrown by the way it was phrased. "How can I solve this problem?" you may have asked yourself. "It doesn't even have numbers in it!"

The key here, as in all ACT questions, is taking control. Take the question (by the throat, if necessary) and wrestle it into a form you can understand. Ask yourself: What's really being asked here? What does it mean when they say something like "the product of n and m^2"?

Well, you might start by putting it into words you might use. You might say something like this: "I've got to take one number times another. One of the numbers is odd and the other is an even number squared. Then I've got to see what kind of number I get as an answer." Once you put the question in your own terms like this, it becomes much less intimidating—and much easier to get right. You'll realize that you don't have to do complex algebraic computations with variables. All you have to do is substitute numbers.

So do it! Try picking some easy-to-use numbers. Say that n is 3 (an odd number) and m is 2 (an even number). Then m^2 would be 4, because 2^2 is 4. And $n \times m^2$ would be 3×4, which is 12—a multiple of four, but not odd, not a noninteger, not an irrational number, and not a perfect square. The only answer that can be right, then, is B.

See what we mean about figuring out the answer creatively rather than passively remembering it? True, there are some things you had to remember here—what even and odd numbers are, how variables and exponents work, and maybe what integers and irrational numbers are. But these are very basic concepts. Most of what you're expected to know on the ACT is like that: basic. (By the way, you'll find such concepts gathered together in the very attractive Math Appendix at the end of this book.)

Of course, basic doesn't always mean easy. Many ACT questions are built on basic concepts, but are tough nonetheless. The problem above, for instance, is difficult because it requires some thought to figure out what's being asked. This isn't only true in Math. It's the same for every part of the ACT.

GET INTO THE ACT MINDSET—TEN TIPS

The creative, take-control kind of thinking we call the ACT Mindset is something you want to bring to virtually every ACT question you encounter. As we'll see, being in the ACT Mindset means reshaping the test-taking experience so that you are in the driver's seat.

It means:

- Answering questions if you want to (by guessing on the impossible questions rather than wasting time on them).
- Answering questions when you want to (by skipping tough but "doable" questions and coming back to them after you've gotten all of the easy questions done).
- Answering questions how you want to (by using "unofficial" ways of getting correct answers fast).

And that's really what the ACT Mindset boils down to: Taking control. Being creative. Solving specific problems to get points as quickly and easily as you can.

What follows are the top ten strategies you need to do just that.

#1—Do Question Triage

In a hospital emergency room, the triage nurse is the person who evaluates each patient and decides which ones get attention first and which ones should be treated later. You should do the same thing on the ACT.

Practicing triage is one of the most important ways of controlling your test-taking experience. It's a fact that there are some questions on the ACT that most students could never answer correctly, no matter how much time or effort they spent on them.

EXAMPLE

57. If $\sec^2 x = 4$, which of the following could be $\sin x$?
   A. 1.73205
   B. 3.14159
   C. $\sqrt{3}$
   D. $\dfrac{\sqrt{3}}{2}$
   E. Cannot be determined from the given information.

Clearly, even if you could manage to come up with an answer to this question, it would take some time (those of you who insist on doing so can refer to the explanation below). But would it be worth the time? We think not.

This question clearly illustrates our point: You should do question triage on the ACT. The first time you look at each question, make a quick decision on how hard and time-consuming it looks. Then decide whether to answer it now or skip it and do it later. Here's how:

- If the question looks comprehensible and reasonably doable, do it right away.

- If the question looks tough and time-consuming, but ultimately doable, skip it, circle the number of the question in your test booklet, and come back to it later.

- If the question looks impossible, forget about it. Guess and move on, never to return.

Food for Thought

Let's say you took two-and-a-half minutes to get a tough question right. That might make you feel good, but you would actually be better off if you had skipped the tough question and, in the same amount of time, answered two or three easier questions correctly.

This triage method is designed to make sure you spend the time needed to do all the easy questions before you risk getting bogged down with a tough problem. Remember, every question on a subject test is worth the same. You get no extra credit for test macho.

Answering easier questions first has another benefit: It gives you confidence to answer harder ones later. Doing problems in the order you choose rather than in the order imposed by the test makers gives you control over the test. Most students don't have time to do all of the problems, so you've got to make sure you do all of the ones you can easily score on!

Do You Know Your Trig?

Okay, since you're reading this, it's obvious that you want to know the answer to the trig question on this page. The answer is D. Here's how we got it:

$$\sec^2 x = 4 \qquad\qquad\qquad \text{given}$$

$$\sec x = 2 \text{ or } -2 \qquad\qquad \text{square root both sides}$$

$$\cos x = \frac{1}{2} \text{ or } -\frac{1}{2} \qquad\qquad \cos x = \frac{1}{\sec x}$$

$$\cos^2 x = \frac{1}{4} \qquad\qquad\qquad \text{square both sides}$$

$$\sin^2 x = 1 - \frac{1}{4} \qquad\qquad \sin^2 x + \cos^2 x = 1$$

$$\sin^2 x = 1 - \cos^2 x$$

$$\sin^2 x = \frac{3}{4}$$

$$\sin x = \sqrt{\frac{3}{4}} \text{ or } -\sqrt{\frac{3}{4}} \qquad\qquad \text{square root both sides}$$

$$\sin x = \frac{\sqrt{3}}{2} \text{ or } -\frac{\sqrt{3}}{2} \qquad\qquad \sqrt{4} = 2$$

So D—$\frac{\sqrt{3}}{2}$—is correct. But if you got it right, don't congratulate yourself quite yet. How long did it take you to get it right? So long that you could have gotten the answers to two easy questions in the same amount of time?

Develop a Plan of Attack

For the English, Reading, and Science Reasoning sections, the best plan of attack is to do each passage as a block. Make a longish first pass through the questions (call it the "triage" pass), doing the easy ones, guessing on the impossible ones, and skipping any that look like they might cause particular trouble. Then, make a second pass (call it the "cleanup pass") and pick up whichever questions you think you can do with harder work.

For Math, you use essentially the same two-pass strategy, except that you move through the whole subject test twice. Work through the doable questions for the whole subject test first. Most of these will probably be toward the beginning, but not all. Then come back and attack the questions that look possible but tough or time-consuming. No matter what subject test you're working on, you should take pains to grid your answers in the right place. It's easy to misgrid when you're skipping around, so be careful. And of course: *Make sure you have an answer gridded for every question by the time the subject test is over!*

#2—Put the Material Into a Form You Can Understand and Use

ACT questions are rarely presented in the simplest, most helpful way. In fact, your main job for many questions is just figuring out what the question means so that you can solve it.

Since the material is presented in such an intimidating way, one of your best strategies for taking control is to recast the material into a form you can handle better. This is what we did in the math problem about "the product of n and m^2." We took the question and reworded it in a way we could understand.

Mark Up Your Test Booklet

This strategy should be employed on all four subject tests. For example, in Reading, many students find the passages overwhelming: 85 to 90 lines of dense verbiage for each one! But the secret is to put the passages into a form you can understand and use. Circle or underline the author's main idea, for one thing. And make yourself a road map of the passage, labeling each paragraph so you understand how it all fits together. That way, you'll also know—later, when you're doing the questions—where in the passage to find certain types of information you need. (We'll show you how to do all of these things later, in the Skill-Building Workouts.)

Reword the Questions

You'll find that you also need to do some recasting of the *questions*. For instance, take this question from a Science Reasoning passage.

EXAMPLE

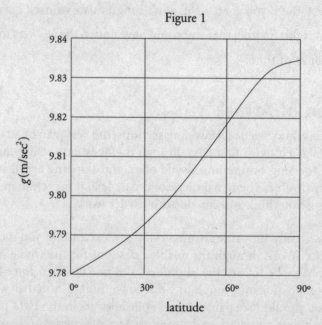

Figure 1

15. According to Figure 1, at approximately what latitude would calculations using an estimated value at sea level of $g = 9.80$ m/sec^2 produce the least error?
    A. 0°
    B. 20°
    C. 40°
    D. 80°

At what latitude would the calculations using a value of $g = 9.80$ m/sec^2 produce the least error? Yikes! What does that mean?

Take a deep breath. Ask yourself: Where would an estimate for g of 9.80 m/sec^2 produce the least error? In a latitude where 9.80 m/sec^2 is the real value of g. If you find the latitude at

KAPLAN

which the real value of g is 9.80 m/sec², then using 9.80 m/sec² as an estimate there would produce no error at all!

So, in other words, what this question is asking is: At what latitude does $g = 9.80$ m/sec²? Now that's a form of the question you can understand. In that form, you can answer it easily: choice C, which you can get just by reading the chart.

Draw Diagrams

Sometimes, putting the material into usable form involves drawing with your pencil. For instance, take a look at the following math problem.

EXAMPLE

2. Jason bought a painting with a frame 1 inch wide.
    If the dimensions of the outside of the frame are 5
    inches by 7 inches, which of the following could
    be the length of one of the sides of the painting
    inside the frame?

    F. 3 inches

    G. 4 inches

    H. $5\frac{1}{2}$ inches

    J. $6\frac{1}{2}$ inches

    K. 7 inches

Just looking at the question the first time, you might be tempted simply to subtract 1 from the outside dimensions and think that the inside dimensions are 4 by 6 (and pick G). Why isn't this correct? Because the frame goes all the way around—both above and below the painting, both to the right and to the left. This would have been clear if you had put the problem in a form you could understand and use.

For instance, you might have made the situation graphic by actually sketching out the painting frame (who says you don't have to be an artist to succeed at the ACT?):

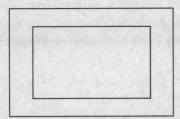

When you draw the picture frame like this, you realize that if the outside dimensions are 5 by 7, the inside dimensions must be 3 by 5. Thus, the correct answer is F.

So remember: On the ACT, you've got to put everything into a form that you can understand and use.

#3—Ignore Irrelevant Issues

It's easy to waste time on ACT questions by considering irrelevant issues. Just because an issue looks interesting, or just because you're worried about something, doesn't make it important. For example, take this English question.

EXAMPLE

...China was certainly one of the cradles

of civilization. It's obvious that, China
                14
has a long history. As is the case with
    14
other ancient cultures, the early history

of China is lost in mythology...

14. **F.** NO CHANGE
    G. It's obvious that China has
        a long history.
    H. Obviously; China has
        a long history.
    J. OMIT the underlined portion.

In this question, the test makers are counting on you to waste time worrying about punctuation. Does that comma belong? Can you use a semicolon here? These issues might be worrisome, but they aren't important. There's a much bigger issue here—namely, does the sentence belong in the passage at all? No, it doesn't. If China has an ancient culture and was a cradle of civilization, it must have a long history, so the sentence really is "obvious." Redundancy is the relevant issue here, not punctuation. Choice J is correct.

Remember, you've got limited time, so don't get caught up in issues that won't get you a point.

#4—Check Back

Remember, the ACT is not a test of your memory, so don't make it one. All of the information you need is in the test itself. You shouldn't be afraid to refer back to it. Much of the information is too complex to accurately remember anyway.

In Reading and Science Reasoning, always refer to the place in the passage where the answer to a question can be found (the question stem will often contain a line reference or a reference to a specific table, graph, or experiment to help you out). Your chosen answer should match the passage—not in exact vocabulary or units of measurement, perhaps, but in meaning.

EXAMPLE

Isaac Newton was born in 1642 in the hamlet of Woolsthorpe in Lincolnshire, England. But he is more famous as a man of Cambridge, where he studied and taught...

7. Which of the following does the author imply is a fact about Newton's birth?
    A. It occurred in Lincoln, a small hamlet in England.
    B. It took place in a part of England known for raising sheep.
    C. It did not occur in a large metropolitan setting.
    D. It caused Newton to seek his education at Cambridge.

You might expect the right answer to be that Newton was born in a hamlet, or in Woolsthorpe, or in Lincolnshire. But none of those is offered as a choice. Choice A is tempting, but wrong. Newton was born in Lincolnshire, not Lincoln. Choice B is actually true, but it's wrong here. As its name suggests, Woolsthorpe was once known for its wool—which comes from sheep. But the question asks for something implied in the passage.

The correct answer here is C, because a hamlet is a small village. That's not a large metropolitan setting. (It's also a famous play, but that's not among the choices.)

Checking back is especially important in Reading and Science Reasoning, because the passages leave many people feeling adrift in a sea of details. Often, the wrong answers will be "misplaced details"—details taken from different parts of the passage. They are things that don't answer the question properly but that might sound good to you if you aren't careful. By checking back with the passage, you can avoid choosing such devilishly clever wrong choices.

There's another important lesson here: Don't pick a choice just because it contains "key words" you remember from the passage. Many wrong choices, like D in the question above, are distortions—they use the right words but say the wrong things about them. Look for answer choices that contain the same ideas you find in the passage.

One of the best ways to avoid choosing misplaced details and distortions is to check back with the passage.

#5—Answer the Right Question

This strategy is a natural extension of the last. As we said, the ACT test makers often include among the wrong choices for a question the correct answer to a different question. Under time pressure, it's easy for you to fall for one of these red herrings, thinking that you know what's being asked for when really you don't.

EXAMPLE

7. What is the value of $3x$ if $9x = 5y + 2$ and $y + 4 = 2y - 10$?
   A. 5
   B. 8
   C. 14
   D. 24
   E. 72

To solve this problem, we need to find y first, even though the question asks about x (because x here is given only in terms of y). You could solve the second equation like this:

$y + 4 = 2y - 10$	given
$4 = y - 10$	by subtracting y from both sides
$14 = y$	by adding 10 to both sides

But choice C, 14, isn't the right answer here, because the question doesn't ask for the value of y—it asks about x. We can use the value of y to find x, however, by plugging the calculated value of y into the first equation:

$9x = 5y + 2$	given
$9x = 5(14) + 2$	because $y = 14$
$9x = 70 + 2$	
$9x = 72$	

But E, 72, isn't the answer either, because the question doesn't ask for $9x$. It doesn't ask for x either, so if you picked B, 8, you'd be wrong as well. Remember to refer to the question! The question asks for $3x$. So we need to divide $9x$ by 3:

$9x = 72$	from above
$3x = 24$	dividing by 3

Thus, the answer is D.

Always check the question again before choosing your answer. Doing all the right work but then getting the wrong answer can be seriously depressing. So make sure you're answering the right question.

#6—Look for the Hidden Answer

On many ACT questions, the right answer is hidden in one way or another. Don't let the answer hide from you.

An answer can be hidden by being written in a way that you aren't likely to expect. For example, you might work out a problem and get .5 as your answer, but then find that .5 isn't among the answer choices. Then you notice that one choice reads "$\frac{1}{2}$." Congratulations, Sherlock. You've found the hidden answer.

But there's another way the ACT can hide answers. Many ACT questions have more than one possible right solution, though only one correct answer choice is given. Often, the ACT will hide that answer by offering one of the less obvious possible answers to a question. For example:

EXAMPLE

2. If $3x^2 + 5 = 17$, which of the following could be the value of x ?
A. −3
B. −2
C. 0
D. 1
E. 4

You quickly solve this very straightforward problem like so:

$3x^2 + 5 = 17$ given
$3x^2 = 12$ by subtracting 5
$x^2 = 4$ dividing by 3
$x = 2$ taking square root of both sides

Having gotten an answer, you confidently look for it among the choices. But 2 isn't a choice. The explanation? This question has two possible solutions, not just one. The square root of 4 can be either 2 or −2. B is thus the answer.

Keep in mind that though there is only one right answer choice for each ACT question, that right answer may not be the one that occurs to you first. A common mistake is to pick an answer that seems "sort of" like the answer you're looking for even when you know it's wrong. Don't settle for second best. If you don't find your answer, don't assume that you're wrong. Try to think of another right way to answer the question.

#7—Guess Intelligently

An unanswered question is always wrong, but even a wild guess may be right. On the ACT, a guess can't hurt you, but it can help. In fact, smart guessing can make a big difference in your score. Always guess on every ACT question you can't answer.

You'll be doing two different kinds of guessing during your two sweeps through any subject test:

- Blind guessing (which you do mostly on questions you deem too hard or time-consuming even to try).

- Considered guessing (which you do mostly on questions that you do some work on, but can't make headway with).

Note

Even the luckiest guessers don't get every guessed question right, of course. But a guesser will get a higher ACT score than a nonguesser, picking up one question here and another there. It all adds up. The most important guessing advice we can give you is never leave any question blank.

Elimination Helps

If you guess blindly, you have one chance in four (or one in five, on the Math) of getting the question right. But if, before guessing, you can eliminate one or two choices as definitely wrong, you can improve those odds to one in three or even one in two. That translates into a higher score.

Smart Guessing

Make sure you get the points you deserve on the questions you can answer. But don't worry about the ones you have to guess on. Odds are good that you'll guess some correctly. And those correct guesses will increase your score just as much as if you'd figured out the answers.

When you guess blindly, you just choose any letter you feel like choosing (Many students like to choose B for Bart; few choose H for Homer). When you guess in a considered way, on the other hand, you've usually done enough work on a question to eliminate at least one or two choices. If you can eliminate any choices, you up the odds that you'll guess correctly.

Here are some fun facts about guessing: If you were to work on only half of the questions on the ACT but get them all right, then guess blindly on the other half of the questions, you would probably earn a composite ACT score of around 23 (assuming you had a statistically reasonable success rate on your guesses). A 23 would put you in roughly the top quarter of all those who take the ACT. It's a good score. And all you had to do was answer half the questions correctly.

On the other hand, if you were to hurry and finish all the questions, but get only half of them right, you'd probably earn only a 19, which is below average.

How? Why are you better off answering half and getting them all right instead of answering all and getting only half right?

Here's the trick. The student who answers half the questions right and skips the others can still take guesses on the unanswered questions—and odds are this student will have enough correct guesses to move up 4 points, from a 19 to a 23. But the student who answers all the questions and gets half wrong doesn't have the luxury of taking guesses.

In short: Guess if you can't figure out an answer for any question!

#8—Be Careful with the Answer Grid

Your ACT score is based on the answers you select on your answer grid. Even if you work out every ACT question correctly, you'll get a low score if you misgrid your answers. So be careful! Don't disdain the process of filling in those little "bubbles" on the grid. Sure, it's pretty mindless, but under time pressure it's easy to lose control and make mistakes. Don't let that happen to you.

Grid in Groups

You should, of course, circle the correct answers in your test booklet as you figure them out. But don't transfer those answers to the grid one by one. That takes too much time. Here's when to grid the answers you've chosen:

• In English, Reading, and Science Reasoning: at the end of each passage.

• In Math: at the end of every page (or every two-page spread).

It's important to develop a disciplined strategy for filling in the answer grid. We find that it's smart to grid the answers in groups rather than one question at a time. What this means is this: Circle the answers you get for each question in the test booklet as you figure them out. Then transfer those answers to the answer grid in groups of five or more (until you get close to the end of the section, when you start gridding answers one by one).

Gridding in groups like this cuts down on errors because you can focus on this one task and do it right. Gridding in groups also saves time you'd otherwise spend moving papers around, finding your place, and redirecting your mind. Answering ACT questions takes deep, hard thinking. Filling out answer grids is easy, but you have to be careful, especially if you do a lot of skipping around. Shifting between "hard thinking" and "careful bookkeeping" takes time and effort.

In English, Reading, and Science Reasoning, the test is divided naturally into groups of questions—the passages. For most students, it makes sense to circle your answers in your test booklet as you work them out. Then, when you're finished with each passage and its questions, grid the answers as a group on your answer grid.

In Math, the strategy has to be different because the Math test isn't broken up into natural groups. For most students, the best strategy for gridding Math questions is to mark your answers in the test booklet and then grid them when you reach the end of each page or every two pages. Since there are usually about five math questions per page, you'll probably be gridding math answers five or ten at a time.

No matter what test you're working on, though, you should start gridding your answers one at a time near the end of the subject test. You don't want to be caught with ungridded answers when time is called.

During the ACT, the proctor should warn you when you have about five minutes left on each subject test. But don't depend on proctors! Yes, they're usually nice people, but they can screw up once in a while. Instead, rely on you own watch. When there's five minutes left in a subject test, start gridding your answers one by one. With a minute or two left, start filling in everything you've left blank. Remember: Even one question left blank could cut your score.

#9—Use the Letters of the Choices to Stay on Track

One oddity about the ACT is that even-numbered questions have F, G, H, J (and, in Math, K) as answer choices, rather than A, B, C, D (and, again, E in Math). This might be a bit confusing at first, but you can make it work for you. A common mistake with the answer grid is to accidentally enter an answer one row up or down. On the ACT, that won't happen if you pay attention to the letter in the answer. If you're looking for an A and you see only F, G, H, J, and K, you'll know you're in the wrong row on the answer grid.

Another advantage of having answers F through K for even-numbered questions is that it makes you less nervous about patterns in the answers. It's common to start worrying if you've picked the same letter twice or three times in a row. Since the questions have different letters, this can't happen on the ACT. Of course, you could pick the first choice (A or F) for several questions in a row. This shouldn't worry you. It's common for the answers in the same position to be correct three times in a row, and even four times in a row isn't unheard of.

The moral of the story is simple: Worrying about patterns in the answers is a waste of time. Don't do it.

#10—Keep Track of Time

It's important to keep track of time while you take the ACT. During your two passes through each subject test, you really have to pace yourself. On average, English, Reading, and Science Reasoning questions should take about a half-minute each. Math questions should average less than one minute each.

Suggested Timings

Below is a list of suggested times for each kind of question and passage on the ACT. These are rough guidelines only! Remember to take into account the fact that you'll probably be taking two passes through the questions.

Passages
English, Reading—about
9 minutes each
(including questions)
Science—about 5 minutes
each (including questions)

Individual Questions
English, Reading, Science—
about 30 seconds each
Math—about 1 minute each

Set your watch to 12:00 at the beginning of each subject test, so it will be easy to check your time. Again, don't rely on proctors, even if they promise you that they will dutifully call out the time every five, ten, or fifteen minutes. Proctors get distracted once in a while.

For English, Reading, and Science questions, it's useful to check your timing as you grid the answers for each passage. English and Reading passages should take about nine minutes each. Science passages should average about five minutes. (In the Strategic Summaries, we've written out suggested checkpoints for each subject test.)

Easier questions should take less time, but harder ones will probably take more. In Math, for instance, you need to go much faster than one per minute during your first sweep. But at the end, you may spend two or three minutes on each of the hardest problems you work out.

TAKE CONTROL

A common thread in all ten strategies above is: Take control. That's Kaplan's ACT Mindset. You are the master of the test-taking experience. Do the questions in the order you want and in the way you want. Use your time for one purpose—to maximize your score. Don't get bogged down or agonize. Remember, you don't earn points for suffering, but you do earn points for moving on to the next question and getting it right.

In the next section of this book—the Skill-Building Workouts—we'll provide you with the arsenal of tools and techniques you need to take control of all four subject tests on the ACT.

BASIC STRATEGY REFERENCE SHEET

The Three Commandments

1. **Thou Shalt Learn the Test**

    *   Learn the directions before test day.
    *   Become familiar with all four subject tests.
    *   Get a sense of the range of difficulty of the questions.

2. **Thou Shalt Learn the Strategies**

    *   Develop a plan of attack for each subject test.
    *   Develop a guessing strategy that works for you.
    *   Find "unofficial" ways of finding answers fast.

3. **Thou Shalt Learn the Material**

    *   Bone up on weak areas.
    *   Find out what is and isn't part of the ACT knowledge base.
    *   Use the Math and English Appendixes to review important concepts.

Taking Control: The Top Ten Strategies

1. Do question triage.

2. Put the material into a form you can understand and use.

3. Ignore irrelevant issues.

4. Check back.

5. Answer the right question.

6. Look for the hidden answer.

7. Guess intelligently.

8. Be careful with the answer grid.

9. Use the letters of the choices to stay on track.

10. Keep track of time.

Skill-Building Workouts

English Workout 1:
When in Doubt, Take It Out

Highlights

- Sample questions

- Tips for answering English questions

- The Kaplan Method

- Practice questions

Think back to the last paper you had to write. Maybe your teacher assigned something like ten pages. You wrote and you wrote, and ended up with six pages. It was the night before the paper had to be turned in. You were out of research and ideas. But you knew what to do: pad it.

You're not alone. Almost all of us have padded papers at one time or another. The recipe for padding, in fact, is practically universal: You repeat yourself a few times. You trade short phrases for long-winded verbiage. You add a few offbeat ideas that don't really belong. And presto! Your six-page paper is transformed into a ten-page paper.

The ACT test makers know that most students pad. And they know how to punish you for it. In fact, almost a third of the English questions on the ACT are testing for the very same bad writing habits—long-windedness, repetitiousness, irrelevance—that padders tend to cultivate.

But there's hope. Once you know what ACT English is testing for, you can easily avoid making these common English mistakes. More than any other part of the exam, the ACT English subject test is predictable.

Emergency Plan

Here's how to use this chapter if you don't have much time. Go to p.48 and learn the Kaplan Method for English questions. Try the practice passage that follows. Check your answers. If you need more help, go back and read the whole chapter.

SAMPLE ECONOMY QUESTIONS

EXAMPLE

On recent ACTs, the shortest answer is <u>correct,</u>
                                              1
<u>and absolutely right</u>, for about half of all English
1

questions. Because this is <u>true</u>, a student who
                                2

knew no English at all could earn<u>—and justly so—</u>an
                                        3
English subject score of about 15. Such a student

could compare the choices carefully, and choose the

<u>single shortest one</u> every time. Where the answers
          4
were the same length, the student could pick at

random. On recent published ACTs, guessing

in this way would have yielded between 35 and

38 correct answers out of 75 questions.

Of course, you're going to <u>be doing</u> much
                                    5

better than that. You actually <u>are capable of</u>
                                        6

<u>speaking the English language</u>. You may not
          6
know every little rule of English usage, but you

certainly know something. Obviously, getting the

1. **A.** NO CHANGE
   B. correct
   C. right, that is, correct,
   D. correct, absolutely, and right,

2. **F.** NO CHANGE
   G. truthfully factual
   H. factually correct
   J. factual—and true too—

3. **A.** NO CHANGE
   B. , and justly so,
   C. and justify
   D. OMIT the underlined portion.

4. **F.** NO CHANGE
   G. singularly shortest one
   H. uniquely short item
   J. shortest one

5. **A.** NO CHANGE
   B. do
   C. achieve
   D. be, achieving,

6. **F.** NO CHANGE
   G. possess the capability of speaking that wonderful language called the language of England
   H. possess the capability of speaking in the land called England
   J. speak English

question right because you know the <u>right answer</u>
7
is better than getting it right because you guessed

well. But you should always remember that the ACT

test makers <u>like</u> the shortest answers.
8
Why? Why should the ACT make life so

easy for you? <u>Why can't History or Science classes</u>
9
<u>in high school be so easy?</u> Because usually, the
9

best way to write something really is the shortest

way to write it. The ACT can't help that, <u>any more</u>
10
<u>than you can help the fact that you must take the</u>
10
<u>ACT to get into college.</u> Good writing is
10

concise and <u>clear.</u> There are many rules of English,
11
but many of them grow from one dominant principle:

use only the words you need to say what you mean. ☐12

7. **A.** NO CHANGE
   B. best choice to select
   C. most correct answer of the choices given
   D. answer considered as correct

8. **F.** NO CHANGE
   G. have a habit of liking
   H. habitually tend to like
   J. are in the habit of liking

9. **A.** NO CHANGE
   B. Why isn't History or Science also easy to master!
   C. History and Science aren't so easy, either!
   D. OMIT the underlined portion.

10. **F.** NO CHANGE
    G. just as you are helpless to avoid the requirement of taking the ACT
    H. whether or not they'd want to
    J. OMIT the underlined portion and end the sentence with a period.

11. **A.** NO CHANGE
    B. clearly better
    C. translucent, like clear water
    D. clear. Thus it is short and to the point.

12. Suppose the author considers adding this final sentence: "Thus, if you can't say something nice, don't say anything at all." Would this be an effective conclusion for the paragraph?
    F. Yes, because this concept is needed to explain the meaning of the previous sentence.
    G. Yes, because it adds an uplifting moral tone to an otherwise depressing, amoral text.
    H. Yes, because this thought is relevant to the next paragraph.
    J. No, because the paragraph is not concerned with being nice.

The shortest answer happens to be correct in all twelve of the questions above. Note that "OMIT," where it is an option, is the shortest answer, since taking the material out leaves a shorter text than leaving anything in. In question 12, answer J is the "shortest" answer, since it leaves the proposed final sentence off entirely.

Think

On recent ACTs, the shortest answer has been correct on about half of all English questions. How can you take advantage of knowing this fact? Stay tuned and we'll tell you.

Redundancy

In questions 1–4 above, the wrong (long) answers are redundant. This means that they make the passage say the same thing twice. The ACT is very strict about redundancy: Never let the passage repeat itself.

Verbosity

The Answers

1. B, 2. F, 3. D, 4. J, 5. B, 6. J, 7. A, 8. F, 9. D, 10. J, 11. A, 12. J

In questions 5–8, the wrong (long) answers are verbose. They force the reader to read more words, but they are no clearer than the short answers and don't add meaning. This is another rule the ACT is very strict about: The best way to write something is the shortest way, as long as the short way doesn't violate any rules of writing mechanics (like grammar or punctuation) or contain vulgarities inappropriate to civilized discourse.

Think

Most ACT English questions test common sense, not tricky rules of grammar or punctuation. Remember: the ACT mindset isn't "Can I remember?" It's "I can figure it out!"

Relevance

Questions 9–12 test relevance. The wrong (long) answers introduce irrelevant concepts. The paragraph is about ACT English questions and how to answer them—it's not about History or Science classes, the necessity of taking the ACT, or that lovely translucence of clear water. Ideas that are not directly and logically tied in with the purpose of the passage should be removed. The ACT is very strict about relevance.

WHEN IN DOUBT . . . AND OTHER TIPS

On a real ACT, more than twenty questions—almost a third of all the English items—test your awareness of redundancy, verbosity, relevance, and similar issues. For these questions—which we call Economy Questions—the shortest answer is correct with great frequency. What that means is:

- If you're not sure whether an idea is redundant, it probably is, so take it out.

- If you're not sure whether a certain way to say something is too verbose, it probably is, so take it out.

- If you're not sure whether an idea is relevant, it probably isn't, so take it out.

  In other words: When in doubt, take it out.

Keep It Short—on All English Questions

Questions in which the lengths of the answers vary greatly, or questions that contain the answer choice "OMIT," are usually Economy Questions. For these questions, you should be especially inclined to choose the shortest choice. For the other questions, the shortest answer is not nearly as often correct. But even for these other questions, the shortest answer is frequently your best bet.

As we'll see in later workouts, the other English questions mostly test your ability to spot nonsense, bad grammar, and bad punctuation. But even in these cases, the rule "when in doubt, take it out" still holds. Most of the time, the best thing to do with nonsense is to take it out. And most grammatical mistakes can be solved by removing the offending words.

Because these issues of writing economy are so important to English questions of all kinds, we've made them the linchpin for our recommended approach to the English subject test. When approaching English questions, the very first question you should ask yourself is: "Does this stuff belong here? Can the passage or sentence work without it?"

Skimming English Questions

Before launching in and starting to correct the prose on an ACT English passage, it usually pays to skim each paragraph to get a sense of how it's shaped and what it's about. For most students, that makes correcting the underlined portions a little easier, since you'll have a better sense of the context. The skimming technique is simple: You skim a paragraph, then do the questions it contains, then skim the next paragraph, do the questions that one contains, etcetera. Some students even find it helpful to skim the entire passage before starting on the questions.

In this preliminary step, you needn't read carefully—you'll be doing that when you tackle the questions—but you should at least get a sense of what the passage is about and, just as important, whether it's written in a formal or informal style (we'll talk more about the tone and style of passages in English Workout 2).

After your brief skim of a paragraph (it should only take a few seconds), it's time to start work on its questions.

THE KAPLAN THREE-STEP METHOD

Here's our three-step (or really, three-question) approach to ACT English questions.

1. Does This Stuff Belong Here?

As we've seen, writing economy is very near to the hearts of ACT test makers. So ask yourself: Does the underlined section belong? Is it expressed as succinctly as possible? If the answer is no, choose the answer that gets rid of the stuff that doesn't belong. If the answer is yes, move on to . . .

2. Does This Stuff Make Sense?

The ACT test makers want simple, easy-to-understand prose. They expect everything to fit together logically. Does the underlined part of the passage make logical sense? If the answer is no, select the choice that turns nonsense into sense. If the answer is yes, go on to . . . .

3. Does This Stuff Sound Like English?

Many grammar errors will sound wrong to your ear. Even the ones that don't will be recognizable to you if you study our twenty Classic Grammar Errors in English Workout 3 and create a "flag list" of the ones you're shaky on. Choose the answer that corrects the error and makes the sentence sound right.

(Note: Steps 2 and 3 will be covered more thoroughly in English Workouts 2 and 3.)

Most ACT English test takers are so worried about grammar and punctuation that they don't think about anything else. That's the wrong mindset. Don't think too much about technical rules. As indicated in the approach above, the first thing to think about is getting rid of unnecessary or irrelevant words. Only after you've decided that the underlined selection is concise and relevant do you go on to Steps 2 and 3. Note that this means you won't necessarily be going through all three steps on any English question. The answer can come at any point in the three-step method.

Practice Being Economical

Now try the next practice passage, keeping in mind the approach you just learned:

EXAMPLE

The Phoenix Cardinals are the <u>oldest,</u>
                   1
<u>most long-established, longest-playing</u> football club
              1
in the National Football League (NFL). They

began as the Racine Avenue Cardinals on Chicago's

1.　**A.** NO CHANGE
  B. oldest
  C. most long-established
  D. longest-playing

South Side sometime in the 1870s or <u>1880s, during</u>
                                    2

<u>the nineteenth century</u>. At that time, the
        2

Cardinals were an amateur team <u>that did not play</u>
                                  3

<u>for money</u>.
   3

There was <u>nothing in the world which so</u>
               4

<u>much as resembled</u> pro football in those
   4

days. The Racine Avenue Cardinals played

amateur ball all through the late 1800s <u>and the game</u>
                                  5

<u>they played was football, no doubt about it</u>.
        5

    None of the other clubs in the NFL was

formed before the league itself was established in

1919. When the NFL was first established, the

Cardinals remained <u>aloof and thumbed their noses at</u>
                         6

<u>it</u>. Professional football had a bad reputation, and
6

the Cardinals were <u>greatly prideful</u> of their record as
                    7

amateurs. But in 1921, the Cardinals decided to

join the NFL. They were required to play a "game

to the death" with the Chicago Tigers <u>(the Detroit</u>
                             8

<u>Tigers are a baseball team)</u>. Whichever team won
       8

would be allowed to stay in Chicago; the other team

2.
- **F.** NO CHANGE
- **G.** 1880s
- **H.** the nineteenth century
- **J.** during the 1880s

3.
- **A.** NO CHANGE
- **B.** that played for the pure joy of the sport
- **C.** that played on a nonprofessional level
- **D.** OMIT the underlined portion and end the sentence with a period.

4.
- **F.** NO CHANGE
- **G.** nothing anything like
- **H.** no such thing as
- **J.** not even a dream of

5.
- **A.** NO CHANGE
- **B.** no doubt about it
- **C.** to be assured it was football
- **D.** OMIT the underlined portion and end the sentence with a period.

6.
- **F.** NO CHANGE
- **G.** aloof.
- **H.** aloof and tried to ignore it.
- **J.** off in their own corner.

7.
- **A.** NO CHANGE
- **B.** full of great pride
- **C.** proud
- **D.** gratefully proud

8.
- **F.** NO CHANGE
- **G.** (not to be confused with the Detroit Tigers, a baseball team)
- **H.** (not the more famous modern-day Detroit Tigers baseball team)
- **J.** OMIT the underlined portion and end the sentence with a period.

would <u>have to move</u>. The Cardinals won.
                9
The Tigers moved away and soon went

bankrupt. The Cardinals are thus the only NFL

team that won their franchise on the football field.

   Ironically, the team that fought to stay in

Chicago eventually moved away. The Cardinals

were rarely as <u>successfully able to win games or</u>
                                 10
<u>make money</u> as the Chicago Bears, their crosstown
   10
rivals. Fans gradually deserted the Cardinals, so the

team moved—to St. Louis in 1958 and to Phoenix in

1986, seeking a more profitable market.

   Maybe Phoenix <u>is the place in which</u> the Cardinals
                          11
are destined to stay. Some people say that the name

"Cardinal" was a nineteenth-century name for a

mythical bird that arose from its own ashes <u>in the</u>
                                              12
<u>fireplace</u>, and that the Cardinals date back to 1871,
   12

the year of the great Chicago fire—which may have

begun on Racine Avenue <u>(or maybe not)</u>. Chicago
                          13
was proud to rise from its ashes like the mythical

9. A. NO CHANGE
B. be forced to move along
C. be legally obliged, by injunction, to relocate their franchise
D. be obligated to be moving out

10. F. NO CHANGE
G. successful at winning
H. winning or profitable, a team,
J. successful

11. A. NO CHANGE
B. is the place at which
C. is where
D. OMIT the underlined portion.

12. F. NO CHANGE
G. that had consumed it
H. created by the fire that had consumed it
J. OMIT the underlined portion.

13. A. NO CHANGE
B. according to ironic legend
C. resulting from violations of the fire code and a cow in a barn
D. OMIT the underlined portion and end the sentence with a period.

Cardinal. The <u>name that is more common</u> for that
14

mythical firebird is—the Phoenix. 15

14. **F.** NO CHANGE
    G. common name
    H. name that is famous
    J. common way of speaking

15. Suppose the author wishes to add a new paragraph at the end of the existing passage quickly summarizing the history of Canadian football. Would this be appropriate, in light of the content and style of the rest of the passage?
    A. Yes, because it is only fair to mention Canadian football at least once in the passage.
    B. Yes, because the Phoenix Cardinals now play Canadian football.
    C. No, because the passage does not focus on sports history.
    D. No, because the passage has nothing to do with Canadian football.

Did you see the point? On every regular format question except number 11, you shouldn't have gotten past the first step of the three-step method, because all of the questions test economy errors. In fact, the shortest answers are correct on every question here except that one. In 11, if you omit the phrase "is the place in which," the sentence doesn't make any sense, meaning that you'd correct it in Step 2 of the three-step approach. (Note: This passage is not typical—most ACT passages don't consist exclusively of Economy Questions—but we used this passage to drive home the point about choosing concise answers on the English subject test.)

The Answers

1. B, 2. G, 3. D, 4. H, 5. D, 6. G, 7. C, 8. J, 9. A, 10. J, 11. C, 12. J, 13. D, 14. G, 15. D

> HINT: Remember that "OMIT," when it is an option, is always the shortest answer. For instance, D is "shorter" than A and B in question 15 because not including a new paragraph makes the passage shorter than including it. (But notice that you still had to decide between C and D in that question.)

Many students might object to answer J in question 10, because the word *successful* alone does not indicate the kind of success meant. But use common sense. What would make a professional football team successful? Winning, and making money. Thus, the concepts of "winning" and "profitability" are implicit in the notion that the Cardinals are (now) a successful team. The ACT expects you to cut anything that isn't absolutely needed.

Remember: *When in doubt, take it out.*

5

Math Workout 1: The End Justifies the Means

Highlights

- The ACT Math Mindset

- The Kaplan Method

- The two-pass plan

- Calculator tips

All that matters on the ACT is correct answers. Your goal on the Math subject test is to get as many correct answers as you can in 60 minutes. It doesn't matter what you do (short of cheating, naturally) to get those correct answers.

You don't have to do every problem the way your math teacher would. Be open to clever and original solution methods. All that matters is that your methods be quick and that they get you a good number of correct answers. How many correct answers you need depends on what kind of score you're aiming for, but chances are you don't have to get so many right as you might think to get a good score. Yes, it's a tough test, but it's graded "on the curve."

As we've pointed out, the ACT is different from the typical high school test. On a typical high school math test, you get a series of problems just like the ones you've been doing in class and for homework over the previous week or so. Since you're being tested on a relatively narrow scope of topics, you're expected to get almost every question right.

ACT math is different. The scope of what's tested is deliberately wide so that every student will get an opportunity to demonstrate his or her strengths, wherever they may lie.

Emergency Plan

Here's how to use this chapter if you don't have much time. Go to p.56 and learn the Kaplan Method for ACT math, trying the sample questions that follow. Read the sidebars throughout the whole chapter for quick ACT strategy tips.

Question Breakdown

Each ACT Math subject test includes:

- 24 Prealgebra and Elementary Algebra questions (corresponding roughly to the Math Appendix, #1–65)

- 10 Intermediate Algebra questions (Math Appendix, #66–70)

- 8 Coordinate Geometry questions (Math Appendix, #71–77)

- 14 Plane Geometry questions (Math Appendix, #78–95)

- 4 Trigonometry questions (Math Appendix, #96–100)

Nobody needs to get all 60 questions right. The average ACT student gets less than half of the math questions right. You need only about 40 correct answers to get your math score over 25—just two right out of every three questions gets you a great score!

THE ACT MATH MINDSET

According to an old legend at M.I.T., a physics professor once asked the following question on a final exam: *How could a barometer be used to determine the height of a tower?*

To answer the question, most students worked out complex equations based on the fact that air pressure (which is what a barometer measures) decreases at higher altitudes. But one student made three suggestions instead:

1. Measure the length of the barometer, then use the barometer as a ruler and measure the tower.

2. Drop the barometer and time its fall, keeping in mind that the acceleration of falling objects is about 32 ft/sec^2.

3. Find the person who built the tower and say, "I'll give you a nice barometer if you tell me how tall your tower is."

Guess which student got an A . . .

On the ACT, as in college and beyond, you'll sometimes be called upon to do more than merely regurgitate memorized facts and unquestioningly follow prepackaged procedures. True, some ACT math questions are straightforward: As soon as you understand what the question's asking, you know what to do. But more challenging—and more fun (really)—are the ACT math questions that aren't what they seem at first glance. These are the questions that call for creative solutions.

Don't Be Obedient

Too often, high school math instruction degenerates into obedience training: You show your work on tests to prove that you did everything the way it was taught in class. If you show the "right" kind of work, you get partial or even full credit, regardless of whether your answers are correct. If you're lucky, your teacher might even give you a nice pat on the back.

Us, Too

When we say to do it your way, that applies to us, too. Don't blindly follow the Kaplan strategies in this book. Use your strengths. If you can think of a good way to do a problem— JUST DO IT!

On the ACT, though, there's no partial credit. All that matters is the right answer. It makes no difference how you find it. In fact, as we'll see, it's sometimes safer and faster if you don't do ACT problems the "right" way—the way you've been taught in school. For a lot of ACT math problems there's more than one way to find the answer. And many of these other ways are faster than the so-called right way.

KAPLAN

Of course, old habits die hard. For years you've been subjected to obedience-training math. You've learned to waste time writing everything out. You've learned to depend on remembering "how you're supposed to do it" instead of finding ways to do it faster and smarter. Maybe you've even learned not to care much about getting right answers. It'll take something pretty drastic to break away. The drastic step we recommend is: Don't show your work.

Don't Show Your Work

No, we don't mean that you should try to do every ACT math problem in your head. Nobody could do that—though most people could and should do a lot less paper calculation than they do. Go ahead and use your pencil to calculate and organize. But don't put stuff down just for the sake of getting it on paper. Don't write out every step. Don't worry about whether you're being neat or whether anybody'd be able to understand your notes. Jot things down for yourself.

Only the Bubbles Count

You will not get credit for anything you write under "DO YOUR FIGURING HERE." You get credit only for correct answers correctly gridded into the "bubbles" on your answer sheet.

If you do every problem the way your algebra teacher would want you to, you may earn his or her undying gratitude, but you won't achieve your goal of getting as many correct answers as possible. You don't have time to use the textbook approach on every question. You don't have time to write out every step.

Be a Thinker—Not a Number Cruncher

One reason you're given limited time for the Math subject test is that the ACT is testing your ability to think, not your willingness to do a lot of mindless calculations. They're looking for creative thinkers, not human calculators. So, one of your guiding principles for ACT math should be: Work less, but think harder.

If you want to get the best score you can, you need to be always on the lookout for quicker ways to solve problems. Here's an example that could take a lot more time than it needs to.

EXAMPLE

1. When $\frac{4}{11}$ is converted to a decimal, the 50th digit after the decimal point is
   A. 2
   B. 3
   C. 4
   D. 5
   E. 6

It seems that when you convert $\frac{4}{11}$ to a decimal, there are at least 50 digits after the decimal point. The question asks for the 50th. One way to answer this question would be to divide 11 into 4, carrying the division out to 50 decimal places. That method would work, but it would take forever. It's not worth spending that much time on one question.

No ACT math question should take more than a minute to take care of, if you know what you're doing. There has to be a faster way to solve this problem. There must be some kind of pattern you can take advantage of. And what kind of pattern might there be with a decimal?

How about a *repeating* decimal?!

In fact, that's exactly what you have here. The decimal equivalent of $\frac{4}{11}$ is a repeating decimal: $\frac{4}{11} = .3636363636\ldots$

Be Creative

Be creative in the process you use to solve problems, not in the answer choices you pick. Don't try to select answers that somehow "look good." The ACT is not a beauty contest.

The 1st, 3rd, 5th, 7th, and 9th digits are each 3. The 2nd, 4th, 6th, 8th, and 10th digits are each 6. Put simply, odd-numbered digits are 3s and even-numbered digits are 6s. The 50th digit is an even-numbered digit, so it's a 6 and the answer is E.

What looked at first glance like a "fractions and decimals" problem turned out to be something of an "odds and evens" problem.

If you don't use creative shortcuts on problems like this one, you'll get bogged down, you'll run out of time, and you won't get a lot of correct answers.

Question 1 demonstrates how the ACT designs problems to reward clever thinking and to punish students who blindly "go through the motions."

But how do you get yourself into a creative mindset on the Math subject test? For one thing, you have to take the time to understand thoroughly each problem you decide to work on. Most students are so nervous about time that they skim each math problem and almost immediately start computing with their pencils. But that's the wrong way of thinking. Sometimes on the ACT, you have to take time to save time. A few extra moments spent understanding a math problem can save many extra moments of computation or other drudgery.

THE THREE-STEP METHOD FOR ACT MATH

At Kaplan, we've developed this take-time-to-save-time philosophy into a three-step method for ACT math problems. The approach is designed to help you find the fast, inventive solutions that the ACT rewards. The steps are:

1. Understand

Focus first on the question stem (the part before the answer choices) and make sure you understand the problem. Sometimes you'll want to read the stem twice, or rephrase it in a way you can better understand. Think to yourself: "What kind of problem is this? What am I looking for? What am I given?" Don't pay too much attention to the answer choices yet, though you may want to give them a quick glance just to see what form they're in.

2. Analyze

Think for a moment and decide on a plan of attack. Don't start crunching numbers until you've given the problem a little thought. Ask: "What's a quick and reliable way to find the correct answer?" Look for patterns and shortcuts, using common sense and your knowledge of the test to find the creative solutions that will get you more right answers in less time. Try to solve the problem without focusing on the answer choices.

3. Select

Once you get an answer—or once you get stuck—check the answer choices. If you got an answer and it's listed as one of the choices, chances are it's right—fill in the appropriate bubble and move on. But if you didn't get an answer, narrow down the choices as best you can by a process of elimination and then guess.

Each of these steps can happen in a matter of seconds. And it may not always be clear when you've finished with one step and moved on to the next. Sometimes you'll know how to attack a problem the instant you read and understand it.

Here's how the Three-Step Method could be applied to Question 1 above.

Step 1: Understand

First, we made sure we understood what the problem was asking for: the 50th digit after the decimal point in the decimal equivalent of a certain fraction. Because we knew what digit and decimal equivalent mean, it took only a second to understand what the problem was asking.

Step 2: Analyze

Second, and most crucially, we analyzed the situation and thought about a plan of attack before we tried to solve the problem. We realized that the "obvious" method would take too long, so we figured out a creative approach that got us an answer of 6 in just a few seconds.

Step 3: Select

Third, we looked at the answer choices, found 6, and selected choice E.

> **Think**
>
> Most students hate it when they solve a problem and their answer isn't among the choices. But actually, not having the answer you want among the choices helps you if you've made a mistake, because it makes you realize that you did something wrong. You can then go back and do the problem right.

The Three-Step Method isn't a rigid procedure; it's a set of guidelines that will keep you on track, moving quickly, and evading pitfalls. Just remember to think before you solve: Focus on the question stem first and save the answer choices for later.

The First Step: Understand

To understand an ACT math problem, you first have to understand the language. Mathematicians are generally very precise in their use of language. They choose their words carefully and mean exactly what they say.

In everyday life we can be a little loose with math terminology. It doesn't really matter that Harvard Square is not a square or that a batting average is not an average.

In an ACT math problem, however, words have precise meanings. You don't need to memorize definitions—you'll never have to recite one on the ACT—but you do need to understand what the question writer means.

Here's an example in which understanding the jargon is half the battle:

EXAMPLE

2. If the sum of five consecutive even integers is equal to their product, what is the greatest of the five integers?
   F. 4
   G. 10
   H. 14
   J. 16
   K. 20

Step 1: Understand

Before you can begin to solve this problem, you have to figure out what it's asking, and to do that you need to know the meanings of *sum*, *product*, *consecutive*, *even*, and *integer*. Remember, take control. Put the question stem into words you can understand. What the question stem is really saying here is that when you add up these five consecutive even integers you get the same thing as when you multiply them.

Step 2: Analyze

How are we going to figure out what these five numbers are? We could set up an equation:

$$x + (x - 2) + (x - 4) + (x - 6) + (x - 8) = x(x - 2)(x - 4)(x - 6)(x - 8)$$

But there's no way you'll have time to solve an equation like this! So don't even try. Come up with a better way.

Let's stop and think logically about this one for a moment. When we think about sums and products, it's natural to think mostly of positive integers. With positive integers, we would generally expect the product to be *greater* than the sum.

But what about negative integers? Hmm. Well, the sum of five negatives is negative, and the product of five negatives is also negative, and generally the product will be "more negative" than the sum, so with negative integers the product will be *less* than the sum.

So when will the product and sum be the same? How about right at the boundary of positive and negative—that is, around 0? The five consecutive even integers with equal product and sum are: –4, –2, 0, 2, and 4.

$$(-4) \times (-2) \times 0 \times 2 \times 4 = (-4) + (-2) + 0 + 2 + 4$$

The product and sum are both 0. Ha! We've done it!

Step 3: Select

The question asks for the greatest of the five integers, which is 4, choice F.

You've probably encountered every math term that appears on the ACT sometime in your high school math career, but you may not remember exactly what every one of them means. The Math Glossary at the back of this book is a complete but compact list of the terminology you need for ACT math problems. Look it over. Mark or jot down the ones you're not so sure of for future reference. And be sure to use the Glossary to look up any unfamiliar term you encounter while practicing with ACT math questions.

Definition Alert

As you refresh your memory of key terminology, watch out for technicalities. Here are a few examples of such technicalities (by the way, these are great for stumping your know-it-all friends):

- "Integers" include 0 and negative whole numbers. If a question says "x and y are integers," it's not ruling out numbers like 0 and -1.

- "Evens and odds" include 0 and negative whole numbers. Zero and -2 are even numbers; -1 is an odd number.

- "Prime numbers" do *not* include 1. The technical definition of a prime number is: "a positive integer with exactly two distinct positive integer factors." Two is prime because it has exactly two positive factors: 1 and 2. Four is not prime because it has three positive factors (1, 2, and 4)—too many! And 1 is not prime because it has only one positive factor (1)—too few!

- "Remainders" are integers. If a question asks for the remainder when 15 is divided by 2, don't say "15 divided by 2 is 7.5, so the remainder is .5." What you should say is: "15 divided by 2 is 7 with a remainder of 1."

- The $\sqrt{}$ symbol represents the positive square root only. The equation $x^2 = 9$ has two solutions: 3 and -3. But when you see $\sqrt{9}$, it means positive 3 only.

- "Rectangles" include squares. The definition of a rectangle is a four-sided figure with four right angles. It doesn't matter if the length and width are the same or not—if it has four right angles, it's a rectangle. When a question refers to "rectangle ABCD," it's not ruling out a square.

The Second Step: Analyze

Now, once you're sure you've gotten a math problem into a form you can understand, you still have to know what to do with the problem. Sometimes you'll know what to do the moment you understand the problem. Here's an example.

EXAMPLE

3. What is the value of $x^2 + 3x - 9$ when $x = -3$?
   A. -27
   B. -9
   C. -6
   D. 0
   E. 9

Step 1: Understand

You've probably seen dozens of problems just like this. If so, then you realize right away that what it's asking is, "What do you get when you plug $x = -3$ into $x^2 + 3x^2 - 9$?"

Step 2: Analyze

So that's what you do—plug it in and "solve":

$$x^2 + 3x - 9 = (-3)^2 + 3(-3) - 9$$
$$= 9 + (-9) - 9$$
$$= -9$$

Step 3: Select

The answer is B.

So this is a case where you knew exactly what to do as soon as you understood what the question was asking. But sometimes you're not so lucky. Let's look at a case where the method of solution is not so obvious, even after you "understand" the stem:

EXAMPLE

4. What is the greatest of the numbers 150, 501, 225, 252, 410?
   F. 150
   G. 501
   H. 225
   J. 252
   K. 410

Step 1: Understand

It's not hard to figure out what the question is asking: Which of five numbers is the greatest? But the five numbers are all written as powers, some of which we don't have time to calculate. Yikes! How are we going to compare them?

Step 2: Analyze

If all the powers had the same base or the same exponent, or if they could all be rewritten with a common base or exponent, we could compare all five at once. As it is, though, we should take two at a time.

Compare 1^{50} and 50^1 to start: $1^{50} = 1$, while $50^1 = 50$, so there's no way choice F could be the biggest.

Next, compare 50^1 and 2^{25}. We don't have time to calculate 2^{25}, but we can see that it doesn't take anywhere near 25 factors of 2 to get over 50. In fact, 2^6 is 64, already more than 50, so 2^{25} is much, much more than 50. That eliminates G.

Choice J, 25^2, doesn't take too long to calculate: $25 \times 25 = 625$. How does that compare to 2^{25}? Once again, with a little thought, we realize that it doesn't take 25 factors of 2 to get over 625. That eliminates J.

The last comparison is easy because choice K, 4^{10}, can be rewritten as $(2^2)^{10} = 2^{20}$, in that form clearly less than 2^{25}. That eliminates K.

Step 3: Select

So the answer is H.

Know When to Skip

At any time during the Three-Step problem-solving process you could choose to cut bait and skip the question. Almost everyone should skip at least some questions the first time through.

If you know your own strengths and weaknesses, you can sometimes choose to skip a question while still in Step 1—"Understand." For example, suppose you never studied trigonometry. Maybe you think that a secant is something that sailors sing while climbing up the yardarms. Well, every form of the ACT includes exactly four trigonometry questions, and it's not hard to spot them. Why waste a second on such a question? Skip it! You don't need those four measly questions to get a great score. And since you know a second visit later won't help any, you might as well go ahead and make some random guesses.

It can be harder to decide when to skip a question if you understand it, but then get stuck in Step 2—"Analyze." Suppose you just don't see how to solve it. Don't give up too quickly. Sometimes it takes a half-minute or so before you see the light. But don't get bogged down either. Never spend more than a minute on a question the first time through the section. No single question is worth it. Be prepared to leave a question and come back to it later. Often, on the second try, you'll see something you didn't see before. That old light bulb will light up over your head and you'll be on your way.

> **Analysis Is Where It's At**
>
> As you can tell already from the few examples we've looked at, Step 2— "Analyze"—is where you'll be doing most of your serious thinking. The other two Math Workouts will address Step 2 in greater detail. Math Workout 2 will focus on analyzing Algebra and Coordinate Geometry problems. Math Workout 3 will focus on analyzing Geometry and Trigonometry problems.

Of course, eventually you're going to grid in an answer choice for every question, even the ones you don't understand. The first time through the section, however, you should concentrate on the questions you understand.

KAPLAN'S TWO-PASS PLAN FOR THE ACT MATH SUBTEST

We recommend that you plan two "passes" through the Math subtest.

- **First Pass:** Examine each problem in order. Do every problem you understand. Don't skip too hastily—sometimes it takes a few seconds of thought before you see how to do it—but don't get bogged down. Never spend more than a minute on any question in the first pass. This first pass should take about 45 minutes.

- **Second Pass:** Use the last 15 minutes to go back to the questions that stumped you the first time through. Sometimes a second look is all you need—after going away and then coming back you'll sometimes suddenly see what to do. In most cases, though, you'll still be stumped by the question stem, so it's time to give the answer choices a try. Work by process of elimination, and guess. Be sure to select an answer for every question, even if it's just a blind guess.

Do the Ones You Can

Don't worry about the ones you can't do. Get your points where you can, and don't expect miracles in the hard problems. Guess and move on.

Never plan on visiting a question a third time. It's inefficient to go back and forth that much. Every time you leave a question and come back to it, you have to take at least a few seconds to refamiliarize yourself with the problem. Always grid in an answer choice on the second pass—even if it's just a wild guess. At the end of the second pass, every question should be answered.

Don't Worry. Be Happy!

If you skip a whole half of the test, you can double the amount of time you have to work on the problems you actually do—virtually making it certain that you make no careless errors.

Don't worry if you don't work on every question in the section. The average ACT test taker gets fewer than half of the problems right. You can score in the top quarter of all ACT test takers if you can do just *half* of the problems on the test, get every single one of them right, and guess blindly on the other half. If you did just *one-third* of the problems and got every one right, then guessed blindly on the other forty problems, you would still earn an average score. And if you had time to make *smart* guesses, eliminating choices that are way off, you'd score even better.

Don't Make Careless Mistakes

Most students don't worry too much about careless errors. Since in school (where you show your work) you can still get partial credit even if you make a careless calculation error, many students think that careless errors somehow "don't count." Not so on the ACT. There are only so many problems you'll know how to do. Some of the problems will be impossible for you. So you make or break your score on the problems you can do. You can't afford to miss one easy problem!

Unless math is a very strong area for you, thereby giving you a real chance at almost every question, the best way to maximize your score is to make sure that you work on the ones you deserve to get correct. Don't worry about getting to every problem (though, of course, you should mark an answer for every problem on your answer grid, even if it's a blind guess).

If math is a strong point for you, don't give up on any of the problems. Don't get complacent on easy problems—that causes careless errors. For strong students, the easy problems may be the most challenging. You have to find a way to answer them quickly and accurately in order to have time for the tougher ones. You won't have time for the hard problems unless you save some time on the easy ones.

Stuck? Try Guesstimates and Estimates

Sometimes when you understand a problem but can't figure out how to solve it, you can at least get a general idea of how big the answer is—what is sometimes called a "ballpark estimate," "guess-estimate," or "guesstimate." You may not know whether you are looking at something the size of an African elephant or the size of an Indian elephant, but you may be pretty sure it isn't the size of a mouse and it isn't the size of a battleship.

Here's a question that's not hard to understand but is hard to solve if you don't remember the rules for simplifying and adding radicals:

EXAMPLE

5. $\dfrac{\sqrt{32} + \sqrt{24}}{\sqrt{8}} = ?$
   A. $\sqrt{7}$
   B. $\sqrt{2} + \sqrt{3}$
   C. $2 + \sqrt{3}$
   D. $\sqrt{2} + 3$
   E. 7

Step 1: Understand

The question wants you to simplify the given expression, which includes three radicals. In other words, turn the radicals into numbers you can use, then work out the fraction.

Step 2: Analyze

The best way to solve this problem would be to apply the rules of radicals— but what if you don't remember them? Don't give up; you can still guesstimate. In the question stem, the numbers under the radicals are not too far away from perfect squares. You could round $\sqrt{32}$ off to $\sqrt{36}$, which is 6. You could round $\sqrt{24}$ to $\sqrt{25}$, which is 5. And you could round $\sqrt{8}$ off to $\sqrt{9}$, which is 3. So the expression is now $\frac{6+5}{3}$, which is $3\frac{2}{3}$. That's just a guesstimate, of course—the actual value might be something a bit less or a bit more than that.

Step 3: Select

Now look at the answer choices. Choice A—$\sqrt{7}$—is less than 3, so it's too small. Choice B—$\sqrt{2} + \sqrt{3}$—is about 1.4 + 1.7, or just barely more than 3, so it seems a little small, too. Choice C—$2 + \sqrt{3}$—is about 2 + 1.7, or about 3.7—that's very close to our guesstimate! We still have to check the other choices. Choice D—$\sqrt{2} + 3$—is about 1.4 + 3, or 4.4—too big. And choice E—7—is obviously way too big. Looks like our best bet is C—and C in fact is the correct answer.

Guesstimating

Guesstimating is much cruder than the kind of estimating and rounding off you are usually taught to do in school. The purpose of using guesstimates is to quickly and easily find the smallest and largest that the answer could possibly be. It's like working on the edges of a puzzle first. Our advice: Don't bother to make a guesstimate if you can't think of an easy way to do it.

NOTE: *To review the traditional textbook methods for adding and simplifying radicals, see the Math Appendix.*

Learn Common Estimates

It pays to learn the approximate value of these three irrational numbers:

$$\sqrt{2} \approx 1.4$$
$$\sqrt{3} \approx 1.7$$
$$\pi \approx 3.14$$

Stuck? Try Eyeballing

There is another simple but powerful strategy that should give you at least a 50-50 chance on almost any diagram question: When in doubt, use your eyes. Trust common sense and careful thinking; don't worry if you've forgotten most of the geometry you ever knew. For almost half of all diagram questions you can get a reasonable answer without solving anything: Just eyeball it.

The math directions say, "Illustrative figures are NOT necessarily drawn to scale," but in fact they almost always are. You're never really *supposed* to just eyeball the figure, but it makes a lot more sense than random guessing. Occasionally, eyeballing can narrow the choices down to one likely candidate.

Here's a difficult geometry question that you might just decide to eyeball:

EXAMPLE

6. In the figure below, points *A*, *B*, and *C* lie on a circle centered at *O*. Triangle *AOC* is equilateral, and the length of *OC* is 3 inches. What is the length, in inches, of arc *ABC*?

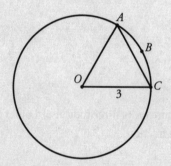

 F. 3
 G. π
 H. 2π
 J. 3π
 K. 6π

Step 1: Understand

There's an "equilateral" triangle that connects the center and two points on the circumference of a circle. You're looking for the length of the arc that goes from A to C.

Step 2: Analyze

What you're "supposed" to do to answer this question is recall and apply the formula for the length of an arc. But suppose you don't remember that formula (most people don't). Should you give up and take a wild guess?

No. You can eyeball it. If you understand the question well enough to realize that "equilateral" means all sides are equal, then you know immediately that side $\overline{AC}$ is 3 inches long. Now look at arc *ABC* compared to side $\overline{AC}$. Suppose you were an ant, and you had to walk from *A* to *C*. If you walked along line segment $\overline{AC}$, it would be a 3-inch trip. About how long a walk would it be along arc *ABC*? Clearly more, but not much more, than 3 inches.

Step 3: Select

Now look at the answer choices. Choice F, 3, is no good: You know the arc is more than 3 inches. All the other choices are in terms of π. Just think of π as "a bit more than 3," and you will quickly see that only one answer choice is in the right ballpark. Choice G—π—would be "a bit more than 3," which sounds pretty good. Choice H—2π—would be "something more than 6." Already that's way too big. Choices J and K are even bigger. It sure looks like the answer has to be G—and it is.

> **NOTE:** *If you want to review the traditional textbook approach to arcs, see the Math Appendix.*

This is a pretty hard question. Not many ACT students would be able to solve question 6 the textbook way. If *you* could, great! That's the way to do it if you know how. Solving the problem is always more reliable than eyeballing.

But when you *don't* know how to solve a diagram problem, or if you think it would take forever to get an answer, eyeballing and eliminating answer choices sure beats wild guessing. Sometimes, as with question 6, you might even be able to narrow the choices down to the one that's probably correct.

In the other two Math Workouts, you'll learn a few special solution methods for some of the more intriguing ACT problems in algebra, coordinate geometry, plane geometry, and trigonometry.

TO CALCULATE OR NOT TO CALCULATE

Since fall 1996, students have been permitted to use calculators on the Math section of the ACT. The good news for noncalculator users is that you never *absolutely need* to use a calculator on the ACT. No math question on the ACT requires messy or tedious calculations. But while the calculator can't answer questions for you, it can keep you from making computational errors on questions you know how to solve. The bad news, however, is that a calculator can actually cost you time if you overuse it. Take a look at this example:

> **Reminder**
>
> If you have forgotten any of the geometry terms discussed in this Workout, look them up in the Math Glossary!

EXAMPLE

7. The sum of all the integers from 1 to 44, inclusive, is subtracted from the sum of all the integers from 7 to 50, inclusive. What is the result?

 A.   6
 B. 44
 C. 50
 D. 264
 E. 300

Trap

If a problem seems to involve a lot of calculation, look for a quicker way.

You could . . . add all the integers from 1 through 44, and then all the integers from 7 through 50, and then subtract the first sum from the second. And then punch in all the numbers into the calculator. And then hope you didn't hit any wrong buttons.

But that's the long way . . . and the wrong way. That way involves hitting over 250 keys on your calculator. It'll take too long, and you're too likely to make a mistake. The amount of computation involved in solving this problem tells you that there must be an easier way. Remember, no ACT problem absolutely requires the use of a calculator.

The Right Way—Think First

Let's look at that problem again:

EXAMPLE

7. The sum of all the integers from 1 to 44, inclusive, is subtracted from the sum of all the integers from 7 to 50, inclusive. What is the result?

 A.   6
 B. 44
 C. 50
 D. 264
 E. 300

A calculator *can* help you on this question, but you have to think first. Both sums contain the same number of consecutive integers, and each integer in the first sum has a corresponding integer 6 greater than it in the second sum. Here's the scratchwork:

```
   1      7
  +2     +8
  +3     +9
   .      .
   .      .
   .      .
 +42    +48
 +43    +49
 +44    +50
```

This means there are 44 pairs of integers which are each 6 apart. So the total difference between the two sums will be the difference between each pair of integers, times the number of pairs. Now you can pull out your calculator, punch "6 × 44 =" and get the correct answer of 264 with little or no time wasted. Mark (D) in your test booklet and move on.

Using the Calculator to Save Time

Of course, there will be many situations on the ACT in which using a calculator can *save* you time. Here's an ACT trig question that's much easier with a calculator:

> ### Find the Pattern, Save Some Time
>
> Spotting the pattern shows you how a calculator can save time.

EXAMPLE

8. sin 495° =

F. $-\dfrac{\sqrt{2}}{2}$

G. $-\dfrac{1}{2}$

H. $\dfrac{1}{2}$

J. $\dfrac{\sqrt{2}}{2}$

K. $\dfrac{3\sqrt{2}}{2}$

Without a calculator this is a very difficult problem. To find a trigonometric function of an angle greater than or equal to 90°, sketch a circle of radius 1 and centered at the origin of the coordinate grid. Start from the point (1, 0) and rotate the appropriate number of degrees counterclockwise. When you rotate counterclockwise 495°, you rotate 360° (which brings you back to where you started), and then an additional 135°. That puts you 45° into the second quadrant. Now you need to know whether sine is positive or negative in the second quadrant. Pretty scary, huh?

With a calculator this problem becomes simple. Just punch in "sin 495°" and you get 0.7071067811865. (A) and (B) are negative, so they're out, and 0.7071067811865 is clearly not equal to $\dfrac{1}{2}$, so (C) is also wrong. That leaves only (D) or (E). Now, is greater than 1, so if you multiply it by another number greater than 1 (namely $\dfrac{3}{2}$), the result is obviously greater than 1. So you can eliminate (E), leaving (D) as the correct answer. With a calculator, you can get this question right without really understanding it.

> ### Calculators NOT Allowed on the Test
>
> Pocket organizers, computers, models with writing pads, computers with QWERTY keyboards, paper tapes, power cords, wireless transmitters, calculators that are noisy, Kray supercomputers.

Calculators: The Game Plan

The key to effective calculator use is practice, so don't run out the night before the test to buy a fancy new calculator. If you don't already have a calculator (and intend to use one on the test), buy one now. Unless you're studying math or science in college, you won't need anything more complex than trig functions. Bear in mind that you're better off bringing a straightforward model you're familiar with than an esoteric model you don't know how to use.

Learning the Do's and Don'ts

Practicing with your calculator is the best way to get a sense of where it can help and save time. It's important to develop a sense of the most effective ways in which to use your calculator on the test. Here's a brief guide to spotting those calculator-friendly Math questions:

EXAMPLE

9. $(7.3 + 0.8) - 3(1.98 + 0.69) =$
    A. −0.99
    B. −0.09
    C.   0
    D.   0.09
    E.   0.99

Know Your Calculator

Some calculators automatically follow the order of operations but others don't. It's important to feel comfortable with your calculator, and know what it can and cannot do.

This problem basically involves straightforward computation, so you'd be right if you reached for your calculator. However, if you just start punching the numbers in as they appear in the question, you might come up with the wrong answer. When you're performing a string of computations, you know that you need to follow the order of operations. The problem is, your calculator might not know this. Some calculators have parentheses keys and do follow PEMDAS, so it's important to know your machine and what its capabilities are.

If your calculator doesn't follow the order of operations, you'd need to perform the operations within parentheses separately. You'd get 8.1 − 3(2.67). Multiplication comes before subtraction, so you'd get 8.1 − 8.01, and then finally .09, choice D.

EXAMPLE

10. A certain bank issues 3-letter identification codes to its customers. If each letter can be used only once per code, how many different codes are possible?
    F.   26
    G.   78
    H.   326
    J.   15,600
    K.   17,576

Backsolve

A calculator can help you in backsolving (plugging the answer choices back into the question stem) and picking numbers (substituting numbers for the variables in the question).

Just manipulating the numbers in this problem will get you nowhere, but once you arrive at the setup, a calculator is very useful.

For the first letter in the code you can choose any of the 26 letters in the alphabet. For the second letter, you can choose from all the letters in the alphabet except the one you used in the first spot, so there are 26 − 1 = 25 possibilities. For the third there are 26 − 2 = 24 possibilities. So the total number of different codes possible is equal to 26 × 25 × 24. Using your calculator you find there are 15,600 codes—choice J.

EXAMPLE

11. Which of the following fractions is greater than 0.68 and less than 0.72 ?

    A. $\frac{5}{9}$

    B. $\frac{3}{5}$

    C. $\frac{7}{11}$

    D. $\frac{2}{3}$

    E. $\frac{5}{7}$

Here you have to convert the fractions in the answer choices to decimals and see which one falls in the range of values given to you in the question. If you're familiar with common decimal/fraction conversions you might know that choice B, $\frac{3}{5} = .6$ (too small) and choice D, $\frac{2}{3}$ is approximately .67 (also too small). But you'd still have to check out the other three choices. Your calculator can make short work of this, showing you that choice A, $\frac{5}{9} = .\overline{55}$, choice C, $\frac{7}{11}$ $= .\overline{63}$, and choice E, $\frac{5}{7}$ is approximately .71. Only 0.71 falls between 0.68 and 0.72, so E is correct.

Summing Up

So, in this first Math Workout, we've laid out a general math strategy for you:

- First, use Kaplan's Three-Step Method for ACT Math Problems to understand them and come up with the creative, fast solutions the ACT is looking for.

- Second, use Kaplan's Two-Pass Strategy for the ACT Math subtest to make sure you get as many correct answers as you can in 60 minutes.

- Third, think before you use your calculator.

In the other two Math Workouts, you'll learn a few special solution methods for some intriguing ACT problems in algebra, coordinate geometry, plane geometry, and trigonometry.

Reading Workout 1:
Know Where You're Going

- The key to ACT Reading

- The Kaplan Method

- Practice questions

Reading skills are crucial on every part of the ACT, not just on the Reading subject test. Savvy ACT-style reading is certainly useful for the English and Science tests, and even your work on many of the Math problems will benefit from the skills discussed below. So don't ignore the Reading Workouts, even if you think you're an ace reader. You may not be an ace *ACT-style* reader.

The kind of reading rewarded by the ACT is special. You probably know how to do it already, but you may be reluctant to do it on a standardized test. You may think that success on a test like the ACT requires that you read very slowly and deliberately, making sure you remember everything before moving on. Well, we at Kaplan have found that this kind of reading won't work on the ACT. In fact, it is a sure way to run out of time halfway through the Reading subtest.

Emergency Plan

Here's how to use this chapter if you don't have much time. Learn the Kaplan Method for ACT Reading on p. 74. Try the sample passage that follows. Check your answers. If you need more help, go back and read the whole chapter.

THE KEY TO ACT READING

The real key to ACT reading is to read quickly but actively, getting a sense of the gist or "main idea" of the passage and seeing how everything fits together to support that main idea. You should constantly try to think ahead. Look for the general outline of the passage—determine how it's structured. Don't worry about the details. You'll come back for those later.

Fast, active reading, of course, requires a little more mental energy than slow, passive reading. But it pays off. Those who dwell on details—who passively let the passage reveal itself at its own pace—are sure to run out of time. Don't be that kind of reader! Again, the key is to *take control*. Make the passage reveal itself to you on *your* schedule, by skimming the passage with

an eye to structure rather than detail. Look for key words that tell you what the author is doing so that you can save yourself time. For instance, read examples very, very quickly, just glancing over the words. When an author says "for example," you know that what follows is an example of a general point. Do you need to understand that specific example? Maybe, maybe not. If you *do*, you can come back and read the verbiage when you're attacking the questions. You'll know exactly where the author gave an example of general point x (or whatever). If you *don't* need to know the example for any of the questions, great! You haven't wasted much time on something that won't get you a point.

You really have to be a "seat-of-the-pants" reader to do well under the stringent time conditions of the ACT Reading test. You must quickly assess what an author's point is, and how he or she is supporting that point. When you get good at this, you can get through passages at an amazing clip.

You actually do this kind of "reading" all the time, and not just when you're reading a book or newspaper. When you watch TV or see a movie, for instance, you can often figure out much of what's going to happen in advance. You see the bad guys run out of a bank with bags of money in their hands, and you can guess that the next thing they'll do is get into a car and drive away in excess of the speed limit. You see a character in an old sitcom bragging to his friends about how great a driver he is, and you know that he's bound to get into a fender bender before the next commercial. This ability to know where something is going is very valuable. Use it on the ACT.

To help you know where an author is going, you should pay careful attention to "structural clues." Words like *but, nevertheless,* and *moreover* help you get a sense of where a piece of writing is going. You also should look for signal phrases (like *clearly, as a result,* or *no one can deny that*) to determine the logic of the passage. The details, remember, you can come back for later, when you're doing the questions. What's important in reading the passage is getting a sense of how those details fit together to express the point or points of the passage.

Practice Knowing Where You're Going

In the following exercise, try to fill in the word or phrase that should come next. For most, there are many possible answers, so don't worry about getting the "right" answer.

Reading Exercise

Fill in the blanks in the following sentences:

1. You'd think that the recipe for a strawberry soufflé would be complicated, but my friend's version was _____.

2. I can't believe my good luck! The one time in my life I buy a lottery ticket, I _____.

3. A parked car burns no fuel and causes no pollution. Once the ignition is turned on, however, _____.

4. As their habitat is destroyed, wild animals _____.

5. The new word-processing program was far easier to use than the old one. Moreover, the accompanying instruction booklet explained the commands in a _____ way.

6. The new word-processing program was far easier to use than the old one. On the other hand, the accompanying instruction booklet explained the commands in a _____ way.

Answers

- In Example #1, the active reader would probably complete the sentence by saying that the friend's version was "actually quite simple" or something similar. How do you know what's coming next here? The structural clue *but* tips you off. *But* tells you that a contrast is coming up. You'd think the recipe would be complicated, *BUT* it's "actually quite simple."

- In Example #2, on the other hand, there's no real structural clue to help you out, but the *meaning* of the sentence should make clear what's coming up. The speaker here is marveling at his good luck, right? That means that he must have won some money. So, a likely completion would be something like: The one time in my life I buy a lottery ticket, I "win the jackpot."

- In Example #3, we have another contrast, signaled by the clue *however*. A parked car doesn't burn fuel or pollute. *HOWEVER*, once you turn on the ignition. . . . The answer has to be something like "the car starts burning gas and polluting." That's the clear contrast that was anticipated by the structural clue *however*.

- Example #4 demonstrates again that you don't need explicit structural clues to stay ahead. Sometimes all you need is common sense. What do you think would happen to animals whose habitat had been destroyed? Would they thrive? Celebrate? Buy a condo in Florida? No, they'd probably "start dying out." They might even "become extinct."

- Examples #5 and #6 show clearly how you can use an author's language to anticipate what point he or she is going to make next. Here, we have identical sentences, except for one small (but very important) difference. In #5, the second sentence begins with the word *moreover*, indicating a continuation, an addition of similar information. In #6, the second sentence starts with *On the other hand*, indicating a contrast, the other side of the coin, something that stands in opposition to what has come before. The blank to #5 should be filled by a phrase like: in a "clear and easy-to-understand" way. That would allow the sentences to make sense together: The program was easy to use; moreover, the instructions were easy to understand. But the sentences in #6 only make sense together if you fill the blank with something like: in a "confusing and unclear" way (to carry out the sense of contrast). To drive the point home, try reversing the suggested completions we just gave you. #5: The program was easier to use; moreover, the instructions were confusing and unclear. Huh? That doesn't make sense. And #6: The program was easier to use; on the other hand, it was easy to understand. Again, that makes no sense.

THE KAPLAN READING METHOD

There are many ways to read, depending on your purpose. When you read your teacher's comments on a paper you wrote, you go very slowly and work out every word to make sure you know what you did right and what you did wrong. When you read for pleasure, you read what you like and skim what you don't. When you cram for most tests, you try to remember the facts you know you'll be asked to recall.

For the ACT, however, you have a special purpose: to answer specific multiple-choice questions. And we've found that the best way to do that is initially to read a passage quickly and actively for general understanding, then refer to the passage to answer individual questions. Not everybody should use the exact same strategy, but we find that almost every ACT test taker can succeed by following these basic steps:

1. Preread the passage
2. Consider the question stem
3. Refer to the passage (before looking at the choices)
4. Answer questions in your own words
5. Match your answer with one of the choices

For most students, these 5 tasks should together take up about nine minutes per passage. Less than three of those nine minutes should be spent prereading. The remaining time should be devoted to considering the questions and referring to the passage to check your answers to the questions. As we mentioned in the ACT Basics section, you'll probably want to take two sweeps through the questions for each passage, getting the doable ones the first time around, coming back for the harder ones.

Step 1: Preread the Passage

Prereading means quickly working through the passage before trying to answer the questions. Remember to "know where you're going," anticipating how the parts of the passage fit together. In this preread, the main goals are to:

- Understand the "gist" of the passage (the "main idea").
- Get an overall idea of how the passage is organized—a kind of road map—so that it will be easier to refer to later.

You may want to underline key points, jot down notes, circle structural clues—whatever it takes to accomplish the two goals above. You may even want to label each paragraph, to fix in your mind how the paragraphs relate to one another and what aspect of the main idea is discussed in each. That could be your road map.

Two important reminders: *Don't* read slowly, and *don't* get bogged down in individual details. Most of the details in the passage aren't required for answering the questions, so why waste time worrying about them?

Common Structural Clues

Indicating a contrast: *but, however, on the other hand, nevertheless*

Indicating a continuation with a similar or complementary thought: *moreover, furthermore, ; (a semicolon)*

Indicating a conclusion: *therefore, thus*

Indicating reasons for a conclusion: *since, because of, due to*

Indicating an example or illustration: *for instance, for example*

Think

As you work on the questions, remember to refer to the passage. Don't trust your memory. But don't confine yourself to the exact words the passage uses. This is a common trap. Think about what they mean.

Step 2: Consider the Question Stem

Approaching the questions requires self-discipline in Reading. Most test takers have an almost irresistible urge to immediately jump to the answer choices to see what "looks okay." That's not a good idea. Don't let the answer choices direct your thinking. The test makers intentionally design the answers to confuse you if they can. So, if you look at the answer choices hoping that they'll suggest something to you, you're just falling into one of their cleverly set traps.

In Reading, you should think about the question stem (the part above the answer choices) without looking at the choices. In most questions, you won't be able to remember exactly what the passage said about the matter in question. That's okay. In fact, even if you *do* think you remember, don't trust your memory. Instead . . .

Answer the Question

In Reading, many students never even try to answer the questions. They just look at the choices and try to "feel" their way to the answer. That won't work. Don't *feel* the answers: Find them in the passage.

Step 3: Refer to the Passage

You won't be rereading the whole passage, of course. But refer by finding the place where the answer to a question can be found (the question stem will sometimes contain a line reference to help you out; otherwise, rely on your road map of the passage). Your chosen answer should match the passage—not in exact vocabulary, perhaps, but in *meaning*.

Fill in the Blanks

One good way to practice self-discipline in Reading questions is to approach the Reading test like a "fill-in-the-blank" test instead of multiple-choice. Spend time thinking about how you'd fill in the blank before you look at the choices.

Step 4: Answer the Question in Your Own Words

It's extremely important in Reading to make a habit of answering the question in your own words (based on your checking of the passage) *before* looking at the answer choices. Most students waste enormous amounts of time thinking about answer choices in Reading. If you do that, you'll never finish, and you'll get so confused you'll probably get many questions wrong.

Step 5: Match Your Answer with One of the Choices

When you look at answer choices in Reading, your mental process should be "matching." You've got an answer in your head based on what you've read and rechecked in the passage. You need to match it to one of the answer choices. Avoid trying to see if they "look right." You don't want to think very hard about the choices if you can help it. They're intended to confuse you, after all, so don't think about them any more than you absolutely have to.

PRACTICING THE KAPLAN METHOD

Now practice the Kaplan method on the full-length ACT passage that follows. We're going to give you added incentive to use it by first showing you the questions *without* answer choices. That way you can't give in to the temptation to look at the choices before you think about the questions. The same questions in ACT style, *with* answer choices, will follow the passage. But try to answer them in "fill-in-the-blank" format first.

Timing

Keep track of time. If you can, try to devote only 9 minutes to each passage and its questions.

EXAMPLE

Questions

Your Answers

1. The author states that "on many manors meadow land was even more valuable than the arable" (lines 79–80) because:

2. According to the passage, the fact that the peasants' individual strips of land were unfenced subdivisions of larger fields required each peasant to:

3. According to the second paragraph (lines 4–33), the fallow part of the arable had to be plowed a total of how many times in any given calendar year?

4. The passage suggests that the practice of peasants owning strips "scattered through the three fields in different parts" (lines 39–40) was instituted in order to:

5. On the basis of the information in the passage, it may be inferred that people in medieval times did not think of sowing hay because:

6. As it is used in line 57, the word "garnered" means:

7. According to the passage, if one of the arable's three great fields were left fallow one year, it would be:

8. Which of the following conclusions is suggested by the fourth paragraph (lines 44–62)?

9. According to the passage, a manor's value might be judged according to the number of its plows because:

10. According to the passage, summer pasture for a manor's geese would be provided:

Passage I

By the tenth century most of northern Europe was divided into farming units known as manors . . . .

Line (5) Almost always a manor comprised four parts: arable, meadow, waste, and the village area itself. The arable was of course the land which grew the crops on which the inhabitants of the manor subsisted. To maintain fertility and keep down weeds it was necessary to fallow a (10) part of the cultivated land each year. It was, therefore, usual (though not universal) to divide the arable into three fields. One such field was planted with winter grain, a second with spring grain, and the third left fallow; the following (15) year, the fallow field would be planted with winter grain, the field in which winter grain had been raised was planted with spring grain, and the third field left fallow. By following such a rotation, the cycle was completed every three (20) years. Since the fallow field had to be plowed twice in the year in order to keep down the weeds, and the others had to be plowed once, work for the plow teams extended almost throughout the year. Plowing stopped only at (25) times when all hands were needed to bring in the harvest, or when the soil was too wet to be plowed, or was frozen. The amount of land that could be tilled was fixed fairly definitely by the number of plows and plow teams which the (30) manor could muster; and official documents sometimes estimated the wealth and value of a manor in terms of the number of plows it possessed.

The three great fields lay open, without (35) fences, but were subdivided into numerous small strips (often one acre in size, i.e., the amount of one day's plowing) which individual peasants "owned." The strips belonging to any one individual were scattered through the three fields (40) in different parts, perhaps in order to assure that each peasant would have strips plowed early and late, in fertile and infertile parts of the arable land.

Custom severely restricted the individual's (45) rights over his land. The time for plowing and planting was fixed by custom and each peasant had to conform, since he needed his neighbor's help to plow his strips and they needed his. Uniform cropping was imperative, since on a (50) given day the village animals were turned into the fields to graze after the harvest had been gathered, and if some individual planted a crop which did not ripen as early as that of his

neighbors, he had no means of defending his (55) field from the hungry animals. If his crop ripened sooner, on the other hand, it could not be garnered without trampling neighboring fields. Moreover, the very idea of innovation was lacking: men did what custom prescribed, (60) cooperated in the plowing and to some extent in the harvesting, and for many generations did not dream of trying to change.

The meadow was almost as important as the arable for the economy of the village. Hay from (65) the meadow supported the indispensable draught animals through the winter. The idea that hay might be sown did not occur to men in medieval times; consequently they were compelled to rely on natural meadows alone. One result was that (70) in many manors shortage of winter fodder for the plow teams was a constant danger. It was common practice to feed oxen on leaves picked from trees, and on straw from the grain harvest; but despite such supplements the draught (75) animals often nearly starved in winter. In some cases oxen actually had to be carried out from their winter stalls to spring pastures until some of their strength was recovered and plowing could begin. Thus on many manors meadow (80) land was even more valuable than the arable and was divided into much smaller strips (often the width of a scythe stroke).

The waste provided summer pasture for various animals of the manor: pigs, geese, cattle, (85) and sheep. The animals of the whole manor normally grazed together under the watchful eyes of some young children or other attendants who could keep them from wandering too far afield, and bring them back to the village at (90) night. The waste also was the source of wood for fuel and for building purposes, and helped to supplement the food supply with such things as nuts, berries, honey, and rabbits. . . .

The fourth segment of the manor was the (95) village itself, usually located in the center of the arable near a source of drinking water, and perhaps along a road or path or footpath leading to the outside world. The cottages of medieval peasants were extremely humble, usually (100) consisting of a single room, with earthen floor and thatched roof. Around each cottage normally lay a small garden in which various vegetables and sometimes fruit trees were planted. In the village streets chickens, ducks, and dogs picked up a precarious living.

From History of Western Civilization, a Handbook, *Sixth Edition, Copyright ©1986 by William H. McNeill; The University of Chicago Press, Chicago.*

1. The author states that "on many manors meadow land was even more valuable than the arable" (lines 79–80) because:
   - **A.** the meadow produced the leaves and straw that fed the manor's various animals through the winter months.
   - **B.** when necessary, the meadow could be used to grow supplementary crops.
   - **C.** the strength of the manor's draught animals depended upon the meadow's production of winter fodder.
   - **D.** profit could be made selling hay to manors with insufficient winter fodder for their draught animals.

   Ⓐ Ⓑ Ⓒ Ⓓ

2. According to the passage, the fact that the peasants' individual strips of land were unfenced subdivisions of larger fields required each peasant to:
   - **F.** follow a fixed planting schedule so as to be able to harvest crops at the same time as the other peasants.
   - **G.** harvest crops independently of his neighbors.
   - **H.** limit the size of strips to what could be plowed in a single day.
   - **J.** maintain small garden plots in order to provide his family with enough food.

   Ⓕ Ⓖ Ⓗ Ⓙ

3. According to the second paragraph (lines 4–33), the fallow part of the arable had to be plowed a total of how many times in any given calendar year?
   - **A.** one
   - **B.** two
   - **C.** four
   - **D.** six

   Ⓐ Ⓑ Ⓒ Ⓓ

4. The passage suggests that the practice of peasants owning strips "scattered through the three fields in different parts" (lines 39–40) was instituted in order to:
   - **F.** divide resources fairly evenly.
   - **G.** preserve the wealth of elite landowners.
   - **H.** protect the three fields from overuse.
   - **J.** force neighbors to work only their own lands.

   Ⓕ Ⓖ Ⓗ Ⓙ

5. On the basis of the information in the passage, it may be inferred that people in medieval times did not think of sowing hay because:
   - **A.** hay sowing had not been done in the past.
   - **B.** the need for more hay was not great enough to warrant the extra work.
   - **C.** northern Europeans did not yet have the necessary farming techniques for successful hay cultivation.
   - **D.** the tight schedule of cultivating the arable meant that the peasants had no time to cultivate extra crops.

   Ⓐ Ⓑ Ⓒ Ⓓ

6. As it is used in line 57, the word "garnered" means:
   F. planted
   G. watered
   H. gathered
   J. plowed

   Ⓕ Ⓖ Ⓗ Ⓙ

7. According to the passage, if one of the arable's three great fields were left fallow one year, it would be:
   A. left fallow for two more years in succession.
   B. planted the next year with winter grain only.
   C. planted the next year with spring grain only.
   D. planted with either winter or spring grain the next year.

   Ⓐ Ⓑ Ⓒ Ⓓ

8. Which of the following conclusions is suggested by the fourth paragraph (lines 44–62)?
   I. An individual was free to cultivate his own land in any way he wished.
   II. The manor was run according to tradition.
   III. Successful farming required cooperative methods.
   F. I and II only
   G. I and III only
   H. II and III only
   J. I, II, and III

   Ⓕ Ⓖ Ⓗ Ⓙ

9. According to the passage, a manor's value might be judged according to the number of its plows because:
   A. the more plows a manor had, the less land had to be left fallow.
   B. plows, while not in themselves valuable, symbolized great wealth.
   C. manors with sufficient plows could continue plowing throughout the year.
   D. the number of plows a manor owned determined how much land could be cultivated.

   Ⓐ Ⓑ Ⓒ Ⓓ

10. According to the passage, summer pasture for a manor's geese would be provided:
    F. next to cottages, within the village.
    G. on the fallow field of the arable.
    H. on the communal ground of the waste.
    J. on the whole of the meadow.

    Ⓕ Ⓖ Ⓗ Ⓙ

What about Roman Numerals?

A small percentage of questions on the ACT—like question 8 in this passage—are Roman numeral questions. You're given three (sometimes four) statements, each labeled with a Roman numeral. The idea is to treat each one as a true-false statement. Decide which statements are true, and then choose the choice that includes those statements and only those statements. Often you can save yourself some time on these questions. For instance, in question 8: Once you decide that Statement I is *false*, you can eliminate choices F, G, and J, all of which include Statement I. Thus, you can get your answer, choice H, without even looking at Statements II and III! Always watch the answer choices in Roman numeral questions.

The Lay of the Land

Well, how'd you do? Did you remember to refer to the passage? You probably found that you had to do a more thorough check for some questions than for others. For relatively easy questions like 3 and 7, for instance, you might have been able to find your answer with real certainty just by reading and understanding the question, with only a quick double-check of the passage. Other questions, like question 5, might have required a more detailed check of the passage. Still other questions, like 1 and 8, might have given you real trouble unless you went back and studied the passage more thoroughly.

This passage, like most nonfiction passages on the ACT, was organized in a fairly logical way around the main idea, which you might have expressed as "the structure and common practices of the medieval manor." Here's one possible road map you might have come up with:

- Paragraph 1 (just a single sentence, really): Intro to the topic of medieval manors (divided, as cited in the first line of next paragraph, into arable, meadow, waste, and village)

- Paragraphs 2, 3, and 4: Discussion of the arable and the practices associated with it

- Paragraph 5: Discussion of the meadow

- Paragraph 6: Discussion of the waste

- Paragraph 7: Discussion of the village

It should be obvious why, in your prereading step, you really need to get some sense of the layout of the passage like this. Many questions don't contain specific line references to help you locate information, and if you don't have a road map of the passage in your head or on paper, you might get lost.

Following is a key to the 10 questions attached to this passage.

Key to Passage I

(Nonfiction—Social Studies)

	ANSWER	REFER TO	TYPE	COMMENTS
1.	C	Lines 63–82	Detail	The entire paragraph supports this claim.
2.	F	Lines 49–55	Detail	"Uniform cropping was imperative . . ."
3.	B	Lines 20–22	Detail	Don't confuse fallow with planted fields.
4.	F	Lines 38–42	Inference	Every peasant got some fertile and some infertile land—inferably, to be fair to each.
5.	A	Lines 58–62, 66–69	Inference	No line reference so you had to have a sense of the structure to find this.
6.	H	Line 55–57	Detail	Use context. The crop is ripe, and so must be ready to be gathered.
7.	B	Lines 14–16	Detail	No line reference; otherwise no problem.
8.	H	Lines 44–62	Inference	I—lines 45–47 says the opposite II—lines 44–49 III—line 49–57
9.	D	Lines 27–30	Detail	No line reference; number of plows = amount of land.
10.	H	Lines 83–85	Detail	Whole paragraph devoted to describing waste.

NOTE: *We'll focus more on the individual question types in Reading Workout 2, at which time we'll show you a fast, effective approach to answering individual questions.*

As you continue in your ACT training, don't forget the very first piece of Reading advice we offered: read actively. Always know where you're going in a passage, and keep an eye on the structure. Use this habit whenever you read on the ACT, not just in the section called Reading. It helps on all four subject tests.

7

Science Workout 1:
Look for Patterns

Highlights

- Reading skills you'll need for Science

- The Kaplan Method

- How to read tables and graphs

- Practice questions

The Science Reasoning subject test causes a lot of unnecessary anxiety among ACT takers. Many people get so overwhelmed by the terminology and technicality of the passages that they just give up. What they fail to realize is that Science Reasoning is a little like the reverse of Math. In Math, you'll remember, we said that many of the questions are difficult problems based on elementary principles. In Science, on the other hand, many of the questions are elementary problems based on difficult material. So it's important that you never panic if you don't understand the passage in Science Reasoning. You can often get many of the questions right on a passage, even if you find it virtually incomprehensible!

Many ACT takers also tend to rely too heavily on what they've learned in school when approaching the Science Reasoning subject test. But as we've said, "remembering" is not the mindset the ACT will reward. You couldn't possibly know the answers to ACT Science Reasoning questions in advance: You have to pull them out of the passages. All the information you need to answer the questions is right on the page. You just have to find it and use it.

Emergency Plan

Here's how to use this chapter if you don't have much time. Learn the Kaplan Method for ACT Reading in Science on the next page. Try the sample passage that follows. Then read the section called Reading Tables and Graphs.

You Don't Need to Know Science

Knowing science is great, and it certainly can help your work in the Science Reasoning subject test. But you don't need to know a truckload of scientific facts to answer ACT Science questions. The questions are answerable from the information in the passage.

Worrying about science knowledge can be a problem no matter how good or bad your science background is. Students who have done poorly in science tend to panic because they think they don't know enough. Students who have done well in science might know too much. Some questions include wrong choices that are scientifically correct but don't relate to the passages. Choosing such answers will get you no points on the ACT. So try not to rely primarily on your knowledge of science. Instead, use your ability to refer to the passages. It's your ability to reason and think critically that's being tested.

Reading Skills You'll Need for Science

ACT Science Reasoning requires many of the same skills that ACT Reading does. The strategies discussed in Reading Workout I will therefore also work well for many Science Reasoning passages. The most important difference between Reading and Science is that the "details" you have to find in the Science Reasoning passages almost all relate to numbers or scientific processes or both, and they are often contained in graphs and tables rather than in paragraph form. The secrets to finding most of these details are explained below.

- **Reading graphs, tables, and research summaries.** Many questions involve only accurately retrieving data from a single graph or table. Others involve combining knowledge from two different graphs or tables. Still others involve understanding experimental methods well enough to evaluate information contained in summaries of experiments.

- **Looking for patterns in the numbers that appear.** Do these numbers get bigger or smaller? Where are the highest numbers? Where are the lowest numbers? At what point do the numbers change? A little calculation is sometimes required, but not much. In Science, you won't be computing with numbers so much as thinking about what they mean.

In Science, as in Reading, it's crucial to consider the questions and at least try to answer them before looking at the answer choices. Refer to the passage to find the answer, and try to match it with one of the choices. Use the process of elimination as a fallback strategy for hard questions—but don't make it your main approach.

The Kaplan Method for Reading in Science

The same Kaplan Method for Reading is also useful in Science. The steps, you'll remember, are:

1. Preread the passage
2. Consider the question stem
3. Refer to the passage (before looking at the choices)
4. Answer the question in your own words
5. Match your answer with one of the choices

But in Science Reasoning, you have seven shorter passages to do instead of the four longer ones in Reading. Each passage should average five minutes. We recommend using just about one minute or so to preread the passage, and then a total of about four minutes to consider the questions and refer to the passage (that's about 40 seconds per question). Notice that this is less time prereading than in the Reading test.

Step One: Preread the Passage

It's especially important in Science Reasoning not to get bogged down in the details (we'll see that this is also critical in the Natural Sciences passage in Reading). Some of the material covered is extremely technical, and you'll just get frustrated trying to understand it completely. So it's crucial that you skim, to get a general idea of what's going on and—just as important—to get a sense of where certain types of data can be found.

Almost all Science Reasoning passages have the same general structure. They begin with an introduction. Always read through the introduction first to orient yourself. Some passages relate to material you may have already studied in high school. If you're familiar with the concepts in the passage, you may not need to do more than skim the introduction. If not, you'll want to read the introduction somewhat more carefully. But remember, don't focus on details. Try to get a sense of the overall situation.

After reviewing the introduction, quickly scan the rest of the passage. How is the information presented? Graphs? Diagrams? Are there experiments? What seems to be important? Size? Shape? Temperature? Speed? Chemical composition? Don't worry about details and don't try to remember it all. Plan to refer to the passage just as you would in Reading.

> **EXAMPLE**
>
> Scientists researching the relationship between birds and dinosaurs have chosen to carefully examine three fossils dating from the Jurassic period: an *archaeopteryx* (the oldest known bird) at the British Museum in London, a *composognathus* (a dinosaur) at the Field Museum in Chicago, and a *teleosaurus* (a crocodile) at the National Museum in Beijing. All three creatures were about the same size as a turkey.

Remember to read actively. Ask yourself: Why would the scientists choose these three creatures? Since the scientists are studying birds and dinosaurs, the first two choices seem natural. But why should they include a crocodile? Maybe the National Museum in Beijing had a special deal on crocodile bones? More likely it's because crocodiles are somewhat like dinosaurs, but not extinct.

As you preread the passage, you also want to make sure you know what any tables and graphs in the passage are meant to represent. Feel free to take notes, mark up the test booklet, or circle important information. Get a sense of what kind of data is contained in each graph and table, but don't read the data carefully yet! You may want to take note of general trends in the data, but don't waste time taking in information that may not be relevant to the questions. Remember, your goal is to answer questions, *not* to learn and remember everything that goes on in the passage.

Answer the Question

As in Reading, it's tempting to avoid the process of actually answering the question and instead to just look at the answer choices and see which sounds best. Don't do it.

Scientific Terms

Scientific terms can be intimidating. But don't worry if you've never heard of things like *archaeopteryx* or *teleosaurus* before. The introduction tells you what they are. On the ACT, if you need to know the meaning of a special scientific term, the test will normally define it for you. If the test doesn't tell you what a word means, you can usually figure it out from the context (or else you won't need to know it).

Step Two: Consider the Question Stem

Most of your time in Science Reasoning will be spent considering questions and referring to the passage to find the answers. Here's where you should do most of your really careful reading. It's essential that you understand exactly what the question is asking. Then, go back to the passage and get a sense of what the answer should be before looking at the choices.

There are really three basic kinds of Science questions:

- **Data Analysis Questions.** For these questions, you'll almost certainly be going back to the graphs and tables in the passage to read and analyze their data. Look for patterns in the data (you'll get some practice reading graphs and tables later in this Workout). And try to get a sense of what the answer should be before looking at the choices.

- **Experiment Questions.** Make sure you understand the purpose of the experiments. What are these scientists trying to prove? Try to identify the control group, if any, in each experiment, and the factor that is being varied from one trial to the next. (Experiments will be covered more fully in Science Workout 2.)

- **Principle Questions.** These questions ask you to apply a scientific principle, or to identify ways of defending or attacking a principle. This includes making predictions based on a given theory, or showing how a hypothesis might be strengthened or weakened by particular findings. (These questions will be especially important for the Conflicting Viewpoints passage, discussed in Science Workout 3.)

As we mentioned, one possible pitfall in answering the questions is relying too heavily on your own knowledge of science. For example, the following question might have appeared with the passage excerpted above:

EXAMPLE

1. The dinosaur studied by the scientists, *composognathus*, was:
   A. definitely a reptile.
   B. definitely a bird.
   C. about the size of a turkey.
   D. larger than *archaeopteryx* or *teleosaurus*.

If you know that dinosaurs are usually classified as reptiles, choice A would be very tempting. But it's wrong. The passage doesn't say that. In fact, if we had read the rest of this passage, we would have learned that the researchers were questioning whether dinosaurs should be classified as reptiles or birds. What the passage *does* say is that all three of the creatures tested are turkey sized, making the correct choice C.

In answering questions, you should use your knowledge of scientific *methods* and *procedures*. But don't rely heavily on any knowledge of specific *facts*.

Step Three: Refer to the Passage

As in Reading, you have to be diligent about referring to the passage. Your prereading of the passage should have given you an idea of where particular kinds of data can be found. Sometimes the questions themselves will direct you to the right place.

KAPLAN

Be careful not to mix up units when taking information from graphs, tables, and summaries. Make sure you don't confuse *decreases* and *increases*. Many questions will hinge on whether you can correctly identify the factors that decrease and the ones that increase. The difference between a correct and an incorrect answer will often be a "decrease" where an "increase" should be. Read the questions carefully!

Step Four: Answer the Question in Your Own Words

The Answers to the Science Reasoning Questions are there in the passage. As we mentioned in Step 2 above, don't rely too much on your own knowledge of science. Instead think of paraprasing the information in the passage.

Step Five: Match Your Answer with One of the Choices

Once you've paraphrased the information and matched it to an answer choice, you might want to double-check the question to make sure that you've actually answered the question asked. Many of the questions in Science Reasoning are reversal questions. Always look for words like *not* and *except* in the questions.

READING TABLES AND GRAPHS

Most of the specific information in ACT Science passages is contained in tables or graphs, usually accompanied by explanatory material. Knowing how to read data from tables and graphs is critical to success on the Science Reasoning subject test!

In order to read most graphs and tables, you have to do four things:

- **Determine what is being represented**
- **Determine what the axes (or columns and rows) represent**
- **Take note of units of measurement**
- **Look for trends in the data**

Let's say you saw the graph on the following page in a Science Reasoning passage.

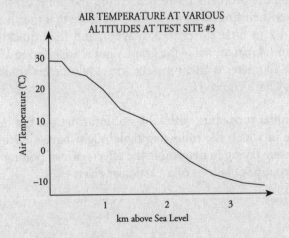

AIR TEMPERATURE AT VARIOUS
ALTITUDES AT TEST SITE #3

- **Determine what is being represented.** Most graphs and tables have titles that tell you what they represent. For some, though, you may have to get that information from the introduction. Here, the graph is representing how cold or hot the air is at various altitudes above a certain Test Site #3.

- **Determine what the axes represent.** These, too, are usually labeled. In the graph above, the x-axis represents distance above sea level in kilometers, while the y-axis represents the air temperature in degrees Celsius.

- **Take note of units of measurement.** Note that distance here is measured in kilometers, not miles or feet. Temperature is measured in degrees *Celsius,* not Fahrenheit.

- **Look for trends in the data.** The "pattern" of the data in this graph is pretty clear. As you rise in altitude, the temperature drops—the higher the altitude, the lower the temperature. (As we'll see later, this kind of trend is called an *inverse variation.*)

The sloping line on the graph represents the various temperatures measured at the various altitudes. To find what the measured temperature was at, say, 2 km above sea level, find the 2 km point on the x-axis and trace your finger directly up from it until it hits the line. It does so at about the level of 3° C. In other words, at an altitude of 2 km above sea level at Test Site #3, the air temperature was about 3° C.

Be careful with units of measurement! Most passages use the metric system, but a few may use traditional or British units of measure. You won't be expected to remember oddball unit conversions like 8 furlongs = 1 mile or 2.54 cm = 1 in, and passages that use special units of measure such as microns or parsecs will define these units if necessary. But don't assume that all the units in the graphs match the units in the questions. For instance, try the following question.

EXAMPLE

2. At what altitude did the meteorologists measure an air temperature of 10° C?
    F. 1.4 m
    G. 140 m
    H. 1400 m
    J. 14 km

Many test takers solving the problem above would find the point on the line at the level of 10° C on the y-axis, trace their fingers down to the x-axis, see that the altitude would be about halfway between 1 and 2 (a little closer to 1, maybe), and then quickly choose F. But F is wrong, since F gives you 1.4 *meters,* while the graph figures are given in *kilometers.* Remember to translate the data! A kilometer is 1,000 meters, so 1.4 kilometers would be 1.4 times 1,000 meters = 1,400 meters. That's choice H.

You should follow a similar procedure with tables of information. For instance, in the introduction to the passage in which the following table might have appeared, you would have learned that scientists were trying to determine the effects of two pollutants (Pb and Hg, lead and mercury) on the trout populations of a particular river:

Location	Water temperature (°C)	Presence of Pb (parts per million)	Presence of Hg (parts per million)	Population Density of Speckled Trout (# per 100 m³)
1	15.4	0	3	7.9
2	16.1	0	1	3.5
3	16.3	1	67	0
4	15.8	54	3	5.7
5	16.0	2	4	9.5

- **Determine what is being represented.** There's no informative title for this table, but the introduction would have told you what the table represents.

- **Determine what the columns and rows represent.** In tables, you get columns and rows instead of x- and y-axes. But the principle is the same. Here, each row represents the data from a different numbered location on the river. Each column represents different data: water temperature, presence of the first pollutant, presence of the second pollutant, population of one kind of trout, population of another kind of trout.

- **Take note of units of measurement.** Temperature is measured in degrees Celsius. The two pollutants are measured in parts per million (or ppm). The trout populations are measured in average number per 100 cubic meters of river.

- **Look for trends in the data.** Glancing at the table, it looks like locations where the Hg concentration is high (as in Location 3), the trout population is virtually nonexistent. This would seem to indicate that trout find a high Hg concentration incompatible. But notice the location where the other pollutant is abundant—in Location 4. Here, both trout populations seem to be more in line with other locations. That would seem to indicate that this other pollutant—Pb—is NOT quite so detrimental to trout populations (though we'd have to do more studies if it turned out that all of the trout in that location had three eyes).

How Tables and Graphs Relate

To really understand tables and graphs, it helps to see how the same information can be represented in both. For instance, look at the following table and graph.

Concentration of *E. coli* in Cooling Pool B	
DISTANCE FROM EFFLUENT PIPE 3	1000s OF *E. COLI* PER CENTILITRE
zero m.	4
5 m.	56
10 m.	276
15 m.	140
20 m.	75

Concentration of *E. coli* in Cooling Pool B

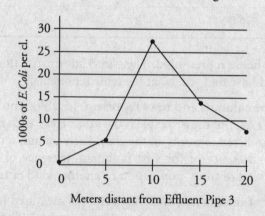

The table and graph above represent the exact same data. And here's yet another way of depicting the same data, in a bar chart.

Concentration of *E. coli* in Cooling Pool B

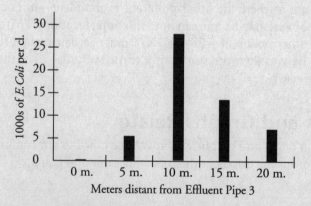

Remember that data can be represented in many different ways. But however it appears in the passage whether it be in tables, graphs, or charts, you'll have to read and translate it to answer the questions.

Look for Patterns and Trends

When you first examine a graph or table, don't focus on exact numbers. Look for *patterns* in the numbers. But don't assume that there is *always* a pattern or trend: Finding that there isn't a pattern is just as important as finding that there *is* one. When looking for patterns and trends, you should keep three specific things in mind:

- **Extremes** (maximums and minimums)
- **Critical points** (or points of change)
- **Direct or inverse variation**

Extremes

Extremes—or maximums and minimums—are merely the highest and lowest points that things reach. In tables, the minimums and maximums will be represented by relatively high and low numbers. In graphs, they will be represented by highs and lows on the *x*- and *y*-axes. In bar charts, they will be represented by the tallest and shortest bars.

In Table 1, what location on the river has the maximum concentration of Hg? Of Pb?

Table 1

Location	Water temperature (°C)	Presence of Pb (parts per million)	Presence of Hg (parts per million)	Population Density of Speckled Trout (# per 100 m^3)
1	15.4	0	3	7.9
2	16.1	0	1	3.5
3	16.3	1	67	0
4	15.8	54	3	5.7
5	16.0	2	4	9.5

A glance at the numbers tells you that Location 3—with 67 ppm—represents the maximum for Hg, while Location 4—with 54 ppm—represents the maximum for Pb.

How can taking note of maximums and minimums help you spot patterns in the data? Look again at Table 1 above. Notice that the maximum concentration of Hg—67 ppm—just happens to coincide with the *minimums* for trout population—0 per 100 m^3 for both. That's a good indication that there's some cause and effect going on here. Somehow, a maximum of Hg concentration correlates with a minimum of trout population. The obvious (though not airtight) conclusion is that a high concentration of Hg is detrimental to trout populations. And this kind of finding is much more readily evident when you look at maximums and minimums.

Critical Points

Critical points—or points of change—are values at which something dramatic happens. For example, at atmospheric pressure water freezes at 0° C and boils at about 100° C. If you examined water at various temperatures below the lower of these two critical points, it would be solid. If you examined water at various temperatures between the two points, it would be liquid. If you examined water above the higher critical point, it would be a gas.

When you scan the numbers in a chart or points on a graph, look for places where values bunch together or where suddenly something special happens. At atmosphere pressure 0° C is a critical point for water—as is 100° C—since something special happens: The substance changes form.

To find out how critical points can help you evaluate data, turn the page and take another look at the graph representing the concentration of *E. coli* (a common type of bacterium) in Cooling Pool B.

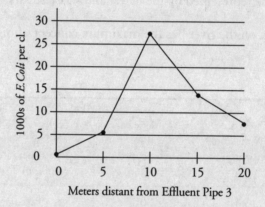

Meters distant from Effluent Pipe 3

Notice how the concentration is low very near Effluent Pipe 3. From there, it rises until about 10 meters away from the pipe, then it falls again, tapering off as you get farther from the pipe. There's a critical point, then, right around 10 meters from Effluent Pipe 3. Somehow, that vicinity is most conducive to the growth of *E. coli*. As you move closer to or farther away from that point, the concentration falls off. So, in looking to explain the data, you'd want to focus on that location—10 meters from the pipe. What is it about that location that's so special? What makes it the hot new place for *E. coli* to see and be seen?

Variation

Variation is a bit more complex than extremes or critical points. Variation refers to the way two different things change *in relation to each other*. Direct variation means that two things vary in the same way: When one gets bigger, the other does too; when one gets smaller, so does the other. Inverse variation means that two things vary in *opposite* ways: When one gets bigger, the other gets smaller, and vice versa. We saw an example of inverse variation in the air temperature graph, where altitude and air temperature varied inversely—as altitude *in*creased, air temperature *de*creased.

But here's a more familiar example for nonscientists: As you walk home from school at a constant rate, time varies directly with the distance from school and indirectly with the distance from home. As time passes (as the amount of time *in*creases) you move farther away from school (the distance from school *increases*). Both *increase* in the same direction. That's direct variation.

But as the amount of time *increases*, the distance to your house *decreases*. The two change in opposite ways. That's inverse variation.

Many of the graphs on the ACT are intended to display variation. As we've just seen, graphs with *x-y* coordinates (horizontal and vertical axes) are used for this purpose. On such a graph, direct variation will be displayed by lines moving upward to the right. Inverse variations will plot out to lines moving downward to the right.

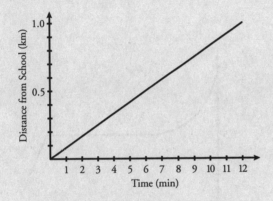

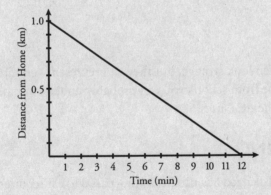

In the two graphs above, both variations make straight lines. This is because the speed at which you walked was constant. Sometimes, direct or inverse variations can be more complicated because the rates are not constant. Such variation could be called "nonlinear," because when plotted on a graph, it produces wavy, zigzag, broken, or curved lines. For example, if you started out from school running, then gradually slowed down as you got tired, then stopped for a while about halfway home to smell some roses before finally continuing home at a steady pace, the variation would not be linear. Distance from school would increase more slowly as time progressed, and for a while the distance wouldn't increase *at all*. Distance to home would decrease more slowly as you slowed down, and would also stop decreasing during the time you stopped to smell the roses.

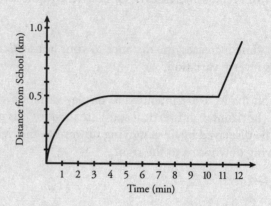

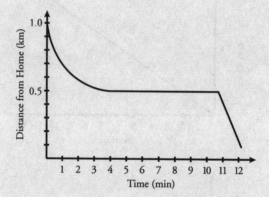

Graphs of this kind often look strange, but they can represent very ordinary activities. If you know how to walk home from school, you can probably understand the kinds of relationships and number patterns the ACT uses.

THE REAL THING

Let's take a look at a full-fledged Science Reasoning passage that requires these skills. Give yourself about seven minutes to do the passage and the questions (on the actual test, you'll want to move a bit faster).

Passage I

Although the effective acceleration due to gravity at the earth's surface is often treated as a constant ($g = 9.80$ m/sec^2) its actual value varies from place to place because of several factors.

First, a body on the surface of any rotating spheroid experiences an effective force perpendicular to the rotational axis and proportional to the speed of rotation. This centrifugal force, which counteracts gravity, varies with latitude, increasing from zero at the poles to a maximum at the equator. In addition, because the earth "bulges" at the equator, a body at equatorial sea level is farther from the center of the earth than is a body at polar sea level. Figure 1 shows the variation of mean values of g at sea level resulting from both effects; the contribution from "bulging" is about half that from rotation.

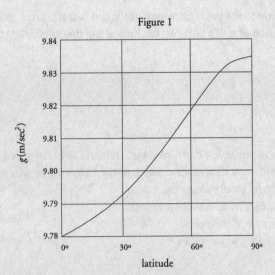

Figure 1

Measurements of *g* also vary depending on local rock density and altitude. Table 1 shows the effect of altitude on *g* at various points above sea level.

Table 1

Change in Altitude (km)	g (m/sec^2)
1	−0.0031
5	−0.0154
10	−0.0309
25	−0.0772
30	−0.1543

EXAMPLE

3. If the earth's density were uniform, at approximately what latitude would calculations using an estimated value at sea level of $g = 9.80$ m/sec^2 produce the least error?
    A. 0°
    B. 20°
    C. 40°
    D. 80°

    Ⓐ Ⓑ Ⓒ Ⓓ

4. According to the passage, the effective acceleration due to gravity at the surface of a rotating but non-"bulging" sphere would tend to be greatest at the:
    F. equator, where the rotation effect is strongest.
    G. equator, where the rotation effect is weakest.
    H. poles, where the rotation effect is strongest.
    J. poles, where the rotation effect is weakest.

    Ⓕ Ⓖ Ⓗ Ⓙ

5. Given the information in the passage, which of the following figures most closely approximates the value of g at a point 10 km high along the equator?
   A. 9.75 m/sec^2
   B. 9.80 m/sec^2
   C. 9.81 m/sec^2
   D. 9.87 m/sec^2

   Ⓐ Ⓑ Ⓒ Ⓓ

6. Given the information presented in the passage, an increase in the speed of the earth's rotation would most likely cause which of the following results at sea level?
      I. An increase in g only along the equator
     II. A decrease in g at all nonpolar points
     III. No change in g at the poles
     IV. An increase in g at the poles
   F. II only
   G. I and III only
   H. II and III only
   J. II and IV only

   Ⓕ Ⓖ Ⓗ Ⓙ

7. Suppose that the earth stopped rotating but still "bulged." Based on information from the passage, the value of g at sea level at the equator would be:
   A. exactly 9.80 m/sec^2.
   B. greater than 9.78 m/sec^2.
   C. exactly 9.78 m/sec^2.
   D. less than 9.78 m/sec^2.

   Ⓐ Ⓑ Ⓒ Ⓓ

8. According to the information in Figure 1, the value of g :
   F. changes by a greater average amount per degree latitude between 30° and 60° than it does near the equator or poles.
   G. changes by a greater average amount per degree latitude near the equator or poles than it does between 30° and 60°.
   H. increases by an average of 5.8 m/sec^2 per degree latitude from the equator to the poles.
   J. decreases by an average of 3.1 x 10^{-3} m/sec^2 per degree latitude from the equator to the poles.

   Ⓕ Ⓖ Ⓗ Ⓙ

Answers and Explanations

This was actually a relatively simple, straightforward Science Reasoning passage, but the terminology may have been intimidating nonetheless. The introduction tells you that the issue here is gravity, and how its pull (in other words, the acceleration due to gravity) changes because of several factors. Those factors—and the changes they cause—are represented in Figure 1 (which deals with the factor of latitude, which has an effect because of global "bulge" and the rotation effect) and Table 1 (which deals with the factor of altitude).

Analyzing Figure 1 as described above, you should have seen that the graph is supposed to show how g (the acceleration due to gravity) is affected by latitude (i.e., north-south location on the globe). The higher the latitude (the greater the distance from the equator), the greater the value of *g*. Thus, there's a *direct variation* between the two, though the variation isn't constant. As the curves at the beginning and ending of the line in Figure 1 tell you, the increase in *g* is "slower" near the equator and near the poles.

Notice how you could have answered **Question 3** just by understanding Figure 1. Question 3 asks, assuming the earth's density were uniform, "at what latitude would calculations using an estimated value at sea level of $g = 9.80$ m/sec^2.produce the least error?" First, figure out what that question is asking. You remember this question; we mentioned it in ACT Basics. It's simply asking you: Where would you get an actual value of *g* closest to 9.80 m/sec^2? Find 9.80 on the *y*-axis of the graph, follow across until you intersect with the curved line, and see where you are on the *x*-axis. That turns out to be about a third of the way from 30° to 60° latitude. In other words, choice C, 40°, is the answer.

Confused?

Remember, you score points by answering the questions right, not by understanding the passages completely. You can get points on a Science Reasoning passage, even if you don't understand it!

Similarly, **Question 4** can be knocked off pretty easily. Where is the "effective acceleration due to gravity"(*g*, in other words) greatest (on a rotating but nonbulging sphere)? To answer this question you need to understand Figure 1. Although Figure 1 includes the effects of both rotation and bulging, it's clear that both factors cause the effective acceleration due to gravity to increase as the latitude increases from 0° to 90°. So the effective acceleration would be the greatest at 90° latitude—the poles. But that only narrows the choices down to H and J. To decide between them, we have to infer further

Answers

3. C, 4. J, 5. A, 6. H 4, 7. B, 8. F

whether the rotation effect is weakest or greatest at the poles. The second paragraph of the introduction gives you the answer: The effect of rotation ("centrifugal force") is zero at the poles. You can't get weaker than zero, so the answer is choice J.

We'll get to **Question 5** below.

To answer **Question 6**, you again need only understand the introduction and Figure 1. This is a Principle question, asking you to apply the principles about rotational effects on *g* to a hypothetical situation in which rotation *in*creased. Well, as you learned in the introduction, the effects of the earth's rotation tend to lessen the effects of gravity, so increasing the speed of rotation would lessen the effects of gravity even more—i.e., a lesser value for *g* except at the poles, where the effect of gravity is zero. So *g* would *de*crease everywhere but at the poles. Statements II and III are true, while Statements I and IV are false. Choice H is correct.

Question 7 requires more applications of principles, and is yet another question that can be answered by simply reading Figure 1. It asks you to suppose that rotation effects (one of the two factors affected by latitude) ceased, but that the earth still bulged at the equator. What would be the value of *g*? Well, again, rotation tends to "counteract" gravity, so it would have a depressing effect on *g*. *Without* rotation, then, *g* would be less depressed—it would go up, in other words. That means (reading from Figure 1 again) that *g* at 0° latitude (the equator) would, in the absence of rotation, go up from its current value of 9.78. That's why B is correct.

Question 8 (not to get monotonous) is still another that can be answered just by a proper reading of Figure 1. It asks you to describe what the graph tells you about the value of *g*. As we saw, the value rises slowly as you head away from 0° latitude (the equator), rises more rapidly in the middle latitudes, and slows down again near 90° latitude (the poles). That's best described by choice F. (Choice G gets it backwards—remember to read the choices carefully!) Choices H and J would involve you in some extensive calculations, at the end of which you'd realize that they were not true. But there's no reason to get that far. If you find yourself doing extensive calculation, you should know that you're on the wrong track. ACT Science Reasoning will involve simple calculation only.

Notice how you could have answered five of the six questions with just a rudimentary grasp of the introduction and an understanding of how to "read" Figure 1.

The other question, **Question 5**, requires that you read both Figure 1 and Table 1 properly. It asks for the value of g at the equator (that information comes from Figure 1), but at an altitude of 10 km above sea level (that information comes from Table 1). Figure 1 tells you that the value of g at the equator *at sea level* would be 9.78 m/sec^2. But at 10 km above sea level, according to Table 1, g *would* be slightly lower—0.0309 m/sec^2 lower, to be precise. So, 9.78 minus 0.0309 would be about 9.75 m/sec^2. That's choice A.

Look for Patterns

The passage and questions above should convince you of one thing: To do well on Science Reasoning, you have to be able to read graphs and tables, paying special attention to trends and patterns in the data. Sometimes, that's ALL you need to do to get most of the points on a passage.

English Workout 2: Make It Make Sense

- Sample "Sense" questions

- Grammar rules tested on the ACT

- Nonstandard format English questions

In English Workout 1, we saw that the ACT expects you to use your words efficiently, and that, in fact, the shortest answer is correct remarkably often. But, obviously, the shortest answer is often wrong. What could make it wrong? It may not mean what it says.

Take this example: "Abraham Lincoln's father was a model of hard-working self-sufficiency. He was born in a log cabin he built with his own hands." Well, that's a cute trick, being born in a cabin you built yourself. Presumably the writer means that Abe was born in a cabin that his father built. But the literal meaning of the example is that the father somehow managed to be born in a cabin that he himself had built.

Don't Take Any Nonsense!

It's possible, of course, to analyze this example in terms of the rules of apostrophe use and pronoun reference. But that's not practical for the ACT, even for a student who has good grammar skills. There isn't time to carefully analyze every question, consider all the rules involved, and decide on an answer. You have to do seventy English questions in only forty minutes—that's almost two questions per minute.

But there *is* plenty of time to approach examples like this one in a more pragmatic way. Ask yourself, *Does this stuff make sense?*

Reminder

Should you always pick the shortest answer in English? NO! All things being equal, lean toward choosing the shortest answer, but don't just pick the shortest answer without thinking.

Think

What you read always has two possible meanings: an intended meaning, and a literal meaning. The intended meaning is what the writer was trying to say. The literal meaning is what the author actually did say. The ACT demands that the intended and literal meanings of every passage be exactly the same.

But for the ACT, it's important to care. You need to adjust your mindset. After deciding whether or not the selection in a question is concise and relevant (Step One in the Three-Step Method), the next step isn't to remember lots of rules; it's to make sure that the sentence *says* exactly what it's supposed to *mean*. If it doesn't, your job is to make it so. Your job, in other words, is to make it make sense.

SAMPLE SENSE QUESTIONS

We at Kaplan have a name for questions that test meaning errors—Sense Questions. Once you get the hang of them, these questions can actually be fun. Errors of meaning are often funny once you see them. The following passage gives examples of the most common kinds of Sense Questions you'll find on the ACT.

EXAMPLE

Passage I

Most people—even those who've never read Daniel Defoe's *Robinson Crusoe*—are familiar with the strange story of the sailor shipwrecked on a far-flung Pacific island. Relatively few of them, however, know that Crusoe's <u>story. It was</u> actually

₁

based on the real-life adventures of a Scottish seaman, Alexander Selkirk. Selkirk came to the Pacific as a member of a 1703 privateering expedition led by a captain named William Dampier. During the voyage, Selkirk became dissatisfied with conditions aboard ship. <u>After a bitter quarrel</u>

₂

<u>with his captain, he put Selkirk ashore</u> on tiny Mas a

₂

Tierra, one of the islands of Juan Fernandez, off the coast of Chile. Stranded, Selkirk lived there alone—in much the <u>same manner as</u> Defoe's

₃

Crusoe—until 1709, when he was finally rescued by another English privateer.

Upon his return to England, Selkirk found himself a <u>celebrity, his</u> strange tale had already

₄

1. **A.** NO CHANGE
    B. story: was
    C. story, was
    D. story was

    Ⓐ Ⓑ Ⓒ Ⓓ

2. **F.** NO CHANGE
    G. Quarreling with his captain, the boat was put ashore
    H. Having quarreled with his captain, Selkirk was put ashore
    J. Having quarreled with his captain, they put Selkirk ashore

    Ⓕ Ⓖ Ⓗ Ⓙ

3. **A.** NO CHANGE
    B. same manner that
    C. identical manner that
    D. identical way as

    Ⓐ Ⓑ Ⓒ Ⓓ

4. **F.** NO CHANGE
    G. celebrity, but his
    H. celebrity. His
    J. celebrity his

    Ⓕ Ⓖ Ⓗ Ⓙ

become the talk of pubs and coffeehouses

throughout the British Isles. The story even

reached the ears of Richard Steele, who featured it

in his periodical, *The Tatler.* Eventually,

he became the subject of a bestselling book,
  5

A Cruizing Voyage Round the World, by Woodes

Rogers. And while there is some evidence
             6
that Defoe, a journalist, may actually have

interviewed Selkirk personally, most literary

historians believe that it was the reprinting of the

Rogers book in 1718 that served as the real stim-

ulus for Defoe's novel.

In *Crusoe*, which has been published in
                           7
1719, Defoe took substantial liberties with the

Selkirk story. For example, while Selkirk's presence

on the island was of course known for many people
                                        8
(certainly everyone in the crew that

stranded him there), no one in the novel is aware

of Crusoe's survival of the wreck and presence

on the island. Moreover, while Selkirk's exile

lasted just six years, Crusoe's goes on for a

much more dramatic, though less credible,

twenty-eight (over four times as long). But Defoe's
                       9
most blatant embellishment of the tale is the

invention of the character of Friday, for whom

there was no counterpart

5. **A.** NO CHANGE
    B. Selkirk became
    C. his became
    D. he becomes

    Ⓐ Ⓑ Ⓒ Ⓓ

6. **F.** NO CHANGE
    G. But since
    H. And therefore
    J. OMIT the underlined portion and start the sentence with "There."

    Ⓕ Ⓖ Ⓗ Ⓙ

7. **A.** NO CHANGE
    B. was published
    C. had been published
    D. will have been published

    Ⓐ Ⓑ Ⓒ Ⓓ

8. **F.** NO CHANGE
    G. widely known among people
    H. known about many people
    J. known to many people

    Ⓕ Ⓖ Ⓗ Ⓙ

9. **A.** NO CHANGE
    B. (much longer)
    C. (a much longer time, of course)
    D. OMIT the underlined portion

    Ⓐ Ⓑ Ⓒ Ⓓ

whatsoever in the real-life story.

    <u>Because of</u> its basis in fact, *Robinson Crusoe*
       10
is often regarded as the first major novel in English

literature. <u>Still popular today, contemporary</u>
                11
<u>audiences enjoyed the book as well</u>. In fact, two
           11
sequels, in which Crusoe returns to the island after

his rescue, were eventually <u>published. Though</u> to
                  12
little acclaim. Meanwhile, Selkirk himself never

<u>gave a hoot about returning</u> to the island that
          13
had made him famous. Legend has it that he never

gave up his eccentric living habits, spending his last

years in a cave teaching alley cats to dance in his

spare time. One wonders if even Defoe himself could

have invented a more fitting end to the bizarre story

of his shipwrecked sailor. ⑭ ⑮

10. **F.** NO CHANGE
   G. Despite
   H. Resulting from
   J. As a consequence of
               Ⓕ Ⓖ Ⓗ Ⓙ

11. **A.** NO CHANGE
   B. Still read today, Defoe's contemporaries
       also enjoyed it.
   C. Viewed by many even then as a classic, the book
       is still popular to this day.
   D. Much read in its day, modern audiences still find
       the book compelling.
               Ⓐ Ⓑ Ⓒ Ⓓ

12. **F.** NO CHANGE
   G. published, though
   H. published although
   J. published; although
               Ⓕ Ⓖ Ⓗ Ⓙ

13. **A.** NO CHANGE
   B. evinced himself as desirous of returning
   C. could whip up a head of steam to return
   D. expressed any desire to return
               Ⓐ Ⓑ Ⓒ Ⓓ

Items 14 and 15 pose questions about the passage as a whole.

---

14. Considering the tone and subject matter of the
preceding paragraphs, is the last sentence an
appropriate way to end the essay?
   F. Yes, because it is necessary to shed some doubt
       on Defoe's creativity.
   G. Yes, because the essay is about the relationship
       between the real Selkirk and Defoe's fictionalized
       version of him.
   H. No, because there is nothing "bizarre" about
       Selkirk's story as it is related in the essay.
   J. No, because the focus of the essay is more on
       Selkirk himself than on Defoe's fictionalized ver-
       sion of him.
               Ⓕ Ⓖ Ⓗ Ⓙ

15. This essay would be most appropriate as part of a:
   A. scholarly study of eighteenth-century
       maritime history.
   B. study of the geography of the islands off of Chile.
   C. history of privateering in the Pacific.
   D. popular history of English literature.
               Ⓐ Ⓑ Ⓒ Ⓓ

Most of the time, we may not notice mistakes in which writers fail to say what they mean because we've taught ourselves to read for intended meaning only. We try to figure out what the author was *trying* to say, and we don't really care much if an author isn't exactly clear.

You may have found these Sense Questions harder than the Economy Questions in English Workout 1. The shortest answers here aren't right nearly as often. But, all other things being equal, the shortest answer is still your best bet. It's correct about half of the time—eight out of fifteen questions: numbers 1, 3, 7, 8, 9, 10, 12, and 13.

On some of the questions in Passage I above, you may not have gotten past Step 1 in the Three-Step Method. Question 9, for example, presented material that was clearly redundant. We certainly know that 28 years is longer than 6 (and if we're really up on our math we can even figure out that 28 is "more than four times" 6), so including any parenthetical aside like the ones given would be unnecessary. Remember, when in doubt, take it out. As we saw in English Workout 1, questions that include an "OMIT" option, and those in which some of the answers are much longer than others, are usually testing writing economy.

In the rest of the questions in this passage, the answers differ in other ways. They may join or fragment sentences, rearrange things, or add words that affect the meaning of the sentences. When the answers are all about the same length, as in most of the questions here, the question is more likely to test sense. Consider the shortest answer first, but don't be as quick to select it and move on. Think about the effect each choice has on the *meaning* of the sentence and pick longer answers if the shortest one doesn't make sense.

> HINT: *Students tend to reject informal writing as "incorrect." But ACT passages are written at various levels of formality. Some are as stiff as textbooks. Others are as casual as a talk with friends. Pay attention to the tone of the words. Are they serious? Are they laid back? Stay with the author's tone. Don't always stay formal.*

GRAMMAR RULES TESTED BY SENSE QUESTIONS

The ACT test makers include questions like those in Passage I to test many different rules of writing mechanics. Though it's not *necessary* to think about rules to answer the questions, familiarity with the rules can give you an alternative approach. The more ways to think about a question you have, the more likely you are to find the right answer.

We'll discuss some of these examples in groups based on what they're designed to test. That way we can briefly discuss the rules, but also show you how the basic strategic approach of "make it make sense" can get you the answers without a lot of technical analysis. Let's start with **Question 1.**

Completeness

> **EXAMPLE**
>
> ...Relatively few of them,
>
> however, know that Crusoe's <u>story. It was</u>
>   1
>
> actually based on the real-life adventures of
>
> a Scottish seaman, Alexander Selkirk.

1. A. NO CHANGE
    B. story: was
    C. story, was
    D. story was

If the underlined section for Question 1 were left as it is, the second sentence of the passage would be incomplete. It wouldn't make sense. "Relatively few people know that Crusoe's story" what? To make it make sense, you've got to continue the sentence so that it can tell us what it is that few people know about Crusoe's story. The three alternatives all do that, but B introduces a nonsensical colon, while C adds a comma when there's no pause in the sentence. D, however, continues the sentence—adding nothing unnecessary, but making it complete.

What Question 1 is testing is something we call completeness—the requirement that every sentence should consist of an entire thought. Don't just blindly judge the completeness of a sentence by whether or not it contains a subject and a verb. The alleged sentence—"Relatively few of them, however, know that Crusoe's story"—actually does contain a subject and a verb, but it's still not complete. It leaves a thought hanging. Don't leave thoughts hanging on the ACT. The test makers don't like it one bit.

Question 12 tests the same concept:

> **EXAMPLE**
>
> ...In fact, two
>
> sequels, in which Crusoe returns to the island
>
> after his rescue, were eventually <u>published</u>.
>   12
> <u>Though to</u> little acclaim.
>   12

12. F. NO CHANGE
    G. published, though
    H. published although
    J. published; although

Here, however, the fragment should be more obvious, since the clause that's trying to pass itself off as a sentence—"Though to little acclaim"—contains neither a subject nor a verb. That's the technical reason it's wrong, and if you recognized this, great. But on a more intuitive level, it just doesn't make sense to say, as a complete thought: "Though to little acclaim." So, you've got to make it make sense.

Clearly, that fragment has to be connected to the sentence before it, so F and J are wrong, since both would leave the fragment isolated. H goes too far in the other direction, omitting any punctuation at all between the fragment and the main body of the sentence, and that's no good. But the correct choice, G, does just what we need it to do: It connects the fragment logically to the main sentence, but it provides a comma to represent the pause between the two.

Again, knowing the rules of grammar certainly helps here, but you could have gotten this answer by just using common sense.

Sentence Structure

Technically, of course, Questions 1 and 12 test sentence structure, which is a broader topic of which completeness is one part. The "rules" of good sentence structure require that every sentence contain a complete thought. A "sentence" without a complete thought is called a *fragment*. A "sentence" with *too many* complete thoughts (usually connected by commas) is called a *run-on*. That's what we find in **Question 4**:

EXAMPLE

…Upon his return to England, Selkirk found

himself a <u>celebrity, his</u> strange tale had   **4. F.** NO CHANGE
              4   **G.** celebrity, but his
already become the talk of pubs and   **H.** celebrity. His
                                              J. celebrity his

coffeehouses throughout the British Isles.

Here we have two complete thoughts: (1) Selkirk found himself a celebrity upon his return, and (2) his tale was bandied about the pubs and coffeehouses. You can't just run these two complete thoughts together with a comma, as the underlined portion does. And you certainly can't just run them together *without* a comma or anything else, as choice J does. You *can* relate the two thoughts with a comma and a linking word (*and*, for instance), but choice G's inclusion of the word *but* makes no sense. It implies a contrast, while the two complete thoughts are actually very similar. Thus, you should create two sentences, one for each thought. That's what correct choice H does.

Remember to make sure all of the sentences in a passage contain at least one, but not more than one, complete thought. Fragments and run-ons appear frequently on the English section of the ACT. Both are sense problems that need to be corrected.

Modifiers

Question 2 tests modifier problems:

> EXAMPLE
>
> ...<u>After a bitter quarrel with his captain, he put</u>
>   2
> <u>Selkirk ashore</u> on tiny Mas a Tierra, one of the
>   2
> islands of Juan Fernandez...

2. **F.** NO CHANGE
    G. Quarreling with his captain, the boat was put ashore
    H. Having quarreled with his captain, Selkirk was put ashore
    J. Having quarreled with his captain, they put Selkirk ashore

In a well-written sentence, it must be clear exactly what words or phrases in the sentence are modifying (or referring to) what other words or phrases in the sentence. In the underlined portion here, the clause "after a bitter quarrel with his captain" should modify the pronoun that follows it—he. But it doesn't. The he who put Selkirk ashore must be the captain, but it can't be the captain who had "a bitter quarrel with his captain." That doesn't make sense (unless the captain quarrels with himself). So put the thing modified next to the thing modifying it. The person who quarreled with his captain was Selkirk—not the boat and not "they," whoever they are—so H is correct.

If you recognized the problem with Question 2 as a "misplaced modifier," that's great. Fantastic, even. But you didn't have to know the technicalities to get the right answer here. You just had to make the sentence make sense.

Question 11 tests a similar problem:

> EXAMPLE
>
> ...<u>Still popular today, contemporary</u>
>   11
> <u>audiences enjoyed the book as well.</u>
>   11

11. **A.** NO CHANGE
    B. Still read today, Defoe's contemporaries also enjoyed it.
    C. Viewed by many even then as a classic, the book is still popular to this day.
    D. Much read in its day, modern audiences still find the book compelling.

The way the sentence is written, it basically means that contemporary audiences are "still popular today." That doesn't make sense. The *intended* meaning is that the *book* is still popular today, as it was then. Choice C fixes the sense problem by putting its modifier—"viewed by many even then as a classic"—next to the thing it modifies—"the book." Notice that the other choices all misplace their modifiers in the same way, making them modify "Defoe's contemporaries" (in B) and "modern audiences" (in D).

As a rule of thumb, you should always make sure that modifiers are as close as possible to the things they modify.

Idiom (Proper Word Form and Choice)

Question 3 tests a rather hazy linguistic concept known as *idiom*. The word "idiomatic" refers to language that, well, uses words in the right way. Many words have special rules. If you're a native speaker of the language, you probably picked up many of these rules by ear before your eighth birthday; if you're not a native speaker, you had to learn them one by one.

EXAMPLE

...Stranded, Selkirk lived there alone—

in much the <u>same manner</u> as Defoe's
           3
Crusoe—until 1709, when he was finally

rescued by another...

3. **A.** NO CHANGE
    B. same manner that
    C. identical manner that
    D. identical way as

The sentence as written actually makes perfect sense. Selkirk lived in "much the same manner as" Defoe's Crusoe. The phrase *much the same* calls for *as* to complete the comparison between Selkirk's and Crusoe's ways of life. Note how B and C would create completeness problems— in much the same (or identical) manner that Defoe's Crusoe *what*? Choice D, meanwhile, is just plain unidiomatic. In English, we just don't say "in much the identical way," because the word *identical* is an absolute. You can't be *more* or *partially* identical; you either are or aren't identical to something else. But even if you didn't analyze D this carefully, it should have just sounded wrong to your ear. (In English Workout 3 we'll show you how "trusting your ear" can be a great way to get correct answers on the English subject test.)

Question 8 tests another idiom problem:

EXAMPLE

...For example, while Selkirk's presence on

the island was of course <u>known for many</u>
                 8
<u>people</u> (certainly everyone in the crew that
 8
stranded him there), no one in the novel is

aware of Crusoe's survival of the wreck and

presence on the island.

8. **F.** NO CHANGE
    G. widely known among people
    H. known about many people
    J. known to many people

The rules of grammar evolved to make sure that language expresses ideas clearly and efficiently. Thus, you can "bypass" the rules by making sure that the writing really does express the meaning. If the words do a good job of expressing meaning, they probably follow the rules. But if the words don't make sense, they probably break a rule somewhere.

The underlined portion as written is unidiomatic. Selkirk's presence wasn't known *for* many people—it was known *by*, or known *to*, many people. When you're "known *for*" something, that means you have a reputation for doing such and such. That makes no sense in this context. But J *does* make sense, since it points out that Selkirk's presence on the island was known *to* many people—that is, it was something that many people knew about. G is unidiomatic; we just wouldn't say "among people" here, since it's not specific enough. That sounds as if we're talking about people as a species. H would have been acceptable if it had read "known about *by* many people," but without the *by* the correction just wouldn't make sense.

Idiom is a tough topic if you're not a native speaker. You have to think very carefully about the meaning of every word. But if you *are* a native speaker, use your many years of hearing English as a guide. Choose the correction that makes sense *and* doesn't sound weird.

Pronouns

Remember, the object of grammar rules is to make sure that the meaning of language is clearly conveyed. Sometimes, the test will throw you a sentence in which the meaning of a pronoun is unclear. You won't be sure whom or what the pronoun is referring to. That's the kind of problem you were given in **Question 5**:

...The story even reached the ears of Richard

Steele, who featured it in his periodical,

The Tatler. Eventually, <u>he became</u> the
                                    5
subject of a best-selling book...

5. **A.** NO CHANGE
    B. Selkirk became
    C. his became
    D. he becomes

HINT: *Mistakes of sense often involve pronouns. Make a habit of checking every underlined pronoun as you go along. What does the pronoun stand for? Can you tell? If not, there's an error. Does it make sense? If not, there's an error.*

The *intended* meaning of the pronoun *he* here is "Selkirk." But what's the closest male name to the pronoun? Richard Steele, the publisher of *The Tatler*. That creates an unclear situation. Make it clear! Choice B takes care of the problem by naming Selkirk explicitly. C would create a sense problem—his *what* became the subject of a book? Meanwhile, D shifts the verb tense into the present, which makes no sense since this book was written over 250 years ago!

Make sure it's perfectly clear to what or to whom all pronouns refer.

Logic

Remember when we talked about structural clues back in Reading Workout 1? (C'mon, it wasn't *that* long ago!) Structural clues are signal words that an author uses to show where he or she is going in a piece of writing. They show how all of the pieces logically fit together. If the author uses the structural clue *on the other hand*, that means a contrast is coming up; if he or she uses the clue *moreover*, that means that a continuation is coming up—an addition that is more or less in the same vein as what came before.

Many ACT English questions mix up the logic of a piece of writing by giving you the wrong structural clue or other logic word. That's what happened in **Question 10**.

EXAMPLE

...<u>Because</u> of its basis in fact, *Robinson*
    10
Crusoe is often regarded as the first major

novel in English literature.

10. F. NO CHANGE
    G. Despite
    H. Resulting from
    J. As a consequence of

As written, this sentence means that *Crusoe* was regarded as the first major novel because it was based on fact. But that makes no sense. If it was based on fact, that would work *against* its being regarded as a novel. There's a contrast between basis in "fact" (which implies nonfiction) and "first major novel" (which implies fiction). To show that contrast logically, you need a contrast word like *despite*. That's why G is correct here. G makes the sentence make sense.

Question 6 also tests logic:

. . . the subject of a best-selling book,

A Cruizing Voyage Round the World,

by Woodes Rogers. <u>And while</u> there is
          6
some evidence that Defoe, a journalist, may

actually have interviewed Selkirk personally,

most literary historians believe that it was

the reprinting of the Rogers book in 1718 that

served as the real stimulus for Defoe's novel.

6. F. NO CHANGE
    G. but since
    H. and therefore
    J. OMIT the underlined portion and start the sentence with "There."

The structural clue should convey a sense of continuation from the preceding sentence (since we're still talking about the book *A Cruizing Voyage*), but also a sense of contrast with the latter part of the sentence of which it's a part (since there is a contrast there between one possible stimulus and another). *And while* does the trick (or both tricks, actually). *And* provides the continuation; *while* provides the needed contrast.

G and H, however, introduce structural clues (*since, therefore*) that imply a cause-and-effect relationship between the two impulses—Defoe's interview and the appearance of *A Cruizing Voyage*—which makes no sense in context. Meanwhile, omitting the portion would create a run-on sentence with two complete thoughts—about Defoe's interview and about the opinion of "most literary historians"—without subordinating one to the other or connecting them with a linking word. Remember, don't always pick "OMIT" just because it's there!

Verb Usage

Verbs have an annoying habit of changing form depending on who's doing the action and when he or she is doing it. Example: "I *hate* verbs; he *hates* verbs; and we both *have hated* verbs ever since we were kids." You have to be very careful to make sure verbs match their subject and the tense of the surrounding context. Take **Question 7**:

> EXAMPLE

...In Crusoe, which <u>has been published in</u>
7
1719, Defoe took substantial liberties with

the Selkirk story.

7. A. NO CHANGE
B. was published
C. had been published
D. will have been published

The publication of *Robinson Crusoe* is something that took place in 1719—the past, in other words. So the underlined portion, which puts the verb in the present perfect tense, is flawed. Choices C and D, meanwhile, would put the verb into several bizarre tenses normally used to convey a complex time relationship. C makes it seem as if publication of the book happened *before* Defoe took his liberties with the story. But that's nonsensical. The liberties were taken in the writing of the book. D, meanwhile, does very strange things with the time sequence. But keep things simple. The book was published in the past; Defoe also took his substantial liberties in more or less the same past. So just use the simple past tense. The book was published in 1719, choice B.

Make sure verbs are in the right case and tense. Put them in the case and tense that make the most sense. The test makers just love to throw verb problems at you.

Tone

As we said earlier, the passages in the English subject test vary in tone. Some are formal; others are informal. Usually, you'll know which is which without having to think about it. If a passage contains slang, a few exclamation points, and a joke or two, the tone is informal; if it sounds like something a Latin instructor would say, it's probably formal.

Good style requires that the tone of a piece of writing be at the same level throughout. Sometimes the underlined portion might not fit the tone of the rest of the passage. If so, it's up to you to correct it.

Look at **Question 13**:

> EXAMPLE

...Meanwhile, Selkirk himself never

<u>gave a hoot about returning</u> to the island that
13
had made him famous.

13. A. NO CHANGE
B. evinced himself as desirous of returning
C. could whip up a head of steam to return
D. expressed any desire to return

Selkirk "never gave a hoot" about going back? No way! Slang doesn't belong in this passage. This isn't the most formally written passage in the world, but it's certainly no place for a phrase like *gave a hoot* or (just as bad) *whip up a head of steam* (that's choice C). B, meanwhile, goes too far in the opposite direction. "Evinced himself as desirous of returning" sounds like something no human being would say. But the rest of the passage sounds human. It makes no sense to shift tonal gears in the middle of a passage. So keep the tone consistent. Choose D.

NONSTANDARD-FORMAT ENGLISH QUESTIONS

> **Watch Out**
>
> Don't pick an answer just because it sounds "fancy." The word "desirous" in Question 13 might be tempting—but don't give in to the temptation. Pick commonsense, everyday words that express the meaning the author intends. Don't worry if it sounds plain.

The Nonstandard-Format questions ask about the passage as a whole. Keep in mind the main point of the passage—the "gist"—as well as the overall tone and style. For an entire passage to "make sense," it has to be consistent throughout, both in content and in tone and style.

Judging the Passage

Question 14 asks you to judge the passage. Was the last sentence an appropriate ending or not? Generally speaking, the correct answer to a question of this type is usually one that approves of the passage. So, unless you're pretty sure that the passage is badly written, give it the "benefit of the doubt." As a rule of thumb, on questions that ask you to judge the passage, lean toward selecting a choice that approves of it.

> EXAMPLE

14. Considering the tone and subject matter of the preceding paragraphs, is the last sentence an appropriate way to end the essay?
    - **F.** Yes, because it is necessary to shed some doubt on Defoe's creativity.
    - **G.** Yes, because the essay is about the relationship between the real Selkirk and Defoe's fictionalized version of him.
    - **H.** No, because there is nothing "bizarre" about Selkirk's story as it is related in the essay.
    - **J.** No, because the focus of the essay is more on Selkirk himself than on Defoe's fictionalized version of him.

Think of the passage as a whole. It's been comparing Selkirk's real life with the one that Defoe made up for the character of Robinson Crusoe. Therefore, ending in this way, with an ironic reference to Defoe as writing a more fitting end to Selkirk's life, is perfectly appropriate. The answer to the question, then, should be yes (eliminating choices H and J). F says yes, but gives a nonsensical reason for saying yes. Why is it necessary to shed doubt on Defoe's creativity? Does the author hold a grudge against Defoe? Not that we can tell. So G is the best answer here.

Reading-Type Questions

If you thought **Question 15** looked like a Reading question hiding in the English part of the exam, you were right. As mentioned in ACT Basics, one reason that you should keep thinking about what the passage means—rather than focusing on picky rules of grammar or punctuation—is that the ACT often asks Reading-type questions.

EXAMPLE

15. This essay would be most appropriate as part of a:
    A. scholarly study of eighteenth-century maritime history.
    B. study of the geography of the islands off of Chile.
    C. history of privateering in the Pacific.
    D. popular history of English literature.

Remember what we said above: Keep the main idea, style, and tone of the whole passage in mind. What was this passage principally about? How Defoe's *Robinson Crusoe* was loosely based on the life of a real shipwrecked sailor, Alexander Selkirk. Would that kind of thing belong in a study of geography (choice B)? No. The focus is on the fictionalization of a historical life, not on the physical features of the islands off Chile. The passage isn't principally about privateering or maritime history either, so C and A are wrong as well. This passage is about the relationship between a true story and a famous fictionalized story. And its tone isn't overly scholarly either. So it probably belongs in a popular history of English literature (choice D).

Structure and Purpose

In English, there will also be questions that test your grasp of overall structure and purpose in a piece of prose. The test makers scramble the order of the sentences in a paragraph (or of the paragraphs in a passage). The question then asks you to decide on the best order for the scrambled parts. Take a look at **Question 16**:

EXAMPLE

[1] Only recently has new evidence led many scientists to question the accepted division between birds and dinosaurs. [2] Traditionally, they have been placed in entirely separate classes within the subphylum *Vertebrata*. [3] Birds and dinosaurs don't have many obvious similarities. [4] Birds formed the class *Aves*, while dinosaurs constituted two orders, *Saurischia* and *Ornithischia*, within the class *Reptilia*.

16. To best fulfill the author's purpose, the order of the sentences in the paragraph above should be:
    F. 1, 2, 3, 4
    G. 2, 3, 4, 1
    H. 3, 2, 4, 1
    J. 3, 2, 1, 4

Here again, the goal is to make it make sense. All of the sentences in this paragraph relate to the differences between birds and dinosaurs. Sentence 3 best introduces this idea. Notice that two of the answer choices begin with Sentence 3—H and J. The other two can be eliminated.

Look again at the logic of the sentences. Clearly, Sentence 4 elaborates on the distinction introduced in Sentence 2, describing the two separate classes into which birds and dinosaurs have traditionally been placed. In order for the paragraph to make sense, then, Sentence 4 must immediately follow Sentence 2. Only H has them in that order, so H looks like the answer.

Just to check, you'll want to read the entire paragraph in the order suggested by H. And if you do, you'll notice that the paragraph makes perfect sense, with Sentence 3 introducing the topic, Sentences 2 and 4 showing how that topic has been traditionally viewed, and Sentence 1 coming in naturally to show how that traditional view is no longer valid.

For questions like this, it's usually a good idea to start by trying to figure out the first (and sometimes the last) sentence, because first and last sentences usually have the most obvious functions in an ACT-style paragraph.

To sum up, the questions in the passage above, as in any ACT English passage, test many specific issues—sentence structure, word form, style, idiom, logic, transitions, modifiers, pronouns, tone, etcetera. But always remember that many of them can be resolved by merely trying to . . . *make it make sense.*

Guessing Hint

In Question 16, two of the answer choices listed Sentence 3 first and two of the choices listed Sentence 1 last. If the same sentence is listed as first or last in two answers, it's actually more likely than the others to belong at the beginning or ending of the passage. If a question had the following answers, what would be the best blind guess?

A. 1, 2, 3, 4, 5
B. 2, 5, 4, 3, 1
C. 3, 1, 2, 5, 4
D. 3, 4, 2, 5, 1

D is the best blind guess. Sentence 3 is the best bet to be first, and Sentence 1 is the best bet to be last, since they appear in these positions most. Note: Questions like this one, in which blind guessing would narrow the choices down to just one, are rare on real ACTs. But you can often narrow the choices to two.

9

Math Workout 2:
Shake It Up!

Highlights

- Ten algebra questions you can expect to see

- How to approach questions that stump you at first

- How to solve some typical story problems

The main idea of Math Workout 1 was: Don't jump in headfirst and start crunching numbers until you've given the problem some thought. Make sure you know what you're doing—*and* that what you're doing won't take too long.

As we saw in Math Workout 1, sometimes you'll know how to proceed as soon as you understand the question. A good number of ACT algebra and coordinate geometry questions are straightforward textbook questions you may already be prepared for.

TEN TEXTBOOK QUESTIONS

When you take the ACT, you can be sure you'll see some of the following questions with only slight variations. You'll find answers and explanations for these questions in the Math Appendix.

1. Evaluate an algebraic expression. (*See Math Appendix, #52*)

   Example: If $x = -2$, then $x^2 + 5x - 6 = ?$

2. Multiply binomials. (*See Math Appendix, #56*)

   Example: $(x + 3)(x + 4) = ?$

KAPLAN 115

3. Factor a polynomial. (*See Math Appendix, #61*)

   Example: What is the complete factorization of $x^2 - 5x + 6$?

4. Simplify an algebraic fraction. (*See Math Appendix, #62*)

   Example: For all $x \neq \pm 3$, $\dfrac{x^2 - x - 12}{x^2 - 9} = ?$

5. Solve a linear equation. (*See Math Appendix, #63*)

   Example: If $5x - 12 = -2x + 9$, then $x = ?$

6. Solve a quadratic equation. (*See Math Appendix, #66*)

   Example: If $x^2 + 12 = 7x$, what are the two possible values of x?

7. Solve a system of equations. (*See Math Appendix, #67*)

   Example: If $4x + 3x = 8$, and $x + x = 3$, what is the value of x?

8. Solve an inequality. (*See Math Appendix, #69*)

   Example: What are all the values of x for which $-5x + 7 < -3$?

9. Find the distance between two points in the (x, y) coordinate plane. (*See Math Appendix, #71*)

   Example: What is the distance between the points with (x, y) coordinates $(-2, 2)$ and $(1, -2)$?

10. Find the slope of a line from its equation. (*See Math Appendix, #73*)

   Example: What is the slope of the line with the equation $2x + 3y = 4$?

These questions are all so straightforward and traditional, they could have come out of a high school algebra textbook. These are the questions you should do the way you were taught.

The techniques you'd use in questions like the ten listed above are the techniques they've been teaching you all along in high school math classes. In case you'd like to review them, you'll find all the standard approaches you might need for the ACT succinctly summarized in the Math Appendix. We're not so concerned in these Workouts with problems you may already know how to solve. Here in Workout 2 we're going to focus on several Algebra and Coordinate Geometry situations where the quick and reliable solution method is not so obvious, where often the best method is one your algebra teacher never told you about.

FOUR WAYS TO SHAKE IT UP

It's bound to happen at some point on Test Day. You look at a math problem and you don't see what to do. Don't freak out at first glance. Think about the problem for a few seconds before you give up. When you don't see the quick and reliable approach right away, shake the problem up a little. Try one of these "shake-it-up" techniques:

1. Restate
2. Remove the disguise
3. Pick numbers
4. Backsolve

#1—Restate

Often, the way to get over that stymied feeling is to change your perspective. Have you ever watched people playing Scrabble®? In their search for high-scoring words that can be formed using the letters on their seven tiles, they continually move the tiles around in their rack. Sometimes a good word becomes apparent only after rearranging the tiles. One might not see the seven-letter word in this arrangement:

REBAGLA

But reverse the tiles and a word almost reveals itself:

ALGABER

The tiles can spell "ALGEBRA."

The same gimmick works a lot on the ACT, too. When you get stuck, try looking at the problem from a different angle. Try rearranging the numbers, or changing fractions to decimals, or factoring, or multiplying out, or redrawing the diagram, or anything that might give you the fresh perspective you need to uncover a good solution method.

Here's a question you might not know what to do with at first glance:

EXAMPLE

1. Which of the following is equivalent to $7^{77} - 7^{76}$?
   A. 7
   B. 7^{77-76}
   C. $7^{77} \div 76$
   D. $7(77-76)$
   E. $7^{76}(6)$

Here's a hint: *Think of an easier problem testing the same principles.* The important thing to look for is the basic relationships involved—here, we have exponents and subtraction. That subtraction sign causes trouble, because none of the ordinary rules of exponents (see Math Appendix, #47–48) seem to apply when there is subtraction of "unlike" terms.

Another hint: How would you work with $x^2 - x$? Most test takers could come up with another expression for $x^2 - x$: they'd factor to $x(x-1)$. Or if the problem asked for $x^{77} - x^{76}$, they'd factor to $x^{76}(x-1)$. The rule is no different for 7 than for x. Factoring out the 7^{76} gives you: $7^{76}(7-1)$, which is $7^{76}(6)$, or choice E.

Sometimes an ACT algebra question will include an expression that isn't of much use in its given form. The breakthrough in such a case may be to restate the expression by either simplifying it or factoring it. For example:

EXAMPLE

2. If $\frac{2}{x} - \frac{6}{x}$ is an integer, which of the following statements must be true?
    F. x is positive.
    G. x is odd.
    H. x is even.
    J. x is a multiple of 3.
    K. x is a multiple of 6.

Reexpress: $\frac{x}{2} - \frac{x}{6} = \frac{3x}{6} - \frac{x}{6} = \frac{2x}{6} = \frac{x}{3}$

This form of the expression tells us a lot more. If $\frac{x}{3}$ is an integer, then x is equal to 3 times an integer:

$\frac{x}{3}$ = an integer

$x = 3 \cdot$ (an integer)

In other words, x is a multiple of 3, choice J.

#2—Remove the Disguise

Sometimes it's hard to see the quick and reliable method immediately because the true nature of the problem is hidden behind a disguise. Look at this example:

3. What are the (x, y) coordinates of the point of intersection of the line representing the equation $5x + 2y = 4$ and the line representing the equation $x - 2y = 8$?
    A. (2, 3)
    B. (–2, 3)
    C. (2, –3)
    D. (–3, 2)
    E. (3, –2)

Coordinate Geometry

Although this question turned out not to be a real coordinate geometry problem, the test makers do have a soft spot in their hearts for coordinate geometry. Typically 8 or more of the 60 math questions involve coordinate geometry. It's hard to get a top score without getting at least some coordinate geometry questions right. Use Math Appendix #71–77 to review the relevant rules and formulas.

This may look like a coordinate geometry question, but do you really have to graph the lines to find the point of intersection? Remember, the ACT is looking for creative thinkers, not mindless calculators! Think about it for a moment—what's the special significance of the point of intersection, the one point that the two lines have in common? That's the one point whose coordinates will satisfy *both* equations.

So what we realize now is that this is not a coordinate geometry question at all, but a "system-of-equations" question. All it's really asking you to do is solve the pair of equations for x and y. The question has *nothing* to do with slopes, intercepts, axes, or quadrants. It's a pure algebra question in disguise.

Now that we know we're looking at a system of equations, the method of solution presents itself more clearly. The first equation has a $+2y$, and the second equation has a $-2y$. If we just "add" the equations, the y terms cancel:

$$5x + 2y = 4$$
$$x - 2y = 8$$
$$\overline{6x \qquad = 12}$$

If $6x = 12$, then $x = 2$. Plug that back into either of the original equations and you'll find that $y = -3$. The point of intersection is $(2, -3)$, and the answer is C.

Here's another disguised question:

EXAMPLE

4. A geometer uses the following formula to estimate the area A of the shaded portion of a circle as shown in the figure below when only the height h and the length of the chord c are known:

$$A = \frac{2ch}{3} + \frac{h^3}{2c}$$

What is the geometer's estimate of the area, in square inches, of the shaded region if the height is 2 inches and the length of the chord is 6 inches?

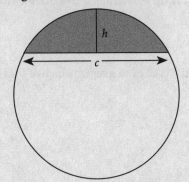

F. 6

G. $6\frac{2}{3}$

H. $7\frac{1}{2}$

J. $8\frac{2}{3}$

K. 12

At first glance, this looks like a horrendously esoteric geometry question. Who ever heard of such a formula?

But when you think about the question a bit, you realize that you don't really have to understand the formula. You certainly don't have to remember it—it's right there in the question.

In fact, this is not really a geometry question at all. It's really just an "evaluate the algebraic expression" question in disguise. All you have to do is plug the given values $h = 2$ and $c = 6$ into the given formula:

$$A = \frac{2ch}{3} + \frac{h^3}{2c}$$

$$= \frac{2(6)(2)}{3} + \frac{(2)^3}{2(6)}$$

$$= 8 + \frac{2}{3} = 8\frac{2}{3}$$

Choice J is correct.

The people who wrote this question wanted you to freak out at first sight and give up. Don't give up on a question too quickly just because it looks like it's testing something you never saw before. In many such cases it's really a familiar problem in disguise.

#3—Pick Numbers

Sometimes you can get stuck on an algebra problem just because it's too general or abstract. A good way to get a handle on such a problem is to bring it down to earth and make it more explicit by temporarily substituting particular numbers for the variables.

EXAMPLE

5. If a is an odd integer and b is an even integer, which of the following must be odd?
   A. $2a + b$
   B. $a + 2b$
   C. ab
   D. a^2b
   E. ab^2

Rather than try to think this one through abstractly, it's easier for most people simply to pick numbers for a and b. There are rules that predict the evenness or oddness of sums, differences, and products, but there's no need to memorize those rules. When it comes to adding, subtracting, and multiplying evens and odds, what happens with one pair of numbers generally happens with all similar pairs.

Just say, for the time being, that $a = 1$ and $b = 2$. Plug those values into the answer choices, and there's a good chance only one choice will be odd:

   A. $2a + b = 2(1) + 2 = 4$
   B. $a + 2b = 1 + 2(2) = 5$
   C. $ab = (1)(2) = 2$
   D. $a^2b = (1)^2(2) = 2$
   E. $ab^2 = (1)(2)^2 = 4$

Choice B was the only odd one for $a = 1$ and $b = 2$, so it *must* be the one that's odd no matter *what* odd number a actually stands for and even number b actually stands for.

#4—Backsolve

With some ACT math problems, rather than try to solve the problem and then look among the choices for the answer, it may actually be easier to take each answer choice and try it out until you find the one that works. Since this approach involves working backwards from the answer choices to the question stem, it's called "backsolving." Here's a good example:

EXAMPLE

6. All 200 tickets were sold for a particular concert. Some tickets cost $10 apiece, and the others cost $5 apiece. If total ticket sales were $1,750, how many of the more expensive tickets were sold?
   F. 20
   G. 75
   H. 100
   J. 150
   K. 175

There are ways to solve this problem by setting up an equation or two, but if you're not comfortable with the algebraic approach to this one, why not just try out each answer choice?

Start with choice H. If 100 tickets went for $10, then the other 100 went for $5. One hundred tickets at $10 is $1,000, and 100 tickets at $5 is $500, for a total of $1,500—too small. There must have been more than one hundred, $10 tickets.

So let's try choice J next. If 150 tickets went for $10, then the other 50 went for $5. So 150 tickets at $10 is $1,500, and 50 tickets at $5 is $250, for a total of $1,750—that's it! The answer is J.

Backsolving your way to the answer may not be a method you'd show your algebra teacher with pride—but your algebra teacher won't be watching on Test Day. Remember, all that matters is right answers—it doesn't matter how you get them.

Backsolving

When backsolving, start with the middle choices—that is, C or H. The answer choices are generally listed in numerical order, and if the first number you try doesn't work, the process of trying out that first number might tell you whether to go for a smaller one or a larger one.

ADVICE FOR SOME SPECIFIC STORY-PROBLEM SITUATIONS

We find that about one-third of the questions in the math subtest are story problems. Although some story problems present unique situations that must be analyzed on the spot, other story problems are just variations on familiar themes. Experience with a few of the more common story problems and their standard solution setups will certainly come in handy on Test Day.

Percent Problems

In percent problems, you're usually given two numbers and asked to find a third. The key is to identify what you have and what you're looking for.

KEY: *Identify the Part, the Percent, and the Whole.*

(Usually the Part is associated with the word *is* and the Whole is associated with the word *of*.)

Put the numbers and the unknown into the general form:

Part = Percent × Whole

EXAMPLE

7. In a group of 250 students, 40 are seniors. What percentage of the group are seniors?
   A. 1.6%
   B. 6.25%
   C. 10%
   D. 16%
   E. 40%

The Percent is what we're looking for ("What percentage . . ."); the Whole is 250 (". . . of the group . . ."); and the Part is 40 (". . . are seniors"). Plug these into the general formula:

$$\text{Part} = \text{Percent} \times \text{Whole}$$
$$40 = 250x$$
$$x = \frac{40}{250} = .16 = 16\%$$

The answer is D.

Percent Change Trap

When a quantity is increased or decreased by a percent more than once, you cannot simply add and subtract the percents to get the answer. In this kind of percent problem:

- The first percent change is a percent of the starting amount, but

- The second percent change is a percent of the new amount.

Percent Increase/Decrease Problems

Many ACT percent problems concern percent change. To increase a number by a certain percent, calculate that percent of the original number and add it on. To decrease a number by a certain percent, calculate that percent of the original number and then subtract. For example, to answer the question, "What number is 30% greater than 80?" first find 30% of 80—that's 24—and add that on to 80: $80 + 24 = 104$.

The ACT has ways of complicating percent change problems. Especially tricky are problems with multiple changes, such as a percent increase followed by another percent increase, or a percent increase followed by a percent decrease.

Here's a question, for example, that's not so simple as it seems at first:

EXAMPLE

8. If a positive number is increased by 70 percent, and then the result is decreased by 50 percent, which of the following accurately describes the net change?
   F. a 20 percent decrease
   G. a 15 percent decrease
   H. a 12 percent increase
   J. a 20 percent increase
   K. a 120 percent increase

To get a handle on this one, pick a number. Suppose the original number is 100. After a 70 percent increase it rises to 170. That number, 170, is decreased by 50 percent, which means it's reduced by half to 85. The net change from 100 to 85 is a 15 percent decrease—choice G.

Average Problems

Instead of giving you a list of values to plug into the average formula, ACT average questions often put a slight spin on the problem. They tell you the average of a group of terms and ask you to find the value of the missing term. Here's a classic example:

EXAMPLE

9. To earn a B for the semester, Linda needs an average of at least 80 on the five tests. Her average for the first four test scores is 79. What is the minimum score she must get on the fifth test to earn a B for the semester?
   A. 80
   B. 81
   C. 82
   D. 83
   E. 84

The key to almost every average question is to use the sum. Sums can be combined much more readily than averages. An average of 80 on five tests is more usefully thought of as a combined score of 400. To get a B for the semester, Linda's five test scores have to add up to 400 or more. The first four scores add up to $4 \times 79 = 316$. She needs another 84 to get that 316 up to 400. The answer is E.

Weighted Average Problems

Another spin ACT test makers put on average problems is to give you an average for part of a group and an average for the rest of the group and then ask for the combined average.

EXAMPLE

10. In a class of 10 boys and 15 girls, the boys' average score on the final exam was 80 and the girls' average score was 90. What was the average score for the whole class?

  F. 83
  G. 84
  H. 85
  J. 86
  K. 87

Probability Trap

The probability of what will happen is not affected by what already has happened. Whenever you flip a fair coin, the probability is $\frac{1}{2}$ that it will be heads. Even if you flip the coin and get heads ten times in a row, the probability is still $\frac{1}{2}$ on the eleventh flip. Of course, the odds against eleven heads in a row are huge, but once the first ten flips are history they're no longer relevant. Only the flips yet to come matter.

Don't just average 80 and 90 to get 85. That would work only if the class had exactly the same number of girls as boys. In this case, there are more girls, so they carry more "weight" in the overall class average. In other words, the class average should be somewhat closer to 90 (the girls' average) than to 80 (the boys' average).

As usual with averages, the key is to use the sum. The average score for the whole class is the total of the 25 individual scores divided by 25. We don't have 25 scores to add up, but we can use the boys' average and the girls' average to get two subtotals.

If 10 boys average 80, then their 10 scores add up to 10 × 80, or 800. If 15 girls average 90, then their 15 scores add up to 15 × 90, or 1,350. Add the boys' total to the girls' total: 800 + 1,350 = 2,150. That's the class total, which can be divided by 25 to get the class average: $\frac{2,150}{25}$ = 86. The answer is J.

Probability Problems

Probabilities are part-to-whole ratios. The whole is the total number of possible outcomes. The part is the number of "favorable" outcomes. For example, if a drawer contains two black ties and five other ties, and you want a black tie, the total number of possible outcomes is 7 (the total number of ties) and the number of "favorable" outcomes is 2 (the number of black ties). The probability of choosing a black tie at random is $\frac{2}{7}$.

WHAT TO DO NEXT

Because more than half the math questions on the ACT involve algebra, it's a good idea to take some time before Test Day to solidify your understanding of the basics. Focus on #52–70 in the Math Appendix. Keep things in perspective. Geometry questions are important, too, but algebra questions are more important.

Reading Workout 2:
Look It Up!

Highlights

- Practice the Kaplan Method
- Looking at the Questions
- Tips for ACT Reading

In Reading Workout 1, we discussed general strategies for approaching ACT Reading. Now let's look more closely at the major types of questions you'll encounter. As we mentioned in ACT Basics, there are really three main types of Reading questions on the test: Specific Detail Questions and Inference Questions (which make up the bulk of any Reading subtest), as well as Big Picture Questions (of which there are usually just a few).

USING THE KAPLAN READING METHOD

Don't forget to use Kaplan's Method for Reading, which we discussed in Reading Workout 1. Here's a reminder of how it works:

Step 1: Preread the Passage

In other words, quickly work through the passage before trying to answer the questions. Read actively, and assemble a mental "road map" or overall idea of how the passage is organized.

Step 2: Consider the Question Stem

Before plunging into the answer choices, take a moment to think about the question. Spend time thinking about the answer to the question before you look at the choices.

Step 3: Refer to the Passage

You don't need to refer to the whole passage. Just refer to the passage by finding the place where the answer to a question can be found. Sometimes a line reference will be included in the question; otherwise, rely on your road map of the passage.

Step 4: Answer the Question in Your Own Words

Do this before looking at the answer choices.

Step 5: Match Your Answer with One of the Choices

With an answer in mind, it'll be easier to spot the best choice

Try the following typical ACT nonfiction passage, this one from the Humanities. Afterward, we'll discuss selected questions from this set as examples of Specific Detail, Inference, and Big Picture Questions.

Passage II

Tragedy was the invention of the Greeks. In their Golden Age, the fifth century before Christ, they produced the world's greatest
Line   dramatists, new forms of tragedy and comedy
(5)   that have been models ever since, and a theatre that every age goes back to for rediscovery of some basic principle....

Since it derived from primitive religious rites, with masks and ceremonial costumes, and
(10)   made use of music, dance, and poetry, the Greek drama was at the opposite pole from the modern realistic stage. In fact, probably no other theatre in history has made fuller use of the intensities of art. The masks, made of paint-
(15)   ed linen, wood, and plaster, brought down from primitive days the atmosphere of gods, heroes, and demons. Our nineteenth- and twentieth-century grandfathers thought masks must have been very artificial. Today, however, we appre-
(20)   ciate their exciting intensity and can see that in a large theatre they were indispensable. If they allowed no fleeting change of expression during a single episode, they could give for each episode in turn more intense expression than
(25)   any human face could. When Oedipus comes back with bleeding eyes, the new mask could be more terrible than any facial makeup the audience could endure, yet in its sculpted intensity more beautiful than a real face.

(30)   Most essential of all intensities, and hardest for us to understand, was the chorus. Yet many playwrights today are trying to find some equivalent to do for a modern play what the chorus did for the Greeks. During the episodes
(35)   played by the actors, the chorus would only provide a background of group response, enlarging and reverberating the emotions of the actors, sometimes protesting and opposing but in general serving as ideal spectators to stir and
(40)   lead the reactions of the audience. But between episodes, with the actors out of the way, the chorus took over. We have only the words, not the music or dance, and some translations of the odes are in such formal, old-fashioned lan-
(45)   guage that it is hard to guess that they were accompanied by vigorous, sometimes even wild dances and symbolic actions that filled an orchestra which in some cities was sixty to ninety feet in diameter. Sometimes the chorus
(50)   expressed simple horror or lament. Sometimes it chanted and acted out, in unison and in precise formations of rows and lines, the acts of violence the characters were enacting offstage. When Phaedra rushes offstage in Hippolytus to
(55)   hang herself from the rafters, the members of the chorus, all fifteen of them, perform in mime and chant the act of tying the rope and swinging from the rafters. Sometimes the chorus tells or reenacts an incident of history or legend that
(60)   throws light on the situation in the play.

Sometimes the chorus puts into specific action what is a general intention in the mind of the main character. When Oedipus resolves to hunt out the guilty person and cleanse the (65) city, he is speaking metaphorically, but the chorus invokes the gods of vengeance and dances a wild pursuit.

On the printed page, the choral odes seem static and formal, lyric and philosophical, (70) emotional letdowns that punctuate the series of episodes, like intermissions between two acts of a play. The reader who skips the odes can get the main points of the play. A few are worth reading as independent poems, notably the (75) famous one in Antigone beginning, "Many are the wonders of the world, but none is more wonderful than man." Some modern acting versions omit the chorus or reduce it to a few background figures. Yet to the Greeks the odes (80) were certainly more than mere poetic interludes: the wild Dionysian words and movements evoked primitive levels of the subconscious and at the same time served to transform primitive violence into charm and beauty and to add (85) philosophical reflections on the meaning of human destiny.

For production today, we can only improvise some partial equivalent. In Athens the entire population was familiar with choral (90) performances. Every year each of the tribes entered a dithyramb in a contest, rehearsing five hundred men and boys for weeks. Some modern composers have tried to write dramatic music for choruses: the most notable examples are the (95) French composer Darius Milhaud, in the primitive rhythms, shouts, and chants of his operatic version of the *Oresteia*; George Gershwin, in the Negro funeral scenes of *Porgy and Bess*; and Kurt Weill, in the African (100) choruses for *Lost in the Stars*, the musical dramatization of Alan Paton's novel, *Cry, the Beloved Country*. For revivals of Greek tragedies we have not dared use much music beyond a few phrases half shouted, half sung, (105) and drumbeats and suggestive melodies in the background.

From Invitation to the Theatre, © *1967 by George Kernodle; Harcourt, Brace, & World Inc., publisher.*

1. Combined with the passage's additional information, the fact that some Greek orchestras were sixty to ninety feet across suggests that:
    A. few spectators were able to see the stage.
    B. no one performer could dominate a performance.
    C. choruses and masks helped overcome the distance between actors and audience.
    D. Greek tragedies lacked the emotional force of modern theatrical productions.

2. Which of the following claims expresses the writer's opinion and not a fact?
    F. The Greek odes contained Dionysian words and movements.
    G. Greek theater has made greater use of the intensities of art than has any other theater in history.
    H. Many modern playwrights are trying to find an equivalent to the Greek chorus.
    J. The chorus was an essential part of Greek tragedy.

3. The description of the chorus' enactment of Phaedra's offstage suicide (lines 54–60) shows that, in contrast to modern theater, ancient Greek theater was:
    A. more violent.
    B. more concerned with satisfying an audience.
    C. more apt to be historically accurate.
    D. less concerned with a realistic portrayal of events.

4. It can be inferred that one consequence of the Greeks' use of masks was that:
    F. the actors often had to change masks between episodes.
    G. the characters in the play could not convey emotion.
    H. the actors wearing masks played nonspeaking roles.
    J. good acting ability was not important to the Greeks.

    Ⓕ Ⓖ Ⓗ Ⓙ

5. Which of the following is supported by the information in the second paragraph (lines 8–29)?
    A. Masks in Greek drama combined artistic beauty with emotional intensity.
    B. The use of masks in Greek drama was better appreciated in the nineteenth century than it is now.
    C. Masks in Greek drama were used to portray gods but never human beings.
    D. Contemporary scholars seriously doubt the importance of masks to Greek theater.

    Ⓐ Ⓑ Ⓒ Ⓓ

6. The author indicates in lines 63–65 that Oedipus's resolution "to hunt out the guilty person and cleanse the city" was:
    F. at odds with what he actually does later in the performance.
    G. misinterpreted by the chorus.
    H. dramatized by the actions of the chorus.
    J. angrily condemned by the chorus.

    Ⓕ Ⓖ Ⓗ Ⓙ

7. According to the passage, when actors were present on stage, the chorus would:
    A. look on as silently as spectators.
    B. inevitably agree with the actors' actions.
    C. communicate to the audience solely through mime.
    D. react to the performance as an audience might.

    Ⓐ Ⓑ Ⓒ Ⓓ

8. The main point of the fourth paragraph (lines 61–67) is that choral odes:
    F. should not be performed by modern choruses.
    G. have a meaning and beauty that are lost in modern adaptations.
    H. can be safely ignored by a modern-day reader.
    J. are only worthwhile in *Antigone*.

    Ⓕ Ⓖ Ⓗ Ⓙ

9. The passage suggests that modern revivals of Greek tragedies "have not dared use much music" (line 103) because:
    A. modern instruments would appear out of place.
    B. to do so would require a greater understanding of how choral odes were performed.
    C. music would distract the audience from listening to the words of choral odes.
    D. such music is considered far too primitive for modern audiences.

    Ⓐ Ⓑ Ⓒ Ⓓ

10. *Porgy and Bess* and *Lost in the Stars* are modern plays that:
    F. are revivals of Greek tragedies.
    G. use music to evoke the subconscious.
    H. perform primitive Greek music.
    J. have made use of musical choruses.

The General Outline of the Passage

A quick preread of the passage should have given you a sense of its general organization:

- First paragraph—introduces the topic of Greek tragedy

- Second paragraph—discusses use of masks (artificial but intense)

- Third paragraph—discusses use of chorus (also artificial but intense)

- Fourth paragraph—expands discussion to choral odes

- Fifth paragraph—concludes with discussion of how Greek tragedy is performed today, and how it has influenced some modern art

That's really all the road map you need going into the questions. Aside from that, you should take a sense of the author's main point: Greek tragedy included many artificial devices, but these devices allowed it to rise to a high level of intensity.

LOOKING AT THE QUESTIONS

Let's take a look at selected questions, which fall into three categories.

Specific Detail Questions

Questions 6 and 7 in the passage above are typical Detail Questions. As you've seen, some Detail Questions (such as 6) give you a line reference to help you out; others (such as 7) don't, forcing you either to start tearing your hair out (if you're an unprepared test taker) or else to seek out the answer based on your own sense of how the passage is laid out (one of the two key reasons to preread the passage). With either type of Detail Question, once you've found the part of the passage that a question refers to, the answer is often (though not always) pretty obvious.

Look It Up

The answers are in the passage. Focus your attention on locating them. Your mindset should be: "Find the answer," not "Remember the answer."

Question 6 provides a line reference (lines 63–65), but to answer the question confidently, you should have also read a few lines before and a few lines after the cited lines. There you would have read: "Sometimes the chorus puts into action what is a general intention in the mind of the main character. When Oedipus resolves . . ." Clearly, the Oedipus example is meant to illustrate the point about the chorus acting out a character's intentions. So H is correct—they are "dramatizing" (or acting out) Oedipus's resolution. (By the way, G might have been tempting, but there's no real evidence that the chorus is "misinterpreting," just that they're "putting a general intention into specific action.")

Question 7 is a Detail Question *without* a line reference. Such questions are common on the ACT, and they require that you have a good sense of the structure of the passage as a whole, so that you can locate the place where the question is answered. This question's mention of the chorus should have sent you to paragraph 3, but that's a long paragraph, so you probably had to skim it to find the answer in line 40, where the author claims that the chorus serves to "lead the reactions of the audience"—captured by correct choice D.

Inference Questions

In ACT Basics, you learned that, in Inference Questions, your job is to combine ideas logically to make an inference—something that's not stated explicitly in the passage but that is definitely said implicitly. Often, Inference Questions have a word like *suggest, infer, inference,* or *imply* in the question stem to tip you off.

To succeed on Inference Questions, you have to "read between the lines." Common sense is your best tool here. You use various bits of information in the passage as evidence for your own logical conclusion.

Like Detail Questions, Inference Questions sometimes do and sometimes don't contain line references. **Question 9** does, referring you to line 103, but you really have to keep the context of the entire paragraph in mind when you make your inference. Why would modern revivals not have "dared" to use much music? Well, the paragraph opens by saying that modern productions "can only improvise some partial equivalent" to the choral odes. Inferably, since we can only improvise the odes, we don't understand very much about them. That's why the use of music would be considered daring, and why choice B is correct.

Question 4 provides no line reference, but the mention of masks should have sent you to the second paragraph of the passage, where (according to your trusty road map) masks are discussed. Lines 22–23 explain that masks "allowed no fleeting change of expression during a single episode." Treat that as your first piece of evidence. Your second comes in lines 23–25: "they [the masks] could give for each episode in turn more intense expression than any human face could." Put those two pieces of evidence together—masks can't change expression *during* a single episode, but they can give expression for each episode in *turn*.

Clearly, the actors must have changed masks between episodes, so that they could express the different emotions that different episodes required. Choice F is correct.

One warning for Inference Questions: Be careful to keep your inferences as "close" to the passage as possible. Don't make wild inferential leaps. An inference should seem to follow naturally and inevitably from the evidence provided in the passage.

Big-Picture Questions

We find that about one-third of the ACT Reading questions are Detail Questions and most of the rest are Inference Questions. But there are also a few questions that test your understanding of the theme, purpose, and organization of the passage as a whole. For these Big-Picture Questions, your main task is different from what it is for Detail or Inference Questions, though you should still plan to find the answer in the passages. Big-Picture Questions tend to look for:

Missing the Big Picture?

If you're still stumped after reading the passage, try doing the Detail and Inference questions first. They can help you fill in the Big Picture.

- Main point or purpose of a passage or part of a passage

- Author's attitude or tone

- Logic underlying the author's argument

- How ideas in different parts of the passage relate to each other

- Difference between fact and opinion

One way to see the Big Picture is to read actively. As you read, ask yourself, "What's this all about? What's the point of this? Why is the author saying this?"

Question 8 asks for the main idea of a particular paragraph—namely, the fourth, which our general outline of the passage indicates as the paragraph about choral odes. Skimming that paragraph, you find reference to how the odes seem to us modern people—"static and formal" (line 69), "like intermissions between two acts of a play" (lines 71–72). Later, the author states, by way of contrast (note the use of the clue word *yet*): "Yet to the Greeks the odes were certainly more than mere poetic interludes." Clearly, the author in this paragraph wants to contrast our modern static view of the odes with the Greeks' view of them as something more. That idea is best captured by choice G.

Question 2, meanwhile, is another common type of Big Picture Question—one that requires that you distinguish between expressions of fact and opinion in the passage. A simple test for fact (versus opinion) is this: Can it be proven objectively? If yes, it's a fact.

The content of Greek odes (choice F) is a matter of fact; you can go to a Greek ode and find out whether it does or doesn't contain Dionysian words. Similarly, the efforts of modern playwrights to find an equivalent to the Greek chorus (choice H), and the central importance of the chorus to Greek tragedy (choice J) can be factually verified.

But the "intensities of art" are a subjective matter. What one person thinks is intense might strike another as boring. So G is the expression of opinion the question is looking for.

A good way to distinguish fact from an author's opinion is to picture yourself as a fact checker for a newspaper or magazine. Is the point in question something you could verify in a book or with an expert? If not, it's probably not a fact.

FIND AND PARAPHRASE . . . AND OTHER TIPS

The examples above show that your real task in Reading is not what you might expect. Your main job is to *find* the answers. Perhaps a better name for the Reading subtest would be "find and paraphrase." But students tend to think that their task in Reading is to "comprehend and remember." That's the wrong mindset.

Here's a key to the Greek tragedy passage, so that you can check the answers to the questions not discussed above.

Key to Passage II

(Nonfiction—Humanities)

	ANSWER	REFER TO	TYPE	COMMENTS
1.	C	Lines 19–21, 34–46	Inference	Q-stem emphasizes distance between audience and stage; masks and choruses help to "enlarge" the action, so that it can be understood from a distance.
2.	G	Throughout	Big Picture	Discussed above.
3.	D	Lines 54–58	Inference	Combine info from lines 8–12, 54–58, 81–86.
4.	F	Lines 21–25	Inference	Discussed above.
5.	A	Lines 8–29	Inference	Combine info from lines 12–14, 25–29.
6.	H	Lines 63–67	Detail	Discussed above.
7.	D	Lines 34–40	Detail	Discussed above.
8.	G	Lines 68–86	Big Picture	Discussed above.
9.	B	Lines 113–117	Inference	Discussed above.
10.	J	Lines 102–106	Detail	"Some modern composers have tried to write dramatic music for choruses."

Don't Be Afraid to Skip

Remember, answer the easy questions for each passage first. Skip the tough ones and come back to them later. Sometimes the thinking you do on an easy question will help you work out a hard one. When students can't finish on time, it's usually because they stubbornly refuse to skip.

Now that you've done a couple of full-length passages and questions, you've probably encountered at least a few questions that you found unanswerable. What do you do if you can't find the answer in the passage, or if you can find it but don't understand, or if you do understand but can't see an answer choice that makes sense? Skip the question. Skipping is probably more important in Reading than in any other ACT question type. Remember to take control. Many students find it useful to skip as many as half of the questions on the first pass through a set of Reading questions. That's fine.

When you come back to a Reading question the second time, it usually makes sense to use the process of elimination. The first time around, you tried to find the *right* answer but you couldn't. So, now try to identify the three *wrong* answers. Eliminating three choices is slower than finding one right choice, so don't make it your main strategy for Reading. But it is a good way to try a second attack on a question.

Another thing to consider when attacking a question for a second time is that the right answer may have been hidden. Maybe it's written in an unexpected way, with different vocabulary. Or maybe there is another good way that you haven't thought of to answer the question. But remember that it's still important to avoid getting bogged down when you come back to a question. Be willing to admit that there are some problems you just can't answer. Guess if you have to.

More Practice with Reading

In the first two Reading Workouts, you've worked on two full-length nonfiction passages—one in Social Studies and one in the Humanities. In Reading Workout 3 we'll talk about some special strategies for the two other kinds of passages—Prose Fiction and (the third nonfiction type) Natural Sciences.

Science Workout 2:
Always Know Your Direction

- How to think like a scientist

- Handling Experiment questions

In Science Workout 1 you learned that to succeed on the ACT Science Reasoning subtest, you've got to be able to spot trends and patterns in the data of graphs and tables. But that's not all you need to do well. You've also got to learn how to think like a scientist. You don't have to know very much science (although it certainly helps), but you should at least be familiar with how scientists go about getting and testing knowledge.

HOW SCIENTISTS THINK

Scientists use two very different kinds of logic, which (to keep things nontechnical) we'll call:

- General-to-Specific Thinking
- Specific-to-General Thinking

General-to-Specific

In some cases, scientists have already discovered a law of nature and wish to apply their knowledge to a specific case. For example, a scientist may wish to know how fast a pebble (call it Pebble A) will be falling when it hits the ground three seconds after being dropped. There is a law of physics from which it can be determined that: On Earth, falling objects accelerate at a rate of about 9.8 m/sec^2. The scientist could use this known general principle to calculate the specific information she needs: After three seconds, the object would be falling at a rate of about 3 sec $\times$ 9.8 m/sec^2, or roughly 30 m/sec. You could think of this kind of logic as *general-to-specific*. The scientist uses a *general* principle (the acceleration of any object falling on Earth) to find a *specific* fact (the speed of Pebble A).

Specific-to-General

But scientists use a different kind of thinking in order to discover a new law of nature. In this case, they examine many specific facts and then draw a general conclusion about what they've seen. For example, a scientist might watch hundreds of different kinds of frogs live and die, and might notice that all of them developed from tadpoles. She might then announce a theory: All frogs develop from tadpoles. You could think of this kind of logic as *specific-to-general*. The scientist looks at many specific frogs to find a *general* rule about all frogs.

This conclusion is called a "theory," not a fact or a truth, because the scientist has not checked every single frog in the universe. She knows that there theoretically *could* be a frog somewhere that grows from pond scum or from a Dalmatian puppy. But until she finds such a frog, it is reasonable for her to think that her theory is correct. Many theories, in fact, are so well documented that they become the equivalent of laws of nature.

Think

When working on ACT Science questions, ask yourself whether you should be doing general-to-specific or specific-to-general thinking.

In your science classes in school, you mostly learn about general-to-specific thinking. Your teachers explain general rules of science to you and then expect you to apply these rules to answer questions and solve problems. Some ACT Science questions are like that as well. But a majority are not. Most ACT Science questions test specific-to-general thinking. The questions test your ability to see the kinds of patterns in specific data that, as a scientist, you would use to formulate your own general theories. We did something like this in Science Workout 1, when we theorized—based on the trends we found in a table of data—that the pollutant Hg was in some way detrimental to trout populations.

HOW EXPERIMENTS WORK

Many ACT passages describe experiments and expect you to understand how they're designed. Experiments help scientists do specific-to-general thinking in a reliable and efficient way. Consider the tadpole researcher above. In a real-world situation, what would probably happen is that she would notice some of the frogs develop from tadpoles and wonder if maybe they all did. Then she'd know what to look for and could check all the frogs systematically. This process contains the two basic steps of any experiment:

Experiments

The experimental method requires that the researcher focus on one factor that varies while other factors remain constant. Experiments often use some sort of control group to make sure that the factor investigated really is significant.

• Forming a theory (guessing that all frogs come from tadpoles)

• Testing a theory (checking the frogs to see if this guess was right)

Scientists are often interested in cause-and-effect relationships. Having formed her theory about tadpoles, a scientist might wonder what *causes* a tadpole to become a frog. To test causal relationships, a special kind of experiment is needed. She must test one possible cause at a time in order to isolate which one actually produces the effect in question. For example, the scientist might inject tadpoles with several different kinds of hormones. Some of these tadpoles might die. Others might turn into frogs normally. But a few—those injected with Hormone X, say—might remain tadpoles for an indefinite time. One reasonable explanation is that Hormone X in some way inhibited whatever causes normal frog development. In other words, the scientist would hypothesize a causal relationship between Hormone X and frog development.

Watch Your Tadpoles' Diets

The relationship between Hormone X and frog development, however, would not be demonstrated very well if the scientist also fed different diets to different tadpoles, kept some in warmer water, or allowed some to have more room to swim than others—or if she didn't also watch tadpoles who were injected with no hormones at all but who otherwise were kept under the same conditions as the treated tadpoles. Why? Because if the "eternal tadpoles" had diets that differed from that of the others, the scientist wouldn't know whether it was Hormone X or the special diet that kept the eternal tadpoles from becoming frogs. Moreover, if their water was warmer than that of the others, maybe it was the warmth that somehow kept the tadpoles from developing. And if she didn't watch untreated tadpoles (a "control group"), she couldn't be sure whether under the same conditions a normal, untreated tadpole would also remain undeveloped.

Thus, a scientist creating a well-designed experiment will:

- Ensure that there's a single factor (like Hormone X) that varies from test to test or group to group

- Ensure that all other factors (diet, temperature, space, etcetera) remain the same

- (Often) ensure that there is a control group (tadpoles who don't get any Hormone X at all) for comparison purposes (though a control group isn't always necessary)

Find What Varies

One of the advantages of knowing how experiments work is that you can tell what a researcher is trying to find out about by checking to see what she allows to vary. That's what is being researched—in this case, Hormone X. Data about things other than hormones and tadpole-to-frog development would be outside the design of the experiment. Information about other factors might be interesting, but could not be part of a scientific proof.

For example, if some of the injected tadpoles that did grow into frogs later actually turned into princes, the data from experiments about the hormone they were given would not prove what causes frogs to become princes, though the data *could* be used to design *another* experiment intended to explore what could make a frog become a prince.

The Varying Factor

Many ACT Science questions ask you to determine the purpose of an experiment or to design one yourself. To figure out the purpose of an experiment, look to see what factor was allowed to change: That's what's being tested. To design an experiment yourself, keep everything constant except the factor you must investigate.

Therefore, whenever you see an experiment in Science Reasoning, you should ask yourself:

- **What's the factor that's being varied?** That is what is being tested.

- **What's the control group?** It's the group that has nothing special done to it (again, there won't *always* be a control group).

- **What do the results show?** What differences exist between the results for the control group and those for the other group or groups? Or between the results for one treated group and those for another, differently treated group?

HANDLING EXPERIMENT QUESTIONS

The following is a full-fledged Science Reasoning passage organized around two experiments. Use the Kaplan as usual (preread the passage; consider the question stem; refer to the passage before looking at the choices), but this time, since this is a passage that centers on experiments, remember to ask yourself the three questions above. Take about 5 or 6 minutes to do the passage and its questions.

Passage II

A *mutualistic* relationship between two species increases the chances of growth or survival for both of them. Several species of fungi form mutualistic relationships called *mycorrhizae* with the roots of plants. The benefits to each species are shown in the figure below.

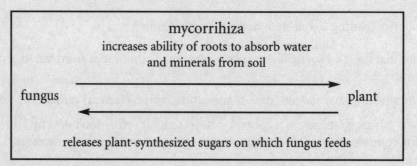

Some of the plant species that require or benefit from the presence of mycorrhizal fungi are noted below.

Cannot survive without mycorrhizae	Grow better with mycorrhizae
All conifers Some deciduous trees (e.g., birch, beech) Orchids	Citrus trees Ericaceae (heath, rhododendrons, azaleas) Grapes Soybeans

Agronomists investigated the effects of mycorrhizae on plant growth and survival in the following studies.

Study 1

Three 4-acre plots were prepared with soil from a pine forest. The soil for Plot A was mixed with substantial quantities of cultured mycorrhizal fungi. The soil for Plot B contained only naturally occurring mycorrhizal fungi. The soil for Plot C was sterilized in order to kill any mycorrhizal fungi. Additionally, Plot C was lined with concrete. After planting, Plot C was covered with a fabric that filtered out microorganisms while permitting air and light to penetrate, as shown below. 250 pine seedlings were planted in each of the 3 plots. All plots received the same amount of water. The 6-month survival rates were recorded in the table below.

Cross-section of Plot C

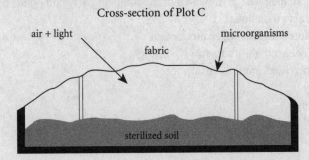

	# Seedlings alive after 6 months	Utilization of available K (average)	Utilization of available P (average)
Plot A	107	18%	62%
Plot B	34	10%	13%
Plot C	0	N/A	N/A

N/A = not applicable

Study 2

The roots of surviving seedlings from Plots A and B were analyzed to determine how efficiently they absorbed potassium (K) and phosphorus (P) from the soil. The results were added to the table above.

1. The most likely purpose of the concrete liner was:
   A. to block the seedlings from sending out taproots to water below the plot.
   B. to prevent mycorrhizal fungi in the surrounding soil from colonizing the plot.
   C. to absorb potassium and phosphorus from the soil for later analysis.
   D. to provide a firm foundation for mycorrhizal fungi in the plot.

2. Mycorrhizae are highly susceptible to acid rain. Given the information from the passage, acid rain is probably most harmful to:
   F. wheat fields.
   G. birch forests.
   H. orange groves.
   J. grape vines.

3. In a third study, pine seedlings were planted in soil from a different location. The soil was prepared as in Study 1. This time, the survival rates for seedlings planted in Plot A and Plot B were almost identical to each other. Which of the following theories would NOT help to explain these results?
   A. Sterilization killed all the naturally occurring mycorrhizal fungi in the new soil.
   B. The new soil was so mineral-deficient that it could not sustain life.
   C. The new soil was naturally more fertile for pine seedlings than that used in Study 1.
   D. Large quantities of mycorrhizal fungi occurred naturally in the new soil.

   Ⓐ Ⓑ Ⓒ Ⓓ

4. According to the passage, in which of the following ways do plants benefit from mycorrhizal associations?
   I. More efficient sugar production
   II. Enhanced ability to survive drought
   III. Increased mineral absorption
   F. I only
   G. III only
   H. II and III only
   J. I, II, and III

   Ⓕ Ⓖ Ⓗ Ⓙ

5. Which of the following generalizations is supported by the results of Study 2?
   A. Mycorrhizal fungi are essential for the survival of pine seedlings.
   B. Growth rates for pine seedlings may be improved by adding mycorrhizal fungi to the soil.
   C. Mycorrhizal fungi contain minerals that are not normally found in pine forest soil.
   D. Pine seedlings cannot absorb all the potassium that is present in the soil.

   Ⓐ Ⓑ Ⓒ Ⓓ

Answers and Explanations

Notice how many diagrams and tables were used here. That's common in experiment passages, where information is given to you in a wide variety of forms. Typically, though, the experiments themselves are clearly labeled, as Study 1 and Study 2 were here.

Answers

1. B, 2. G, 3. A, 4. H, 5. D

A quick prereading of the introduction would have revealed the topic of the experiments here—the "mutualistic relationship" between some fungi and some plant roots, the relationship called mycorrhiza ("myco" for short). The first diagram just shows you who gets what out of this relationship. The benefit accruing to the plant (the arrow pointing to the word plant) is an increased ability to absorb water and minerals. The benefit accruing to the fungus (the other arrow) is the plant-synthesized sugars on which the fungus feeds. That's the mutual benefit that the myco association creates.

Notice, by the way, that reading this first diagram alone is enough to answer **Question 4**, which we'll do right now. The question is asking: What do the plants get out of the association? And we just answered that—increased ability to absorb water and minerals. Statement III is obviously correct, but so is Statement II, since increased water absorption would indeed enhance the plant's ability to survive drought (a drought is a shortage of water, after all). Statement I, though, is a distortion. We know that the *fungi* benefit from sugars produced by the plants, but we don't have any evidence that the association actually causes plants to produce sugar more efficiently. So I is out; II and III are in, making H the answer to question 4.

Can't Live Without Those Fungi

But let's get back to the passage. We've just learned who gets what out of the myco association. Now we get a chart that shows what *kind* of plants enter into such associations. Some (those in the first column) are so dependent on myco associations that they can't live without them. Others (those in the second column) merely grow better with them; presumably they could live without them.

Here again, there's a question we can answer based solely on information in this one table. **Question 2** tells us that mycos are highly susceptible to acid rain, and then asks what kind of plant communities would be most harmed by acid rain. Well, if acid rain hurts mycos, then the plants that are most dependent on myco fungi (that is, the ones listed in the first column) would be the most harmed by acid rain. Of the four choices, only birch forests—choice G—correspond to something in column 1 of the table. Birch trees can't even *survive* without myco fungi, so anything that hurts myco fungi would inferably hurt birch forests. (Grapevines and orange groves—which are citrus trees—would *also* be hurt by acid rain, but not as much, since they *can* survive without myco fungi; meanwhile, we're told nothing about wheat in the passage.)

Well, we've answered two of the five questions already and we haven't even gotten to the first experiment. That brings up an important point—namely, that even in passages that center around experiments, there are plenty of Data Analysis questions. Don't expect there to be passages that have only Data Analysis Questions, other passages that have only Experiment Questions, and others that have only Principle Questions. Most passages will have a mixture of all three.

> ### Some Points Are Quicker Than Others
>
> Many questions on experiment passages will be answerable based solely on the data contained in a single graph or table. You can get these points with relative ease, even if you don't have time for, or don't fully understand, the experiments.

Study 1

Now look at the first experiment. Three plots, each with differently treated soil, are planted with pine seedlings. Plot A gets soil with cultivated myco fungi; Plot B gets untreated soil with only naturally occurring myco fungi; and Plot C gets no myco fungi at all, since the soil has been sterilized and isolated (via the concrete lining and the fabric covering). Now ask yourself the three important experiment questions.

- **What's the factor being varied?** The factor being varied is the amount of myco fungi in the soil. Plot A gets lots; Plot B gets just the normal amount; Plot C gets none at all. It's clear, then, that the scientists are testing the effects of myco fungi on the growth of pine seedlings.

- **What's the control group?** The plants in Plot B, since they get untreated soil. To learn the effects of the fungi, the scientists will then compare the results from fungi-rich Plot A with the control, and the results from fungi-poor Plot C with the same control.

- **What do the results show?** The results are listed in the first column of the table below the illustration of Plot C. And they are decisive: No seedlings at all survived in Plot C; 34 did in Plot B; and 107 did in Plot A. The minimums and maximums coincide. Minimum fungi = minimum number of surviving seedlings; maximum fungi = maximum number of surviving seedlings. Clearly there's a cause-and-effect relationship here. Myco fungi probably help pine seedlings survive.

Questions 1 and 3 can be answered solely on the basis of Study 1. **Question 1** is merely a procedural question: Why the concrete liner in Plot C? Well, in the analysis of the experiment above, we saw that the factor being varied was the amount of myco fungi. Plot C was designed to have none at all. Thus, one can safely assume that the concrete liner was probably there to prevent any stray myco fungi from entering the sterilized soil—choice B.

Question 3 actually sets up an extra experiment based on Study 1. The soils were prepared in the exact same way, except that the soil came from a different location. The results? The number of surviving seedlings from Plots A and B were almost identical. What can that mean? Well, Plot A was supposed to be the fungi-rich plot, whereas Plot B (the control) was supposed to be the fungi-normal plot. But here they have the same results. However, notice that we're *not* told what those results are; it could be that no seedlings survived in any plots this time around.

The question—a reversal question—is phrased so that the three wrong choices are things that *could* explain the results; the correct choice will be the one that *can't*. Choices B, C, and D all *can* explain the results, since they all show how similar results could have been obtained from Plots A and B. If the new soil just couldn't support life—fungi or no fungi—well, Plots A and B would have gotten similar results; namely, no seedlings survive. On the other end of the spectrum, choices C and D show how the two plots might have gotten similar *high* survival rates. If there were lots of myco fungi naturally in this soil (that's choice D), then there wouldn't be all that much difference between the soils in Plots A and B. And if the soil were naturally extremely fertile for the pine seedlings (that's choice C), there must have been lots of fungi naturally present in the soil because pine tress (conifers) don't grow without fungi. So all three of these answers would help to explain similar results in Plots A and B.

Choice A, however, wouldn't help, since it talks about the sterilized soil that's in Plot C. The soil in Plot C won't affect the results in Plots A and B, so choice A is the answer here—the factor that *doesn't* help to explain the results.

Watch for Reversals

Some questions on the ACT are reversal questions—that is, they ask for the one choice that isn't true. Question 3 is a classic example. The wrong choices are things that could explain the results; the correct answer is the one that can't. It's easy to get mixed up on these questions. Remember: Always double-check the question stem to make sure you're answering the right question!

Study 2

This study takes the surviving seedlings from Plots A and B in Study 1 and just tests how much potassium (K) and phosphorus (P) the roots have used. The results are listed in the second and third columns of the table. (Notice the "N/A"—not applicable—for Plot C in these columns, since there were no surviving seedlings to test in Plot C!) The data show much better utilization of both substances in the Plot A seedlings, the seedlings that grew in a fungi-rich soil. This data would tend to support a theory that the myco fungi aid in the utilization of K and P, and that this in turn aids survival in pine seedlings.

The only question that hinges on Study 2 is Question 5. It asks what generalization would be supported by the specific results of Study 2. Notice that Study 2 involved only measuring K and P. It did not involve survival rates (that was Study 1), so Choice A can't be right. And *neither* study measured growth rates, so B is out. The minerals K and P were in the control group's soil, which was natural, untreated pine forest soil, so choice C is clearly unsupported.

But the *data* did show that not all of the potassium (K) could be absorbed by pine seedlings. Only 18 percent was absorbed in Plot A, while only 10 percent was absorbed in Plot B. That's a long way from 100 percent, so choice D seems a safe generalization to make.

PRACTICE WITH EXPERIMENT QUESTIONS

Now that we've taken you step by step through a Science Reasoning passage based on an experiment, it's time to try one on your own. Give yourself about 6 minutes for the following passage and questions. This time the explanations at the end will be very short:

Passage III

The following flowchart shows the steps used by a chemist in testing sample solutions for positive ions of silver (Ag), lead (Pb), and mercury (Hg).

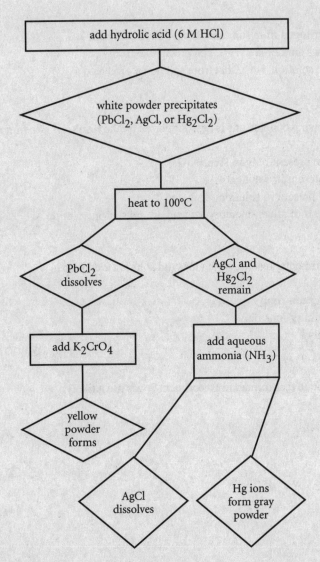

The following experiments were performed by the chemist:

Experiment 1

Hydrochloric acid (6 M HCl) was added to samples of four unknown solutions labeled 1, 2, 3, and 4. A white powder precipitated out of solutions 1, 2, and 3; no precipitate formed in solution 4.

Experiment 2

Each of the sample solutions from Experiment 1 was placed in a 100°C water bath for 15 minutes. The precipitate in solution 1 redissolved completely; solutions 2 and 3 still contained a white powder; solution 4 was unchanged. Solutions 2 and 3 were centrifuged to remove the precipitates, which were retained for further testing. Potassium chromate (K_2CrO_4) was then added to each sample. A bright yellow precipitate formed in solutions 1 and 2; none formed in solutions 3 or 4.

Experiment 3

The white powder centrifuged from solutions 2 and 3 in Experiment 2 was treated with aqueous ammonia (NH_3). The precipitate from solution 2 returned into solution, while that from solution 3 produced a gray powder.

6. Which of the following conclusions is best supported by the results of Experiment 1 alone?
    F. Silver ions are present only in solution 3.
    G. No ions are present in solution 4.
    H. Lead ions are present in solutions 1, 2, and 3.
    J. No positive ions of silver, mercury, or lead are present in solution 4.

    Ⓕ Ⓖ Ⓗ Ⓙ

7. Based on the experimental results, which ions did solution 2 contain?
    A. Lead ions only
    B. Lead and silver ions only
    C. Silver and mercury ions only
    D. Silver ions only

    Ⓐ Ⓑ Ⓒ Ⓓ

8. The yellow precipitate that formed in Experiment 2 was most likely:
    F. AgCl
    G. Hg_2Cl_2
    H. $PbCrO_4$
    J. Ag_2CrO^4

    Ⓕ Ⓖ Ⓗ Ⓙ

9. The experimental results suggest that if lead chloride ($PbCl_2$) were treated with aqueous ammonia (NH_3), the results would be:
   A. a bright yellow precipitate.
   B. a light gray precipitate.
   C. a powdery white precipitate.
   D. impossible to determine from the information given.

10. A student proposed that the analysis could be carried out more efficiently by heating the samples to 100° C before adding the 6 M HCl. This suggestion is:
   F. a bad idea; since $PbCl_2$ will not precipitate out of solution at this temperature, lead ions would be undetectable.
   G. a bad idea; the hot solutions could not be safely centrifuged.
   H. a good idea; the number of steps would be reduced from 3 to 2, saving much time and effort.
   J. a good idea; the chloride-forming reaction would proceed faster, eliminating the necessity for a 15-minute water bath.

Answers and Explanations

This experiment passage was somewhat different from the preceding one. In the mycorrhiza experiment, the scientists were thinking in specific-to-general terms (observing the growth of *specific* pine seedlings to come to a conclusion about the *general* effect of myco fungi on pine seedlings). In this series of experiments, the general principle is known—silver, lead, and mercury will precipitate or dissolve when certain things are done to them—and the scientists are using this principle to test certain specific substances in order to identify them. In fact, this is more like a procedure than an experiment, since there's no control group. But the same kind of experimental thinking—using the results of varying procedures to make reasonable inferences about what's happening—will get you your answers.

This passage also introduces the idea of a flowchart. Basically, the flowchart indicates an order of procedures. You follow the flowchart from top to bottom. The things in squares indicate what's done to a specimen; the things in diamonds indicate possible results.

So, let's say you have an unknown substance. Following the flowchart, the first thing you do is add hydrochloric acid. If a white powder precipitates, that means there are positive ions of silver, lead, and/or mercury. (If nothing precipitates, the experiment is over; the substance is not of interest here.)

But, assuming you do get a white powder, how do you identify exactly which kind of white powder you have? You do the next procedure—heat it to 100°C. When you do this, any lead ions will dissolve, but any silver or mercury ions will remain as a powder. So, the flowchart has to divide here.

Answers

6. J, 7. B, 8. H, 9. D, 10. F

Flowcharts

Flowcharts are just what their name implies—charts depicting the "flow" of procedures. Follow a flowchart, either across or down, to find out what procedures come first, which come next, etcetera. Where flowcharts branch into two or more different arms, these represent alternative results. If one result occurs, you follow that "arm"; if the other result occurs, you follow the other "arm."

If part of your specimen dissolved when heated, that doesn't necessarily mean you have lead ions. To test for that, you add K_2CrO_4. If a yellow powder forms, then you know you've got lead; if not, you've got something else.

But what about the other branch? That tells you what has to be done if you *do* have some powder remaining after heating. And what you do is add NH_3. If the powder dissolves, you've got silver ions. If it forms a gray powder, on the other hand, what you've got are mercury (Hg) ions.

The Experiments

The three experiments here are actually three parts of a single experiment or procedure, each one using the results of the former in the way outlined in the flowchart. The questions ask for results at various points in the procedure, so let's look at them briefly now:

Key to Passage III

	ANSWER	REFER TO	COMMENTS
6.	J	Experiment 1 only	If any Ag, Pb, or Hg ions were present, they would have precipitated out as powder. Note that G is too extreme (could be ions of a fourth type not within scope of the experiment). Not enough testing in Exp. 1 to determine F or H.
7.	B	All 3 experiments	Heating left powder, so has to have Ag or Hg or both, so cut A. Addition of K_2CrO_4 left yellow precipitate, so must contain Pb (cut C and D).
8.	H	Experiment 2	Must be lead-based, because Ag and Hg precipitates were already removed (cut F, G, and J).
9.	D	Flowchart	No evidence for what would happen—two different branches of the flowchart.
10.	F	Flowchart	If the solutions were heated first, and then the HCl was added, the $PbCl_2$ would never form, and the chemist would not know whether lead ions were present.

As you've seen, not all experiments on the ACT Science Reasoning subject test are specific-to-general experiments; some are general-to-specific procedures. But the same kind of strict thinking—manipulating factors to narrow down possibilities—can get you points, no matter what direction you're thinking in.

English Workout 3: Trust Your Ear—Make It All Match

- How to get the right answer by "listening" to the choices

- 20 ACT grammar hot spots

In the first two English workouts, we discussed English questions that hinged mostly on common sense. But there are also some English questions—we call them Technicality Questions—that may seem harder because they test for the technical rules of grammar, requiring you to correct errors that don't necessarily harm the economy or sense of the sentence. But don't worry. You don't have to be a grammar whiz to get these questions right. Luckily, you can often detect these errors because they "sound funny." Most of the time on the ACT, it's safe to trust your ear.

For example, which of the following "sounds right" and which "sounds funny"?

- Bob doesn't know the value of the house he lives in.

- Bob don't know the value of the house he lives in.

The first sounds a lot better, right? And for many of these questions, all you need to do is "listen" carefully in this way. You may not know the formal rules of grammar, punctuation, and diction, but you communicate in English every day. You wouldn't be communicating unless you had a decent feel for the rules.

HINT: In questions testing specific rules of grammar, the answers tend to all be about the same length. "OMIT" is not usually a choice.

Think

Technicality Questions test specific rules of grammar. With questions of this type, there's no strong bias toward shorter answers, so trust your ear, not your eyes, on these questions.

Is the Passage Formal or Informal?

Some of you may have caught an apparent error in both of the examples above—ending a sentence with a preposition such as "in." This is undesirable in extremely formal writing. But ACT passages aren't usually that formal. The ACT test writers expect you to have a feel for the level of formality in writing. If the passage is informal, pick informal answers. If the passage is slightly formal (as most ACT passages are), pick slightly formal answers. If the passage is extremely formal, pick extremely formal answers. For example, if the passage starts off "You'll just love Bermuda—great beaches, good living . . . ." it won't end like this: "and an infinitely fascinating array of flora and fauna which may conceivably exceed, in range and scope, that of any alternative . . . ." It's too formal. Pick something like this: "You'll just love Bermuda—great beaches, good living, and lots of awesome plants and animals."

Think

Some students are offended that the ACT expects them to talk like somebody else. That feeling is justified, but it won't help improve your ACT score. Don't stubbornly pick an answer that "sounds" right to you but which you know wouldn't sound right to a "standard" English speaker. Your goal should be to get the best ACT score you can, not to prove a point about regional or ethnic biases.

Do You Have a Regional or Ethnic Dialect?

Although ACT passages differ in level of formality, they all are designed to test "standard" English—the kind used by middle-class people in most of America. Test takers who speak regional or ethnic dialects may therefore find it more difficult to follow their ears on some ACT questions. In much of the South, for instance, it's common to use the word "in" with the word "rate," like this: "Mortality declined *in* a rate of almost 2 percent per year." Most speakers of English, however, use the word "at" with "rate," like this: "Mortality declined *at* a rate of . . . ." Fortunately, ACT questions testing issues like this are rare. And even if you do speak a "nonstandard" dialect, you probably know what standard English sounds like. The dialect used on most television and radio programs would be considered "standard."

Listen Carefully

In the following short passage, many students will be able to determine a large number of correct answers by "listening" carefully to each choice.

EXAMPLE

Passage II

Halloween was first celebrated <u>among various</u>
1
Celtic tribes in Ireland in the fifth century B.C. It

traditionally took place on the official last day of

summer—October <u>31, and</u> was named "All-Hallows'
2
Eve." It was believed that all persons who had

died during the previous year returned on this

day to select persons or animals to inhabit for the

1. **A.** NO CHANGE
   B. among varied
   C. between the various
   D. between various

   Ⓐ Ⓑ Ⓒ Ⓓ

2. **F.** NO CHANGE
   G. 31—and
   H. 31. And
   J. 31; and

   Ⓕ Ⓖ Ⓗ Ⓙ

next twelve months, until they could <u>pass peaceful</u>
                                          3
into the afterlife.

On All-Hallows' Eve, the Celts <u>were dressing</u> up
                                      4
as demons and monsters to frighten the spirits

away, and tried to make their homes <u>as coldest</u> as
                                        5
possible to prevent any stray hosts from crossing

their thresholds. Late at night, the townspeople

typically gathered outside the village, where a

druidic priest would light a huge bonfire to

frighten away ghosts and to honor the sun god for

the past summer's harvest. Any villager <u>whom was</u>
                                            6
suspected of being possessed would be captured,

after which <u>they</u> might be sacrificed in the
              7
bonfire as a warning to other spirits seeking to

possess the living. When the Romans invaded

the British Isles, they adopted Celtic—not

Saxon—Halloween rituals, but outlawed

human sacrifice in A.D. 61. Instead, they used

effigies for their sacrifices. In time, as <u>belief in</u>
                                              8
spirit possession waned, Halloween rituals lost

their serious aspect and <u>had been</u> instead
                            9
performed for amusement.

Irish immigrants, fleeing from the potato

famine in the 1840s, <u>brought there</u> Halloween
          10
customs to the United States. In New England,

Halloween became a night of costumes and

practical jokes. Some favorite

3. **A.** NO CHANGE
     B. pass peacefully
     C. passed peacefully
     D. be passing peaceful

Ⓐ Ⓑ Ⓒ Ⓓ

4. **F.** NO CHANGE
     G. were dressed
     H. dressed
     J. are dressed

Ⓕ Ⓖ Ⓗ Ⓙ

5. **A.** NO CHANGE
     B. colder
     C. coldest
     D. as cold

Ⓐ Ⓑ Ⓒ Ⓓ

6. **F.** NO CHANGE
     G. whom were
     H. who was
     J. who were

Ⓕ Ⓖ Ⓗ Ⓙ

7. **A.** NO CHANGE
     B. it
     C. he or she
     D. those

Ⓐ Ⓑ Ⓒ Ⓓ

8. **F.** NO CHANGE
     G. belief for
     H. believing about
     J. belief of

Ⓕ Ⓖ Ⓗ Ⓙ

9. **A.** NO CHANGE
     B. having been
     C. have been
     D. were

Ⓐ Ⓑ Ⓒ Ⓓ

10. **F.** NO CHANGE
      G. brought they're
      H. brought their
      J. their brought-in

Ⓕ Ⓖ Ⓗ Ⓙ

pranks <u>included unhinging</u> front gates
11
and overturning outhouses. The Irish also

introduced the custom of carving jack-o'-

lanterns. The ancient Celts probably began

the tradition by hollowing out a large turnip, carving it

with a demon's face, and lighting it from inside

with a candle. Since there were <u>far less</u> turnips in
12
New England than in Ireland, the Irish

immigrants were forced to settle for pumpkins.

Gradually, Halloween celebrations spread to

other regions of the United States. Halloween has

been a popular holiday ever since, <u>although these</u>
13
<u>days it's</u> principal celebrants are children
13
<u>rather than</u> adults.
14

11. **A.** NO CHANGE
    B. include unhinging
    C. had included unhinged
    D. includes unhinged

    Ⓐ Ⓑ Ⓒ Ⓓ

12. **F.** NO CHANGE
    G. lots less
    H. not as much
    J. far fewer

    Ⓕ Ⓖ Ⓗ Ⓙ

13. **A.** NO CHANGE
    B. although these days its
    C. while now it's
    D. while not it is

    Ⓐ Ⓑ Ⓒ Ⓓ

14. **F.** NO CHANGE
    G. rather then
    H. rather
    J. else then

    Ⓕ Ⓖ Ⓗ Ⓙ

Key

	ANSWER	PROBLEM	EXPLANATION
1.	A	*among/between* distinction	See Error 18 below
2.	G	commas and dashes mixed	See Error 6 below
3.	B	use of adjectives and adverbs	See Error 7 below
4.	H	unnecessary-*ing* ending	See Error 16 below
5.	D	comparative/superlative	See Error 17 below
6.	H	*who/whom* confusion	See Error 11 below
7.	C	pronoun usage error	See Error 1 below
8.	F	preposition error	See Error 10 below
9.	D	tense problem with *to be*	See Error 15 below
10.	H	*they're/there/their* mixup	See Error 13 below
11.	A	verb tense problem	See Error 14 below
12.	J	*less/fewer* confusion	See Error 19 below
13.	B	*it's/its* confusion	See Error 12 below
14.	F	*then/than* confusion	See Error 17 below

Many students could rely almost exclusively on their ear to correct many of the above errors. But there are a few English questions on every ACT that test errors your ear probably won't or can't catch. If you've got a good ear for English, there might be only a handful of such questions on the test. If not, there might be many more. For these, you'll have to think about the rules more formally. But fortunately, only a small number of rules are typically involved, and we'll discuss them all in this workout. Even more fortunately, most of the technicalities tested on the ACT boil down to one general principle: *Make it all match.*

CLASSIC GRAMMAR ERRORS

The rest of this workout is designed to help you build your own "flag list" of common errors on the ACT that your ear might not catch. Consider each classic error. If it seems like common sense to you (or, better, if the error just sounds like bad English to you, while the correction sounds like good English), you probably don't have to add it to your flag list. On the other hand, if it doesn't seem obvious, add it to your list.

As we'll see, making things match works in two ways. Some rules force you to match one part of the sentence with another part. Other rules force you to match the right word or word form with the intended meaning.

Error 1: *They* and *It* (Singulars and Plurals)

The most tested "matching" rule on the ACT is this: Singular nouns must match with singular verbs and pronouns, and plural nouns must match with plural verbs and pronouns. The most common error in this area involves the use of the word *they*. It's plural, but in everyday speech, we often use it as a singular.

> *Sentence*—"If a student won't study, they won't do well."
>
> *Problem*—A *student* (singular) and *they* (plural) don't match.
>
> *Correction*—"If students won't study, they won't do well," or "If a student won't study, he or she won't do well."

Error 2: *And* (Compound Subjects)

Another common matching error concerns "compound subjects" (lists).

> *Sentence*—"The fool gave the wrong tickets to Bob and I."
>
> *Problem*—*I* is a subject; it can't be the object of the preposition *to*.
>
> *Correction*—"The fool gave the wrong tickets to Bob and me."
>
> **HINT:** *Try dropping the rest of the list (Bob and). "The fool gave the wrong tickets to I" should sound funny to you.*

Error 3: Commas or Dashes (Parenthetical Phrases)

One rule of punctuation is tested far more often than any other on the ACT. Parenthetical phrases must begin and end with the same punctuation mark. Such phrases can be recognized because without them the sentence would still be complete. For instance: "Bob, on his way to the store, saw a large lizard in the street." If you dropped the phrase "on his way to the store," the sentence would still be complete. Thus, this phrase is parenthetical. It could be marked off with commas, parentheses, or dashes. But the same mark is needed at both ends of the phrase.

> Sentence—"Bob—on his way to the store, saw a lizard."
>
> Problem—The parenthetical phrase starts with a dash but finishes with a comma.
>
> Correction—"Bob, on his way to the store, saw a lizard."

Error 4: Commas (Run-Ons and Comma Splices)

The ACT test makers expect you to understand what makes a sentence and what doesn't. You can't combine two sentences into one with a comma (though you can with a semicolon or conjunction).

Sentence—"Ed's a slacker, Sara isn't."

Problem—Two sentences are spliced together with a comma.

Correction—"Ed's a slacker, but Sara isn't." or "Ed's a slacker; Sara isn't." or "Ed, unlike Sara, is a slacker."

Usually, only one thing should happen in each sentence. There should be one "major event." There are only a few ways to put more than one event in a sentence. One way is to connect the sentences with a conjunction (a word like *and* or *but*), as in the first correction. Or, as in the second, a semicolon can stand for such a word. The other way is to "subordinate" one event to the other in a clause, as in the third correction.

Error 5: Fragment

This rule goes hand in hand with the one above. A sentence must have at least one "major event." A "fragment" is writing that could be a subordinate part of a sentence, but not a whole sentence itself.

Sentence—"Emily listened to music. While she studied."

Problem—"She studied" would be a sentence, but *while* makes this a fragment.

Correction—"Emily listened to music while she studied."

Error 6: Any Punctuation Mark

The ACT doesn't test tricky rules of punctuation. But it does expect you to know what the punctuation marks mean and to match their use to their meanings. Here are some common punctuation marks and their meanings:

Period (.)—means "full stop" or "end of sentence."

Question mark (?)—serves the same purpose, but for questions.

Exclamation mark (!)—can be used instead of a period, but is generally inappropriate for all but very informal writing because it indicates extreme emotion.

Comma (,)—means "little stop." In many cases a comma is optional. But never use a comma where a stop would be confusing, as in: "I want to go, to the, store."

Semicolon (;)—used to separate two complete, but closely related thoughts.

Colon (:)—works like an "=" sign, connecting two equivalent things. Colons are usually used to begin a list.

Dash (—)—can be used for any kind of pause, usually a long one or one indicating a significant shift in thought.

Error 7: -ly Endings (Adverbs and Adjectives)

The ACT expects you to understand the difference between adverbs (the -ly words) and adjectives. The two are similar because they're both "modifiers." They modify, or refer to, or describe, another word or phrase in the sentence. The trick is that nouns and pronouns must be modified by adjectives, while other words, especially verbs and adjectives themselves, must be modified by adverbs.

Sentence—"Anna is an extreme gifted child, and she speaks beautiful too."

Problem—*Extreme* and *beautiful* are adjectives, but they're supposed to modify an adjective (*gifted*) and a verb (*speaks*) here, so they should be adverbs.

Correction—"Anna is an extremely gifted child, and she speaks beautifully too."

Error 8: *Good* or *Well*

In everyday speech, we often confuse the words *good* and *well*. But *good* is an adjective (it modifies a noun or pronoun); *well* is an adverb (it can modify verbs and adjectives).

Sentence—"Joe did good on the ACT."

Problem—Good is an adjective, but here it's modifying a verb (*did*), so use an adverb.

Correction—"Joe did well on the ACT."

One exception: *Well* can also be used as an adjective, when it means "healthy." So: "Joe was well again by the morning of the ACT" is correct, even though *well* is modifying the noun *Joe*.

Error 9: *Lie, Lay, Laid, Lain*

The words *lay* and *lie* are easy to confuse because they look alike and have similar meanings. The key difference in meaning is point of view. If the speaker is doing something without a direct object, he is "lying." If the speaker is doing it to something else, he is "laying." So, for example, "I will go lie down" (not *lay down*), but "I will lay this pencil on the desk" (not *lie* it).

It gets worse. The past tense of *lay* is *laid*. That's not too hard. The confusing word is *lie*. The past tense of *lie* is *lay*; when used for special tenses (with the words *had*, *have*, or *been*, for example), the form is *lain*. Thus, you'd say "I lay down" (meaning you, yourself, took a rest at some time in the past), or "I have lain down for a nap every afternoon for years now." But you'd say, "I laid that pencil on the desk yesterday, just as I have laid it on the desk every day for years now."

Don't confuse *lie* with the word *lie* that relates to dishonesty. The past tense of *lie* (meaning to tell an untruth) is *lied*.

Sentence—"I lied. I said that I had lain down, but I hadn't. In fact, I had just laid the pencil down. After I lied, though, I lay down to repent for having lied."

Problem—None. All uses of *lie, lied, lay, laid,* and *lain* above are correct.

Try not to get bogged down with *lie* and *lay*. If you don't get it, don't sweat it. It will account for one point if it appears at all.

Error 10: *In, of, to, for* (Idiomatic Preposition Use)

Whenever you see a preposition, double check to make sure it makes sense and that it "matches" the other words. Many words require particular prepositions.

Sentences—"She tried to instill on me a respect to the law." "I want to protect you in all dangers."

Problem—The prepositions don't match the verbs.

Corrections—"She tried to instill in me a respect for the law." "I want to protect you from all dangers."

Error 11: *Who* or *Whom*

Many students fear the words *who* and *whom* more than any other grammatical conundrum. Fear no more. There's an easy way to remember when to use them: They work the same way he and him work. Turn the sentence into a question as we've done in the example below. If the answer to the question is *he*, the form should be *who*. If the answer is *him*, the form should be *whom*. Notice that the *m*'s go together.

Sentence—"Always remember who you're speaking to."

Problem—*Who* is wrong. Ask: Speaking to who? Speaking to him, not to he. So, it should be *whom*.

Correction—"Always remember whom you're speaking to."

Some students try to avoid the who/whom problem by using the word *which* instead. Nope. It's not nice to call people "whiches." Never use the word *which* for a person.

Error 12: *Its* or *It's* (Apostrophe Use)

Probably the trickiest rule on the ACT is the proper use of apostrophes. Apostrophes are used primarily for two purposes: possessives and contractions. When you make a *noun* (not a pronoun) possessive by adding an "s," you use an apostrophe. Examples: *Bob's, the water's, a noodle's.* You NEVER use an apostrophe to make a pronoun possessive—pronouns have special possessive forms. You'd never write "her's." When you run two words together to form a single word, you use an apostrophe to join them. For example: *You'd, he's, they're.*

Apostrophes also have a few unusual uses, but luckily they're almost never tested on the ACT. So, master the basics and you're in good shape. The most common apostrophe issue on the ACT is usage of the words *its* and *it's*. A good way to remember which is which is that *its* and *it's* follow the same rule as do *his* and *he's*. Both *its* and *his* are possessive pronouns—so they have *no* apostrophes. Both *it's* and *he's* are contractions—so they *do* have apostrophes.

Sentence—"The company claims its illegal to use it's name that way."

Problem—*It's* is a contraction of *it is*; *its* is the possessive form of *it*.

Correction—"The company claims it's illegal to use its name that way."

Error 13: *There, Their,* or *They're* and *Are* or *Our* (Proper Word Usage)

Some students confuse the words *there*, *their*, and *they're*. A good way to remember which is *they're* is to remember that contractions use apostrophes—so *they're* is the contraction for *they are*. You can tell which is *there* because it's spelled like *here*, and the words *here* and *there* match. (*Their* means "of or belonging to them"; you'll just have to remember that one the old-fashioned way.)

Students also frequently confuse the words *are* (a verb) and *our* (a possessive). You can remember that *our* is spelled like *your*, another, less confusing possessive.

Error 14: *Sang, Sung, Brang, Brung,* etcetera (Verb Forms)

When the answers differ because of different forms of the same or similar verbs (for example, *live, lives, lived*), ask yourself *who* did it and *when* did they do it? We would say "I now live" but "he now lives." In these sentences, the who is different—and so the verb changes. Similarly, we would say "I now live" but "I lived in the past." In these sentences, the *when* is different—so the verb changes.

Most verbs are "regular" in this way, with only the endings "s" and "d" to worry about. You use the "s" when the point of view is "he," "she," or "it" and the time is now (present tense). You use the "d" for times in the past. For times in the future, or several steps backward in time, there are no special endings. You use the words *will, will have, have,* and *had* for these time sequences. "I *will* live. I *will have* lived for twenty-five years by the time the next century begins. I *had* lived in Nebraska, but we moved. I *have* lived in Indiana since then."

But a few verbs are irregular. They have special forms. For example, we say "sang" rather than "singed" and "have sung" rather than "have singed" or "have sang." Each of these verbs must be learned separately.

One irregular verb commonly tested on the ACT is *bring*.

> *Sentence*—"I've brung my umbrella to work."

> *Problem*—*Brang* and *brung* aren't used in standard English.

> *Correction*—"I've brought my umbrella to work."

Error 15: *Be* and *Was* (Forms of the Verb to Be)

The ACT tests the use of proper verb forms, especially of the verb to be. You must use the following forms. Memorize them if you have to:

PRESENT TENSE:	I *am*, we *are*, you *are*, they *are*, he *is*, she *is*, it *is*
PAST TENSE:	I *was*, we *were*, you *were*, they *were*, he/she/it *was*
FUTURE TENSE:	I/we/you/they/he/she/it *will be*
PERFECT TENSE:	I/we/you have been, he/she/it *has been*
PAST PERFECT:	I/we/you/he/she/it *had been*
FUTURE PERFECT:	I/we/you/he/she/it *will have been*

Notice that different forms of the verb (*am, are, is, were, was, will be, have been, had been, will have been*) are used depending on point of view (called "case" in grammar) and whether the action is now, in the past, or in the future (called "tense" in grammar). In many dialects, the words *be* and *was* are used instead of the special forms given. For example, many speakers might say "They *be* going home," or "They *was* going home." But the ACT would require you to write "They *are* (or *were*) going home."

Error 16: *-ing* Endings (Unidiomatic Verb Use)

Don't use *-ing* endings where they aren't needed. They are used to indicate repeated or continuous action and shouldn't be used for a single action that occurs once.

Sentence—"When I left for the store, I was forgetting my list."

Problem—The *-ing* ending isn't necessary.

Correction—"When I left for the store, I forgot my list."

Error 17: *-er* and *-est, More,* and *Most* (Comparatives and Superlatives)

Whenever you see the endings *-er* or *-est*, or the words *more* or *most*, double-check to make sure they're used logically. Words with *-er* or with *more* should be used to compare two only things. If there are more than two things involved, use *-est* or *most*.

Sentence—"Bob is the fastest of the two runners."

Problem—The comparison is between just two things, so *-est* is inappropriate.

Correction—"Bob is the faster of the two runners."

Don't use the words *more* or *most* if you can use the endings instead. Say "I think vanilla is tastier than chocolate," not "I think vanilla is more tasty than chocolate." Never use both *more* or *most and* an ending. Don't say "Of the five flavors of frozen yogurt I've eaten, strawberry delight is the most tastiest." Just say it's "the tastiest."

Error 18: *Between* or *Among*

Make sure that you use the word *between* only when there are two things involved. When there are more than two things, or an unknown number of things, use *among*.

Sentence—"I will walk among the two halves of the class." "I will walk between the many students in class."

Problem—Use *between* for two things; *among* for more than two.

Correction—"I will walk between the two halves of the class." "I will walk among the many students in class."

Error 19: *Less* or *Fewer*

Make sure that you use the word *less* only for uncountable things. When things can be counted, they are *fewer*.

Sentence—"I have fewer water than I thought, so I can fill less buckets."

Problem—You can count buckets; you can't count water.

Correction—"I have less water than I thought, so I can fill fewer buckets."

HINT: *People are always countable, so use* fewer *when writing about them.*

Error 20: *Hopefully*

Don't use the word *hopefully* to mean "I hope" or "let's hope." *Hopefully* means only "in a manner full of hope," and can be used only as an adverb.

Sentence—"Hopefully, I'll remember every item on my flag list."

Problem—*Hopefully* is not a substitute for *I hope*.

Correction—"I hope I'll remember every item on my flag list."

And let's hope that you do. As we've seen in the three English Workouts, common sense is all you need for most English questions, but some rules it pays to learn cold.

For a more thorough account of the grammar points you should know for the ACT, refer to the English Appendix.

13

Math Workout 3: Figuring It Out

Highlights

- Ten geometry questions you can expect to see on the test

- How to handle tough geometry questions

Every ACT Math subject test has 14 geometry questions and 4 trigonometry questions. Depending on what kind of score you're aiming for, you might be able to blow off those few trigonometry questions. But you probably don't want to blow off that many geometry questions.

Fortunately, a good number of the geometry questions are straightforward textbook questions. Nothing's distorted or disguised: They are what they seem. You know what to do with these questions—if you know your geometry—the instant you understand them.

TEN TEXTBOOK QUESTIONS

Here's a set of ten such questions. When you take the ACT you will see quite a few questions just like these—possibly reworded and certainly with different numbers and figures. Use these questions to find out how well you remember your geometry.

EXAMPLE

1. In the figure below, line *t* crosses parallel lines *m* and *n*. What is the degree measure of ∠*x* ?

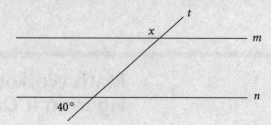

   A. 40
   B. 50
   C. 60
   D. 130
   E. 140

   Ⓐ Ⓑ Ⓒ Ⓓ Ⓔ

2. In the figure below, △*ABC* is isosceles with *AB* = *BC*. What is the degree measure of ∠*x* ?

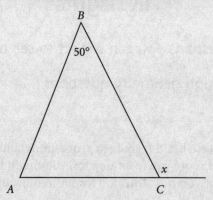

   F. 50
   G. 65
   H. 100
   J. 115
   K. 130

   Ⓕ Ⓖ Ⓗ Ⓙ Ⓚ

3. In the figure below, ∠B is a right angle and the lengths of $\overline{AB}$, $\overline{BC}$, and $\overline{CD}$ are given in units. What is the area of △ACD, in square units?

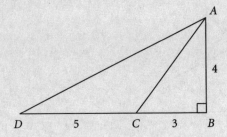

A. 10
B. 12
C. 16
D. 20
E. 32

Ⓐ Ⓑ Ⓒ Ⓓ Ⓔ

4. In the figure below, △ABC is similar to △DEF. ∠A corresponds to ∠D, ∠B corresponds to ∠E, and ∠C corresponds to ∠F. If the given lengths are of the same unit of measure, what is the value of x ?

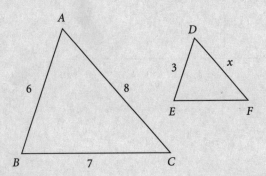

F. 3
G. 3.5
H. 4
J. 5
K. 6

Ⓕ Ⓖ Ⓗ Ⓙ Ⓚ

5. In △ABC below, ∠B is a right angle. If $\overline{AB}$ is 1 unit long and $\overline{BC}$ is 2 units long, how many units long is $\overline{AC}$?

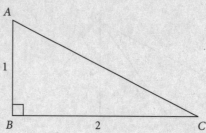

    A. $\sqrt{2}$
    B. $\sqrt{3}$
    C. 2
    D. $\sqrt{5}$
    E. 3

Ⓐ Ⓑ Ⓒ Ⓓ Ⓔ

6. In the figure below, $\overline{AC}$ is perpendicular to $\overline{BD}$, the measure of ∠D is 30° and the measure of ∠B is 45°. If $\overline{AD}$ is 6 units long, how many units long is $\overline{AB}$?

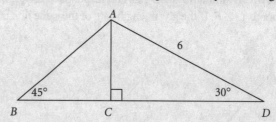

    F. 3
    G. $3\sqrt{2}$
    H. $2\sqrt{6}$
    J. $3\sqrt{3}$
    K. 6

Ⓕ Ⓖ Ⓗ Ⓙ Ⓚ

7. In the figure below, $\overline{BE}$ is perpendicular to $\overline{AD}$, and the lengths of $\overline{AB}$, $\overline{BC}$, CD, and $\overline{BE}$ are given in inches. What is the area, in square inches, of trapezoid *ABCD* ?

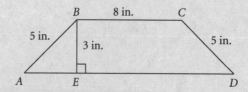

    A. 24
    B. 30
    C. 32
    D. 34
    E. 36

Ⓐ Ⓑ Ⓒ Ⓓ Ⓔ

KAPLAN

8. What is the area, in square inches, of a circle with a diameter of 8 inches?
   F. 4π
   G. 8π
   H. 16π
   J. 32π
   K. 64π

   Ⓕ Ⓖ Ⓗ Ⓙ Ⓚ

9. In the circle centered at O in the figure below, the measure of $\angle AOB$ is 40°. If $\overline{OA}$ is 9 units long, how many units long is minor arc AB ?

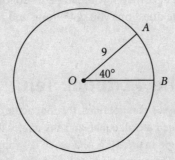

   A. π
   B. 2π
   C. 9
   D. 9π
   E. 40

   Ⓐ Ⓑ Ⓒ Ⓓ Ⓔ

10. In the figure below, $ABCD$ is a square and $\overline{AB}$ is a diameter of the circle centered at O. If $\overline{AD}$ is 10 units long, what is the area, in square units, of the shaded region?

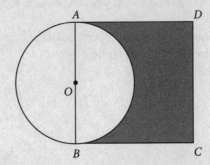

   F. $100 - 50\pi$
   G. $100 - 25\pi$
   H. $100 - \dfrac{25\pi}{2}$
   J. $100 - 10\pi$
   K. $100 - 5\pi$

   Ⓕ Ⓖ Ⓗ Ⓙ Ⓚ

Scoring

10 correct: You have a solid grounding in geometry. Straightforward textbook geometry questions are no problem for you. Skip ahead to the section called More Complex Geometry Questions.

8–9 correct: You have a pretty good—if not perfect—grasp of the geometry you need to know for the ACT. Before moving on to the discussion of more complex geometry, read the explanations below of the questions you got wrong, and study the pages of the Appendix they direct you to.

0–7 correct: You have gaps in your knowledge of geometry. Before you can hope to get much out of our discussion of more complex geometry, you had better solidify your geometry foundations. Look at the explanations below of the questions you got wrong and study the pages of the Appendix they direct you to.

Explanations for the Textbook Ten

1. When a transversal crosses parallel lines, the four acute angles formed are all equal, the four obtuse angles formed are all equal, and any angles that are not equal are supplementary. The angle marked x is obtuse, so it's supplementary to the given 40° angle. $180 - 40 = 140$. The answer is E. (*Math Appendix, #79*)

2. The three angles of any triangle add up to 180°. Furthermore, the two angles opposite the equal sides of an isosceles triangle are equal. The given angle measures 50°, so the other two angles split the remaining 130°. Since those other two angles are equal, they each measure 65°. The angle marked x is adjacent and supplementary to a 65° angle, so $x = 180 - 65 = 115$. The answer is J. (*Math Appendix, #80*)

3. The formula for the area of a triangle is $A = \frac{1}{2}bh$. To apply this formula, you need the base and the height. Here you can use $\overline{CD}$ for the base and $\overline{AB}$ for the height. So: Area = $\frac{1}{2}(CD)(AB) = 12(5)(4) = 10$. The answer is A. (*Math Appendix, #83*)

4. In similar triangles, corresponding sides are proportional. $\overline{DE}$ corresponds to $\overline{AB}$, and $\overline{DF}$ corresponds to $\overline{AC}$, so we can set up this proportion:

$$\frac{DA}{BE} = \frac{DA}{CF}$$
$$\frac{6}{3} = \frac{8}{x}$$
$$6x = 3 \times 8$$
$$6x = 24$$
$$x = 4$$

The answer is H. (*Math Appendix, #82*)

5. The Pythagorean theorem says: $(\text{leg}_1)^2 + (\text{leg}_2)^2 = (\text{hypotenuse})^2$. Here the legs have lengths of 1 and 2, so plug them into the formula:

$$(1)^2 + (2)^2 = (\text{hypotenuse})^2$$
$$1 + 4 = x^2$$
$$x^2 = 5$$
$$x = \sqrt{5}$$

The answer is D. (*Math Appendix, #84*)

6. The indicated angles tell you that $\triangle ABC$ is a 45-45-90 triangle and that $\triangle ACD$ is a 30-60-90 triangle. $\overline{AD}$ is the hypotenuse and $\overline{AC}$ is the shorter leg of the 30-60-90 triangle, so $AC = \frac{1}{2}(AD) = 3$. $\overline{AC}$ is also the shorter leg of the 45-45-90, and $\overline{AB}$, the side we're looking for, is the hypotenuse. Therefore, $AB = (AC)\sqrt{2} = 3\sqrt{2}$. The answer is G. (*Math Appendix, #85*)

7. The formula for the area of a trapezoid is $A = (\frac{b_1 + b_2}{2})h$, where b_1 and b_2 are the lengths of the parallel sides. You could think of it as the height times the average of the bases. In this case you're given the height (3 inches), one base (8 inches), and enough information to figure out the other base. Notice that $\triangle ABE$ is a 3-4-5 triangle, so $AE = 4$ inches. And if you were to drop an altitude down from point C, you'd get another 3-4-5 triangle on the right:

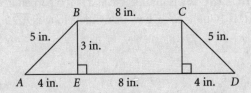

Now you can see that the bottom base is 16 inches. Plug these numbers into the formula:

$$A = (\frac{b_1 + b_2}{2})h$$
$$= (\frac{8 + 16}{2}) \times 3$$
$$= 12 \times 3 = 36$$

The answer is E. (Math Appendix, #87)

8. The formula for the area of a circle is $A = \pi r^2$, where r is the radius. If the diameter is 8 inches, then the radius is 4 inches, which we plug into the formula:
$$A = \pi r^2$$
$$= \pi(4)^2$$
$$= 16\pi$$

The answer is H. (*Math Appendix, #91*)

9. The central angle of minor arc AB is 40°, which is $\frac{1}{9}$ of the whole circle's 360°. The length of minor arc AB, therefore, is $\frac{1}{9}$ of the whole circle's circumference.

$$C = 2\pi r = 2\pi(9) = 18\pi$$
$$\frac{1}{9}C = \frac{1}{9}(18\pi) = 2\pi$$

The answer is B. (*Math Appendix, #90*)

10. The shaded region is equal to the area of the square minus the area of the semicircle. The area of the square is $10 \times 10 = 100$. The radius of the circle is half of 10, or 5, so the area of the whole circle is $\pi(5)^2 = 25\pi$, and the area of the semicircle is $\frac{25\pi}{2}$. The square minus the semicircle, then, is:

$100 - \frac{25\pi}{2}$. The answer is H. (*See Math Appendix, #87, #91.*)

THE MORE COMPLICATED GEOMETRY QUESTIONS

ACT geometry questions are not all as straightforward as the above. As if it weren't hard enough to remember all the facts and formulas needed for problems like the Textbook Ten above, the test writers have ways of further complicating geometry questions.

ACT geometry questions are not all what they seem. It's not always obvious at first what the question is getting at. Sometimes you really have to think about the figure and the given information before that light bulb goes on in your head. Often the inspiration that brings illumination is finding the hidden information.

Here's an example that doesn't come right out and say what it's all about.

EXAMPLE

1. In the figure below, $\triangle ABC$ is a right triangle and $\overline{AC}$ is perpendicular to $\overline{BD}$. If $\overline{AB}$ is 6 units long, and $\overline{AC}$ is 10 units long, how many units long is $\overline{AD}$?

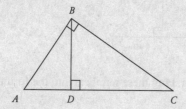

    A. 3
    B. $2\sqrt{3}$
    C. 3.6
    D. 4
    E. $3\sqrt{2}$

At first this looks like a Pythagorean theorem question. In fact, the two given sides of $\triangle ABC$ identify it as the 6-8-10 version of the 3-4-5 special right triangle. (*Math Appendix, #85*) So we know that $BC = 8$. So what? What good does that do us? How's that going to help us find AD ?

The inspiration here is to realize that this is a "similar triangles" problem. We don't see the word similar anywhere in the question stem, but the stem and the figure combined actually tell us that all three triangles in the figure—$\triangle ABC$, $\triangle ADB$, and $\triangle BDC$—are similar. We know the triangles are similar because they all have the same three angles. Here are the three triangles separated and oriented to show the correspondences:

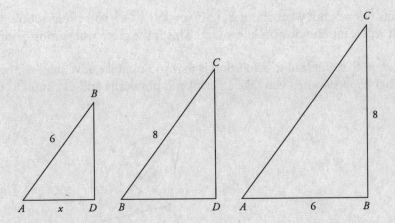

In this orientation it's easy to see the proportion setup that will solve the problem:

$$\frac{10}{6} = \frac{6}{x}$$

$$10x = 36$$

$$x = 3.6$$

The answer is C.

Here's another example with hidden information:

EXAMPLE

2. In the figure below, the area of the circle centered at O is 25π, and $\overline{AC}$ is perpendicular to $\overline{DB}$. If $\overline{AC}$ is 8 units long, how many units long is $\overline{BD}$?

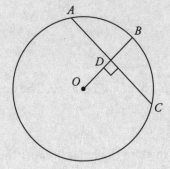

   F. 2
   G. 2.5
   H. 3
   J. 3.125
   K. 4

This is a tough one. It's not easy to see how to get $\overline{BD}$ from the given information. You can use the area—25π—to figure out the radius, and then you'd know the length of $\overline{OB}$:

$$\text{Area} = \pi r^2$$

$$25\pi = \pi r^2$$

$$25 = r^2$$

$$r = 5$$

So you know $\overline{OB}$ = 5, but what about $\overline{BD}$? If you knew $\overline{OD}$, you could subtract that from $\overline{OB}$ to get what you want. But do you know $\overline{OD}$? This is the place where most people get stuck.

The inspiration that will lead to a solution is that you can take advantage of the right angle at D. Look what happens when you take a pencil and physically add $\overline{OA}$ and $\overline{OC}$ to the figure:

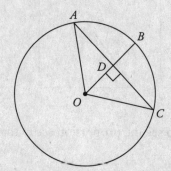

$\triangle OAD$ and $\triangle OCD$ are right triangles. And when we write in the lengths, we discover some special right triangles:

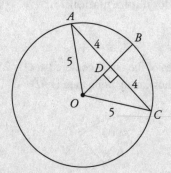

Now it's apparent that *OD* = 3. Since *OB* =5, *BD* is 5 – 3 = 2. The answer is F.

Figureless Problems

Some ACT geometry problems present an extra challenge because they don't provide a figure. You have to "figure it out" for yourself. Try this one:

EXAMPLE

3. If one side of a right triangle is 3 units long, and a second side is 4 units long, which of the following could be the length, in units, of the third side?
    A. 1
    B. 2
    C. $\sqrt{7}$
    D. $3\sqrt{2}$
    E. $3\sqrt{3}$

The key to solving most figureless problems is to sketch a diagram, but sometimes that's not so easy because the test makers deliberately give you less information than you might like.

KAPLAN

Question 3 is the perfect example. It gives you two sides of a right triangle and asks for the third. Sounds familiar. And the two sides it gives you—3 and 4—*really* sound familiar. It's a 3-4-5, right?

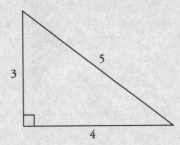

So the answer's 5 . . .

Whoops! There's no 5 among the answer choices! What's going on?!

Better check back. Notice that the question asks, "Which of the following *could* be the length . . . ." That *could* is crucial. It suggests that there's more than one possibility. Our answer of 5 was too obvious. There's another one somewhere.

Can you think of another way of sketching the figure with the same given information? Who says that the 3 and 4 have to be the two legs? Look at what happens when you make one of them—the larger one, of course—the *hypotenuse:*

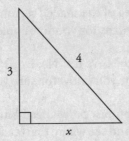

This is not a 3-4-5 triangle, because in a 3-4-5, the 3 and the 4 are the legs. This is no special right triangle; to figure out the length of the third side, resort to the Pythagorean theorem:

$$(\text{leg}_1)^2 + (\text{leg}_2)^2 = (\text{hypotenuse})^2$$
$$3^2 + x^2 = 4^2$$
$$9 + x^2 = 16$$
$$x^2 = 7$$
$$x = \sqrt{7}$$

The answer is C.

Many Steps and Many Concepts

Some of the toughest ACT geometry questions are ones that take many steps to solve and combine many different geometry concepts. The following is an example.

EXAMPLE

4. In the figure below, $\overline{AB}$ is tangent to the circle at A. If the circumference of the circle is 12π units and $\overline{OB}$ is 12 units long, what is the area, in square units, of the shaded region?

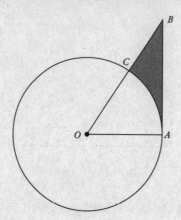

F. $18\sqrt{3} - 6\pi$

G. $24\sqrt{3} - 6\pi$

H. $18\sqrt{3} - 2\pi$

J. $12\pi - 12$

K. $24\sqrt{3} - 2\pi$

Trigonometry

It's always obvious when you've come to one of the trigonometry questions. There are only four of them, so you can still get a good score without them. But trigonometry questions are generally among the most straightforward and predictable math questions on the ACT. "SOHCAHTOA" alone is usually enough to get you two right answers. If you can master Math Appendix #96–100, you can get all four. It's up to you. You are in control. No one knows your strengths and weaknesses better than you. If you've never studied trigonometry, or if you know you never "got" it, SKIP THE TRIG QUESTIONS. If trigonometry is your favorite math topic, go for it! If, like most people, you're somewhere between those extremes, pick your spots. Do the ones you understand; guess on the ones you don't.

This is about as hard as they come on the ACT. It is by no means clear how the given information—the circumference of the circle and the length of $\overline{OB}$—will lead you to the area of the shaded region. The way through this problem has too many twists and turns for you to be able to see straight through it.

So what do you do? Give up? No. *Don't* give up immediately unless you're really short on time or you know for sure you can't do the problem.

So then should you just plow ahead blindly and figure out every length, angle, and area you can and see where that leads you? *Well, not exactly.* It would be better to be more systematic.

The key to success with a circuitous problem like question 4 is to focus on your destination—what you're looking for—and think about what you need to get there. Then go back to the given information and see what you can do with it to get you going in the right direction. Think about where you're headed before you take even one step; otherwise you may just have to backtrack.

Your destination in question 4 is "the area of the shaded region." That region is a shape that has no name, let alone an area formula. Like most shaded regions, this one is in fact the difference between two familiar shapes with names and area formulas. Think of the shaded region in question 4 as:

(the area of $\triangle AOB$) – (the area of sector AOC)

With that in mind, you know you need to figure out the area of the triangle and the area of the sector.

First, the triangle. You are explicitly given $OB = 12$. You are also given that $\overline{AB}$ is tangent to the circle at A, which tells you that $\overline{OA}$ is a radius and that $\angle OAB$ is a right angle. So if you can figure out the radius of the circle, you'll have two sides of a right triangle, which will enable you to figure out the third side, and then figure out the area.

You can get the radius from the given circumference. Plug what you know into the formula and solve for r :

$$\text{Circumference} = 2\pi r$$
$$12\pi = 2\pi r$$
$$r = \frac{12\pi}{2\pi} = 6$$
$$OA = 6$$

Aha! So it turns out that $\triangle AOB$ is no ordinary right triangle. Since one leg—6—is exactly half the hypotenuse—12—you're looking at a 30-60-90 triangle. By applying the well-known side ratios ($1:\sqrt{3}:2$) for a 30-60-90 triangle (*Appendix B, #85*), you determine that $AB = 6\sqrt{3}$. Now you can plug the lengths of the legs in for the base and altitude in the formula for the area of a triangle, and this is what you'll get:

$$\text{Area} = \frac{1}{2}bh$$
$$= \frac{1}{2}(6\sqrt{3})(6)$$
$$= 18\sqrt{3}$$

Already it looks like the answer is going to be F or H—they're the choices that begin with $18\sqrt{3}$. You could just guess F or H and move on, but if you've come this far, you might as well go all the way.

Next, you need to determine the area of the sector. Fortunately, while working on the triangle, you figured out the two things you need to get the area of the sector: the radius of the circle (6) and the measure of the central angle (60°). The radius tells you that the area of the whole circle (πr^2) is 36π. And the central angle tells you that the sector is $\frac{60}{360}$ or $\frac{1}{6}$ of the circle. One sixth of 36π is 6π. So the area of the shaded region is $18w - 6\pi$, choice F.

WHAT TO DO NEXT

If you worked through this chapter and you discovered any rusty areas in your geometry knowledge, check out Math Appendix #78–95. If you have time, you should also review trigonometry in Math Appendix #96–100.

Reading Workout 3: Arts and Sciences

> ## Highlights

- Handling Prose Fiction passages

- Handling Natural Sciences passages

- What to do in an emergency

Now that you've learned the general approach to ACT Reading (in Reading Workout 1) and the approach for each of the specific question-types (in Reading Workout 2), let's look more closely at the two kinds of the chapter called ACT passage that give students the most trouble—the Prose Fiction passage and the Natural Sciences passage.

As shown in the ACT Basics Chapter, the passage breakdown for every ACT Reading test is as follows:

Prose Fiction—one passage per test.

Nonfiction—three passages per test, one each in:

- Social Studies

- Natural Sciences

- Humanities

Your approach will be essentially the same for all three nonfiction passages, since they're all well-organized essays. Your approach to the Prose Fiction passage, however, will be somewhat different.

What follows are two full ACT Reading passages—one Prose Fiction passage and one Natural Sciences passage (which, for convenience, we'll call just Science)—complete with questions. We'll talk about specific strategies for each, but, just as important, we'll talk about how you can bring together everything you've learned so far and combine this knowledge into a plan of attack for *all* Reading passages. At the end of the Workout, we'll also show you how to salvage a few extra points if you find yourself near the end of the test with not enough time to read the final passage.

HANDLING THE PROSE FICTION PASSAGE

The Prose Fiction passage differs from the three nonfiction passages in that it is not a well-structured essay designed to communicate ideas in a logical, orderly way. It is, usually, a story in which characters fully equipped with their own motivations and emotions interact with each other in revealing ways. For that reason, the Prose Fiction passage won't break down into an orderly outline or road map, so don't even try to characterize the function of each paragraph. Pay attention instead to the *story*.

In the Prose Fiction passage, almost all of the questions relate to the characters. Your job is to find the answers to the following questions:

- **Who are these people?** What are they like? How are they related to each other?

- **What is their state of mind?** Are they angry? Sad? Reflective? Excited?

- **What's going on?** What's happening on the surface? What's happening *beneath* the surface?

Most of the passages focus on one person, or are written from the point of view of one of the characters. Figure out who this main character is and pay special attention to what he or she is like. Read between the lines to determine unspoken emotions and attitudes. Little hints—a momentary frown, a pointed or sarcastic comment—are sometimes all you have to go on, so *pay attention*. In fact, you'll probably want to spend more time prereading the Prose Fiction passage than you do any of the other three passages. It's important to get a good feel for the tone and style of the passage as a whole before going to the questions.

Fortunately, the questions in these passages tend to go quicker than in the other passages, so you'll be able to make up some of that extra time you spend on the passage.

Make It a Movie in Your Head

Try to make the passage into a movie! Imagine the scenes, the characters, the events. In the Prose Fiction passage, it should be easy to imagine the story unfolding like a movie. Pay careful attention not only to what the characters say but how they say it as well.

And don't forget to read actively, as always. Don't just read and then react. Once you have an idea of the personality of the characters, you should be able to anticipate how they will react to the events of the passage.

Without a Map

Prose Fiction passages aren't constructed in an orderly way, as the nonfiction passages are. So don't try to construct a mental road map for the Prose Fiction passage. Instead, pay attention to the story and the characters.

What a Character!

In the Prose Fiction passage, you want to focus on the characters. Who are they? What are they like? The author won't usually tell you outright. You have to figure it out for yourself, judging from what they say and do.

PRACTICE WITH THE PROSE FICTION PASSAGE

What follows is a typical ACT Prose Fiction passage, complete with questions. Before trying it, you might want to glance back at the techniques discussed in our first Reading Workout. Review the Kaplan Reading Method. Recall that you should probably plan to spend about three minutes prereading (a little more, actually, since this is the Prose Fiction passage). Then do whichever questions you can figure out quickly. Skip any hard or time-consuming problems and come back for them later.

When you work on the questions, constantly refer to the passage. Plan to spend much more time with your eyeball pointed at the passage than at the questions. And don't forget to answer the questions in your own words (based on what you've preread and reread in the passage) before you look at the answers.

Passage III

I recall a mist starting in as I crossed the lawn that afternoon. I was making my way up to the summer house for the purpose of
Line clearing away the remains of his lordship's
(5) taking tea there with some guest a little while earlier. I can recall spotting from some distance . . . . Miss Kenton's figure moving about inside the summerhouse. When I entered she had seated herself on one of the
(10) wicker chairs scattered around its interior, evidently engaged in some needlework. On closer inspection, I saw she was performing repairs to a cushion. I went about gathering up the various items of crockery from amidst
(15) the plants and the cane furniture, and as I did so, I believe we exchanged a few pleasantries, perhaps discussed one or two professional matters. For the truth was, it was extremely refreshing to be out in the summerhouse after
(20) many continuous days in the main building and neither of us was inclined to hurry with our tasks . . . . In fact, I was looking out over the lawn to where the mist was thickening down around the poplar trees planted along
(25) the cart-track, when I finally introduced the topic of the previous year's dismissals. Perhaps a little predictably, I did so by saying:

"I was just thinking earlier, Miss Kenton. It's rather funny to remember now, but you
(30) know, only this time a year ago, you were still insisting you were going to resign. It rather amused me to think of it." When I finally turned to look at her, she was gazing through the glass at the great expanse of fog outside.

(35) "You probably have no idea, Mr.

Stevens," she said eventually, "how seriously I really thought of leaving this house. I felt so strongly about what happened. Had I been anyone worthy of any respect at all, I dare say
(40) I would have left Darlington Hall long ago."
She paused for a while, and I turned my gaze back out to the poplar trees down in the distance. Then she continued in a tired voice: "It was cowardice, Mr. Stevens. Simple
(45) cowardice. Where could I have gone? I have no family. Only my aunt. I love her dearly, but I can't live with her for a day without feeling my whole life is wasting away. I did tell myself, of course, I would soon find some
(50) situation.

"But I was so frightened, Mr. Stevens. Whenever I thought of leaving, I just saw myself going out there and finding nobody who knew or cared about me. There, that's all
(55) my high principles amount to. I feel so ashamed of myself. But I just couldn't leave, Mr. Stevens. I just couldn't bring myself to leave."

Miss Kenton paused again and seemed to
(60) be deep in thought. I thus thought it opportune to relate at this point, as precisely as possible, what had taken place earlier between myself and Lord Darlington. I proceeded to do so and concluded by saying:

(65) "What's done can hardly be undone. But it is at least a great comfort to hear his lordship declare so unequivocally that it was all a terrible misunderstanding. I just thought you'd like to know, Miss Kenton, since I
(70) recall you were as distressed by the episode as I was."

"I'm sorry, Mr. Stevens," Miss Kenton said behind me in an entirely new voice, as though she had just been jolted from a dream, (75) "I don't understand you." Then as I turned to her, she went on: "As I recall, you thought it was only right and proper that Ruth and Sarah be sent packing. You were positively cheerful about it."

(80)   "Now really, Miss Kenton, that is quite incorrect and unfair. The whole matter caused me great concern, great concern indeed. It is hardly the sort of thing I like to see happen in this house."

(85)   "Then why, Mr. Stevens, did you not tell me so at the time?"

I gave a laugh, but for a moment was rather at a loss for an answer. Before I could formulate one, Miss Kenton put down her (90) sewing and said:

"Do you realize, Mr. Stevens, how much it would have meant to me if you had thought to share your feelings last year? You knew how upset I was when my girls were dismissed. Do (95) you realize how much it would have helped me? Why, Mr. Stevens, why, why, why do you always have to pretend?"

I gave another laugh at the ridiculous turn the conversation had suddenly taken. (100) "Really, Miss Kenton," I said, "I'm not sure I know what you mean. Pretend? Why, really . . . ."

"I suffered so much over Ruth and Sarah leaving us. And I suffered all the more (105) because I believed I suffered alone."

From *The Remains of the Day*, © 1989 by Kazuo Ishiguro; Alfred A. Knopf, Inc., publisher.

1. Based on the details in the passage, it can be inferred that Mr. Stevens and Miss Kenton are Lord Darlington's:
    A. guests.
    B. relatives.
    C. acquaintances.
    D. employees.

    Ⓐ Ⓑ Ⓒ Ⓓ

2. The statement "Had I been anyone worthy of any respect at all, I dare say I would have left Darlington Hall long ago" (lines 38–40) can be interpreted to mean:
    F. no one at Darlington Hall truly respects Miss Kenton.
    G. Miss Kenton has little respect for Mr. Stevens.
    H. Miss Kenton feels she betrayed her principles by staying.
    J. Miss Kenton senses that Mr. Stevens feels superior to her.

    Ⓕ Ⓖ Ⓗ Ⓙ

3. According to the passage, the intent of Mr. Stevens's recollection of Miss Kenton's desire to resign (lines 28–32) is most likely to:
    A. open up a discussion of an event that had upset Miss Kenton.
    B. turn the conversation to the professional topic of furniture repair.
    C. indulge in nostalgic reminiscences of happier days.
    D. irritate Miss Kenton by mocking the seriousness of that desire.

    Ⓐ Ⓑ Ⓒ Ⓓ

4. Mr. Stevens gives "a laugh" (line 87) because he is suddenly:
    F. amused.
    G. insecure.
    H. suspicious.
    J. sarcastic.

    Ⓕ Ⓖ Ⓗ Ⓙ

5. The main point of Miss Kenton's references to her own family (lines 45–48) is that:

    A. she would have nowhere to turn if she left her job.
    B. children often reject those they should love.
    C. she was afraid of discovering that she did not love her aunt.
    D. life becomes very tedious when one visits relatives.

    Ⓐ Ⓑ Ⓒ Ⓓ

6. What is it that Mr. Stevens describes as "done" (line 59)?

    F. Lord Darlington's earlier conversation with him
    G. Miss Kenton's talk of leaving Darlington hall
    H. Ruth and Sarah's dismissal
    J. Any talk of Miss Kenton's dismissal

    Ⓕ Ⓖ Ⓗ Ⓙ

7. As he is revealed in the passage, Mr. Stevens is:

    A. bored with their conversation in the summer house.
    B. increasingly hostile to Miss Kenton's depiction of his actions.
    C. uncomfortable with expressing his deep affection for Miss Kenton.
    D. unaware of how his past behavior had affected Miss Kenton.

    Ⓐ Ⓑ Ⓒ Ⓓ

8. Which of the following would be out of character for the narrator?

        I. Pointing out to Miss Kenton why she was unfairly characterizing his actions
        II. Spending time thinking about Miss Kenton's accusations
        III. Ridiculing Miss Kenton for poorly repairing the cushion

    F. I only
    G. II only
    H. I and II only
    J. III only

    Ⓕ Ⓖ Ⓗ Ⓙ

9. Miss Kenton interacts with Mr. Stevens in a way that can best be described as:

    A. sincere but formal.
    B. indifferent but polite.
    C. timid but angry.
    D. patronizing but kindly.

    Ⓐ Ⓑ Ⓒ Ⓓ

10. At the end of the passage, Miss Kenton asks "Why, Mr. Stevens, why, why, why do you always have to pretend?" (lines 96–97) What specific action of Mr. Stevens does she have in mind?

    F. His apparent cheerfulness at Ruth and Sarah's dismissal
    G. His simulation of great affection for her
    H. His phony concern for her own future employment
    J. His empty expressions of sympathy for her own suffering

    Ⓕ Ⓖ Ⓗ Ⓙ

Answers and Explanations

It should be clear now why trying to build a mental road map of the Prose Fiction passage is not such a good idea. Unlike the paragraphs in the nonfiction passages, those in the Prose Fiction passage tend not to be organized around a single topic. They just move the story forward. Instead of building a road map, then, your prereading step should have been spent finding answers to the important questions about character and action.

- **Who are these people?** The first paragraphs of the passage are peppered with hints about who these people are. Lines 4–5 discuss Mr. Stevens "clearing away the remains of his lordship's taking tea." Lines 12–13 describes Miss Kenton "performing repairs to a cushion." Line 31 discusses her previous plans for resigning. Clearly, Mr. Stevens and Miss Kenton are servants (we later learn—in line 63—that their employer is Lord Darlington). Notice how, by answering this basic question, you've already answered Question 1.

- **What is their state of mind?** We read of "the previous year's dismissals" (line 26) and Miss Kenton's intentions to leave the house (lines 39–40) as a result of them. She "felt so strongly about what happened" (lines 37–38) but she was afraid to take the step of actually leaving in protest ("It was cowardice," she admits in line 44). It sounds like some other servants were dismissed unfairly last year, and that this upset Miss Kenton. Apparently, Mr. Stevens also found the incident distressing (lines 81–82), but Miss Kenton hadn't realized this at the time.

- **What's going on?** These are obviously very formal people, but there are strong emotions rumbling beneath the surface. It's clear that Miss Kenton is very upset because she didn't realize that Mr. Stevens disapproved of the dismissals, too ("Do you realize, Mr. Stevens, how much it would have meant to me if you had thought to share your feelings last year?"—lines 91–93. And later: "Why, Mr. Stevens, why, why, why do you always have to *pretend*?"—lines 96–97). We get the impression that Mr. Stevens is not a man who very readily shows his feelings and emotions—as Miss Kenton puts it, he always *pretends*.

As for the questions, notice how many inference-type questions there are. This is typical of the Prose Fiction passage, where so much information is conveyed implicitly—"between the lines." In most cases, you have to read around the specific line references in order to find your answer. If you've done your prereading step properly, however, you should be able to knock off most of the questions quickly.

Key to Passage III
(Prose Fiction)

	ANSWER	REFER TO	TYPE	COMMENTS
1.	D	First 2 paragraphs	Inference	Discussed above.
2.	H	Lines 38–40, 48–50	Inference	"There, that's all my high principles amount to," she says.
3.	A	Lines 28–33, 60–63	Inference	Lines 60–63 show that Mr. Stevens has just been discussing this subject with Lord Darlington, and now wants to discuss it with Miss Kenton.
4.	G	Lines 87–88	Inference	He is "at a loss for an answer," and clearly not laughing out of amusement.
5.	A	Lines 45–50	Detail	"Where could I have gone? I have no family."
6.	H	Lines 65–71	Detail	Refers to "the previous year's dismissals," first mentioned in lines 25–26.
7.	D	Throughout	Big Picture	Mr. Stevens' nervous laughs hint that he had no idea how deeply Miss Kenton was affected.
8.	J	Throughout	Inference	I—He does this in lines 80–84. II—He wishes to respond to the accusations in lines 76–79. III—This kind of blatant harshness would be uncharacteristic of so discreet and proper a man.
9.	A	Throughout	Big Picture	Miss Kenton freely expresses her feelings to him throughout, so she is sincere. But she never loses her formal language and demeanor.
10.	F	Lines 91–96, 72–79	Inference	She wishes that he "had thought to share [his] feelings;" she was under the impression that he was "positively cheerful about [the dismissals]."

THE NATURAL SCIENCES PASSAGE

The Science passage in the Reading subject test is often similar in outward appearance to a passage on the Science Reasoning subject test. Illustrations, graphs, and tables of information may be included. Usually, though, the emphasis in Reading is more on understanding ideas rather than reading and analyzing experiments and data.

Approaching the Science passage is really not any different from approaching the other nonfiction passages, since all are well-organized essays that lay out ideas in a straightforward, logical way. But you may be more likely to find unfamiliar vocabulary in Science passages. *Don't panic.* Any unfamiliar terms will usually be defined explicitly in the passage, or else will have definitions inferable from context.

You Don't Have to Be an Einstein

As in the Science Reasoning subject test, you don't have to be a science whiz to get a decent score. The same advice that helps on the other passages—know where you're going; look it up—will get you points on the Science passage.

Weak in Science?

Don't freak out if you find yourself in a fog as you read the Science passage. Keep your head, and quickly get to the questions. Focus on the detail questions with line references. You can score points on the Science passage, even if you don't get it.

Don't Get Lost!

In the Science passage, it's easy to lose yourself in complex details. Don't do it. It's *especially* important not to get bogged down in the Science passage! Many students try to understand and remember everything as they read. But that's not the right ACT mindset. In your prereading of the passage, just get the "gist" and the outline; don't sweat the details. As always, use line references in the questions when possible. They will lead you back to the details that are important. You'd be surprised how many questions you can answer on a passage you don't really understand.

PRACTICE WITH THE NATURAL SCIENCES PASSAGE

The next passage is a typical ACT-style Science passage with questions. Try to attack it with the same Kaplan Method you use for other passages. Remember: Don't get bogged down in the details! And don't worry if you don't understand everything, particularly just after prereading. Your only goal is to get a sense of the passage and its outline.

Passage IV

Atoms can be excited in many ways other than by absorbing a photon. The element phosphorous spontaneously combines with
Line oxygen when exposed to air. There is a
(5) transfer of energy to the phosphorous electrons during this chemical reaction which excites them to sufficiently high energy states that they can subsequently emit light when dropping into a lower state. This is an
(10) example of what is termed chemiluminescence, the emission of light as a result of chemical reaction.

A related effect is bioluminescence, when light is produced by chemical reactions
(15) associated with biological activity. Bioluminescence occurs in a variety of life forms and is more common in marine organisms than in terrestrial or freshwater life. Examples include certain bacteria, jellyfish,
(20) clams, fungi, worms, ants, and fireflies. There is considerable diversity in how light is produced. Most processes involve the reaction of a protein with oxygen, catalyzed by an enzyme. The protein varies from one
(25) organism to another, but all are grouped under the generic name luciferin. The enzymes are known as luciferase. Both words stem from the Latin lucifer meaning light-bearing. The various chemical steps leading to
(30) bioluminescence are yet to be explained in detail, but in some higher organisms the process is known to be activated by the nervous system.

The firefly is best understood. Its light
(35) organ is located near the end of the abdomen.
Within it luciferin is combined with other
atomic groups in a series of processes in
which oxygen is converted into carbon
dioxide. The sequence culminates when the
(40) luciferin is split off from the rest, leaving it in
an excited state. The excess energy is released
as a photon. The peak in the emission
spectrum lies between 550 and 600 nm
depending on the type of luciferase. This flash
(45) produced by the simultaneous emission of
many photons serves to attract mates, and
females also use it to attract males of other
species, which they devour.

Certain bacteria also produce light when
(50) stimulated by motion. This is why the
breaking sea or a passing boat generate the
greenish light seen in some bodies of water
such as Phosphorescent Bay in Puerto Rico.
Some fish have a symbiotic relationship with
(55) bacteria. The "flashlight fish" takes advantage
of the light created by bacteria lodged beneath
each eye. Certain other fish produce their own
bioluminescence, which serves as
identification. However, the biological
(60) advantage if any of bioluminescence in some
other organisms such as fungi remains a
mystery.

Triboluminescence is the emission of
light when one hard object is sharply struck
(65) against another. This contact, when atom
scrapes against atom, excites electrons and
disrupts electrical bonds. Light is then
created when the electrons find their way to
lower states. Triboluminescence is not to be
(70) confused with the glow of small particles that
may be broken off by the impact. Such

"sparks" are seen as a result of their high
temperature. Light given off by hot objects is
known as thermoluminescence, or
(75) incandescence.

Another form of thermoluminescence is
the basis for dating ancient ceramic objects.
Quartz and other constituents of clay are
continually irradiated by naturally occurring
(80) radioactive elements (e.g., uranium and
thorium) and by cosmic rays. This produces
defects in the material where electrons may
be trapped. Heating pottery to 500°C releases
the trapped electrons, which can then migrate
(85) back to their original atoms, where on
returning to an atomic orbit they then emit a
photon. The intensity of thermoluminescence
is therefore a measure of the duration of
irradiation since the time when the pottery
(90) had been previously fired.

Excitation is also possible by other
means. The passage of an electrical current
(electroluminescence) is one. The impact of
high energy particles is another. The *aurora*
(95) *borealis* and its southern counterpart the
aurora australis arise when a stream of high
energy particles from the sun enters the
earth's upper atmosphere and literally shatters
some of the molecules of the air. This leaves
(100) their atoms in excited states, and the light
subsequently given off is characteristic of the
atoms. Although the oxygen molecule, a
major constituent of our atmosphere, has no
emission in the visible, the oxygen atom can
(105) emit photons in either the red or green
portions of the spectrum. Other atoms
contribute to light at other wavelengths.

From Light and Color in Nature and Art, © *1983 by*
Samuel J. Williamson; John Wiley & Sons, publisher.

11. According to the information in the sixth paragraph (lines 76–90),
the brighter the thermoluminescence of a heated piece of ancient pottery:
   A. the younger the piece is.
   B. the older the piece is.
   C. the less irradiation has occurred within the piece's clay.
   D. the fewer electrons have become trapped within the clay.

Ⓐ Ⓑ Ⓒ Ⓓ

12. If an ancient ceramic bowl is heated to 500° C, light is emitted when certain electrons:
    F. release radioactive elements found in the clay.
    G. scrape against other electrons.
    H. become superheated.
    J. return to their former atoms.

    Ⓕ Ⓖ Ⓗ Ⓙ

13. Compared to bioluminescence, chemiluminescence is NOT produced by:
    A. organic proteins that have been catalyzed.
    B. a chemical reaction.
    C. any reaction involving oxygen.
    D. a change in energy states.

    Ⓐ Ⓑ Ⓒ Ⓓ

14. It can be inferred from the passage that the description of the firefly's production of light is a good example of the degree to which researchers understand:
    F. why light attracts fireflies.
    G. how a chemical process can trigger bioluminescence.
    H. how female fireflies attack male fireflies.
    J. how to measure the intensity of a firefly's bioluminescence.

    Ⓕ Ⓖ Ⓗ Ⓙ

15. In both chemiluminescence and bioluminescence, photons are emitted:
    A. as excess energy.
    B. only by certain marine organisms.
    C. only when luciferase are present.
    D. only when phosphorous is present.

    Ⓐ Ⓑ Ⓒ Ⓓ

16. Based on details in the passage, the word "excited" as used in line 1 means:
    F. split off from a molecule.
    G. agitated until glowing.
    H. raised to a higher energy level.
    J. heated to the point of disintegration.

    Ⓕ Ⓖ Ⓗ Ⓙ

17. In discussing the creation of the two kinds of aurora, the passage asserts that the oxygen molecule "has no emission in the visible [spectrum]" (line 104) but also states that "the oxygen atom can emit photons in either the red or the green portions of the spectrum" (lines 104–106). Is the passage logically consistent?
    A. Yes, because visible light is emitted after the oxygen molecules have been broken apart into oxygen atoms.
    B. Yes, because the passage presents factual information and therefore cannot be illogical.
    C. No, because the oxygen molecule forms the largest part of the atmosphere and scientific theories must account for its invisible emissions.
    D. No, because the writer has failed to adequately differentiate between the oxygen molecule's behavior and that of the oxygen atom.

    Ⓐ Ⓑ Ⓒ Ⓓ

18. Assume that two meteors have collided and shattered. Astronomers see both a burst of light and then a subsequent glow. Such a visual phenomenon could best be explained as the result of:

      I. chemiluminescence
     II. triboluminescence
   III. thermoluminescence

  F. II only
  G. II and III only
  H. I and III only
  J. I, II, and III

Ⓕ Ⓖ Ⓗ Ⓙ

19. Based on information presented in the passage, which of the following is a hypothesis, rather than a fact?

  A. Fireflies use bioluminescence to attract mates.
  B. Thermoluminescence and triboluminescence are two distinctly different kinds of light emission.
  C. A firefly's type of luciferase determines the peak of its light emission's intensity.
  D. All organisms that produce bioluminescence do so for some biological advantage.

Ⓐ Ⓑ Ⓒ Ⓓ

20. According to the last paragraph (lines 91–107), both the *aurora borealis* and the *aurora australis:*

  F. demonstrate the effects on atoms of high energy particles.
  G. occur in the presence of oxygen.
  H. emit light due to the presence of electrical currents.
  J. are visible from the surface of the earth.

Ⓕ Ⓖ Ⓗ Ⓙ

Answers and Explanations

Feeling a little numb? Unless you're a real science buff, you probably found this passage a lot less exciting than the atoms did. And you may have found yourself adrift in a sea of bewildering terms—*chemiluminescence, luciferin, aurora australis.*

We hope, though, that you didn't panic. You could still get points—and lots of them—from this passage even if all that you took away from your prereading was a sense that the passage was mainly about things in nature glowing when their atoms are excited. That, and a sense of a road map, was really all you needed. Most of the questions were answerable by referring back to the appropriate lines in the passage and paraphrasing what you read there.

Here's a possible road map for the passage:

- First paragraph: Introduction of idea of excited atoms releasing photons (i.e., luminescence). Discusses *chemiluminescence* (resulting from a chemical reaction).

- Second paragraph: Discusses *bioluminescence* (associated with biological activity—that is, with things that are alive).

- Third paragraph: Example of *bioluminescence*—fireflies.

- Fourth paragraph: More examples of *bioluminescence*—sea life.

- Fifth paragraph: Discusses *triboluminescence* (things hitting each other) and *thermoluminescence* (hot objects).

- Sixth paragraph: Example of *thermoluminescence*—refired ceramic objects.

- Seventh paragraph: Concludes with discussion of *electroluminescence* (associated with electrical currents).

Basically, the author is giving us a rundown on the various kinds of luminescence in nature. When the questions ask about one kind or another, you simply refer to the appropriate paragraph and lines.

Below is a key to the answers for this passage. Notice how you could have gotten an answer to number 12, for instance, *even if you were totally confused*. If you found "500°" in the passage (line 83), the sentence more or less spelled out the answer for you, requiring a minimum of paraphrasing. Again, never panic if you don't understand the passage as a whole! Just find the questions you can understand, and find the answers in the passage.

Key to Passage IV

(Nonfiction—Natural Sciences)

	ANSWER	REFER TO	TYPE	COMMENTS
11.	B	Lines 76–90	Inference	More time since last firing to trap more electrons, creating brighter glow.
12.	J	Lines 84–85	Detail	"migrate back to their original atoms"
13.	A	Paragraph 2	Detail	Be careful with the reversal word "NOT" in the question. "Organic" means "having to do with life."
14.	G	Lines 22–33, 34–48	Inference	Remember, passage is about luminescence, not fireflies.
15.	A	Lines 5–12, 45–48	Inference	B and C aren't chemi-; D isn't bio-. Only A is both.
16.	H	Line 2–12, 65–77	Detail	Lines 5–9 say it all.
17.	A	Lines 91–108	Big Picture	Remember, you should usually select a choice that approves of the passage. Note difference between oxygen molecule and oxygen atom.
18.	G	Lines 63–75	Inference	I—No, since no chemical reaction II—Yes, since impact reaction III—Yes, since "subsequent glow" (probably a heat reaction)

| 19. | D | Throughout | Big Picture | Any statement about "all organisms" is probably a hypothesis, since no one can verify what's true of every organism in existence. |
| 20. | F | Lines 91–108 | Detail | "a stream of high energy particles from the sun." |

EMERGENCY STRATEGY FOR TEST DAY

If you're nearly out of time and you've still got an entire passage untouched, you need to shift to last-minute strategies. Don't try to preread the passage; you'll just run out of time before you answer any questions. Instead, scan the questions without reading the passage and look first for the ones that mention line numbers or specific paragraphs. You can often get quick points on these questions by referring back to the passage as the question stem directs, reading a few lines around the reference, and taking your best shot.

Of course, the most important thing is to make sure you have gridded in at least a random guess on every question. If some of your blind guesses are right (as some of them statistically *should* be), they'll boost your score just as much as well-reasoned, thought-out answers would!

Finishing Isn't That Important

Don't worry if you don't have time to look at all the questions. You can earn scores in the top 15 percent of all ACT test takers even if you never look at a whole passage in Reading—if almost all the questions you do answer on the other three passages are right and if you remember to guess on the rest.

15

Science Workout 3:
Keep Your Viewpoints Straight

Science Workout 3:
Keep Your Viewpoints Straight

Highlights

- Handling the conflicting viewpoints passage

- A really scary practice passage

On every Science Reasoning subject test you'll find one "Conflicting Viewpoints" passage, in which two scientists propose different theories about a particular scientific phenomenon. Often, the two theories are just differing interpretations of the same data; other times, each scientist offers his own data to support his own opinion. In either case, it's essential that you know more or less what theory each scientist is proposing, and that you pay careful attention to how and where their theories differ.

In Science Workout 2, we talked about how scientists think, and you should bring all of that information to bear on the Conflicting Viewpoints passage. Since the scientists are disagreeing on interpretation, it's usually the case that they're engaging in specific-to-general thinking. They're each using specific data, sometimes the *same* specific data, but they're coming to very different general conclusions.

It's important to remember that your job is *not* to figure out which scientist is right and which is wrong. Instead, you'll be tested on whether you *understand* each scientist's position and the thinking behind it. That's what the questions will hinge on.

Point and Viewpoints

Sometimes you may find yourself understanding one scientist's viewpoint but not the other's. Don't let that upset you. Many of the questions will involve just one scientist's theory, so even if Scientist 2 has totally lost you, you can still do well on questions that involve Scientist 1 only. Remember: You get points for answering individual questions, not for understanding everything!

PREREADING THE CONFLICTING VIEWPOINTS PASSAGE

When tackling the Conflicting Viewpoints passage, you'll probably want to spend a little more time than usual on the prereading step of the Kaplan Reading Method. As we saw on other Science Reasoning passages, your goal in prereading is to get a general idea of what's going on so that you can focus when you do the questions. But we find that it pays to spend a little extra time with the Conflicting Viewpoints passage in order to get a clearer idea of the opposing theories and the data behind them

The passage will usually consist of a short introduction laying out the scientific issue in question, followed by two different viewpoints on that issue. Sometimes these viewpoints are presented under the headings Scientist 1 and Scientist 2, or else the headings might be Theory 1 and Theory 2, Hypothesis 1 and Hypothesis 2, or something similar.

A scientific viewpoint on the ACT will typically consist of two parts:

- A statement of the general theory

- A summary of the data behind the theory

Usually, the very first line of each viewpoint expresses the geneal theory. So, for instance, Scientist 1's first sentence might be something like: *The universe will continue to expand indefinitely*. This is Scientist 1's viewpoint boiled down to a single statement. Scientist 2's first sentence might be: *The force of gravity will eventually force the universe to stop expanding and to begin contracting*. This is Scientist 2's viewpoint, and it is clearly in direct contradiction to Scientist 1's opinion.

It's very important that you understand these basic statements of theory, and, just as important, that you see how they're opposed to each other. In fact, you might want to circle the theory statement for each viewpoint, right there in the test booklet, to fix the two positions in your mind.

After each statement of theory will come the data that's behind it. As we said, sometimes the scientists are just drawing different interpretations from the same data. But usually, each will have different supporting data. There are two different kinds of data:

- Data that support the scientist's own theory

- Data that weaken the opposing scientist's theory

It's normally a good idea to identify the major points of data for each theory. You might underline a phrase or sentence that crystallizes each, or even take note of whether it primarily supports the scientist's own theory or shoots holes in the opposing theory.

Once you understand each scientist's theory and the data behind it, you'll be ready to move on to the questions. Remember that some of the questions will refer to only one of the viewpoints. Whatever you do, *don't mix up the two viewpoints*! A question asking about the data supporting Theory 2 may have wrong answers that perfectly describe the data for Theory *1*. If you're careless, you can easily fall for one of these wrong answers.

THE REAL THING

What follows is a full-fledged, ACT-style Conflicting Viewpoints passage. Give yourself six minutes or so to do the passage and all seven questions.

Passage IV

Tektites are natural, glassy objects that range in size from the diameter of a grain of sand to that of a human fist. They are found in only a few well-defined areas, called strewn fields. Two theories about the origin of tektites are presented below.

Scientist 1

Tektites almost certainly are extraterrestrial, probably lunar, in origin. Their forms show the characteristics of air-friction melting. In one study, flanged, "flying saucer" shapes similar to those of australites (a common tektite form) were produced by ablating lenses of tektite glass in a heated airstream that simulated atmospheric entry.

Atmospheric forces also make terrestrial origin extremely improbable. Aerodynamic studies have shown that because of atmospheric density, tektite-like material ejected from the earth's surface would never attain a velocity much higher than that of the surrounding air, and therefore would not be shaped by atmospheric friction. Most likely, tektites were formed either from meteorites or from lunar material ejected in volcanic eruptions.

Analysis of specimen #14425 from the *Apollo 12* lunar mission shows that the sample strongly resembles some of the tektites from the Australasian strewn field. Also, tektites contain only a small fraction of the water that is locked into the structure of terrestrial volcanic glass. And tektites never contain unmelted crystalline material; the otherwise similar terrestrial glass produced by some meteorite impacts always does.

Scientist 2

Nonlocal origin is extremely unlikely, given the narrow distribution of tektite strewn fields. Even if a tightly focused jet of lunar matter were to strike the earth, whatever was deflected by the atmosphere would remain in a solar orbit. The next time its orbit coincided with that of the earth, some of the matter would be captured by earth's gravity and fall over a wide area.

There are striking similarities not only between the composition of the earth's crust and that of most tektites but between the proportions of various gases found in the earth's atmosphere and in the vesicles of certain tektites.

Tektites were probably formed by meteorite impacts. The shock wave produced by a major collision could temporarily displace the atmosphere above. Terrestrial material might then splatter to suborbital heights and undergo air-friction melting upon reentry. And tektite fields in the Ivory Coast and Ghana can be correlated with known impact craters.

1. The discovery that many tektites contain unmelted, crystalline material would:
    A. tend to weaken Scientist 1's argument.
    B. tend to weaken Scientist 2's argument.
    C. be incompatible with both scientists' views.
    D. be irrelevant to the controversy.

2. Which of the following is a reason given by Scientist 2 for believing that tektites originate on the earth?
    F. The density of the earth's atmosphere would prevent any similar lunar or extraterrestrial material from reaching the earth's surface.
    G. Tektites have a composition totally unlike that of any material ever brought back from the Moon.
    H. Extraterrestrial material could not have been as widely dispersed as tektites are.
    J. Material ejected from the Moon or beyond would eventually have been much more widely distributed on Earth.

3. Scientist 1 could best answer the point that some tektites have vesicles filled with gases in the same proportion as the earth's atmosphere by:
    A. countering that not all tektites have such gas-filled vesicles.
    B. demonstrating that molten material would be likely to trap some gases while falling through the terrestrial atmosphere.
    C. suggesting that those gases might occur in the same proportions in the Moon's atmosphere.
    D. showing that similar vesicles, filled with these gases in the same proportions, are also found in some terrestrial volcanic glass.

4. How did Scientist 2 answer the argument that tektitelike material ejected from the earth could not reach a high enough velocity relative to the atmosphere to undergo air-friction melting?
    F. By asserting that a shock wave might cause a momentary change in atmosphere density, permitting subsequent aerodynamic heating
    G. By pointing out that periodic meteorite impacts have caused gradual changes in atmospheric density over the eons
    H. By attacking the validity of the aerodynamic studies cited by Scientist 1
    J. By referring to the correlation between tektite fields and known impact craters in the Ivory Coast and Ghana

5. The point of subjecting lenses of tektite glass to a heated airstream was to:
   A. determine their water content.
   B. see if gases became trapped in their vesicles.
   C. reproduce the effects of atmospheric entry.
   D. simulate the mechanism of meteorite formation.

6. Researchers could best counter the objections of Scientist 2 to Scientist 1's argument by:
   F. discovering some phenomenon that would quickly remove tektite-sized objects from orbit.
   G. proving that most common tektite shapes can be produced by aerodynamic heating.
   H. confirming that active volcanoes once existed on the moon.
   J. mapping the locations of all known tektite fields and impact craters.

7. Which of the following characteristics of tektites is LEAST consistent with the theory that tektites are of extraterrestrial origin?
   A. Low water content
   B. "Flying saucer" shapes
   C. Narrow distribution
   D. Absence of unmelted material

Answers and Explanations

Your prereading of the introduction should have revealed the issue at hand—namely, tektites, which are small glassy objects found in certain areas known as strewn fields. The conflict is about the *origin* of these objects: In other words, where did they come from?

Answers

1. A, 2. J, 3. B, 4. F, 5. C, 6. F, 7. C

Scientist 1's theory is expressed in his first sentence: "Tektites almost certainly are extraterrestrial, probably lunar, in origin." Put that into a form you can understand: In other words, Scientist 1 believes that tektites come from space, probably the moon. Scientist 2, on the other hand, has an opposing theory, also expressed in her first sentence: "Nonlocal origin is extremely unlikely." In other words, it's unlikely that tektites came from a nonlocal source; instead, they probably came from a *local* source, i.e., right here on Earth. The conflict is clear. One says that tektites come from space; the other says they come from Earth. You might have even labeled the two positions: "space origin" and "Earth origin."

But how do these scientists support their theories? Scientist 1 presents three points of data:

1. Tektite shapes show characteristics of "air-friction melting" (supporting the theory of space origin).
2. "Atmospheric forces" wouldn't be great enough to shape tektitelike material ejected from Earth's surface (weakening the theory of earth origin).
3. Tektites resemble moon rocks gathered by *Apollo 12* but not Earth rocks (strengthening the theory of space origin).

Scientist 2 also presents three points of data:

1. Any matter coming from space would "fall over a wide area" instead of being concentrated in strewn fields (weakening the theory of space origin).
2. There are "striking similarities" between tektites and the composition of the earth's crust (strengthening the theory of Earth origin).
3. "Meteorite impacts" could create shock waves, explaining how terrestrial material could undergo air-friction melting (strengthening the theory of Earth origin by counteracting Scientist 1's first point).

Obviously, you wouldn't want to write out the supporting data for each theory the way we've done above. But it probably would be a good idea to underline the key phrases in the data descriptions ("air-friction melting," "*Apollo 12*," etcetera) and number them. What's important is that you have an idea of what data supports which theory. The questions, once you get to them, will then force you to focus.

Question 1 asks how it would affect the scientists' arguments if it were discovered that many tektites contain unmelted crystalline material. Well, Scientist 1 says that tektites never contain unmelted crystalline material, and that the terrestrial glass produced by some meteorite impacts *always* does. Therefore, by showing a resemblance between tektites and earth materials, this discovery would weaken Scientist 1's argument for extraterrestrial origin. Choice A is correct.

For **Question 2**, you had to identify which answer choice was used by Scientist 2 to support the argument that tektites are terrestrial in origin. You should have been immediately drawn to choice J, which expresses what we've identified above as Scientist 2's first data point. Notice how choice F is a piece of evidence that Scientist 1 cites. (Remember not to confuse the viewpoints!) As for G, Scientist 2 says that tektites *do* resemble earth materials, but never says that they *don't* resemble lunar materials. And choice H gets it backwards; Scientist 2 says that extraterrestrial material *would* be widely dispersed, and that the tektites are *not* widely dispersed, rather than vice versa.

For **Question 3**, you need to find the best way for Scientist 1 to counter the point that some tektites have vesicles filled with gases in the same proportion as the earth's atmosphere. First, make sure you understand the meaning of that point. The idea that these gases must have been trapped in the vesicles (little holes) while the rock was actually being formed is being used by Scientist 2 to suggest that tektites are of terrestrial origin. Scientist 1 *could* say that not all tektites have such gas-filled vesicles—Choice A—but that's not a great argument. If any reasonable number of them *do*, Scientist 1 would have to come up with an alternative explanation (Scientist 2 never claimed that *all* tektites contained these vesicles). But if, as B suggests, Scientist 1 could demonstrate that molten material would be likely to trap some terrestrial gases while falling through earth's atmosphere, this would explain how tektites might have come from beyond the earth and still contain vesicles filled with Earthlike gases. Choice C is easy to eliminate if you know that the moon's atmosphere is extremely thin and totally different in composition from the earth's atmosphere, so it doesn't make much sense to suggest that those gases might occur in the same proportions as in the moon's atmosphere. Finally, since it's Scientist 2 who claims that tektites are terrestrial in origin, choice D, showing that similar gas-filled vesicles occur in some terrestrial volcanic glass, wouldn't help Scientist 1 at all.

In **Question 4**, you're asked how Scientist 2 answered the argument that tektitelike material ejected from the earth could not reach a high enough velocity to undergo air-friction melting. Well, that was Scientist 2's third data point. The shock wave produced by a major meteorite collision could momentarily displace the atmosphere right above the impact site (meaning the air moved out of the way for a brief time). So, when the splattered material reentered the atmosphere, it would undergo air-friction melting. That's basically what choice F says, so F is correct.

In **Question 5**, the concept of subjecting lenses of tektite glass to a heated airstream was mentioned toward the beginning of Scientist 1's argument. The point was to simulate the entry of extraterrestrial tektite material through Earth's atmosphere, and that's closest to choice C.

Question 6 shows again why it pays to keep each scientist's viewpoint straight. You can't counter the objections of Scientist 2 to Scientist 1's argument unless you know what Scientist 2 was objecting to. Scientist 2's first data point is the only one designed to shoot holes in the opposing viewpoint. There, Scientist 2 takes issue with the idea that lunar material could strike the earth without being dispersed over a far wider area than the known strewn fields. But if, as correct choice F says, researchers found some force capable of removing tektite-sized objects from orbit *quickly*, it would demolish the objection that Scientist 2 raises in her first paragraph. The tektite material would strike the earth or be pulled away quickly, instead of remaining in a solar orbit long enough to be captured by the earth's gravity and subsequently be distributed over a wide area of the earth.

Question 7 wasn't too tough if you read the question stem carefully. You want to find the tektite characteristic that is LEAST consistent with the theory that tektites came from the moon or beyond. This is Scientist 1's theory, so you want to pick the answer choice that doesn't go with his argument. Scientist 1's evidence *does* include tektites' low water content, "flying saucer" shapes, and absence of unmelted material. The only answer choice that he didn't mention was the narrow distribution of the strewn fields. And with good reason. That's part of Scientist 2's argument *against* an extraterrestrial origin. So the correct answer is choice C.

Know Your Evidence

As you can see, many questions on the Conflicting Viewpoints passage involve evidence: what evidence was presented, what evidence would hurt or help one scientist's views, what evidence was used for what purpose. It's important that you take note of the evidence (data) each scientist uses.

THE DEEP END

Now we're going to do something very cruel. We're going to to throw you a Science Reasoning passage of such technical difficulty that many of you will want to go screaming for the exits before you finish reading it.

But we're doing this for a reason. Sometimes on the ACT Science Reasoning test, you'll find yourself encountering a bear of a passage—one that seems entirely incomprehensible. The secret to success with these passages is: *Don't panic*. As we'll show you, you can get points on even the most difficult Science Reasoning passage in the entire history of the ACT—as long as you keep your cool and approach it in a savvy, practical way. Here's the passage.

Passage V

Neutrinos (*n*) are subatomic particles that travel at approximately the speed of light. They can penetrate most matter, because they are electrically neutral and effectively massless.

Generally accepted theory holds that the nuclear reactions that power the Sun create vast quantities of neutrinos as byproducts. Three proposed stages (PPI, PPII, and PPIII) of the most important solar reaction are shown in Figure 1, along with their neutrino-producing subpaths. Equations for the subpaths are shown in Table 1, as are the predicted neutrino energies and fluxes.

Figure 1

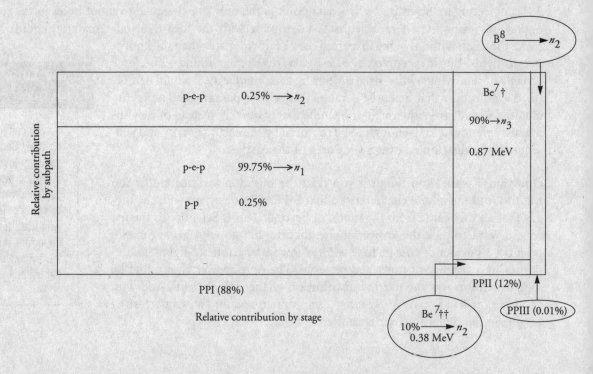

Table 1

Subpath name	Subpath equation	Neutrino energy (MeV)	Expected flux on Earth ($10^{10}\text{cm}^{-2}\text{sec}^{-1}$)
p-p	$_1H^1 + {}_1H^1 \longrightarrow {}_1H^2 + \beta^+ + n$	0.42	6.06781
p-e-p	$_1H^1 + \beta^- + {}_1H^1 \longrightarrow {}_1H^2 + n$	1.44	0.01524
Be^7†	$_4Be^7 + \beta^- \longrightarrow {}_3Li^7 + n$	0.87	0.43924
Be^7††	$_4Be^7 + \beta^- \longrightarrow {}_3Li^7 + n$	0.38	0.04880
B^8	$_5B^8 \longrightarrow {}_4Be^8 + \beta^+ + n$	14.05*	0.00054

†Be^7 subpath 1   *Maximum
††Be^7 subpath 2

8. According to the information presented in the passage, which of the following stages or subpaths should contribute the smallest portion of the total solar neutrino flux on Earth?
   - F. p-p
   - G. PPI
   - H. PPII
   - J. PPIII

   Ⓕ Ⓖ Ⓗ Ⓙ

9. Of the neutrinos that are produced in the subpaths described in the passage, which type can have the greatest energy?
   - A. n_1
   - B. n_2
   - C. n_3
   - D. n_4

   Ⓐ Ⓑ Ⓒ Ⓓ

10. Based on the information presented in the passage, the percentage of solar neutrinos produced by Be^7 subpath 2 is approximately:
   - F. 1.2%
   - G. 10%
   - H. 12%
   - J. 90%

   Ⓕ Ⓖ Ⓗ Ⓙ

11. Solar neutrinos are detected through a reaction with $_{37}Cl$ for which the minimum neutrino energy is approximately 0.8 MeV. Of the neutrinos discussed in the passage, this method would detect:
   - A. all of the neutrinos produced in PPI and PPII.
   - B. some of the neutrinos produced in PPI, PPII, and PPIII.
   - C. only neutrinos produced in Be^7 subpath 1 of PPII.
   - D. only neutrinos produced in PPIII.

   Ⓐ Ⓑ Ⓒ Ⓓ

12. The symbol β represents a beta particle, a particle emitted during nuclear decay. Beta particles may be positively or negatively charged. During which of the following subpaths are beta particles emitted?

  I. p-p

  II. p-e-p

  III. B^8

F. II only
G. I and III only
H. II and III only
J. I, II, and III

Ⓕ Ⓖ Ⓗ Ⓙ

Answers and Explanations

Confused? If you aren't, you should stick close to your phone, because the Nobel Prize committee will probably be calling sometime soon! On the other hand, if you *were* confused, don't sweat it. As we said in ACT Basics, some ACT questions are so hard that even your *teachers* would have a hard time getting them correct.

Answers

8. J, 9. D, 10. F, 11. B, 12. G

The good news is that you don't have to understand a passage to get a few questions right. For instance, here's how you might have approached the passage above.

Getting Points Even if You Don't Get the Point

Your prereading of the introduction should have told you that the passage is about neutrinos coming from the sun. But that may be all you were able to get from this gibberish. You may have been in a total fog looking at Figure 1 and Table 1. But if you didn't panic, you might have noticed a few things: First, that whatever Figure 1 illustrates, there are some really big parts and some really small parts. If you look at the *x*-axis of the chart, you'll see that, whatever PPI, PPII, and PPIII are, the first is 88%, the second only 12%, and the third only .01%.

Is that tiny, vague insight enough to get a point? Yes! Look at **Question 8**. It asks which stage or subpath contributes the *smallest* portion of flux. Well, look for a small portion. PPIII's figure of 0.01% is a very small number, whatever it's supposed to be referring to, so PPIII would be a good guess here. And indeed, choice J is correct for Question 8.

You could have gotten a point here without even understanding what the passage was all about!

What about Table 1? This is a little easier to understand, especially if you ignore the column about subpath equations. But "neutrino energy" sounds like something we can comprehend. Apparently, each subpath produces a different level of neutrino energy. Some have high energy (like B^8, with 14.06) and some have low energy (like B^7++, with only 0.38). Energy is mentioned in **Question 9**. Which type of neutrinos can have the greatest energy? Well, if B^8 were a choice, we'd pick that. But the choices are these funny *v*s, not Bs. Well, try to find B^8 somewhere in the other chart—Figure 1. There we find it somehow associated with v_4 neutrinos. So take a gamble; choose v_4—which is choice D—for this question. If you did that, you'd still have gotten another point, still without really understanding much more than before.

You're hot; keep it going. **Question 10** refers to Be^7 subpath 2. You may have noticed in the note under Table 1 that the Be^7 with two little dagger marks signifies subpath 2. So far, so good. Notice that the choices are all percentages. Where are percentages mentioned? In Figure 1. So find Be^7 with two dagger marks in Figure 1. You find it in the area of PPII, which is 12 percent of the x-axis in that chart. But notice that Be^7 with two dagger marks represents only *part* of that part of the figure—10 percent, to be exact. So, 10 percent of 12 percent would be 1.2%. That's choice F. It's also the correct answer.

Things get a little harder with **Question 11**, but you still might have gotten the answer if you used common sense. Here we get some mumbo jumbo about $_{37}$Cl, but the part of the question that should have caught your eye was the bit about a minimum neutrino energy of 0.8 MeV. Neutrino energy was represented in the third column of Table 1. According to that table, only three subpaths have an energy greater than 0.8—p-e-p (with 1.44), Be^7 with one dagger mark (with 0.87), and B^8 (the champion, with 14.06). Unfortunately, the answer choices aren't expressed in those terms; they're expressed in terms of PPI, II, and III, so we're going to have to translate from table to figure again, just as we did with Question 9.

Take p-e-p first. That's part (but not all) of the PPI portion of Figure 1. Be^7 with one dagger mark, similarly, is part (but not all) of the PPII portion. And B8 is all of the PPIII portion. So there are at least parts of PPI, PPII, and PPIII implicated here. That should have led you to Choice B, which would have gotten you yet another point. Notice that choice A is inaccurate because it talks about *all* of something in PPI and PPII, and doesn't mention PPIII at all. Choices C and D, meanwhile, seem too limited, since they only mention one of the PP areas (whatever they are). So B was definitely the closest answer choice.

Finally, **Question 12** talks about beta particles. Well, that little beta symbol appears only in the subpath column of Table 1. There we find beta symbols in the equations for *all* of the subpaths in the table. That may have led you to believe that all three Roman numerals should be included, and no one would have blamed you for choosing choice J (I, II, and III). You would have been wrong, but you can't win them all when you're winging questions you don't really understand.

Of course, if you noticed that the question was asking for beta particles *emitted*, and if you knew that in the subpath equations everything *before* the arrow is what you start with while everything *after* the arrow is what you finish with, you might have been able to make a better guess. You would have realized that those equations with a beta symbol *before* the arrow were ones in which a beta particle was *absorbed*, while those with a beta symbol *after* the arrow were ones in which a beta particle was *emitted*. In that case, then, you would have seen that the equations for p-p and B^8 *do* have beta particles emitted, while the equation for p-e-p does not. That might have led you to choice G—I and III only—which *is* the correct answer.

Six questions, six points—and all without understanding the passage in any deep or thorough way. Of course, if you understand the mysteries of neutrino flux and p-e-p subpaths, congratulations. You're probably enough of a science whiz to ace the subject test anyway. But if you're like most ACT test takers, you won't understand everything the passages talk about. Sometimes you'll even find yourself totally lost.

Finishing Isn't That Important

Don't worry if you don't have time to look at all the questions. You can earn high scores in the ACTScience Reasoning section—even if you never look at a whole passage—if almost all the questions you do answer are right and if you remember to guess on the rest.

The moral of the story, of course, is don't give up on a passage just because you don't understand it. You may not be able to get *every* point associated with the passage, but you may be able to get at least one or two (or three or four). Remember: The test is designed in such a way that you can *figure out* many of the questions, even if you don't know the subject area.

Let's conclude now with another quick point about getting quick points. If you're nearly out of time and you've still got a whole Science Reasoning passage left, you need to shift to last-minute strategies. As in Reading, don't try to preread the passage, or you'll just run out of time before you answer any questions. Instead, scan the questions without reading the passage and look first for the ones that require only reading data off of a graph or table. You can often get a couple of quick points just by knowing how to find data quickly.

Again, the most important thing is to make sure you have gridded in at least a random guess on every question.

Ready, Set, Go

16

Strategic Summaries

Highlights

Everything you need to know for each of the subject tests:

- An overview

- The mindset you need to succeed

- The Kaplan Method

- Special strategies

- Tips on timing

- What to do when you're running out of time

ENGLISH TEST STRATEGIC SUMMARY

The English subject test:

- Is 45 minutes long.

- Includes 5 passages, representing a range of writing styles and levels of formality.

- Consists of 75 questions, divided among the 5 passages. They test many different points of grammar, punctuation, writing mechanics, usage, and rhetorical skills, by proposing ways of expressing information underlined at various points in the passages. We divide the questions strategically into three groups:

Emergency Plan

If you have two weeks or fewer to prep for the ACT, read this chapter. It reviews the key facts and strategies for the English, Math, Reading, and Science Reasoning tests.

 201

1. Economy Questions

2. Sense Questions

3. Technicality Questions

There are also a few *Out-of-Format* Questions that require different strategies, as outlined in Special Strategies below.

The questions do NOT get harder as you proceed through the section.

The Mindset for the English Test

- When in doubt, take it out. Make sure that everything is written as concisely as possible. If you think something doesn't belong in a sentence, it probably doesn't, so choose an answer that leaves it out.

- Make it make sense. Grammar allows language to communicate meaning clearly. Most grammatically faulty sentences on the ACT don't say what the author obviously intended to say. If a sentence has more than one possible meaning, figure out what the author intended to say, and fix the sentence so it conveys that meaning properly.

- Trust your ear. Mistakes in grammar often sound bad to your ear. Trust that instinct. Don't choose the answer that "sounds fancy," choose the one that "sounds right." But keep in mind that there are some errors your ear won't catch. For these errors, use your flag list.

The Method

For each question, ask yourself three things. Note that you may actually have your answer before getting to all three questions:

1. Ask: Does this stuff belong here? Is it redundant? Is it relevant? Is this a long way to say a short idea? If so, choose an answer that gets rid of the stuff that doesn't belong.

2. Ask: Does this stuff make sense? The ACT test makers want short, simple, easy-to-understand prose. They expect everything to fit together logically. Choose the answer that turns nonsense into sense.

3. Ask: Does this stuff sound like English? If not, choose the answer that does. Recognize items on your "flag list" from English Workout 3 and let them help out when your ear isn't sure. These classic errors appear again and again on ACT English subject tests.

Special Strategies: Out of Format Questions

A few questions will require you to rearrange the words in a sentence, the sentences in a paragraph, or even the paragraphs in a passage. Others may ask questions about the meaning of all or part of the passage, or to describe its structure. Your approach to these questions should be:

1. Determine your task. What is the question asking you to do?

2. Consider the passage as a whole. Most passages will have a well-defined theme, laid out in a logical way. Choose the answer that expresses this theme, or the arrangement of elements that best continues the logical "flow" of the passage.

3. Prephrase your answer. As in Reading, you should have an idea of what the answer is before looking at the choices.

Timing

We recommend that you NOT skip around in the English subject test. Although you can certainly use the usual Two-Pass Approach, you might prefer to go straight from beginning to end, answering all of the questions as you go. Unlike in other sections, in English you'll usually have at least a sense of what the right answer should be right away. Remember, even the correct answer will start to sound wrong if you think about it too much!

Set your watch to 12:00 at the beginning of the subject test. Although you should go faster if you can, here's roughly where you should be at the following checkpoints:

12:09	One passage finished and answers gridded in
12:18	Two passages finished and answers gridded in
12:27	Three passages finished and answers gridded in
12:36	Four passages finished and answers gridded in
12:45	Five passages finished and answers for the entire section gridded in.

Note that you should do at least some work on all 75 English questions, and make sure you have at least one guess gridded in for every question when time is called.

When You're Running out of Time

If you have no time left even to read the last few questions, choose the shortest answer for each one. Remember that "OMIT," when it appears, counts as the shortest answer.

Scoring

Your performance on the English subject test will be averaged into your ACT Composite Score, weighted equally with your scores on the other three subject tests. You will also receive:

*   English subject score—from 1 to 36—for the entire English subject test

*   Usage/Mechanics subscore—from 1 to 18—based on your performance on the questions testing grammar, usage, punctuation, and sentence structure

*   Rhetorical Skills subscore—from 1 to 18—based on your performance on the questions testing strategy, organization, and style

MATH TEST STRATEGIC SUMMARY

The Math subject test:

- Is 60 minutes long.

- Consists of 60 questions, which test your grasp of prealgebra, algebra, coordinate geometry, plane geometry, and trigonometry. We breakdown the questions into the following strategic categories:

    1. Diagram Questions

    2. Story Questions

    3. Concept Questions

The questions tend to test more advanced math concepts as you proceed through the section.

The Mindset for the Math Test

- The end justifies the means. Remember that what's important on the ACT is getting as many correct answers as quickly as possible. If that means doing straightforward questions in a straightforward way, that's fine. But many questions can be solved faster by unorthodox methods.

- Take time to save time. It sounds paradoxical, but to go your fastest on the ACT Math test you've got to slow down. Never dive in headlong, wildly crunching numbers, manipulating equations, or filling out figures without first giving the problem a few seconds of thought.

- When in doubt, shake it up. ACT Math questions are not always what they seem at first sight. Sometimes all you need is a new perspective to break through the disguise.

The Method

1. Understand. First focus on the question stem and make sure you understand the problem. Sometimes you'll want to read the stem twice, or rephrase it in a way you can better understand. Think to yourself: "What kind of problem is this? What am I looking for? What am I given?" When you begin, don't pay too much attention to the answer choices, though you may want to give them a quick glance just to see what form they're in.

2. Analyze. Think for a moment and decide on a plan of attack. Don't start crunching numbers until you've given the problem a little thought. "What's a quick and reliable way to find the correct answer?" Look for patterns and shortcuts, using common sense and your knowledge of the test to find the creative solutions that will get you more right answers in less time. Try to solve the problem without focusing on the answer choices.

3. Select. Once you get an answer—or once you get stuck—check the answer choices. If you got an answer and it's listed as one of the choices, chances are it's right—fill in the appropriate bubble and move on. But if you didn't get an answer, narrow down the choices as best you can by a process of elimination, and then guess.

Special Strategies

We offer several recommendations for what to do when you get stuck. If after a few moments of thought you find you still can't come up with a reasonable way of doing the problem, try one of these techniques:

1. Backsolve. We recommend that you normally attempt to solve a problem before looking at the answer choices. But when you're stuck, take advantage of the multiple-choice format. In some of the questions, you can just try out each answer choice until you find the one that works.

2. Pick numbers. Some problems are hard because they're general or abstract. Bring these down to earth by temporarily replacing variables with specific numbers.

3. Guesstimate. Sometimes you'll understand what a problem is asking for, but you just won't know what algorithm, formula, or theorem to apply. If you can figure out some ballpark estimate for the correct answer, you'll probably be able to eliminate at least one or two answer choices.

4. Eyeball. Even though the directions warn you that diagrams are "not necessarily" drawn to scale, eyeballing is a surprisingly effective guessing strategy. When you don't fully fathom the geometry of a situation, but you do have a diagram to work with, see how many answer choices you can eliminate just by sizing things up with your eyes.

Timing

Remember the Two-Pass Approach. Spend about 45 minutes on your first pass through the Math subject test, doing the easier questions, guessing on the questions you know you'll never get, and marking the tough ones that you'll want to come back to. Spend the last 15 minutes picking up those questions that you skipped on the first pass.

We recommend that you grid your answers at the end of every page or every two-page spread. In the last five minutes or so, start gridding your answers one by one. And make sure that you have an answer (even if it's a blind guess) gridded for every question by the time the subject test is over.

Don't worry if you have to guess on a lot of the math questions. You can miss a lot of questions on the subject test and still get a great score. Remember that the average ACT test taker gets less than half the math questions right!

When You're Running out of Time

If at some point you realize you have more questions left than you have time for, be extra willing to skip around, looking for questions you understand right away. Pick your spots. Concentrate on the questions you have the best chance of correctly answering. Just be sure to grid an answer—even if it's just a wild guess—for every question.

Scoring

Your performance on the Math subject test will be averaged into your ACT Composite Score, equally weighted with your scores on the other three subject tests. You will also receive:

- Math subject score—from 1 to 36—for the entire Math subject test
- Prealgebra/Elementary Algebra subscore—from 1 to 18
- Intermediate Algebra/Coordinate Geometry subscore—from 1 to 18
- Plane Geometry/Trigonometry subscore—from 1 to 18

READING TEST STRATEGIC SUMMARY

The Reading subject test:

- Is 35 minutes long.
- Includes four passages:
- Three Nonfiction passages (one each in Social Studies, Natural Sciences, and Humanities, though there is no significant difference among them except subject matter)
- One Prose Fiction passage (an excerpt from a short story or novel)
- Consists of 40 questions, 10 on each passage. They include:
  1. Specific Detail Questions
  2. Inference Questions
  3. Big Picture Questions

The questions do NOT get harder as you go through the section.

The Mindset for the Reading Test

- Know where you're going. Try to read passages actively, anticipating where the author is going by paying attention to structural clues and common sense. Pay attention to the structure of each passage and don't get bogged down in the details.
- Look it up. Find the answers, don't remember them. Think of the passages as reference books, not textbooks. Refer.

The Method

1. Preread the passage. Try to understand the "gist" of the passage. Get a sense of the overall structure of the passage. Create a mental road map (except on the Prose Fiction passage) to make referring back easier.
2. Consider the question stem. Understand the question first, without looking at the array of answer choices. Remember that many wrong choices are designed to mislead test takers who just jump past the question stem and start comparing choices to each other.

3. Refer to the passage before looking at the choices. Always refer to the passage before answering the question. If the question includes a line reference, use it. Only then look at the choices. Make sure your answer matches the passage in meaning, and that it doesn't just use the same words as the passage.

4. Answer the question in your own words before looking at the choices.

5. Match your answer with one of the choices. Having an answer in mind will keep you from getting bogged down.

Special Strategies

Prose Fiction Passage

When you preread the passage, pay attention to the characters, especially the main character. Read between the lines to determine unspoken emotions and attitudes. Ask yourself:

- Who are these people? What are they like? How are they related to each other?

- What is their state of mind? Are they angry, sad, reflective, excited?

- What's going on? What's happening on the surface? What's happening beneath the surface?

Nonfiction Passages

Don't be thrown by unfamiliar vocabulary. If you find a difficult term, odds are the definition will be given to you in context (or else it simply might not matter what the word means). Remember, you can still get lots of questions right, even if you don't fully understand the passage. The answers to all of the questions can be found.

Timing

You might want to take a few seconds at the beginning of the subject test to page through the passages, gauging the difficulty of each one. At first glance you may wish to skip an entire passage if it seems very difficult.

We recommend that you treat each passage and its questions as a block. Take two passes through each block before moving on to the next (skip around if you like, but watch your answer grid if you do!). Get the easy questions on the first pass through and save the tougher ones for the second pass. Just make sure to keep track of time.

Set your watch to 12:00 at the beginning of the subject test. Although you should go faster if you can, here's roughly where you should be at the following checkpoints.

12:09 . . . . .One passage finished and answers gridded in

12:18 . . . . .Two passages finished and answers gridded in

12:27 . . . . .Three passages finished and answers gridded in

12:35 . . . . .Four passages finished and answers for entire section gridded in

Don't spend time agonizing over specific questions. Avoid thinking long and hard about the answer choices. Once you've spent a minute or so on a question, make your best guess and keep moving on.

Don't panic if you can't finish all four passages. Make sure you do a good job on at least three passages—and remember to grid answers (even if they're blind guesses) for all questions by the end. Even if you try all four passages, you probably won't really work on all forty questions. For many questions, you'll just have to guess. Just make sure you guess on the tough ones and actually work on the easy ones!

When You're Running out of Time

If you have less than 5 minutes left for the last passage, do the following:

1. Skip the prereading step.

2. Look for questions with specific line references and do them.

3. Refer to the cited location in the passage and answer the question as best you can, based on what you see there.

4. Make sure you have gridded in an answer for every question before time is called.

Scoring

Your performance on the Reading subject test will be averaged into your ACT Composite Score, weighted equally with your scores on the other three subject tests. You will also receive:

- Reading subject score—from 1 to 36—for the entire Reading subject test

- Social Science/Sciences subscore—from 1 to 18—based on your performance on the nonfiction passages drawn from Social Studies and Natural Sciences

- Arts/Literature subscore—from 1 to 18—based on your performance on the nonfiction passage (drawn from the Humanities) and on the Prose Fiction passage

SCIENCE REASONING TEST STRATEGIC SUMMARY

The Science Reasoning subject test:

- Is 35 minutes long.

- Includes 7 "passages," or sets of scientific information, involving graphs, tables, and research summaries. Typically, one of the passages involves two conflicting viewpoints on a single scientific issue.

- Consists of 40 questions, divided among the 7 passages. We divide the questions strategically into three categories:

  1. Data Analysis Questions

  2. Experiment Questions

  3. Principle Questions

The questions do NOT get harder as you proceed through the section.

The Mindset for the Science Reasoning Test

- Look for patterns. Usually, the exact data contained in Science Reasoning passages are not as important as are changes in the data. Look for extremes (maximums and minimums), critical points (points of change), and variation (direct and inverse).

- Know your direction. There are two kinds of scientific reasoning—general-to-specific and specific-to-general. Always be aware of when scientists are inferring a specific case from a general rule, and when they are using specific data to form a (general) theory.

- Refer, don't remember. Don't even think of trying to remember data. It's always there, right on the page, for you to refer to when needed.

The Method

1. Preread the passage. Look for the overall topic. What is being researched? Look for the purpose of each experiment. How do the experiments differ? Don't get bogged down in details and don't worry about understanding everything.

2. Consider the question stem. Make sure you understand exactly what the question is asking. Get a sense of what the answer should be without looking at the choices, many of which are designed to mislead you if you're indecisive.

3. Refer to the passage before looking at the choices. Always refer back to the passage before looking at the choices and selecting one. Make sure you read charts and graphs accurately, and that you do not confuse different kinds of units.

4. Answer the question in your own words. Don't rely too much on your knowledge of science. Paraphrase the information in the passage.

5. Match your answer with one of the choices. Having an answer in mind will help you to avoid falling for a wrong answer.

Special Strategies

Reading Tables and Graphs

When reading tables and graphs, you should:

- Determine what is being represented

- Determine what the axes (or columns and rows) represent

- Take note of units of measurement

- Look for trends in the data

Experiments

Remember how experiments work. There is typically (though not always) a control group plus an experimental group or groups. In a well-designed experiment, the only difference between the groups will be a variation in the factor that's being tested. Ask yourself:

- What's the factor that's being varied?

- What's the control group, if any?

- What do the results show? What differences exist between the results for one group and those for another?

Conflicting Viewpoints Passage

Spend a little more time than usual on the pre-reading step of this passage. Focus on the two points of view. What are the scientists arguing about? What do they agree on, if anything? What do they differ on? Identify the following for each scientist:

- Basic theory statement (usually the first sentence of each scientist's presentation)

- Major pieces of data behind the theory (keeping in mind whether each supports the scientist's own theory or weakens the opposing scientist's theory)

Timing

Some Science Reasoning passages are a lot harder than others, and they're not arranged in order of difficulty, so you might want to take a few seconds at the beginning of the subject test to page through the passages, gauging the difficulty of each one. You may wish to skip an entire passage if it seems very difficult (but remember that a very difficult passage may have very easy questions).

As in Reading, treat each passage and its questions as a block, taking two passes through each block before moving on to the next. Get the easy questions on the first pass through and save the tougher ones for the second pass. Some questions will probably be impossible for you to answer; take an intuitive guess on these.

Set your watch to 12:00 at the beginning of the subject test. Although you should go faster if you can, here's where you should be at the following checkpoints:

12:05 . . . . .One passage finished and answers gridded in

12:10 . . . . .Two passages finished and answers gridded in

12:15 . . . . .Three passages finished and answers gridded in

12:20 . . . . .Four passages finished and answers gridded in

12:25 . . . . .Five passages finished and answers gridded in

12:30 . . . . .Six passages finished and answers gridded in

12:35 . . . . .Seven passages finished and answers for the entire section gridded in

Don't spend time agonizing over specific questions. Avoid thinking long and hard about the answer choices. If you've spent a minute or so on a question and don't seem to be making any headway, make your best guess and move on.

Don't panic if you can't finish all seven passages, but try to do a good job on at least five of them. And make sure you remember to grid answers (even if they're blind guesses) for all questions by the end.

When You're Running out of Time

If you have fewer than three minutes left for the last passage, do the following:

1. Skip the prereading step.

2. Look for questions that refer to specific experiments or to specific graphs or tables.

3. Refer to the cited location in the passage and answer the question as best you can, based on what you see there.

4. Make sure you have gridded in an answer for every question before time is called.

Scoring

Your performance on the Science Reasoning subject test will be averaged into your ACT Composite Score, weighted equally with your scores on the other three subject tests. You will also receive:

- Science Reasoning subject score—from 1 to 36—for the entire Science Reasoning subject test

Unlike the other three subject scores, the Science Reasoning score is not divided into sub-scores.

Last-Minute Tips

Highlights

Training tips for putting in a peak performance

- Before the test

- On Test Day

- After the test

Is it starting to feel like your whole life is a buildup to the ACT? You've known about it for years, you've worried about it for months, and now you've spent at least a few hours in solid preparation for it. As the test gets closer, you may find your anxiety is on the rise. But you really shouldn't worry. After the preparation you've received from this book, you're in good shape for Test Day.

COUNTDOWN TO TEST DAY

To calm any pretest jitters you may have (and assuming you've left yourself at least some breathing time before your ACT), let's go over a few last-minute strategies for the couple of days before and after the test.

Emergency Plan

If you have two weeks or fewer to prep for the ACT, read this chapter. It tells you how to use your time wisely before, during, and after the test.

Three Days Before the Test

- If you haven't already done so, take one of the the full-length practice tests in this book under timed conditions or take one of the practice tests on the *Higher Score CD-*

ROM, if you've bought the version of this book with the CD-ROM. If you have already worked through all the tests in the book and on the CD, try an actual published ACT (your guidance counselor might have one).

- Try to use all of the techniques and tips you've learned in this book. Take control. Approach the test strategically and creatively.

WARNING: Don't take a full practice ACT unless you have at least forty-eight hours left before the test! Doing so will probably exhaust you, hurting your scoring potential on the actual test! You wouldn't run a marathon the day before the real thing, would you?

Two Days Before the Test

- Go over the results of your practice test. Don't worry too much about your score or whether you got a specific question right or wrong. Remember the practice test doesn't count. But do examine your performance on specific questions with an eye to how you might get through each one faster and with greater accuracy on the actual test to come.

- After reviewing your test, look over the Strategic Summaries. If you feel a little shaky about any of the areas mentioned, quickly read the relevant workouts.

- This is the day to do your last studying—review a couple of the more difficult principles we've covered, do a few more practice problems, and call it quits. It doesn't pay to make yourself crazy right before the test. Besides, you've prepared. You'll do well.

The Day Before the Test

- Don't study.
- Get together an "ACT survival kit" containing the following items:
- Watch
- At least three sharpened No. 2 pencils
- Pencil sharpener
- two erasers
- Photo ID card (if you're not taking the test at your high school, make sure your ID is official)
- Your admission ticket
- Snack—there's a break, and you'll probably get hungry
- Your lucky rabbit's foot
- Know exactly where you're going and how you're getting there. It's probably a good idea to visit your test center sometime before test day, so that you know what expect on the big day.
- Relax the day before the test. Read a good book, take a bubble bath, watch TV. Exercise can be a good idea early in the afternoon. Working out makes it easier to sleep when you're nervous, and it also makes many people feel better. Of course, don't work so hard that you can't get up the next day!

- Get a good night's sleep. Go to bed early and allow for some extra time to get ready in the morning.

TEST DAY TIPS

The Morning of the Test

- Eat breakfast. Make it something substantial, but not anything too heavy or greasy. Don't drink a lot of coffee if you're not used to it; bathroom breaks cut into your time, and too much caffeine—or any other kind of drug—is a bad idea.

- Dress in layers so that you can adjust to the temperature of the test room.

- Read something. Warm up your brain with a newspaper or a magazine. You shouldn't let the ACT be the first thing you read that day.

- Be sure to get there early. Allow yourself extra time for traffic, mass-transit delays, and any other possible problems.

- If you can, go to the test with a friend (even if he or she isn't taking the test). It's nice to have somebody supporting you right up to the last minute.

During the Test

- Don't get rattled. If you find your confidence slipping, remind yourself how well you've prepared. You've followed the Three Commandments of ACT Success. You know the test; you know the strategies; you know the material tested. You're in great shape, as long as you relax!

- Even if something goes really wrong, don't panic. If the test booklet is defective—two pages are stuck together or the ink has run—try to stay calm. Raise your hand, and tell the proctor you need a new book. If you accidentally misgrid your answer page or put the answers in the wrong section, again don't panic. Raise your hand, and tell the proctor. He or she might be able to arrange for you to regrid your test after it's over, when it won't cost you any time.

After the Test

Once the test is over, put it out of your mind. If you don't plan to take the ACT again, shelve this book and start thinking about more interesting things.

You might walk out of the ACT thinking that you blew it. This is a normal reaction. Lots of people—even the highest scorers—feel that way. You tend to remember the questions that stumped you, not the many that you knew. If you're really concerned, call us for advice. Also call us if you had any problems with your test experience—a proctor who called time early, a testing room whose temperature hovered just below freezing. We'll do everything we can to make sure that your rights as a test taker are preserved!

But remember, unless you've ignored our recommendation about NOT listing any schools to receive your scores automatically, you've got nothing to worry about (provided that there is still time to get the scores there before the deadline). If you really did blow the test, you can take it again and no admissions officer will be the wiser.

Odds are, though, you didn't really blow it. Most people only remember their disasters on the test; they don't remember the numerous small victories that kept piling up the points.

But for Now . . .

Just relax. You've prepared for the ACT with Kaplan. You're going to do well.

Practice Tests and Explanations

ACT Practice Test 1
Answer Sheet

ENGLISH TEST

	10 Ⓕ Ⓖ Ⓗ Ⓙ	20 Ⓕ Ⓖ Ⓗ Ⓙ	30 Ⓕ Ⓖ Ⓗ Ⓙ	40 Ⓕ Ⓖ Ⓗ Ⓙ	50 Ⓕ Ⓖ Ⓗ Ⓙ	60 Ⓕ Ⓖ Ⓗ Ⓙ	70 Ⓕ Ⓖ Ⓗ Ⓙ
1 Ⓐ Ⓑ Ⓒ Ⓓ	11 Ⓐ Ⓑ Ⓒ Ⓓ	21 Ⓐ Ⓑ Ⓒ Ⓓ	31 Ⓐ Ⓑ Ⓒ Ⓓ	41 Ⓐ Ⓑ Ⓒ Ⓓ	51 Ⓐ Ⓑ Ⓒ Ⓓ	61 Ⓐ Ⓑ Ⓒ Ⓓ	71 Ⓐ Ⓑ Ⓒ Ⓓ
2 Ⓕ Ⓖ Ⓗ Ⓙ	12 Ⓕ Ⓖ Ⓗ Ⓙ	22 Ⓕ Ⓖ Ⓗ Ⓙ	32 Ⓕ Ⓖ Ⓗ Ⓙ	42 Ⓕ Ⓖ Ⓗ Ⓙ	52 Ⓕ Ⓖ Ⓗ Ⓙ	62 Ⓕ Ⓖ Ⓗ Ⓙ	72 Ⓕ Ⓖ Ⓗ Ⓙ
3 Ⓐ Ⓑ Ⓒ Ⓓ	13 Ⓐ Ⓑ Ⓒ Ⓓ	23 Ⓐ Ⓑ Ⓒ Ⓓ	33 Ⓐ Ⓑ Ⓒ Ⓓ	43 Ⓐ Ⓑ Ⓒ Ⓓ	53 Ⓐ Ⓑ Ⓒ Ⓓ	63 Ⓐ Ⓑ Ⓒ Ⓓ	73 Ⓐ Ⓑ Ⓒ Ⓓ
4 Ⓕ Ⓖ Ⓗ Ⓙ	14 Ⓕ Ⓖ Ⓗ Ⓙ	24 Ⓕ Ⓖ Ⓗ Ⓙ	34 Ⓕ Ⓖ Ⓗ Ⓙ	44 Ⓕ Ⓖ Ⓗ Ⓙ	54 Ⓕ Ⓖ Ⓗ Ⓙ	64 Ⓕ Ⓖ Ⓗ Ⓙ	74 Ⓕ Ⓖ Ⓗ Ⓙ
5 Ⓐ Ⓑ Ⓒ Ⓓ	15 Ⓐ Ⓑ Ⓒ Ⓓ	25 Ⓐ Ⓑ Ⓒ Ⓓ	35 Ⓐ Ⓑ Ⓒ Ⓓ	45 Ⓐ Ⓑ Ⓒ Ⓓ	55 Ⓐ Ⓑ Ⓒ Ⓓ	65 Ⓐ Ⓑ Ⓒ Ⓓ	75 Ⓐ Ⓑ Ⓒ Ⓓ
6 Ⓕ Ⓖ Ⓗ Ⓙ	16 Ⓕ Ⓖ Ⓗ Ⓙ	26 Ⓕ Ⓖ Ⓗ Ⓙ	36 Ⓕ Ⓖ Ⓗ Ⓙ	46 Ⓕ Ⓖ Ⓗ Ⓙ	56 Ⓕ Ⓖ Ⓗ Ⓙ	66 Ⓕ Ⓖ Ⓗ Ⓙ	
7 Ⓐ Ⓑ Ⓒ Ⓓ	17 Ⓐ Ⓑ Ⓒ Ⓓ	27 Ⓐ Ⓑ Ⓒ Ⓓ	37 Ⓐ Ⓑ Ⓒ Ⓓ	47 Ⓐ Ⓑ Ⓒ Ⓓ	57 Ⓐ Ⓑ Ⓒ Ⓓ	67 Ⓐ Ⓑ Ⓒ Ⓓ	
8 Ⓕ Ⓖ Ⓗ Ⓙ	18 Ⓕ Ⓖ Ⓗ Ⓙ	28 Ⓕ Ⓖ Ⓗ Ⓙ	38 Ⓕ Ⓖ Ⓗ Ⓙ	48 Ⓕ Ⓖ Ⓗ Ⓙ	58 Ⓕ Ⓖ Ⓗ Ⓙ	68 Ⓕ Ⓖ Ⓗ Ⓙ	
9 Ⓐ Ⓑ Ⓒ Ⓓ	19 Ⓐ Ⓑ Ⓒ Ⓓ	29 Ⓐ Ⓑ Ⓒ Ⓓ	39 Ⓐ Ⓑ Ⓒ Ⓓ	49 Ⓐ Ⓑ Ⓒ Ⓓ	59 Ⓐ Ⓑ Ⓒ Ⓓ	69 Ⓐ Ⓑ Ⓒ Ⓓ	

MATH TEST

	8 Ⓕ Ⓖ Ⓗ Ⓙ Ⓚ	16 Ⓕ Ⓖ Ⓗ Ⓙ Ⓚ	24 Ⓕ Ⓖ Ⓗ Ⓙ Ⓚ	32 Ⓕ Ⓖ Ⓗ Ⓙ Ⓚ	40 Ⓕ Ⓖ Ⓗ Ⓙ Ⓚ	48 Ⓕ Ⓖ Ⓗ Ⓙ Ⓚ	56 Ⓕ Ⓖ Ⓗ Ⓙ Ⓚ
1 Ⓐ Ⓑ Ⓒ Ⓓ Ⓔ	9 Ⓐ Ⓑ Ⓒ Ⓓ Ⓔ	17 Ⓐ Ⓑ Ⓒ Ⓓ Ⓔ	25 Ⓐ Ⓑ Ⓒ Ⓓ Ⓔ	33 Ⓐ Ⓑ Ⓒ Ⓓ Ⓔ	41 Ⓐ Ⓑ Ⓒ Ⓓ Ⓔ	49 Ⓐ Ⓑ Ⓒ Ⓓ Ⓔ	57 Ⓐ Ⓑ Ⓒ Ⓓ Ⓔ
2 Ⓕ Ⓖ Ⓗ Ⓙ Ⓚ	10 Ⓕ Ⓖ Ⓗ Ⓙ Ⓚ	18 Ⓕ Ⓖ Ⓗ Ⓙ Ⓚ	26 Ⓕ Ⓖ Ⓗ Ⓙ Ⓚ	34 Ⓕ Ⓖ Ⓗ Ⓙ Ⓚ	42 Ⓕ Ⓖ Ⓗ Ⓙ Ⓚ	50 Ⓕ Ⓖ Ⓗ Ⓙ Ⓚ	58 Ⓕ Ⓖ Ⓗ Ⓙ Ⓚ
3 Ⓐ Ⓑ Ⓒ Ⓓ Ⓔ	11 Ⓐ Ⓑ Ⓒ Ⓓ Ⓔ	19 Ⓐ Ⓑ Ⓒ Ⓓ Ⓔ	27 Ⓐ Ⓑ Ⓒ Ⓓ Ⓔ	35 Ⓐ Ⓑ Ⓒ Ⓓ Ⓔ	43 Ⓐ Ⓑ Ⓒ Ⓓ Ⓔ	51 Ⓐ Ⓑ Ⓒ Ⓓ Ⓔ	59 Ⓐ Ⓑ Ⓒ Ⓓ Ⓔ
4 Ⓕ Ⓖ Ⓗ Ⓙ Ⓚ	12 Ⓕ Ⓖ Ⓗ Ⓙ Ⓚ	20 Ⓕ Ⓖ Ⓗ Ⓙ Ⓚ	28 Ⓕ Ⓖ Ⓗ Ⓙ Ⓚ	36 Ⓕ Ⓖ Ⓗ Ⓙ Ⓚ	44 Ⓕ Ⓖ Ⓗ Ⓙ Ⓚ	52 Ⓕ Ⓖ Ⓗ Ⓙ Ⓚ	60 Ⓕ Ⓖ Ⓗ Ⓙ Ⓚ
5 Ⓐ Ⓑ Ⓒ Ⓓ Ⓔ	13 Ⓐ Ⓑ Ⓒ Ⓓ Ⓔ	21 Ⓐ Ⓑ Ⓒ Ⓓ Ⓔ	29 Ⓐ Ⓑ Ⓒ Ⓓ Ⓔ	37 Ⓐ Ⓑ Ⓒ Ⓓ Ⓔ	45 Ⓐ Ⓑ Ⓒ Ⓓ Ⓔ	53 Ⓐ Ⓑ Ⓒ Ⓓ Ⓔ	
6 Ⓕ Ⓖ Ⓗ Ⓙ Ⓚ	14 Ⓕ Ⓖ Ⓗ Ⓙ Ⓚ	22 Ⓕ Ⓖ Ⓗ Ⓙ Ⓚ	30 Ⓕ Ⓖ Ⓗ Ⓙ Ⓚ	38 Ⓕ Ⓖ Ⓗ Ⓙ Ⓚ	46 Ⓕ Ⓖ Ⓗ Ⓙ Ⓚ	54 Ⓕ Ⓖ Ⓗ Ⓙ Ⓚ	
7 Ⓐ Ⓑ Ⓒ Ⓓ Ⓔ	15 Ⓐ Ⓑ Ⓒ Ⓓ Ⓔ	23 Ⓐ Ⓑ Ⓒ Ⓓ Ⓔ	31 Ⓐ Ⓑ Ⓒ Ⓓ Ⓔ	39 Ⓐ Ⓑ Ⓒ Ⓓ Ⓔ	47 Ⓐ Ⓑ Ⓒ Ⓓ Ⓔ	55 Ⓐ Ⓑ Ⓒ Ⓓ Ⓔ	

READING TEST

	6 Ⓕ Ⓖ Ⓗ Ⓙ	12 Ⓕ Ⓖ Ⓗ Ⓙ	18 Ⓕ Ⓖ Ⓗ Ⓙ	24 Ⓕ Ⓖ Ⓗ Ⓙ	30 Ⓕ Ⓖ Ⓗ Ⓙ	36 Ⓕ Ⓖ Ⓗ Ⓙ
1 Ⓐ Ⓑ Ⓒ Ⓓ	7 Ⓐ Ⓑ Ⓒ Ⓓ	13 Ⓐ Ⓑ Ⓒ Ⓓ	19 Ⓐ Ⓑ Ⓒ Ⓓ	25 Ⓐ Ⓑ Ⓒ Ⓓ	31 Ⓐ Ⓑ Ⓒ Ⓓ	37 Ⓐ Ⓑ Ⓒ Ⓓ
2 Ⓕ Ⓖ Ⓗ Ⓙ	8 Ⓕ Ⓖ Ⓗ Ⓙ	14 Ⓕ Ⓖ Ⓗ Ⓙ	20 Ⓕ Ⓖ Ⓗ Ⓙ	26 Ⓕ Ⓖ Ⓗ Ⓙ	32 Ⓕ Ⓖ Ⓗ Ⓙ	38 Ⓕ Ⓖ Ⓗ Ⓙ
3 Ⓐ Ⓑ Ⓒ Ⓓ	9 Ⓐ Ⓑ Ⓒ Ⓓ	15 Ⓐ Ⓑ Ⓒ Ⓓ	21 Ⓐ Ⓑ Ⓒ Ⓓ	27 Ⓐ Ⓑ Ⓒ Ⓓ	33 Ⓐ Ⓑ Ⓒ Ⓓ	39 Ⓐ Ⓑ Ⓒ Ⓓ
4 Ⓕ Ⓖ Ⓗ Ⓙ	10 Ⓕ Ⓖ Ⓗ Ⓙ	16 Ⓕ Ⓖ Ⓗ Ⓙ	22 Ⓕ Ⓖ Ⓗ Ⓙ	28 Ⓕ Ⓖ Ⓗ Ⓙ	34 Ⓕ Ⓖ Ⓗ Ⓙ	40 Ⓕ Ⓖ Ⓗ Ⓙ
5 Ⓐ Ⓑ Ⓒ Ⓓ	11 Ⓐ Ⓑ Ⓒ Ⓓ	17 Ⓐ Ⓑ Ⓒ Ⓓ	23 Ⓐ Ⓑ Ⓒ Ⓓ	29 Ⓐ Ⓑ Ⓒ Ⓓ	35 Ⓐ Ⓑ Ⓒ Ⓓ	

SCIENCE TEST

	6 Ⓕ Ⓖ Ⓗ Ⓙ	12 Ⓕ Ⓖ Ⓗ Ⓙ	18 Ⓕ Ⓖ Ⓗ Ⓙ	24 Ⓕ Ⓖ Ⓗ Ⓙ	30 Ⓕ Ⓖ Ⓗ Ⓙ	36 Ⓕ Ⓖ Ⓗ Ⓙ
1 Ⓐ Ⓑ Ⓒ Ⓓ	7 Ⓐ Ⓑ Ⓒ Ⓓ	13 Ⓐ Ⓑ Ⓒ Ⓓ	19 Ⓐ Ⓑ Ⓒ Ⓓ	25 Ⓐ Ⓑ Ⓒ Ⓓ	31 Ⓐ Ⓑ Ⓒ Ⓓ	37 Ⓐ Ⓑ Ⓒ Ⓓ
2 Ⓕ Ⓖ Ⓗ Ⓙ	8 Ⓕ Ⓖ Ⓗ Ⓙ	14 Ⓕ Ⓖ Ⓗ Ⓙ	20 Ⓕ Ⓖ Ⓗ Ⓙ	26 Ⓕ Ⓖ Ⓗ Ⓙ	32 Ⓕ Ⓖ Ⓗ Ⓙ	38 Ⓕ Ⓖ Ⓗ Ⓙ
3 Ⓐ Ⓑ Ⓒ Ⓓ	9 Ⓐ Ⓑ Ⓒ Ⓓ	15 Ⓐ Ⓑ Ⓒ Ⓓ	21 Ⓐ Ⓑ Ⓒ Ⓓ	27 Ⓐ Ⓑ Ⓒ Ⓓ	33 Ⓐ Ⓑ Ⓒ Ⓓ	39 Ⓐ Ⓑ Ⓒ Ⓓ
4 Ⓕ Ⓖ Ⓗ Ⓙ	10 Ⓕ Ⓖ Ⓗ Ⓙ	16 Ⓕ Ⓖ Ⓗ Ⓙ	22 Ⓕ Ⓖ Ⓗ Ⓙ	28 Ⓕ Ⓖ Ⓗ Ⓙ	34 Ⓕ Ⓖ Ⓗ Ⓙ	40 Ⓕ Ⓖ Ⓗ Ⓙ
5 Ⓐ Ⓑ Ⓒ Ⓓ	11 Ⓐ Ⓑ Ⓒ Ⓓ	17 Ⓐ Ⓑ Ⓒ Ⓓ	23 Ⓐ Ⓑ Ⓒ Ⓓ	29 Ⓐ Ⓑ Ⓒ Ⓓ	35 Ⓐ Ⓑ Ⓒ Ⓓ	

KAPLAN

Practice Test 1

HOW TO TAKE THESE PRACTICE TESTS

Practice Tests 1 and 2 are Kaplan-created tests, similar to the actual ACT test booklet. Before taking a practice test, find a quiet room where you can work uninterrupted for two and a half hours. Make sure you have a comfortable desk, your calculator, and several No. 2 pencils. Use the answer sheet to record your answers. Once you start a practice test, don't stop until you've finished. Remember: You can review any questions within a section, but you may not jump from one section to another.

You'll find the answers and explanations to the test questions immediately following each test.

ENGLISH TEST

45 Minutes—75 Questions

Directions: In the following five passages, certain words and phrases have been underlined and numbered. You will find alternatives for each underlined portion in the right-hand column. Select the one that best expresses the idea, that makes the statement acceptable in standard written English, or that is phrased most consistently with the style and tone of the entire passage. If you feel that the original version is best, select "NO CHANGE." You will also find questions asking about a section of the passage or about the entire passage. For these questions, decide which choice gives the most appropriate response to the given question. For each question in the test, select the best choice, and fill in the corresponding space on the answer folder. You may wish to read each passage through before you begin to answer the questions associated with it. Most answers cannot be determined without reading several sentences around the phrases in question. Make sure to read far enough ahead each time you choose an alternative.

Passage I

Many people enjoy the hobby of aquarium keeping.

It has several advantages. <u>As pets they are very quiet, not worrying too much about pats on the head or 4:00 A.M. walks.</u> Yet even many avid aquarists are unaware
1

of the fact that their hobby has a fascinating history.

Fish keeping actually has ancient origins, <u>who beginning with</u> the Sumerians over 4,500 years ago.
2

They kept fish in artificial ponds. The ancient

Assyrians and Egyptians also kept fish. In addition to

<u>keeping and having</u> fish as pets, the Chinese used them
3

for practical purposes, raising carp for food as early as

100 B.C. They were probably the first people to <u>breeds</u>
4

fish with any degree of success. Their selective breed-

ing of ornamental goldfish was introduced in Japan,

where the breeding of ornamental carp was perfected.

<u>The ancient Romans</u> kept fish for food and
5

entertainment. They were the were the first known

1. A. NO CHANGE
    B. Fish make quiet pets; they do not need to be patted on the head or walked at 4:00 A.M.
    C. Their owner who did not pat them on the head is not worried about walking these quiet pets at 4:00 A.M.
    D. These quiet pets without a pat on the head from their owners are not to be walked at 4:00 A.M. by necessity.

2. F. NO CHANGE
    G. which begins with
    H. beginning with
    J. who, beginning at

3. A. NO CHANGE
    B. keeping and possessing
    C. keep and have
    D. keeping

4. F. NO CHANGE
    G. breeded
    H. breed
    J. bred

5. A. NO CHANGE
    B. These are the ancient Romans
    C. Yes, one can find ancient Romans which
    D. The ancient Romans, nevertheless,

GO ON TO THE NEXT PAGE ➡

KAPLAN

seawater aquarists, constructing ponds supplied with

fresh ocean water. The Romans were also the first to use

open-air tanks to preserve and fatten fish for market.

In seventeenth-century England, goldfish were

<u>being</u> kept in glass containers, but aquarium keeping did
  6

not become well established until the relationship among

animals, oxygen, and plants <u>became known</u> a century
                7

later. In the eighteenth century, France's importation of

goldfish from the Orient created a need for small

aquariums. Ceramic bowls, occasionally fitted with

transparent panels, were produced. 8

By 1850, the keeping of fish, reptiles, and

amphibians had become a useful method of study for

naturalists. Philip Gosse, a British ornithologist, first

coined the term "aquarium." The first display aquariums

opened in 1853 at Regent's Park in <u>London aquariums</u>
                         9

soon appeared in Naples, Berlin, and Paris. The first

aquarium to serve as a financial enterprise was opened by

the circus entrepreneur P. T. Barnum at the American

Museum in New York City. By 1928, forty-five public or

commercial aquariums were open. <u>Then it slowed and</u>
                              10

<u>few new large aquariums appeared until after World</u>
                      10

<u>War II</u>. Marineland of Florida, built in 1956, was the first
  10

oceanarium. <u>*Flipper* was a popular television show about</u>
                      11

<u>a dolphin.</u>
  11

6. F. NO CHANGE
    G. to have been
    H. sometimes being
    J. OMIT the underlined portion.

7. A. NO CHANGE
    B. which became known
    C. becoming known
    D. were known almost

8. The purpose of the preceding sentence is to:
    F. emphasize the inappropriateness of the aquariums produced at that time.
    G. illustrate the fact that the importation of goldfish produced a corresponding need for small containers.
    H. contradict the assertion made earlier in the paragraph that the English kept goldfish in glass containers.
    J. explain why goldfish could not live for long in small containers.

9. A. NO CHANGE
    B. London, which
    C. London, where it
    D. London, and

10. F. NO CHANGE
    G. Then its growth having slowed; few new large ones appeared until after World War II.
    H. Then having slowed, few new large ones appeared until after World War II was over.
    J. Then growth slowed, and few new large aquariums appeared until after World War II.

11. A. NO CHANGE
    B. A popular television show about a dolphin was *Flipper.*
    C. (A popular television show, *Flipper,* was about a dolphin.)
    D. OMIT the underlined portion.

GO ON TO THE NEXT PAGE ➡

So next time you meet an aquarist you might share

some of this <u>"fish trivia." For</u> fish keeping is not only an
                    12
entertaining hobby; it also has a rich and long history,

<u>have playing</u> a role in many diverse cultures since ancient
   13
times.

> Items 14–15 pose questions about the passage as a
> whole.

14. Which of the following best summarizes the conclusion
made by the essay as a whole?
  F. The study of history is a valuable task.
  G. People who keep aquariums must learn "fish
trivia."
  H. The hobby of keeping aquariums has an intriguing
past.
  J. Maintaining an aquarium is a big responsibility.

12. **F.** NO CHANGE
  G. —fish trivia. For
  H. "fish trivia," and
  J. "fish trivia! For

13. **A.** NO CHANGE
  B. having played
  C. has
  D. had played

15. The essay is made up of five paragraphs. Which of the
following is the best description of how the paragraphs
are organized?
  A. First example, second example, third example,
definition, argument.
  B. Introduction, earliest examples, later examples,
most recent examples, conclusion.
  C. Historical survey, first example, second example,
third example, fourth example.
  D. Introduction, background information, argument,
counterargument, personal account.

Passage II

The late twentieth century may well be remembered

as the Age of the "Yuppie" (young urban professional).

Our society seems obsessed with the notion of social

mobility. There are two different types of social <u>mobility:</u>
                                                    16
<u>horizontal and vertical.</u> If there is a change in occupation,
     16
but no change in social class, it is called "horizontal

mobility." One example of this would be a lawyer who

changes law firms that are comparable <u>in pay salary and</u>
                                            17
<u>prestige.</u> A change in role involving a change in social
   17

standing <u>is called "vertical mobility"</u> and can be either
                    18
upward or downward.

   The extent of change can vary greatly. At one pole,

social mobility may affect only one member of a society.

16. **F.** NO CHANGE
  G. mobility horizontal, and vertical.
  H. mobility; horizontal and vertical.
  J. mobility: being horizontal and vertical.

17. **A.** NO CHANGE
  B. in pay and prestige.
  C. with pay, salary and prestige.
  D. pay in terms of salary and prestige.

18. **F.** NO CHANGE
  G. it's called "vertical mobility"
  H. they're called "vertical mobility"
  J. it is called "vertical mobility"

GO ON TO THE NEXT PAGE ➡

At the other extreme, it may change the entire social system.

The Russian Revolution of 1917, <u>therefore</u>, altered an entire
                                     19
class structure.

[1] <u>In addition to involving degrees of change,</u> social
                        20
mobility occurs at a variety of rates. [2] The "American

dream" is based in part on the notion of rapid social

mobility, in which an unknown individual becomes an

"overnight success." [3] One example of rapid social

mobility would be the young guitar player who becomes

an instant rock star. [4] The athlete who wins an Olympic

gold medal <u>too</u> [5] For instance, each generation in a
                     21
family may be a little better off than the generation

before it. [6] Social mobility may also be accomplished

by more gradual changes. 22

The results of mobility are difficult to measure <u>in</u>
                                                    23
<u>that.</u> Some view large-scale mobility in a negative light,
 23
claiming that it disintegrates class structure and puts an

end to meaningful traditions. <u>Accordingly</u> others claim
                                   24

that <u>they're</u> attempting to rise validate and therefore
      25
reinforce the class system. They see mobility as a

positive thing, enabling individuals to improve their own

19. **A.** NO CHANGE
B. nonetheless
C. for instance
D. consequently

20. **F.** NO CHANGE
G. In addition, it involved differing degrees of change,
H. In addition to the fact that it involved change's differing degrees,
J. It involves degrees of change,

21. **A.** NO CHANGE
B. is another example.
C. is too.
D. OMIT the underlined portion and end with a period.

22. For the sake of unity and coherence, sentence 6 should be placed:
F. where it is now.
G. after sentence 2.
H. after sentence 4.
J. at the beginning of the next paragraph.

23. **A.** NO CHANGE
B. in.
C. on.
D. OMIT the underlined portion and end the sentence with a period.

24. **F.** NO CHANGE
G. (Begin new paragraph) Similarly,
H. (Begin new paragraph) Likewise,
J. (Do NOT begin new paragraph) On the other hand,

25. **A.** NO CHANGE
B. they
C. those who are
D. their

GO ON TO THE NEXT PAGE ➡

lives and the lives of their families. 26

Still others see social mobility as destroying, rather

than <u>reinforced—the class system yet</u> they feel this is a
                        27
positive change. According to them, society will benefit

from the breakdown <u>like a flat tire</u> of a social system in
                         28
which material wealth is given so much importance.

Whether we view it positively or negatively, social

mobility is a basic fact of modern industrial society. The

crowd of yuppies hitting the shopping malls, credit cards

in hand, <u>show</u> that vertical mobility is very much with us
         29

<u>and so will a lot of other things be</u>.
        30

26. Suppose that at this point in the passage the writer wanted to add more information. Which of the following additions would be most relevant to the paragraph?
   F. A discussion of the problems of the educational system in America
   G. A listing of average salaries for different occupations
   H. Some examples of the benefits of social mobility
   J. A discussion of a rock star's new video

27. A. NO CHANGE
   B. reinforcing, the class system; yet
   C. reinforced. The class system; and
   D. that it reinforces the class system

28. F. NO CHANGE
   G. (such as a flat tire)
   H. (like the kind a flat tire gets)
   J. OMIT the underlined portion.

29. A. NO CHANGE
   B. shows
   C. showing
   D. to show

30. F. NO CHANGE
   G. and there they will be for some time to come.
   H. and will be for some time to come.
   J. OMIT the underlined portion and end the sentence with a period.

GO ON TO THE NEXT PAGE ➡

Passage III

> The following paragraphs may or may not be in the most logical order. Each paragraph is numbered in parentheses, and item 45 will ask you to choose the sequence of paragraph numbers that is in the most logical order.

[1]

The critic George Moore once said of this artist <u>that</u>
                                                    31
<u>is</u> "her pictures are the only pictures painted by a woman
31
that could not be destroyed without creating a blank, a

hiatus in the history of art." In part a tribute to Morisot,

Moore's <u>statement are also one</u> that shows the prejudices
            32
Morisot faced as a woman in a male-dominated

discipline.

[2]

The Impressionist painter Berthe Morisot was born

in1841 to a wealthy family that had connections to the

French government. Yet it was no surprise to anyone

when Morisot <u>showed little interest in it, and instead took</u>
                                    33
<u>after her grandfather</u> the painter Jean Honoré Fragonard.
            33

<u>Being her earliest</u> childhood, she had the desire to be an
            34
artist. At the age of twenty-one, she began seven years of

study with Corot. She had her first work accepted at the

Paris Salon in 1864. In 1868 she met the Impressionist

painter Edouard <u>Manet and</u> served as his model for
                        35
several portraits. She was actively involved with the

Impressionist exhibiting society of the 1870s and 1880s.

31. **A.** NO CHANGE
    B. that being that
    C. is
    D. that

32. **F.** NO CHANGE
    G. statement's is also one
    H. statement is also one
    J. statements are also among those

33. **A.** NO CHANGE
    B. showed little interest in politics and instead took after her grandfather,
    C. with little interest in it—politics—took up after her grandfather instead
    D. was little interested in it, taking after her grandfather

34. **F.** NO CHANGE
    G. From, her being in earliest
    H. Being in early
    J. From her earliest

35. **A.** NO CHANGE
    B. Manet (who was neither Belgian nor Dutch) and
    C. Manet (a man not Belgian and not Dutch) and
    D. Manet—a man of neither Belgian nor Dutch extraction, and

GO ON TO THE NEXT PAGE ➡

[3]

Either Morisot's subject matter nor her style is
                        36
distinctive. As a woman, she lacked the freedom enjoyed

by her male colleagues, who face no threat of social
                        37
disapproval in their journeys through Parisian cafes,

theaters, and parks. Therefore, Morisot turned her
                      38
limitations to her advantage, creating a unique vantage

point. Unlike her fellow Impressionists, who painted

scenes of Parisian night life, Morisot concentrated on her

own private sphere. Portraying women performing
                     39

domestic and social activities. 40

[4]

Morisot's paintings frequently feature female

members of her family, especially her daughter. She

often captures her models at thoughtful moments in their

chores. In contrast to the vast landscapes of her male

colleagues, Morisot's figures are generally enclosed by

some device: such as a balustrade, balcony, veranda, or
                41
embankment. The sense of confinement conveyed by

many of her paintings may be in part a reflection of the

barriers Morisot faced as a woman artist. But despite the

36. F. NO CHANGE
    G. Neither Morisot's subject matter nor her style is
    H. Neither Morisot's subject matter or her style are
    J. Neither Morisot's subject matter nor her style

37. A. NO CHANGE
    B. colleagues, whom faced
    C. colleagues, who faced
    D. colleagues, and faced

38. F. NO CHANGE
    G. Similarly,
    H. Likewise,
    J. However,

39. A. NO CHANGE
    B. sphere. She began to portray
    C. sphere insofar portraying
    D. sphere, which were

40. Paragraph 3 makes the point that Morisot's painting did not include subject matter available to her male colleagues. The author wants to revise the whole paragraph to emphasize a more positive judgment of her work's value and a less negative view of its limitations. Which of the following revisions of the paragraph's first sentence would best allow her to express this changed perspective?
    F. While Morisot's subject matter lacks originality, her style, in fact, is quite suited to expressing her distinctive interests.
    G. Morisot's subject matter and style are somewhat limited by her society's confining standards, but her work takes on a greater meaning in its social context.
    H. Morisot's subject matter may not appear particularly distinctive, but her work has great meaning in its social context.
    J. Few can say that Morisot is one of the great Impressionists, but there are not many great Impressionists in any case.

41. A. NO CHANGE
    B. some device—
    C. some device:
    D. some such device such as,

obstacles, Morisot managed to achieve the recognition

she deserved, helping to ease the way for her successors

<u>the people who followed after her.</u>
 42

42. **F.** NO CHANGE
 G. those who came after.
 H. which followed her.
 J. OMIT the underlined portion and end the sentence with a period.

Items 43–45 pose questions about the passage as a whole.

---

43. The writer could best continue this essay by:
 A. discussing how Morisot's success influenced social attitudes toward later women artists.
 B. comparing several Impressionist landscape paintings by various artists.
 C. providing background information on the art critic George Moore.
 D. listing, by title and author, a series of articles on important Impressionists.

44. In the second paragraph, is the writer's reference to specific dates appropriate?
 F. No, because the information interferes with the biographical purpose of this essay.
 G. No, because the information, while it does not interfere with the biographical purpose of the essay, is out of place, since the rest of the essay does not cite dates.
 H. Yes, because the information helps to make the story of Morisot believable.
 J. Yes, because the information helps to carry out the biographical purpose of this essay.

45. Choose the sequence of paragraph numbers that will make the passage's structure most logical.
 A. NO CHANGE
 B. 2, 1, 3, 4
 C. 2, 3, 1, 4
 D. 3, 2, 4, 1

GO ON TO THE NEXT PAGE ➡

Passage IV

It used to be that when people wanted to see a scary movie they could choose from films such as *Dracula* and *Frankenstein*. But these classic monster movies, with an occasional exception, <u>has been replaced</u> by a new breed
46

of horror <u>film the</u> slasher movie. It is interesting and
47
perhaps somewhat disturbing to examine what such changes in taste may indicate about some of the values at work in our nation.

    <u>First:</u> commercially successful low-budget chiller
48
was *Halloween*, and in its wake psycho-slasher films

have the movie market <u>glutted.</u> The formula for these
49
movies consists of the serial murder of teenagers by a

ruthless psychotic, with some humor thrown in. <u>The fact</u>
50
<u>of the matter being that the popularity of the series</u> of
50
Friday the Thirteenth movies and of their hundreds of

silly imitators indicates that there is a huge market for

such portrayals of random violence. Indeed, filmgoers

appear to cast their votes for more and more graphic

forms of violence. As a result, filmmakers<u>—those who</u>
51
<u>actually made films</u>—generate
51

<u>increasing gory</u> productions.
52

46. **F.** NO CHANGE
    G. have been replaced
    H. were being replaced
    J. replaced

47. **A.** NO CHANGE
    B. film, which is the
    C. film: the
    D. film known, as the

48. **F.** NO CHANGE
    G. First;
    H. The first
    J. First—

49. **A.** NO CHANGE
    B. (Place after *have*)
    C. (Place after *movie*)
    D. (Place after *wake*)

50. **F.** NO CHANGE
    G. The fact of the matter being
    H. The popularity of the
    J. Factually speaking, in terms of popularity,

51. **A.** NO CHANGE
    B. —those making the films, actually
    C. (which are the people making the films)
    D. OMIT the underlined portion.

52. **F.** NO CHANGE
    G. increasing, gory,
    H. increasingly full of gore,
    J. increasingly gory

GO ON TO THE NEXT PAGE ➡

As a result of this <u>trend</u>, slasher films now represent
53
mainstream Hollywood movies. Once limited only to the

<u>periphery (fringe)</u> of the movie industry, the exploitation
54
of gore has become a major box office attraction. Older

slasher films, such as *Psycho* and *The Texas Chainsaw*

Massacre, actually seem like classics in comparison to

the countless imitators filling video stores and movie

screens. <u>They're</u> so many of these low-budget imitators
55
in distribution that, in 1981 alone, they accounted for half

of the fifty top-grossing movies. That's a big wad of

cash! 56

Although the popularity of such films has declined

somewhat as their novelty has worn <u>off. However,</u> they
57
remain a standard feature of the yearly production

schedule. Even many high-budget horror films have

adopted the slasher formula of chills and violence. Are

these movies a means of harmless fun, as some fans

claim? Are they a reflection of an <u>increasingly and</u>
58
<u>evermore violent?</u> Or do such movies perhaps even
58
encourage violence? Considering the great changes both

within the movie industry and in <u>public (human)</u> taste,
59
these are questions that we must begin to consider. 60

53. **A.** NO CHANGE
B. trend:
C. trend—
D. —trend—

54. **F.** NO CHANGE
G. periphery
H. periphery (that is, the fringe)
J. periphery, fringe,

55. **A.** NO CHANGE
B. They are
C. There's
D. There are

56. Is the final sentence of this paragraph appropriate?
F. No, because its reference to money is irrelevant to the topic of the paragraph.
G. No, because its reference to money, while relevant to the topic of the paragraph, is conveyed through an inappropriate image.
H. Yes, because the exclamation with which the sentence ends heightens the drama of the paragraph.
J. Yes, because its specific image helps to clarify the preceding sentence.

57. **A.** NO CHANGE
B. off, and they
C. off, so
D. off, they

58. **F.** NO CHANGE
G. more, and more, and more violent society
H. increasingly violent society
J. increasingly violent society, full of anger, blood and shooting

59. **A.** NO CHANGE
B. public, and human
C. public
D. human's

GO ON TO THE NEXT PAGE ➡

60. How can the tone and purpose of this essay best be described?
  - F. The tone is serious; the purpose is to point out a significant change in entertainment.
  - G. The tone is lighthearted; the purpose is to recommend a new form of entertainment.
  - H. The tone is sarcastic; the purpose is to show how contemporary movies lack value.
  - J. The tone is harsh; the purpose is to urge people not to attend slasher films.

Passage V

> The following paragraphs may or may not be in the most logical order. Each paragraph is numbered in parentheses, and item 75 will ask you to choose the sequence of paragraph numbers that is in the most logical order.

[1]

The strangest of these events all involve <u>unexplained</u>
                                              61
<u>disappearances—the kind that haven't been fully</u>
                      61
<u>explained.</u> Ships have been found
   61

<u>abandoned and deserted</u> for no apparent reason.
          62

<u>Without transmitting distress signals, some ships having</u>
                         63
<u>vanished forever.</u> Planes have reported their position and
       63
then disappeared. Even rescue missions are said to have

vanished while flying in the area. Theories accounting for

such occurrences <u>ranging towards</u> the interference of
                        64
UFOs to the existence of powerful fields of some

unknown force. So far, no conclusions <u>have been reached.</u>
                                               65

61. A. NO CHANGE
  - B. unexplained disappearances, which haven't been explained, fully.
  - C. unexplained disappearances.
  - D. unexplained disappearances that have not been explained.

62. F. NO CHANGE
  - G. abandoned
  - H. abandoned, including left
  - J. abandoned (deserted)

63. A. NO CHANGE
  - B. They've not transmitted distress signals, and they've vanished forever, never to return.
  - C. Transmitting no distress signals, having vanished forever, have been some ships.
  - D. Some ships have vanished forever without transmitting any distress signal.

64. F. NO CHANGE
  - G. range to
  - H. ranging from
  - J. range from

65. A. NO CHANGE
  - B. have (yet) been reached.
  - C. having yet been reached.
  - D. yet reached.

GO ON TO THE NEXT PAGE ➡

[2]

In the North Atlantic Ocean, the Bermuda Islands—a

jumble of 300 islets, rocks, and islands—form part of a

roughly triangular <u>region (England is roughly triangular,</u>
66
<u>too)</u> whose other boundaries are the southern U.S.
66

<u>coast and</u> the Greater Antilles. Perhaps the first
67
European to explore this area was Juan de Bermudez in

1515. <u>They wonder who</u> whether he ever experienced
68
anything strange back then, for this is the region known

today as the Bermuda Triangle. Extremely strange events

<u>had been</u> frequently reported from this area. ☐70
69

[3]

Others are critical of the claims posed about the

Bermuda Triangle. They point out that wreckage has not

been found and that scientific searches have uncovered

nothing to substantiate the strange events attributed to the

region. Also, they question <u>so it can be</u> that boaters and
71
fliers continue to travel through the region unharmed. ☐72

66. F. NO CHANGE
    G. region (like England)
    H. region
    J. England-like region

67. A. NO CHANGE
    B. coast (but not rivers) and
    C. coast, but not rivers, and
    D. coast—but not rivers—and

68. F. NO CHANGE
    G. We are those who wonder
    H. Some wonder
    J. Some of them are wondering

69. A. NO CHANGE
    B. has been
    C. is
    D. have been

70. Is the mention of Juan de Bermudez appropriate?
    F. No, because it connects two dissimilar things, exploration and the Bermuda Triangle.
    G. Yes, because it provides background information while introducing the main subject of the passage.
    H. Yes, because the passage suggests that exploration is more significant than the supernatural.
    J. Yes, because Juan de Bermudez is the only person named in the passage.

71. A. NO CHANGE
    B. which
    C. how
    D. OMIT the underlined portion.

72. Suppose that at this point the writer wanted to add more information. Which of the following additions would be most relevant?
    F. A geographical description of the Bermuda Triangle
    G. A brief allusion to other well-known supernatural phenomena
    H. More evidence disputing the occurrence of supernatural forces
    J. A discussion of Bermuda's tourist trade

GO ON TO THE NEXT PAGE ➡

[4]

We may never be <u>certain in the way a judge is</u> of the

73

truth about the Bermuda Triangle. Yet people will

continue to be intrigued by the supernatural and the

strange. One thing we can be sure of is that this enigmatic

place will continue to fascinate the public and stir up

controversy for years to come.

73. **A.** NO CHANGE
B. absolutely certain
C. certain like a judge
D. certain as a judge is

Items 74–75 pose questions about the passage as a whole.

---

74. Suppose the editor of a travel magazine had requested that the writer give an account of one specific disappearance that has occurred in the Bermuda region. Does this essay successfully fulfill that request?
   F. Yes, because the disappearances described are actual events.
   G. Yes, because the essay focuses on mysterious disappearances in the Bermuda Triangle.
   H. No, because the writer has relied on generalities in discussing the nature of disappearances in the region.
   J. No, because the essay lacks factual information of any sort.

75. For the sake of unity and coherence, Paragraph 1 should be placed:
   A. where it is now.
   B. after Paragraph 2.
   C. after Paragraph 3.
   D. after Paragraph 4.

END OF ENGLISH TEST

IF YOU FINISH BEFORE TIME IS CALLED, YOU MAY CHECK YOUR WORK ON THIS SECTION ONLY. DO NOT TURN TO ANY OTHER SECTION IN THE TEST. **STOP**

234 **KAPLAN**

MATHEMATICS TEST

60 Minutes—60 Questions

Directions: Solve each of the following problems, select the correct answer, and then fill in the corresponding space on your answer sheet.

Don't linger over problems that are too time-consuming. Do as many as you can, then come back to the others in the time you have remaining.

Note: Unless otherwise noted, all of the following should be assumed.

1. Illustrative figures are *not* necessarily drawn to scale.

2. All geometric figures lie in a plane.

3. The term *line* indicates a straight line.

4. The term *average* indicates arithmetic mean.

---

1. If $5x + 3 = -17$, then $x = $?

   DO YOUR FIGURING HERE.

   A. -25

   B. $-7\frac{1}{3}$

   C. -4

   D. 4

   E. $6\frac{1}{3}$

2. John wants to make fruit salad. He has a recipe that serves 6 people and uses 4 oranges, 5 pears, 10 apples, and 2 dozen strawberries. If he wants to serve 18 people, how many pears will John need?

   F. 5

   G. 10

   H. 15

   J. 20

   K. 25

3. What is the greatest integer that is a factor of both 8×10^9 and 6×10^3?

   A. 1×10^9

   B. 2×10^6

   C. 6×10^3

   D. 2×10^3

   E. 1×10^3

4. What is the area of the rectangle in the standard (x, y) coordinate plane shown in the figure below?

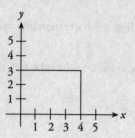

DO YOUR FIGURING HERE.

F.   4
G.   7
H.   10
J.   12
K.   14

5. A costume designer wants to put a white silk band around a cylindrical top hat. If the radius of the cylindrical part of the top hat is 4 inches, how long, in inches, should the white silk band be to just fit around the top hat?

A. 8π
B. 25π
C. 50π
D. 100π
E. 200π

6. A large jar holds 48 olives while a small jar holds only 32 olives. Which of the following expressions represents the number of olives needed to fill x large jars and y small jars?

F. $48x + 32y$
G. $\dfrac{x}{48} + \dfrac{y}{32}$
H. $\dfrac{xy}{80}$
J. $80xy$
K. $\dfrac{1536}{xy}$

7. If $f(x) = 3x^2 + 4$, $f(x + 1) = ?$

A. $3x^2 + 5$
B. $3x^2 + x + 4$
C. $3x^2 + 4$
D. $3x^2 + 2x + 5$
E. $3x^2 + 6x + 7$

GO ON TO THE NEXT PAGE ➡

8. $5\frac{5}{6} + 3\frac{5}{8} + 1\frac{1}{3} = ?$

DO YOUR FIGURING HERE.

F. $9\frac{11}{17}$

G. $9\frac{19}{24}$

H. $10\frac{9}{24}$

J. $10\frac{4}{5}$

K. $10\frac{19}{24}$

9. Jimmy's school is 10 miles from his house, on the same street. If he walks down his street directly from the school to his house he passes a candy store and a grocery store. The candy store is 2.35 miles from the school and the grocery store is 3.4 miles from the candy store. How many miles is it from the grocery store to Jimmy's house?

A. 3.75
B. 4.25
C. 4.75
D. 5.25
E. 5.75

10. Harry is a piano student who can learn 2 new pieces in a week. If his piano teacher gives him 3 new pieces every week for 4 weeks, how many weeks will it take Harry to learn all these pieces?

F. 6
G. 7.5
H. 8
J. 12
K. 15

11. In $\triangle DEF$ below, the measure of $\angle EDF$ is 35° and the measure of $\angle DFE$ is 65°. What is the measure of $\angle DEF$?

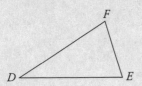

A. 35°
B. 45°
C. 75°
D. 80°
E. 100°

GO ON TO THE NEXT PAGE ➡

12. Randy scored 150, 195, and 160 in 3 bowling games. What should she score on her next bowling game if she wants to have an average score of exactly 175 for the 4 games?

F. 205
G. 195
H. 185
J. 175
K. 165

DO YOUR FIGURING HERE.

13. Which of the following best describes a triangle in the standard (x, y) coordinate plane with vertices having coordinates $(0, 0)$, $(3, 5)$, and $(0, 2)$?

A. All three angles measure less than 90°.
B. All three sides are the same length.
C. Exactly two sides are the same length.
D. One angle measures 90°.
E. One angle measures more than 90°.

14. What is the sum of the solutions of the equation $2y^2 - 4y - 6 = 0$?

F. −4
G. −2
H. −1
J. 2
K. 4

15. Which of the following is the decimal equivalent of $\frac{7}{8}$?

A. 1.125
B. 1.120
C. 0.875
D. 0.870
E. 0.625

16. June, Maria, and Billy each have a collection of marbles. June has 20 more marbles than Billy, and Maria has 3 times as many marbles as Billy. If altogether they have 100 marbles, how many marbles does Billy have?

F. 16
G. 20
H. 25
J. 30
K. 32

GO ON TO THE NEXT PAGE ➡

17. The equation $3x - 2y = 4$ can be graphed in the standard (x, y) coordinate plane. What is the y-coordinate of a point on the graph whose x-coordinate is 6?

    A.   11
    B.   7
    C.   5
    D.   3
    E. −11

DO YOUR FIGURING HERE.

18. In the figure below, parallel lines r and s are cut by transversal t. The measure of $\angle p$ is 20° less than three times the measure of $\angle q$. What is the value of $p - q$?

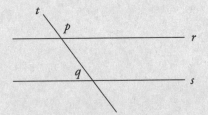

    F.   80°
    G.   90°
    H. 100°
    J. 130°
    K. 160°

19. Which of the following systems of equations does NOT have a solution?

    A. $x + 3y = 19$
        $3x + y = 6$

    B. $x + 3y = 19$
        $x - 3y = 13$

    C. $x - 3y = 6$
        $3x - y = 7$

    D. $x - 3y = 19$
        $3x + y = 6$

    E. $x + 3y = 6$
        $3x + 9y = 7$

GO ON TO THE NEXT PAGE ➡

20. In the figure below, L, M, R, and S are collinear. $\overline{LS}$ is 50 units long; $\overline{MS}$ is 38 units long; and $\overline{MR}$ is 13 units long. How many units long is $\overline{LR}$?

F. 13
G. 20
H. 23
J. 25
K. 37

DO YOUR FIGURING HERE.

21. If $33\frac{1}{3}\%$ of t is 9, what is $133\frac{1}{3}\%$ of t ?

A. 12
B. 18
C. 27
D. 36
E. 42

22. In $\triangle DEF$ below, $\overline{DE} = 1$ and $\overline{DF} = \sqrt{2}$ What is the value of tan x ?

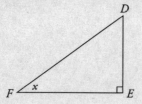

F. $\frac{\sqrt{2}}{2}$
G. 1
H. $\sqrt{2}$
J. $\sqrt{3}$
K. 2

23. A circle with center at the origin and radius 7 is graphed in the standard (x, y) coordinate plane. Which of the following is NOT a point on the circumference of the circle?

A. $(7, 0)$
B. $(-3, 2\sqrt{10}\,)$
C. $(\sqrt{7}, 3)$
D. $(0, -7)$
E. $(-\sqrt{26}\,, -\sqrt{23}\,)$

GO ON TO THE NEXT PAGE ➡

KAPLAN

DO YOUR FIGURING HERE.

24. Points *A* and *B* have integral coordinates in the standard (*x*, *y*) coordinate plane below. What is the product of the *y*-coordinates of *A* and *B* ?

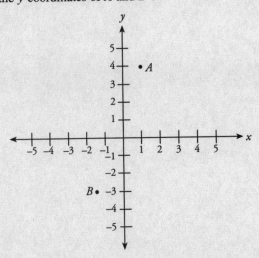

  F.   12
  G.   6
  H.   −2
  J.   −6
  K. −12

25. In the figure below, line *m* is parallel to line *n*, point *A* lies on line *m*, and points *B* and *C* lie on line *n*. If ∠*BAC* is a right angle, what is the measure of ∠*y* ?

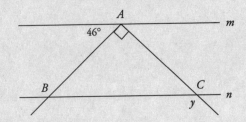

  A.   54°
  B.   90°
  C. 124°
  D. 136°
  E. 154°

26. If $s = -3$, then $s^3 + 2s^2 + 2s = $?

  F. −15
  G. −10
  H.   −5
  J.   5
  K.   33

GO ON TO THE NEXT PAGE ➡

27. For all r, s, t, and u, $r(t+u) - s(t+u) = ?$
    A. $(r+s)(t+u)$
    B. $(r-s)(t-u)$
    C. $(r+s)(t-u)$
    D. $(r-s)(t+u)$
    E. 0

DO YOUR FIGURING HERE.

28. In the figure below, $\angle ABC$ is a right angle and $\overline{DF}$ is parallel to $\overline{AC}$. If $\overline{AB}$ is 8 units long, $\overline{BC}$ is 6 units long and $\overline{DB}$ is 4 units long, what is the area in square units of $\triangle DBF$?

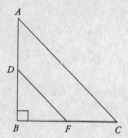

    F. 6
    G. 12
    H. 16
    J. 24
    K. 48

29. What is the value of cos 225°?

    A. $-\dfrac{\sqrt{2}}{2}$

    B. $-\dfrac{\sqrt{3}}{3}$

    C. $-\dfrac{1}{2}$

    D. $\dfrac{1}{2}$

    E. $\dfrac{\sqrt{2}}{2}$

30. In triangle $\triangle XYZ$ below, $\overline{XS}$ and $\overline{SZ}$ are 3 and 12 units long, respectively. If the area of $\triangle XYZ$ is 45 square units, how many units long is altitude $\overline{YS}$?

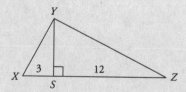

    F. 3
    G. 6
    H. 9
    J. 12
    K. 15

GO ON TO THE NEXT PAGE ➡

31. In the figure below, *O* is the center of the circle, *C* and *D* are points on the circle, and *C*, *O*, and *D* are collinear. If the length of $\overline{CD}$ is 10 units, what is the circumference, in units, of the circle?

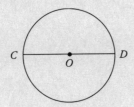

   A. 10π
   B. 20π
   C. 25π
   D. 40π
   E. 100π

32. The formula for the surface area of a right circular cone, including the base, is $A = \pi rs + \pi r^2$, where *A* is the surface area, *r* is the radius, and *s* is the length from the vertex to the edge of the cone. Which of the following represents an equivalent formula for *A* ?

   F. $A = 2\pi rs$
   G. $A = 2\pi r^2 s$
   H. $A = \pi r(1 + s)$
   J. $A = \pi r^2(1 + s)$
   K. $A = \pi r(r + s)$

33. What is the slope of the line determined by the equation $5x + 3y = 13$?

   A. -15
   B. $-\dfrac{5}{3}$
   C. $-\dfrac{3}{5}$
   D. $\dfrac{3}{5}$
   E. $\dfrac{5}{3}$

34. Given any two real numbers *a* and *b*, which of the following is true about the quantity $|a - b| + \sqrt{b - a}$?

   F. It is always equal to an integer.
   G. It is positive if $b > a$.
   H. It is always positive.
   J. It is negative if $a = b$.
   K. It is always real.

DO YOUR FIGURING HERE.

GO ON TO THE NEXT PAGE ➡

35. One of the solutions of the equation $x^2 - 7x + 8 = 0$ is $x = \frac{7 - \sqrt{17}}{2}$. What is the other solution?

DO YOUR FIGURING HERE.

A. $-\frac{7}{2} - \sqrt{17}$

B. $\frac{-7 - \sqrt{17}}{2}$

C. $\frac{-7 + \sqrt{17}}{2}$

D. $7 - \frac{\sqrt{17}}{2}$

E. $\frac{7 + \sqrt{17}}{2}$

36. How many units long is one of the sides of a square that has diagonal 20 units long?

F. 10

G. $10\sqrt{2}$

H. 15

J. 20

K. $15\sqrt{2}$

37. For all a, $(3a - 4)(a + 2) = ?$

A. $3a^2 - 8$

B. $3a^2 + 7a - 8$

C. $3a^2 + 2a - 8$

D. $3a^2 - 2a - 8$

E. $3a^2 + 5a - 8$

38. The midpoint of line segment $\overline{AC}$ in the standard (x, y) coordinate plane has coordinates $(4, 8)$. The (x, y) coordinates of A and C are $(4, 2)$ and $(4, s)$, respectively. What is the value of s ?

F. 4

G. 5

H. 10

J. 12

K. 14

39. In a group of 3 numbers, the second number is 3 less than 4 times the first number, and the third number is 5 more than twice the first. If s represents the first number, which of the following expressions represents the sum of the three numbers in terms of s ?

A. $5s$

B. $5s + 2$

C. $6s + 8$

D. $7s - 1$

E. $7s + 2$

GO ON TO THE NEXT PAGE ➡

40. In the figure below, line $\overline{PQ}$ intersects $\triangle ABC$ at points E and D. $\angle B$ measures 80°, $\angle SAB$ measures 130°, and $\angle CDQ$ measures 110°. What is the measure of $\angle DEC$?

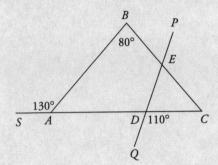

   F. 40°
   G. 50°
   H. 60°
   J. 70°
   K. 80°

41. Jack bought a painting for $200. A year later a friend bought it from him for $170. What percent of the original price did Jack lose in the overall transaction?

   A. 10%
   B. 12%
   C. 15%
   D. 22%
   E. 25%

42. Which of the following is the set of all values of x such that $0 \le x \le 2\pi$ and $\cos x = -\frac{1}{2}$?

   F. $\{\frac{\pi}{6}, \frac{5\pi}{6}\}$
   G. $\{\frac{\pi}{3}, \frac{5\pi}{6}\}$
   H. $\{\frac{\pi}{2}, \frac{3\pi}{2}\}$
   J. $\{\frac{2\pi}{3}, \frac{4\pi}{3}\}$
   K. $\{\frac{2\pi}{3}, \frac{5\pi}{3}\}$

43. The roots of the equation $5x^2 + 2x - 7 = 0$ are $x = 1$ and $x = ?$

   A. -7
   B. $-\frac{7}{5}$
   C. -1
   D. 0
   E. $\frac{7}{5}$

GO ON TO THE NEXT PAGE ➡

44. In the figure below, $\overline{PS}$ is parallel to $\overline{QR}$, and $\overline{PR}$ intersects $\overline{SQ}$ at T. If the measure of $\angle PST$ is 65° and the measure of $\angle QRT$ is 35°, then what is the measure of $\angle PTQ$?

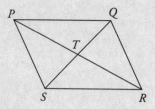

DO YOUR FIGURING HERE.

- **F.** 55°
- **G.** 75°
- **H.** 90°
- **J.** 100°
- **K.** 115°

45. Ms. Rodriguez leaves her office and drives east. At the same time, Ms. Green leaves the same office and drives west at a rate of speed that is 15 miles per hour faster than Ms. Rodriguez. At the end of 5 hours, the two cars are 475 miles apart. How many miles were traveled by the faster car?

- **A.** 200
- **B.** 250
- **C.** 275
- **D.** 300
- **E.** 350

46. Line ℓ is graphed in the standard (x, y) coordinate plane as shown below. If the equation for line ℓ is written in the form $y = mx + b$, which of the following is true about m and b ?

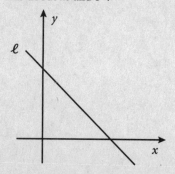

- **F.** m and b are both positive.
- **G.** m is negative and b is positive.
- **H.** m is positive and b is negative.
- **J.** Either m or b must equal 0.
- **K.** m and b are both negative.

GO ON TO THE NEXT PAGE ➡

KAPLAN

47. Which of the following must be true of the fraction $\frac{x^2}{y^2}$ if $|y| < |x|$, and $xy \neq 0$?

   A. $\frac{x^2}{y^2}$ must be greater than or equal to 2.

   B. $\frac{x^2}{y^2}$ must be greater than 1.

   C. $\frac{x^2}{y^2}$ could equal 1.

   D. $\frac{x^2}{y^2}$ must be less than 1.

   E. $\frac{x^2}{y^2}$ cannot equal $\frac{3}{2}$.

DO YOUR FIGURING HERE.

48. What is the value of $a^2 - 2ab + b^2$ if $a - b = 12$?

   F.   0
   G.   24
   H.   48
   J.   144
   K.   288

49. In $\triangle DEF$, x represents the measure of $\angle EDF$. The measure of $\angle DEF$ is 30° greater than the measure of $\angle EDF$, and the measure of $\angle EFD$ is 15° less than the sum of the measures of $\angle EDF$ and $\angle DEF$. Which of the following expressions represents the measure of $\angle EFD$?

   A. $-2x + 15°$
   B. $-x + 15°$
   C. $x + 15°$
   D. $2x - 15°$
   E. $2x + 15°$

GO ON TO THE NEXT PAGE ➡

50. In the figure below, $\overline{CD}$ is parallel to $\overline{AB}$, and $\overline{PQ}$ intersects $\overline{CD}$ at R and $\overline{AB}$ at T. If the measure of $\angle CRP = 110°$, then what is the measure of $\angle ATQ$?

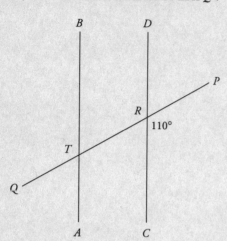

DO YOUR FIGURING HERE.

- **F.** 30°
- **G.** 50°
- **H.** 70°
- **J.** 90°
- **K.** 110°

51. If $x = \sin\ \theta$, $y = \cos\ \theta$, and $z = \tan\ \theta$, then $x^2 + y^2 = ?$

- **A.** z^2
- **B.** $(x + y)^2$
- **C.** $2y$
- **D.** 0
- **E.** 1

52. Line T in the standard (x, y) coordinate plane has y-intercept -3 and is parallel to the line determined by the equation $3x - 5y = 4$. Which of the following is an equation for line T ?

- **F.** $y = -\frac{3}{5}x + 3$
- **G.** $y = -\frac{5}{3}x - 3$
- **H.** $y = \frac{3}{5}x + 3$
- **J.** $y = \frac{5}{3}x + 3$
- **K.** $y = \frac{3}{5}x - 3$

GO ON TO THE NEXT PAGE ➡

KAPLAN

53. On the number line below, what is the distance from A to B ?

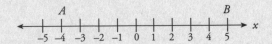

DO YOUR FIGURING HERE.

A. 1
B. 4
C. 5
D. 9
E. 18

54. In the standard (x, y) coordinate plane shown in the figure below, points A and B lie on line m, and point C lies below it. The coordinates of points A, B, and C are (0, 5), (5, 5), and (3, 3), respectively. What is the shortest distance from point C to line m ?

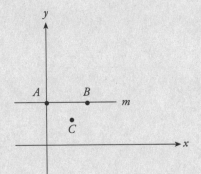

F. 2

G. $2\sqrt{2}$

H. 3

J. $\sqrt{13}$

K. 5

55. Which of the following inequalities is equivalent to $-2 - 4x \leq -6x$?

A. $x \geq -2$
B. $x \geq 1$
C. $x \geq 2$
D. $x \leq -1$
E. $x \leq 1$

GO ON TO THE NEXT PAGE ➡

56. In the figure below, each corner of the polygon is a right angle. What is the area of the polygon?

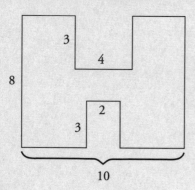

DO YOUR FIGURING HERE.

- **F.** 50
- **G.** 56
- **H.** 62
- **J.** 72
- **K.** 80

57. In the standard (x, y) coordinate plane shown below, two circles of the same radius r are enclosed by rectangle $ABCD$. Which of the following expressions is equal to $a - b$?

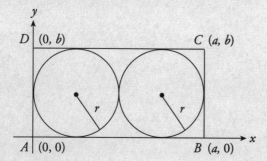

- **A.** $-r$
- **B.** 0
- **C.** r
- **D.** $2r$
- **E.** $4r$

58. Each one of the 60 teenagers in an after-school club is 14, 15, 16, 17 or 18 years old. 20 teenagers are 15 years old, 8 are 18 years old, and 20% are 14 years old. There are twice as many 16-year-olds as there are 18-year-olds. What percent of the teenagers are either 17 or 18 years old?

- **F.** 10%
- **G.** 15%
- **H.** 20%
- **J.** 25%
- **K.** 30%

GO ON TO THE NEXT PAGE ➡

59. Darryl has 5 blue T-shirts and 7 orange T-shirts. If he picks one T-shirt at random, what is the probability that it will NOT be blue?

   A. 1

   B. $\frac{7}{12}$

   C. $\frac{1}{2}$

   D. $\frac{5}{12}$

   E. $\frac{1}{6}$

60. What is the equation of the ellipse graphed in the standard (x, y) coordinate plane below?

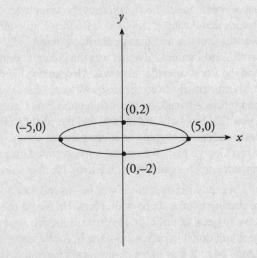

   F. $\frac{x^2}{25} + \frac{y^2}{4} = 1$

   G. $\frac{x^2}{25} - \frac{y^2}{9} = 1$

   H. $\frac{x^2}{25} - \frac{y^2}{4} = 1$

   J. $\frac{x^2}{25} + \frac{y^2}{9} = 1$

   K. $\frac{x^2}{20} + \frac{y^2}{4} = 1$

DO YOUR FIGURING HERE.

END OF MATH TEST

IF YOU FINISH BEFORE TIME IS CALLED, YOU MAY CHECK YOUR WORK ON THIS SECTION ONLY. DO NOT TURN TO ANY OTHER SECTION IN THE TEST. **STOP**

KAPLAN 251

READING TEST

35 Minutes—40 Questions

Directions: This test contains four passages, each followed by several questions. After reading a passage, select the best answer to each question and fill in the corresponding oval on your answer sheet. You are allowed to refer to the passages while answering the questions.

Passage I

It was late afternoon and the shadows were slanting swiftly eastward when George Webber came to his senses somewhere in the wilds of the upper
Line Bronx. How he got there he never knew. All he could
(5) remember was that suddenly he felt hungry and stopped and looked about him and realized where he was. His dazed look gave way to one of amazement and incredulity, and his mouth began to stretch into a broad grin. In his hand he still held the rectangular
(10) slip of crisp yellow paper, and slowly he smoothed out the wrinkles and examined it carefully.

It was a check for five hundred dollars. His book had been accepted, and this was an advance against his royalties.

(15) So he was happier than he had ever been in all his life. Fame, at last, was knocking at his door and wooing him with her sweet blandishments, and he lived in a kind of glorious delirium. The next weeks and months were filled with the excitement of the
(20) impending event. The book would not be published till the fall, but meanwhile there was much work to do. Foxhall Edwards had made some suggestions for cutting and revising the manuscript, and, although George at first objected, he surprised himself in the
(25) end by agreeing with Edwards, and he undertook to do what Edwards wanted.

George had called his novel *Home to Our Mountains,* and in it he had packed everything he knew about his home town in Old Catawba and the
(30) people there. He had distilled every line of it out of his own experience of life. And, now that the issue was decided, he sometimes trembled when he thought that it would only be a matter of months before the whole world knew what he had written. He loathed
(35) the thought of giving pain to anyone, and that he might do so had never occurred to him until now. But now it was out of his hands, and he began to feel uneasy. Of course it was fiction, but it was made as all honest fiction must be, from the stuff of human
(40) life. Some people might recognize themselves and be offended, and then what would he do? Would he have to go around in smoked glasses and false whiskers? He comforted himself with the hope that his characterizations were not so true as, in another mood, he

(45) liked to think they were, and he thought that perhaps no one would notice anything.

Rodney's Magazine, too, had become interested in the young author and was going to publish a story, a chapter from the book, in their next number. This
(50) news added immensely to his excitement. He was eager to see his name in print, and in the happy interval of expectancy he felt like a kind of universal Don Juan, for he literally loved everybody—his fellow instructors at the school, his drab students, the little
(55) shopkeepers in all the stores, even the nameless hordes that thronged the streets. Rodney's, of course, was the greatest and finest publishing house in all the world, and Foxhall Edwards was the greatest editor and the finest man that ever was. George had liked
(60) him instinctively from the first, and now, like an old and intimate friend, he was calling him Fox. George knew that Fox believed in him, and the editor's faith and confidence, coming as it had come at a time when George had given up all hope, restored his self-
(65) respect and charged him with energy for new work.

Already his next novel was begun and was beginning to take shape within him. He would soon have to get it out of him. He dreaded the prospect of buckling down in earnest to write it, for he knew the
(70) agony of it. It was like a demoniacal possession, driving him with alien force much greater than his own. While the fury of creation was upon him, it meant sixty cigarettes a day, twenty cups of coffee, meals snatched anyhow and anywhere and at whatever time
(75) of day or night he happened to remember he was hungry. It meant sleeplessness, and miles of walking to bring on the physical fatigue without which he could not sleep, then nightmares, nerves, and exhaustion in the morning. As he said to Fox:
(80)
"There are better ways to write a book, but this, God help me, is mine, and you'll have to learn to put up with it."

When *Rodney's Magazine* came out with the story, George fully expected convulsions of the earth,
(85) falling meteors, suspension of traffic in the streets, and a general strike. But nothing happened. A few of his friends mentioned it, but that was all. For several

GO ON TO THE NEXT PAGE ➡

(90) days he felt let down, but then his common sense reassured him that people couldn't really tell much about a new author from a short piece in a magazine. The book would show them who he was and what he could do. It would be different then. He could afford to wait a little longer for the fame which he was certain would soon be his.

Excerpt from *You Can't Go Home Again* by Thomas Wolfe. Copyright © 1934, 1937, 1938, 1939, 1940 by Maxwell Perkins as Executor of the Estate of Thomas Wolfe. Reprinted by permission of HarperCollins Publishers.

1. Why does George think he would "have to go around in smoked glasses and false whiskers" (lines 42)?
   A. Famous authors have to protect their privacy from admiring strangers.
   B. A disguise would help him gather information for a new book.
   C. If he were going to be a famous writer he had better look the part.
   D. People he had offended might otherwise confront him.

2. According to George's description, the process of writing a novel:
   F. was similar to being overwhelmed by an alien spirit.
   G. was a time filled with unspoken rage.
   H. was best carried out during times when other people were asleep.
   J. could only be performed when he was physically exhausted.

3. By saying to Foxhall Edwards that "There are better ways to write a book, but this, God help me, is mine, and you'll have to learn to put up with it," (lines 80–82) George sought to:
   A. reassure Foxhall that the next book would, in fact, be completed.
   B. emphasize that the process, though difficult, could not be avoided.
   C. rebuke Foxhall for not having enough faith in his new project.
   D. suggest that his own approach to writing was really superior to other approaches.

4. Given George's expectations concerning the publication of his story in *Rodney's Magazine,* the public's response to the story can best be described as:
   F. sour.
   G. appropriate.
   H. ironic.
   J. enthusiastic.

5. According to the passage, Foxhall Edwards' belief in George's ability was important primarily because:
   A. George needed a friend he could confide in.
   B. *Home to Our Mountains* required extensive revision.
   C. George needed a friend he could look up to.
   D. Foxhall restored George's faith in his own work.

6. What was George's ultimate response to his story's publication in *Rodney's Magazine*?
   F. He refused to accept that the story had few readers.
   G. He expected that fame would come eventually anyway.
   H. He convinced himself that he had never wished for fame.
   J. He lost confidence in himself as a writer.

7. As it is used in the passage, the word *wooing* (line 17) means:
   A. courting.
   B. confusing.
   C. admiring.
   D. bothering.

8. The fact that George "sometimes trembled" (line 32) when he thought of his novel's publication indicates that he:
   F. secretly disliked Foxhall's suggestions.
   G. was eager to meet the people back in his home town.
   H. worried that some people would be hurt by his novel.
   J. feared that critics would denounce his novel.

9. George's estimation of his novel's achievement can best described as:
   A. vain but bitter.
   B. proud but concerned.
   C. modest but hopeful.
   D. angry but resigned.

10. The first paragraph suggests that, just prior to the moment at which this passage begins, George has most likely been:
   F. wandering in dazed excitement after learning that his book would be published.
   G. walking off nervous tension brought on by working on his second novel.
   H. trying to find his way home from his book publisher's office.
   J. in a joyous dream state as a result of being relieved of his financial difficulties.

GO ON TO THE NEXT PAGE ➡

Passage II

In the 500 years since Leonardo, two ideas about man have been especially important. The first is the emphasis on the full development of the human
Line personality. The individual is prized for himself. His
(5) creative powers are seen as the core of his being. The unfettered development of individual personality is praised as the ideal, from the Renaissance artists through the Elizabethans, and through Locke and Voltaire and Rousseau. This vision of the freely
(10) developing man, happy in the unfolding of his own gifts, is shared by men as different in their conceptions as Thomas Jefferson and Edmund Burke. . . .

Thus the fulfillment of man has been one of the two most formative grand ideas. . . . Men have seen
(15) themselves entering the world with a potential of many gifts, and they have hoped to fulfill these gifts in the development of their own lives. This has come to be the unexpressed purpose of the life of individuals: fulfilling the special gifts with which a man is
(20) endowed.

The self-fulfillment of the individual has itself become part of a larger, more embracing idea, the self-fulfillment of man. We think of man as a species with special gifts, which are the human gifts. Some of these
(25) gifts, the physical and mental gifts, are elucidated for us explicitly by science; some of them, the aesthetic and ethical gifts, we feel and struggle to express in our own minds; and some of them, the cultural gifts, are unfolded for us by the study of history. The total of
(30) these gifts is man as a type or species, and the aspiration of man as a species has become the fulfillment of what is most human in these gifts.

This idea of human self-fulfillment has also inspired scientific and technical progress. We
(35) sometimes think that progress is illusory, and that the devices and gadgets which have become indispensable to civilized men in the last 500 years are only a self-propagating accumulation of idle luxuries. But this has not been the purpose in the minds of scientists and
(40) technicians, nor has it been the true effect of these inventions on human society. The purpose and the effect has been to liberate men from the exhausting drudgeries of earning their living, in order to give them the opportunity to live. From Leonardo to Franklin, the
(45) inventor has wanted to give, and has succeeded in giving, more and more people the ease and leisure to find the best in themselves which was once the monopoly of princes.

Only rarely has a thinker in the last 500 years
(50) gone back from the ideal of human potential and fulfillment. Calvin was perhaps such a thinker who went back, and believed as the Middle Ages did, that man comes into this world as a complete entity, incapable of any worthwhile development. And it is
(55) characteristic that the state which Calvin organized was, as a result, a totalitarian state. For if men cannot develop, and have nothing in them which is personal and creative, there is no point in giving them freedom.

The second of the two grand formative ideas is the
(60) idea of freedom. We see in fact that human fulfillment is unattainable without freedom, so that these two main ideas are linked together. There could be no development of the personality of individuals, no fulfillment of those gifts in which one man differs
(65) from another, without the freedom for each man to grow in his own direction.

What is true of individuals is true of human groups. A state or a society cannot change unless its members are given freedom to judge, to criticize, and
(70) to search for a new status for themselves. Therefore the pressure of ideas has been toward freedom as an expression of individuality. Sometimes men have tried to find freedom along quiet paths of change, as the humanists did on the eve of the Reformation, and as
(75) the dissenting manufacturers of the eighteenth century did. At other times, the drive for freedom has been explosive: intellectually explosive in the Elizabethan age and the Scientific Revolution, economically explosive in the Industrial Revolution, and politically
(80) explosive in the other great revolutions of our period, from Puritan times to the age of Napoleon.

…Freedom is a supple and elusive idea, whose advocates can at times delude themselves that obedience to tyranny is a form of freedom. Such a
(85) delusion ensnared men as diverse as Luther and Rousseau, and Hegel and Marx. Philosophically, there is indeed no unlimited freedom. But we have seen that there is one freedom which can be defined without contradiction, and which can therefore be an end in
(90) itself. This is freedom of thought and speech: the right to dissent.

Excerpt from *The Western Intellectual Tradition: From Leonardo to Hegel* by J. Bronowski and Bruce Mazlish. Copyright © 1960 by J. Bronowski and Bruce Mazlish; reprinted by permission of HarperCollins Publishers.

GO ON TO THE NEXT PAGE ➡

11. The authors mention Calvin in the fifth paragraph (lines 49–58) in order to:

   A. introduce the topic of the Middle Ages.

   B. praise an unusual thinker.

   C. present a counterexample.

   D. illustrate a point made in the previous paragraph.

12. As it is used in line 25, the word "elucidated" means:

   F. decided.

   G. revealed.

   H. invented.

   J. judged.

13. The passage implies that, in the past 500 years, history has revealed two intellectual traditions that are:

   A. equally important, even though mutually exclusive.

   B. similarly important and closely tied together.

   C. only now being seen as particularly important.

   D. less important than freedom of thought and speech.

14. In the fourth paragraph (lines 33–48) the authors' point about "devices and gadgets" is that:

   F. all technological progress is an illusion.

   G. all inventors attain self-fulfillment.

   H. these inventions have allowed people to work less.

   J. these inventions are a necessary evil.

15. What do the authors suggest was "once the monopoly of princes" (line 48)?

   A. Political power to create totalitarian states

   B. Vast amounts of wealth for personal use

   C. Leisure time for self-fulfillment

   D. Brilliant inventions to spur human progress

16. In the final paragraph, the authors indicate that the idea of freedom:

   F. always involves some element of political dissent.

   G. is actually a delusion.

   H. has, at times, been defined as obedience to tyranny.

   J. is sometimes seriously flawed.

17. Which of the following opinions concerning "the self-fulfillment of the individual" (line 21) would the authors most likely reject?

   A. Self-fulfillment requires a degree of leisure.

   B. Self-fulfillment is a praiseworthy but unreachable goal.

   C. Self-fulfillment is an ideal shared by diverse thinkers.

   D. Self-fulfillment means pursuing one's creative potential.

18. The authors clearly indicate that they believe freedom is:

   F. essential if societies are to progress.

   G. the product of stable societies only.

   H. a prerequisite for world peace.

   J. only attainable through revolution.

19. According to the passage, Luther, Rousseau, Hegel, and Marx have in common that they were:

   A. misled by a false idea of freedom.

   B. believers in unlimited freedom.

   C. supporters of the right to dissent.

   D. opponents of tyranny.

20. The authors' attitude toward intellectual, economic, and political revolutions is best characterized as:

   F. detached.

   G. concerned.

   H. suspicious.

   J. approving.

GO ON TO THE NEXT PAGE ➡

Passage III

Italy emerged from World War I battered and humiliated. Although it was one of the victorious Allies, Italy's armies had made a poor showing, and
Line Italy had realized few of the grandiose ambitions for
(5) which it had entered the war. In the Paris peace settlements Italy had been awarded the adjacent Italian-speaking areas of Austria-Hungary but had been denied further acquisitions east of the Adriatic and in Asia and Africa, some of which it ardently
(10) desired. These frustrations were severe blows to Italian national pride.

Italy's weak economy emerged from the war acutely maladjusted. The national debt was huge and the treasury empty. The inflated currency, together
(15) with a shortage of goods, raised prices ruinously. Hundreds of thousands of demobilized veterans could find no jobs. In the summer of 1919, there was widespread disorder. Veterans began seizing and squatting on idle, and sometimes on cultivated, lands.
(20) Sit-down strikes developed in the factories. During the winter of 1920–1921, several factories were seized by the workers, and Marxism seemed to be gaining strength. The Italian government, torn by factions, seemed too weak to prevent the disorder and protect
(25) private property. Although the strife diminished and the Marxist threat waned before the end of 1921, the landlords and the factory owners were thoroughly frightened. Many of them, and indeed many small-business and professional people, longed for vigorous
(30) leadership and a strong government. The vigorous leader who stepped forward was Benito Mussolini. The strong government was his Fascist dictatorship.

Mussolini was a dynamic organizer and leader. The son of a blacksmith, he became first a teacher and
(35) later a radical journalist and agitator. Before World War I he was a pacifistic socialist, but during the war he became a violent nationalist. After the war he began organizing unemployed veterans into a political action group with a socialistic and extremely nationalistic
(40) program. During the labor disturbances of 1919–1921, Mussolini stood aside until it became apparent that the radical workers' cause would lose; then he threw his support to the capitalists and the landlords. Crying that he was saving Italy from communism and waving the
(45) flag of nationalism, Mussolini organized his veterans into terror squads of black-shirted "Fascisti," who beat up the leaderless radical workers and their liberal supporters. He thereby gained the support of the frightened capitalists and landed aristocracy. By 1922
(50) Mussolini's Fascist party was strong enough to "march on Rome" and seize control of the faction-paralyzed government. Appointed premier by the weak and distraught King Victor Emmanuel III, Mussolini acquired extraordinary powers. Between 1924 and
(55) 1926 Mussolini turned his premiership into a dictatorship. All opposition was silenced. Only the Fascist party could engage in organized political activity. The press and the schools were turned into propaganda agencies. The secret police were
(60) everywhere. Eventually, the Chamber of Deputies itself was replaced by Mussolini's handpicked Fascist political and economic councils.

Italy's economic life was strictly regimented but in such a way as to favor the capitalistic classes.
(65) Private property and profits were carefully protected. All labor unions were abolished except those controlled by the Fascist party. Strikes and lockouts were forbidden. Wages, working conditions, and labor management disputes were settled by compulsory
(70) arbitration under party direction. An elaborate system of planned economy was set up to modernize, coordinate, and increase Italy's production of both industrial and agricultural goods. The very complicated economic and political machinery that
(75) Mussolini created for these purposes was called the corporate state. On the whole there was probably a small decline in per capita income under Italian fascism despite some superficial gains. The budget was balanced and the currency stabilized. But Italy's
(80) taxes were the highest in the world, and labor's share of economic production was small.

Fascism, however, was primarily political in character, not economic. The essence of its ideology was nationalism run wild. Although Italy never
(85) became such a full-blown, viciously anti-Semitic police state as Germany, Mussolini understood the dynamic, energizing quality of militant nationalism. His writings and speeches rang with such words as *will, discipline, sacrifice, decision,* and *conquest.*
(90) "The goal," he cried, "is always—empire! To build a city, to found a colony, to establish an empire, these are the prodigies of the human spirit…We must resolutely abandon the whole liberal phraseology and way of thinking. …Discipline. Discipline at home in
(90) order that we may present the granite block of a single national will. War alone brings up the highest tension, all human energy and puts the stamp of nobility upon the people who have the courage to meet it."

From *A Short History of Western Civilization*, by John B. Harrison, Richard E. Sullivan, Dennis Sherman. Copyright © 1990 by McGraw-Hill Inc.; reprinted by permission of McGraw-Hill, Inc.

GO ON TO THE NEXT PAGE ➡

21. According to information presented in the passage, "grandiose ambitions" (line 4) refers to Italy's desire for:

A. territorial expansion.

B. complete victory at the end of World War I.

C. peacetime employment for all its veterans.

D. a supremely powerful army.

22. The passage suggests that Mussolini came to power in 1922 largely as a result of:

    I. a desire for stability among property-owning middle classes.

    II. a lack of strong opposition from the government in Rome.

    III. his violent opposition to radical workers.

F. I and II only

G. I and III only

H. II and III only

J. I, II, and III

23. In which of the following ways does the passage support the theory that fascism arises after periods of diminished national pride?

A. It attributes the fascists' seizure of power from the King to Mussolini's abilities as a leader.

B. It demonstrates that Mussolini achieved national fame largely because of his eagerness to fight communism.

C. It shows a connection between the growth of the corporate state and Mussolini's rise to power.

D. It links Mussolini's ascendancy to the fact that Italy gained less than it hoped for after World War I.

24. The author suggests that, during the disturbances of 1919–1921, "Mussolini stood aside until it became apparent that the radical workers' cause would lose" (lines 40–41) because he was:

F. secretly hoping the radical workers would win.

G. an opportunist, waiting for his chance to seize power.

H. unaware of the importance of the radicals' challenge.

J. basically a pacifist at that time in his life.

25. A dictatorship is commonly defined as a form of government that has absolute authority over its citizens. Which of the following statements from the passage supports the view that Mussolini's government was a dictatorship?

A. "Mussolini was a dynamic organizer and leader."

B. "All labor unions were abolished except those controlled by the Fascist party."

C. "Veterans began seizing and squatting on idle, and sometimes on cultivated, lands."

D. "The budget was balanced and the currency stabilized."

26. It can be inferred from the passage that, to Mussolini, nationalism was a:

F. way to protect Italy from German aggression.

G. method to bring economic prosperity to war-ravaged Italy.

H. powerful political tool.

J. threat to his rise to power.

27. The passage suggests that if the rights of factory workers in 1920 were compared to their rights in 1926, one could accurately say that:

A. while workers' per capita income rose, workers lost their rights to collective bargaining.

B. labor's share of economic production grew.

C. workers' collective action was increasingly disallowed.

D. labor management disputes were completely suppressed.

28. The passage suggests that under the Italian fascists, economic rebuilding was:

F. undermined by labor disturbances.

G. resisted by the corporate state.

H. marred by excessively high taxation.

J. slowed by a failure to balance the budget.

29. Based on information in the passage, the "corporate state" can best be defined as a:

A. system of structuring government according to business practices.

B. series of economic programs aimed at ending an inflated currency.

C. negotiating team that arbitrated worker-management disputes.

D. complex, planned economy designed to maximize the production of goods.

30. It can be inferred that the author quotes Mussolini's words in the last paragraph (lines 82–93) for the purpose of:

F. illustrating the nationalistic element in his words.

G. praising his abilities as a public speaker.

H. condemning the ideas that Mussolini advances.

J. demonstrating the difference between Italian and German fascism.

GO ON TO THE NEXT PAGE ➡

Passage IV

Tornadoes have long been an enigma, striking sporadically and violently, generating the strongest of all surface winds, and causing more deaths annually in
Line the United States than any other natural phenomenon
(5) other than lightning. It is estimated that tornadoes can generate a maximum wind speed of 300 miles per hour, based on analysis of motion pictures and damage to structures.

Tornadoes are formed in the updrafts of a thun-
(10) derstorm or are associated with hurricanes when they pass over land. They are tightly wound vortexes of air, rarely more than several hundred feet across. They rotate in a counterclockwise direction in the Northern Hemisphere and a clockwise direction in the Southern
(15) Hemisphere. Drawn by the greatly reduced atmospheric pressure in the central core, air streams into the base of the vortex from all directions. The air then turns abruptly to spiral upward around the core, and finally merges with the airflow in the parent cloud at the upper
(20) end of the tornado. The pressure within the core might be as little as 10 percent lower than the surrounding atmosphere, which would be equivalent to a sudden drop in pressure from that at sea level to an altitude of 3000 feet.

(25) The vortex frequently becomes visible as a wide, dark funnel cloud hanging partway or all the way to the ground. A funnel cloud can only form if the pressure drop in the core reaches a critical value, which depends on the temperature and humidity of the inflowing air.
(30) As air flows into the area of lower pressure, it expands and cools, causing water vapor to condense and form water droplets.

Sometimes, no condensation cloud forms, and the only way a tornado can reveal itself is by the dust and
(35) debris it carries aloft over land or water spray over the ocean. In that case, it becomes a waterspout, which often frequent the Florida coast and the Bahamas.

The funnel is usually cone shaped, but short, broad, cylindrical pillars up to a mile wide are formed
(40) by very strong tornadoes, and often, long, ropelike tubes dangle from the storm cloud. Over the tornado's brief lifetime, usually no more than a few hours, the size, shape, and color of the funnel might change markedly, depending on the intensity of the winds, the
(45) properties of the inflowing air, and the type of ground over which it hovers. The color varies from a dirty white to a blue gray when it consists mostly of water droplets, but if the core fills with dust, it takes on the color of the soil and other debris. Tornadoes are also
(50) noisy, often roaring, like a laboring freight train or a jet plane taking off. The sound results from the interaction of the concentrated high winds with the ground.

The world's tornado hot spot, with about 700 tornadoes yearly, is the United States, particularly the
(55) central and southeastern portions of the country, known as tornado alley. The states most frequently visited by tornadoes are Texas, Arkansas, Oklahoma, Kansas, Nebraska, and Missouri, with a high occurrence of tornadoes continuing on up into Canada.

(60) Tornadoes develop in the spring and to a lesser extent in the fall, when conditions are ripe for the formation of tornado-generating thunderstorms. These conditions include a highly unstable distribution of temperature and humidity in the atmosphere, strong
(65) cold fronts that provide the lift needed to start convection, and winds in the upper atmosphere favorable for the formation of strong updrafts.

For a tornado to form, the air in the updraft must begin to rotate. This is accomplished by a wind shear
(70) where the wind speed increases with height and veers from southeast to west. Once rotation begins, the tornado builds down toward the ground, although not all tornadoes actually reach the ground. When on the ground, the tornado funnel sucks up air at its lower
(75) end, like the hose of a vacuum cleaner.

Tornadoes are steered by the jet stream, and generally travel in a northeasterly direction for about 5 to 15 miles. Their forward ground speed is normally slow enough (30 to 60 miles per hour) for them to be
(80) outrun by an automobile, although this is not always a recommended practice because of the unpredictable nature of tornadoes, which often hop about from place to place. Members of NOAA's National Severe Storms Laboratory at the University of Oklahoma actually
(85) chase tornadoes in vehicles carrying an instrument package known as TOTO which stands for Totable Tornado Observatory. This package is placed in the path of the tornado. TOTO is equipped to measure a tornado's behavior such as wind speed, wind direc-
(90) tion, atmospheric temperature and pressure, and electric field strength.

Reprinted, with permission, from book #2942 *Violent Storms*, by Jon Erickson; Copyright © 1988 by TAB Books, a division of McGraw-Hill, Inc., Blue Ridge Summit, PA 17294-0850 (1-800-233-1128).

GO ON TO THE NEXT PAGE ➡

31. The author refers to tornadoes as "vortexes of air" (line 11) to emphasize the fact that the air is:

    A. moving downward.

    B. expanding.

    C. dispersing.

    D. whirling.

32. The inspection of films showing the action of tornadoes allowed researchers to determine that tornadoes:

    F. are often accompanied by lightning.

    G. gain maximum size when they pass over land.

    H. are caused by the updrafts of thunderstorms.

    J. reach wind speeds of up to 300 miles per hour.

33. The passage suggests that the direction of a tornado's rotation is influenced chiefly by:

    A. whether a hurricane or a thunderstorm has caused it to form.

    B. the difference in pressure between air in the core and air in the surrounding atmosphere.

    C. the direction of the airflow in its parent cloud.

    D. where the tornado is located on the earth's surface.

34. Researchers often have difficulty getting TOTO to record the information they need. Based on the information in the last paragraph, this is most likely true because:

    F. no scientific instruments can withstand a tornado's force.

    G. it is difficult to predict precisely the path a tornado will take.

    H. tornadoes' characteristics vary too much to measure accurately.

    J. the majority of tornadoes occur over water and are thus unapproachable.

35. If a tornado is to form, which of the following must occur first?

    A. Powerful updrafts and wind shear

    B. Movement of the funnel toward the ground

    C. Movement of air up the funnel from the ground

    D. Uniform distribution of temperature and humidity in the atmosphere

36. The expression "wind shear" (line 69) means that, while gaining altitude, wind:

    F. direction changes, while wind speed stays the same.

    G. speed changes, while wind direction stays the same.

    H. speed and wind direction both change.

    J. is sucked up the lower end of a funnel.

37. The passage suggests that it should be possible to predict when tornadoes are likely to form if:

    A. certain key atmospheric conditions are known.

    B. "tornado alley" can be accurately identified.

    C. the movement of warm fronts can be predicted.

    D. TOTO's readings are accurate.

38. According to the passage, a condensation cloud is created when:

    F. water vapor entering the funnel is affected by changes in air pressure.

    G. the funnel passes over a body of water.

    H. cool air rushes into the funnel and immediately forms droplets.

    J. dust and debris are sucked into the funnel.

39. The main purpose of the third and fourth paragraphs (lines 25–37) is to describe:

    A. how funnels are formed.

    B. how a condensation cloud is formed.

    C. the main factors that make tornadoes visible.

    D. how funnel clouds can vary in color, shape, and size.

40. Based on information presented in the passage, it is a fact that all tornadoes:

    F. are colored by the dust and debris they carry.

    G. touch the earth's surface.

    H. occur in the spring.

    J. are steered by the jet stream.

END OF READING TEST

IF YOU FINISH BEFORE TIME IS CALLED, YOU MAY CHECK YOUR WORK ON THIS SECTION ONLY. DO NOT TEURN TO ANY OTHER SECTION IN THE TEST.

STOP

 259

SCIENCE REASONING TEST

35 Minutes—40 Questions

Directions: Each of the following seven passages is followed by several questions. After reading each passage, decide on the best answer to each question and fill in the corresponding oval on your answer sheet. You are allowed to refer to the passages while answering the questions.

Passage I

Medical researchers and technicians can track the characteristic radiation patterns emitted by certain inherently unstable isotopes as they spontaneously decay into other elements. The half-life of a radioactive isotope is the amount of time necessary for one-half of the initial amount of its nuclei to decay. The decay curves of isotopes $_{39}Y^{90}$ and $_{39}Y^{91}$ are graphed below as functions of the ratio of N, the number of nuclei remaining after a given period, to N_0, the initial number of nuclei.

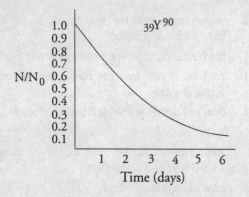

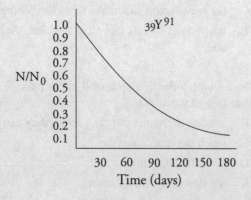

1. The half-life of $_{39}Y^{90}$ is approximately:

   A. 2.7 days.
   B. 5.4 days.
   C. 27 days.
   D. 58 days.

2. What will the approximate ratio of $_{39}Y^{90}$ to $_{39}Y^{91}$ be after 2.7 days if the initial samples of the two isotopes contain equal numbers of nuclei?

   F. 1:1
   G. 1:2
   H. 2:1
   J. 10:1

3. When inhaled by humans, $_{39}Y^{90}$ accumulates in the gastrointestinal tract, whereas $_{39}Y^{91}$ accumulates in the bones. If the total amount of each isotope inhaled goes to the specified area, which of the following situations will exist three days after a patient inhales these substances, assuming none of the isotopes leave the specified areas due to physiological factors?

   A. The amount of $_{39}Y^{91}$ in the gastrointestinal tract will be approximately equal to the total amount inhaled.
   B. The amount of $_{39}Y^{90}$ in the bones will be approximately one-half of the total amount inhaled.
   C. The amount of $_{39}Y^{90}$ in the gastrointestinal tract will be approximately one-half of the total amount inhaled.
   D. None of the $_{39}Y^{91}$ inhaled will be left in the bones.

GO ON TO THE NEXT PAGE ➡

4. Approximately how many $_{39}Y^{91}$ nuclei will exist after three half-lives have passed, if there are 1,000 nuclei to begin with?

   F.   50
   G. 125
   H. 250
   J. 500

5. Which of the following conclusions is/are supported by the information given in the passage?

   I. $_{39}Y^{90}$ is less stable than $_{39}Y^{91}$
   II. Only one-quarter of the original amount of $_{39}Y^{90}$ will remain after 116 days.
   III. $_{39}Y^{90}$ and $_{39}Y^{91}$ are both radioactive.

   A. I only
   B. III only
   C. I and II only
   D. I and III only

GO ON TO THE NEXT PAGE ➡

Passage II

Recently, college teams from all over the country sent tennis players to participate in a series of experiments conducted by the Physical Education Department of a major university. A variety of coaching methods was used to improve the players' serves, as described below.

Experiment 1

Two groups of 50 tennis players worked on the speed of their basic serves for two weeks. One group consisted solely of right-handed players; the other consisted solely of left-handed players. Half of each group watched videos of a right-handed tennis coach, while the other half watched videos of a left-handed coach. Each player was told to pattern his or her serve on that of the coach in the video. The players received no verbal or physical guidance. The average speed of each player's serve was measured at the beginning and end of the two-week period, and changes were recorded in Table 1.

Table 1

Players' handedness	Average Coach's handedness	change in speed (mph)
Right	Right	+5
Right	Left	+2
Left	Right	−1
Left	Left	+8

Experiment 2

For two weeks, a second group of 100 right-handed tennis players watched the same videos of the right-handed tennis coach. The coach also physically guided 50 of those players through the motions of the serve. Again, no verbal instruction was given during the experiment. The average speed and accuracy of each player's serves were recorded at the beginning and end of this two-week period. The results are recorded in Table 2.

Table 2

Guided	Average Change in Speed (mph)	Average Change in Accuracy
No	+5	+15%
Yes	+9	+25%

Experiment 3

For two weeks, a third group of 100 right-handed tennis players worked on their basic serves. 50 players received no verbal instruction; they watched the same video of the right-handed tennis coach, who also physically guided them through the motions of the serve. The other 50 players did not observe the video but received verbal instruction from the coach, who then physically guided them through the motions of the serve. The results are shown in Table 3.

Table 3

Guidance Plus	Average Change in Speed (mph)
Video	+7
Verbal Coaching	+10

6. Which of the following results would be expected if Experiment 3 were repeated using left-handed tennis players and a left-handed coach?

   F. The average service accuracy of all the players would increase by at least 30%.

   G. The average service speed of all the players would decrease slightly.

   H. Verbal coaching would improve average service speed less than would watching the video.

   J. The average service speed of the players who watched the video would increase by at least 8 mph.

GO ON TO THE NEXT PAGE ➡

7. Which of the following conclusions could NOT be supported by the results of Experiment 1?

   A. Imitating someone whose handedness is the opposite of one's own will cause one's skills to deteriorate.

   B. Left-handed people are better than right-handed people at imitating the movement of someone with similar handedness.

   C. People learn more easily by observing someone with similar handedness than by observing someone with handedness opposite their own.

   D. Right-handed people are better than left-handed people at imitating the movement of someone whose handedness is opposite their own.

8. Which of the following hypotheses is best supported by the results of Experiment 2?

   F. Instructional videos are more helpful for right-handed tennis players than is verbal instruction.

   G. Instructional videos are more helpful for left-handed tennis players than for right-handed tennis players.

   H. Physical guidance by a coach improves both speed and accuracy of service for right-handed tennis players.

   J. Physical guidance by a coach improves service accuracy for right-handed tennis players more than for left-handed players.

9. Suppose 50 left-handed tennis players watch a video of a left-handed coach and are also physically guided by that coach. The results of the experiments suggest that the players' average change in service speed will most closely approximate:

   A. −1 mph.

   B. +5 mph.

   C. +8 mph.

   D. +12 mph.

10. Which of the following hypotheses is best supported by the results of Experiment 1 alone?

    F. Tennis players improve less by observing coaches whose handedness is the opposite of their own than by observing those with similar handedness.

    G. Right-handed tennis players are coached by left-handed coaches more frequently than left-handed players are coached by right-handed coaches.

    H. Right-handed coaches are better models for all tennis players than are left-handed coaches.

    J. People learn much better from physical contact plus a visual stimulus than from the visual stimulus alone.

11. What change in procedure would allow a researcher to best determine the effects of verbal instruction on the average service speed of tennis players?

    A. Repeating Experiment 3 with left-handed players

    B. Repeating Experiment 2 with an instructional audio tape instead of a video

    C. Measuring the service speed of 100 tennis players before and after they listened to an instructional audio tape

    D. Verbally coaching 50 left-handed and 50 right-handed tennis players and then measuring their service speed

Passage III

The temperature of any stellar body causes it to emit a characteristic spectrum of radiation. The apparent color of the star corresponds to the wavelength at which most of its radiation is emitted. Stars are assigned to spectral classes according to these characteristic wavelengths, with O as the bluest/warmest and M as the reddest/coolest. The Hertzsprung-Russell (H-R) diagram below plots each known star within 5 parsecs of the Sun by spectral class and absolute magnitude. Absolute magnitude is a measure of luminosity as viewed from a distance of 10 parsecs. An absolute magnitude of +1.0 indicates maximum brightness. (1 parsec = 3.23 light years.)

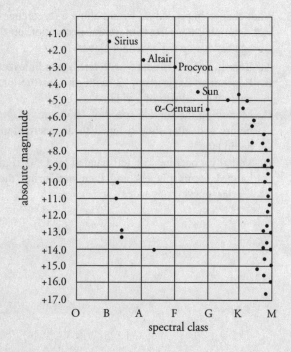

12. According to the data shown, most stars within 5 parsecs of the Sun have:

    F. a spectral class of M.
    G. an absolute magnitude of +11.0.
    H. a mass similar to that of the Sun.
    J. a bluish color.

13. According to the information given, which of the following stars—Sirius, Altair, α-Centauri—are likely to be hotter than the Sun?

    A. Sirius, Altair, and α-Centauri
    B. Sirius and Altair
    C. Sirius
    D. α-Centauri

14. The faintest stars that are visible to the naked eye are of the 6th magnitude. On the basis of this information and the data given, which of the following conclusions is most likely to be valid?

    F. The majority of stars within 5 parsecs of the Sun are visible from a distance of 10 parsecs.
    G. The majority of stars within 5 parsecs of the Sun are not visible from a distance of 10 parsecs.
    H. Stars in spectral classes K and M are visible from a distance of 10 parsecs.
    J. Stars in spectral class B are visible from a distance of 10 parsecs.

15. The data given in the passage support which of the following conclusions?

    I. α-Centauri is redder in color than Sirius.
    II. The Sun has a higher surface temperature than does Altair.
    III. If both the Sun and Procyon were viewed at a distance of 10 parsecs, the Sun would appear brighter.

    A. I only
    B. III only
    C. I and II only
    D. II and III only

16. In which of the following ways would a Hertzsprung-Russell diagram that included all of the known stars within 10 parsecs of the Sun differ from the one shown here?

    F. The number of points on the graph would approximately double, while the shape would remain the same.
    G. Most of the additional stars would fall in the portion of the graph between Sirius and α-Centauri.
    H. Most of the additional stars would be in spectral class M with an absolute magnitude of less than +16.0
    J. It cannot be determined from the information given.

GO ON TO THE NEXT PAGE ➡

Passage IV

The reaction of a certain cobalt complex with sodium nitrite ($NaNO_2$) can yield two different products. Product A is a light orange solid with a melting point measured at approximately 90.5° C; Product B is a dark pink solid with a melting point of 68° C. A series of experiments was performed to determine the reaction conditions that favor each product.

Experiment 1

Two separate solutions of the cobalt complex were prepared as follows. Solution 1 was acidified to pH 5.5; Solution 2 was made basic to pH 8.5. All other conditions were identical for the two solutions. When $NaNO_2$ was added to Solution 1, a dark pink solid with a melting point of 68° C was formed. Adding $NaNO_2$ to Solution 2 produced a white solid with a melting point of 81° C.

Experiment 2

Two separate solutions of the cobalt complex were prepared as above. After addition of $NaNO_2$, the solutions were heated to 110° C for 20 minutes. Solution 1 produced a dark pink solid with a melting point of 68° C. Solution 2 produced a light orange solid which melted at 91° C.

Experiment 3

Two separate solutions were prepared as in the previous experiments. After the addition of $NaNO_2$, each solution was treated with a small amount of citrate ion and then heated as in Experiment 2. Solution 1 remained a clear purple liquid. Solution 2 produced a light orange solid which melted at 90° C.

17. The experimental results indicate that Product B is most likely to form when one heats:

    A. a basic solution with added citrate ion.

    B. an acidic solution with added citrate ion.

    C. an acidic solution with no added citrate ion.

    D. a basic solution with no added citrate ion.

18. Which of the following conclusions is NOT supported by the experimental results?

    F. The formation of Product B is not affected by the presence of citrate ion.

    G. The formation of Product B is not affected by the heating of the solution.

    H. Products A and B form under different conditions.

    J. The formation of Product A is affected by the heating of the solution.

19. Which of the following additional experiments would yield the most useful data concerning the reaction conditions that favor each product?

    A. Varying the concentration of the solutions

    B. Testing with pH levels of 7.0

    C. Heating the solutions to 175° C

    D. Freezing the solutions

20. Which of the following hypotheses is supported by the results of Experiment 2 only?

    F. Products A and B can both be formed in solutions heated to 110° C.

    G. Solution 1 must be heated to yield any product.

    H. Citrate ion prevents the formation of Product A.

    J. Product B forms more readily at lower temperatures.

21. Which of the following conditions remain(s) constant in all three experiments?

    A. The temperature of the solutions during the experiments

    B. The initial amount of cobalt complex present

    C. The amount of citrate ion present

    D. The amount of cobalt complex and the amount of citrate ion present

22. It is suggested that Product B may react to form other, more readily dissolved compounds in the presence of certain ions. Such a hypothesis is best supported by the fact that:

    F. Product A forms at a different pH than Product B.

    G. Solution 2 yields a different color solid when heated.

    H. Product B is unstable in the presence of Product A.

    J. no solid forms in Solution 1 when citrate ion is added prior to heating.

GO ON TO THE NEXT PAGE ➡

Passage V

Two scientists present various grounds for classifying the giant panda (*Ailuropoda melanoleuca*) as a raccoon or as a bear.

Scientist 1

Although the giant panda superficially resembles a bear (*Ursidae*), many of its anatomical, behavioral, and genetic characteristics are closer to those of raccoons (*Procyonidae*). The bones and teeth of *Ailuropoda melanoleuca,* for example, are very similar in structure to those of the raccoon. While male bears can be up to 100% larger than females of the same species, male giant pandas and raccoons differ very little in size from females of their species. Like the raccoon, the giant panda has a friendly greeting which consists of bleating and barking. When intimidated, both animals cover their eyes with their front paws. Most bears do not exhibit these behaviors. Finally, *Ailuropoda melanoleuca* and the *Procyonidae* have 21 and 19 pairs of chromosomes, respectively, while the *Ursidae* have 36 pairs.

Scientist 2

Giant pandas should be classified as *Ursidae*. Research studies have shown that the ancestors of *Ailuropoda melanoleuca* had about 40 chromosomal pairs, and geneticists theorize that the reduction occurred when the chromosomes underwent head-to-head fusion. Other research has shown that the DNA of the giant panda is far more similar to that of the *Ursidae* than to that of any other family. Furthermore, giant pandas and other bears are not only of similar size, but also have very similar body proportions and walk with the same pigeon-toed gait. Giant pandas display aggressive behavior in the same manner as do other bears, by swatting and trying to grab adversaries with their forepaws.

23. Which of the following, if true, would provide additional support for the hypothesis of Scientist 2?

   A. The blood proteins of giant pandas are very similar to those of several bear species.

   B. Giant pandas and raccoons have similar markings, including dark rings around their eyes.

   C. Giant pandas have 21 pairs of chromosomes while raccoons have only 19 pairs.

   D. There is little difference in size between male and female giant pandas.

24. Scientist 1 and Scientist 2 would agree on which of the following points?

   F. Giant pandas should be classified in a separate family.

   G. The giant panda should not be classified as a raccoon.

   H. Raccoons and bears are physically and behaviorally very similar.

   J. Animals should be classified into families based on their physical, behavioral, and genetic characteristics.

25. Which of the following characteristics would support the classification of a mammal as a member of the *Ursidae*?

   I. 36 pairs of chromosomes and DNA similar to that of many bear species

   II. Raccoonlike markings and 19 pairs of chromosomes

   III. 62% greater average size among males than among females

   A. I only

   B. II only

   C. I and III only

   D. II and III only

GO ON TO THE NEXT PAGE ➡

26. According to Scientist 1, which of the following is the giant panda most likely to do when frightened?

    F. Bleat and bark
    G. Cover its eyes with its paws
    H. Swat and grab with its forepaws
    J. Walk away pigeon-toed

27. According to Scientist 2, the giant panda should be classified as a bear because:

    A. there is little disparity in the size of male and female giant pandas.
    B. the greeting rituals of the giant panda resemble those of bears.
    C. both bears and giant pandas are herbivorous.
    D. the DNA of giant pandas is similar to that of bears.

28. Suppose that giant pandas have glandular scent areas. This fact could be used to support the viewpoint of:

    F. Scientist 1, if it were also shown that raccoons also have glandular scent areas.
    G. Scientist 2, if it were also shown that bears do not have glandular scent areas.
    H. Scientist 1, if it were also shown that raccoons have a very poor sense of smell.
    J. Scientist 2, if it were also shown that bears urinate to lay down their scent.

29. Which of the following arguments could Scientist 1 use to counter Scientist 2's claim about the behavior of giant pandas and bears?

    A. The giant panda walks with a pigeon-toed gait.
    B. Unlike most bears, but like raccoons, an aggressive giant panda bobs its head up and down.
    C. The giant panda swats and grabs at its adversaries.
    D. Unlike most bears, the giant panda has only 19 pairs of chromosomes.

GO ON TO THE NEXT PAGE ➡

Passage VI

The graph below shows different primary energy sources as percentages of energy consumption in the United States during selected years from 1850 to 1985.

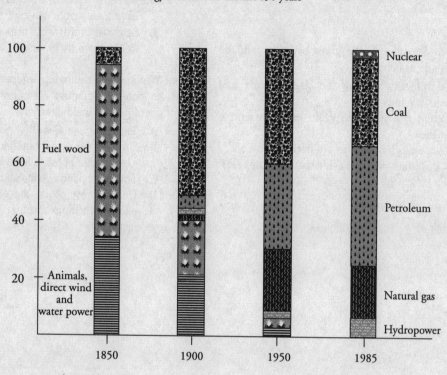

Energy sources over the last 150 years

30. As the relative importance of petroleum as a primary energy source increased, the use of coal:

F. also increased.

G. decreased.

H. remained constant.

J. stopped completely.

31. The data shown support the hypothesis that the ability to utilize coal as an energy source:

A. was developed during the 1900s.

B. was dependent on the development of mechanized mining techniques.

C. predated the ability to utilize natural gas.

D. was predated by the ability to utilize natural gas.

GO ON TO THE NEXT PAGE ➡

32. As the consumption of alternate energy sources increased, the use of farm animals:

   F. decreased to below 1% of the total.
   G. increased to over 30% of the total.
   H. increased, then decreased.
   J. remained the same.

33. Which of the following conclusions concerning energy consumption from 1900 to 1950 is supported by the information given in the graph?

   A. Energy sources became more diverse.
   B. Work animals became more important.
   C. Natural gas became the major energy source.
   D. Coal remained the largest single source of energy.

34. The data on the graph support which of the following conclusions?

   I. Energy consumption in 1985 relied in part on technologies that did not exist in 1850.
   II. The largest source of energy in the United States has always been coal.
   III. The short supply of available petroleum will lead to a decrease in its use.

   F. I only
   G. III only
   H. I and II only
   J. II and III only

GO ON TO THE NEXT PAGE ➡

Passage VII

The regenerative powers of *Asterias rubens,* a common starfish, were investigated in the following experiments.

Experiment 1

Randomly selected starfish were divided into five groups of 25 each. The individuals in one group were left intact. Members of the other four groups were subjected to selective amputation, as indicated in the table below. The starfish were kept in laboratory tanks simulating the natural environment of *Asterias rubens* for nine months. The results of periodic observations are recorded in Table 1.

Table 1

fully regenerated after[†]:

Removed Portion	3 mos.	6 mos.	9 mos.	# of starfish dead after 9 mos.
None	—	—	—	3
Outer arm	20	23	23	2
Whole arm	15	22	22	3
Arm & 1/5 body	6	21	23	2
2 arms & 1/3 body	5	12	24	1

[†]cumulative total

Experiment 2

The regenerative powers of portions of *Asterias rubens* were investigated next. Five groups of pieces of *Asterias rubens* were selected at random, placed in separate laboratory tanks under the same conditions as in Experiment 1, and observed for one year. The combined results from all five tanks are presented in Table 2.

Table 2

# of starfish fully regenerated after[†]:

Remaining Body Portion	3 mos.	6 mos.	9 mos.	1 yr.	# dead after 1 yr.
Lower arm	0	0	0	0	3
Arm & 1/5 body	0	0	8	20	2
2 arms & 1/3 body	0	2	13	22	2

[†]cumulative total

35. According to the experimental results, approximately what percentage of *Asterias rubens* specimens can regenerate two entire arms and part of the central body within six months?

A. 25%
B. 50%
C. 75%
D. 100%

36. Which of the following conclusions is supported by the results of Experiment 2 only?

F. Starfish are only capable of regenerating arms.
G. Starfish with larger portions removed regenerate at faster rates.
H. Some starfish die as a result of confinement in laboratory tanks.
J. Regeneration is dependent upon the existence of a portion of the central body.

GO ON TO THE NEXT PAGE ➡

37. The information given supports which of the following conclusions?

    I. *Asterias rubens* are often found in very deep water.

    II. *Asterias rubens* can regenerate limbs lost due to attack by other marine animals.

    III. The population of *Asterias rubens* would probably increase if body parts were broken off.

  A. I only

  B. III only

  C. II and III only

  D. I, II, and III

38. The first group of starfish was used in Experiment 1:

  F. as a control to see how many starfish were likely to die under the conditions of the experiment.

  G. as a control for the second experiment.

  H. to test the natural recuperative powers of *Asterias rubens*.

  J. to determine the effect of a fresh water environment on *Asterias rubens*.

39. In Experiment 2, the sum of fully regrown and dead starfish after one year did not always equal 25. The hypothesis which best explains this is that:

  A. some of the starfish were lost during the experiment.

  B. the researchers miscalculated somewhere during the course of the experiment.

  C. some body parts fused together to form single starfish.

  D. some of the starfish were alive but not fully regenerated.

40. Starfish prey on abalone. At one time it was common practice for abalone fishermen to chop starfish into pieces and throw them back into the ocean. What was the most probable result of this practice?

  F. The starfish population immediately skyrocketed.

  G. The starfish population increased over a period of time as some pieces underwent regeneration.

  H. The starfish population decreased drastically.

  J. Every piece that was returned to the ocean eventually became a complete starfish again.

END OF SCIENCE REASONING TEST

IF YOU FINISH BEFORE TIME IS CALLED, YOU MAY CHECK YOUR WORK ON THIS SECTION ONLY. DO NOT TURN TO ANY OTHER SECTION IN THE TEST.

STOP

To find a score for Practice Test 1, refer to the instructions in the section called "Compute Your Score," beginning on page 371.

Practice Test 1:
Answers and Explanations

English Answer Key

1. B	21. B	41. C	61. C
2. H	22. H	42. J	62. G
3. D	23. D	43. A	63. D
4. H	24. J	44. J	64. J
5. A	25. C	45. B	65. A
6. J	26. H	46. G	66. H
7. A	27. B	47. C	67. A
8. G	28. J	48. H	68. H
9. D	29. B	49. B	69. D
10. J	30. J	50. H	70. G
11. D	31. D	51. D	71. C
12. F	32. H	52. J	72. H
13. B	33. B	53. A	73. B
14. H	34. J	54. G	74. H
15. B	35. A	55. D	75. B
16. F	36. G	56. G	
17. B	37. C	57. D	
18. F	38. J	58. H	
19. C	39. B	59. C	
20. F	40. H	60. F	

The questions fall into the following categories, according to the skills they test. If you notice that you're having trouble with particular categories, review the following:

1. REDUNDANCY—English Workout 1

2. RELEVANCE—English Workout 1

3. VERBOSITY—English Workout 1

4. LOGIC—English Workout 2

5. SENTENCE STRUCTURE—English Workouts 2 and 3

6. COMPLETENESS—English Workouts 2 and 3

7. IDIOM—English Workouts 2 and 3

8. TONE—English Workout 2

9. PUNCTUATION—English Workout 3

10. VERB USAGE—English Workout 2

11. PRONOUNS—English Workouts 2 and 3

12. JUDGING THE PASSAGE—English Workout 2

13. READING-TYPE QUESTIONS—English Workout 2

14. STRUCTURE AND PURPOSE—English Workout 2

Passage I

1. (B)—Pronouns

A plural pronoun must logically refer to the closest plural noun that came before it. Choice A is incorrect because the word *they* can't logically stand for *people* here. It must mean *fish,* but *fish* hasn't been used yet in the sentence. Choices C and D make the same error but use *these* and *them.* They also suffer from wordiness.

2. (H)—Pronouns

Trust your ear. In original version F, you wouldn't say "origins who." *Who* can refer only to people. Choice G correctly uses *which,* but its singular verb, *begins,* can't go with the plural origins. Along with the faulty pronoun *who,* J contains the unidiomatic *beginning at.*

3. (D)—Redundancy

The words *keep(ing), possess(ing), having* and *have* all essentially mean the same thing. Using two of them together (choices A, B, and C) adds redundancy, not meaning, to the sentence.

4. (H)—Verb Usage

Trust your ear. The infinitive form of the verb is *to breed,* so the correct choice is H. The other options produce the incorrect verb forms *to breeds* (choice F), *to breeded* (choice G), and *to bred* (choice J).

5. (A)—Logic

Trust your ear, and make it make sense. Choices B, C, and D don't add anything to the sentence that isn't already expressed in correct choice A. In fact, the sentence makes no sense when B or C is plugged into it. The "nevertheless" in choice D suggests some sort of contrast, but there is none; the Romans are just another example of fish keepers.

6. (J)—Verb Usage

What happened in seventeenth-century England? Goldfish "were kept" in glass containers. The verb tense is wrong in choices F, G, and H.

7. (A)—Verb Usage

Ask yourself how the underlined verb is being used. It's the main verb for the subject *relationship*. A is the only choice that works. In choice B, the sentence won't make sense if we insert *which*. C is wrong because a main verb can never have an *-ing* form unless there is some form of the verb *to be* in front of it. You can say "I am running," but not "I running."

8. (G)—Reading-Type Question

The preceding sentence tells you how the need for small aquariums was met. It does not indicate that the container was inappropriate (choice F), contradict a statement about English containers (choice H), or talk about goldfish life spans (choice J).

9. (D)—Sentence Structure

The full sentence from which this question is taken is actually two short but complete sentences: "The first display aquariums opened . . . in London" and "aquariums soon appeared in Naples, Berlin, and Paris." When two short sentences are joined into one, and linked by a comma, the comma must be followed by a conjunction—a word like *and, but*, or *or*. In this case, the word is *and*.

10. (J)—Pronouns

Choices F and G are incorrect because they use *it* or *its* to refer *to the growth in aquariums* without having first used the longer phrase. Choice H is incorrect because it does not say what has been slowed.

11. (D)—Relevance

It is irrelevant to mention a television show about dolphins (choices A, B, and C) in a passage that discusses aquariums, even though dolphins are sometimes found in aquariums.

12. (F)—Logic

The two ideas here are *causally* related: You would share fish trivia *because* fish keeping has an interesting history. "For" (choice F) illustrates this connection. Choice G illogically sets "fish trivia" apart from the rest of the sentence. Choice J uses one set of quotation marks, but quotation marks always come in pairs.

13. (B)—Verb Usage

Trust your ear. *Have playing* sounds weird, and it doesn't mean anything. Choices C and D also sound odd. Whenever a sentence has more than one verb, there must be a conjunction between them. ("Fish keeping is [verb] . . . but [conjunction] . . . it also has [verb] . . .") There is no conjunction before the underlined phrase, so it cannot be a verb [choices C and D]. It's really a descriptive phrase [choice B].

14. (H)—Reading-Type Question

This passage is about the history of aquariums. It doesn't discuss the study of history in general (choice F) or the responsibility involved in maintaining an aquarium (choice J). It mentions that an aquarist might enjoy "fish trivia," but doesn't state that such trivia must be learned (choice G).

15. (B)—Structure and Purpose

Look at the first and last paragraphs. The first paragraph of the passage leads into, or introduces, the discussion of the history of aquariums. It's not an example (choice A) or a historical survey (choice C). The last paragraph is a wrap-up for the passage, not a personal account (choice D).

Passage II

16. (F)—Punctuation

The sentence is correct as it stands. There is clearly a pause between *mobility* and *horizontal*, so we need some form of punctuation between the two words. Choice H uses a semicolon, but semicolons connect two phrases that could be sentences by themselves. The phrase *horizontal and vertical* could not be a sentence. F and J correctly use a colon, which introduces a list or definition. However, J unnecessarily inserts the word *being*. Don't add what you don't need.

17. (B)—Redundancy

The words *pay* and *salary* have approximately the same meaning. It is redundant to use both (choices A and C). Choice D produces the phrase *firms that are comparable pay in terms of salary and prestige*, which makes no sense.

18. (F)—Pronouns

Think about what the sentence is saying. G, H, and J add unnecessary pronouns to the sentence. The subject, *change,* is right there, so it's wrong to throw in the pronoun *they* or *it.*

19. (C)—Logic

The mention of the Russian Revolution illustrates the point made in the preceding sentence, that social mobility "may change the entire social system." *For instance* (choice C) correctly indicates this. A, B, and D are wrong because this sentence does not offer a conclusion based on the preceding sentence.

20. (F)—Completeness

We hope your ear told you that G and J sound funny. Since choices G and J are complete sentences in themselves, you can't connect them to another complete sentence, "social mobility occurs at a variety of rates," with a comma. We also hope you steered clear of choice H, with its incorrect and confusing phrase *change's differing degrees.*

21. (B)—Completeness

The underlined word occurs in an incomplete sentence that lacks a verb. Choices A, C, and D are incorrect because they do not create complete sentences. C adds the verb *is,* but doesn't tell us *what* the athlete is. Choice B, however, adds a verb and completes the meaning.

22. (H)—Structure and Purpose

Sentence 6 says that gradual changes can accomplish social mobility, so it makes most sense before sentence 5, which gives an example of a gradual change. Choice H is correct.

23. (D)—Completeness

The phrase *in that* (choice A) sounds funny and makes the sentence incomplete. Changing the phrase to *in* (choice B) or *on* (choice C) still doesn't complete the sentence. Omitting the phrase, however, leaves a complete sentence.

24. (J)—Logic

The preceding sentence stated that some people view large-scale mobility negatively. This sentence offers a contrasting opinion. The words *accordingly* (choice F), *similarly* (choice G), and *likewise* (choice H) are incorrect because they imply agreement. The phrase *on the other hand* (choice J) correctly introduces a differing thought.

25. (C)—Pronouns

Your ear can help on this one. You might say *they attempt*, but not *they attempting* (choice B). In choice A, *they are attempting* sounds okay until you keep reading. Ask yourself what *they are attempting to rise validate* means.

26. (H)—Relevance

The main theme of the passage is social mobility. The American educational system (choice F), salary ranges (choice G), or a rock video (choice J) have nothing to do with this. The correct choice is H, since it talks about some benefits of social mobility.

27. (B)—Verb Usage

The sentence compares two verbs: *destroy* and *reinforce*. Things that are compared need to be in the same form. *Destroying* ends in *-ing*, so we need the *-ing* form of *reinforce*. Only choice B uses this form.

28. (J)—Logic

OMIT the underlined portion (choice J). It's not clear how a flat tire benefits anyone. G and H don't help.

29. (B)—Verb Usage

The subject of the sentence is *crowd*, not *yuppies*. A crowd is singular, no matter how many yuppies are in it, so we need the singular *shows* instead of *show*.

30. (J)—Verbosity

The point of the sentence is that vertical mobility is not a passing phenomenon. The underlined portion is not necessary and only distracts from this point.

Passage III

31. (D)—Sentence Structure

D is the simplest version, and it's right. Use your ear, or ask yourself what the subject of *is* or *being* is in choices A, B, and C. It can't be *that* because *that* isn't a pronoun here; so *is* or *being* doesn't refer to anything here. Rather, *that* is a conjunction, a word which combines one phrase, "The critic George Moore once said of this artist," with another, *her pictures are the only pictures. . . .*

32. (H)—Verb Usage

Use your ear: *statement are* sounds funny. That's because a singular noun must have a singular verb. *Statement* is singular, but *are* is plural. Choice H corrects the problem by making the verb singular. Choice J corrects it by making the noun plural, but *statement* also has to agree with *shows,* so we need the singular form in choice H.

33. (B)—Pronouns

A pronoun must refer to something. In A and D, we can guess that *it* refers to politics, but this isn't made clear in the sentence. Choice C adds the word *politics,* but the construction is clumsy. Correct choice B is simplest and clearest.

34. (J)—Logic

Trust your ear. *Being her earliest childhood* (choice F) sounds odd, and it is. It means that she *was* her earliest childhood. Choice G starts with the word *from* set off with a comma. The only time this construction is used is when someone is signing a letter.

35. (A)—Relevance

The passage is talking about the painters Morisot studied with, not about their nationalities. Manet's heritage, no matter how it is phrased, is not relevant. Choice A is correct.

36. (G)—Idiom

Make it all match. *Either* goes with *or. Neither* goes with *nor.* The two *n* words go together. Choices G and J use a correct pair, but J leaves out the verb. Choice G correctly uses a singular verb form. (Although *either/or* and *neither/nor* compare two things, they treat each thing separately, as a singular subject.)

37. (C)—Pronouns

Who is doing the facing? Morisot's male colleagues are, so they should be referred to by the pronoun *who.* The passage is talking about Morisot's lifetime, which was in the *past.* So we use the past tense, *faced.*

38. (J)—Logic

The previous sentence talks about Morisot's setbacks. This sentence talks about the way she overcame them. We are looking for a connecting word that implies *contrast:* Morisot did well *in spite of* her hardships. *However* (choice J) provides the contrast we are looking for.

39. (B)—Completeness

In choice A, *Portraying women performing domestic and social activities* is not a complete sentence. It has no subject. Choice C uses the word *insofar* incorrectly. Choice D says "her sphere *were*." Since *sphere* is singular, we would have to say "her sphere *was*." Correct choice B makes the fragment into a sentence by giving it the subject *she* and using an appropriate form of the verb (began to portray).

40. (H)—Structure and Purpose

We're looking for a statement that will present Morisot in a more positive light. Choice H suggests that while her subject matter may *appear* limited, it could *actually* be considered quite meaningful, given the social context in which it was produced. Choices F, G, and J, in contrast, are all somewhat negative in tone.

41. (C)—Punctuation

We can introduce a list of examples with a colon or with the words *such as*, but not with both, so choice A is wrong. A dash doesn't introduce a list of examples, so choice B is wrong. Choice D is wrong because it uses a comma after the phrase *such as*. If you read the sentence with a pause after *such as*, it sounds awkward.

42. (J)—Redundancy

Choices F, G, and H are redundant. By definition, successors are the people who follow in order or sequence someone else.

43. (A)—Structure and Purpose/Relevance

Ask yourself: What is the main point of the passage? The passage is about Morisot's experience as a female artist. Only choice A is relevant to that topic. Choice C refers to George Moore, who is mentioned in the passage in relation to Morisot. To devote a section of the passage to him, however, would change its focus. Likewise, a discussion of Impressionism would divert the focus of the passage away from Morisot.

44. (J)—Judging the Passage/Relevance

Does the inclusion of dates seem appropriate? Well, the passage is a biography, and dates are generally appropriate in a biography, so the correct answer is J. The story of Morisot isn't unbelievable, so the author would have no reason to introduce something just to make us believe it (choice H).

45. (B)—Structure and Purpose

First, try to find an appropriate beginning. Paragraph 1 is especially easy to eliminate, since it refers to "this artist" without ever telling us her name. Paragraph 3 is less obvious, but it talks about Morisot's subject matter and style without telling us who she is. The passage can't start with paragraph 4, because none of the answer choices does. Paragraph 2 provides general background information on Morisot, so it should be first. That leaves choices B and C. Paragraph 3 introduces Morisot's subject matter, which paragraph 4 talks about in greater detail. So it makes sense to put paragraph 3 immediately before 4.

Passage IV

46. (G)—Verb Usage

Make sure everything matches. Ask, *what is the subject?* Even though *exception* occurs right before the verb, the subject is *movies. Movies* is plural, so we need a plural verb. *Were being replaced* (choice H) is plural, but it illogically changes the tense. We're talking about a change in movies right now, not in the distant past. Use your ear. You should be able to tell that choice H sounds funny.

47. (C)—Punctuation

"The slasher movie" is the "new breed of horror film." We need something to connect a thing and its definition: either punctuation or a connecting phrase. Choice D inserts an unnecessary comma, and both B and D are wordy. A colon, in choice C, works just fine.

48. (H)—Completeness

The subject of the sentence is *the first commercially successful low-budget chiller.* Choices F, G, and J separate *first* from *commercially successful low-budget chiller.* The sentence doesn't make sense this way. *The first* tells us *which* "commercially successfully low budget film" we are talking about, so it must be connected to that phrase.

49. (B)—Verb Usage

Plug the choices in. Choices A, C, and D don't make sense. That's because the verb is *have glutted,* and the whole verb has to go in one place.

50. (H)—Verbosity

Choices F and J sound funny. That's because they use complicated expressions. Not only does G use an awkward construction, it also eliminates the subject (popularity). Simpler is better. Choice H is the right answer.

51. (D)—Redundancy

The word *filmmakers* is all that's needed.

52. (J)—Verbosity

Trust your ear. *Increasing gory* sounds a bit off. Choice J adds an *ly* which makes it correct. Notice that *increasingly* describes *gory. Gory* is an adjective, and if you want to describe anything that's not a noun, you need an adverb. Most adverbs (like *increasingly*) are formed by adding *ly* to an adjective (like *increasing*).

53. (A)—Punctuation

Ask yourself what job the punctuation is doing. In this sentence, the punctuation indicates a slight pause. Since commas do that, the comma (choice A) is correct.

54. (G)—Redundancy

When in doubt, take it out. *Periphery* means *fringe,* so using both words is unnecessary.

55. (D)—Verb Usage

They're may sound like *there are* but it means *they are*, which doesn't make sense here. Also, *they're* is the same as *they are* in choice B. There can't be two correct answers, so whenever two answers mean the same thing they must both be wrong.

56. (G)—Tone

Try to decide on appropriateness first. "That's a big wad of cash!" sounds out of place because it is very informal, while the passage is relatively formal. So we can decide that the statement is not appropriate, and look for an answer that gives us this reason. The correct choice G refers to the passage's tone.

57. (D)—Sentence Structure

Conjunctions are words that combine one phrase with another. Using two conjunctions, like *although* and *however* in choice A, is redundant, illogical, and wrong. Choices B and C make this same mistake. You should be able to hear these errors, but be careful! You have to read the entire sentence in order to notice the *although*.

58. (H)—Redundancy

Increasingly, evermore, and *more, and more, and more* all mean the same thing, just as *violent* and *full of anger, blood and shooting* mean the same thing. Say each once.

59. (C)—Redundancy

The public is, by definition, made up of human beings, so choices A and B are redundant. In choice D, *human's* refers to one specific being, but the passage is talking about the general taste.

60. (F)—Tone

Answer one part of the question first. Look at the tone. People who make sarcastic remarks are being harsh, derisive, and often ironic—that is, they mean the opposite of what they say. The passage does not do this, nor is it light-hearted, so we can eliminate choices G and H. The author is serious, and does discuss a change in entertainment, so F is correct.

Passage V

61. (C)—Redundancy

"Unexplained" things *are* things that haven't been explained yet. When in doubt, take it out.

62. (G)—Redundancy

Abandoned means "deserted," so don't say both.

63. (D)—Verb Usage

Listen to the sentence as it stands. It sounds odd, because *having* can't be the main verb of a sentence. You can say "I am going," or "I go," but not, "I going." Choice D is simple and it has a subject (*some ships*) and an acceptable verb (*have vanished*).

64. (J)—Idiom

Trust your ear. English speakers use certain idioms or expressions, just because that's the way we say things. Something ranges "from the interference of UFOs to the existence of powerful fields," *not* "to or toward the interference of UFOs to the existence of powerful fields," as in choices F and G.

65. (A)—Redundancy

So far means the same as *yet*, so B, C, and D are all redundant. Also, if you read choice D back into the sentence, you'll hear that it leaves out the verb (*have been*). Choice A is correct.

66. (H)—Relevance

It's not important to the passage that England is also triangular. When in doubt, take it out.

67. (A)—Logic

Think about it: If a country's coast is a boundary, why bring rivers into the discussion?

68. (H)—Verbosity

Say it simply. Choices F, G, and J are all wordy and awkward. Those qualities are not admired by the ACT test makers.

69. (D)—Verb Usage

The first problem here is verb tense. The meaning of the sentence as it stands is that strange events were reported in the *past*, but people are wondering about the region *now*. If the events "had" been reported (choice A) the author would be talking about a *past* conception of the Bermuda Triangle. The second problem is number. *Events* is plural. *Is* (choice C) and *has* (choice B) are singular.

70. (G)—Relevance

Inappropriate statements usually stick out. You stop reading and wonder why you were told something. That doesn't happen here, so the mention of Juan de Bermudez is probably appropriate. Now consider *why* it is appropriate. Choice H is incorrect and choice J has nothing to do with why the mention of Bermudez is appropriate. Choice G is correct. (If you're not sure the statement is relevant, look at the reason given for saying it's not: Exploration and the Bermuda Triangle are not dissimilar, since we are talking about the exploration of Bermuda.)

71. (C)—Sentence Structure

Trust your ear. What are they questioning?

72. (H)—Relevance

What new information would be a continuation of the topic? The passage at this point isn't talking about geography (choice F), the tourist trade (choice J), or other supernatural phenomena (choice G). It is discussing doubts about whether there have been supernatural occurrences in the Bermuda Triangle.

73. (B)—Redundancy

We know what *certain* means. Adding a definition is redundant.

KAPLAN

74. (H)—Structure and Purpose

Answer the question first. The passage talks about many events, not just one, so the answer to the question is "no." Now look at the reasons. The passage does contain factual information, so choice J is wrong. Choice H is correct because the writer does not focus on one specific disappearance.

75. (B)—Structure and Purpose

Paragraph 1 is a discussion of the *types* of strange events that have been reported. It should logically come after the introduction of the fact that strange events have been reported. Choice B is correct since paragraph 2 introduces the fact that strange events have been reported.

Math Answer Key			
1. C	16. F	31. A	46. G
2. H	17. B	32. K	47. B
3. D	18. F	33. B	48. J
4. J	19. E	34. G	49. E
5. A	20. J	35. E	50. H
6. F	21. D	36. G	51. E
7. E	22. G	37. C	52. K
8. K	23. C	38. K	53. D
9. B	24. K	39. E	54. F
10. F	25. D	40. H	55. E
11. D	26. F	41. C	56. H
12. G	27. D	42. J	57. D
13. E	28. F	43. B	58. H
14. J	29. A	44. J	59. B
15. C	30. G	45. C	60. F

1. (C)—Solving a Linear Equation

Math Appendix, #63. Find x by getting it by itself on one side of the equation:

$$5x + 3 = -17$$

Subtract 3 from both sides. $\qquad 5x = -20$

Divide both sides by 5. $\qquad x = \frac{-20}{5}$

Simplify. $\qquad x = -4$

Alternatively, use backsolving. $5x + 3 = -17$ will be true for the correct value of x only. Since the answer choices are in numerical order, try C first.

$$x = -4, \text{ then } 5(-4) + 3 = -17$$

$$-20 + 3 = -17$$

$$-17 = -17$$

This is true, so C must be correct.

2. (H)—Solving a Proportion

Math Appendix, #38. Six people are served by 4 oranges, 5 pears, 10 apples, and 24 strawberries. Eighteen people—that is, 3 3 6 people—will need 3 times as much, that is, 3 times as many of each ingredient. So John needs $3 \times 5 = 15$ pears.

3. (D)—Greatest Common Factor

Math Appendix, #15. Factor both numbers:

$8 \times 10^9 = 2 \times 2 \times 2 \times 10 \times 10 \times 10 \times 10 \times 10 \times 10 \times 10 \times 10 \times 10$
$6 \times 10^3 = 2 \times 3 \times 10 \times 10 \times 10$

Since both numbers have a factor of 2 and three factors of 10, the greatest integer that is a factor of both will be $2 \times 10 \times 10 \times 10 = 2 \times 10^3$.

4. (J)—Areas of Special Quadrilaterals

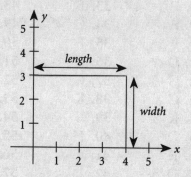

Math Appendix, #87. Area of a rectangle = length 3 width

From the diagram, length = 4 and width = 3. Therefore area = $4 \times 3 = 12$.

5. (A)—Circumference of a Circle

Math Appendix, #89. Draw a diagram to help visualize the situation:

As can be seen from the diagram, the length of the band is the same as the circumference of the cylinder. The circumference of a cylinder and the circumference of a circle are determined in the same way:

Circumference = $2\pi r = 2 \times \pi \times 4 = 8\pi$.

6. (F)—Translating from English into Algebra

Math Appendix, #65. For every large jar there are 48 olives, so x large jars hold $48x$ olives.

For every small jar there are 32 olives, so y small jars hold $32y$ olives.

The total number of olives needed is $48x + 32y$.

This problem could also be attacked by picking numbers. Let $x = 1$ and $y = 2$. Then there is one large jar needing 48 olives, and two small jars needing $2 \times 32 = 64$ olives, for a total of $48 + 64 = 112$ olives. Any answer choice which does not result in 112 when $x = 1$ and $y = 2$ may be eliminated.

(F) $48x + 32y = 48 \times 1 + 32 \times 2 = 112$ —This may be correct.

(G) $\frac{x}{48} + \frac{y}{32} = \frac{1}{48} + \frac{2}{32} \neq 112$ —Discard.

(H) $\frac{xy}{80} = \frac{1 \times 2}{80} = \frac{2}{80} \neq 112$ —Discard.

(J) $80xy = 80 \times 1 \times 2 \neq 112$ —Discard.

(K) $\frac{1536}{xy} = \frac{1536}{1 \times 2} = 768 \neq 112$ —Discard.

Since answer choice (A) was the only one to give the appropriate number, it is correct.

7. (E)—Evaluating an Algebraic Expression

Math Appendix, #52. Substitute $x + 1$ for x in the expression $3x^2 + 4$:

$$3(x + 1)^2 + 4$$

Expand $(x + 1)^2$. $= 3(x^2 + 2x + 1) + 4$

Multiply out parentheses. $= 3x^2 + 6x + 3 + 4$

Gather like terms. $= 3x^2 + 6x + 7$

8. (K)—Converting a Mixed Number to an Improper Fraction, Adding/Subtracting Fractions

Math Appendix, #25, 22.

$$5\frac{5}{6} + 3\frac{5}{8} + 1\frac{1}{3} = 5 + 3 + 1 + \frac{5}{6} + \frac{5}{8} + \frac{1}{3}$$

$$= 9 + \frac{5}{6} + \frac{5}{8} + \frac{1}{3}$$

$$= 9 + \frac{20}{24} + \frac{15}{24} + \frac{8}{24}$$

$$= 9 + \frac{43}{24}$$

$$= 9 + 1\frac{19}{24}$$

$$= 10\frac{19}{24}$$

9. (B)—Miscellaneous Line Segments

Draw a diagram:

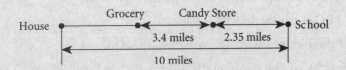

It is 2.35 + 3.4 = 5.75 miles from the school to the grocery store. The distance from the grocery store to home is the remaining portion of the 10 miles between school and home. That is, (10 miles) − (5.75 miles) = 4.25 miles.

10. (F)—Rate

Math Appendix, #39. That is 3 pieces every week for 4 weeks, for a total of 3 × 4 = 12 pieces.

He can learn 2 new pieces per week. To learn 12 pieces will take him 12 ÷ 2 = 6 weeks.

11. (D)—Interior Angles of a Triangle

Math Appendix, #80. The sum of the interior angles of any triangle is 180°. So:

$$\angle EDF + \angle DFE + \angle DEF = 180°$$
$$35° + 65° + \angle DEF = 180°$$
$$\angle DEF = 180° - 35° - 65°$$
$$\angle DEF = 80°$$

12. (G)—Averages—Finding the Missing Number

Math Appendix, #44. $\text{Average} = \dfrac{\text{Sum of Terms}}{\text{Number of Terms}}$

In this case she needs an average of 175. Let the score on the next game be x.

$$\text{Then } 175 = \frac{150 + 195 + 160 + x}{4}$$
$$175 \times 4 = 150 + 195 + 160 + x$$
$$700 = 505 + x$$
$$700 - 505 = x$$
$$195 = x$$

So she must score 195 on the next game for an average of 175.

13. (E)—Miscellaneous Coordinate Geometry and Triangles

Draw a diagram:

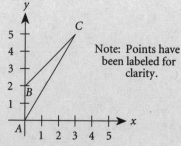

Note: Points have been labeled for clarity.

Run through the answer choices to see which one works.

(A) ∠ABC is *greater* than 90°—Discard.

(B) All three sides are *not* the same length—Discard.

(C) *No* sides are the same length—Discard.

(D) *No* angle measures 90°—Discard.

(E) One angle, $\angle ABC$, is greater than 90°—This is correct.

14. (J)—Solving a Quadratic Equation

Math Appendix, #66. $2y^2 - 4y - 6 = 0$ is of the form $ax^2 + bx + c = 0$, and so its roots can be found by the quadratic formula.

$$x = \frac{-b \pm \sqrt{b^2 - 4ac}}{2a}$$

$$= \frac{-(-4) \pm \sqrt{(-4)^2 - 4 \times 2 \times (-6)}}{4}$$

$$= \frac{4 \pm \sqrt{16 + 48}}{4} = 1 \pm 2, \text{ which is 3 or } -1. \text{ The sum of 3 and } -1 \text{ is 2.}$$

15. (C)—Converting Fractions and Decimals

Math Appendix, #29. Eliminate answer choices (A) and (B) straight off, since the numerator is less than the denominator, $\frac{7}{8}$ must be less than 1.

$$\frac{1}{8} = 0.125, \text{ so } \frac{7}{8} = 7 \times 0.125 = 0.875$$

16. (F)—Translating from English into Algebra, Solving a System of Equations

Math Appendix, #65, 67. Translate:

"June has 20 marbles more than Billy."	$J = B + 20$
"Maria has 3 times as many marbles as Billy."	$M = 3B$
"Altogether they have 100 marbles."	$J + M + B = 100$

We need B, the number of marbles Billy has.

Substitute the expressions in terms of B for J and M.

$$B + 20 + 3B + B = 100$$

Gather like terms.	$5B + 20 = 100$
Subtract 20.	$5B = 80$
Divide by 5.	$B = 16$

So Billy has 16 marbles.

17. (B)—Solving a Linear Equation

Math Appendix, #63: Rather than graphing the equation, the quickest way to solve this is to substitute 6 for x in the equation, and to solve for y.

	$3x - 2y = 4$
Substitute $x = 6$.	$3(6) - 2y = 4$
Multiply out parentheses.	$18 - 2y = 4$
Subtract 18 from both sides.	$-2y = -14$
Divide both sides by -2.	$y = \frac{-14}{-2}$
Simplify.	$y = 7$

18.(F)—Parallel Lines and Transversals

Math Appendix, #79. When a transversal cuts parallel lines, all acute angles formed are equal and all obtuse angles formed are equal. So here all obtuse angles have measure p and all acute angles measure q. The question says that "the measure of $\angle p$ is 20° less than three times the measure of $\angle q$." That is, $p = 3q - 20$. Also $p + q = 180$, since p and q are supplementary angles; that is, they form a straight line.

Solve for q:

$$p + q = 180$$

Substitute $3q - 20$ for p.	$3q - 20 + q = 180$
Gather like terms.	$4q - 20 = 180$
Add 20 to both sides.	$4q = 200$
Divide both sides by 4.	$q = 50$

So $p = 3q - 20 = 3(50) - 20 = 150 - 20 = 130$

$p - q = 130 - 50 = 80$

(*Note:* By eyeballing you could have eliminated answer choices J and K as too large.)

19.(E)—Solving a System of Equations

Math Appendix, #67. Do not solve all the systems of equations—this would be too time consuming. Think about the problem first. The solution of a system of equations is the point these equations intersect—if the lines are parallel, they will not intersect, and there will be no solution. The lines that are parallel will have the same slope. The answer choices are all in the form $Ax + By = C$. You could find the slopes if the equations were in the slope-intercept form. This can be done by subtracting Ax from both sides, and dividing by B to get $y = -\frac{A}{B}x + \frac{C}{B}$, so here slope $= -\frac{\text{coefficient of } x}{\text{coefficient of } y} = -\frac{A}{B}$.

(A) Slope of 1st equation $= -\frac{1}{3}$

Slope of 2nd equation $= \frac{3}{-1} = -3$

The slopes are different—Discard.

(B) Slope of 1st equation $= -\frac{1}{3}$

Slope of 2nd equation $= \frac{1}{3}$

The slopes are different—Discard.

(C) Slope of 1st equation $= -\frac{1}{-3} = \frac{1}{3}$

Slope of 2nd equation $= \frac{3}{-1} = 3$

The slopes are different—Discard.

(D) Slope of 1st equation $= -\frac{1}{-3} = \frac{1}{3}$

Slope of 2nd equation $= -\frac{3}{1} = -3$

The slopes are different—Discard.

(E) Slope of 1st equation $= -\dfrac{1}{3}$

Slope of 2nd equation $= -\dfrac{3}{9} = -\dfrac{1}{3}$

Since these slopes are the same, there is no solution to this system of equations.

20. (J)—Miscellaneous Line Segments

Mark in the lengths:

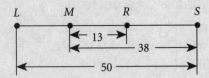

The distance *LR* is the distance *LM* plus the distance *MR*.

The distance *MR* is 13.

The distance *LM* is the distance *LS* minus the distance *MS*. That is $50 - 38 = 12$.

Therefore $LR = 12 + 13 = 25$.

(*Note:* You could have discarded answer choice *F* straight away—*LR* must be longer than *MR*.)

21. (D)—Percent Formula

Math Appendix, #32. $133\frac{1}{3}\%$ is 4 times $33\frac{1}{3}\%$.

So, if $33\frac{1}{3}\% = 9$, then $133\frac{1}{3}\% = 4 \times 9 = 36$.

22. (G)—Sine, Cosine, and Tangent of Acute Angles—SOHCAHTOA

Math Appendix, #96. Since $\tan = \frac{\text{opposite}}{\text{adjacent}}$, you need to know the lengths of the side opposite *x*, $\overline{DE}$, and the side adjacent to *x*, $\overline{FE}$.

Since $DE = 1$ and $DF = \sqrt{2}$, this must be an isosceles right triangle with sides in the ratio $1 : 1 : \sqrt{2}$. (You could also show this by using the Pythagorean theorem.) So $DE = FE = 1$.

$\tan x = \frac{\text{opposite}}{\text{adjacent}} = \frac{DE}{FE} = \frac{1}{1} = 1$

23. (C)—Equation for a Circle

Math Appendix, #75: Draw a diagram:

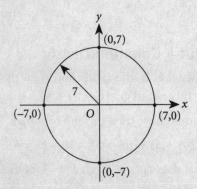

Obviously A and D lie on the circle—Eliminate these answer choices.

The formula for a circle is $(x-a)^2 + (y-b)^2 = r^2$, where a and b are the x- and y-coordinates of the center, and r is the radius. In this case the center is $(0, 0)$ and r is 7. Therefore the equation of this circle is $x^2 + y^2 = 49$, and any point that is not on the circle will not satisfy this equation.

(B) $(-3, 2\sqrt{10})$: $(-3)^2 + (2\sqrt{10})^2 = 9 + 40 = 49$—Discard.

(C) $(\sqrt{7}, 3)$: $(\sqrt{7})^2 + 3^2 = 7 + 9 = 16 \neq 49$—This point is not on the circle, and so C is correct.

24. (K)—Miscellaneous Coordinate Geometry

Point A is 4 units above the x-axis, so its y-coordinate is 4.

Point B is 3 units below the x-axis, so its y-coordinate is –3.

The product of the y-coordinates is $4 \times (-3) = -12$.

25. (D)—Intersecting Lines, Parallel Lines and Transversals

Math Appendix, #78, #79. Since y is greater than 90°, answer choices A and B can be eliminated by eyeballing.

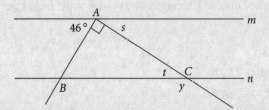

Since the angle marked 46°, the right angle, and angle s make up a straight line, they sum to 180°. So $46 + 90 + s = 180$, or $s = 44$. Both s and t are acute angles formed by the same transversal, $\overline{AC}$, so t also has a measure of 44°.

Since y and t are supplementary, $y + t = 180$. That is $y = 180 - 44 = 136$.

26. (F)—Evaluating an Algebraic Expression

Math Appendix, #52. Plug in (-3) for s :

$$s^3 + 2s^2 + 2s = (-3)^3 + 2(-3)^2 + 2(-3)$$
$$= -27 + 2(9) + (-6)$$
$$= -27 + 18 - 6$$
$$= -15$$

27. (D)—Factoring Out a Common Divisor

Math Appendix, #58. Notice that in the expression $r(t + u) - s(t + u)$ both r and s are being multiplied by $t + u$. Factor this out to get $(r - s)(t + u)$.

If you didn't see this, you could have tried picking numbers. Let $r = 2$, $s = 3$, $t = 4$, and $u = 5$.

Then $r(t + u) - s(t + u) = 2(4 + 5) - 3(4 + 5) = 18 - 27 = -9$.

Any of the answer choices that does not give a value of –9 for these values of r, s, t, and u may be discarded.

(A) $(r + s)(t + u) = (2 + 3)(4 + 5) = (5)(9) = 45$—Discard.

(B) $(r - s)(t - u) = (2 - 3)(4 - 5) = (-1)(-1) = 1$—Discard.

(C) $(r + s)(t - u) = (2 + 3)(4 - 5) = (5)(-1) = -5$—Discard.

(D) $(r - s)(t + u) = (2 - 3)(4 + 5) = (-1)(9) = -9$—This may be correct.

(E) 0 —Discard.

So answer choice D is the only one that gives a value of –9 for the chosen values, and so it must be correct.

28. (F)—Similar Triangles; and Math Appendix, #83: Area of a Triangle

Math Appendix, #82. ΔABC and ΔDBF are similar, since corresponding angles are of the same measure. Therefore their sides are proportional.

That is, $\frac{AB}{BC} = \frac{DB}{BF}$, or $\frac{8}{6} = \frac{4}{BF}$, so $BF = 3$.

The area of a triangle is $\frac{1}{2}$(base $\times$ height) $= \frac{1}{2}(3 \times 4) = 6$.

Note: You could have discarded answer choices J and K by logic—the area of the smaller triangle must be less than the area of the larger triangle, which is $\frac{1}{2}(6 \times 8) = 24$.

29. (A)—Trigonometric Functions of Other Angles

Math Appendix, #98. Consider the unit circle:

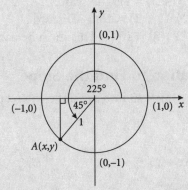

The cosine of any value is the x-coordinate when plotted on the unit circle, so cos 225° is the x-coordinate of A. Note that this point is below the x-axis, so the x-coordinate must be negative—eliminate answer choices D and E. Also notice that x is the length of the leg of the right triangle formed by dropping a line perpendicular to the x-axis from A. This is an isosceles right triangle, since it has interior angles of 45° and 90°. The ratio of side lengths in such a triangle is $1 : 1 : \sqrt{2}$. Since the hypotenuse has a length of 1, the legs must have lengths of $\frac{1}{\sqrt{2}} = \frac{1}{\sqrt{2}} \times \frac{\sqrt{2}}{\sqrt{2}} = \frac{\sqrt{2}}{2}$. So cos 225° $= -\frac{\sqrt{2}}{2}$.

30. (G)—Area of a Triangle

Math Appendix, #83. The area of a triangle is $\frac{1}{2}$ (base $\times$ height). In this case the area is 45 square units, and the base is XZ, which is $3 + 12 = 15$. The height is YS.

So $45 = \frac{1}{2}(15 \times YS)$

$45 \times 2 = 15 \times YS$

$$90 \div 15 = YS$$
$$6 = YS$$

Since this diagram looks to be drawn to scale, you could also have eliminated answer choices J and K as too large, and answer choice F as too small.

31. (A)—Circumference of a Circle

Math Appendix, #89. The circumference of a circle is πd, where d is the diameter. Here the diameter is 10, so the circumference is 10π.

32. (K)—Factoring Out a Common Divisor

Math Appendix, #58. Rearrange the formula:

$$A = \pi rs + \pi r^2$$
Factor out π. $\quad A = \pi(rs + r^2)$
$$A = \pi(rs + rr)$$
Factor out an r. $\quad A = \pi r(s + r)$

Alternatively, pick numbers. Let $r = 2$ and $s = 3$. Then $A = \pi rs + \pi r^2 = \pi(2)(3) + \pi(2)^2 = 10\pi$

Any answer choice which does not give a result of 10π can be eliminated.

(F) $A = 2\pi rs = 2\pi(2)(3) = 12\pi$—Discard.
(G) $A = 2\pi r^2 s = 2\pi(2)^2(3) = 24\pi$—Discard.
(H) $A = \pi r(1 + s) = \pi(2)(1 + 3) = 8\pi$—Discard.
(J) $A = \pi r^2(1 + s) = \pi(2)^2(1 + 3) = 16\pi$—Discard.
(K) $A = \pi r(r + s) = \pi(2)(2 + 3) = 10\pi$—This must be correct.

33. (B)—Using an Equation to Find the Slope

Math Appendix, #73. Get $5x + 3y = 13$ into the slope-intercept form, $y = mx + b$. Then m will be the slope.

$$5x + 3y = 13$$

Subtract $5x$. $\quad 3y = -5x + 13$

Divide by 3. $\quad y = -\frac{5}{3}x + \frac{13}{3}$

So $\quad\quad\quad\quad\quad m = \text{slope} = -\frac{5}{3}$.

34. (G)—Miscellaneous Number Properties

Try to disprove the statements by picking numbers. Let $a = b = 1$. Then:

$|a - b| + \sqrt{b - a} = |1 - 1| + \sqrt{1 - 1} = 0 + 0 = 0$. So if $a = b$, the answer is not always negative, so discard answer choice J. Since 0 is neither positive nor negative, also discard H.

Try fractions. Let $a = \frac{1}{2}$ and $b = \frac{3}{4}$. Then $|a - b| + \sqrt{b - a} = |\frac{1}{2} - \frac{3}{4}| + \sqrt{\frac{3}{4} - \frac{1}{2}} = |-\frac{1}{4}| + \sqrt{\frac{1}{4}} = \frac{1}{4} + \frac{1}{2} = \frac{3}{4}$. Now this is not equal to an integer, so discard answer choice F.

What if $a = -1$ and $b = -2$? Then $|a - b| + \sqrt{b - a} =$
$|(-1) - (-2)| + \sqrt{(-2) - (-1)} = |1| + \sqrt{-1}$

Now the square root of −1 is not real, so discard answer choice K. That leaves only answer choice G, which must then be correct.

35. (E)—Solving a Quadratic Equation

Math Appendix, #66: The quadratic formula states that the roots of an equation in the form $ax^2 + bx + c = 0$ are

$$\frac{-b \pm \sqrt{b^2 - 4ac}}{2a}$$

In this case $a = 1$, $b = -7$ and $c = 8$, so the roots are:

$$\frac{-(-7) \pm \sqrt{(-7)^2 - 4 \times 1 \times 8}}{2 \times 1} = \frac{7 \pm \sqrt{17}}{2} = \frac{7 + \sqrt{17}}{2} \text{ or } \frac{7 - \sqrt{17}}{2}$$

That is, answer choice E.

36. (G)—Special Right Triangles

Math Appendix, #85. Draw a diagram:

The sides of the square are the legs of a right triangle. By the Pythagorean theorem:

$$\text{leg}_1{}^2 + \text{leg}_2{}^2 = \text{hypotenuse}^2$$
$$x^2 + x^2 = 20^2$$
$$2x^2 = 400$$
$$x^2 = 200$$
$$x = \sqrt{200}$$

Get the radical into the form of the answer choices:

$$x = \sqrt{200} = \sqrt{100} \times \sqrt{2} = 10\sqrt{2}$$

37. (C)—Multiplying Binomials—FOIL

Math Appendix, #56. $(3a - 4)(a + 2)$:

First	$3a \times a = 3a^2$
Outer	$3a \times 2 = 6a$
Inner	$-4 \times a = -4a$
Last	$-4 \times 2 = -8$

Combine: $3a^2 + 6a - 4a - 8 = 3a^2 + 2a - 8$

38. (K)—Finding the Distance Between Two Points

Math Appendix, #71. Draw a diagram:

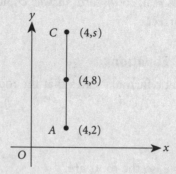

The midpoint must be the same distance from A as from C. Since it is 6 units above point A it must be 6 units below point C; i.e., C must have a y-coordinate of 14.

39. (E)—Translating from English into Algebra

Math Appendix, #65. Translate into math.

The question says s represents the first number.
"The second number is 3 less than 4 times the first number," i.e., $4s - 3$
"The third number is 5 more than twice the first," i.e., $2s + 5$
The sum of all three numbers is then

$$s + 4s - 3 + 2s + 5 = 7s + 2$$

40. (H)—Intersecting Lines, Interior Angles of a Triangle, Exterior Angles of a Triangle

Math Appendix, #78, 80, 81. Since $\angle SAB$ and $\angle BAC$ are supplementary, $\angle SAB + \angle BAC = 180°$. Since $\angle SAB = 130°$, $\angle BAC = 50°$. We now have two of the interior angles of $\triangle ABC$. Since the sum of the interior angles in a triangle is 180°, $\angle BAC + \angle ABC + \angle ACB = 180°$. That is 50° + 80° + $\angle ACB$ = 180°. Therefore $\angle ACB = 50°$.

$\angle EDC$ is supplementary to $\angle QDC$. Since $\angle QDC = 110°$, $\angle EDC = 70°$. We now have two interior angles of $\triangle DEC$. The third is $\angle DEC$. Since the sum of the interior angles in a triangle is 180°, $\angle DEC + \angle DCE + \angle EDC = 180°$. That is $\angle DEC$ + 50° + 70° = 180°. Therefore $\angle DEC = 60°$.

41. (C)—Percent Increase and Decrease

Math Appendix, #33. Jack lost $200 - $170 = $30.

$$\text{Percent} = \frac{\text{Part}}{\text{Whole}} \times 100\%$$

$$= \frac{\$30}{\$200} \times 100\% = 15\%$$

42.—(J)—Trigonometric Functions of Other Angles

Math Appendix, #98. Consider the unit circle:

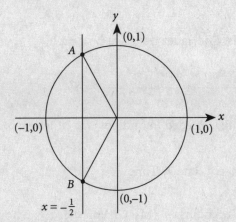

Cosine $x = -\frac{1}{2}$ for those values where $x = -\frac{1}{2}$ on the unit circle, in this case A and B. From the diagram, it can be seen that this occurs at $\frac{2\pi}{3}$ and $\frac{4\pi}{3}$.

43. (B)—Solving a Quadratic Equation

Math Appendix, #66. The fastest way to solve is by backsolving. Plug the answer choices into $5x^2 + 2x - 7$ and see which one equals 0:

(A) $5(-7)^2 + 2(-7) - 7 = 245 - 14 - 7 = 224$—Discard.

(B) $\qquad 5(-\frac{7}{5})^2 + 2(-\frac{7}{5}) - 7 = 5(\frac{49}{25}) - \frac{14}{5} - 7$

$$= \frac{49}{5} - \frac{14}{5} - 7$$

$$= \frac{35}{5} - 7$$

$$= 0$$

This is the correct answer.

44. (J)—Intersecting Lines, Parallel Lines and Transversals, Interior Angles of a Triangle, and Exterior Angle of a Triangle

Math Appendix, 78–81. It might help to redraw the diagram, extending lines:

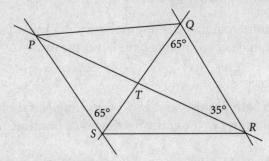

What you have is two parallel lines and two transversals. Since all acute angles that are formed by a transversal are the same size, $\angle PST = \angle TQR$. So $\triangle QRT$ has an interior angle of $65°(\angle TQR)$, and another of $35°(\angle QRT)$. Since the sum of interior angles in a triangle is $180°$, $\angle QTR = 180° - 65° - 35° = 80°$. Since $\angle QTR$ and $\angle PTQ$ are supplementary, that is, form a straight line, $\angle PTQ = 180° - \angle QTR = 180° - 80° = 100°$.

45. (C)—Rate

Math Appendix, #39. Let the rate that Ms. Rodriguez travels at be x mph.

The speed at which the cars were traveling is needed to find how far either car traveled.

Use the distance formula to find x:

$$\text{Distance} = \text{Rate} \times \text{Time}$$

In this case:

Distance $= (\text{Ms. Rodriguez's speed} \times 5 \text{ hours}) + (\text{Ms. Green's speed} \times 5 \text{ hours})$

475 miles $= (x \text{ mph} \times 5 \text{ hours}) + [(x + 15)\text{mph} \times 5 \text{ hours}]$

475 miles $= 5x$ miles $+ 5x$ miles $+ 75$ miles

475 miles $= 10x$ miles

$40 = x$

So Ms. Rodriguez drives at 40 mph, and Ms. Green at 55 mph.

In 5 hours the faster car will travel 55 mph $\times$ 5 hours $= 275$ miles.

46. (G)—Using an Equation to Find the Slope, Using an Equation to Find an Intercept

Math Appendix, #73, 74. If the equation of a line is expressed in the form $y = mx + b$, then m is the slope and b is the y-intercept. From the graph it can be seen that the slope is negative, since y decreases as x increases (any line that rises as you move right has a positive slope; any that falls off as you go right has a negative slope). So m is negative. Also from the graph, it can be seen that the line crosses the y-axis above the x-axis—that is, the y-intercept is positive—so b, the y-intercept, is positive. The only answer choice that agrees with this is answer choice G.

47. (B)—Solving an Equation that Includes Absolute Value Signs

Math Appendix, #68. If $xy \neq 0$ then $x \neq 0$ and $y \neq 0$.

The square of any nonzero number is positive, so x^2 and y^2 are positive.
The larger the magnitude of any number, the larger the square of that number.

So if $|y| < |x|$, that means $y^2 < x^2$.

Since x^2 and y^2 are also both positive, and $x^2 > y^2$, the numerator of the fraction $\frac{x^2}{y^2}$ will be greater than the denominator; i.e., the entire fraction must be greater than 1.

48. (J)—Evaluating an Algebraic Expression, Factoring the Square of a Binomial

Math Appendix, #52, 60. If you did not recognize the common quadratic $a^2 - 2ab + b^2 = (a - b)^2$, you could factor the expression $a^2 - 2ab + b^2$ using FOIL in reverse.

$a^2 - 2ab + b^2 = (a - b)(a - b) = (12)(12) = 144$

49. (E)—Translating From English Into Algebra; and Interior Angles of a Triangle

Math Appendix, #65, 80.

$\angle EDF = x$.

"$\angle DEF$ has a measure of 30° more than $\angle EDF$" means that $\angle DEF = x + 30$.

"$\angle EFD$ is 15° less than the sum of the measures of $\angle EDF$ and $\angle DEF$" means that $\angle EFD = (x + x + 30) - 15 = 2x + 15$.

50. (H)—Parallel Lines and Transversals

Math Appendix, #79. When a transversal cuts parallel lines, all acute angles formed are equal and all obtuse angles formed are equal.

So $\angle ATR = \angle CRP = 110°$

Since $\angle ATQ$ and $\angle ATR$ form a straight line, their sum is 180°.

So $\angle ATQ + 110° = 180°$

$\angle ATQ = 70°$

51. (E)—Simplifying Trigonometric Expressions

Math Appendix, #99. Since $\sin^2\theta + \cos^2\theta = 1$, for all values of θ, and $x = \sin\theta$ and $y = \cos\theta$, then $x^2 + y^2 = 1$.

52. (K)—Using an Equation to Find the Slope, Using an Equation to Find an Intercept

Math Appendix, #73, 74. All answer choices are in the slope-intercept form, $y = mx + b$, where m is the slope and b is the y-intercept.

Line T has a y-intercept of −3, so in this case $b = -3$. Discard answer choices F, H, and J.

Since T is parallel to $3x - 5y = 4$, they have the same slope. Find the slope of $3x - 5y = 4$:

$$3x - 5y = 4$$
$$-5y = -3x + 4$$
$$y = \frac{3}{5}x - \frac{4}{5}$$

So the slope is $\frac{3}{5}$ and line T has equation $y = \frac{3}{5}x - 3$.

53. (D)—Adding/Subtracting Signed Numbers

Math Appendix, #5. Simply count the number of spaces between A and B on the number line. If the distance is too great to count, in general the distance between any two points, A and B, is $|A - B|$.

54. (F)—Finding the Distance Between Two Points

Math Appendix, #71.

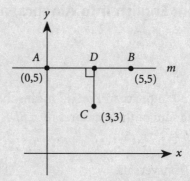

As can be seen from the diagram above, the shortest distance between C and line m is segment $\overline{CD}$. Since $\overline{CD}$ is parallel to the y-axis, the length of $\overline{CD}$ is the difference between the y-coordinates of D and C. Since line m is parallel to the x-axis, and passes through point $(0, 5)$, all points on line m have a y-coordinate of 5. Since C has a y-coordinate of 3, the distance CD is $5 - 3$, or 2.

55. (E)—Solving an Inequality

Math Appendix, #69. Rearrange the inequality:

$$-2 - 4x \leq -6x$$

Add 2 to both sides.	$-4x \leq -6x + 2$
Add $6x$ to both sides.	$2x \leq 2$
Divide both sides by 2.	$x \leq 1$

56. (H)—Areas of Special Quadrilaterals

Math Appendix, #87. The figure is a rectangle with two smaller rectangles cut out of it. The total area is the area of the large rectangle minus the area of the cutouts.

The area of any rectangle is length × width.
The area of the large rectangle = $8 \times 10 = 80$.
The area of the top cutout rectangle = $3 \times 4 = 12$.
The area of the bottom cutout rectangle = $3 \times 2 = 6$.
Total area = $80 - 12 - 6 = 62$.

57. (D)—Miscellaneous Quadrilaterals and Circles

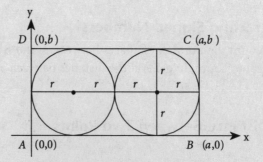

As can be seen from the above diagram, a is the distance between A and B, that is, the length of the rectangle $ABCD$. This is equal to $4r$.

Similarly, b is the distance between A and D, that is, $2r$.
So $a - b = 4r - 2r = 2r$.

58. (H)—Percent Formula

Math Appendix, #32. Find the number of teenagers in each age group:

"20 teenagers are 15 years old"—20, 15-year-olds

"8 teenagers are 18 years old"—8, 18-year-olds

"20% are 14 years old"—20% of $60 = \frac{1}{5} \times 60 = 12$—12, 14-year-olds

"There are twice as many 16-year-olds as 18-year-olds"—There are 8, 18-year-olds, so there are $2 \times 8 = 16$, 16-year-olds

Since there are 60 teenagers total, the remainder are 17 years old.

$60 - 20 - 8 - 12 - 16 = 4$, 17-year-olds.

There is a total of $4 + 8 = 12$, 17- and 18-year-olds.

Since Percent $= \frac{\text{Part}}{\text{Whole}} \times 100\%$, in this case Percent $= \frac{12}{60} \times 100\% = 20\%$.

59. (B)—Probability

Math Appendix, #46. Probability of an event occurring $= \frac{\text{Number of favorable outcomes}}{\text{Number of possible outcomes}}$

In this case, a favorable outcome is not picking a blue T-shirt. Since 7 T-shirts are not blue, the number of favorable outcomes is 7.

The number of outcomes is the total number of t-shirts that could be picked, that is, $5 + 7$, or 12.

So the probability of not picking a blue T-shirt $= \frac{7}{12}$.

60. (F)—Equation for an Ellipse

Math Appendix, #77. The correct equation will be true for all the points on the ellipse. Four points are given in the diagram. Run them through the equations in the answer choices; if the equation is not true for any one of these points, it may be discarded.

(F) Try $(0, 2)$; $\frac{x^2}{25} + \frac{y^2}{4} = \frac{0^2}{25} + \frac{2^2}{4} = \frac{4}{4} = 1$

Now try $(5, 0)$; $\frac{x^2}{25} + \frac{y^2}{4} = \frac{5^2}{25} + \frac{0^2}{4} = \frac{25}{25} = 1$

Now try $(-5, 0)$; $\frac{x^2}{25} + \frac{y^2}{4} = \frac{(-5)^2}{25} + \frac{0^2}{4} = \frac{25}{25} = 1$

Now try $(0, -2)$; $\frac{x^2}{25} + \frac{y^2}{4} = \frac{0^2}{25} + \frac{(-2)^2}{4} = \frac{4}{4} = 1$

Since the equation is true for all 4 points, this is the correct answer.

Reading Answer Key

1. D	11. C	21. A	31. D
2. F	12. G	22. J	32. J
3. B	13. B	23. D	33. D
4. H	14. H	24. G	34. G
5. D	15. C	25. B	35. A
6. G	16. H	26. H	36. H
7. A	17. B	27. D	37. A
8. H	18. F	28. H	38. F
9. B	19. A	29. D	39. C
10. F	20. J	30. F	40. J

PASSAGE I

Prose Fiction

This is a Prose Fiction passage, so remember to ask yourself the three important questions:

- *Who are these people?*

  George Webber is a young writer who has just heard that his novel has been accepted for publication.

- *What is their state of mind?*

  George is feeling many things at once: happiness about having a novel accepted for publication; fear that parts of the novel might offend some people; eagerness to see a chapter of his novel published in a magazine; dread at the prospect of writing a second novel; and disappointment when people did not react to his writing in the way he had expected.

- *What's going on?*

  George is going through some very mixed feelings. Although he is extremely excited about realizing his dream of becoming a writer, at the same time he's realizing that what is so momentous to him—the publication of his novel—is not really all that important to the rest of the world.

1. (D)—Inference Question

Remember to check back to the passage to make sure that your answer works in context. Lines 39–41 explain that George was concerned that "some people might recognize themselves and be offended." This is what made him think he might have "to go around in smoked glasses and false whiskers."

2. (F)—Detail Question

The sixth paragraph (lines 66–79) discusses George's feelings about writing his next novel. Lines 69–70 state that writing for him is "like a demoniacal possession, driving him with alien force much greater than his own." This idea is paraphrased by choice F.

3. (B)—Inference Question

The paragraph (lines 66–79) preceding the quote by George Webber to Foxhall Edwards explains the difficult, tortuous process that George goes through in writing. George probably sensed that his agony and fatigue would be obvious to Fox and others, but he knew that without this agony he would not be able to do good work. Line 68 especially shows that George knew that the act of writing would be painful—he would "get it out of him." Therefore, choice B best describes George's reason for offering the quote in question.

4. (H)—Inference Question

George "expected convulsions of the earth" (line 84) when his story was published. He had worried that "people might recognize themselves and be offended" (lines 40–41). Instead, "nothing happened. A few of his friends mentioned it, but that was all" (lines 86–87). No one was offended. For all the worrying and wondering that George did, the contrast between this calm public response and the anticipated response could be best characterized as "ironic."

5. (D)—Detail Question

Lines 59–63 discuss the very positive impact that Fox had on George. The text says that "the editor's faith and confidence, coming as it had come at a time when George had given up all hope, restored his self-respect and charged him with energy for new work." This idea is best summarized by choice D.

6. (G)—Detail Question

The last paragraph (lines 88–93) describes what happened when *Rodney's Magazine* came out with George's story. After an initial letdown (lines 86–87), George decided that "people couldn't really tell much about a new author from a short piece in a magazine. . . . He could afford to wait a little longer for the fame which he was certain would soon be his" (lines 88–93). Therefore, choice G best answers the question.

7. (A)—Detail Question

"Fame, at last, was knocking at his door and wooing him with her sweet blandishments" (lines 16–17). Typically, a suitor *woos* the object of his desire with gifts. In the previous paragraph we learned that George had just received a check for $500 as "an advance against his royalties" (lines 13–14) on a book he had written. This money could be considered fame's gift. The word *courting* in choice A best captures this concept of *wooing*.

8. (H)—Inference Question

The source of George's trembling (line 32) is explained in subsequent sentences. "He loathed the thought of giving pain to anyone. . . . But…some people might recognize themselves and be offended" (lines 36–41).

9. (B)—Inference Question

To select the correct choice for this difficult question, you must analyze George's behavior. George is very proud of his work. This can be inferred from several parts of the passage. Lines 30–31 are worded to convey his pride of authorship when they say, "He had distilled every line of it out of his own experiences of life." His extremely high (and unrealistic) expectations about the effect of having his story published in *Rodney's Magazine* (lines 83–85) also convey

George's belief that his work was very important. George did have concerns, though. The fourth paragraph discusses his worry that his fictional characterizations might offend the real people on which they were based. This pride mixed with concern is expressed in choice B.

10. (F)—Inference Question

When George is described early in this passage, the word *dazed* is used (in line 7). In lines 2–4 the reader learns that George has come "to his senses somewhere in the wilds of the Upper Bronx." In lines 12–14 the reader learns that the paper George was happily looking at earlier is a $500 royalty check. Therefore, you can infer that George has been wandering around dazed after learning that his book has been accepted for publication—choice F. Choice J might have been tempting, but it's the fact that his book will be published, not the money he'll earn from it, that makes George dazed and happy.

PASSAGE II

Humanities

This rather confusing passage deals with the connection between two "grand ideas": human self-fulfillment and freedom. Here's a road map to the passage:

- The **first and second paragraphs** provide some historical perspective about the ideal of human self-fulfillment.

- The **third paragraph** explains what the authors have in mind when they speak of human self-fulfillment.

- The **fourth paragraph** mentions that self-fulfillment has led to scientific and technical progress, which, in turn, has made individual self-fulfillment easier.

- The **fifth paragraph** discusses one thinker, Calvin, who did not believe in human self-fulfillment, and the consequences of this attitude.

- The **sixth and seventh paragraphs** tie together the ideals of human self-fulfillment and freedom, saying that the former is not possible without the latter, and introduces some historical examples to support this thesis.

- Finally, the **eighth paragraph** mentions some thinkers who distorted the idea of freedom, and the importance of freedom of thought and speech.

11. (C)—Big Picture Question

The passage talks about self-fulfillment and freedom and what these great ideas have inspired. Paragraph five begins with the sentence: "Only rarely has a thinker...gone back from the ideal of human potential and fulfillment." The next sentence, which introduces Calvin, says "Calvin was perhaps such a thinker who went back and believed. . . . that man [is]. . . . incapable of any worthwhile development" (lines 53–54). Calvin, therefore, is a counterexample offered to show that not everyone over the past five hundred years has believed in the ideals of self-fulfillment and human potential.

12. (G)—Detail Question

Reread the lines surrounding the word *elucidated* in line 25 to get its meaning. Lines 26–28 say "aesthetic and ethical gifts, we feel and struggle to express in our own minds." Lines 28–29 say "cultural gifts, are unfolded for us by the study of history." Considering this, "revealed," choice G, best captures this idea of unfolding and struggling to express gifts.

13. (B)—Big Picture Question

Lines 60–62 explain that "human fulfillment is unattainable without freedom, so that these two main ideas are linked together." The sixth paragraph begins talking about freedom by describing it as "the second of the two grand formative ideas." This follows the first five paragraphs which discuss fulfillment. This information supports B as the correct answer.

14. (H)—Detail Question

Lines 41–43 explain that, "The purpose and the effect [of devices and gadgets] has been to liberate men from the exhausting drudgeries of earning their living." Choice H best paraphrases these ideas.

15. (C)—Inference Question

Lines 46–47 indicate that, before the development of all sorts of work-saving devices and gadgets, princes alone had the "leisure to find the best in themselves."

16. (H)—Inference Question

In lines 82–84 the authors explain that "freedom . . . advocates can at times delude themselves that obedience to tyranny is a form of freedom." Therefore, the author's ideas are best expressed by choice H.

17. (B)—Big Picture Question

You can find the answer to this question by a process of elimination (remember, you're looking for the choice that the authors would *reject*). Choice A is supported by the discussion in paragraph four (lines 33–48): People are able to find the best in themselves when they have more leisure time. Choice C is supported by paragraph one (lines 1–12): The authors mention various people in diverse professions in various eras who have all praised the development of the individual. Choice D is supported in lines 57–58, where the authors contend that men develop by having something in them "which is personal and creative." This leaves choice B—nowhere in the text do the authors say or imply that "self-fulfillment is a praiseworthy but unreachable goal." Indeed the authors seem to believe that self-fulfillment is possible.

18. (F)—Big Picture Question

Lines 60–61 say that freedom is necessary for human fulfillment. Lines 33–34 talk about self-fulfillment inspiring progress. The final paragraph talks about the importance of freedom of thought and speech. Thus, the authors would undoubtedly contend that freedom is necessary for a society to make progress.

19. (A)—Detail Question

Lines 82–86 talk about the delusion that "ensnared" Luther, Rousseau, Hegel, and Marx. According to the authors, all of them confused freedom with obedience to tyranny. Choice A, therefore, is the answer.

20. (J)—Big Picture Question

The authors make it clear throughout the passage that they feel freedom is a valuable ideal. In the seventh paragraph, they suggest that revolutions have often made societies more free. Considering this, choice J is the best answer.

PASSAGE III

Social Studies

This well-organized passage is about Mussolini's rise to power in postwar Italy. A road map:

- The **first two paragraphs** discuss the territorial and economic problems that set the stage for Mussolini's rise to power.

- The **third paragraph** outlines the events that resulted in Mussolini's dictatorship.

- The **fourth and fifth paragraphs** explore Mussolini's economic and political philosophy.

21. (A)—Detail Question

Lines 5–9 talk about the lands that Italy obtained and hoped to obtain as it emerged from World War I. The author explains that in spite of being given land in Austria-Hungary, the Italians were disappointed not to be awarded "further acquisitions east of the Adriatic and in Asia and Africa." "Grandiose ambitions," therefore, refers to the desire for more land.

22. (J)—Big Picture Question

There is evidence in this passage to support all three of the statements. Lines 25–30 explain the reaction of landlords, factory owners, small businesses and professional people to the economic unrest in Italy following the war—they "longed for vigorous leadership and a strong government." In other words, they desired the stability that Mussolini's regime seemed to offer, as statement I suggests. Statement II also contributed to Mussolini's rise to power. Lines 51–52 explain that he seized "control of the faction-paralyzed government" in Rome. Statement III also was important. Lines 45–48 explain that Mussolini's veterans terrorized "the leaderless radical workers and their liberal supporters." The answer is choice J, which states that Statements I, II, and III were all important factors in Mussolini's rise to power.

23. (D)—Big Picture Question

The authors describe the rise of fascism in paragraphs 1 through 3. Paragraph 1 explains how the peace settlements following World War I resulted in "severe blows to Italian national pride" because Italy was awarded less land than it hoped for. This is discussed as the first of many problems that laid the groundwork for a new nationalistic, fascist leader like Mussolini to rise to power. So the way that the passage supports the theory (that fascism arises after periods of diminished national pride) is best stated by choice D.

24. (G)—Inference Question

From the text it seems that Mussolini had organized unemployed veterans into a political action group (lines 37–40) before the end of the labor disturbances in 1921. Mussolini eventually sent his veterans to beat up the radical workers and their supporters (lines 45–48) in an effort to get the support of the capitalists and the landlords (lines 43–44). However, he waited to do so until it became clear that the workers would lose (lines 41–42). The reason he waited to commit his group of veterans was that he wanted to join up with the side that would ultimately be victorious. This certainly sounds opportunistic to us.

25. (B)—Inference Question

The correct answer should convey the idea that Mussolini had absolute power over the citizens of Italy. Choice B—abolishing all non-Fascist unions—is the only choice that conveys Mussolini's control over the lives of individuals.

26. (H)—Inference Question

Lines 82–89 describe the role of nationalism in Mussolini's Italy. The authors explain that Mussolini used the "energizing quality" of militant nationalism for political purposes—to attract support for his new regime. Choice H paraphrases this idea best.

27. (D)—Inference Question

One aspect of Mussolini's rise that comes across in paragraphs 2 through 4 is his hard-line policy towards labor. Line 20 indicate that Italian workers were conducting sit-down factory strikes in 1920. By 1926 these workers were forbidden to strike and were subject to compulsory arbitration (lines 68–70). Choice D best states this crackdown on workers' rights.

28. (H)—Inference Question

The fourth paragraph talks about Italy's economic life under Mussolini's corporate state. Lines 76–81 describe the economic effects of Mussolini's policies—even though he balanced Italy's budget and stabilized its currency, taxes reached record levels, leading to a decline in per capita income. Choice H is the correct answer here—excessively high taxation disrupted economic rebuilding.

29. (D)—Detail Question

Lines 71–73 describe the corporate state as a "planned economy [that] was set up to modernize, coordinate, and increase Italy's production of both industrial and agricultural goods." Choice D best paraphrases this information.

30. (F)—Inference Question

In the final paragraph in lines 83–84 the authors contend that fascism was nationalism "run wild." The subsequent quotes are intended to provide an illustration of those nationalistic ideas.

Passage IV

Natural Sciences

The title of this wide-ranging passage could be: "Everything You Ever Wanted to Know About Tornadoes." Or perhaps "Everything You Never Wanted to Know About Tornadoes." In any case, it's all here:

- The **first paragraph** mentions the destructive power of tornado winds.

- The **second, third, fourth, and fifth paragraphs** talk about the formation, structure, and physical appearance of tornadoes.

- The **sixth paragraph** discusses where tornadoes are most likely to form, in a place called (appropriately enough) "tornado alley."

- The **seventh and eighth paragraphs** explain when and under what conditions tornadoes are likely to emerge.

- The **ninth paragraph** talks about the unpredictable movements of tornadoes and why this makes them difficult to track and study.

31. (D)—Detail Question

The term *vortexes of air* appears in line 11. The text immediately following the use of this term discusses the rotation of tornadoes, mentioning that air streams into the base and then spirals upward (lines 12–20).

32. (J)—Detail Question

Lines 5–8 explain that the wind speeds of tornadoes have been determined "based [in part] on analysis of motion pictures."

33. (D)—Inference Question

Tornado rotation is discussed in lines 12–15. The direction of rotation is based on the hemisphere in which the tornado occurs.

34. (G)—Inference Question

Lines 81–83 in the last paragraph describe "the unpredictable nature of tornadoes, which often hop about from place to place." Since scientists operate the TOTO device by placing it "in the path of the tornado," you can infer that the unpredictable movements of tornadoes might make TOTO hard to use.

35. (A)—Detail Question

Paragraphs seven and eight (lines 60–75) discuss the conditions required for tornadoes to form. Lines 66–67 explain the need for strong updrafts. Lines 69–72 explain the effect of wind shear on the initiation of tornado rotation. These two factors are listed in choice A.

36. (H)—Detail Question

Lines 70–72 explain what happens during wind shear—"wind speed increases with height and veers from southeast to west." Choice H accurately rewords this information.

37. (A)—Inference Question

Paragraphs seven and eight (lines 60–75) discuss the factors that determine the formation of tornadoes. These factors are based on weather conditions in the sky. You can infer from this information that it would be possible to predict the formation of tornadoes if these atmospheric conditions were known.

38. (F)—Detail Question

This question requires a careful reading of the text. At the end of paragraph three, the author describes the formation of funnel clouds—we're told that a pressure drop in the core of the cloud causes air to flow in, where it hits an area of lower pressure, and causes water vapor to condense into droplets. The term *condensation cloud* is never used to describe a funnel cloud in paragraph three. However, the terms are synonymous. This becomes clear when you read the beginning of paragraph four: "Sometimes, no condensation cloud forms" (line 33). So correct choice F accurately describes the formation of condensation clouds.

39. (C)—Big Picture Question

Paragraph three (lines 25–32) begins "The vortex frequently becomes visible" (line 25). Paragraph four begins "Sometimes . . . the only way a tornado can reveal itself" (lines 33–34). So both paragraphs address what makes a tornado visible. The answer is Choice C.

40. (J)—Big Picture Question

Line 76 states that tornadoes "are steered by the jet stream." Choice J is the answer. Based on information in the passage choices F, G, and H are not true of *all* tornadoes.

Science Reasoning Answer Key			
1. A	11. C	21. B	31. C
2. G	12. F	22. J	32. F
3. C	13. B	23. A	33. D
4. G	14. G	24. J	34. F
5. D	15. A	25. C	35. B
6. J	16. J	26. G	36. J
7. A	17. C	27. D	37. C
8. H	18. F	28. F	38. F
9. D	19. B	29. B	39. D
10. F	20. F	30. G	40. G

Passage I

The first passage mostly requires an ability to read the two given graphs, each of which traces the rate of decay in a different radioactive isotope. The *y*-axis of each graph represents the proportion of remaining (undecayed) nuclei to original nuclei, while the *x*-axis of each represents time. Notice, though, that the first graph runs from 0 days to just 6 days, while the second graph runs from 0 days to 180 days. That's a big difference, indicating that the second isotope—$_{39}Y^{91}$—decays at a much slower rate.

1. (A)

In the introduction to the passage, the "half-life" of an isotope is defined as the amount of time needed for one-half of the initial number of nuclei to decay. To figure out the half-life of $_{39}Y^{90}$, look at the first graph. When half of the nuclei have decayed, the N/N_0 ratio would be .5 (since there'd be half as many nuclei after the half-life as there were originally). Draw a horizontal line across the graph at the level of .5. The horizontal line will intersect the curve at a specific point; from this point, draw a vertical line down to the *x*-axis. The vertical line intersects the *x*-axis somewhere between 2.5 and 3 days, which means that the amount of time it takes for half of the nuclei to decay is between 2.5 and 3 days. Choice A is the only answer that falls in this range.

2. (G)

Since N_0 is the same for both samples, you can use the two graphs to figure out the ratio of $_{39}Y^{90}$ to $_{39}Y^{91}$ after 2.7 days. You know from having done the previous question that after 2.7 days about .5 of $_{39}Y^{90}$ still remains. Take a look at the graph for $_{39}Y^{91}$: After 2.7 days, hardly any will have decayed at all. Therefore, the ratio of $_{39}Y^{90}$ to $_{39}Y^{91}$ will be .5 to 1, or 1 to 2 (G).

3. (C)

This is a rather strange, convoluted question, but what it means is that one isotope $(_{39}Y^{90})$ will accumulate in the gastrointestinal tract while the other $(_{39}Y^{91})$ will accumulate in the bones. Since none of the isotopes leave the bones or the gastrointestinal tract as a result of processes that normally occur in the human body, you can use the values for the half-lives given in the graphs. So after three days, a little over half of the original $_{39}Y^{90}$ will be left (in the gastrointestinal tract), but just about all of the $_{39}Y^{91}$ will be left (in the bones). With this information in hand, you just have to examine the choices. Choice A is incorrect because $_{39}Y^{91}$ accumulates in the bones, not the gastrointestinal tract. Choice B is incorrect since $_{39}Y^{90}$ accumulates in the gastrointestinal tract, not in the bones. Choice C is correct because, as we said, about half of the nuclei of $_{39}Y^{90}$ decay after 3 days, so about half of the inhaled amount will be in the gastrointestinal tract after 3 days. Choice D is out because after 3 days, almost all of the $_{39}Y^{91}$ will be left in the bones.

4. (G)

After one half-life has passed, half of the original 1,000 nuclei will have decayed, leaving 500. After the second half-life has passed, half of the 500 will be gone, leaving 250. When the third half-life has passed, half of the 250 will have decayed, leaving 125, choice G.

5. (D)

Statement I is true: $_{39}Y^{90}$ is less stable than $_{39}Y^{91}$ because $_{39}Y^{90}$ decays more rapidly (remember that the *x*-axes are scaled differently). This rules out choice B. Statement II is wrong because a very small fraction (much less than a quarter) of $_{39}Y^{90}$ would remain after 116 days. Choice C can thus also be eliminated. Statement III is obviously true, given the fact that they decay in this manner, making D the correct answer.

Passage II

This passage involves three tennis-training experiments, the results of each being summarized in a table. Remember to look for patterns in the data. Notice, for instance, that in Table 1 the greatest increases in serving speed were obtained when right-handed players watched a right-handed coach and when left-handed players watched a left-handed coach. Similarly, in Table 2, coach guidance caused higher increases in *both* serving speed and serving accuracy. This kind of observation about the data should help you to formulate theories (e.g., that training is more effective when the coach uses the same hand as the player).

6. (J)

In Experiment 1, left-handed video watchers watching a left-handed coach improved their service speed by 8 mph. Since right-handed players in Experiment 3 (the one asked about here) improved even more with a combination of videos and physical instruction than with videos alone, lefties will probably improve at least as much in Experiment 3 as they did in Experiment 1, making choice J the right answer.

7. (A)

Choice A is the only conclusion that cannot be supported by the data of Experiment 1. Imitating someone with opposite handedness does not always cause a deterioration of skills: Right-handed players actually improved somewhat when they watched videos of left-handed coaches.

8. (H)

Experiment 2 was designed to determine whether right-handed players improve more with videos alone or with videos and physical guidance combined. The players given a combination of videos and guidance clearly showed greater improvement in both service speed and service accuracy as compared to those who just used videos. This supports the hypothesis (choice H) that physical guidance by a coach improves both speed and accuracy of service for right-handed players. (Note: There is nothing in Experiment 2 to support any conclusion whatsoever about left-handed players, since none were involved in the experiment.)

9. (D)

In Experiments 1 and 2, right-handed players who watched a right-handed coach on video improved 5 mph in speed. According to Experiment 2, right-handed players who watched videos and received physical guidance improved by 9 mph (4 mph more than with videos alone). Guidance appears to further improve service speed. Since left-handers improve by 8 mph with videos alone (Experiment 1), adding physical guidance to their training should make their overall improvement in service speed greater than 8 mph. The only choice greater than 8 mph is D.

10. (F)

Experiment 1 investigated the effect of watching videos of left- or right-handed coaches on the service speed of left- or right-handed players. The results support the conclusion in choice F. Players watching videos of coaches with the same handedness improved their speeds by 5 mph (righties) and 8 mph (lefties), whereas players watching videos of coaches with the opposite handedness improved their speed only a little (2 mph for righties) or not at all (for lefties). Tennis players seem to improve less when observing coaches whose handedness is opposite to their own.

11. (C)

Choice C is the best procedure to determine the effects of verbal instruction on average service speed because it measures he amount of improvement that is due solely to verbal instruction. In addition, all of the players receive the exact same verbal instruction, since the instructions have been recorded (personal verbal instruction may vary considerably). Choice A's procedure is not optimal because Experiment 3 involves the factors of videos and physical guidance as well as verbal instruction. Choice B's procedure involves physical guidance so it is also not ideal. Choice D's procedure does not measure the players' service speed before instruction, so there is no way to gauge improvement.

Passage III

This passage hinges on the Hertzsprung-Russell diagram, which plots individual stars in terms of their absolute magnitude (brightness, in other words) on the y-axis, and their spectral class (which is a measure of color/temperature) on the x-axis. What does this mean? It means that stars that are high on the chart are brighter than those that are low on the chart (because the greater the number for absolute magnitude, the dimmer the star). It also means that stars that are on the right side of the chart (which most of them are) are M class (i.e., the reddest and coolest), while those toward the left side of the chart are the bluest and warmest.

12. (F)

Nearly all of the stars on the diagram fall in the spectral class M, so choice F is correct.

13. (B)

The text explains that the spectral classes of stars on the diagram go from warmest on the left (O) to coolest on the right (M). Therefore, any stars in a spectral class to the left of G, the Sun's spectral class, are warmer than the Sun. Of the three named stars, only two are in a spectral class to the left of G: Sirius and Altair.

14. (G)

Most of the stars on the diagram fall below the absolute magnitude of 6; that is, they would not be visible to the naked eye from a distance of 10 parsecs. (Remember that 1.0 is the maximum brightness and that stars with absolute magnitudes of 15.0 to 17. 0 are very dim.)

15. (A)

A quick review: Moving across the spectral classes from left to right, the stars go from warm to cool and from blue to red. Statement I is correct because α-Centauri is in a spectral class to the right of Sirius' spectral class. This means that you can eliminate choices B and D, which do not contain Statement I. Statement II is incorrect because the Sun is to the right of Altair on the diagram, indicating that the Sun is cooler. This eliminates choice C. Choice A is the correct answer, and you don't even have to look at Statement III (though if you do, you'll find that it's incorrect, since the Sun is lower on the diagram than is Procyon).

16. (J)

It's impossible to know what the diagram of stars within 10 parsecs of the Sun would look like, even though you have the graph of the stars within 5 parsecs of the sun in front of you. It may be tempting to assume that by doubling the distance the number of stars would be doubled as well (F). However, when you double the distance from the Sun, you more than double the volume of space; there may be, for all you know, many more than double the original number of stars on the new diagram. There is similarly no basis on which to judge the absolute magnitude or the spectral class of the additional stars (G and H).

Passage IV

This passage is based around three different experiments, all designed to determine what conditions favor Product A and what conditions favor Product B when a particular cobalt complex reacts with sodium nitrite. Remember to note the differences in the procedures of the three experiments. Experiment 2 differs from Experiment 1 in that the solutions were heated after $NaNO_2$ was added. Experiment 3 differs from Experiment 1 in that after $NaNO_2$ was added, citrate ion was added and the solutions were heated.

17. (C)

To answer this question, look at the conditions in which Product B was formed. Solution 1 in Experiment 1 and Solution 1 in Experiment 2 both yielded Product B. These solutions were both acidic, so the correct answer must be either choice B or choice C. The next step is to determine whether Product B was formed when citrate ion was added. The results of Experiment 3 show that there is no yield of Product B with added citrate ion, so choice C is the correct answer.

18. (F)

Choice F is the conclusion that is not supported by the experimental results. As you know from the previous question, Product B is not formed when citrate ion is added to the solution. Since it does form in the same solution if no citrate ion is added (Experiment 2), the presence of citrate ion does indeed affect the formation of Product B. All of the other choices are legitimate conclusions based on the experimental data.

19. (B)

Varying the pH (choice B) may well show that different degrees of acidity or basicity will have a marked impact on product formation. Heating the solutions has been tried already, and freezing the solutions should stop the reactions altogether. Varying the concentration, meanwhile, won't alter the ability of the known compound to react.

20. (F)

When you're answering a question that's based on only part of the data, make sure that the answer you choose is based only on the relevant data. In Experiment 2, it was found that when the solutions were heated to 110° C, both Product A and Product B were formed. Therefore, choice F is supported by the results of Experiment 2. All of the other choices are hypotheses that could only be supported or refuted using the results of Experiments 1 and 3 along with the results of Experiment 2.

21. (B)

This question asks you to identify the condition or conditions that are held constant through all three experiments. The temperature was varied, ruling out choice A, and the amount of citrate ion was not the same in all three experiments, so you can eliminate choices C and D. Only choice B remains. You are never told the specific quantity of cobalt complex used, but you can assume it was the same in all three experiments since the solutions of Experiments 2 and 3 were prepared just as they were in Experiment 1.

22. (J)

The fact that Product B is formed in Solution 1 when heated but is not formed when citrate ion is added prior to heating (J) is evidence to support the hypothesis that Product B may react to form other more readily dissolved compounds in the presence of certain ions. None of the other choices involves the presence of any type of ion.

Passage V

This is the conflicting viewpoints passage; the viewpoints that are in question are different suggested classifications for the giant panda—as a raccoon or as a bear. Examine the scientists' positions carefully. Scientist 1 votes for a raccoon classification, citing as evidence anatomical similarities, comparable size among males and females, similar noises and eye-covering behavior, and certain chromosomal similarities. Scientist 2 votes for a bear classification, citing evidence such as DNA similarities, similar body proportions, and aggressive behavior.

23. (A)

In this question you are asked to determine which of the four choices would provide additional support for the viewpoint expressed by Scientist 2. Similarities between the blood proteins of giant pandas and several bear species (A) would certainly indicate that pandas should be classified as bears, which is Scientist 2's viewpoint. Watch out for choices that support the other position in questions like this: Choices B and D, for instance, are wrong because they support Scientist 1's argument that pandas should be classified as raccoons, not bears. Choice C, meanwhile, is inconclusive.

24. (J)

Both scientists make their arguments by comparing the physical, behavioral, and genetic characteristics of the giant panda to the characteristics of either the bear or the raccoon family. They would definitely agree that animals should be classified into families based on these criteria.

25. (C)

Let's take a look at the statements. You know from Scientist 1's statement that *Ursidae* (bears) have 36 pairs of chromosomes, so Statement I would support the classification of the mammal as a bear. This narrows the possible choices down to A and C. You also know from Scientist 1 that male bears can be twice the size of female bears, whereas male and female raccoons are the same size. Statement III, therefore, also supports the classification of the mammal as a bear. Choice C is the right choice, and you don't even have to look at Statement II (which would argue *against* a classification as a bear).

26. (G)

Scientist 1 explains that both raccoons and pandas cover their eyes with their front paws whenever intimidated.

27. (D)

Scientist 2 mentions that research has shown that the giant panda's DNA is far more similar to a bear's DNA than to that of any other family. Choice D paraphrases this idea.

28. (F)

If giant pandas and raccoons both had glandular scent areas, this would be evidence to support the viewpoint of Scientist 1, who thinks that giant pandas should be classified as raccoons.

29. (B)

Scientist 2 contends that giant pandas display the same aggressive behavior as bears do: They swat and try to grab adversaries with their forepaws. The only choice that is a counter argument to this claim is B: An aggressive panda's behavior is like a raccoon's behavior, not a bear's, in that the panda bobs its head up and down like a raccoon.

Passage VI

This passage consists almost exclusively of a complex bar graph recording primary energy sources at various times in history—namely, 1850, 1900, 1950, and 1985. Notice the changing proportions. Fuel wood, which was an extremely important source of energy in 1850, virtually disappeared by 1950 and 1985. Petroleum, on the other hand, which barely registers on the 1900 graph (and not at all on the 1850 graph) has by 1985 become the dominant source of energy. One reasonable conclusion to be drawn from these data trends? As technology changes over time, the fuels of choice seem to change as well.

30. (G)

Petroleum first appears on the graph as an energy source in 1900 and accounts for an increasingly greater percentage of total energy consumption in 1950 and 1985, judging by the increasing size of the petroleum portion of the bar. The portion of the bar representing coal, on the other hand, decreases from 1900 to 1950 and again from 1950 to 1985.

31. (C)

Focus on the coal portion of each bar. Coal was an energy source in 1850, so the ability to utilize it was developed well before the 1900s—choice A is wrong. The graph tells you nothing about mechanized mining techniques, so choice B is out, too. To choose between choices C and D you have to determine if the use of coal predated natural gas or vice versa. The first time coal appears on the graph is 1850, while the first time natural gas appears on the graph is 1900. Therefore, the use of coal must have predated the use of natural gas, making C the correct choice.

32. (F)

The portion of the bar that includes farm animals as an energy source is over 30 percent of the total in 1850, but it gets smaller in 1900 and 1950 until it disappears altogether by 1985. Choice F is the correct answer.

33. (D)

Compare the bars for 1900 and 1950. Choice A is wrong because the number of major energy sources was the same (six) in 1900 as in 1950. Choice B is out for reasons discussed in the previous question. Since coal, not natural gas, has the largest portion of the bar for 1950 (as it did for 1900), choice D is the correct answer.

34. (F)

Statement I is supported by the graph because nuclear power, natural gas, and petroleum were all energy sources in 1985 that did not exist in 1850. The graph does not support Statements II or III, however. Coal was not the largest source of energy in 1850 or 1985, which rules out

II, and there is no way to know from the graph whether there is indeed a short supply of petroleum, so III is out. This makes choice F the correct answer.

Passage VII

The scientists conducting the two experiments in this last passage might have a little trouble with animal-rights advocates if they're not careful. They apparently spend their days chopping body parts off of starfish and watching what happens. The results are recorded in two tables. Basically, the data in Table 1 seem to indicate that the bigger the chunk of a starfish you cut off, the longer it takes for the remaining starfish to regenerate the missing part (nothing surprising there). But starfish are strange creatures, and sometimes their missing parts themselves can regenerate into full starfish. That's what Table 2 records. Here, the data indicate that the smaller the chopped-off body part, the less likely it is to regenerate into a full starfish (and the more likely it is to be dead after a year). The general lesson to be learned here is that the bigger the chunk of starfish you have left, the more likely it is that it will eventually regenerate into a whole, live starfish. Now aren't you glad to know that?

35. (B)

According to the bottom row of Table 1, 12 of the starfish that had 2 arms and 1/3 of their body removed were fully regenerated after 6 months. Since each group started out with 25 starfish, 12 out of 25 starfish, or roughly 50 percent, regenerated 2 entire arms and part of the central body after 6 months. Choice B is correct.

36. (J)

In Experiment 2 certain body portions of *Asterias rubens* were allowed to regenerate. The number of whole starfish was recorded at 3-month intervals over the course of a year. According to the table of the results, no starfish was regenerated when only the lower arm was present. This would support the conclusion in choice J—that regeneration is dependent upon the existence of a portion of the central body. The results of Experiment 1 are not relevant to this conclusion, so choice J is the correct answer. The conclusion in choice H, that some starfish die from confinement in lab tanks, is not supported by the results of Experiment 2, since no healthy starfish were studied. In order to conclude that starfish die from confinement in lab tanks and not as a result of amputating portions of their bodies, the scientists would have to study starfish with intact bodies as they did in Experiment 1. You are only supposed to consider the results of Experiment 2 here, so choice H is not correct.

37. (C)

There is no mention of water depth in the passage, the experiments, or the results, so Statement I is out. This means that you can eliminate choices A and D since both of them include Statement I. Statement II is supported by the experimental results that show starfish can regenerate limbs they have lost (how they lose them doesn't matter). Since Statement II is true, choice C must be the answer. Although it would not be necessary at this point to verify that Statement III is true, the data indicate that if a body part that includes some of the central body is broken off from a starfish, the part will regenerate to become an entirely new, separate starfish. This would increase the population of starfish, so Statement III is correct.

38. (F)

Look back quickly at Table 1. The starfish in the first group were whole throughout the experiment—nothing was chopped off, in other words. The group acted as a control for the experiment in that the effect of the artificial environment could be measured apart from the effect of amputation. Three intact starfish in Group 1 died solely from being kept in lab tanks. If this group had not been included in the experiment, the deaths of starfish in other groups would have been attributed solely to the effect of amputation. Choice F is the correct answer.

39. (D)

As the question indicates, the sum of fully regenerated starfish plus dead starfish does not equal 25 for the last two rows of Table 2. Partially regenerated, living starfish would be omitted from this count, which makes choice D the correct explanation.

40. (G)

You know from Experiment 2 that starfish body parts can regenerate into whole starfish over time as long as there is a portion of the central body present. Immediate skyrocketing of the population (F) is not possible due to the amount of time it takes for starfish to regenerate. Choice J is wrong because some pieces will not contain portions of the central body and therefore will not regenerate. Choice G takes the time factor into account as well as the evidence from Experiment 2 that some pieces do not undergo regeneration, so choice G is the correct answer.

ACT Practice Test 2
Answer Sheet

ENGLISH TEST

	10 Ⓕ Ⓖ Ⓗ Ⓙ	20 Ⓕ Ⓖ Ⓗ Ⓙ	30 Ⓕ Ⓖ Ⓗ Ⓙ	40 Ⓕ Ⓖ Ⓗ Ⓙ	50 Ⓕ Ⓖ Ⓗ Ⓙ	60 Ⓕ Ⓖ Ⓗ Ⓙ	70 Ⓕ Ⓖ Ⓗ Ⓙ
1 Ⓐ Ⓑ Ⓒ Ⓓ	11 Ⓐ Ⓑ Ⓒ Ⓓ	21 Ⓐ Ⓑ Ⓒ Ⓓ	31 Ⓐ Ⓑ Ⓒ Ⓓ	41 Ⓐ Ⓑ Ⓒ Ⓓ	51 Ⓐ Ⓑ Ⓒ Ⓓ	61 Ⓐ Ⓑ Ⓒ Ⓓ	71 Ⓐ Ⓑ Ⓒ Ⓓ
2 Ⓕ Ⓖ Ⓗ Ⓙ	12 Ⓕ Ⓖ Ⓗ Ⓙ	22 Ⓕ Ⓖ Ⓗ Ⓙ	32 Ⓕ Ⓖ Ⓗ Ⓙ	42 Ⓕ Ⓖ Ⓗ Ⓙ	52 Ⓕ Ⓖ Ⓗ Ⓙ	62 Ⓕ Ⓖ Ⓗ Ⓙ	72 Ⓕ Ⓖ Ⓗ Ⓙ
3 Ⓐ Ⓑ Ⓒ Ⓓ	13 Ⓐ Ⓑ Ⓒ Ⓓ	23 Ⓐ Ⓑ Ⓒ Ⓓ	33 Ⓐ Ⓑ Ⓒ Ⓓ	43 Ⓐ Ⓑ Ⓒ Ⓓ	53 Ⓐ Ⓑ Ⓒ Ⓓ	63 Ⓐ Ⓑ Ⓒ Ⓓ	73 Ⓐ Ⓑ Ⓒ Ⓓ
4 Ⓕ Ⓖ Ⓗ Ⓙ	14 Ⓕ Ⓖ Ⓗ Ⓙ	24 Ⓕ Ⓖ Ⓗ Ⓙ	34 Ⓕ Ⓖ Ⓗ Ⓙ	44 Ⓕ Ⓖ Ⓗ Ⓙ	54 Ⓕ Ⓖ Ⓗ Ⓙ	64 Ⓕ Ⓖ Ⓗ Ⓙ	74 Ⓕ Ⓖ Ⓗ Ⓙ
5 Ⓐ Ⓑ Ⓒ Ⓓ	15 Ⓐ Ⓑ Ⓒ Ⓓ	25 Ⓐ Ⓑ Ⓒ Ⓓ	35 Ⓐ Ⓑ Ⓒ Ⓓ	45 Ⓐ Ⓑ Ⓒ Ⓓ	55 Ⓐ Ⓑ Ⓒ Ⓓ	65 Ⓐ Ⓑ Ⓒ Ⓓ	75 Ⓐ Ⓑ Ⓒ Ⓓ
6 Ⓕ Ⓖ Ⓗ Ⓙ	16 Ⓕ Ⓖ Ⓗ Ⓙ	26 Ⓕ Ⓖ Ⓗ Ⓙ	36 Ⓕ Ⓖ Ⓗ Ⓙ	46 Ⓕ Ⓖ Ⓗ Ⓙ	56 Ⓕ Ⓖ Ⓗ Ⓙ	66 Ⓕ Ⓖ Ⓗ Ⓙ	
7 Ⓐ Ⓑ Ⓒ Ⓓ	17 Ⓐ Ⓑ Ⓒ Ⓓ	27 Ⓐ Ⓑ Ⓒ Ⓓ	37 Ⓐ Ⓑ Ⓒ Ⓓ	47 Ⓐ Ⓑ Ⓒ Ⓓ	57 Ⓐ Ⓑ Ⓒ Ⓓ	67 Ⓐ Ⓑ Ⓒ Ⓓ	
8 Ⓕ Ⓖ Ⓗ Ⓙ	18 Ⓕ Ⓖ Ⓗ Ⓙ	28 Ⓕ Ⓖ Ⓗ Ⓙ	38 Ⓕ Ⓖ Ⓗ Ⓙ	48 Ⓕ Ⓖ Ⓗ Ⓙ	58 Ⓕ Ⓖ Ⓗ Ⓙ	68 Ⓕ Ⓖ Ⓗ Ⓙ	
9 Ⓐ Ⓑ Ⓒ Ⓓ	19 Ⓐ Ⓑ Ⓒ Ⓓ	29 Ⓐ Ⓑ Ⓒ Ⓓ	39 Ⓐ Ⓑ Ⓒ Ⓓ	49 Ⓐ Ⓑ Ⓒ Ⓓ	59 Ⓐ Ⓑ Ⓒ Ⓓ	69 Ⓐ Ⓑ Ⓒ Ⓓ	

MATH TEST

	8 Ⓕ Ⓖ Ⓗ Ⓙ Ⓚ	16 Ⓕ Ⓖ Ⓗ Ⓙ Ⓚ	24 Ⓕ Ⓖ Ⓗ Ⓙ Ⓚ	32 Ⓕ Ⓖ Ⓗ Ⓙ Ⓚ	40 Ⓕ Ⓖ Ⓗ Ⓙ Ⓚ	48 Ⓕ Ⓖ Ⓗ Ⓙ Ⓚ	56 Ⓕ Ⓖ Ⓗ Ⓙ Ⓚ
1 Ⓐ Ⓑ Ⓒ Ⓓ Ⓔ	9 Ⓐ Ⓑ Ⓒ Ⓓ Ⓔ	17 Ⓐ Ⓑ Ⓒ Ⓓ Ⓔ	25 Ⓐ Ⓑ Ⓒ Ⓓ Ⓔ	33 Ⓐ Ⓑ Ⓒ Ⓓ Ⓔ	41 Ⓐ Ⓑ Ⓒ Ⓓ Ⓔ	49 Ⓐ Ⓑ Ⓒ Ⓓ Ⓔ	57 Ⓐ Ⓑ Ⓒ Ⓓ Ⓔ
2 Ⓕ Ⓖ Ⓗ Ⓙ Ⓚ	10 Ⓕ Ⓖ Ⓗ Ⓙ Ⓚ	18 Ⓕ Ⓖ Ⓗ Ⓙ Ⓚ	26 Ⓕ Ⓖ Ⓗ Ⓙ Ⓚ	34 Ⓕ Ⓖ Ⓗ Ⓙ Ⓚ	42 Ⓕ Ⓖ Ⓗ Ⓙ Ⓚ	50 Ⓕ Ⓖ Ⓗ Ⓙ Ⓚ	58 Ⓕ Ⓖ Ⓗ Ⓙ Ⓚ
3 Ⓐ Ⓑ Ⓒ Ⓓ Ⓔ	11 Ⓐ Ⓑ Ⓒ Ⓓ Ⓔ	19 Ⓐ Ⓑ Ⓒ Ⓓ Ⓔ	27 Ⓐ Ⓑ Ⓒ Ⓓ Ⓔ	35 Ⓐ Ⓑ Ⓒ Ⓓ Ⓔ	43 Ⓐ Ⓑ Ⓒ Ⓓ Ⓔ	51 Ⓐ Ⓑ Ⓒ Ⓓ Ⓔ	59 Ⓐ Ⓑ Ⓒ Ⓓ Ⓔ
4 Ⓕ Ⓖ Ⓗ Ⓙ Ⓚ	12 Ⓕ Ⓖ Ⓗ Ⓙ Ⓚ	20 Ⓕ Ⓖ Ⓗ Ⓙ Ⓚ	28 Ⓕ Ⓖ Ⓗ Ⓙ Ⓚ	36 Ⓕ Ⓖ Ⓗ Ⓙ Ⓚ	44 Ⓕ Ⓖ Ⓗ Ⓙ Ⓚ	52 Ⓕ Ⓖ Ⓗ Ⓙ Ⓚ	60 Ⓕ Ⓖ Ⓗ Ⓙ Ⓚ
5 Ⓐ Ⓑ Ⓒ Ⓓ Ⓔ	13 Ⓐ Ⓑ Ⓒ Ⓓ Ⓔ	21 Ⓐ Ⓑ Ⓒ Ⓓ Ⓔ	29 Ⓐ Ⓑ Ⓒ Ⓓ Ⓔ	37 Ⓐ Ⓑ Ⓒ Ⓓ Ⓔ	45 Ⓐ Ⓑ Ⓒ Ⓓ Ⓔ	53 Ⓐ Ⓑ Ⓒ Ⓓ Ⓔ	
6 Ⓕ Ⓖ Ⓗ Ⓙ Ⓚ	14 Ⓕ Ⓖ Ⓗ Ⓙ Ⓚ	22 Ⓕ Ⓖ Ⓗ Ⓙ Ⓚ	30 Ⓕ Ⓖ Ⓗ Ⓙ Ⓚ	38 Ⓕ Ⓖ Ⓗ Ⓙ Ⓚ	46 Ⓕ Ⓖ Ⓗ Ⓙ Ⓚ	54 Ⓕ Ⓖ Ⓗ Ⓙ Ⓚ	
7 Ⓐ Ⓑ Ⓒ Ⓓ Ⓔ	15 Ⓐ Ⓑ Ⓒ Ⓓ Ⓔ	23 Ⓐ Ⓑ Ⓒ Ⓓ Ⓔ	31 Ⓐ Ⓑ Ⓒ Ⓓ Ⓔ	39 Ⓐ Ⓑ Ⓒ Ⓓ Ⓔ	47 Ⓐ Ⓑ Ⓒ Ⓓ Ⓔ	55 Ⓐ Ⓑ Ⓒ Ⓓ Ⓔ	

READING TEST

	6 Ⓕ Ⓖ Ⓗ Ⓙ	12 Ⓕ Ⓖ Ⓗ Ⓙ	18 Ⓕ Ⓖ Ⓗ Ⓙ	24 Ⓕ Ⓖ Ⓗ Ⓙ	30 Ⓕ Ⓖ Ⓗ Ⓙ	36 Ⓕ Ⓖ Ⓗ Ⓙ
1 Ⓐ Ⓑ Ⓒ Ⓓ	7 Ⓐ Ⓑ Ⓒ Ⓓ	13 Ⓐ Ⓑ Ⓒ Ⓓ	19 Ⓐ Ⓑ Ⓒ Ⓓ	25 Ⓐ Ⓑ Ⓒ Ⓓ	31 Ⓐ Ⓑ Ⓒ Ⓓ	37 Ⓐ Ⓑ Ⓒ Ⓓ
2 Ⓕ Ⓖ Ⓗ Ⓙ	8 Ⓕ Ⓖ Ⓗ Ⓙ	14 Ⓕ Ⓖ Ⓗ Ⓙ	20 Ⓕ Ⓖ Ⓗ Ⓙ	26 Ⓕ Ⓖ Ⓗ Ⓙ	32 Ⓕ Ⓖ Ⓗ Ⓙ	38 Ⓕ Ⓖ Ⓗ Ⓙ
3 Ⓐ Ⓑ Ⓒ Ⓓ	9 Ⓐ Ⓑ Ⓒ Ⓓ	15 Ⓐ Ⓑ Ⓒ Ⓓ	21 Ⓐ Ⓑ Ⓒ Ⓓ	27 Ⓐ Ⓑ Ⓒ Ⓓ	33 Ⓐ Ⓑ Ⓒ Ⓓ	39 Ⓐ Ⓑ Ⓒ Ⓓ
4 Ⓕ Ⓖ Ⓗ Ⓙ	10 Ⓕ Ⓖ Ⓗ Ⓙ	16 Ⓕ Ⓖ Ⓗ Ⓙ	22 Ⓕ Ⓖ Ⓗ Ⓙ	28 Ⓕ Ⓖ Ⓗ Ⓙ	34 Ⓕ Ⓖ Ⓗ Ⓙ	40 Ⓕ Ⓖ Ⓗ Ⓙ
5 Ⓐ Ⓑ Ⓒ Ⓓ	11 Ⓐ Ⓑ Ⓒ Ⓓ	17 Ⓐ Ⓑ Ⓒ Ⓓ	23 Ⓐ Ⓑ Ⓒ Ⓓ	29 Ⓐ Ⓑ Ⓒ Ⓓ	35 Ⓐ Ⓑ Ⓒ Ⓓ	

SCIENCE TEST

	6 Ⓕ Ⓖ Ⓗ Ⓙ	12 Ⓕ Ⓖ Ⓗ Ⓙ	18 Ⓕ Ⓖ Ⓗ Ⓙ	24 Ⓕ Ⓖ Ⓗ Ⓙ	30 Ⓕ Ⓖ Ⓗ Ⓙ	36 Ⓕ Ⓖ Ⓗ Ⓙ
1 Ⓐ Ⓑ Ⓒ Ⓓ	7 Ⓐ Ⓑ Ⓒ Ⓓ	13 Ⓐ Ⓑ Ⓒ Ⓓ	19 Ⓐ Ⓑ Ⓒ Ⓓ	25 Ⓐ Ⓑ Ⓒ Ⓓ	31 Ⓐ Ⓑ Ⓒ Ⓓ	37 Ⓐ Ⓑ Ⓒ Ⓓ
2 Ⓕ Ⓖ Ⓗ Ⓙ	8 Ⓕ Ⓖ Ⓗ Ⓙ	14 Ⓕ Ⓖ Ⓗ Ⓙ	20 Ⓕ Ⓖ Ⓗ Ⓙ	26 Ⓕ Ⓖ Ⓗ Ⓙ	32 Ⓕ Ⓖ Ⓗ Ⓙ	38 Ⓕ Ⓖ Ⓗ Ⓙ
3 Ⓐ Ⓑ Ⓒ Ⓓ	9 Ⓐ Ⓑ Ⓒ Ⓓ	15 Ⓐ Ⓑ Ⓒ Ⓓ	21 Ⓐ Ⓑ Ⓒ Ⓓ	27 Ⓐ Ⓑ Ⓒ Ⓓ	33 Ⓐ Ⓑ Ⓒ Ⓓ	39 Ⓐ Ⓑ Ⓒ Ⓓ
4 Ⓕ Ⓖ Ⓗ Ⓙ	10 Ⓕ Ⓖ Ⓗ Ⓙ	16 Ⓕ Ⓖ Ⓗ Ⓙ	22 Ⓕ Ⓖ Ⓗ Ⓙ	28 Ⓕ Ⓖ Ⓗ Ⓙ	34 Ⓕ Ⓖ Ⓗ Ⓙ	40 Ⓕ Ⓖ Ⓗ Ⓙ
5 Ⓐ Ⓑ Ⓒ Ⓓ	11 Ⓐ Ⓑ Ⓒ Ⓓ	17 Ⓐ Ⓑ Ⓒ Ⓓ	23 Ⓐ Ⓑ Ⓒ Ⓓ	29 Ⓐ Ⓑ Ⓒ Ⓓ	35 Ⓐ Ⓑ Ⓒ Ⓓ	

ENGLISH TEST

45 Minutes—75 Questions

Directions: In the following five passages, certain words and phrases have been underlined and numbered. You will find alternatives for each underlined portion in the right-hand column. Select the one that best expresses the idea, that makes the statement acceptable in standard written English, or that is phrased most consistently with the style and tone of the entire passage. If you feel that the original version is best, select "NO CHANGE." You will also find questions asking about a section of the passage or about the entire passage. For these questions, decide which choice gives the most appropriate response to the given question. For each question in the test, select the best choice, and fill in the corresponding space on the answer folder. You may wish to read each passage through before you begin to answer the questions associated with it. Most answers cannot be determined without reading several sentences around the phrases in question. Make sure to read far enough ahead each time you choose an alternative.

Passage I

[1]

If you are like most visitors to Athens, you will make your way to the <u>Acropolis, the hill</u> that once served as a
[1]
fortified, strategic position overlooking the Aegean Sea to see the Parthenon. This celebrated temple was dedicated in the fifth century B.C. to the goddess Athena. There is no more famous building in all of Greece; to climb up its marble steps is <u>to have beheld</u> a human creation that has
[2]
attained the stature of a natural phenomenon like the Grand Canyon. <u>You should also make an attempt to sample</u>
[3]
<u>Athenian cuisine while you're there.</u>
[3]

[2]

Generations of architects <u>have proclaimed</u> the Parthenon
[4]
to be the most brilliantly conceived structure in the Western world. The genius of its construction is <u>subtle for example</u>
[5]
the temple's columns were made to bulge outward slightly in order to compensate for the <u>fact, viewed from a distance, that</u>
[6]
<u>straight columns appear concave.</u>
[6]

1. A. NO CHANGE
   B. Acropolis. The hill
   C. Acropolis — the hill
   D. Acropolis

2. F. NO CHANGE
   G. to behold
   H. beholding
   J. to be holding

3. A. NO CHANGE
   B. Also make an attempt to sample Athenian cuisine while you're there.
   C. While you're there, you should also make an attempt to sample Athenian cuisine.
   D. OMIT the underlined portion.

4. F. NO CHANGE
   G. has proclaimed
   H. proclaims
   J. are proclaiming

5. A. NO CHANGE
   B. subtle; for example
   C. subtle. For example
   D. subtle. For example,

6. F. NO CHANGE
   G. fact that straight columns, viewed from a distance, appear concave.
   H. view from a distance: straight columns appearing concave.
   J. fact, when viewed from far away, that straight columns appear concave.

GO ON TO THE NEXT PAGE ➡

Using this and other techniques, the architects strove to create an optical <u>illusion of: uprightness,</u> solidity and permanence.

₇

[3]

<u>Because of this,</u> the overall impression you'll get of the Parthenon will be far different from the one the ancient Athenians had. Only by standing on the marble steps of the Parthenon and allowing your imagination to transport you back to the Golden Age of <u>Athens. You will</u> be able to see the temple's main attraction, the legendary statue of Athena Parthenos. It was 38 feet high and made of ivory and over a ton of pure gold. <u>Removed from the temple in the fifth century</u> <u>A.D.,</u> all that remains is the slight rectangular depression on the floor where it stood.

[4]

Many of the ornate carvings and sculptures that adorned the walls of the Acropolis <u>is</u> no longer there, either. In the early nineteenth century, the British diplomat Lord <u>Elgins decision to</u> "protect" the ones that survived by removing them from the Parthenon and carrying them back to Britain (he had the permission of the Ottoman Turks, who controlled Greece at the time, to do so).

[5]

After they gained independence from the Turks, <u>they</u> began to demand the sculptures and carvings back from the British, to no avail. Thus, if you want to gain a complete picture of what the Parthenon once looked like, you'll have to visit not only the Acropolis of Athens, but the British Museum in London as well.

7. **A.** NO CHANGE
   B. illusion of: uprightness,
   C. illusion of, uprightness,
   D. illusion of uprightness,

8. **F.** NO CHANGE
   G. Thus,
   H. Rather,
   J. Of course,

9. **A.** NO CHANGE
   B. Athens; you will
   C. Athens will you
   D. Athens. You may

10. **F.** NO CHANGE
    G. Having been removed from the temple in the 5th century A.D.,
    H. Given its removal from the temple in the 5th century A.D.,
    J. The statue was removed from the temple in the 5th century A.D.;

11. **A.** NO CHANGE
    B. will be
    C. have been
    D. are

12. **F.** NO CHANGE
    G. Elgin's deciding that
    H. Elgin decided to
    J. Elgin's decision to

13. **A.** NO CHANGE
    B. the Turks
    C. the Greeks
    D. who

GO ON TO THE NEXT PAGE ➡

Items 14 and 15 pose questions about the passage as a whole.

14. The writer wishes to insert the following material into the essay:
"Some of them were destroyed in 1687 when attacking Venetians bombarded the Acropolis, setting off explosives that had been stored in the Parthenon."
The new material best supports, and therefore would most logically be placed in, Paragraph:
F. 1
G. 2
H. 3
J. 4

15. Suppose the editor of an architecture journal had requested that the writer focus primarily on the techniques the ancient Greek architects used in constructing the Parthenon. Does the essay fulfill this request?
A. Yes, because the essay makes it clear that the Parthenon was an amazing architectural achievement.
B. Yes, because the essay explains in the second paragraph the reason the temple's columns bulge outward slightly.
C. No, because the Parthenon's construction is only one of several topics covered in the essay.
D. No, because the author never explains what the architects who designed the Parthenon were trying to accomplish.

Passage II

Although there is no conclusive evidence that a man named Robin Hood ever actually existed, the story of Robin Hood and his band of merry men has become one of the most popular traditional tales in English literature. Robin is the hero in a series of ballads dating from at least the 14th century. These ballads are telling of discontent
16
among the lower classes in the north of England during a turbulent era culminating in the Peasants' Revolt of 1381. A good deal of the rebellion against authority stemmed from restriction of hunting rights. These early ballads reveal the cruelty that was a part of medieval life. Robin Hood was a rebel, and many of the most striking episodes depict him and his companions robbing and killing representatives of authority, and they gave the gains to the poor. Their most
17   18
frequentest enemy was the Sheriff of Nottingham, a local
18
agent of the central government. Other enemies included wealthy ecclesiastical landowners.

16. F. NO CHANGE
G. telling
H. tell
J. they are telling

17. A. NO CHANGE
B. they were giving
C. giving
D. gave

18. F. NO CHANGE
G. even more frequenter
H. frequent
J. frequentl

GO ON TO THE NEXT PAGE ➡

While Robin could be ruthless with those who abused their power, he was kind to the oppressed. He was a people's hero as King Arthur was a noble's.

(The Broadway musical *Camelot* and Walt Disney's *The Sword in the Stone* are based on the legend of King Arthur.)
19

Some scholars have sought to prove that there was an actual Robin Hood. However, references to the Robin Hood legends by medieval writers make it clear that the ballads were the only evidence for Robin's existence available to them. A popular modern belief that Robin was
20
of the time of Richard I probably stems from the antiquary Richard Stukely's fabrication of a "pedigree." 22
21

19. **A.** NO CHANGE
     B. (The Broadway musical and the movie, respectively, *Camelot* and Walt Disney's *The Sword in the Stone*, are based on the legend of King Arthur.)
     C. (Movies and musicals, including *The Sword in the Stone* and *Camelot*, are derived from the legend of King Arthur.)
     D. OMIT the underlined portion.

20. **F.** NO CHANGE
     G. him.
     H. it.
     J. those writing ballads about him.

21. **A.** NO CHANGE
     B. Stukelys fabrication
     C. Stukelys fabrication,
     D. Stukely's, fabrication

22. Suppose that at this point in the passage the writer wanted to add more information about Richard Stukely. Which of the following additions would be most relevant to the passage as a whole?
     F. A discussion of relevant books on England during the realm of Richard I
     G. A definition of the term *antiquary*
     H. An example of Stukely's interest in King Arthur
     J. A description of the influence Stukely's fabricated pedigree has had on later versions of the Robin Hood tale

GO ON TO THE NEXT PAGE ➡

In the 18th century, the nature of the legend was distorted by the suggestion that Robin was as a fallen
₂₃
nobleman. Writers adopted this new element as eagerly as
₂₄
puppies. Robin was also given a love interest; Maid Marian.
₂₄   ₂₅
Some critics say that these ballads lost much of their vitality and poetic value by losing the social impulse that prompted their creation.

Consequently, in the twentieth century, the legend of
₂₆
Robin Hood has inspired several movies and a television series. Even a Broadway musical basing on the tale. So,
₂₇
whether or not a Robin Hood actually lived in ancient Britain, and the legendary Robin has lived in the popular
₂₈
imagination for more than six hundred years.

23. **A.** NO CHANGE
    B. was like as if he was
    C. was a
    D. is as a

24. **F.** NO CHANGE
    G. eagerly.
    H. eagerly, like a puppy.
    J. like a puppy's eagerness.

25. **A.** NO CHANGE
    B. interests—Maid
    C. interest: Maid,
    D. interest—Maid

26. **F.** NO CHANGE
    G. (Do NOT begin new paragraph) In the twentieth century, on the one hand,
    H. (Begin new paragraph) In the twentieth century,
    J. (Begin new paragraph) In the twentieth century, therefore,

27. **A.** NO CHANGE
    B. has been based
    C. to base
    D. OMIT the underlined portion.

28. **F.** NO CHANGE
    G. Britain,
    H. Britain, therefore
    J. Britain;

Items 29 and 30 pose questions about the passage as a whole.

29. Suppose this passage were written for an audience that was unfamiliar with the legend of Robin Hood. The writer could most effectively strengthen the passage by:
    A. citing examples of legendary rebels from Spanish and French literature.
    B. including further evidence of Robin Hood's actual existence.
    C. quoting a few lines from a Broadway musical about ancient Britain.
    D. including a brief summary of the Robin Hood legend.

30. This passage was probably written for readers who:
    F. are experts on how legends are handed down.
    G. are authorities on ancient British civilization and culture.
    H. are convinced that Robin Hood was an actual historical personage.
    J. have some familiarity with the Robin Hood legends.

GO ON TO THE NEXT PAGE ➡

Passage III

> The following paragraphs may or may not be in the most logical order. Each paragraph is numbered in brackets, and item 45 will ask you to choose the sequence of paragraph numbers that is in the most logical order.

[1]

When Mt. St. Helens erupted, my training as a private pilot paid off. My editor asked me to write a feature story on the volcano. Only scientists and reporters were allowed within a <u>ten-mile radius</u> of the mountain. Eager to see Mt.
₃₁
St. Helens for himself, my brother Jeff volunteered to accompany me as an assistant on the flight. He had never flown with me before, <u>and I looked forward at the</u>
₃₂
<u>opportunity to show off my skills.</u>
₃₂

[2]

<u>If I could read a newspaper</u>, I entertained thoughts of
₃₃
becoming a photo journalist. I always envisioned <u>myself</u> in
₃₄
some faraway exotic place performing dangerous deeds as a foreign correspondent. I was thrilled when I was hired for my first job as a cub reporter for the local newspaper in my rural hometown. However, some of the glamour began to fade after covering the umpteenth garden party. Then one day Mother Nature <u>intervened</u>, giving me the opportunity
₃₅
to cover an international event.

31. **A.** NO CHANGE
    B. radius, consisting of ten miles,
    C. measurement of a ten mile radius
    D. radius, measuring ten miles,

32. **F.** NO CHANGE
    G. but looked forward to the opportunity of showing off my skills.
    H. and I looked forward to the opportunity to show off my skills.
    J. nevertheless I anticipated being able to show off my skills.

33. **A.** NO CHANGE
    B. Since I found it easy to read a newspaper,
    C. Although I could read a newspaper,
    D. Ever since I could read a newspaper,

34. **F.** NO CHANGE
    G. I
    H. me
    J. it

35. **A.** NO CHANGE
    B. intervened:
    C. intervened;
    D. —intervened—

GO ON TO THE NEXT PAGE ➡

KAPLAN

[3]

When we arrived at the airport <u>filing my flight plan;</u>

<u>giving</u> my credentials as a reporter for the Gresham
36

Outlook. As we departed Troutdale airport, my Cessna 152

ascended slowly on its way towards Mt. St. Helens. As we

neared the crater, I kept a <u>careful</u> watch for other airplanes
37

in the vicinity. A few other pilots were also circling around

the crater. I had to maintain a high enough altitude to avoid

both the smoke being emitted <u>from: the crater</u> and the ashen
38

residue already in the atmosphere. Too much exposure to

the volcanic particles could put my plane out of service.

This element of danger served to increase not only my

awareness, but also my excitement.

[4]

Jeff and I were at first speechless <u>and mute</u> at the
39

awesome sight below us as we circled the crater. It was as

if the spectacular beauty of a Fourth of July celebration

were contained in one natural phenomenon. Jeff helped

me, <u>steadying the plane and took notes</u>, while I shot
40

pictures and dictated story ideas to him. 41

[5]

My story appeared as the front-page feature the

following day. <u>However</u>, I have realized many of my early
42

dreams, working as a foreign correspondent in many

different countries. And yet none of my experiences has

surpassed that special pride and excitement I felt covering

my first "international" story.

36. F. NO CHANGE
    G. I filed my flight plan, and gave
    H. filing my flight plan, giving
    J. my flight plan was filed by me, and I gave

37. A. NO CHANGE
    B. (place before airplanes)
    C. (place before neared)
    D. (place before crater)

38. F. NO CHANGE
    G. (from: the crater)
    H. from, the crater,
    J. from the crater

39. A. NO CHANGE
    B. and also mute
    C. —and mute—
    D. OMIT

40. F. NO CHANGE
    G. steadying the plane and taking notes,
    H. steadied the plane and taking notes,
    J. steadies the plane and takes notes

41. The writer could most effectively strengthen the passage
    at this point by adding which of the following?
    A. A description of Mt. St. Helens
    B. The sentence, "Jeff, take this plane lower!" to add
        excitement
    C. The statement, "A volcano is a vent in the earth's
        crust through which lava is expelled," to inform
        the reader
    D. A discussion of other recent volcanic eruptions to
        provide a contrast

42. F. NO CHANGE
    G. Since that time,
    H. Furthermore,
    J. Nevertheless,

GO ON TO THE NEXT PAGE ➡

Items 43-45 pose questions about the passage as a whole.

43. Readers are likely to regard the passage as best described by which of the following terms?
  A. Optimistic
  B. Bitter
  C. Nostalgic
  D. Exhausted

44. Is the author's use of the pronoun "I" appropriate in the passage?
  F. No, because, as a rule, one avoids "I" in formal writing.
  G. No, because it weakens the passage's focus on volcanoes.
  H. Yes, because it gives immediacy to the story told in the passage.
  J. Yes, because "I" is, as a rule, appropriate in writing.

45. Choose the sequence of paragraph numbers that will make the passage's structure most logical.
  A. NO CHANGE
  B. 2, 1, 3, 4, 5
  C. 3, 4, 5, 1, 2
  D. 4, 5, 1, 2, 3

Passage IV

Sherlock Holmes, the <u>ingenious and extremely clever</u> [46] detective with the deer-stalker hat, pipe and magnifying glass, is a universally recognizable character. Everyone knows of Holmes's ability to solve even the most bizarre mysteries through the application of cold logic. <u>Therefore, everyone</u> [47] is familiar with the phrase "elementary, my dear Watson," Holmes's perennial response to the requests of his baffled sidekick, Dr. Watson, for an explanation of his amazing deductions. <u>Strictly speaking, of course, Holmes's</u> [48] <u>"deductions" were not deductions at all, but inductive</u> [48] <u>inferences.</u> [48]

But how many people know anything about the creator of Sherlock Holmes, Sir Arthur Conan Doyle? Fans of Holmes might be surprised to discover that <u>he</u> [49] did not want <u>to be engraved forever in the memory of the people</u> [50] as the author of the Sherlock Holmes stories.

46. F. NO CHANGE
  G. ingenious
  H. ingenious, extremely clever
  J. cleverly ingenious

47. A. NO CHANGE
  B. Although everyone
  C. For this reason, everyone
  D. Everyone

48. F. NO CHANGE
  G. (Strictly speaking, of course, Holmes's "deductions" were not deductions at all, but inductive inferences.)
  H. Holmes's "deductions" were, strictly speaking, not deductions at all, but inductive inferences.
  J. OMIT the underlined portion.

49. A. NO CHANGE
  B. Conan Doyle
  C. they
  D. the detective

50. F. NO CHANGE
  G. to go down in the annals of history
  H. to be permanently thought of forever
  J. to be remembered

GO ON TO THE NEXT PAGE ➡

In fact, Conan Doyle sent Holmes to his death at the end of
51
the second book of short stories and subsequently felt a

great sense of relief. Having had enough of his famous

character by that time, Sherlock Holmes would never
52
divert him again from more serious writing, he promised
52
himself. It took eight years and the offer of a princely sum
52
of money before Conan Doyle could be persuaded to revive

the detective. Soap opera characters are sometimes brought
53
back to life after they've been pronounced dead, too.
53

[1]

Admirers of Holmes's coldly scientific approach to his

detective work may also be taken aback when they learn

that Conan Doyle has been deeply immersed in
54
spiritualism.

[2]

Convinced by these experiences of the validity of

paranormal phenomena, that he lectured on spiritualism in
55
towns and villages throughout Britain.

[3]

For example, he and his family attempted to

communicate with the dead by automatic writing, thought
56
to be a method of talking with those no longer among the
56
living, and through a spiritual medium, an individual who
56
supposedly could contact those in the world beyond.

[4]

Conan Doyle claimed to have grasped materialized

hands and watched heavy articles swimming through the air

during sessions led by the medium. 57

51. A. NO CHANGE
  B. Despite this,
  C. Regardless,
  D. Yet

52. F. NO CHANGE
  G. the diversion of Sherlock Holmes, he promised
    himself, would never again keep him from more
    serious writing.
  H. more serious writing consumed all his time from
    then on.
  J. he promised himself that Sherlock Holmes would
    never again divert him from more serious writing.

53. A. NO CHANGE
  B. (Soap opera characters are sometimes brought
    back to life after they've been pronounced dead,
    too.)
  C. Sometimes you'll see soap opera characters who
    were dead being brought back to life, just like
    Holmes.
  D. OMIT the underlined portion.

54. F. NO CHANGE
  G. is deeply immersed
  H. was deeply immersed
  J. has been immersed deeply

55. A. NO CHANGE
  B. phenomena, he lectured
  C. phenomena was he that he lectured
  D. phenomena. He lectured

56. F. NO CHANGE
  G. a means of getting in touch with those beyond the
    grave
  H. thought to be a method of talking with the dead
  J. OMIT the underlined portion.

57. For the sake of unity and coherence, Sentence 2 should
  be placed:
  A. where it is now.
  B. before Sentence 1.
  C. after Sentence 3.
  D. after Sentence 4.

GO ON TO THE NEXT PAGE ➡

Doyle seems never to have asked himself: why they
would manifest themselves in such curious ways, or to have
reflected on the fact that many of these effects are the
standard trappings of cheating mediums. One has to
wonder, what would Sherlock Holmes have to say? ⬚60
                                                    59

58. F. NO CHANGE
  G. himself — why they
  H. himself why those in the other world
  J. himself why they

59. A. NO CHANGE
  B. what would Sherlock Holmes have said?
  C. what is Sherlock Holmes going to say?
  D. what had Sherlock Holmes said?

60. Which of the following would be the best title for the passage?
  F. Cheating Mediums: The Truth about Spiritualists.
  G. Conan Doyle and Spiritualism.
  H. The Secret Life of Sherlock Holmes.
  J. Writers and Their Religious Beliefs.

Passage V

During the summer of 1988, I watched Yellowstone
National Park go up in flames. Fires ignited by lightning, in
                                                    61
June, had been allowed to burn unsuppressed because park
officials expected that the usual summer rains would douse
them. But the rains never came, a more plentiful supply of
                                         62
fuel (fallen logs, branches, and pine needles were available,
          63
and winds of up to 100 MPH whipped the spreading fires
along and carried red-hot embers to other areas, creating
new fires.

By the time park officials succumbed to the pressure of
public opinion and decided to try to extinguish the flames. Its
                                                         64
too late. The situation remained out of control in spite of
                                            65
the efforts of 9,000 fire fighters employed state-of-the-art
                                       66
equipment. By September, more than 720,000 acres of
Yellowstone had been affected by fire. Nature was only able
                                              67
to curb the destruction; the smoke did not begin to clear
     67
until the first snow arrived on September 11.

61. A. NO CHANGE
  B. Fires having been ignited by lightning, in June,
  C. Fires ignited by lightning in June
  D. Fires ignited by lightning, in June,

62. F. NO CHANGE
  G. very much
  H. much more
  J. OMIT the underlined portion.

63. A. NO CHANGE
  B. (fallen logs, branches, and pine needles) was
  C. (fallen logs, branches, and pine needles needles) were
  D. (fallen logs, branches, and pine needles had been

64. F. NO CHANGE
  G. flames. It's
  H. flames, it's
  J. flames, it was

65. A. NO CHANGE
  B. control. In spite of
  C. control; despite
  D. control; in spite of

66. F. NO CHANGE
  G. who were employing
  H. which were employing
  J. which employed

67. A. NO CHANGE
  B. Nature able only to curb the destruction;
  C. Nature was able to curb only the destruction;
  D. Only nature was able to curb the destruction;

GO ON TO THE NEXT PAGE ➡

Having been an ecologist who has studied forests for
68
20 years, I knew that this was not nearly the tragedy it

seemed to be. Many more acres of forest burned in Alaska
69
in 1988 than in Yellowstone Park. Large fires are, after all,
69
necessary in order that the continued health in the forest
70
ecosystem be maintained. Fires thin out overcrowded areas
70
and allow the sun to reach species of plants stunted by

shade. Ash fertilizes the soil, and fire smoke kills forest

bacteria. In the case of the lodgepole pine, fire is essential

to reproduction: the pines' cone has only opened when
71
exposed to temperatures greater than 112 degrees.

The fires in Yellowstone did result in some loss of

wildlife, but overall the region's animals proved to be fire-

tolerant and fire-adaptive. However large animals such as
72
bison were often seen grazing and bedding down in

meadows near burning forests. Also, the fire posed little

threat to the members of any endangered animal species in

the park. [73]

My confidence in the natural resilience of the forest has

been borne out in the years since the fires ravaged

Yellowstone. Judging from the recent pictures of the park,
74
the forest was not destroyed; it was rejuvenated.

68. F. NO CHANGE
    G. An ecologist
    H. I'm an ecologist
    J. Being an ecologist,

69. A. NO CHANGE
    B. The amount of acreage that burned in Yellowstone
        in 1988 was nowhere near as great as in Alaska.
    C. Many more acres of forest burned in Alaska in
        1988, than in Yellowstone Park.
    D. OMIT the underlined portion.

70. F. NO CHANGE
    G. for the continued health of the forest ecosystem to
        be maintained.
    H. in order that the continued health of the forest
        ecosystem can persevere.
    J. for the continued health of the forest ecosystem.

71. A. NO CHANGE
    B. pine's cone has only opened
    C. pine's cone only opens
    D. pines' cones have only opened

72. F. NO CHANGE
    G. Clearly,
    H. In fact,
    J. Instead,

73. The writer has decided that a better transition is needed
    between the previous paragraph and this one. Which of
    the following sentences could be added at the
    beginning of this paragraph to do that best?
    A. Although fire is an integral part of the long-term
        life of the forest, animals suffer in the short term.
    B. Since forest fires play such a natural role, I
        expected the impact on animal life to be minimal.
    C. One never knows what toll a fire will take on the
        wildlife, though.
    D. Temperatures greater than 112 degrees is indeed
        rather hot.

74. F. NO CHANGE
    G. Recent pictures of the park show that
    H. Judging by the recent pictures of the park,
    J. As judged according to pictures taken of the park
        recently,

75. If the writer wished to provide support for the claim
    that the fire posed little threat to the members of any
    endangered animal species in the park, he or she would
    most likely:
    A. list the endangered animal species known to
        inhabit the park.
    B. discuss the particular vulnerability of endangered
        species of birds to forest fires.
    C. cite the reports of biologists who monitored
        animal activity in the park during the fire.
    D. explain how infrequent such an extensive series of
        forest fires really is.

**IF YOU FINISH BEFORE TIME IS CALLED, YOU MAY CHECK YOUR WORK ON
THIS SECTION ONLY. DO NOT TURN TO ANY OTHER SECTION IN THE TEST.**   STOP

   329

MATHEMATICS TEST

60 Minutes—60 Questions

Directions: Solve each of the following problems, select the correct answer, and then fill in the corresponding space on your answer sheet. Don't linger over problems that are too time-consuming. Do as many as you can, then come back to the others in the time you have remaining.

Note: Unless otherwise noted, all of the following should be assumed.
1. Illustrative figures are not necessarily drawn to scale.
2. All geometric figures lie in a plane.
3. The term *line* indicates a straight line.
4. The term *average* indicates arithmetic mean.

---

1. The regular price for a certain bicycle is $125.00. If that price is reduced by 20%, what is the new price?

   A. $100.00

   B. $105.00

   C. $112.50

   D. $120.00

   E. $122.50

DO YOUR FIGURING HERE.

2. If $x = -5$, then $2x^2 - 6x + 5 = ?$

   F. -15

   G. 15

   H. 25

   J. 85

   K. 135

3. How many distinct prime factors does the number 36 have?

   A. 2

   B. 3

   C. 4

   D. 5

   E. 6

4. In the figure below, what is the value of x ?

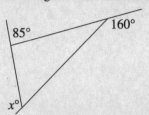

DO YOUR FIGURING HERE.

F. 105°

G. 115°

H. 135°

J. 245°

K. 255°

5. What is the average of $\frac{1}{20}$ and $\frac{1}{30}$?

A. $\frac{1}{25}$

B. $\frac{1}{24}$

C. $\frac{2}{25}$

D. $\frac{1}{12}$

E. $\frac{1}{6}$

6. The toll for driving a segment of a certain freeway is $1.50 plus 25 cents for each mile traveled. Joy paid a $25.00 toll for driving a segment of the freeway. How many miles did she travel?

F. 10

G. 75

H. 94

J. 96

K. 100

7. For all x, $3x^2 \cdot 5x^3 = ?$

A. $8x^5$

B. $8x^6$

C. $15x^5$

D. $15x^6$

E. $15x^8$

GO ON TO THE NEXT PAGE ➡

8. How many units apart are the points $P(-1,-2)$ and $Q(2,2)$ in the standard (x,y) coordinate plane?

   F. 2

   G. 3

   H. 4

   J. 5

   K. 6

9. In a group of 25 students, 16 are female. What percentage of the group are female?

   A. 16%

   B. 40%

   C. 60%

   D. 64%

   E. 75%

10. For how many integer values of x will $\dfrac{7}{x}$ be greater than $\dfrac{1}{4}$ and less than $\dfrac{1}{3}$?

    F. 6

    G. 7

    H. 12

    J. 28

    K. infinitely many

11. Which of the following is a polynomial factor of $6x^2 - 13x + 6$?

    A. $2x + 3$

    B. $3x - 2$

    C. $3x + 2$

    D. $6x - 2$

    E. $6x + 2$

12. What is the value of a if $\dfrac{1}{a} + \dfrac{2}{a} + \dfrac{3}{a} + \dfrac{4}{a} = 5$?

    F. $\dfrac{1}{2}$

    G. 2

    H. 4

    J. $12\dfrac{1}{2}$

    K. 50

DO YOUR FIGURING HERE.

GO ON TO THE NEXT PAGE ➡

KAPLAN

13. In the figure below, $\overline{AD}$, $\overline{BE}$, and $\overline{CF}$ all intersect at point G. If the measure of $\angle AGB$ is 40° and the measure of $\angle CGE$ is 105°, what is the measure of $\angle AGF$?

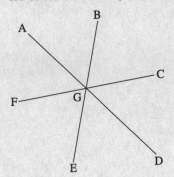

A. 35°

B. 45°

C. 55°

D. 65°

E. 75°

14. Which of the following is the solution statement for the inequality $-3 < 4x - 5$?

F. $x > -2$

G. $x > \frac{1}{2}$

H. $x < -2$

J. $x < \frac{1}{2}$

K. $x < 2$

GO ON TO THE NEXT PAGE ➡

15. In the figure below, $\overline{BD}$ bisects $\angle ABC$. The measure of $\angle ABC$ is 100° and the measure of $\angle BAD$ is 60°. What is the measure of $\angle BDC$?

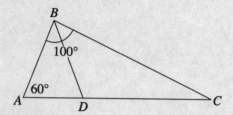

DO YOUR FIGURING HERE.

A. 80°

B. 90°

C. 100°

D. 110°

E. 120°

16. If $x + 2y - 3 = xy$, where x and y are positive, then which of the following equations expresses y in terms of x ?

F. $y = \dfrac{3 - x}{2 - x}$

G. $y = \dfrac{3 - x}{x - 2}$

H. $y = \dfrac{x - 3}{2 - x}$

J. $y = \dfrac{x - 2}{x - 3}$

K. $y = \dfrac{6 - x}{x - 2}$

17. In a group of 50 students, 28 speak English and 37 speak Spanish. If everyone in the group speaks at least one of the two languages, how many speak both English and Spanish?

A. 11

B. 12

C. 13

D. 14

E. 15

GO ON TO THE NEXT PAGE ➡

18. A car travels 288 miles in 6 hours. At that rate, how many miles will it travel in 8 hours?

   F. 216

   G. 360

   H. 368

   J. 376

   K. 384

19. When $\frac{4}{11}$ is written as a decimal, what is the 100th digit after the decimal point?

   A. 3

   B. 4

   C. 5

   D. 6

   E. 7

20. What is the solution for x in the system of equations below?

   $$3x + 4y = 31$$
   $$3x - 4y = -1$$

   F. 4

   G. 5

   H. 6

   J. 9

   K. 10

21. In the standard (x,y) coordinate plane, points P and Q have coordinates (2,3) and (12,–15), respectively. What are the coordinates of the midpoint of $\overline{PQ}$?

   A. (6,–12)

   B. (6,–9)

   C. (6,–6)

   D. (7,–9)

   E. (7,–6)

DO YOUR FIGURING HERE.

GO ON TO THE NEXT PAGE ➡

22. In the figure below, ∠B is a right angle, and the measure of ∠C is θ. What is the value of cos θ ?

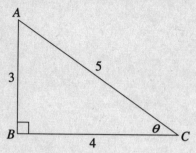

DO YOUR FIGURING HERE.

F. $\frac{3}{4}$

G. $\frac{3}{5}$

H. $\frac{4}{5}$

J. $\frac{5}{4}$

K. $\frac{4}{3}$

23. In the figure below, the circle centered at P is tangent to the circle centered at Q. Point Q is on the circumference of circle P. If the circumference of circle P is 6 inches, what is the circumference, in inches, of circle Q ?

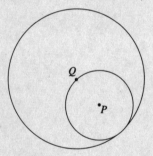

A. 12

B. 24

C. 36

D. 12π

E. 36π

GO ON TO THE NEXT PAGE ➡

KAPLAN

24. If $f(x) = x^3 - x^2 - x$, what is the value of $f(-3)$?

    F.   −39

    G.   −33

    H.   −21

    J.   −15

    K.   0

25. If the lengths, in inches, of all three sides of a triangle are integers, and one side is 7 inches long, what is the least possible perimeter of the triangle, in inches?

    A.   9

    B.   10

    C.   15

    D.   21

    E.   24

26. What is the complete factorization of $2x + 3x^2 + x^3$?

    F. $x(x^2 + 2)$

    G. $x(x - 2)(x + 3)$

    H. $x(x - 1)(x + 2)$

    J. $x(x + 1)(x + 2)$

    K. $x(x + 2)(x + 3)$

27. If $xyz \neq 0$, which of the following is equivalent to $\dfrac{x^2 y^3 z^4}{(xyz^2)^2}$?

    A. $\dfrac{1}{y}$

    B. $\dfrac{1}{z}$

    C. y

    D. $\dfrac{x}{yz}$

    E. xyz

28. As a decimal, what is the sum of $\frac{2}{3}$ and $\frac{1}{12}$?

    F.   0.2

    G.   0.5

    H.   0.75

    J.   0.833

    K.   0.875

DO YOUR FIGURING HERE.

GO ON TO THE NEXT PAGE ➡

29. The formula for converting a Fahrenheit temperature reading to Celsius is $C = \frac{5}{9}(F - 32)$, where C is the reading in degrees Celsius and F is the reading in degrees Fahrenheit. Which of the following is the Fahrenheit equivalent to a reading of 95° Celsius?

   A. 35° F

   B. 53° F

   C. 63° F

   D. 203° F

   E. 207° F

30. A jar contains 4 green marbles, 5 red marbles, and 11 white marbles. If one marble is chosen at random, what is the probability that it will be green?

   F. $\frac{1}{3}$

   G. $\frac{1}{4}$

   H. $\frac{1}{5}$

   J. $\frac{1}{16}$

   K. $\frac{1}{55}$

31. What is the average of the expressions $2x + 5$, $5x - 6$, and $-4x + 2$?

   A. $x + \frac{1}{3}$

   B. $x + 1$

   C. $3x + \frac{1}{3}$

   D. $3x + 3$

   E. $3x + 3\frac{1}{3}$

32. The line that passes through the points $(1, 1)$ and $(2, 16)$ in the standard (x, y) coordinate plane is parallel to the line that passes through the points $(-10, -5)$ and $(a, 25)$. What is the value of a ?

   F. -8

   G. 3

   H. 5

   J. 15

   K. 20

DO YOUR FIGURING HERE.

GO ON TO THE NEXT PAGE ➡

KAPLAN

33. In the figure below, $\overline{QS}$ and $\overline{PT}$ are parallel, and their lengths, in units, are as marked. If the perimeter of $\triangle QRS$ is 11 units, how many units long is the perimeter of $\triangle PRT$?

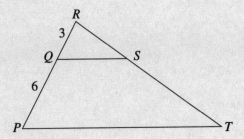

DO YOUR FIGURING HERE.

   A. 22

   B. 33

   C. 66

   D. 88

   E. 99

34. The figure shown below belongs in which of the following classifications?

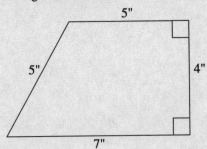

   I. Polygon

   II. Quadrilateral

   III. Rectangle

   IV. Trapezoid

   F. I only

   G. II only

   H. IV only

   J. I, II, and III only

   K. I, II, and IV only

GO ON TO THE NEXT PAGE ➡

35. If one solution to the equation $2x^2 + (a - 4)x - 2a = 0$ is $x = -3$, what is the value of a ?

A. 0

B. 2

C. 4

D. 6

E. 12

36. A menu offers 4 choices for the first course, 5 choices for the second course, and 3 choices for dessert. How many different meals, consisting of a first course, a second course, and a dessert, can one choose from this menu?

F. 12

G. 24

H. 30

J. 36

K. 60

37. If an integer is divisible by 6 and by 9, then the integer must be divisible by which of the following?

   I.   12

   II. 18

   III. 36

A. I only

B. II only

C. I and II only

D. I, II, and III

E. None

38. For all $x \neq 0$, $\dfrac{x^2 + x^2 + x^2}{x^2} = ?$

F.   3

G. $3x$

H. x^2

J. x^3

K. x^4

DO YOUR FIGURING HERE.

GO ON TO THE NEXT PAGE ➡

39. Joan has q quarters, d dimes, n nickels, and no other coins in her pocket. Which of the following represents the total number of coins in Joan's pocket?

A. $q + d + n$

B. $5q + 2d + n$

C. $.25q + .10d + .05n$

D. $(25 + 10 + 5)(q + d + n)$

E. $25q + 10d + 5n$

40. Which graph below represents the solutions for x of the inequality $5x - 2(1 - x) \geq 4(x + 1)$?

F.

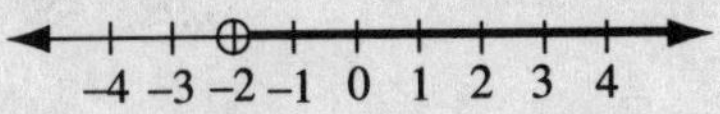

G.

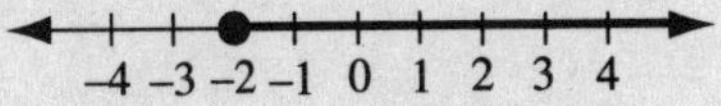

H.

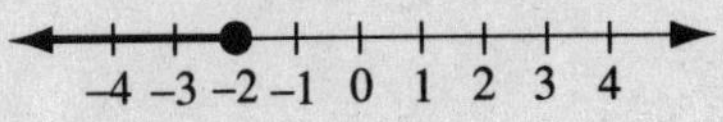

J.

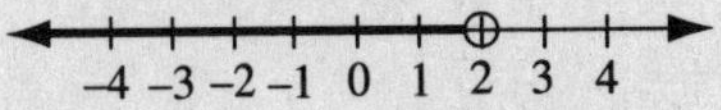

K.

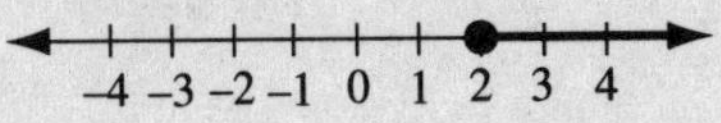

41. In the standard (x, y) coordinate plane, line m is perpendicular to the line containing the points $(5, 6)$ and $(6, 10)$. What is the slope of line m ?

A. -4

B. $-\dfrac{1}{4}$

C. $\dfrac{1}{4}$

D. 4

E. 8

GO ON TO THE NEXT PAGE ➡

42. In the right triangle below, sin θ = ?

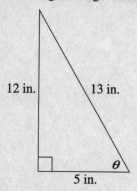

12 in.   13 in.

5 in.

θ

DO YOUR FIGURING HERE.

F. $\dfrac{5}{13}$

G. $\dfrac{5}{12}$

H. $\dfrac{12}{13}$

J. $\dfrac{13}{12}$

K. $\dfrac{13}{5}$

43. If $9^{2x-1} = 3^{3x+3}$, then $x = ?$

A. -4

B. $-\dfrac{7}{4}$

C. $-\dfrac{10}{7}$

D. 2

E. 5

44. From 1970 through 1980, the population of City Q increased by 20%. From 1980 through 1990, the population increased by 30%. What was the combined percent increase for the period 1970–1990 ?

F. 25%

G. 26%

H. 36%

J. 50%

K. 56%

GO ON TO THE NEXT PAGE ➡

DO YOUR FIGURING HERE.

45. Martin's average score after 4 tests is 89. What score on the 5th test would bring Martin's average up to exactly 90?

A. 90
B. 91
C. 92
D. 93
E. 94

46. Which of the following is an equation for the circle in the standard (x,y) coordinate plane that has its center at $(-1,-1)$ and passes through the point $(7,5)$?

F. $(x - 1)^2 + (y - 1)^2 = 10$
G. $(x + 1)^2 + (y + 1)^2 = 10$
H. $(x - 1)^2 + (y - 1)^2 = 12$
J. $(x - 1)^2 + (y - 1)^2 = 100$
K. $(x + 1)^2 + (y + 1)^2 = 100$

47. Which of the following is an equation for the graph in the standard (x,y) coordinate plane below?

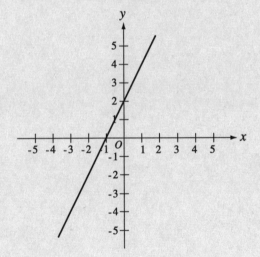

A. $y = -2x + 1$
B. $y = x + 1$
C. $y = x + 2$
D. $y = 2x + 1$
E. $y = 2x + 2$

GO ON TO THE NEXT PAGE ➡

48. What is $\frac{1}{4}$% of 16 ?

DO YOUR FIGURING HERE.

   F.   0.004

   G.   0.04

   H.   0.4

   J.   4

   K.   64

49. For all s, $(s + 4)(s - 4) + (2s + 2)(s - 2) = ?$

   A. $s^2 - 2s - 20$

   B. $3s^2 - 12$

   C. $3s^2 - 2s - 20$

   D. $3s^2 + 2s - 20$

   E. $5s^2 - 2s - 20$

50. Which of the following is an equation of the parabola graphed in the (x,y) coordinate plane below?

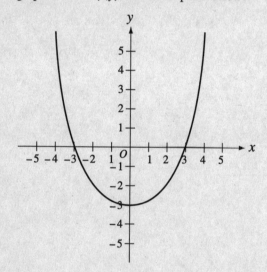

   F. $y = \frac{x^2}{3} - 3$

   G. $y = \frac{x^2 - 3}{3}$

   H. $y = \frac{x^2}{3} + 3$

   J. $y = \frac{x^2 + 3}{3}$

   K. $y = 3x^2 - 3$

GO ON TO THE NEXT PAGE ➡

KAPLAN

51. In the figure below, $\sin \alpha = \frac{4}{5}$. What is $\cos \beta$?

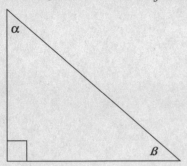

DO YOUR FIGURING HERE.

A. $\frac{3}{4}$

B. $\frac{3}{5}$

C. $\frac{4}{5}$

D. $\frac{5}{4}$

E. $\frac{4}{3}$

52. For all $x \neq 0$, $\dfrac{x^2 + x^2 + x^2}{x} = ?$

F. $3x$

G. x^3

H. x^5

J. x^7

K. $2x^2 + x$

53. One can determine a student's score S on a certain test by dividing the number of wrong answers (w) by 4 and subtracting the result from the number of right answers (r). This relation is expressed by which of the following formulas?

A. $S = \dfrac{r - w}{4}$

B. $S = r - \dfrac{w}{4}$

C. $S = \dfrac{r}{4} - w$

D. $S = 4r - w$

E. $S = r - 4w$

GO ON TO THE NEXT PAGE ➡

54. What is the volume, in cubic inches, of the cylinder shown in the figure below?

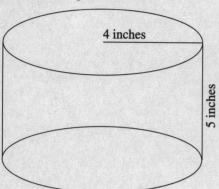

DO YOUR FIGURING HERE.

- **F.** 20π
- **G.** 40π
- **H.** 60π
- **J.** 80π
- **K.** 100π

55. In the figure below, $\overline{AB}$ is perpendicular to $\overline{BC}$. The lengths of $\overline{AB}$ and $\overline{BC}$, in inches, are given in terms of x. Which of the following represents the area of $\triangle ABC$, in square inches, for all $x > 1$?

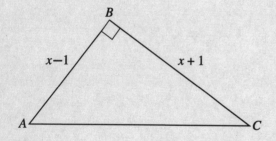

- **A.** x
- **B.** $2x$
- **C.** x^2
- **D.** $x^2 - 1$
- **E.** $\dfrac{x^2 - 1}{2}$

GO ON TO THE NEXT PAGE ➡

56. In 1990, the population of Town *A* was 9,400 and the population of Town *B* was 7,600. Since then, each year, the population of Town *A* has decreased by 100, and the population of Town *B* has increased by 100. Assuming that in each case the rate continues, in what year will the two populations be equal?

F. 1998

G. 1999

H. 2000

J. 2008

K. 2009

57. In a certain club, the average age of the male members is 35 and the average age of the female members is 25. If 20% of the members are male, what is the average age of all the club members?

A. 26

B. 27

C. 28

D. 29

E. 30

DO YOUR FIGURING HERE.

GO ON TO THE NEXT PAGE ➡

58. To determine the height h of a tree, Roger stands b feet from the base of the tree and measures the angle of elevation to be θ, as shown in the figure below. Which of the following relates h and b ?

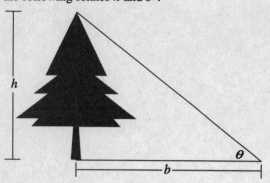

DO YOUR FIGURING HERE.

   F. $\sin \theta = \dfrac{h}{b}$

   G. $\sin \theta = \dfrac{b}{h}$

   H. $\sin \theta = \dfrac{b}{\sqrt{b^2 + h^2}}$

   J. $\sin \theta = \dfrac{h}{\sqrt{b^2 + h^2}}$

   K. $\sin \theta = \dfrac{\sqrt{b^2 + h^2}}{b}$

59. The formula for the lateral surface area S of a right circular cone is $S = \pi r \sqrt{r^2 + h^2}$, where r is the radius of the base and h is the altitude. What is the lateral surface area, in square feet, of a right circular cone with base radius 3 feet and altitude 4 feet?

   A. $3\pi\sqrt{5}$

   B. $3\pi\sqrt{7}$

   C. 15π

   D. 21π

   E. $\dfrac{75\pi}{2}$

GO ON TO THE NEXT PAGE ➡

60. In the figure below, line *t* crosses parallel lines *m* and *n*. Which of the following statements must be true?

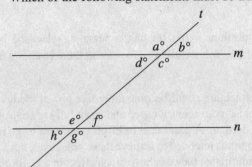

DO YOUR FIGURING HERE.

F. $a = b$

G. $a = d$

H. $b = e$

J. $c = g$

K. $d = g$

IF YOU FINISH BEFORE TIME IS CALLED, YOU MAY CHECK YOUR WORK ON THIS SECTION ONLY. DO NOT TURN TO ANY OTHER SECTION IN THE TEST.   **STOP**

KAPLAN   349

READING TEST

35 Minutes—40 Questions

Directions: This test contains four passages, each followed by several questions. After reading a passage, select the best answer to each question and fill in the corresponding oval on your answer sheet. You are allowed to refer to the passages while answering the questions.

Passage I

Men and women for whom economic security is the prime consideration do not usually choose a career in architecture. College graduates who focus on the
Line issue of opportunity are more likely to get an MBA or a
(5) law or medical degree. The image of these other professions and how much better their members fare financially haunts architects. Not only do architects generally have lower incomes than those in other professions, but the demand for services of lawyers and
(10) physicians is more stable, and they are able to exercise more control over the domains in which they work. The differences are very apparent now as the privileged position of lawyers and physicians has come under scrutiny. Critics, however, are finding it difficult to
(15) reduce the autonomy of these professions, while architects are continually losing out to clients and other parties in the building industry in the battle for hegemony.

The use of these other professions as a reference
(20) group for architects in judging their own status in the hierarchy of social influence is a relatively new development. It begins in the middle of the nineteenth century, when a large number of middle-class occupations in Europe and America pressed
(25) governments to grant them special protected status, through a system of licensing. As a way of making sure they would be included under the licensing umbrella, architects began emphasizing those aspects of their work that most nearly resembled the thinking and skills
(30) of other fields. For example, architects, like physicians, argued that their work affected public health and safety. The result was a shift in the definition of architecture from a focus on artistic accomplishment to expertise in dealing with the structural integrity of buildings,
(35) ventilation requirements, and the ability to interpret building and housing codes. The registration examinations still emphasize this component of architecture, even though this emphasis defines architecture in a way that parallels what others in the
(40) building industry are better at handling than architects.

Should architects keep berating themselves because they do not enjoy many of the social and economic rewards of the other major professions? It might be worthwhile if there were a good chance that

(45) architecture could become more like law or medicine, that is, more science-based and more fully in control of its domain. A great deal of effort continues to go into programs intended to achieve these objectives, but I am doubtful that they can have much effect in transforming
(50) the fundamental existential condition of architecture. For example, even when architecture emphasizes its regard for the pragmatics of building, it still remains linked to the fate of the construction industry. Yet, as the current condition of the industry indicates,
(55) construction is notoriously volatile. Physicians face a much different situation, since illness and disease do not diminish during economic depression; indeed there is reason to believe that morbidity increases. And lawyers, like accountants, provide service to a wide
(60) range of industries, so that when business diminishes in one sector, they are supported by others.

At the same time, however, the attributes that first earned architecture its place as "the mother of all arts" are those that continue to set it apart today. There is no
(65) other profession that is able to achieve what architects have historically accomplished in the realm of building. No other building profession is so learned about how to relate light, mass and structure to produce memorable visual and spatial experiences. Rare is the
(70) building not produced by an architect, that represents the supreme values of civilization. The design of the great seminal monumental buildings is the unique province of architecture, its "natural market."

But many practitioners seem embarrassed to
(75) present themselves as artists. They seem to fear it may encourage clients to regard them as no different from painters, sculptors, and other visual artists. They also appear worried that to promote this image will create the impression that architecture is a luxury service,
(80) which, as the history of the profession's achievement shows, it usually is. Routine, ordinary buildings can be constructed without the benefit of architects. But instead of trying to compete in this market, where it is not particularly successful anyway, the profession
(85) should be making more effort to broaden what I have called its natural market. The question is how to stretch the profession's capacity, without at the same time injuring its fundamental strengths and its

GO ON TO THE NEXT PAGE ➡

KAPLAN

(90) acknowledged cultural role. The strategy of emphasizing their skills in building, which so many firms have adopted, puts architects in competition with other professions and parties that can do it just as well, if not better. It also just discourages clients and the profession itself from recollecting the primary skill of the architect for which there is no peer; the design of
(95) buildings that have some value as art. This is the direction in which the profession must move if it is going to find greater employment in the decades ahead.

From "Architects and Power, the Natural Market for Architecture," Prof. Robert Gutman, *Progressive Architecture,* December, 1992.

1. According to the passage, architects do not like being regarded as:
   A. doctors.
   B. artists.
   C. builders.
   D. accountants.

2. As it is used in the passage, the word *privileged* (line 13) most likely means:
   F. authorized.
   G. confidential.
   H. superior.
   J. aristocratic.

3. The passage suggests that architects were granted special protected status through a system of licensing partly because:
   A. their market was threatened by other workers in the construction industry.
   B. their work affected public health and safety.
   C. many other middle-class occupations enjoyed similar protection.
   D. fewer great monumental buildings were being designed.

4. According to the passage, doctors and lawyers fare better financially than architects because:
   I. the demand for architects' services is less stable.
   II. doctors and lawyers are more able to exercise control over their fields.
   III. architects are forced to compete with other parties in building industry.
   F. I and II
   G. II and III
   H. I and III
   J. I, II and III

5. The main point the passage makes about architecture is that:
   A. architects should focus on designing buildings that have some artistic value.
   B. architects should possess as much economic security as doctors and lawyers do.
   C. architects should work to abolish the traditional system of licensing.
   D. architects should work to compete more with other building professions.

6. According to the passage, architecture is described as the "mother of all arts" (line 64) because:
   F. architects have been designing buildings since the beginnings of civilization.
   G. architecture is similar in nature to painting, sculpture and other visual arts.
   H. architects relate light, mass and structure to produce memorable artistic effects.
   J. architecture has survived the passage of time better than other art forms.

7. According to the passage, all of the following professionals thrive during periods of economic depressions EXCEPT:
   A. physicians.
   B. architects.
   C. lawyers.
   D. accountants.

8. Which of the following statements is best supported by the fifth paragraph?
   F. Architects want their clients to acknowledge their status as artists.
   G. Architects are not required in the construction of ordinary buildings.
   H. Architects would like their profession to be regarded as a luxury service.
   J. Architects have been most successful in the housing market.

GO ON TO THE NEXT PAGE ➡

9. According to the passage, college graduates are unlikely to choose a career in architecture because:
   A. there are fewer degrees offered in architecture than in other professions.
   B. architects are lower paid than those in other professions.
   C. rising costs in education make architecture a less practical choice.
   D. other professions have a more glamorous image.

10. According to the passage, law and medicine are different from architecture in that they are:
    F. less based on scientific knowledge.
    G. more dependent on economic conditions.
    H. better protected by a licensing system.
    J. more fully in control of their domain.

GO ON TO THE NEXT PAGE ➡

Passage II

Enlightenment ideas were put forth by a variety of intellectuals who in France came to be known as the *philosophes*. *Philosophes* is French for philosophers, and
Line in a sense these thinkers were rightly considered
(5) philosophers, for the questions they dealt with were philosophical: How do we discover truth? How should life be lived? What is the nature of God? But on the whole the term has a meaning different from the usual meaning of "philosopher." The *philosophes* were intellectuals,
(10) often not formally trained or associated with a university. They were usually more literary than scientific. They generally extended, applied, popularized, or propagandized ideas of others rather than originating those ideas themselves. The *philosophes* were more
(15) likely to write plays, satires, pamphlets or simply participate in verbal exchanges at select gatherings than to write formal philosophical books.

It was the *philosophes* who developed the philosophy of the Enlightenment and spread it to much of
(20) the educated elite in Western Europe (and the American colonies). Although the sources for their philosophy can be traced to the Scientific Revolution in general, the *philosophes* were most influenced by their understanding of Newton, Locke, and English institutions.

(25) The *philosophes* saw Newton as the great synthesizer of the Scientific Revolution who rightly described the universe as ordered, mechanical, material, and only originally set in motion by God, who since then has remained relatively inactive. Newton's synthesis
(30) showed to the *philosophes* that reason and nature were compatible: Nature functioned logically and discernibly, and what was natural was also reasonable. Newton exemplified the value of reasoning based on concrete experience. The *philosophes* felt that his empirical
(35) methodology was the correct path to discovering truth.

John Locke (1632–1704) agreed with Newton but went further. This English thinker would not exempt even the mind from the mechanical laws of the material universe. In his *Essay Concerning Human*
(40) *Understanding* (1691), Locke pictured the human brain at birth as a blank sheet of paper on which nothing would ever be written except sense perception and reason. What human beings become depends on their experiences — on the information received through the senses. Schools
(45) and social institutions could therefore play a great role in molding the individual from childhood to adulthood. Human beings were thus by nature far more malleable than had been assumed. This empirical psychology of Locke rejected the notion that human beings were born
(50) with innate ideas or that revelation was a reliable source of truth. Locke also enunciated liberal and reformist political ideas in his *Second Treatise of Civil Government*

(1690), which influenced the *philosophes*. On the whole Locke's empiricism, psychology and politics were
(55) appealing to the *philosophes*.

England, not coincidentally the country of Newton and Locke, became the admired model for many of the *philosophes*. They tended to idealize it, but England did seem to allow greater individual freedom, tolerate
(60) religious differences, and evidence greater political reform than other countries, especially France. England seemed to have gone furthest in freeing itself from traditional institutions and accepting the new science of the seventeenth century. Moreover, England's approach
(65) seemed to work, for England was experiencing relative political stability and prosperity. The *philosophes* wanted to see in their own countries much of what England already seemed to have.

Many *philosophes* reflected the influence of Newton,
(70) Locke, and English institutions, but perhaps the most representative in his views was Voltaire (1778). Of all leading figures of the Enlightenment, he was the most influential. Voltaire, the son of a Paris lawyer, became the idol of the French intelligentsia while still in his early
(75) twenties. His versatile mind was sparkling; his wit was mordant. An outspoken critic, he soon ran afoul of both church and state authorities. First he was imprisoned in the Bastille; later he was exiled to England. There he encountered the ideas of Newton and Locke and came to
(80) admire English parliamentary government and tolerance. In *Letters on the English* (1732), *Elements of the Philosophy of Newton* (1738), and other writings, he popularized the ideas of Newton and Locke, extolled the virtues of English society, and indirectly criticized French
(85) society. Slipping back into France, he was hidden for a time and protected by a wealthy woman who became his mistress. Voltaire's facile mind and pen were never idle. He wrote poetry, drama, history, essays, letters, and scientific treatises—ninety volumes in all. The special targets of his
(90) cynical wit were the Catholic church and Christian institutions. Few people in history have dominated their age intellectually as did Voltaire.

From *A Short History of Western Civilization,* by John Harrison, Richard Sullivan, Dennis Sherman. Copyright 1990 by McGraw-Hill. Reprinted by permission.

GO ON TO THE NEXT PAGE ➡

11. The *philosophes* can best be described as:
   A. writers swept up by their mutual admiration of John Locke.
   B. professors who lectured in philosophy at French universities.
   C. intellectuals responsible for popularizing Enlightenment ideas.
   D. scientists who furthered the work of the Scientific Revolution.

12. Which of the following would most likely have been written by Voltaire?
   F. A treatise criticizing basic concepts of the Scientific Revolution.
   G. A play satirizing religious institutions in France.
   H. A collection of letters mocking the English Parliament.
   J. A sentimental poem expounding the virtues of courtly love.

13. According to the passage, Locke felt that schools and social institutions could "play a great role in molding the individual" (lines 45–46) primarily because:
   A. human beings were born with certain innate ideas.
   B. human nature becomes more malleable with age.
   C. society owes each individual the right to an education.
   D. the human mind is chiefly influenced by experience.

14. Based on the information in the passage, which of the following best describes Newton's view of the universe?
   I. The universe was initially set in motion by God.
   II. Human reason is insufficient to understand the laws of nature.
   III. The universe operates in a mechanical and orderly fashion.
   F. I only
   G. I and II only
   H. I and III only
   J. II and III only

15. According to the passage, which of the following works questioned the idea that revelation was a reliable source of truth?
   A. *Letters on the English.*
   B. *Second Treatise of Civil Government.*
   C. *Elements of the Philosophy of Newton.*
   D. *Essay Concerning Human Understanding.*

16. The passage supports which of the following statements concerning the relationship between Newton and Locke?
   F. Locke's psychology contradicted Newton's belief in an orderly universe.
   G. Locke maintained that Newton's laws of the material universe also applied to the human mind.
   H. Newton eventually came to accept Locke's revolutionary ideas about the human mind.
   J. Newton's political ideas were the basis of Locke's liberal and reformist politics.

17. According to the passage, the *philosophes* believed that society should:
   I. allow individuals greater freedom.
   II. free itself from traditional institutions.
   III. tolerate religious differences.
   A. I only
   B. I and II only
   C. II and III only
   D. I, II, and III

18. It can be inferred from the passage that the author regards England's political stability and economic prosperity as:
   F. the reason why the *philosophes* did not idealize England's achievement.
   G. evidence that political reforms could bring about a better way of life.
   H. the result of Voltaire's activities after he was exiled to England.
   J. an indication that the Scientific Revolution had not yet started there.

19. The passage suggests that the French political and religious authorities during the time of Voltaire:
   A. allowed little in the way of free speech.
   B. overreacted to Voltaire's mild satires.
   C. regarded the *philosophes* with indifference.
   D. accepted the model of English parliamentary government.

20. How does the passage support the point that the *philosophes* were "more literary than scientific" (line 11)?
   F. It demonstrates how the *philosophes'* writings contributed to the political change.
   G. It compares the number of works that Voltaire authored to Newton's output.
   H. It traces the influences of English literary works on French scientists.
   J. It describes the kinds of literary activities the *philosophes* commonly engaged in.

GO ON TO THE NEXT PAGE ➡

KAPLAN

Passage III

Rosemary sat at her kitchen table, working at a crossword puzzle. Crosswords were nice; they filled the time, and kept the mind active. She needed just one word
Line to complete this morning's puzzle; the clue was "a Swiss
(5) river," and the first of its three letters was "A." Unfortunately, Rosemary had no idea what the name of the river was, and could not look it up. Her atlas was on the desk, and the desk was in the guest room, currently being occupied by her grandson Victor. Looking up over the tops
(10) of her bifocals, Rosemary glanced at the kitchen clock: it was almost 10 A.M. *Land sakes!* Did the boy intend to sleep all day? She noticed that the arthritis in her wrist was throbbing, and put down her pen. At eighty-seven years of age, she was glad she could still write at all. She
(15) had decided long ago that growing old was like slowly turning to stone; you couldn't take anything for granted. She stood up slowly, painfully, and started walking to the guest room.

The trip, though only a distance of about twenty-five
(20) feet, seemed to take a long while. Late in her ninth decade now, Rosemary often experienced an expanded sense of time, with present and past tense intermingling in her mind. One minute she was padding in her slippers across the living room carpet, the next she was back on the farm
(25) where she'd grown up, a sturdy little girl treading the path behind the barn just before dawn. In her mind's eye, she could still pick her way among the stones in the darkness, more than seventy years later... Rosemary arrived at the door to the guest room. It stood slightly ajar, and she
(30) peered through the opening. Victor lay sleeping on his side, his arms bent, his expression slightly pained. *Get up, lazy bones,* she wanted to say. Even in childhood, Rosemary had never slept past 4 A.M.; there were too many chores to do. How different things were for Victor's
(35) generation! Her youngest grandson behaved as if he had never done a chore in his life. Twenty-one years old, he had driven down to Florida to visit Rosemary in his shiny new car, a gift from his doting parents. Victor would finish college soon, and his future appeared bright—if he ever
(40) got out of bed, that is.

Something Victor had said last night over dinner had disturbed her. Now what was it? Oh yes; he had been talking about one of his college courses—a "gut," he had called it. When she had asked him to explain the term,
(45) Victor had said it was a course that you took simply because it was easy to pass. Rosemary, who had not even had a high school education, found the term repellent. If she had been allowed to continue her studies, she would never have taken a "gut".... The memory flooded back
(50) then, still painful as an open wound all these years later. It was the first day of high school. She had graduated from grammar school the previous year, but her father had

forbidden her to go on to high school that fall, saying that she was needed on the farm. After much tearful pleading,
(55) she had gotten him to promise that next year, she could start high school. She had endured a whole year of chores instead of books, with animals and rough farmhands for company instead of people her own age. Now, at last, the glorious day was at hand. She had put on her best dress
(60) (she owned two), her heart racing in anticipation. But her father was waiting for her as she came downstairs.

"Where do you think you're going?" he asked.

"To high school, Papa."

"No you're not. Take that thing off and get back to
(65) work."

"But Papa, you promised!"

"Do as I say!" he thundered.

There was no arguing with Papa when he spoke that way. Tearfully, she had trudged upstairs to change
(70) clothes. Rosemary still wondered what life would have been like if her father had not been waiting at the bottom of the stairs that day, or if somehow she had found the strength to defy him...

Suddenly, Victor stirred, without waking, and
(75) mumbled something unintelligible. Jarred from her reverie, Rosemary stared at Victor. She wondered if he were having a nightmare.

From "Graduation," by Jon Krupp.

21. According to the passage, Victor is Rosemary's:
    A. nephew.
    B. son.
    C. grandson.
    D. great grandson.

22. It can be inferred from the passage that Rosemary is disturbed by Victor's:
    F. intention to drop out of college.
    G. disregard of her harsh upbringing.
    H. willingness to take courses that are easy to pass.
    J. inability to get out of bed in the morning.

GO ON TO THE NEXT PAGE ➡

23. The passage suggests that in the year after she finished grammar school, Rosemary most wanted:
    A. an escape from her father's company.
    B. the opportunity to go to college.
    C. the chance to study challenging subjects.
    D. the company of people her own age.

24. The passage suggests that Rosemary's attitude towards the physical afflictions of old age is generally one of:
    F. sadness.
    G. acceptance.
    H. resentment.
    J. optimism.

25. According to the passage, Rosemary does crossword puzzles in order to:
    A. keep her mind active.
    B. practice her handwriting.
    C. learn new geographical facts.
    D. make her more aware of time.

26. The focus of the passage as a whole is on:
    F. Rosemary's concern at Victor's lack of motivation.
    G. the harsh treatment Victor received from his father.
    H. the contrast between Victor's and Rosemary's attitudes towards education.
    J. Rosemary's struggle to suppress painful memories.

27. It can be inferred from the passage that Victor's "shiny new car" (line 37–38) is mentioned in order to illustrate:
    A. the excessive generosity of Rosemary's parents.
    B. the contrast between Rosemary's generation and his.
    C. the strength of Victor's prospects for the future.
    D. the lack of physical hardship in Victor's life.

28. The third paragraph (lines 41-61) primarily portrays Rosemary in her youth as:
    F. resentful of her father's conduct.
    G. eager to continue her education.
    H. undecided about her future career.
    J. proud of her appearance.

29. Rosemary's recollection of growing up on the farm (lines 24–28) is mentioned as an example of her:
    A. nostalgia for her childhood experiences.
    B. determination to overcome her physical disabilities.
    C. ability to recall past and present events at the same time.
    D. disappointment at being denied an education.

30. The statement that Victor's "future appeared bright" (line 39) most likely reflects the opinion of:
    F. Rosemary.
    G. Victor.
    H. Victor's parents.
    J. Rosemary's father.

GO ON TO THE NEXT PAGE ➡

Passage IV

The ozone layer, the tenuous layer of gas that surrounds our planet between twelve and forty-five kilometers above our surface is being rapidly depleted.
Line Seasonally occurring holes have appeared in it over the Poles,
(5) and, more recently, over the temperate regions of the northern hemisphere. The threat is a serious one since the ozone layer traps almost all in-coming ultraviolet radiation, which is harmful to all living organisms — humans, animals and plants.

(10) Even though the ozone layer is twenty-five kilometers thick, the atmosphere in it is very tenuous and the total amount of ozone, compared with other atmospheric gases, is quite small. If all of the ozone in a vertical column reaching up through the atmosphere were
(15) to be compressed to sea-level pressure, it would form a layer only a few millimeters thick...

Detailed study of the ozone layer began comparatively recently, in 1930, the earliest observations being made by the English scientist Sydney Chapman.
(20) These initial observations were taken up by the World Meteorological Organization (WMO) which established the Dobson network consisting of one hundred observation stations. Since 1983, on the initiative of WMO and the United Nations Environment Programme
(25) (UNEP), seven of these stations have been entrusted with the task of making long-term forecasts of the likely evolution of our precious shield.

In 1958, the researchers who permanently monitor the ozone content of the layer above the South Pole began
(30) to observe several seasonal variations. From June there was a slight reduction in ozone content which reached a minimum in October. In November there was a sudden increase in the ozone content. The fluctuations appeared to result from the natural phenomena of wind effects and
(35) temperature change.

However, although the October minimum remained constant until 1979, the total ozone content over the Pole was steadily diminishing until, in 1985, public opinion was finally roused by reports of a "hole" in the ozone
(40) layer and observations were intensified.

The culprits responsible for the hole had already been identified as being supersonic aircraft, such as Concorde, (although these have now been exonerated) and the notorious compounds known as chlorofluorocarbons, or
(45) CFCs. Synthesized in 1928 by chemists working at General Motors in the United States, CFCs are compounds of atoms of chlorine and fluorine. Having the advantage of being non-flammable, non-toxic and non-corrosive, they came into widespread use in the 1950s.
(50) They are widely used in refrigerators, air-conditioners, and to make the "bubbles" in the foam plastic used, for example, in car seats and as insulation in buildings...

In 1989 they represented a market valued at over $1.5 billion and a labor force of 1.6 million. Of the twenty-five
(55) countries producing CFCs, the United States, France, the United Kingdom, Japan and Germany account for three-quarters of the total world production of some 1.2 million tons.

These figures give some idea of the importance of the
(60) economic interests that are at stake in any decision to ban the industrial use of CFCs. But, with CFCs incriminated by scientists, the question arose as to whether we were prepared to take the risk of seeing an increase in the number of cases of skin cancer, eye ailments such as cataracts, or
(65) even a lowering of the human immune defense system, all effects that would follow further depletion of the ozone layer...

In 1987, twenty-four industrialized countries signed the Montreal Protocol on Substances that Deplete the Ozone
(70) Layer, the first world agreement aimed at halting the production of CFCs. As more evidence emerged concerning the seriousness of the threat, it became apparent that the protocol was not stringent enough and, year by year, its severity was increased until in 1990 in London, seventy
(75) countries agreed to stop all production of CFCs by the year 2000...

Unfortunately, even if the entire world were to agree today to halt all production and use of CFCs, this would not provide an immediate solution to the problem. A single
(80) molecule of chlorine can destroy from 10,000 to 100,000 molecules of ozone. Furthermore, CFCs have a lifespan of between 75 and 400 years and they take ten years to reach the ozone layer. In other words, what we are experiencing now results from CFCs emitted ten years ago.

(85) Industrialists are now urgently searching for substitute products. Some, such as propane, are too dangerous because they are inflammable; others, the HCFCs, might prove to be toxic and to contribute to the greenhouse effect, i.e. to the process of global warming.
(90) Nevertheless, nobody can say that the situation will not right itself, whether in the short term or long term, if we ourselves lend a hand.

From "Earth's Ozone Shield Under Threat", France Bequette, the *UNESCO Courier*, June 1990.

31. As it is used in the passage, the term *tenuous* most likely means:
    A. thin.
    B. dangerous.
    C. substantial.
    D. fragile.

32. According to the passage, the public first became aware of the depletion of ozone layer in:
    F. 1930
    G. 1958
    H. 1979
    J. 1985

33. According to the passage, all of the following contribute to fluctuations in the content of the ozone layer EXCEPT:
    A. supersonic aircraft.
    B. chlorofluorocarbons.
    C. temperature changes.
    D. wind effects.

34. The main point of the seventh paragraph (lines 53–58) is to:
    F. highlight the amount of CFCs produced every year.
    G. criticize the countries responsible for producing CFCs.
    H. indicate the economic interests at stake in the CFC debate.
    J. list the most important members of the Montreal Protocol.

35. According to the passage, alternatives to using CFCs may be difficult to find because substitute products:
    I. may prove to be toxic.
    II. are too dangerous to use.
    III. contribute to global warming.

    A. II only
    B. II and III only
    C. I and II only
    D. I, II, and III

36. According to the passage, forecasts about the future of the ozone layer are made by:
    F. the WMO.
    G. the Dobson network.
    H. the Montreal Protocol.
    J. the UNEP.

37. Which of the following would be the most likely result if all production of CFCs were to end today?
    A. Scientists would have to replace the quantities of ozone already lost.
    B. The ozone layer would only return to normal levels after 75 years.
    C. Scientists would also have to destroy all chlorine molecules in the atmosphere.
    D. The benefits would not be experienced for another ten years.

38. According the passage, the ozone layer is:
    F. a few millimeters thick.
    G. twelve kilometers thick.
    H. twenty-five kilometers thick.
    J. over forty kilometers thick.

39. Which of the following statements is best supported by the fourth paragraph (lines 28–35)?
    A. The ozone layer undergoes seasonal variations in density.
    B. The number of CFCs in the atmosphere increases from June to October.
    C. The ozone layer over the South Pole is more at risk than in other areas.
    D. The first studies of ozone layer depletion underestimated its severity.

40. The main conclusion reached in the passage about the threat to the ozone layer is that:
    F. the cost of banning CFCs altogether may make it an impractical answer.
    G. finding alternative products to CFCs may provide a long-term remedy to the situation.
    H. halting production of CFCs is unlikely to produce a solution to the problem.
    J. agreements between CFC-producing countries need to be more strictly enforced.

END OF READING TEST

IF YOU FINISH BEFORE TIME IS CALLED, YOU MAY CHECK YOUR WORK ON THIS SECTION ONLY. DO NOT TEURN TO ANY OTHER SECTION IN THE TEST. STOP

SCIENCE REASONING TEST

35 Minutes—40 Questions

Directions: Each of the following seven passages is followed by several questions. After reading each passage, decide on the best answer to each question and fill in the corresponding oval on your answer sheet. You are allowed to refer to the passages while answering the questions.

Passage I

Optical fibers are strands of highly transparent glass used for communication transmissions. When light is transmitted through optical fibers, power is lost along the way. The power lost depends on the distance travelled, the wavelength of the light transmitted, the glass used, and any impurities present. The following attenuation (power loss in db/km) curve, which was recorded for a fluoride glass optical fiber, includes the attenuation caused by three different impurities commonly present in fluoride glass fibers.

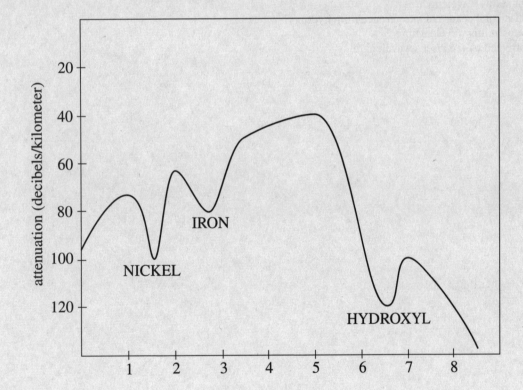

1. In this fiber, copper impurities can lead to an attenuation of roughly 95 decibels per kilometer at wavelengths near 1.6 microns. Such impurities, if graphed as above, would produce an attenuation response similar to that of:
   A. nickel.
   B. iron.
   C. hydroxyl.
   D. none of the impurities in the graph.

2. According to the graph, in a fiber without any impurities, as wavelength increases, power loss will:
   F. decrease then increase.
   G. increase then decrease.
   H. remain the same.
   J. fluctuate randomly.

3. If a researcher using a 6.6 micron laser wished to limit power loss, this fluoride glass fiber would be:
   A. ideal, because attenuation is at a minimum at this wavelength.
   B. impossible, because the fiber does not conduct light at this wavelength.
   C. inefficient, because of interference from hydroxyl groups at this wavelength.
   D. unaffected by the laser's wavelength.

4. Suppose a scientist were able to develop a fluoride glass fiber without any hydroxyl impurities. Which of the following predictions would most likely be true?
   I. There will be less power lost in the range between six and seven microns.
   II. The attenuation due to iron impurities would increase.
   III. The fiber's overall power loss would decrease.

   F. I only
   G. I and III only
   H. II and III only
   J. I, II, and III

5. A certain computer communications system requires a cable five kilometers long. Based on the data in the table, what is the minimum power loss that can be achieved using a fluoride glass fiber?
   A. 5 decibels
   B. 12.5 decibels
   C. 25 decibels
   D. 125 decibels

GO ON TO THE NEXT PAGE ➡

Passage II

A *binary star system* consists of two stars that are gravitationally bound to each other. If two stars that orbit each other are viewed along a line of sight that is not perpendicular to the orbital plane, they will alternately appear to eclipse each other. The orbit of *eclipsing binary* system *Q* is shown in Figure 1 below.

Astronomers deduce that a given "star" is an eclipsing binary from its *light curve*—the plot of its surface brightness (observed from a fixed position) against time. The light curve of an eclipsing binary typically displays a deep primary minimum and a shallower secondary minimum. Figure 2 shows the light curve of System *Q*.

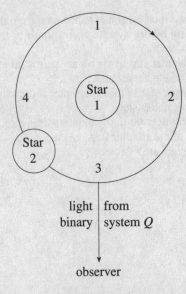

Figure 1

Notes: Diagram is not drawn to scale. Star 1 is brighter than Star 2.

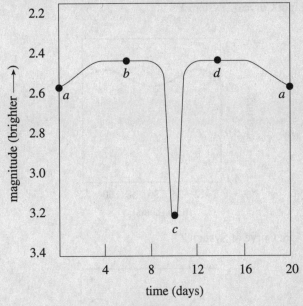

Figure 2

6. The point on the light curve labeled *c* corresponds to the position in Figure 1 labeled:
    F. 1.
    G. 2.
    H. 3.
    J. 4.

7. The period of revolution for eclipsing binary *Q* is about:
    A. 4 days.
    B. 10 days.
    C. 12 days.
    D. 20 days.

8. The stars in eclipsing binary *Q* alternately eclipse each other for periods of approximately:
    F. 2 days and 4 days.
    G. 2 days and 5 days.
    H. 2 days and 8 days.
    J. 5 days each.

GO ON TO THE NEXT PAGE ➡

Light Curve of System *X*

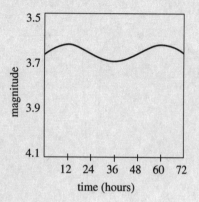

Light Curve of System *Z*

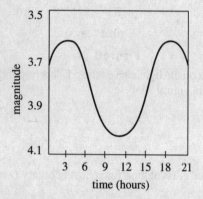

9. The light curves for two eclipsing binaries, Systems *X* and *Z*, are shown. Which of the following hypotheses would account for the deeper primary minimum of System *Z* ?

   A. There is a more extreme difference between the magnitudes of the two stars of System *X* than between those of the two stars of System *Z*.

   B. There is a more extreme difference between the magnitudes of the two stars of System *Z* than between those of the two stars of System *X*.

   C. System *X* has a longer period of revolution than does System *Z*.

   D. System *Z* has a longer period of revolution than does System *X*.

10. The greatest total brightness shown on the light curve of an eclipsing binary system corresponds to the point in the orbit when:

   F. the brighter star in the binary pair is directly in front of the darker star.

   G. the larger star in the binary pair is directly in front of the smaller star.

   H. the brighter star in the binary pair is directly in front of the smaller star.

   J. both stars are visible.

GO ON TO THE NEXT PAGE ➡

Passage III

The utilization and replenishing of the Earth's carbon supply is a cyclic process involving all living matter. This cycle is shown below.

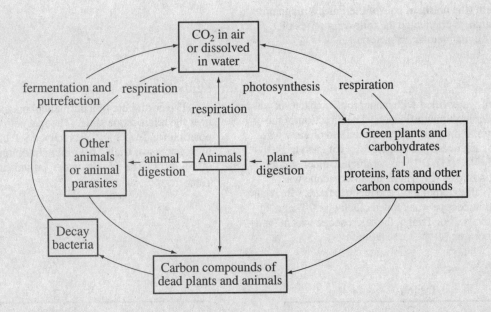

11. What effect would a sudden drop in the amount of the Earth's decay bacteria have on the amount of carbon dioxide in the atmosphere?
   A. The CO_2 level will drop to a life-threatening level since the bacteria is the sole source of CO_2.
   B. The CO_2 level will rise because the bacteria usually consume CO_2.
   C. The CO_2 level may decrease slightly, but there are other sources of CO_2.
   D. The CO_2 level will increase slightly due to an imbalance in the carbon cycle.

12. Which of the following statements are consistent with the carbon cycle as presented in the diagram?
   I. A non plant-eating animal does not participate in the carbon cycle.
   II. Both plant and animal respiration contribute CO_2 to the Earth's atmosphere.
   III. All CO_2 is released into the air by respiration.

   F. I only
   G. II only
   H. I and II only
   J. II and III only

13. A direct source of CO_2 in the atmosphere is:
   A. the fermentation of green-plant carbohydrates.
   B. the photosynthesis of tropical plants.
   C. the digestion of plant matter by animals.
   D. the respiration of animal parasites.

14. Which of the following best describes the relationship between animal respiration and photosynthesis?
   F. Respiration and photosynthesis serve the same function in the carbon cycle.
   G. Animal respiration provides vital gases for green plants.
   H. Animal respiration prohibits photosynthesis.
   J. There is no relationship between respiration and photosynthesis.

15. The elimination of which of the following would cause the earth's carbon cycle to grind to a complete halt?
   A. Green plants
   B. Animals
   C. Animal predation
   D. Decay bacteria

GO ON TO THE NEXT PAGE ➡

Passage IV

Microbiologists have observed that certain species of bacteria are magnetotactic, i.e., sensitive to magnetic fields. Several species found in the bottom of swamps in the Northern Hemisphere tend to orient themselves towards magnetic north (the northern pole of the Earth's magnetic field). Researchers conducted the following series of experiments on magnetotactic bacteria.

Study 1

A drop of water filled with magnetotactic bacteria was observed under high magnification. The direction of the first 500 bacterial migrations across the field of view was observed for each of 5 trials and the tally for each trial recorded in Table 1. Trial 1 was conducted under standard laboratory conditions. In Trial 2, the microscope was shielded from all external light and electric fields. In Trials 3 and 4, the microscope was rotated clockwise 90° and 180°, respectively. For Trial 5, the microscope was moved to another laboratory at the same latitude.

Study 2

The north pole of a permanent magnet was positioned near the microscope slide. The magnet was at the 12:00 position for Trial 1 and was moved 90° clockwise for each of 3 successive trials. All other conditions were as in Trial 1 of Study 1. The results were tallied and recorded in Table 2.

Table 1

Trial #	Direction			
	North	East	South	West
1	474	7	13	6
2	481	3	11	5
3	479	4	12	5
4	465	9	19	7
5	484	3	11	6

Table 2

Trial #	Direction			
	12:00	3:00	6:00	9:00
1	472	6	15	9
2	8	483	3	6
3	17	4	474	5
4	5	19	9	467

16. The theory that light was not the primary stimulus affecting the direction of bacterial migration is:
   F. supported by a comparison of the results of Studies 1 and 2.
   G. supported by a comparison of the results of Trials 1 and 2 of Study 1.
   H. supported by a comparison of the results of Trials 3 and 4 of Study 1.
   J. not supported by any of the results noted in the passage.

17. If the south pole of the permanent magnet used in Study 2 had been placed near the microscope slide, what would the most likely result have been?
   A. The figures for each trial would have remained approximately the same, since the strength of the magnetic field would be unchanged.
   B. The bacteria would have become disoriented, with approximately equal numbers moving in each direction.
   C. The major direction of travel would have shifted by 180° because of the reversed direction of the magnetic field.
   D. The bacteria would still have tended to migrate towards Earth's magnetic north, but would have taken longer to orient themselves.

GO ON TO THE NEXT PAGE ➡

18. It has been suggested that magnetic sensitivity helps magnetotactic bacteria orient themselves downwards. Such an orientation would be most advantageous from an evolutionary standpoint if:

   F. organisms that consume magnetotactic bacteria were mostly bottom-dwellers.

   G. the bacteria could only reproduce by migrating upwards to the water's surface.

   H. bacteria that stayed in the top layers of water tended to be dispersed by currents.

   J. the nutrients necessary for the bacteria's survival were more abundant in bottom sediments.

19. Researchers could gain the most useful new information about the relationship between magnetic field strength and bacterial migration by repeating Study 2 with:

   A. incremental position changes of less than 90°.

   B. a magnet that rotated slowly around the slide in a counterclockwise direction.

   C. more and less powerful magnets.

   D. larger and smaller samples of bacteria.

20. Which of the following statements is supported by the results of Study 1?

   F. The majority of magnetotactic bacteria migrate toward the Earth's magnetic north pole.

   G. The majority of magnetotactic bacteria migrate toward the north pole of the nearest magnet.

   H. The majority of magnetotactic bacteria migrate toward the 12:00 position.

   J. The effect of the Earth's magnetic field on magnetotactic bacteria is counteracted by electric fields.

21. What is the control in Study 1?

   A. Trial 1

   B. Trial 2

   C. Trial 3

   D. Trial 5

GO ON TO THE NEXT PAGE ➡

Passage V

A process has been developed by which plastic bottles can be recycled into a clear, colorless material. This material, called *nu-PVC*, can be used to form park benches and other similar structures. A series of experiments was performed to determine the weathering abilities of nu-PVC.

Experiment 1

Fifteen boards of *nu-PVC*, each $150 \times 25 \times 8$ cm in size, were sprayed with distilled water for ten hours a day for 32 weeks. All fifteen boards remained within 0.1 cm of their original dimensions. The surfaces of the boards displayed no signs of cracking, bubbling, or other degradation.

Experiment 2

Fifteen sheets of *nu-PVC*, each 2 m $\times 2$ m $\times 5$ cm, were hung in a chamber in which the humidity and temperature were held constant. The sheets were irradiated with ultraviolet light for 12 hours a day for 32 weeks. At the end of the experiment, the sheets' flexibility had decreased by an average of 17.5%. The surface of the sheets showed no signs of degradation, but they had all become milky white in color.

Experiment 3

Fifteen boards, as in Experiment 1, were each found to be capable of supporting an average of 963 pounds for 15 days without breaking or bending. These same boards were then kept for 32 weeks at temperatures ranging from 5° C to –15° C. At the end of the experiment, the boards were able to support an average of only 400 pounds without bending or breaking.

22. Based on the results of Experiment 1, which of the following conclusions concerning the effect of rain on *nu-PVC* is valid?
   F. The material absorbs water over time causing it to permanently swell.
   G. The material will be useful only in areas where there is no acid rain.
   H. The material's surface does not appear to require a protective coating to avoid water damage.
   J. The material loses flexibility after prolonged exposure to precipitation.

23. Park benches in an often snow-covered region of Minnesota are to be replaced with new ones, made of *nu-PVC*. The experimental results indicate that:
   A. the benches will suffer little degradation due to weathering.
   B. the benches would have to be stored indoors during the winter to remain usable.
   C. the benches should be varnished to prevent rain from seeping into the material.
   D. the benches will lose flexibility.

24. A reasonable control for Experiment 1 would be:
   F. a *nu-PVC* board submerged in distilled water.
   G. a *nu-PVC* board stored in a dry warehouse.
   H. a wooden board subjected to the same conditions.
   J. a wooden board stored in a dry warehouse.

25. The purpose of the ultraviolet radiation used in Experiment 2 was to:
   A. simulate the effects of sunlight.
   B. avoid damage to the material's finish.
   C. turn the boards a uniform color.
   D. test the strength of the *nu-PVC*.

26. From the information given, it can be inferred that *nu-PVC's* advantage over standard building materials such as wood is that it:
   F. is heavier and denser than other materials.
   G. can be developed in different colors and textures.
   H. is less subject to structural cracking and failure.
   J. is made from recycled plastic wastes.

27. Which of the following experiments would be the most likely to provide useful information concerning the weathering of *nu-PVC*?
   I. Repeating Experiment 1, increasing the length of the experiment from 32 weeks to 64 weeks
   II. Investigating of the effects of sea water and salt-rich air on the material
   III. Repeating Experiment 3, decreasing the minimum temperature from –15° C to –40° C
   A. II only
   B. III only
   C. I and II only
   D. I, II, and III

GO ON TO THE NEXT PAGE ➡

Passage VI

Preliminary research indicates that dietary sugar may react with proteins in the body, damaging the proteins and perhaps contributing to the aging process. The chemical effects of glucose on lens proteins in the eye were investigated in the following experiments.

Experiment 1

A human tissue protein sample was dissolved in a glucose and water solution, resulting in a clear yellow solution. After 30 minutes, the solution became opaque. Spectrographic analysis revealed that an *Amadori product* had formed on the protein. It was determined that the Amadori products on one protein had combined with free amino groups on nearby proteins, forming brown pigmented cross-links between the two proteins. The cross-links are termed *Advanced Glycosylation End products (AGE)*.

Experiment 2

Forty-six samples of human lens proteins taken from subjects ranging in age from 12–80 years were studied under an electron microscope. The lens proteins in the samples from older subjects occured much more often in aggregates formed by cross-linked bonds than did the lens proteins in the samples from younger subjects. Fluorescent characteristics revealed the cross-links to be of two types: di-sulfide bonds and an indeterminate formation with brownish pigmentation.

Experiment 3

Two solutions containing lens proteins from cow lenses were prepared, one with glucose and one without. Only the glucose solution turned opaque. Analysis revealed that the lens proteins in the glucose solution had formed pigmented cross-links with the brownish color and fluorescence characteristics of those observed in Experiment 2.

28. It was assumed in the design of Experiment 3 that cow lens proteins:
    F. have a brownish pigment.
    G. react with sulfides.
    H. remain insoluble in water.
    J. react similarly to human lens proteins.

29. Based on the results in Experiment 1 only, it can be concluded that:
    A. proteins can form di-sulfide cross-links.
    B. glucose dissolved in water forms AGE.
    C. glucose can react with proteins to form cross-links.
    D. Amadori products are a result of glucose metabolism.

30. As people age, the lenses in their eyes sometimes turn brown and cloudy (known as senile cataracts). Based on this information and the results of Experiment 2, which of the following hypotheses is the most likely to be valid?
    F. As people age, the amount of sulfur contained in lens proteins increases.
    G. Senile cataracts are caused by cross-linked bonds between lens proteins.
    H. Lens proteins turn brown with age.
    J. Older lens proteins are more fluorescent than younger lens proteins.

31. Which of the following hypotheses about the brown pigmented cross-links observed in Experiment 2 is best supported by the results of the three experiments?
    A. Their brownish color is caused by di-sulfide bonds.
    B. They are a natural formation which can be found at birth.
    C. They are caused by glucose in the diet reacting with lens proteins.
    D. They form when proteins are dissolved in water.

32. Based on the experimental results, lens proteins from a 32-year-old man would most likely have:
    F. more cross-links than lens proteins from a 32-year-old woman.
    G. more cross-links than lens proteins from an 18-year-old cow.
    H. more cross-links than lens proteins from an 18-year-old man.
    J. more cross-links than lens proteins from an 80-year-old man.

33. People with uncontrolled diabetes have excess levels of blood glucose. Based on this information and the results of the experiments, a likely symptom of advanced diabetes would be:
    A. senile cataracts, due to an increase of free amino groups in the urine.
    B. senile cataracts, due to glucose interacting with di-sulfide cross-links on lens proteins.
    C. senile cataracts, due to AGE cross-links of lens proteins.
    D. kidney failure, due to high levels of free amino groups in the urine.

GO ON TO THE NEXT PAGE ➡

Passage VII

Two scientists discuss their views about the Quark Model.

Scientist 1

According to the Quark Model, each proton consists of three quarks: two up quarks, which carry a charge of +2/3 each, and one down quark, which carries a charge of –1/3. All mesons, one of which is the π^+ particle, are composed of one quark and one antiquark, and all baryons, one of which is the proton, are composed of three quarks. The Quark Model explains the numerous different types of mesons that have been observed. It also successfully predicted the essential properties of the Υ meson. Individual quarks have not been observed because they are absolutely confined within baryons and mesons. However, the results of deep inelastic scattering experiments indicate that the proton has a substructure. In these experiments, high-energy electron beams were fired into protons. While most of the electrons incident on the proton passed right through, a few bounced back. The number of electrons scattered through large angles indicated that there are three distinct lumps within the proton.

Scientist 2

The Quark Model is seriously flawed. Conventional scattering experiments should be able to split the proton into its constituent quarks, if they existed. Once the quarks were free, it would be easy to distinguish quarks from other particles using something as simple as the Millikan oil drop experiment, because they would be the only particles that carry fractional charge. Furthermore, the lightest quark would be stable because there is no lighter particle for it to decay into. Quarks would be so easy to produce, identify, and store that they would have been detected if they truly existed. In addition, the Quark Model violates the Pauli exclusion principle which originally was believed to hold for electrons, but was found to hold for all particles of half-integer spin. The Pauli exclusion principle states that no two particles of half-integer spin can occupy the same state. The Δ^{++} baryon which supposedly has three up quarks violates the Pauli exclusion principle because two of those quarks would be in the same state. Therefore, the Quark Model must be replaced.

34. Which of the following would most clearly strengthen Scientist 1's hypothesis?
    F. Detection of the Δ^{++} baryon
    G. Detection of a particle with fractional charge
    H. Detection of mesons
    J. Detection of baryons

35. Which of the following are reasons why Scientist 2 claims quarks should have been detected, if they existed?
    I. They have a unique charge
    II. They are confined within mesons and baryons
    III. They are supposedly fundamental particles, and therefore could not decay into any other particle
    A. I only
    B. II only
    C. I and III only
    D. I, II, and III

36. Which of the following could Scientist 1 use to counter Scientist 2's point about the Pauli exclusion principle?
    F. Evidence that quarks do not have half-integer spin
    G. Evidence that the Δ^{++} baryon exists
    H. Evidence that quarks have fractional charge
    J. Evidence that quarks have the same spin as electrons

37. If Scientist 1's hypothesis is correct, the Δ^{++} baryon should have a charge of:
    A. –1
    B. 0
    C. 1
    D. 2

38. According to Scientist 2, the Quark Model is flawed:
    F. because the existence of individual baryons cannot be experimentally verified.
    G. because the existence of individual quarks cannot be experimentally verified.
    H. because particles cannot have fractional charge.
    J. because it doesn't include electrons as elementary particles.

39. Scientist 1 believes that some of the high-energy electrons that were aimed into the proton in the deep inelastic scattering experiments bounced back because:
    A. they hit quarks.
    B. they hit other electrons.
    C. they were repelled by the positive charge on the proton.
    D. they hit baryons.

GO ON TO THE NEXT PAGE ➡

40. The fact that deep inelastic scattering experiments revealed a proton substructure of three lumps supports the Quark Model because:

    F. protons are mesons, and meson supposedly consist of three quarks.

    G. protons are mesons, and mesons supposedly consist of a quark and an antiquark.

    H. protons are baryons, and baryons supposedly consist of three quarks.

    J. protons are baryons, and baryons supposedly consist of one quark and one antiquark.

END OF SCIENCE TEST

IF YOU FINISH BEFORE TIME IS CALLED, YOU MAY CHECK YOUR WORK ON THIS SECTION ONLY. DO NOT TURN TO ANY OTHER SECTION IN THE TEST. **STOP**

Compute Your Score

To score your results for Practice Tests 1 and 2, follow the directions on the following pages.

Compute Your Score

1 **Figure out your score in each section.** Refer to the answer keys to figure out the number right in each test section. Enter the results below:

		Test 1	Test 2			Test 1	Test 2
RAW SCORES	English:			Reading:			
	Math:			Science Reasoning:			

2 **Find your practice test scores.** Find your raw score on each section in the table below. The score in the far left column indicates your estimated scaled score if this were an actual ACT.

SCALED SCORE	RAW SCORES			
	TEST 1 ENGLISH	TEST 2 MATHEMATICS	TEST 3 READING	TEST 4 SCIENCE REASONING
36	75	60	40	40
35	74	60	40	40
34	73	59	39	39
33	72	58	39	39
32	71	57	38	39
31	70	55–56	37	38
30	69	53–54	36	37
29	68	50–52	35	36
28	67	48–49	34	35
27	65–66	45–47	33	34
26	63–64	43–44	32	33
25	61–62	40–42	31	32
24	58–60	38–39	30	30–31
23	56–57	35–37	29	28–29
22	53–55	33–34	28	26–27
21	49–52	31–32	27	24–25
20	46–48	28–30	25–26	21–23
19	44–45	26–27	23–24	19–20
18	41–43	23–25	21–22	17–18
17	39–40	20–22	19–20	16
16	36–38	17–19	17–18	15
15	34–35	15–16	15–16	14
14	30–33	13–14	13–14	13
13	28–29	11–12	12–13	12
12	25–27	9–10	10–11	11
11	23–24	8	9	10
10	20–22	7	8	9
9	17–19	6	7	8
8	14–16	5	6	7
7	12–13	4	5	6
6	9–11	3	4	5
5	7–8	2	3	4
4	4–6	1	2	3
3	3	1	1	2
2	2	0	1	1
1	1	0	0	0

		Test 1	Test 2			Test 1	Test 2
SCALED	English:				Reading:		
SCORES	Math:				Science Reasoning:		

3 **Find your estimated composite score.** To calculate your estimated composite score, simply add together your scaled scores on each subsection and divide by four.

COMPOSITE SCORE:

Test 1   Test 2

Practice Test 2:
Answers and Explanations

English Answer Key

1. C	20. F	39. D	58. H
2. G	21. A	40. G	59. B
3. D	22. J	41. A	60. G
4. F	23. C	42. G	61. C
5. D	24. G	43. C	62. J
6. G	25. D	44. H	63. B
7. D	26. H	45. B	64. J
8. J	27. B	46. G	65. A
9. C	28. G	47. D	66. G
10. J	29. D	48. J	67. D
11. D	30. J	49. B	68. G
12. H	31. A	50. J	69. D
13. C	32. H	51. A	70. J
14. J	33. D	52. J	71. C
15. C	34. F	53. D	72. H
16. H	35. A	54. H	73. B
17. C	36. G	55. B	74. G
18. H	37. A	56. J	75. C
19. D	38. J	57. D	

The questions fall into the following categories, according to the skills they test. If you notice that you're having trouble with particular categories, review the following:

1. REDUNDANCY—English Workout 1

2. RELEVANCE—English Workout 1

3. VERBOSITY—English Workout 1

 375

4. LOGIC—English Workout 2

5. SENTENCE STRUCTURE—English Workout 2

6. COMPLETENESS—English Workouts 2 and 3

7. IDIOM—English Workouts 2 and 3

8. TONE—English Workout 2

9. PUNCTUATION—English Workout 3

10. VERB USAGE—English Workout 2

11. PRONOUNS—English Workouts 2 and 3

12. JUDGING THE PASSAGE—English Workout 2

13. READING-TYPE QUESTIONS—English Workout 2

14. STRUCTURE AND PURPOSE—English Workout 2

15. MODIFIERS—English Workout 2

Passage I

1. (C)—Punctuation

At first glance, there may not seem to be anything wrong here. However, the dash after "Aegean Sea" alerts you that the writer has chosen to set off the parenthetical phrase describing "Acropolis" with dashes instead of commas. This means that you have to replace the comma after "Acropolis" with a dash, in order to have a matching pair. If there were a comma after "Aegean Sea," this underlined part of the sentence would not need to be changed. Knowing that you need to "make it all match" will help you score points on ACT English.

2. (G)—Sentence Structure

This question tests your sense of parallelism. Your ear can often help you identify unparallel constructions. "To climb . . . is to have beheld" is unparallel. They should be in the same form: "to climb . . . is to behold."

3. (D)—Relevance

You have the option to OMIT in this question, an option that you should definitely take. Athenian cuisine has nothing to do with the subject of the paragraph or the passage, which is the Parthenon.

4. (F)—Verb Usage

This verb is appropriately plural—the subject, "generations," is plural—and in the present perfect tense. Choices **G** and **H** are singular verbs, while **J** is wrong because generations of architects can't all be proclaiming at the present time.

5. (D)—Sentence Structure

Run-on sentences are common in the English section. There are a couple of ways to deal with this run-on sentence. You could put a semicolon after "subtle" to separate the clauses, or you could put a period after "subtle" and make the clauses into separate sentences. Since the choices offer you both options, there must be something more. And there is: you need a comma after "For example" to set it off from the rest of the sentence. Choice **D** fixes both errors.

6. (G)—Modification

This part of the sentence sounds strange; it seems that the "fact" is what is being "viewed from a distance," not the "straight columns." "Viewed from a distance" is a misplaced modifier that has to be moved to a position where it clearly modifies "columns." Choice **G** accomplishes this.

7. (D)—Punctuation

Read the sentence out loud and you'll hear that it has punctuation problems. There is no need for a semicolon or any other kind of punctuation mark between "of" and "uprightness." Don't place a comma before the first element of a series (**C**), and don't place a colon between a preposition and its objects (**B**).

8. (J)—Logic

The phrase "because of this" doesn't make sense here. The optical illusion the architects created is not the reason you'll get a different impression of the Parthenon from the one the ancient Athenians had; the reason is that the statue of Athena Parthenos isn't there anymore. The introductory phrase that makes sense is "Of course" (**J**).

9. (C)—Completeness

"Only by standing . . . Golden Age of Athens" is a sentence fragment that has to be hooked up somehow to the sentence after it. You can't just use a semicolon to join the two (**B**) because then the first clause of the new sentence will still be only a fragment. You have to reverse the subject and verb of the second sentence to attach the fragment to it, as **C** does.

10. (J)—Modification

What was removed from the Temple? The underlined part of the sentence is an introductory modifying phrase that you know describes the statue, but the word "statue" isn't anywhere in the sentence. As a result, the sentence doesn't make sense at all; it's impossible that "all that remains" in the temple was removed in the fifth century A.D. Choice **J** makes the sentence make sense.

11. (D)—Verb Usage

Quite a few words come between the subject and the verb of this sentence. You shouldn't be fooled, though; "many" is the subject of the sentence, not "carvings," "walls," or "Acropolis." Since "many" is plural, the verb of the sentence has to be plural as well. "Is" has to be changed to "are."

12. (H)—Completeness

This sentence is really only a sentence fragment; it has a subject, "decision," but no verb. Choice (**H**) rewords the underlined portion to make "Lord Elgin" the subject and "decided" the verb.

13. (C)—Pronouns

"They" is an ambiguous pronoun because it's not immediately clear what group "they" refers to. You can figure out from the context that "they" is the Greeks; no other group could have won independence from the Turks and demanded the carvings back from the British. To make the first sentence clear, you have to replace "they" with "the Greeks."

14. (J)—Reading-Type

What could have been destroyed by explosions in the Parthenon? Carvings. The fact that some of the carvings were destroyed during a war is another good reason that many of them can no longer be found in the Parthenon, as Paragraph 4 states. Therefore, the new material belongs in Paragraph 4.

15. (C)—Judging the Passage

The answer to the question is clearly "no," the writer did not fulfill the request, because only the second paragraph discusses techniques of construction at all; even then, only one technique, the bulging of the columns, is described in any detail. The author covers several topics in the essay in addition to construction techniques, including the statue of Athena Parthenos and the fate of the carvings.

Passage II

16. (H)—Verb Usage

The previous sentence tells you that "Robin is the hero"; look for a verb form that matches the present tense "is," since the sentence continues the discussion of the ballads. **H**'s "tell" is in the right tense. **F** switches to another tense, the present progressive, which makes it sound as if the ballads were literally speaking. **G** lacks a main verb, creating a sentence fragment. **J** has the same tense problem as **F**, and compounds it by adding an extra, unnecessary subject, "they."

17. (C)—Verb Usage

Make it all match. You need a verb that is parallel to "robbing" and "killing," so "giving" **C** is the correct choice.

18. (H)—Modification

The adjective "frequent" is the correct choice to modify "enemy." The underlined choice uses the both the word "most" and the suffix "-est" to indicate the highest degree, or superlative form. Use one or the other, but not both. Likewise, **G** incorrectly uses "more" and the suffix *-er* together. Both of these express the comparative form—but again, you'd use one or the other, not both at once. In **J**, "frequently" is an adverb and so can't describe a noun.

19. (D)—Relevance

When you see the OMIT option, ask yourself if the underlined portion is really necessary. The parentheses were a clue that the underlined part wasn't really essential. It goes off on a tangent about modern adaptations of the King Arthur legend whereas Robin Hood is the focus of the passage. **A**, **B**, and **C** all reword the irrelevant sentence.

20. (F)—Pronouns

This is correct as is. "Them" matches the plural noun it's standing in for: "writers." **G** "him" and **H** "it" are singular, so they don't.

21. (A)—Punctuation

This is correct because we want the *possessive* apostrophe. **B** and **C** are wrong because they are the plural, not the possessive, form of Stukely. And there obviously aren't a lot of Stukelys running around. **D** is wrong because if you read it out loud you can tell that no pause—and so no comma—is called for.

22. (J)—Reading-Type

Since this passage is aimed at discussing the historical development of the Robin Hood legend, choice **J** would be most in keeping with the subject matter. **A** goes way off track; you're asked to add more information on *Stukely*, not on English history. **G** and **H** do relate their points to Stukely but they pursue details. The main topic of the passage is Robin Hood, not antiquaries (**G**). (Remember, you want a choice that is most relevant to the passage *as a whole*.) As for **H**, King Arthur was mentioned earlier in the passage, but then only to make a point about Robin Hood. A discussion of Stukely's interest in King Arthur would stray from the topic of the passage.

23. (C)—Logic

The shortest answer is the best choice. Choices **A** and **D** wrongly imply a comparison between Robin and a nobleman, when the claim was that Robin *was* a nobleman. **B** is incoherent.

24. (H)—Tone

The comparison with a puppy is silly in this context since it jars with the matter-of-fact tone of this passage; all choices except **G** can be eliminated. The ACT will often try to fool you like this by sticking in a phrase that just doesn't go with the passage's tone.

25. (D)—Punctuation

The only choice that will tie in both parts of the sentence is **D**. A dash in this context correctly makes an emphatic pause between "love interest" and its appositive, "Maid Marian." All the rest of the choices have punctuation errors. Semicolons are used between independent clauses, and the part that would follow the semicolon in **A** isn't a clause. The plural form of the noun, "interests" (**B**), doesn't agree with the singular article. **C** can be ruled out because there is no reason to pause in the middle of a name, and so the comma is incorrectly placed.

26. (H)—Logic

All the choices, with the exception of **H**, have inappropriate connecting words. Since the passage moves to a discussion of a new time period, you *should* begin a new paragraph, ruling out **G**. In addition, "on the one hand" should be followed by "on the other hand." "Consequently" (**F**) and "therefore" (**J**) wrongly imply that what follows is a result of something in the previous sentence.

27. (B)—Verb Usage

The correct verb tense, and the only choice that doesn't create a sentence fragment, is **B**. "Basing" (**A**) and "to base" (**C**) create sentence fragments. Of course the omission of the verb would also result in a sentence fragment, so **D** is incorrect.

28. (G)—Logic

G is the only choice that fits the rest of the sentence both logically and grammatically. "And" doesn't make sense as a connecting word in the original. **H** also uses a connecting word that doesn't logically fit; "therefore" inaccurately suggests a cause and effect relationship. **J** is wrong because a semicolon should be used between independent clauses, and the first clause can't stand alone.

29. (D)—Reading-Type

Since we're told that the audience is unfamiliar with the story, it would make sense to include a summary of the Robin Hood legend (**D**), something the passage lacks. **A** and **C** would do nothing for a reader curious about Robin Hood, since they go off on tangents about other issues. As the passage states that Robin Hood's existence is questionable ("legendary"), **B** doesn't fit in with the stance of the writer.

30. (J)—Reading-Type

Rarely are ACT English passages written for authorities or experts; they're usually written for the general public, as **J** correctly states in this question. If the passage were directed towards "experts" (**F**) or "authorities" (**G**), much of the basic information it presents would be unnecessary and not included. Since the passage states that the existence of Robin Hood is legendary, the passage can't be aimed at readers craving confirmation that he "was an actual historical personage," so **H** is wrong.

Passage III

31. (A)—Verbosity

The shortest answer is correct. "Ten-mile" is correctly punctuated—the hyphen makes it an adjective modifying "radius." The other answers are wordy and awkward.

32. (H)—Idiom

You don't look forward *at* something. You look forward *to* something. **G** wrongly implies that it is the brother who looks forward to the opportunity to show off the narrator's skills. **J** wrongly implies a contrast between the two parts of the sentence. Actually, it is precisely because she hasn't flown with her brother that the writer anticipates showing off her skills to him. In addition, **J** is punctuated incorrectly: you need a semicolon or a period before "nevertheless."

33. (D)—Logic

"Ever since" means from the time the narrator first could read to the present time of the narrative. This span of time makes sense, since the writer is telling us how long she had planned on a journalism career. "If" in **A** signals a hypothetical situation, rather than a period of time. "Since" in **B** implies a cause and effect relationship that doesn't hold up. Why would her ability to easily read a newspaper be a reason for her career decision? "Although" in **C** signals a contrast, but there isn't one.

34. (F)—Pronouns

It's true that you use "I" and "me," in **G** and **H**, when you're writing about yourself. However, you can't say "I always envisioned I," or "I always envisioned me." You have to say "I always envisioned myself."

35. (A)—Punctuation

A is correct because all you need to do is pause before the word "giving," and this pause is signaled by the comma. You don't need a colon, in **B**. Colons signal lists or definitions. You don't need a semicolon in **C** either—a semicolon should be placed between clauses that could stand alone as sentences, but the second part of this sentence can't. **D** creates a sentence with no verb.

36. (G)—Modification

This is an example of a misplaced modifier. **F** and **H** make it sound as if it is the airport, and not the pilot, that is filing the flight plan. **J** is awkward (it uses a passive construction) and wordy. **G** is concise, and the verbs "filed" and "gave" are parallel.

37. (A)—Modification

The adjective "careful" should be placed next to "watch," the noun it modifies. **B** is wrong because the reference is not to "careful airplanes." "Neared" requires an adverb such as "carefully" before it, not an adjective. **D** is wrong because it is the people, not the crater, that are "careful."

38. (J)—Punctuation

The colon in the original interrupts the flow of the sentence. Colons often function like equals signs. ("Here's what we need for the picnic: salami, ham, cheese, and bread.") Colons signal lists or definitions, but nothing needs to be equated in this sentence.

39. (D)—Redundancy

Since "speechless" and "mute" mean the same thing, it's redundant to use both of them.

40. (G)—Verb Usage

"Steadying" and "took" should be in parallel form. This makes **G** right. The verbs in **J** are parallel but they're in the present tense, which doesn't fit with the past tense verbs "shot" and "dictated" in the nonunderlined part of the sentence.

41. (A)—Tone

Since Jeff and the narrator are circling the mountain, "a description of Mt. St. Helens" would be appropriate. **B** contradicts the information in the passage; we're told that the plane must stay high enough to avoid smoke and ash. In any case, the tone of **B** doesn't suit the calm tone of the rest of the passage. **C** sounds as if it belongs in a science textbook rather than in a story. **D** wanders too far from the direct observation of the Mt. St. Helens volcano, which is the paragraph's focus.

42. (G)—Logic

"Since that time" is an appropriate transition. It makes clear the time shift between the day at Mt. St. Helens and the present. The other choices contain inappropriate connecting words. "However" in **F** and "nevertheless" in **J** signal contrasts, but there isn't one in the passage. "Furthermore" suggests an elaboration of what came before, but there is none in the passage.

43. (C)—Reading-Type Question

Since the author is favorably recalling a memorable past experience, "nostalgic" in **C** is the best choice. The passage is positive in tone. It's definitely not "bitter," **B**, or "exhausted," **D**. "Optimistic" is close but wrong. "Optimistic" means "hopeful." The passage focuses on the excitement of the past, not on the good things that might happen.

44. (H)—Judging the Passage

The use of "I" is appropriate because this is a firsthand account. First-person narratives do tend to draw the reader in. **J** is not true, since "I" is not appropriate in all types of writing. The passage is personal and chatty; it's not an example of "formal writing." The passage isn't focused on "volcanoes" in general, as **G** says, but on the Mt. St. Helens eruption, the narrator's first international story.

45. (B)—Structure and Purpose

The passage reads best if the first and second paragraphs are switched. **A, C,** and **D** confuse the time sequence of the narrative, which follows the narrator from her early dreams of becoming a photojournalist, to the memorable Mt. St. Helens story, to her present experience as a foreign correspondent.

Passage IV

46. (G)—Redundancy

The description of Sherlock Holmes as "ingenious and extremely clever" is redundant because "ingenious" and "extremely clever" mean the same thing. You only need to use one of the two to get the point across.

47. (D)—Logic

"Therefore" is supposed to be a signal that the sentence that follows is a logical conclusion based on information from the preceding sentence or sentences. The use of "therefore" doesn't make any sense here because you can't conclude that everyone knows the phrase "elementary, my dear Watson" just because everyone knows of Holmes's detective abilities. Choice **C** is wrong for the same reason—"for this reason" and "therefore" mean the same thing in this context. "Although" (choice **B**) indicates some sort of contrast; this would be wrong because there is no contrast within this sentence or between this sentence and the previous one. Really, there is no need for a structural signal here at all. Choice **D** is correct.

48. (J)—Relevance

Note that this question has an OMIT option—a strong clue that the underlined portion is irrelevant to the paragraph. The theme of the first paragraph is "everyone knows who Sherlock Holmes is (or was)." The last sentence has absolutely nothing to do with this main idea, so it should be omitted. Putting parentheses around the sentence (choice **G**) will not make it more relevant, so that is not the way to solve the problem.

49. (B)—Pronouns

"He" is an ambiguous pronoun because it's unclear whether "he" refers to Conan Doyle or to Sherlock Holmes. You know after reading the entire sentence that "he" is Conan Doyle, so you have to replace "he" with "Conan Doyle" for the sake of clarity.

50. (J)—Verbosity

From a grammatical point of view, there is nothing wrong here; it's just unnecessarily wordy. The ACT prizes clarity and simplicity in style, which often means that the shortest answer is the best one. "To be remembered" is the most concise, and therefore the correct, answer.

51. (A)—Logic

"In fact" is the appropriate signal phrase here. "Despite this," "regardless," and "yet" would all indicate a contrast between this sentence and the previous one. There is no contrast, however; Conan Doyle did not want to be remembered as the author of Sherlock Holmes stories, so he killed the detective off (at least for a while).

52. (J)—Modification

A modifying phrase that begins a sentence refers to the noun or pronoun immediately following the phrase. According to that rule, the phrase "having had enough of his famous character by that time" modifies "Sherlock Holmes," which doesn't make sense at all. The sentence has to be rearranged so that the introductory phrase describes Conan Doyle. **J** is the choice that accomplishes this.

53. (D)—Relevance

Once again, take note of the OMIT choice. What do soap opera characters have to do with Arthur Conan Doyle and Sherlock Holmes? Nothing. This sentence disrupts the flow of the paragraph by being almost completely irrelevant, so it has to be omitted.

54. (H)—Verb Usage

The verb is in the wrong tense. "Has been deeply immersed" is in the present perfect tense, which is used to describe an action that started in the past and continues to the present or that happened a number of times in the past and may happen again in the future. Since Conan Doyle's immersion in spiritualism is over and done with, you have to use the simple past: "was deeply immersed."

55. (B)—Completeness

This is a sentence fragment because there is no subject and verb; all you have is an introductory phrase and a subordinate clause starting with "that." By omitting "that," you can turn the subordinate clause into a main clause, making "he lectured" the subject and verb (choice **B**). Choice **C** would work if the sentence began with "so convinced." **D** is wrong because the introductory phrase can't stand alone as a sentence.

56. (J)—Redundancy

Since this sentence says that Conan Doyle and his family attempted to communicate with the dead by automatic writing, it's redundant to explain that automatic writing was thought to be a means of communicating with "those no longer among the living." Omit the underlined portion of the sentence.

57. (D)—Structure and Purpose

The second sentence refers to "these experiences," so it should come directly after the sentence that describes the paranormal experiences Conan Doyle seemed to have had. The fourth sentence is the one that talks about materialized hands and heavy articles swimming through the air, so the second sentence should come after the fourth.

58. (H)—Pronouns

There are two problems with the underlined portion of the sentence: the colon does not belong there, and the pronoun "they" is ambiguous because it doesn't refer to anything in particular in the previous sentence. Choice **H** takes care of both of these problems by dropping the colon and by spelling out what the pronoun was supposed to refer to.

59. (B)—Logic

Here you just have to pick the choice that makes sense. Sherlock Holmes is only a fictional character, so choices **A**, **C**, and **D** are wrong; Holmes could not possibly have said anything about Conan Doyle's spiritualism, nor will he ever. You can still wonder, however, what the esteemed detective would have said, if he were real. This is the idea behind the last sentence.

60. (G)—Reading-Type

The correct answer has to express the focus on Conan Doyle's spirituality. Choice G does this; no other choice captures the scope of the passage.

Passage V

61. (C)—Punctuation

Read this sentence to yourself, pausing whenever you hit a comma. It doesn't sound right, does it? Now read the sentence again without pausing for the two commas. It should sound as though it flows a lot more smoothly and naturally. There is no reason to set off "in June" from the rest of the sentence, because it is not a parenthetical phrase. The commas should be omitted.

62. (J)—Modification

There is no reason to use the comparative form of plentiful ("more plentiful") because nothing is being compared here. In fact, no sort of adjective is needed in front of plentiful at all, so the OMIT choice is the correct one.

63. (B)—Verb Usage

A look at the answer choices would have helped you spot the errors in this part of the sentence. There is no parenthesis after "needles" to match the parenthesis in front of "fallen." Once you put the second parenthesis where it belongs, you can see that the subject of this clause is not "fallen logs, branches, and pine needles," but rather "supply." Since "supply" is singular, the verb should be singular also—"were" has to be changed to "was."

64. (J)—Completeness

There are two problems here. One, the first "sentence" of this paragraph is really just a fragment because it doesn't have a subject or a verb. It should be the introductory phrase for the second sentence. Two, the second sentence uses "its," the possessive form of "it," when it should use "it was." Merely adding an apostrophe to "its" (as choices **G** and **H** do) would be wrong because "it's" means "it is," not "it was"; you have to have the past tense here. Choice **J** takes care of both of these problems.

65. (A)—Punctuation

This part of the sentence is okay. No punctuation is necessary. It would be a mistake to try to break the sentence up into two parts with a period or semicolon after "control" because the part that started with "in spite of" would only be a fragment. Likewise, choice **C** creates a fragment.

66. (G)—Pronoun

The phrase "of 9,000 firefighters employed state-of-the-art equipment" doesn't make sense at all. You need a relative clause after firefighters; for example, "who employed state-of-the-art equipment." It is not correct to use the relative pronoun "which" when referring to a person or a group of people, so choice **G** is correct.

67. (D)—Modification

As you can see from the choices, the question here is where to put the modifier "only" so that the sentence makes sense. Since the fires did not stop until the first snow, you can infer that "only nature" was able to curb the destruction (choice **D**). All of the other choices state that nature had just a limited ability to curb the destruction, which is not what the writer means to say.

68. (G)—Sentence Structure

The introductory modifying phrase is unnecessarily wordy; drop the "having been" and the phrase becomes clearer and more concise. Choice **H** is wrong because it would produce a run-on sentence. Choice **J** is out because there is no reason to put a comma between "ecologist" and "who."

69. (D)—Relevance

It seems at first that this sentence belongs in the paragraph because it follows the first sentence pretty naturally. Read further in the paragraph, however, and you realize that the fact that more acres burned in Alaska than in Yellowstone in 1988 is really irrelevant to the writer's argument in this paragraph. The writer is explaining that forest fires can be good for a forest, and that's why the Yellowstone fires were not such a great tragedy.

70. (J)—Redundancy

It's redundant to say "in order that continued health . . . be maintained"; if the health of the forest is maintained, obviously it will continue. **J** is the choice that avoids redundancy. Remember, the shortest choice is often the correct one.

71. (C)—Verb Usage

Use the present tense to describe things that are always true—"the sun comes up in the morning," "the cone only opens when exposed to great heat." Also, since the writer is talking about the cone of the lodgepole pine (which is singular), the possessive should be "pine's," not "pines."

72. (H)—Logic

"However" is the wrong transition signal to use here because there is no contrast between this sentence and the previous one. This sentence actually supports the previous one. The fact that large animals were grazing and bedding down near the fire shows that they were indeed fire tolerant and fire adaptive so the appropriate signal phrase would be "in fact."

73. (B)—Sentence Structure and Purpose

The third paragraph describes how the plant life of a forest benefits from a forest fire, while the fourth paragraph explains that the wildlife of Yellowstone survived the 1988 fires relatively well, as expected. A transition sentence between the two paragraphs is not going to say that "animals suffer" from a forest fire or that "one never knows what toll a fire will take"; these choices contradict the author's tone and opinion. **D** is an irrelevant statement. This leaves **B**, which is correct because it reflects the author's opinion in both paragraphs and provides a good introduction to the fourth.

74. (G)—Modification

The problem with "judging from the recent pictures of the park" is that the phrase is modifying "forest," and a forest obviously can't judge anything. The phrase would have been okay if the sentence read "judging from the recent pictures of the park, I think that the forest was not destroyed." In this case the phrase modifies "I," the author, who is capable of judging. Choice **G** takes care of the problem by rewriting the sentence so that the modifying phrase is gone.

75. (C)—Reading-Type

Simply listing the endangered animal species in the park (**A**) would not show the fire to be relatively harmless to those species. Discussing the vulnerability of endangered birds to forest fires (**B**) would make the fire seem dangerous, so it's out, too. **D** may seem like an attractive choice, but it's not correct: even if the fires are infrequent, they could still be harmful to the endangered animals. **C** is the correct answer. Reports of park biologists that the endangered animals were okay during the fire would be good evidence that they were not significantly threatened.

Math Answer Key

1. A	20. G	39. A	58. J
2. J	21. E	40. K	59. C
3. A	22. H	41. B	60. J
4. G	23. A	42. H	
5. B	24. G	43. E	
6. H	25. C	44. K	
7. C	26. H	45. E	
8. J	27. C	46. K	
9. D	28. H	47. E	
10. F	29. D	48. G	
11. B	30. H	49. C	
12. G	31. A	50. F	
13. D	32. F	51. C	
14. G	33. B	52. F	
15. D	34. K	53. B	
16. F	35. D	54. J	
17. E	36. K	55. E	
18. K	37. B	56. G	
19. D	38. F	57. B	

1. (A)—Percent Increase/Decrease

Math Appendix, #33. To reduce a number by 20%, you could take 20% of the original number and subtract the result, or you could just take 80% of the original number:

New price = 80% of Original price
$$= (.80)(\$125)$$
$$= \$100$$

2. (J)—Evaluating an Algebraic Expression

Math Appendix, #52. Plug in $x = -5$ and see what you get:
$$2x^2 - 6x + 5 = 2(-5)^2 - 6(-5) + 5$$
$$= 2 \cdot 25 - (-30) + 5$$
$$= 50 + 30 + 5$$
$$= 85$$

3. (A)—Prime Factorization

Math Appendix, #11. The prime factorization of 36 is $2 \times 2 \times 3 \times 3$. That factorization includes 2 distinct prime factors, 2 and 3.

4. (G)—Exterior Angles of a Triangle

Math Appendix, #81. The exterior angles of a triangle (or *any* polygon, for that matter) add up to 360°:
$$x + 85 + 160 = 360$$
$$x = 115$$

5. (B)—Average Formula and Adding/Subtracting Fractions

Math Appendix, #41, #22. Don't jump to hasty conclusions—don't just average the denominators. Do it right—add the fractions and divide by 2:

$$\text{Average of 2 numbers} = \frac{\text{Sum}}{2}$$

$$\frac{\frac{1}{20}+\frac{1}{30}}{2} = \frac{\frac{3}{60}+\frac{2}{60}}{2} = \frac{\frac{5}{60}}{2} = \frac{\frac{1}{12}}{2} = \frac{1}{12}\cdot\frac{1}{2} = \frac{1}{24}$$

6. (H)—Rate

Math Appendix, #39. Everyone pays $1.50, and the rest of the toll is based on the number of miles traveled. Subtract $1.50 from Joy's toll to see how much is based on distance traveled: $25.00 – $1.50 = $23.50. Then divide that amount by 25 cents per mile:

$$\frac{\$23.50}{\$0.25 \text{ per mile}} = 94 \text{ miles}$$

7. (C)—Multiplying and Dividing Powers and Multiplying Monomials

Math Appendix, #47. #55. Multiply the coefficients and add the exponents:

$$3x^2 \cdot 5x^3 = 3\cdot 5 \cdot x^{2+3} = 15x^5$$

8. (J)—Finding the Distance Between Two Points

Math Appendix, #71. You could use the distance formula, but it's easier here to think about a right triangle. One leg is the difference between the x's, which is 3, and the other leg is the difference between the y's, which is 4, so you're looking at a 3-4-5 triangle, and the hypotenuse, which is the distance from P to Q is 5.

9. (D)—Percent Formula

Math Appendix, #32. Percent times Whole equals Part:

$$(\text{Percent}) \times 25 = 16$$

$$\text{Percent} = \frac{16}{25} = 0.64 = 64\%$$

10. (F)—Comparing Fractions

Math Appendix, #28. For $\frac{7}{x}$ to be greater than $\frac{1}{4}$, the denominator x has to be less than 4 times the numerator, or 28. And for $\frac{7}{x}$ to be less than $\frac{1}{3}$, the denominator x has to be greater than 3 times the numerator, or 21. Thus x could be any of the integers 22 through 27, of which there are 6.

11. (B)—Factoring Other Polynomials

Math Appendix, #61. To factor $6x^2 - 13x + 6$, you need a pair of binomials whose "first" terms will give you a product of $6x^2$ and whose "last" terms will give you a product of 6. And since the middle term of the result is negative, the two last terms must both be negative. You know that one of the factors is among the answer choices, so you can use them in your trial-and-error effort to factor. You know you're looking for a factor with a minus sign in it, so the answer's either **B** or **D**.

Try **B** first: Its first term is $3x$, so the other factor's first term would have to be $2x$ (to get that $6x^2$ in the product). **B**'s last term is -2, so the other factor's last term would have to be -3. Check to see if $(3x - 2)(2x - 3)$ works:

$$(3x - 2)(2x - 3)$$
$$= (3x \cdot 2x) + [3x\,(-3)] + [(-2)(2x)] + [(-2)(-3)]$$
$$= 6x^2 - 9x - 4x + 6$$
$$= 6x^2 - 13x + 6$$

It works. There's no need to check **D**.

12. (G)—Adding/Subtracting Fractions

Math Appendix, #22. The four fractions on the left side of the equation are all ready to be added, because they already have a common denominator: a.

$$\frac{1}{a} + \frac{2}{a} + \frac{3}{a} + \frac{4}{a} = 5$$
$$\frac{1 + 2 + 3 + 4}{a} = 5$$
$$\frac{10}{a} = 5$$
$$10 = 5a$$
$$a = 2$$

13. (D)—Intersecting Lines

Math Appendix, #78. $\angle CGE$ and $\angle BGF$ are vertical angles, so they're equal, and $\angle BGF$ measures $105°$. If you subtract $\angle AGB$ from $\angle BGF$, you're left with $\angle AGF$, the angle you're looking for. So, $\angle AGF$ measures $105° - 40°$, or $65°$.

14. (G)—Solving an Inequality

Math Appendix, #69. You solve an inequality much the way you solve an equation: Do the same things to both sides until you've isolated what you're solving for. (Just remember to flip the sign if you ever multiply or divide both sides by a negative number.) Here you want to isolate x:

$$-3 < 4x - 5$$
$$2 < 4x$$
$$\frac{2}{4} < x$$
$$x > \frac{1}{2}$$

15. (D)—Interior Angles of a Triangle, Exterior Angles of a Triangle

Math Appendix, #80, #81. Because $\overline{BD}$ bisects $\angle ABC$, the measure of $\angle ABD$ is $50°$. Now you know 2 of the 3 angles of $\triangle ABD$, so the third angle measures $180° - 60° - 50° = 70°$.

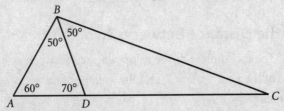

$\angle BDC$, the angle you're looking for, is supplementary to the 70° angle, so $\angle BDC$ measures $180° - 70° = 110°$.

16. (F)—Solving "In Terms Of" and Factoring out a Common Divisor

Math Appendix, #64, #58. To express y in terms of x, isolate y:

$$x + 2y - 3 = xy$$
$$2y - xy = -x + 3$$
$$y(2 - x) = 3 - x$$
$$y = \frac{3 - x}{2 - x}$$

17. (E)—Parts and Whole

Math Appendix, Miscellaneous. If you add the number of English-speakers and the number of Spanish-speakers, you get $28 + 37 = 65$. But there are only 50 students, so $65 - 50 = 15$ of them are being counted twice—because those 15 speak both languages.

18. (K)—Rates

Math Appendix, #39. Set up a proportion:

$$\frac{288 \text{ miles}}{6 \text{ hours}} = \frac{x \text{ miles}}{8 \text{ hours}}$$
$$6x = 288 \cdot 8$$
$$6x = 2,304$$
$$x = 384$$

19. (D)—Repeating Decimals

Math Appendix, #30. To convert a fraction to a decimal, you divide the denominator into the numerator. Clearly you don't have time to take the division out to 100 places after the decimal point. There must be a pattern you can take advantage of. Start dividing and continue just until you see what the pattern is:

$$11 \overline{)\ 4.000000...} \quad .363636...$$

The 1st, 3rd, 5th, etc. digits are 3; and the 2nd, 4th, etc. digits are 6. In other words, every odd-numbered digit is a 3 and every even-numbered digit is a 6. The 100th digit is an even-numbered digit, so it's a 6.

20. (G)—Solving a System of Equations

Math Appendix, #67. Since it's x you're looking for, eliminate y. Fortunately, the equations are all ready for you—just add them and the $+4y$ cancels with the $-4y$:

$$3x + 4y = 31$$
$$\underline{3x - 4y = -1}$$
$$6x \qquad = 30$$
$$x = 5$$

21. (E)—Finding the Distance Between Two Points

Math Appendix, #71. The coordinates of the midpoint are the averages of the coordinates of the endpoints. The average of the x's is $\frac{2 + 12}{2} = 7$, and the average of the y's is $\frac{3 + (-15)}{2} = -6$, so the coordinates of the midpoint are $(7, -6)$.

22. (H)—Sine, Cosine, and Tangent of Acute Angles

Math Appendix, #96. Cosine is "adjacent over hypotenuse." Here the leg adjacent to θ is 4 and the hypotenuse is 5, so $\cos \theta = \frac{4}{5}$.

23. (A)—Circumference of a Circle

Math Appendix, #89. The radius of circle Q is twice the radius of circle P. You could use the circumference of circle P to find the radius of circle P, then double that radius to get the radius of circle Q, and finally use that radius to calculate the circumference of circle Q. It's much easier and faster, however, if you realize that "double the radius means double the circumference." If the circumference of circle P is 6, then the circumference of circle Q is twice that, or 12.

24. (G)—Evaluating an Algebraic Expression

Math Appendix, #52: This looks like a functions question, but in fact it's just a "plug-in-the-number-and-see-what-you-get" question.

$$f(x) = x^3 - x^2 - x$$
$$f(-3) = (-3)^3 - (-3)^2 - (-3)$$
$$= -27 - 9 + 3$$
$$= -33$$

25. (C)—Integer/Noninteger, and Miscellaneous Triangles

Math Appendix, #3: If the 2 unknown side lengths are integers, and the sum of the 2 lengths has to be greater than 7, then the least amount the 2 unknown sides could add up to would be 8, which would make the perimeter $7 + 8 = 15$.

26. (H)—Factoring other Polynomials—FOIL in Reverse and Factoring out a Common Divisor

Math Appendix, #61. First factor out an x from each term, then factor what's left:
$$2x + 3x^2 + x^3 = x(2 + 3x + x^2)$$
$$= x(x^2 + 3x + 2)$$
$$= x(x + 1)(x + 2)$$

27. (C)—Simplifying an Algebraic Fraction, Multiplying and Dividing Powers, Raising Powers to Powers

Math Appendix, #62, #47, #48. Get rid of the parentheses in the denominator, and then cancel factors the numerator and denominator have in common:
$$\frac{x^2\, y^3\, z^4}{(xyz^2)^2} = \frac{x^2\, y^3\, z^4}{x^2\, y^2\, z^4} = \frac{x^2}{x^2}\, \frac{y^3}{y^2}\, \frac{z^4}{z^4} = y$$

28. (H)—Adding/Subtracting Fractions, Converting Fractions to Decimals

Math Appendix, #22, #29. Normally you would have a choice: Either convert the fractions to decimals first and then add, or add the fractions first and then convert the sum to a decimal. In this case, however, both fractions would convert to endlessly repeating decimals, which might be a bit unwieldy when adding. In this case it seems to make sense to add first, then convert:
$$\frac{2}{3} + \frac{1}{12} = \frac{8}{12} + \frac{1}{12} = \frac{9}{12} = \frac{3}{4} = 0.75$$

29. (D)—Solving a Linear Equation

Math Appendix, #63. This looks like a physics question, but in fact it's just a "plug-in-the-number-and-see-what-you-get" question. Be sure you plug 95 in for C (not F):

$$C = \frac{5}{9}(F - 32)$$

$$95 = \frac{5}{9}(F - 32)$$

$$\frac{9}{5} \cdot 95 = F - 32$$

$$F - 32 = 171$$

$$F = 171 + 32 = 203$$

30. (H)—Probability

Math Appendix, #46. Probability equals the number of favorable outcomes divided by the total number of possible outcomes. In this problem, a "favorable outcome" is choosing a green marble—that's 4. The "total number of possible outcomes" is the total number of marbles, or 20:

$$\text{Probability} = \frac{\text{Favorable Outcomes}}{\text{Total Outcomes}}$$

$$= \frac{4}{20}$$

$$= \frac{1}{5}$$

31. (A)—Adding and Subtracting Polynomials, Average Formula

Math Appendix, #54, #41. To find the average of three numbers—even if they're algebraic expressions—add them up and divide by 3:

$$\text{Average} = \frac{\text{Sum of terms}}{\text{Number of terms}}$$

$$= \frac{(2x + 5) + (5x - 6) + (-4x + 2)}{3}$$

$$= \frac{3x + 1}{3}$$

$$= x + \frac{1}{3}$$

32. (F)—Using Two Points to Find the Slope

Math Appendix, #72. Parallel lines have the same slope. Use the first pair of points to figure out the slope:

$$\text{Slope} = \frac{y_2 - y_1}{x_2 - x_1} = \frac{16 - 1}{2 - 1} = 15$$

Then use the slope to figure out the missing coordinate in the second pair of points:

$$\text{Slope} = \frac{y_2 - y_1}{x_2 - x_1}$$

$$15 = \frac{(25 - (-5)}{a - (-10))}$$

$$15 = \frac{30}{a + 10}$$

$$15a + 150 = 30$$

$$15a = -120$$

$$a = -8$$

33. (B)—Similar Triangles

Math Appendix, #82. When parallel lines make a big triangle and a little triangle as they do here, the triangles are similar (because they have the same angle measurements). Side $\overline{PR}$ is three times the length of $\overline{QR}$, so each side of the big triangle is three times the length of the corresponding side of the smaller triangle, and therefore the ratio of the perimeters is also 3:1. So the perimeter of ΔPRT is 3 times 11, or 33.

34. (K)—Characteristics of Special Quadrilaterals

Math Appendix, #86. It *is* a polygon because it's composed of straight line segments. It *is* a quadrilateral because it has *four* sides. It is *not* a rectangle because opposite sides are not equal. It *is* a trapezoid because it has one pair of parallel sides.

35. (D)—Evaluating an Algebraic Expression and Solving a Linear Equation

Math Appendix, #52, #63. Plug in $x = -3$ and solve for a:

$$2x^2 + (a - 4)x - 2a = 0$$

$$2(-3)^2 + (a - 4)(-3) - 2a = 0$$

$$18 - 3a + 12 - 2a = 0$$

$$30 - 5a = 0$$

$$-5a = -30$$

$$a = 6$$

36. (K)—Counting the Possibilities

Math Appendix, #45. The total number of combinations of a first course, second course, and dessert is equal to the product of the 3 numbers:

Total possibilities = $4 \times 5 \times 3 = 60$

37. (B)—Prime Factorization, Least Common Multiple

Math Appendix, #11, #14. An integer that's divisible by 6 has at least one 2 and one 3 in its prime factorization. An integer that's divisible by 9 has at least two 3's in its prime factorization. Therefore, an integer that's divisible by both 6 and 9 has at least one 2 and two 3's in its prime factorization. That means it's divisible by 2, 3, $2 \times 3 = 6$, $3 \times 3 = 9$, and $2 \times 3 \times 3 = 18$. It's *not* necessarily divisible by 12 or 36, each of which includes *two* 2's in its prime factorization.

You could also do this one by **picking numbers**. Think of a common multiple of 6 and 9 and use it to eliminate some options. $6 \times 9 = 54$ is an obvious common multiple—and it's not divisible by 12 or 36, but it is divisible by 18. The *least* common multiple of 6 and 9 is 18, which is also divisible by 18. It looks like every common multiple of 6 and 9 is also a multiple of 18.

38. (F)—Simplifying an Algebraic Fraction

Math Appendix, #62.

$$\frac{x^2 + x^2 + x^2}{x^2} = \frac{3x^2}{x^2} = 3$$

39. (A)—Translating from English into Algebra

Math Appendix, #65. Read carefully. This question's a lot easier than you might think at first. It's asking for the total *number* of coins, not the total value. q quarters, d dimes, and n nickels add up to a total of $q + d + n$ coins.

40. (K)—Solving an Inequality and Graphing Inequalities

Math Appendix, #69, #70. You solve an inequality much the way you solve an equation: Do the same things to both sides until you've isolated what you're solving for. (Just remember to flip the sign if you ever multiply or divide both sides by a negative number.)

$$5x - 2(1 - x) \geq 4(x + 1)$$
$$5x - 2 + 2x \geq 4x + 4$$
$$5x + 2x - 4x \geq 4 + 2$$
$$3x \geq 6$$
$$x \geq 2$$

The "greater-than-or-equal-to" symbol is graphed as a solid circle.

41. (B)—Using Two Points to Find the Slope

Math Appendix, #72. First find the slope of the line that contains the given points:

$$\text{Slope} = \frac{y_2 - y_1}{x_2 - x_1} = \frac{10 - 6}{6 - 5} = 4$$

Line m is perpendicular to the above line, so the slope of m is the negative reciprocal of 4, or $-\frac{1}{4}$.

42. (H)—Sine, Cosine, and Tangent of Acute Angles

Math Appendix, #96. Sine is "opposite over hypotenuse." Here the leg opposite θ is 12 and the hypotenuse is 13, so

$$\sin \theta = \frac{12}{13}.$$

43. (E)— Raising Powers to Powers, Solving a Linear Equation

Math Appendix, #48, #63. Reexpress the left side of the equation so that both sides have the same base:

$$9^{2x - 1} = 3^{3x + 3}$$
$$(3^2)^{2x - 1} = 3^{3x + 3}$$
$$3^{4x - 2} = 3^{3x + 3}$$

Now that the bases are the same, just set the exponents equal:

$$4x - 2 = 3x + 3$$
$$4x - 3x = 3 + 2$$
$$x = 5$$

44. (K)—Combined Percent and Decrease

Math Appendix, #35. Be careful with combined percent increase. You generally cannot just add the 2 percents, because they're generally percents of different wholes. In this instance, the 20% increase is based on the 1970 population, but the 30% increase is based on the larger 1980 population. If you just added 20% and 30% to get 50%, you fell into the test maker's trap.

The best way to do a problem like this one is to **pick a number** for the original whole and just see what happens. And, as usual, the best number to pick here is 100. (That may be a small number for the population of a city, but verisimilitude is not important—all that matters is the math.)

If the 1970 population was 100, then a 20% increase would put the 1980 population at 120. Now, to figure the 30% increase, multiply 120 by 130%:

New # = (Original #) + (30% of Original #)
New # = 130% of Original #
$$x = 1.3(120)$$
$$= 156$$

Since the population went from 100 to 156, that's a 56% increase.

45. (E)—Finding the Missing Number

Math Appendix, #44: The best way to deal with changing averages is go by way of the sums. Use the old average to figure out the total of the first 4 scores:

Sum of first 4 scores = $4 \times 89 = 356$

And use the new average to figure out the total he needs after the 5th score:

Sum of 5 scores = $5 \times 90 = 450$

To get his sum up from 356 to 450, Martin needs to score $450 - 356 = 94$.

46. (K)—Equation for a Circle

Math Appendix, #75. If you find the distance from the center to the given point on the circle, you'll have the radius. The difference between the x's is 8, and the difference between the y's is 6. If 8 and 6 are the lengths of the legs of a right triangle, then the hypotenuse is 10. The radius, then, is 10. Now you can plug the radius and the coordinates of the center point into the general form of the equation of a circle:

$$(x - h)^2 + (y - k)^2 = r^2$$
$$(x + 1)^2 + (y + 1)^2 = 10^2$$
$$(x + 1)^2 + (y + 1)^2 = 100$$

47. (E)—Using Two Points to Find the Slope, Using an Equation to Find the Slope, and Using an Equation to Find the Intercept

Math Appendix, #72, #73, #74. Use the points where the line crosses the axes—(−1,0) and (0,2)—to find the slope:

$$\text{Slope} = \frac{y_2 - y_1}{x_2 - x_1} = \frac{2 - 0}{0 - (-1)} = 2$$

The y-intercept is 2. Now plug $m = 2$ and $b = 2$ into the slope-intercept equation form:

$y = mx + b$

$y = 2x + 2$

48. (G)—Percent Formula

Math Appendix, #32. Be careful. The question is not asking, "What is $\frac{1}{4}$ of 16?" It's asking, "What is $\frac{1}{4}$ *percent* of 16?" One-fourth of 1 percent is 0.25%, or 0.0025:

$\frac{1}{4}$% of $16 = 0.0025 \cdot 16 = 0.04$

49. (C)—Multiplying Binomials—FOIL

Math Appendix, #56. Use FOIL to get rid of the parentheses, and then combine like terms:

$$(s + 4)(s - 4) + (2s + 2)(s - 2)$$
$$= (s^2 - 16) + (2s^2 - 2s - 4)$$
$$= s^2 + 2s^2 - 2s - 16 - 4$$
$$= 3s^2 - 2s - 20$$

50. (F)—Equation for a Parablola and Evaluating an Algebraic Expression

Math Appendix, #76, #56. The easiest way to find the equation of a given parabola is to take a point or two from the graph and plug the coordinates into the answer choices, eliminating the choices that don't work. Start with a point with coordinates that are easy to work with. Here you could start with (3,0). Plug $x = 3$ and $y = 0$ into each answer choice and you'll find that only **F** works.

51. (C)—Sine, Cosine, and Tangent of Acute Angles

Math Appendix, #96. Since $\sin a = \frac{4}{5}$, you could think of this as a 3-4-5 triangle:

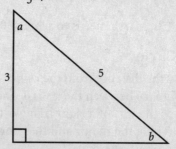

Cosine is "adjacent over hypotenuse." Here the leg adjacent to b is 4, and the hypotenuse is 5, so $\cos b = \frac{4}{5}$. (Notice that the sine of one acute angle in a right triangle is equal to the cosine of the other acute angle.)

52. (F)—Adding and Subtracting Monomials, Simplifying an Algebraic Fraction

Math Appendix, #53, #62. Add the like terms in the numerator and then divide by the denominator:

$$\frac{x^2 + x^2 + x^2}{x} = \frac{3x^2}{x} = 3x$$

53. (B)—Translating from English to Algebra

Math Appendix, #65. When you divide w by 4, you get $\frac{w}{4}$. When you subtract that result from r, you get $r - \frac{w}{4}$.

54. (J)—Volume of Other Solids

Math Appendix, #95. The formula for the volume of a cylinder is $V = \pi r^2 h$, where r is the radius of the circular base and h is the height. Here $r = 4$ and $a = 5$, so:

$$\text{Volume} = \pi r^2 h$$
$$= \pi(4)^2(5)$$
$$= \pi(16)(5)$$
$$= 80\pi$$

55. (E)—Area of a Triangle and Multiplying Binomials—FOIL

Math Appendix, #83, #56. With a right triangle you can use the 2 legs as the base and the height to figure out the area. Here the leg lengths are expressed algebraically. Just plug the 2 expressions in for b and h in the triangle area formula:

$$\text{Area} = \frac{1}{2}(x-1)(x+1) = \frac{1}{2}\left(x^2 - 1\right) = \frac{x^2 - 1}{2}$$

56. (G)—Rate

Math Appendix, #39. The difference between the populations in 1990 was $9,400 - 7,600 = 1,800$. Each year, as the larger population goes down by 100 and the smaller population goes up by 100, the difference decreases by <u>200</u>. Thus it will take $1,800 \div 200 = 9$ years to erase the difference.

57. (B)—Miscellaneous Averages: Weighted Average

The overall average is not simply the average of the 2 average ages. Because there are a lot more women than men, women carry more weight, and the overall average will be a lot closer to 25 than 35.

This problem's easiest to deal with if you pick particular numbers for the females and males. The best numbers to pick are the smallest: Say there are 4 females and 1 male. Then the ages of the 4 females total 4 times 25, or 100, and the age of the 1 male totals 35. The average, then, is $(100 + 35)$ divided by 5, or 27.

58. (J)—Sine, Cosine, and Tangent of Acute Angles and Pythagorean Theorem

Math Appendix, #96, #84. The height h of the tree is the leg opposite θ. The distance b from the base of the tree is the leg adjacent to θ. "Opposite over adjacent" is tangent, but all the answer choices are in terms of the sine. Sine is "opposite over hypotenuse," so you're going to have to figure out the hypotenuse. Use the Pythagorean theorem:

$$(\text{hypotenuse})^2 = (\text{leg}_1)^2 + (\text{leg}_2)^2$$
$$(\text{hypotenuse})^2 = b^2 + h^2$$
$$\text{hypotenuse} = \sqrt{b^2 + h^2}$$

Now, to get the sine, put the opposite h over the hypotenuse $\sqrt{b^2 + h^2}$:

$$\sin \theta = \frac{h}{\sqrt{b^2 + h^2}}$$

59. (C)—Evaluating an Algebraic Expression

Math Appendix #52. This looks like a solid geometry question, but in fact it's just a "plug-in-the-number-and-see-what-you-get" question.

$$S = \pi r \sqrt{r^2 + h^2}$$
$$= \pi(3) \sqrt{3^2 + 4^2}$$
$$= 3\pi \sqrt{9 + 16}$$
$$= 3\pi \sqrt{25}$$
$$= 3\pi \cdot 5$$
$$= 15\pi$$

60. (J)—Parallel Lines and Transversals

Math Appendix #79. When a transversal crosses parallel lines, all the resulting acute angles are equal and all the resulting obtuse angles are equal. You can generally tell at sight which angles are equal. In this problem's figure, $a = c = e = g$, and $b = d = f = h$. Only J is true: c and g are both obtuse. In all the other choices you'll find an obtuse and an acute.

Reading Answer Key			
1. B	11. C	21. C	31. A
2. H	12. G	22. H	32. J
3. B	13. D	23. D	33. A
4. J	14. H	24. G	34. H
5. A	15. D	25. A	35. D
6. H	16. G	26. H	36. G
7. B	17. D	27. B	37. D
8. G	18. G	28. G	38. H
9. B	19. A	29. C	39. A
10. J	20. J	30. F	40. G

Passage I—Social Studies

Here's a road map to this social studies passage on architecture:

Paragraph 1 compares architects to other professionals, noting that in an economic and social sense they are worse off than doctors and lawyers.

Paragraph 2 goes into the historical background of architecture as a profession.

Paragraphs 3, 4, and 5 discuss the passage's big idea—whether architects should try to improve their professional status. This question is posed in paragraph 3, while in paragraphs 4 and 5, the author argues that architects should emphasize the artistic value of their profession (rather than try to improve their economic and social standing).

1. (B)—Detail Question

The first sentence in paragraph 5 says that architects "seem embarrassed to present themselves as artists," choice **B**. Choice **A** is wrong because paragraphs 1 and 2 show that architects want to be thought of in the *same* way as doctors. Although the passage mentions both builders (**C**) and accountants (**D**), there is no information that indicates that architects resent comparisons to them.

2. (H)—Detail Question

To determine the meaning of a word in the passage, it's necessary to understand the context in which that word appears. The word "privileged" comes up in the context of the author's point that doctors and lawyers, professionally speaking, are in a stronger position than architects. Thus, "privileged" in this case means "superior," choice **H**.

3. (B)—Inference Question

Since the question asks about how architects came to be regarded as professionals, your mental road map of the passage should have sent you to paragraph 2, the only paragraph that discusses historical matters. Lines 26–31 say that architects convinced governments to grant them a professional license by emphasizing architecture's affect on "public health and safety," choice **B**. Choices **A**, **C**, and **D** play on details that aren't linked to the licensing process.

4. (J)—Detail Question

The question asks why doctors and lawyers are in a better economic position than architects, so it's back to paragraph 1, where this issue is examined. The second half of the paragraph brings up three reasons why doctors and lawyers are better off: The demand for their services is "more stable," option I; they have more control over their fields, option II; and they aren't forced to deal with competitors, option III. Thus, **J** is correct.

5. (A)—Big Picture Question

The first part of the passage argues that architects are worse off economically and socially than other professionals. The second part of the passage argues that architects should concentrate on their art rather than try to improve their status. Choice **A**, therefore, is correct. Choice **B**, in contrast, goes against the spirit of the passage, which says that it isn't likely that architects will be able to achieve the status of doctors and lawyers. Choices **C** and **D**, finally, distort details in the passage.

6. (H)—Big Picture Question

Architecture is described as the "mother of all arts" because of the "attributes" that "set it apart." These attributes include its unrivaled ability to "relate light, mass, and structure to produce memorable visual and spatial experiences," choice **H**. Choice **G** runs counter to the thrust of the passage, which indicates that architecture is different from other arts. And choices **F** and **J** introduce issues not taken up in the text.

7. (B)—Detail Question

The effect of economic downturns on professionals is brought up towards the end of paragraph 3. Line 55 notes that the construction industry is "notoriously volatile," a clear indication that architects (**B**) face trouble in times of economic hardship. To the contrary, lines 56–62 say that doctors (**A**), lawyers (**C**), and accountants (**D**) are all assured of business in hard times.

8. (G)—Inference Question

Lines 84–86 state explicitly that architects aren't needed "in the construction of ordinary buildings," choice **G**. Choices **F** and **H** are flatly contradicted by lines 76–78 and lines 78–80, respectively; and choice **J** is not dealt with in the passage at all.

9. (B)—Detail Question

The information you need is in the first two sentences of the passage. These sentences say that college students who are interested in economic prosperity are probably not going to seek a career in architecture because other professions offer more opportunity for advancement. In other words, these professions pay better than architecture. So, choice **B** is correct. Choice **D** distorts a detail in paragraph 1, while choices **A** and **C** bring up issues that the passage does not deal with at all.

10. (J)—Detail Question

Lines 46–47 indicate that law and medicine are "more fully in control of [their] domain" than architecture, choice **J**. Choices **F** and **G** are flatly contradicted by paragraph 3, which says that law and medicine are more science-based and less dependent on economic conditions than architecture. Choice **H** is contradicted by paragraph 2, which strongly implies that law, medicine, and architecture are all protected by a licensing system.

Passage II—Social Studies

This passage tackles the *philosophes,* a group of mainly French intellectuals. Here's a road map:

Paragraph 1 defines the term *philosophes*—they were a group of thinkers who took the ideas of others and spread them through literary works.

Paragraph 2 says that the *philosophes* developed and spread the philosophy of the Enlightenment throughout Western Europe and the American colonies.

Paragraphs 3, 4, and 5 discuss the influence of Newton, Locke, and English institutions on the *philosophes'* thinking.

Paragraph 6 describes the ideas and career of perhaps the most famous *philosophe*, Voltaire.

11. (C)—Detail Question

This question asks for a description of the *philosophes,* so it's back to the first two paragraphs. Lines 11–14 say that they took the ideas of others and popularized them. The first sentence of paragraph 2 goes on to state that they "developed the philosophy of the Enlightenment and spread it to much of the educated elite in Western Europe (and the American colonies)." Thus, choice **C** is correct. Choices **B** and **D** are contradicted by information in the first paragraph, which states that the *philosophes* were generally neither professors nor scientists. Choice **A**, on the other hand, is too narrow in scope: True, the *philosophes* were influenced by Locke, but they were also influenced by Newton and English institutions.

12. (G)—Inference Question

Your mental road map of the passage should have sent you directly to the last paragraph, where Voltaire is discussed. This paragraph says that Voltaire criticized both French society and religious institutions, so you can infer that he might have attacked French religious institutions, choice **G**. Choice **H** is contradicted by information in the paragraph, which states that Voltaire "came to admire" English government. It's unlikely that he would have criticized the Scientific Revolution (**F**) because the *philosophes* were disciples of this revolution. Finally, the passage says nothing about Voltaire's views of "courtly love" (**J**), so you can't infer what his position on this issue would have been.

13. (D)—Detail Question

The answer to a question that contains a line reference is found in the lines around that reference. Locke's idea that "schools and social institutions could . . . play a great role in molding the individual" comes up right after his belief that humans are shaped by their experiences, choice **D**. Choice **A** is contradicted by lines 49–50, while choices **B** and **C** distort details in paragraph 4.

14. (H)—Inference Question

Your mental road map should have pointed you to paragraph 3, where Newton is discussed. This paragraph says that Newton believed that "the universe [was] . . . originally set in motion by God," option I, and that "the universe operates in a mechanical and orderly fashion," option III. But this paragraph doesn't say that Newton believed that "human reason is insufficient to understand the laws of nature," option II; if anything, it implies just the opposite. Choice **H**, options I and III only, is correct.

15. (D)—Detail Question

Lines 49–51 reveal that it was Locke who questioned the notion that "revelation was a reliable source of truth." Thus, you're looking for a work written by him, so you can immediately eliminate choices **A**, *Letters on the English,* and **C**, *Elements of the Philosophy of Newton,* both of which were authored by Voltaire. The remaining two works, *Second Treatise of Civil Government* (**B**) and *Essay Concerning Human Understanding* (**D**) were both written by Locke; but *Second Treatise of Civil Government* (**B**) is a political, not a philosophical, work, so it can be eliminated as well. That leaves choice **D** as the correct answer.

16. (G)—Inference Question

The first sentence of paragraph 4 states that Locke "agreed with Newton but went further." Specifically, Locke also thought that the human mind was subject to "the mechanical laws of the material universe," choice **G**. The other choices distort details in paragraphs 3 and 4.

17. (D)—Big Picture Question

The *philosophes*—as paragraph 5 shows—were greatly influenced by an England that allowed more individual freedom, was more tolerant of religious differences, and was freer of traditional political institutions than other countries, particularly France. Indeed, the *philosophes* wanted other countries to adopt the English model. Thus, choice **D**, options I, II, and III, is correct.

18. (G)—Big Picture Question

Since this question also asks about England, it's right back to paragraph 5. In the second-to-last sentence of the paragraph, the *philosophes* cite England's political stability and prosperity as evidence that England's system worked. The last sentence of the paragraph goes on to say that the *philosophes* "wanted to see in their own countries much of what England already seemed to have." Choice **G**, therefore, is correct. Choice **F**, on the other hand, flatly contradicts the gist of paragraph 5. Finally, choices **H** and **J** distort details from the wrong part of the passage.

19. (A)—Inference Question

The French political and religious authorities during the time of Voltaire are discussed in paragraph 6. Voltaire got in hot water with the authorities over his outspoken views, so it's safe to assume that they weren't advocates of free speech, choice **A**. Since they first imprisoned and then exiled him, they clearly didn't regard the *philosophes* with indifference, choice **C**. The passage doesn't say *precisely* what Voltaire was imprisoned and exiled for, so you can't infer that the authorities "overreacted to Voltaire's mild satires" (**B**), which, in any case, weren't that mild. Finally, since Voltaire was an advocate of the English system of government, it's also safe to assume that the French hadn't accepted this model. So **D**'s out as well.

20. (J)—Big Picture Question

The notion that the *philosophes* were "more literary than scientific" appears in the middle of paragraph 1. A few lines further down, the paragraph furnishes a list of the types of literary works produced by the *philosophes,* so choice **J** is correct. The passage never mentions any "political change" (**F**). Nor does it compare the literary outputs of Newton and Voltaire (**G**). Finally, choice **H** is out because the *philosophes* were not scientists.

Passage III—Fiction

This passage, about an older woman called Rosemary and her grandson Victor, is essentially a story about the generation gap. Here's a road map:

In Paragraph 1, Rosemary's awareness of the easy life Victor seems to be leading spurs a series of flashbacks in which she remembers her childhood experiences growing up on a farm.

Paragraph 2 relates her memories of getting up early in the morning.

In paragraph 3, Rosemary remembers her father preventing her from going to high school because he needed help on the farm. The author contrasts Rosemary's painful recollections with Victor's casual attitude towards education.

21. (C)—Detail Question

Line 9 explicitly states that Victor is Rosemary's grandson (**C**).

22. (H)—Inference Question

Rosemary's unease with Victor's behavior is the topic of paragraph 3. She is disturbed by his willingness to take a college course simply because it's "easy to pass," choice **H**. Choices **G** and **J** distort details from the wrong paragraph, while choice **F** brings up an idea that's not in the passage.

23. (D)—Inference Question

The answer is strongly implied in the passage. Paragraph 3 notes that Rosemary wanted to go to high school after finishing grammar school. Her father would not permit her to go, so she had to spend time "with animals and rough farmhands for company instead of people her own age" (**D**). Choice **B** is flatly contradicted by paragraph 3, which indicates that Rosemary wanted to go to high school, not college. Choices **A** and **C** make inferences that are not supported by the passage.

24. (G)—Inference Question

Lines 15–16 say that Rosemary "had decided long ago that growing old was like slowly turning to stone." This sentiment suggests that she is resigned to the physical problems that accompany old age. "Acceptance" (**G**), therefore, is correct. "Sadness" (**F**) and "resentment" (**H**) are too negative in tone, while "optimism" (**J**) is too positive: Rosemary, in short, isn't at all emotional about the aging process.

25. (A)—Detail Question

Rosemary's interest in crossword puzzles is discussed in the opening sentences of paragraph 1. She does them for two reasons: to pass the time and to keep her mind active, choice **A**. The other choices distort details in paragraphs 1 and 2. Choice **B** plays on Rosemary's happiness at still being able to write at 87; choice **C** plays on her need to consult an atlas to look up the Swiss river; and choice **D** plays on her experience of "an expanded sense of time" as she grows older.

26. (H)—Big Picture Question

Most of the passage is about the different attitudes of Rosemary and Victor towards education (**H**). The first two paragraphs serve as a lead-in to this topic, while the remainder of the passage concentrates on Rosemary's thoughts and memories about education. Rosemary mentions Victor's laziness (**F**), but this isn't the main focus of the passage. Education is the primary focus. There's no information at all to suggest that Victor's father has mistreated him (**G**). Indeed, just the opposite is implied: Victor's "doting parents," after all, have given him a new car. Finally, choice **J** doesn't mention education. Moreover, Rosemary doesn't try to suppress her memories.

27. (B)—Inference Question

The answer to a question that contains a line reference requires you to understand the context in which the reference appears. In the lines that precede the mention of Victor's "shiny new car," Rosemary considers his easy upbringing, how he looks as if he's never done a chore. In other words, Victor's car is a symbol of his generation, which has had a much easier time of it than Rosemary's. So **B** is correct. Rosemary's parents (**A**)—her father anyway—can't be described as generous. Besides, her parents have nothing to do with Victor's car. Similarly, while Rosemary seems to feel that Victor's future prospects are bright (**C**), and that his life lacks hardship (**D**), neither has anything to do with his car.

28. (G)—Detail Question

Paragraph 3 says that Rosemary is disturbed by Victor's dismissive attitude towards his education. She doesn't like the idea that his only reason for taking a course is that he can pass it. In contrast to Victor's attitude, in other words, Rosemary, in her youth, was eager to continue her education (**G**). Choices **F** and **J** refer to details from the wrong paragraphs, while choice **H** introduces an issue that the passage never tackles.

29. (C)—Detail Question

A few lines before Rosemary recalls what it was like growing up on the farm, the passage says that "Rosemary often experienced an expanded sense of time, with present and past tense intermingling in her mind." (**C**). Choice **D**, on the other hand, alludes to recollections from the wrong paragraphs. Choices **A** and **B** distort details in paragraph 2.

30. (F)—Inference Question

The reference to Victor's bright future comes at the end of paragraph 2. It's clear from the text that it's Rosemary (**F**) who thinks that he has a good future. The passage never says what Victor thought about his own future (**G**). Nor does it say what his parents thought about his future (**H**). And it's extremely unlikely that Victor and Rosemary's father (**J**) were even alive at the same time.

Passage IV—Science

Here's a road map to this passage on the ozone layer:

Paragraph 1 introduces us to the problem of the ozone layer's depletion—the passage's big idea.

Paragraph 2 describes the nature of the ozone layer.

Paragraphs 3–5 discuss the study of the ozone layer, mentioning in particular that scientists have been carefully monitoring its depletion.

Paragraphs 6–10 explain what is responsible for the depletion of the ozone layer—CFCs—and what is being done to stem their use around the world.

The passage ends on a cautiously optimistic note in paragraph 11, implying that a solution to the problem can be found if people work to find it.

31. (A)—Detail Question

The term "tenuous" is used twice in the passage—in the first sentences of paragraphs 1 and 2. In the first instance, "tenuous" appears in the context of a discussion about the ozone layer's depletion. In the second instance, it appears in the context of a discussion about the tiny amount of ozone in the atmosphere. In this passage, then, "tenuous" means "thin" (**A**). "Substantial" (**C**) suggests just the opposite of what "tenuous" means in this passage. Finally, "dangerous" (**B**) and "fragile" (**D**) simply don't convey the correct idea.

32. (J)—Detail Question

In passages that contain a lot of different dates, check back with the text to make sure that you know what each one represents. Lines 38–40 say that the public first took notice of the depletion of the ozone layer in *1985*, choice **J**. 1930 (**F**) was the year that scientists first began to observe the ozone layer. 1958 (**G**) was the year when scientists first began to notice seasonal variations in the content of the ozone layer. And 1979 (**H**) was the year in which the October minimum in the ozone layer diminished.

33. (A)—Detail Question

The last sentence of paragraph 4 identifies temperature changes (**C**) and wind effects (**D**) as phenomena that *cause* fluctuations in the content of the ozone layer. Similarly, paragraph 6 identifies CFCs (**B**) as a *cause* of fluctuations in content. That leaves choice (**A**), supersonic aircraft, as the correct answer)—and, indeed, paragraph 6 relates that supersonic aircraft, originally thought to have contributed to fluctuations in the content of the ozone layer, have now been *ruled out* as a cause of these fluctuations.

34. (H)—Inference Question

Paragraph 7 mentions such issues as market value, labor force, and production levels. In other words, it's all about economic matters related to CFCs. So (**H**) is correct. Choice **F** focuses on a detail in the paragraph, not its overall purpose. There's no criticism leveled at CFC producers (**G**). Finally, the Montreal Protocol (**J**) is dealt with in paragraph 8.

35. (D)—Inference Question

Alternatives to CFCs are discussed in the last paragraph, which states that it may be difficult to find alternatives to CFCs because substitute products may be toxic, option I; dangerous, option II; and contributors to global warming, option III. Choice **D**, therefore, is correct.

36. (G)—Detail Question

The last two sentences of paragraph 3 make clear that it's Dobson network stations (**G**) that forecast the future of the ozone layer. The WMO (**F**) and the UNEP (**J**) entrusted this task to the Dobson network. The Montreal Protocol (**H**) concerns the preservation of the ozone layer by controlling the production of CFCs.

37. (D)—Inference Question

There is no information in the passage to suggest either that scientists could replace lost ozone (**A**) or that they could destroy existing chlorine molecules (**C**). Choice **B** distorts a detail in paragraph 10, which states that CFCs have a lifespan of between 75 and 400 years. This doesn't mean that the ozone level in the atmosphere returns to "normal" after 75 years. But the last two sentences of this paragraph do say that it takes ten years for the effects of these CFCs to make themselves felt. You can infer from this information that the world would start to see benefits ten years from now if CFC production were banned today, choice **D**.

38. (H)—Detail Question

The first sentence of paragraph 2 states that the ozone layer itself is 25 kilometers thick (**H**). Choice **F** refers to the compression of ozone gas at sea level, not the actual ozone layer itself. Choices **G** and **J** refer to the height of the ozone layer above the surface.

39. (A)—Big Picture Question

The first sentence of paragraph 4 brings up the issue of seasonal variations in the ozone layer. The rest of the paragraph then goes on to describe these variations in more detail. Choice **A**, therefore, is correct. Choice **B** flatly contradicts information in paragraph 4. Choice **C** distorts a detail in paragraph 5. And choice **D** introduces an idea that the passage doesn't support.

40. (G)—Big Picture Question

In the last sentence of the passage, the author ends on a somewhat optimistic note, saying that a solution to the ozone problem might be found if people "lend a hand." He says this even though he acknowledges that today's substitute products present problems of their own. Choice **G** reflects this partially optimistic assessment. The other choices are either too pessimistic or distort the author's point of view.

Science Answer Key

1. A	12. G	23. B	34. G
2. F	13. D	24. G	35. C
3. C	14. G	25. A	36. F
4. G	15. A	26. J	37. D
5. D	16. G	27. A	38. G
6. H	17. C	28. J	39. A
7. D	18. J	29. C	40. H
8. H	19. C	30. G	
9. B	20. F	31. C	
10. J	21. A	32. J	
11. C	22. H	33. C	

Passage I

The first passage describes the power loss (attenuation) in optical fibers due to impurities. The graph shows the attenuation curve for fluoride glass fibers. At certain ranges in wavelength, as you can see, impurities cause a sharp increase in attenuation; for example, nickel causes a power loss of about 95 db/km at 1.5 microns. The thing to note about this graph is that attenuation in db/km (the y-axis) increases as you move downward. This means, for example, that hydroxyl causes greater power loss than either of the other two impurities.

1. (A)

Take a look at the graph and locate the point that corresponds to 1.6 microns and 95 db/km. As it turns out, this is precisely where the line dips—and attenuation sharply increases—due to the presence of nickel impurities. Therefore, copper impurities have an attenuation response similar to that of nickel (**A**).

2. (F)

In order to answer this question, you have to envision what the attenuation curve would look like without the sharp dips due to the impurities. It looks as though the curve would rise steadily going from left to right until it reached 5 microns and 20 db/km, at which point it would start to fall. Once you saw this, you might have been tempted to answer that power loss will "increase then decrease," but remember that the power loss increases as you go down the y-axis. This means that power loss is actually decreasing and then increasing (**F**) as you move along the curve from left to right.

3. (C)

At 6.6 microns, according to the graph, hydroxyl impurities in a fluoride glass fiber cause an attenuation of nearly 120 db/km. That's quite a considerable loss of power. Someone who wished to limit power loss at this wavelength would not choose to use fluoride glass fiber because of "the interference from the hydroxyl groups at this wavelength" (**C**). This does not mean, though, that a fluoride glass fiber does not conduct any light at this wavelength at all, as (**B**) suggests; it's just that a lot of power is lost.

4. (G)

This question is a follow-up to the last one. You already know that hydroxyl impurities in fluoride glass fibers cause power loss in the range between six and seven microns. It stands to reason, then, that if you could get rid of these impurities there would be less power loss both in the range of six to seven microns (Statement I) and in the fiber overall (Statement III). There is no reason to think that the attenuation due to iron impurities would increase, however, so Statement II is false. That makes (**G**) correct.

5. (D)

There are two steps to solving this problem. First, you have to figure out from the graph what the lowest attenuation could be for a fluoride glass fiber. The highest point on the curve—and the point of least power loss—is in the range of 5 microns, where the power loss is roughly 25 db/km. You could therefore transmit light at a wavelength of 5 microns and lose only 25 db/km. The second step to the problem is to multiply the power loss per kilometer (25 db/km) by 5 kilometers to determine what the power loss would be for a five-kilometer cable. The answer is 125 db (**D**).

Passage II

This Data Representation passage is about binary star systems. Figure 1 shows how one star orbits around the other so that each appears to eclipse the other to the observer. The diagram is drawn so that you, the reader, are looking "down" on the system from "above"—from this vantage point you wouldn't see an eclipse. But the "observer" in the diagram is looking at the system "from the side"; from the observer's vantage point, one star can get in the way of the other and cause an eclipse.

Figure 2 is a light curve of the system. Note that the beginning and end points of the graph are the same point. In other words, when the system reaches the twentieth day it is right back where it started from, and it embarks on the cycle all over again. You can ignore the numbers on the y-axis; all you have to know is that as you go up the y-axis, brightness increases. The sharp drop in brightness between the ninth and eleventh days is what the text refers to as a deep primary minimum. The secondary minimum is the shallower dip in brightness that goes from the sixteenth day all the way around to the fourth day of the cycle.

6. (H)

Point c is the point on the light curve at which the eclipsing binary is the darkest. Take a look at Figure 1. From the point of view of the observer, System Q is going to be darkest when the light from the brighter star, Star 1, is being blocked by the light from the less bright Star 2. Star 2 interposes itself between Star 1 and the observer when Star 2 is in position 3 (**H**).

7. (D)

According to the x-axis of the light curve, the complete cycle of changes in the system's surface brightness (from point a through points b, c, and d, and back to point a again) lasts twenty days. This means that it takes Star 2 twenty days to complete its orbit around Star 1 (it is this orbit, after all, that is causing the changes in the system's brightness). **D** is the correct answer.

8. (H)

The drops in brightness on the light curve (Figure 2) indicate when one star is eclipsing the other. The sharp drop known as the primary minimum—when the darker star eclipses the brighter star—lasts approximately two days. The secondary minimum—when the brighter star eclipses the darker star—goes from day 16 through day 20 to day 4, a total of eight days.

9. (B)

This question introduces two new light curve graphs. What gives System Z a deeper primary minimum than X? Well, the reason Q had a deep primary minimum was that one star was brighter than the other; during the time that the brighter star's light was eclipsed by the darker star, the whole system became much darker. You can safely assume that this is the reason Z has a deep primary minimum as well. X's lack of a deep primary minimum must mean, then, that neither of its stars is significantly brighter than the other. As you can see from X's light curve, the drop in brightness of the system is about the same no matter which star is being eclipsed, so the two stars must be equally bright. Since the more extreme difference in the magnitudes of System Z's stars is the reason for Z's deeper primary minimum, (**B**) is correct.

10. (J)

If either star in an eclipsing binary system is in front of the other, the brightness of the system is going to be reduced. The only time the system reaches maximum brightness is when both stars are completely visible—when the full brightness of one star is added to the full brightness of the other (**J**).

Passage III

This is a passage with practically no text and one diagram that illustrates the carbon cycle. Each box of the diagram is a state in which naturally occurring carbon can be found (e.g., in carbon dioxide in air or in animals) and the arrows show how carbon can move from one state to another. For example, the carbon found in carbon dioxide can, through the process of photosynthesis, be taken up by green plants and incorporated into various carbon compounds (in fact, according to the diagram, this is the only way that the carbon in carbon dioxide can enter the carbon cycle). Pay attention to the direction of the arrows.

11. (C)

Decay bacteria, according to the diagram, get carbon from the carbon compounds of dead plants and animals and add to the supply of carbon dioxide in air and water through fermentation and putrefaction. Since there is no other way to get carbon from dead plants and animals back to carbon dioxide, you know that a drop in decay bacteria will reduce the amount of carbon available for forming carbon dioxide. The carbon dioxide level will not be greatly affected, though, because there are three other sources of carbon for carbon dioxide. (**C**) is correct.

12. (G)

Let's take each of the statements one by one. Statement I is false because the diagram shows that the carbon in "animals" can move to "other animals" through the process of "animal digestion." An animal that only eats other animals is participating in the carbon cycle when it digests its prey. Statement II is clearly true; there are arrows labeled "respiration" going from the "green plants," the "animals," and the "other animals" stages back to the carbon dioxide stage. Statement III, however, is not true, because some carbon dioxide is released into the air by fermentation and putrefaction. Since only Statement II is true, (G) is correct.

13. (D)

There are four direct sources of atmospheric carbon dioxide, according to the diagram: fermentation by decay bacteria and respiration by green plants, by animals, and by "other animals or animal parasites." (D) correctly cites the respiration of animal parasites. If you were tempted by (B), note the direction of the arrow for photosynthesis. Photosynthesis removes atmospheric carbon dioxide, using it as a source for carbon.

14. (G)

The arrow signifying animal respiration and the arrow signifying photosynthesis are linked in the diagram by the "carbon dioxide in air or dissolved in water" box. Animal respiration is one of the sources of carbon for carbon dioxide, and the carbon dioxide in turn provides carbon for the process of photosynthesis. In this sense, "animal respiration provides vital gases for green plants" (G).

15. (A)

Look closely at the diagram. The only way that carbon dioxide can enter the carbon cycle is through the process of photosynthesis in which it is taken up by green plants. Note that green plants also emit carbon dioxide back into the air via the process of respiration. Therefore, if green plants were eliminated the carbon cycle would come to a complete stop and (A) is correct.

Passage IV

The first paragraph of this Research Summary passage explains that the experiments were conducted on bacteria that are sensitive to magnetic fields. Study 1 tested to see whether these bacteria will migrate in the direction of magnetic north in various experimental conditions. The table of results indicates that the vast majority of bacterial migrations were in the direction of magnetic north no matter whether the microscope was in standard lab conditions, shielded, rotated, or moved to another laboratory.

Study 2 was conducted to determine whether the position of a nearby magnet would affect the direction of bacterial migration. In each experimental condition, according to the data, most of the bacterial migrations were in the direction of the north pole of the magnet. Clearly, you can conclude based on the evidence from this study and the previous one that the bacteria are sensitive to magnetic fields and tend to migrate in the direction of a magnet's north pole.

16. (G)

In order to be able to tell whether light was the stimulus affecting the direction of bacterial migration, you have to compare two trials, one with the light on and one with the light off. If there is no difference in the direction of bacterial migration in the two trials, then light does not have an effect and is not the primary stimulus. The two trials you need to compare are Trial 1 and Trial 2 of Study 1, because Trial 1 was conducted under standard lab conditions (with the light on) and in Trial 2 the microscope was shielded from all external light. Since the results of the trials differed only minimally, they support the theory that light was not the primary stimulus. (**G**) is correct.

17. (C)

As we saw from the data, the bacteria are sensitive to magnetic fields and tend to migrate in the direction of magnetic north. In Study 2 this meant that the bacteria moved toward the magnet because the magnet's north pole was near the slide. If the magnet's south pole were placed near the slide, the magnetic field would be reversed and the bacteria would migrate in exactly the opposite direction, away from the magnet. That makes **C** the correct answer.

18. (J)

You don't need experimental data to answer this question; you just have to figure out which answer choice provides the best reason a bacteria should be able to move downward. (**F**) and (**G**) are out immediately because both are good reasons a bacteria should move upward, not downward. While it may have been somewhat advantageous for bacteria not to be dispersed by currents (**H**), it would have been much more important for them to move downward to find food, so (**J**) is the best answer.

19. (C)

Here you have to determine which new study would yield new and useful information about the relationship between magnetic field strength and bacterial migrations. You should try to determine the experimental condition that the researchers should vary before you look at the answer choices. To gain new information about magnetic field strength and bacterial migrations, the researchers should vary the magnetic field strength and observe the effect on bacterial migrations. (**C**) is correct because it suggests using more and less powerful magnets which would produce stronger and weaker magnetic fields than that of the magnet in Study 2.

20. (F)

In each of the trials of Study 1, bacterial migrations were largely found to be in the direction of magnetic north. Shielding from light and electric fields, rotation of the microscope, and movement of the microscope to another lab all had no distinct effect on the direction of migration. It is fairly easy to conclude from Study 1 that "the majority of magnetotactic bacteria migrate toward the Earth's magnetic north pole" (**F**).

21. (A)

In any experiment, the control condition is the one used as a standard of comparison in judging the experimental effects of the other conditions. In Study 1, there would be no way to know what the effect of, say, rotating the microscope was on bacterial migration if you didn't know how the bacteria migrated before you rotated the microscope. The control condition is the trial that is run without any experimental manipulations: in this case, Trial 1 (**A**).

Passage V

This Research Summary presents the results of three experiments that were done on the material *nu-PVC*. The purpose of the experiments was to "determine the weathering abilities of *nu-PVC*," so you can assume that each of the experimental conditions was designed to simulate some aspect of extreme weather. The method in Experiment 1 was to spray fifteen boards of *nu-PVC* with distilled water fourteen hours a day for 32 weeks; the boards were unaffected. The second experiment tested the ability of *nu-PVC* sheets to withstand ultraviolet light. Sheet flexibility decreased by 17.5% on average, and the sheets also turned white. In the third experiment, *nu-PVC* boards were tested for their ability to support weight before and after they were exposed for 32 weeks to cold temperatures. More than half of the boards' strength was lost as a result of this exposure.

22. (H)

According to the results of Experiment 1, *nu-PVC* does not suffer any kind of damage when exposed to water for a long period of time. It seems safe to say, then, that *nu-PVC* would not need a protective coating to avoid water damage (**H**).

23. (B)

The results that are relevant here are those from Experiment 3, in which *nu-PVC*'s ability to withstand cold temperatures was tested. The *nu-PVC* boards did not fare well during this experiment; they lost more than half of their capacity to support weight without bending or breaking. In a cold environment, the benches could not be kept outside during the winter without sustaining damage. (**B**) is correct.

24. (G)

Remember that a control is an experimental condition in which nothing special is done to the thing being tested. The control serves as a standard of comparison for the experimental effects found in other conditions. In Experiment 1, the *nu-PVC* boards were sprayed with distilled water for a long period of time to see what effect the water would have. In order to assess the water's effects accurately, though, you have to compare the results of Experiment 1 to the results of a condition in which *nu-PVC* boards are not exposed to water (**G**).

25. (A)

Although at first this question seems to require outside knowledge, it can be answered by the process of elimination using the information in the introduction. The introduction of the passage states that the series of experiments was performed to test the weathering abilities of *nu-PVC*. The only weather phenomenon in the answer choices is sunlight (**A**).

26. (J)

You know nothing in particular about standard building materials from the passage—you don't know how well they stand up to rain or ultraviolet radiation or how well they support weight after exposure to cold weather. This means you cannot compare *nu-PVC* to other materials at all, which rules out (**F**) and (**H**). (**G**) is out because there is no information in the passage about the "different colors and textures" of *nu-PVC*. That leaves (**J**). (**J**) is correct because it is an advantage of *nu-PVC* (perhaps the only one) that it is made of recycled plastic wastes. Nu-PVC helps to solve the garbage problem at the same time that it fills the need for building materials; wood and other standard building materials don't do that.

27. (A)

The conditions of the original experiments were clearly chosen so that *nu-PVC* would be subjected to extremes of water, radiation and cold. There is little point in making the conditions even more extreme when a park bench would never have to survive such weather. It is unlikely, for example, that a park bench will be exposed to 32 weeks of continuous rain, much less 64 weeks, or that a bench will have to endure 8 months of −40° C temperature. Thus Statements I and III are not going to provide useful information. Statement II, on the other hand, is an important experiment, because sea water and salt-rich air may well have a corrosive effect on *nu-PVC* whereas distilled water did not. (**A**) is correct.

Passage VI

The purpose of the three experiments described in this Research Summary was to investigate the effect of glucose on lens proteins in the eye. You should expect, after reading the first paragraph, that glucose would be found to react adversely with the lens proteins and damage them.

Experiment 1 showed that when human tissue protein is dissolved in glucose, an Amadori product forms that causes one protein to bind with another in a brown pigmented cross-link called an Advanced Glycosylation End product. Experiment 2 demonstrated that the lens proteins in older subjects are often bound to each other by cross-links; the cross-links are either di-sulfide bonds or "an indeterminate formation with brownish pigmentation" (you can guess from the color that it is the same type of cross-link as was found in Experiment 1). In Experiment 3, it was found that the lens proteins of cow lenses form brown cross-links when dissolved in glucose—the same type of brown cross-links found in Experiment 2 (and, you can infer, in Experiment 1).

28. (J)

The researcher who designed the experiments was interested in the effect of dietary glucose on lens proteins in the human eye, not the cow eye. There would be no reason to use cow lens proteins in Experiment 3 if cow lens proteins were expected to react any differently from human lens proteins, especially when human lens proteins were readily available for use— they were used, after all, for Experiment 1. Therefore, you know that the researcher assumed that cow lens proteins would react the same as human lens proteins (**J**).

29. (C)

Make sure that you stick to the results of Experiment 1 only when you answer this question. All you know from Experiment 1 is that when a human tissue protein was dissolved in a glucose and water solution, the proteins formed Amadori products that combined with other proteins to make brown cross-links. You can conclude from this that the glucose reacted with the proteins to form cross-links (**C**). Based on Experiment 1, though, you know nothing about di-sulfide cross links (**A**) or glucose metabolism (**D**). (**B**) contradicts the results of Experiment 1 because it is protein, not glucose, that forms AGE.

30. (G)

Take another look at the results of Experiment 2. It was found that in the samples from older subjects the lens proteins often formed cross-linked bonds, some of which were brown. The senile cataracts in the lenses of older people are also brown. The conclusion suggested by the identical colors of the cataracts and the cross-linked bonds is that the senile cataracts are made up of, or caused by, cross-linked bonds (**G**).

31. (C)

You don't know from the results of Experiment 2 how the brown pigmented cross-links developed among the lens proteins of older humans. Experiments 1 and 3 indicate, however, that glucose reacts with lens proteins in such a way that brown pigmented cross-links form among the proteins. And remember the main purpose of the experiments: the researcher is investigating the effects of glucose on lens proteins in order to see whether dietary sugar (glucose) damages proteins. The hypothesis that dietary sugar reacted with lens proteins to cause the brown pigmented cross-links found in older subjects would seem to be supported by the results of the three experiments (**C**).

32. (J)

The relevant results are those from Experiment 2: the lens proteins of younger subjects were found to have formed cross-linked aggregates much less frequently than the lens proteins of older subjects were. So you would expect that the lens proteins of a 32-year-old man would have fewer cross-links than the lens proteins of an 80-year-old man (**J**).

33. (C)

String together the hypotheses that were the correct answers from questions 30 and 31, and you have the following overall hypothesis: Dietary glucose causes brown pigmented (AGE) cross-links to form among lens proteins, and these brown cross-links in turn cause the formation of brown senile cataracts. According to this hypothesis, the excess glucose in an uncontrolled diabetic's blood should cause the formation of AGE cross-links among lens proteins and subsequently the development of senile cataracts (**C**).

Passage VII

This passage contains a lot of scientific information and terms that you probably have never seen before. Just remember that you are not expected to recognize or understand everything in the passage. Your job is to answer questions, not to learn particle physics.

Scientist 1 explains the Quark Model—the structure of the proton, the structure of mesons and baryons in general—and then proceeds to give the reasons she thinks the Quark Model is correct. It explains the existence of the many different types of mesons, and it predicted the properties of at least one meson. Although individual quarks have not been observed, the deep inelastic scattering experiments indicated that the proton did indeed have a substructure of "three distinct lumps," which agrees with the Quark Model.

Scientist 2 asserts, however, that the Quark Model is flawed. He argues that if Quarks really existed, they would have been found already; since they haven't been found, they don't exist. In addition, he says, the quark Model violates the Pauli exclusion principle, the rule that no two identical particles of half-integer spin can occupy the same state. The Δ^{++} baryon is cited as an example of a particle predicted by the Quark Model that violates the Pauli exclusion principle.

34. (G)

Scientist 1 is a proponent of the Quark Model, which says that baryons (including the proton) and mesons are made up of quarks, which have fractional charge. Quarks have never been observed, however. You find out from Scientist 2 that quarks should be easy to distinguish from other particles because they would be the only ones with fractional charge. If a particle with fractional charge was detected, then, it would most likely be a quark, and this would strengthen Scientist 1's hypothesis that the Quark Model is correct. Mesons, baryons and the Δ^{++} baryon have all been detected, but mere detection of them does not tell us anything about their substructure, so it cannot be used to support the Quark Model.

35. (C)

Scientist 2 says that it should be easy to split the proton into quarks; that the quarks should be easy to distinguish because of their unique charge (Statement I); and that they should be stable, because they can't decay into lighter particles (Statement III). Statement II is wrong because it is Scientist 1's explanation of why quarks cannot be detected. Therefore, (C) is correct.

36. (F)

Scientist 2 says that the Quark Model is wrong because it violates the Pauli exclusion principle, which states that no two particles of half-integer spin can occupy the same state. He says that in the Δ^{++} baryon, for example, the presence of two up quarks in the same state would violate the principle, so the model must be incorrect. If Scientist 1 were able to show, however, that quarks do not have half-integer spin (F), she could argue that the Pauli exclusion principle does not apply to quarks and thus counter Scientist 2's objections. Evidence that the Δ^{++} baryon exists (G) or that quarks have fractional charge (H) isn't going to help Scientist 1 because neither has anything to do with the Pauli exclusion principle. Evidence that quarks have the same spin as electrons (J) would only support Scientist 2's position.

37. (D)

According to Scientist 2, the Δ^{++} baryon has three up quarks. Each up quark has a charge of +2/3 each, so the three quarks together have a total charge of 2 (D).

38. (G)

Scientist 2 thinks that the Quark Model is flawed for two reasons: 1) quarks have not been detected experimentally, and they would have been if they existed, and 2) the Quark Model violates the Pauli exclusion principle. The first reason is paraphrased in (G), the correct answer. (F) is wrong because the existence of individual baryons, including protons, has been verified experimentally. Scientist 2 never says that he thinks particles cannot have fractional charge, nor does he complain that the Quark Model doesn't include electrons as elementary particles, so (**H**) and (**J**) are wrong as well.

39. (A)

The deep inelastic scattering experiments, according to Scientist 1, showed that the proton has a substructure. The three distinct lumps that were found to bounce high-energy electrons back and scatter them through large angles were the three quarks that make up the proton (at least in Scientist 1's view), so **A** is correct.

40. (H)

This question is a follow-up of the last one. If the three lumps were indeed quarks, then this supports the Quark Model because in the Quark Model the proton consists of three quarks. "Protons supposedly consist of three quarks" is not one of the choices, though, so you have to look for a paraphrase of this idea. Protons are baryons and not mesons, so (**F**) and (**G**) are out. Baryons, like the proton, are all supposed to consist of three quarks, so this rules out (**J**) and makes (**H**) the correct answer.

Appendixes

English Review for the ACT

PUNCTUATION REVIEW

Commas

1. Use commas to separate items in a series

If more than two items are listed in a series, they should be separated by commas. The final comma—the one that precedes the word "and"—may be omitted. An omitted final comma would not be considered an error on the ACT.

> Example: My recipe for buttermilk biscuits includes flour, baking soda, salt, shortening, and buttermilk.

> ALSO RIGHT: My recipe for buttermilk biscuits includes flour, baking soda, salt, shortening and buttermilk.

Be watchful for commas placed **before** the first element of a series or **after** the last element.

> WRONG: My recipe for chocolate cake includes, flour, baking soda, sugar, eggs, milk and chocolate.

> WRONG: Flour, baking soda, sugar, eggs, milk and chocolate, are the ingredients in my chocolate cake.

2. Use commas to separate two or more adjectives before a noun

Example: I can't believe you sat through that long, dull movie three times in a row.

> It is **incorrect** to place a comma **after** the last adjective in a series.

> WRONG: The manatee is a blubbery, bewhiskered, creature.

3. Use commas to set off parenthetical clauses and phrases

If a phrase or clause is not necessary to the main idea expressed by a sentence, it should be set off by commas.

> Example: Phillip, who never had any formal chef's training, bakes excellent cheesecake.

The main idea here is that Phillip bakes an excellent cheesecake. The intervening clause merely serves to further identify Phillip; it should therefore be enclosed in commas.

4. **Use commas after introductory phrases**

   Example: Having watered his petunias every day during the drought, Harold was disappointed when his garden was destroyed by aphids.

   Example: After the banquet, Harold and Melissa went dancing.

5. **Use commas to separate independent clauses**

Use a comma before a conjunction (*and, but, nor, yet, etcetera*) that connects two independent clauses.

   Example: Marta is good at basketball, but she's better at soccer.

Semicolons

Like commas, semicolons can be used to separate independent clauses. As we saw above, two related independent clauses that are connected by a conjunction such as *and, but, nor,* or *yet* should be punctuated by a comma. If the words *and, but, nor, or yet* aren't used, the clauses should be separated by a semicolon.

   Example: Whooping cranes are an endangered species; there are only fifty of them alive today.

   Example: Whooping cranes are an endangered species, and they are unlikely to survive if we continue to pollute their habitat.

Semicolons may also be used between independent clauses connected by words like *therefore, nevertheless,* and *moreover.* For more on this topic, see the section on "Sentence Structure" in this Appendix.

Colons

In Standard Written English, the colon is used only as a means of signaling that what follows is a list, definition, explanation, or restatement of what has gone before. A word or phrase such as *like the following, as follows, namely,* or *this* is often used along with the colon to make it clear that a list, summary, or explanation is coming up.

   Example: This is what I found in her refrigerator: a moldy lime and a jar of peanut butter.

   Example: Your instructions are as follows: Read the passage carefully, answer the questions, and turn over your answer sheet.

The Dash

The dash has two uses. One is to indicate an abrupt break in thought.

   Example: The alligator, unlike the crocodile, will usually not attack humans—unless, that is, she feels that her young are in danger.

The dash can also be used to set off a parenthetical expression from the rest of the sentence.

   Example: At 32° Fahrenheit—which is zero on the Celsius scale—water will freeze.

The Apostrophe

The apostrophe has two distinct functions. It is used with contracted verb forms to indicate that one or more letters have been eliminated:

   Example: The **boy's** an expert at chess. (The boy is an expert at chess.)

   Example: The **boy's** left for the day. (The boy has left for the day.)

The apostrophe is also used to indicate the possessive form of a noun.

> Example: The **boy's** face was covered with mosquito bites after a day in the swamp.

GRAMMAR REVIEW

Subject-Verb Agreement

The form of a verb must match, or agree with, its subject in two ways: person and number.

1. Agreement of Person

When we talk about person, we're talking about whether the subject and verb of a sentence show that the author is making a statement about himself (first person), about the person he is speaking to (second person), or about some other person, place, or thing (third person).

- *First Person Subjects: I, we.*

  Example: **I am** going to Paris. **We are** going to Rome.

- *Second Person Subject: you.*

  Example: **Are you** sure you weren't imagining that flying saucer?

- *Third Person Subjects: he, she, they, it, and names of people, places and things.*

  Example: **He is driving** me crazy.

2. Agreement of Number

When we talk about number, we're talking about whether the subject and verb show that one thing is being discussed (singular) or that more than one thing is being discussed (plural).

> **HINT:** *Subjects and verbs must agree in number. Subjects and verbs that don't agree in number appear very frequently on the ACT.*

WRONG: The **children catches** the school bus every morning.

RIGHT: The **children catch** the school bus every morning.

Be especially careful of subject-verb agreement when the subject and verb are separated by a long string of words.

WRONG: **Wild animals** in jungles all over the world is endangered.

RIGHT: **Wild animals** in jungles all over the world **are** endangered.

Pronouns

A pronoun is a word that is used in place of a noun. The antecedent of a pronoun is the word to which the pronoun refers.

> Example: <u>Mary</u> was late for work because
> ANTECEDENT
>
> <u>she</u> forgot to set the alarm.
> PRONOUN

Occasionally, an antecedent will appear in a sentence *after* the pronoun.

> Example: Because <u>he</u> sneezes so often, <u>Arthur</u>
> PRONOUN   ANTECEDENT
>
> always thinks <u>he</u> might have the flu.
> PRONOUN

1. Pronouns and Agreement

In clear, grammatical writing, a pronoun must clearly refer to and agree with its antecedent.

Number agreement of pronouns is more frequently tested on the ACT than person agreement, although you may see a question that tests person agreement.

Number and Person

	Singular	Plural
First Person	I, me	we, us
	my, mine	our, ours
Second Person	you	you
	your, yours	your, yours
Third Person	he, him	they, them
	she, her	
	it	
	one	
	his	their, theirs
	her, hers	
	its	
	one's	

Number Agreement

Pronouns must agree in number with their antecedents. A singular pronoun should stand in for a singular antecedent. A plural pronoun should stand in for a plural antecedent. Here's a typical ACT pronoun error.

> WRONG: The bank turned Harry down when he applied for a loan because **their** credit department discovered that he didn't have a job.

What does the plural possessive *their* refer to? The singular noun *bank*. The singular possessive *its* is what we need here.

> RIGHT: The bank turned Harry down for a loan because **its** credit department discovered that he didn't have a job.

Person Agreement

Pronouns must agree with their antecedents in person too. A first-person pronoun should stand in for a first-person antecedent, and so on.

One more thing to remember about *which* pronoun to use with which antecedent: Never use the relative pronoun *which* to refer to a human being. Use *who* or *whom* or *that*.

> WRONG: The woman **which** is standing at the piano is my sister.

> RIGHT: The woman **who** is standing at the piano is my sister.

2. Pronouns and Case

A more subtle type of pronoun problem is one in which the pronoun is in the wrong case. Look at the following chart:

Case

	Subjective	Objective
First Person	I	me
	we	us
Scond Person	you	you
Third Person	he	him
	she	her
	it	it
	they	them
	one	one
Relative Pronouns	who	whom
	that	that
	which	which

When to Use Subjective Case Pronouns

- Use the subjective case for the subject of a sentence.

Example: **She** is falling asleep.

WRONG: Nancy, Claire, and **me** are going to the ballet.

RIGHT: Nancy, Claire, and **I** are going to the ballet.

- Use the subjective case after a linking verb like *to be*.

Example: It is **I**.

- Use the subjective case in comparisons between the subject of verbs that are not stated, but understood.

Example: Gary is taller than **they** (are).

When to Use Objective Case Pronouns

- Use the objective case for the object of a verb.

Example: I called **her**.

- Use the objective case for the object of a preposition.

Example: I laughed at **him**.

- Use the objective case after infinitives and gerunds.

Example: Asking **him** to go was a big mistake.

Example: To give **him** the scare of his life, we all jumped out of his closet.

- Use the objective case in comparisons between objects of verbs that are not stated but understood.

Example: She calls you more than (she calls) **me**.

3. ***Who* and *Whom***

Another thing you'll need to know is when to use the relative pronoun *who* (subjective case) and when to use the relative pronoun *whom* (objective case: *whom* goes with *him* and *them*). The following method is very helpful when you're deciding which one to use.

Example: Sylvester, (*who* or *whom*?) is afraid of the dark, sleeps with a Donald Duck night-light on.

- Look only at the relative pronoun in its clause. Ignore the rest of the sentence.

(Who or Whom?) is afraid of the dark.

- Turn the clause into a question. Ask yourself:

Who or Whom is afraid of the dark?

- Answer the question with an ordinary personal pronoun.

He is.

- If you've answered the question with a subjective case pronoun (as you have here), you need the subjective case who in the relative clause.

Sylvester, **who** is afraid of the dark, sleeps with a Donald Duck night-light on.

If you answer the question with an objective case pronoun, you need the objective case *whom* in the relative clause.

Try answering the question with he *or* him. Who *goes with* he *(subjective case) and* whom *goes with* him *(objective case)*.

Sentence Structure

A sentence is a group of words that can stand alone because it expresses a complete thought. To express a complete thought, it must contain a subject, about which something is said, and a verb, which says something about the subject.

Example: Dogs bark.

Example: The explorers slept in yak-hide tents.

Example: Looking out of the window, John saw a flying saucer.

Every sentence consists of at least one clause. Many sentences contain more than one clause (and phrases, too).

A **clause** is a group of words that contains a subject and a verb. "Dogs bark," "The explorers slept in a yak-hide tent," and "John saw a flying saucer" are all clauses.

A **phrase** is a group of words that does not have both a subject and a verb.

Looking out of the window is a phrase.

1. Sentence Fragments

On the ACT, some of those innocent-looking groups of words beginning with capital letters and ending with periods are only masquerading as sentences. In reality, they're sentence fragments.

A sentence fragment is a group of words that seems to be a sentence but which is *grammatically* incomplete because it lacks a subject or a verb, **or** which is *logically* incomplete because other elements necessary for it to express a complete thought are missing.

> WRONG: Eggs and fresh vegetables on sale at the farmers' market.

This is not a complete sentence because there's no verb to say something about the subject, *eggs and fresh vegetables*.

> WRONG: Because Richard likes hippopotamuses.

Even though this contains a subject (Richard) and a verb (likes), it's not a complete sentence because it doesn't express a complete thought. We don't know what's true "*because* Richard likes hippopotamuses."

> WRONG: Martha dreams about dinosaurs although.

This isn't a complete sentence because it doesn't express a complete thought. What makes Martha's dreaming about dinosaurs in need of qualification or explanation?

2. Run-On Sentences

Just as unacceptable as an incomplete sentence is a "too-complete" sentence, a run-on sentence.

A run-on sentence is actually two complete sentences stuck together either with just a comma or with no punctuation at all.

> WRONG: The children had been playing in the park, they were covered with mud.

> WRONG: The children had been playing in the park they were covered with mud.

There are a number of ways to fix this kind of prob-lem. They all involve a punctuation mark or a con-necting word that can properly connect two clauses.

- Join the clauses with a semicolon.

RIGHT: The children had been playing in the park; they were covered with mud.

- Join the clauses with a coordinating conjunc-tion and a comma.

RIGHT: The children had been playing in the park, and they were covered with mud.

(Coordinating Conjunctions: *and, but, for, nor, or, so, yet*)

- Join the clauses with a subordinating conjunc-tion.

RIGHT: Because the children had been playing in the park, they were covered with mud.

OR

RIGHT: The children were covered with mud because they had been playing in the park.

(Subordinating Conjunctions: *after, although, if, since, while.*)

- And, of course, the two halves of a run-on sen-tence can be written as two separate, complete sentences.

RIGHT: The children had been playing in the park. They were covered with mud.

Verbs

On the ACT you'll find items that are wrong because a verb is in the wrong tense. To spot this kind of prob-lem, you need to be familiar both with the way each tense is used **and** with the ways the tenses are used together. English has six tenses, and each has a simple form and a progressive form.

	Simple	Progressive
PRESENT	I work	I am working
PAST	I worked	I was working

FUTURE	I will work	I will be working
PRESENT PERFECT	I have worked	I have been working
PAST PERFECT	I had worked	I had been working
FUTURE PERFECT	I will have worked	I will have been working

1. Using the Present Tense

Use the present tense to describe a state or action occurring in the present time.

> Example: I **am** a student.

> Example: They **are studying** the Holy Roman Empire.

Use the present tense to describe habitual action.

> Example: They **eat** at Joe's Diner every night.

> Example: My father never **drinks** coffee.

Use the present tense to describe things that are always true.

> Example: The earth **is** round.

> Example: Grass **is** green.

2. Using the Past Tense

Use the simple past tense to describe an event or state that took place at a specific time in the past and is now over and done with.

> Example: Norman **broke** his toe when he tripped over his son's tricycle.

3. Using the Future Tense

> Use the future tense for actions expected in the future.

> Example: I **will call** you on Wednesday.

> We often express future actions with the expression *to be going to*:

> Example: I **am going to move** to another apartment soon.

4. Using the Present Perfect Tense

Use the present perfect tense for actions and states that started in the past and continue up to and into the present time.

> Example: I **have been living** here for the last two years.

Use the present perfect for actions and states that happened a number of times in the past and may happen again in the future.

> Example: I **have heard** that song several times on the radio.

Use the present perfect for something that happened at an unspecified time in the past.

> Example: Anna **has seen** that movie already.

5. Using the Past Perfect Tense

The past perfect tense is used to represent past actions or states that were completed before other past actions or states. The more recent past event is expressed in the simple past, and the earlier past event is expressed in the past perfect.

> Example: When I turned my computer on this morning, I realized that I **had exited** the program yesterday without saving my work.

6. Using the Future Perfect Tense

Use the future perfect tense for a future state or event that will take place before another future event.

> Example: By the end of the week, I **will have worked** four hours of overtime.

Adjectives and Adverbs

On the ACT, you may find an occasional item that's wrong because it uses an adjective where an adverb is called for, or vice versa.

An adjective modifies, or describes, a noun or pronoun.

Example: A woman in a **white** dress stood next to the **old** tree.

Example: The boat, **leaky** and **dirty**, hadn't been used in years.

An adverb modifies a verb, an adjective, or another adverb. Most, but not all, adverbs end in *-ly*. (Don't forget that some **adjectives**—*friendly, lovely*—also end in *-ly*.)

Example: The interviewer looked *approvingly* at the *neatly* dressed applicant.

STYLE REVIEW

Pronouns and Reference

When we talk about pronouns and their antecedents, we say pronouns refer to or refer back to their antecedents. We talked earlier about pronouns that didn't agree in person or number with their antecedents. But a different kind of pronoun reference problem exists when a pronoun either doesn't refer to any antecedent at all or doesn't refer clearly to one, and only one, antecedent.

Sometimes an incorrectly used pronoun has no antecedent.

POOR: Joe doesn't like what **they play** on this radio station.

Who are they? We can't tell, because there is no antecedent for they. On the ACT, this sort of usage is an error.

RIGHT: Joe doesn't like what **the disc jockeys play** on this radio station.

Don't use pronouns without antecedents when doing so makes a sentence unclear. Sometimes a pronoun seems to have an antecedent until you look closely and see that the word that appears to be the antecedent is not a noun, but an adjective, a possessive form, or a verb. The antecedent of a pronoun must be a noun.

WRONG: When you are painting, make sure you don't get **it** on the floor.

RIGHT: When you are painting, make sure you don't get **paint** on the floor.

Other examples of pronoun reference problems:

WRONG: I've always been interested in astronomy and finally have decided to become **one**.

RIGHT: I've always been interested in astronomy and finally have decided to become an **astronomer**.

Don't use pronouns with remote references. A pronoun that is too far away from what it refers to is said to have a remote antecedent.

WRONG: Jane quit smoking and, as a result, temporarily put on a lot of weight. **It** was very bad for her health.

RIGHT: Jane quit smoking because **it** was very bad for her health, and, as a result, she temporarily gained a lot of weight.

Don't use pronouns with faulty broad reference. A pronoun with broad reference is one that refers to a whole idea instead of to a single noun.

WRONG: He built a fence to stop people from looking into his backyard. **That's** not easy.

RIGHT: He built a fence to stop people from looking into his backyard. The fence was not easy **to build**.

Redundancy

This type of style error is frequently tested on the ACT. Words or phrases are redundant when they have basically the same meaning as something already stated in the sentence. Don't use two phrases when one is sufficient.

WRONG: The school was **established and founded** in 1906.

RIGHT: The school was **established** in 1906.

Relevance

Irrelevant asides, even when set off in parentheses, are to be avoided on the ACT. Everything in the sentence should serve to get across the point in question. Something unrelated to that point should be cut.

POOR: No one can say for sure just how successful the new law will be in the fight against crime (just as no one can be sure whether he or she will ever be a victim of a crime).

BETTER: No one can say for sure just how successful the new law will be in the fight against crime.

Verbosity

Sometimes having extra words in a sentence results in a style problem. Conciseness is something that is valued on the ACT.

WORDY: The supply of **musical instruments that are antique** is limited, so they become more valuable each year.

BETTER: The supply of **antique musical instruments** is limited, so they become more valuable each year.

WORDY: We **were in agreement with each other** that Max was an unsuspecting old fool.

BETTER: We **agreed** that Max was an unsuspecting old fool.

COMMONLY MISUSED WORDS

among/between

In most cases, you should use *between* for two items and *among* for more than two.

Example: The competition **between** Anne and Michael has grown more intense.

Example: He is always at his best **among** strangers.

But use common sense. Sometimes *among* is not appropriate.

Example: Plant the trees in the area **between** the road, the wall, and the fence.

amount/number

Amount should be used to refer to a uncountable quantity. *Number* should refer to a countable quantity.

Example: The **amount** of food he threw away would feed a substantial **number** of people.

as/like

Like is a preposition; it takes a noun object. *As*, when functioning as a conjunction, introduces a subordinate clause. Remember, a clause is a part of a sentence containing a subject and verb.

Example: He sings **like** an angel.

Example: He sings **as** an angel sings.

as . . . as . . .

The idiom is *as . . . as . . .*, **not** *as . . . than . . .*

WRONG: That suit is **as** expensive **than** this one.

RIGHT: That suit is **as** expensive as this one.

fewer/less

Use *fewer* before a plural noun; use *less* before a singular one.

Example: There are **fewer** apples on this tree than there were last year.

Example: He makes **less** money than she does.

neither . . . nor . . .

The correlative conjunction is *neither . . . nor . . .*, **not** *neither . . . or . . .*

Example: He is *neither* strong *nor* flexible.

Avoid the redundancy caused by using *nor* following a negative.

> WRONG: Alice's departure was **not** noticed by Debby **nor** Sue.

> RIGHT: Alice's departure was **not** noticed by Debby **or** Sue.

its/it's

Many people confuse *its* and *it's*. Its is possessive; *It's* is a contraction of it is:

> Example: The cat licked **its** paws.

> Example: **It's** raining cats and dogs.

their/they're/there

Many people confuse *their*, *there*, and *they're*. Their is possessive; *they're* is a contraction of *they are*:

> Example: The girls rode **their** bikes home.

> Example: **They're** training for the big race.

There has two uses: It can indicate place and it can be used as an expletive—a word that doesn't do anything in a sentence except delay the subject.

> Example: Put the book over **there**.

> Example: **There** will be fifteen runners competing for the prize.

ABSOLUTE VALUE—the magnitude of a number, irrespective of its sign. Written as a number inside vertical lines: $|3|=3$ *and* $|-3| = 3$.

ACUTE ANGLE—an angle measuring less than 90°. *A triangle with three acute angles is called an acute triangle.*

ADJACENT ANGLES—two angles having a common side and a common vertex.

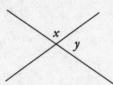

In the figure above, angles x and y are adjacent. (They are also supplementary.)

ALGEBRAIC EXPRESSION—one or more algebraic terms connected with plus and minus signs. *An algebraic expression is not an equation because it has no equal sign.*

ALTITUDE—a perpendicular segment whose length can be used in calculating the area of a triangle or other polygon.

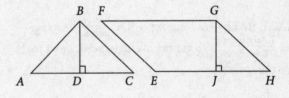

In the figure above, $\overline{BD}$ is an altitude of $\triangle ABC$, and $\overline{GJ}$ is an altitude of parallelogram EFGH.

ANGLE—two line segments coming together at a point called the vertex.

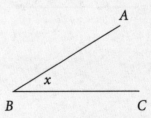

The angle pictured above could be called $\angle ABC$, $\angle B$, or $\angle x$.

ARC—a portion of the circumference of a circle.

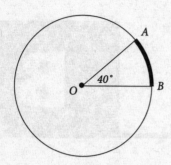

Because the central angle is $\frac{1}{9}$ of a full circle's 360°, the length of minor arc AB is $\frac{1}{9}$ the circumference.

AREA—a measure, in square units, of the size of a region in a plane. *Finding the area of a figure invariably involves multiplying two dimensions, such as length and width, or base and height.*

AVERAGE—the sum of a group of numbers divided by the number of numbers in the group. *To find the average of 2, 7, and 15, divide the sum (2 + 7 + 15 = 24) by the number of numbers (3): 24 ÷ 3 = 8.*

AVERAGE RATE—Average A per $B = \frac{\text{Total } A}{\text{Total } B}$. Average speed $= \frac{\text{Total distance}}{\text{Total time}}$. *To get the average speed, don't just average the speeds.*

AXES—the perpendicular "number lines" in the coordinate plane.

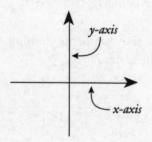

BASE—a side of a polygon that will be used with an altitude in calculating the area; a face of a solid, the area of which will be used with an altitude in calculating the volume.

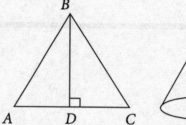

In the figure above, $\overline{AC}$ is the base of the triangle, and circle O is the base of the cone.

BINOMIAL—an algebraic expression with two terms. *The FOIL method of multiplying works only for a pair of binomials.*

BISECTOR—a line or line segment that divides an angle in half. *The bisector of a 90° angle divides it into two 45° angles.*

CENTRAL ANGLE—an angle formed by two radii of a circle.

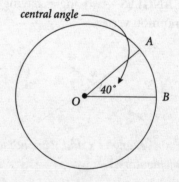

In the figure above, ∠AOB is a central angle.

CHORD—a line segment connecting two points on a circle.

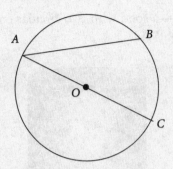

In the figure above, $\overline{AB}$ and $\overline{AC}$ are chords of circle O. Because it passes through the center, $\overline{AC}$ is also a diameter.

CIRCLE—the set of points in a plane at a particular distance from a central point. *A circle is not a polygon because it is not made up of straight sides.*

CIRCUMFERENCE—the distance around a circle. *The circumference of a circle is analogous to the perimeter of a polygon.*

CIRCUMSCRIBED—drawn outside another figure with as many points touching as possible.

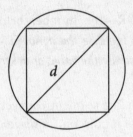

In the figure above, the circle is circumscribed about the square; d is both a diagonal of the square and a diameter of the circle.

COEFFICIENT—the numerical or "constant" part of an algebraic term. *In the monomial $-4x^2y$, the coefficient is -4. In the expression ax^2+bx+c, a, b, and c are the coefficients.*

COMMON DENOMINATOR—a number that can be used as the denominator for two or more fractions so that they can be added or subtracted. *Before you can add the fractions $\frac{5}{6}$ and $\frac{5}{8}$, you must first re-express the fractions with a common denominator, such as 24: $\frac{5}{6} = \frac{20}{24}$ and $\frac{5}{8} = \frac{15}{24}$.*

COMMON FACTOR—a factor shared by two integers. *Any two integers will have at least 1 for a common factor.*

COMMON MULTIPLE—a multiple shared by two integers. *You can always get a common multiple for two integers by multiplying them, though that will not necessarily be the least common multiple.*

COMPLEMENTARY ANGLES—two angles whose measures add up to 90°. *A 30° angle and a 60° angle are complementary.*

CONE—a solid with a circle at one end and a single point at the other.

CONGRUENT—identical; of the same size and shape. *Congruent polygons have the same angles and side lengths.*

CONSECUTIVE—one after another, in order, without skipping any. *The numbers 6, 9, 12, 15, 18, and 21 are consecutive multiples of 3.*

COORDINATES—the pair of numbers, written inside parentheses, that specifies the location of a point in the coordinate plane. *The first number is the x-coordinate and the second number is the y-coordinate.*

COSECANT—the ratio of the hypotenuse to the opposite leg. *The cosecant of ∠A in the figure below is* $\frac{\text{hypotenuse}}{\text{opposite}} = \frac{13}{5}$.

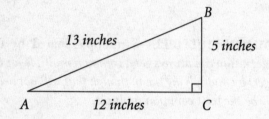

COSINE—the ratio of the adjacent leg to the hypotenuse. *The cosine of ∠A in the figure above is* $\frac{\text{adjacent}}{\text{hypotenuse}} = \frac{12}{13}$.

COTANGENT—the ratio of the adjacent leg to the opposite leg. *The cotangent of ∠A in the figure above is* $\frac{\text{adjacent}}{\text{opposite}} = \frac{12}{5}$.

CUBE—a rectangular solid whose faces are all squares.

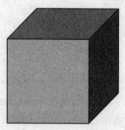

CUBE (of a number)—the third power. *The cube of a negative number is negative.*

CYLINDER—a solid with two circular ends connected by "straight" sides.

DECIMAL—a noninteger written with digits and a decimal point. *A decimal is equivalent to a common fraction whose denominator is 10, 100, or 1,000, etcetera.*

DEGREE OF AN EQUATION—the greatest exponent in a single-variable equation. *The equation $x^3 - 9x = 0$ is a third-degree equation because the biggest exponent is 3.*

DEGREE—one 360th of a full rotation. *A right angle measures 90 degrees—often written 90°.*

DENOMINATOR—the number below the fraction bar. *When you increase the denominator of a positive fraction, you decrease the value of the fraction: $\frac{7}{11}$ is less than $\frac{7}{10}$.*

DIAGONAL—a line segment connecting two nonadjacent vertices of a polygon. *A diagonal divides a rectangle into two right triangles.*

DIAMETER—(the length of) a line segment connecting two points on a circle and passing through the center. *A diameter is a chord of maximum length.*

DIFFERENCE—the result of subtraction. *The positive difference between 3 and 7 is 4.*

DIGIT—one of the numbers from 0 through 9. *In the 3-digit number 355, the hundreds' digit is 3, the tens' digit is 5, and the ones' digit is 5.*

DISTINCT—different, distinguishable. The number *355 has 2 distinct digits: 3 and 5.*

EDGE—a line segment formed by the intersection of two faces.

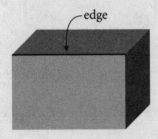

A rectangular solid has 12 edges.

ELLIPSE—a set of points in a plane for which

the sum of the distances from two points (called *foci*) is constant.

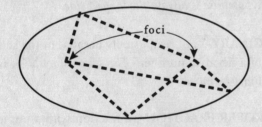

EQUATION—a statement of equality between two quantities. *It's an equation if it includes an equal sign.*

EQUATION OF A LINE—an equation that describes the relationship between the *x*- and *y*-coordinates of every point on the line in the coordinate plane. *The equation of the x-axis is y = 0, and the equation of the y-axis is x = 0.*

EQUILATERAL TRIANGLE—a triangle with three equal sides.

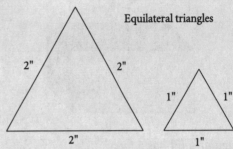

Equilateral triangles

All equilateral triangles are similar—they all have three 60° angles,

EVEN NUMBER—a multiple of 2. *The set of even numbers includes not only 2, 4, 6, etcetera, but also 0, –2, –4, –6, etcetera.*

EXPONENT—the small, raised number written to the right of a variable or number, indicating the number of times that variable or number is to be used as a factor. *In the expression $-4x^3$, the exponent is 3, so $-4x^3 = -4 \cdot x \cdot x \cdot x$.*

EXTERIOR ANGLE—the angle created outside a polygon when one side is extended. *The exterior angles of any polygon add up to 360°.*

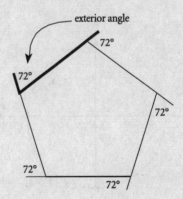

The exterior angles of a regular pentagon each measure 72°.

FACE—a polygon formed by edges of a solid.

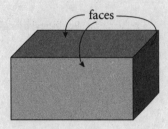

faces

A rectangular solid has 6 faces.

FACTOR (of *n*)—a positive integer that divides into *n* with no remainder. *The complete list of factors of 18 is: 1, 2, 3, 6, 9, and 18.*

FACTORING (a polynomial)—re-expressing a polynomial as the product of simpler expressions. *The complete factorization of $2x^2 + 7x + 3$ is $(2x + 1)(x + 3)$.*

FRACTION—a number expressed as a ratio. *In everyday speech, the word* fraction *implies something less than 1, but to a mathematician, any number written in the form $\frac{A}{B}$ is a fraction.*

GRAPH OF AN EQUATION—a line or curve in the coordinate plane that represents all the ordered pair solutions of an equation.

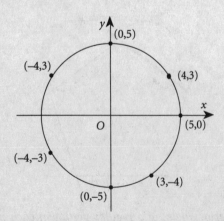

The figure above shows the graph of the equation $x^2 + y^2 = 25$.

GREATEST COMMON FACTOR—the greatest integer than is a factor of both numbers under consideration. *The greatest common factor (GCF) of relative primes is 1.*

HEXAGON—a six-sided polygon.

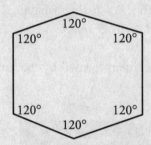

120° 120° 120° 120° 120° 120°

The six angles of a regular hexagon each measure 120°.

HYPOTENUSE—the side of a right triangle opposite the right angle.

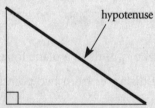

hypotenuse

The hypotenuse is always the longest side.

IMAGINARY—not real, usually because of the square root of a negative number. *The square root of –4 is an imaginary number.*

IMPROPER FRACTION—a fraction with a numerator that's greater than the denominator. $\frac{35}{8}$ *is an improper fraction and is therefore greater than 1.*

INEQUALITY—a statement that compares the size of two quantities. *There are four inequality symbols:* < *("less than"),* ≤ *"(less than or equal to"),* > *("greater than"), and* ≥ *("greater than or equal to").*

INSCRIBED—drawn inside another figure with as many points touching as possible.

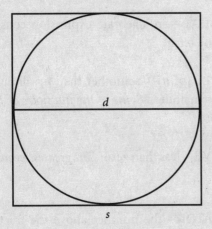

When a circle is inscribed within a square, the diameter d of the circle is the same as a length of a side s of the square.

INTEGER—a whole number; *325, 0, and −29 are integers.*

INTERCEPT—the point where a given line crosses the *x*-axis or *y*-axis.

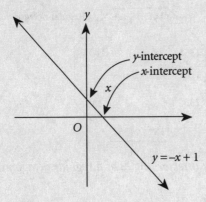

The y-intercept is the b in the slope-intercept form y = mx + b.

INTERIOR ANGLE—an angle inside a polygon formed by two adjacent sides. *Every polygon has the same number of interior angles as sides.*

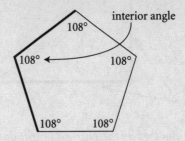

The interior angles of a regular pentagon each measure 108°.

IRRATIONAL—real, but not capable of being expressed as a ratio of integers. $\sqrt{2}$, $\sqrt{3}$, *and* π *are irrational numbers.*

ISOSCELES TRIANGLE—a triangle with two sides of equal length.

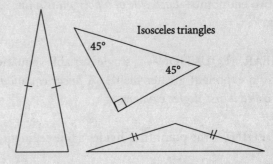

The angles opposite the equal sides of an isosceles triangle are also equal.

LEAST COMMON MULTIPLE—the smallest number that is a multiple of both given numbers. *The least common multiple of relative primes is their product.*

LEGS (of a right triangle)—the sides that make up the right angle.

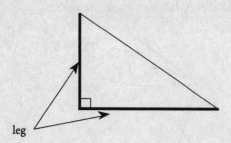

leg

You can use the legs as the base and altitude to find the area of a right triangle.

LIKE TERMS—algebraic terms in which the elements other than the coefficients are alike. *2ab and 3ab are like terms, and so they can be added: 2ab + 3ab = 5ab.*

LINE—a straight row of points extending infinitely in both directions. *A line has only one dimension.*

LINE SEGMENT—a straight row of points connecting two endpoints. *Each side of a polygon is a line segment.*

LINEAR EQUATION—a single-variable equation with no exponent greater than 1. *A linear equation is also called a first-degree equation.*

MIDPOINT—the point that divides a line segment in half.

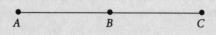

A   B   C

In the figure above, B is the midpoint of $\overline{AC}$, so AB = BC.

MIXED NUMBER—a noninteger greater than 1 written with a whole number part and a fractional part. *The mixed number $4\frac{2}{3}$ can also be expressed as the improper fraction $\frac{14}{3}$.*

MONOMIAL—an algebraic expression consisting of exactly one term.

MULTIPLE (of n)—a number than *n* will divide into with no remainder. *Some of the multiples of 18 are: 0, 18, and 90.*

NEGATIVE—less than zero. *The greatest negative integer is –1.*

NUMERATOR—the number above the fraction bar. *When you increase the numerator of a positive fraction, you increase the value of the fraction: $\frac{13}{17}$ is greater than $\frac{12}{17}$.*

OBTUSE ANGLE—an angle measuring more than 90° and less than 180°. *An obtuse triangle is one that has one obtuse angle.*

OCTAGON—an eight-sided polygon.

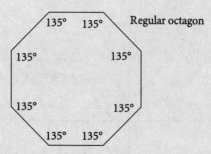

Each of the interior angles of a regular octagon measures 135°.

ODD NUMBER—an integer that is *not* a multiple of 2. *Any integer that's not even is odd.*

ORIGIN—the point where the *x*- and *y*-axes intersect. *The origin represents the point (0,0).*

PARABOLA—the set of points in a plane that are the same distance from a point called the *focus* and a line called the *directrix*.

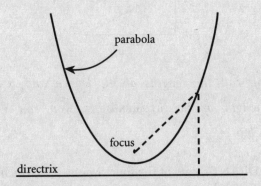

PARALLEL LINES—coplanar lines that never intersect. *Parallel lines are the same distance apart at all points.*

PARALLELOGRAM—a quadrilateral with two pairs of parallel sides.

Parallelogram

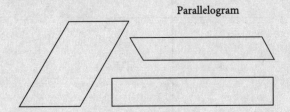

Opposite sides of a parallelogram are equal; opposite angles of a parallelogram are also equal.

PENTAGON—a five-sided polygon.

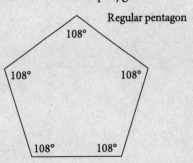

The interior angles of any pentagon add up to 540°. Each of the interior angles of a regular pentagon measures 108°.

PERCENT—one hundredth. *20% means 20 hundredths, or $\frac{20}{100} = \frac{1}{5}$*

PERCENT INCREASE/DECREASE—amount of increase or decrease expressed as a percent of the original amount. *A decrease from 100 to 83 is a 17% decrease.*

PERIMETER—the sum of the lengths of the sides of a polygon. *Two polygons with the same area do not necessarily have the same perimeter.*

PERPENDICULAR—intersecting at a right angle. *The altitude and base of a triangle are perpendicular.*

PI—an irrational number, approximately 3.14, which is equal to the ratio of the circumference of any circle to its diameter. The symbol for pi is π. *Pi appears in the formulas for the circumference and area of a circle, as well for the volumes of a sphere, a cylinder, and a cone.*

POINT—a precise position in space. *A point has no length, breadth, or thickness.*

POLYGON—a closed figure composed of any number of straight sides.

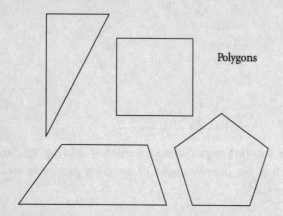

Polygons

Triangles, squares, trapezoids, and pentagons are all polygons, but circles and ellipses are not.

POLYNOMIAL—an algebraic expression that is the sum of two or more terms. *Binomials and trinomials are just two types of polynomials.*

POSITIVE—greater than zero. *Zero is not a positive number.*

POWER—a product obtained by multiplying a quantity by itself one or more times. *The fifth power of 2 is 32.*

PRIME FACTORIZATION—an integer expressed as the product of prime numbers. *The prime factorization of 60 is 2 × 2 × 3 × 5.*

PRIME NUMBER—an integer greater than 1 that has no factors other than 1 and itself. *The first 10 prime numbers are: 2, 3, 5, 7, 11, 13, 17, 23, 29, and 31. Notice that 2 is the only even prime number.*

PROBABILITY—the likelihood of a particular event, expressed as the ratio of the number of "favorable" occurrences to the total number of possible occurrences. *Probability is a part-to-whole ratio and can therefore never be greater than 1.*

PRODUCT—the result of multiplication. *The product of 3 and 4 is 12.*

PROPORTION—an expression of the equality of ratios. *Corresponding sides of similar figures are proportional.*

PYTHAGOREAN THEOREM—the rule that states, "for any right triangle, the sum of the squares of the legs is equal to the square of the hypotenuse."

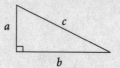

If you call the lengths of the legs a and b and the length of the hypotenuse c, you can write "$a^2 + b^2 = c^2$."

QUADRANT—one of the four regions into which the axes divide the coordinate plane.

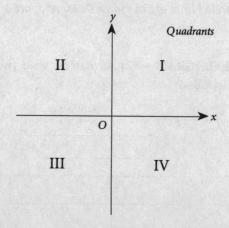

Quadrants

When you know the signs of the coordinates, you know which quadrant contains that point. For any point in Quadrant IV, for example, the x-coordinate is positive and the y-coordinate is negative.

QUADRATIC EQUATION—a second-degree equation. *Quadratic equations with one unknown often have two solutions.*

QUADRILATERAL—a four-sided polygon. *Squares, rectangles, parallelograms, and trapezoids are all quadrilaterals.*

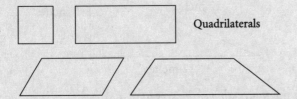

Quadrilaterals

QUOTIENT—the result of division. *When 12 is divided by 3, the quotient is 4.*

RADIAN—a unit for expressing the measure of an angle.

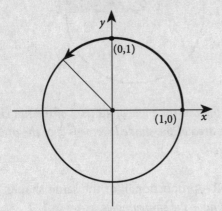

The angle shown in the figure above measures $\frac{3\pi}{4}$ radians, which is the same as 135°. It's no coincidence that $\frac{3\pi}{4}$ is also the length of the arc shown.

RADICAL—the symbol $\sqrt{}$, which by itself represents the positive square root, and with a little number written in—as in $\sqrt[5]{32}$—represents a higher root. *By convention, $\sqrt{}$ represents the positive square root only.*

RADIUS—(the length of) a line segment connecting the center and a point on a circle. *The radius is half the diameter.*

RATE—a ratio of quantities measured in different units. *The most familiar rates have units of time after the word "per," such as: meters per second, pages per hour, inches per year.*

RATIO—a fraction that expresses the relative sizes of two quantities. *A ratio is generally ex-pressed with the words "of" and "to": as in "the ratio of girls to boys."*

RATIONAL—capable of being expressed as a ratio of integers. *The repeating decimal .074074074074 . . . is a rational number because it can be written as $\frac{2}{27}$.*

REAL—having a place on the number line. *π is a real number because it has a location—somewhere just to the right of 3.14—on the number line.*

RECIPROCALS—a pair of numbers whose product is 1. *To get the reciprocal of a fraction, switch the numerator and denominator: the reciprocal of $\frac{2}{7}$ is $\frac{7}{2}$.*

RECTANGLE—a quadrilateral with four right angles. *All rectangles are parallelograms, but not all parallelograms are rectangles.*

RECTANGULAR SOLID—a solid whose faces are all rectangles.

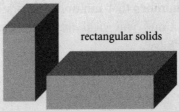

rectangular solids

REDUCING A FRACTION—expressing a fraction in lowest terms by factoring out and canceling common factors. $\frac{6}{8}$ reduces to $\frac{3}{4}$.

REGULAR POLYGON—a polygon with all equal sides and all equal angles. *Equilateral triangles and squares are regular polygons.*

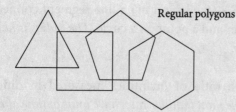

Regular polygons

RELATIVE PRIMES—positive integers that have no factors in common. *Thirty-five and 54 are relative primes because their prime factorizations (35 = 5 × 7, and 54 = 2 × 3 × 3 × 3) have nothing in common.*

REPEATING DECIMAL—a decimal with a digit or cluster of digits that repeats indefinitely. *The fraction $\frac{1}{7}$ is equivalent to the repeating decimal .142857142857142857. . . , which can be written as .$\overline{142857}$.*

RHOMBUS—a quadrilateral with four equal sides.

Rhombi

 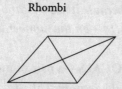

The diagonals of a rhombus are perpendicular.

RIGHT ANGLE—an angle measuring 90°. *A rectangle is a polygon with four right angles.*

RIGHT TRIANGLE—a triangle with a right angle. *Every right triangle has exactly two acute angles.*

ROOT—a number that multiplied by itself a certain number of times will yield the given quantity. *The third root of 8 is 2.*

SCALENE TRIANGLE—a triangle with sides of different lengths. *A 3-4-5 triangle is a scalene triangle.*

SECANT—the ratio of the hypotenuse to the adjacent leg. *The secant is the reciprocal of the cosine.*

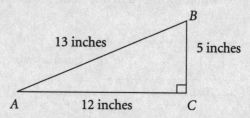

In the figure above, the secant of $\angle A$ is $\frac{13}{12}$.

SECTOR—a region bounded by two radii and an arc.

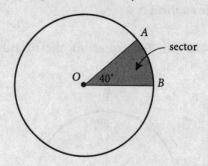

Because the central angle of 40° is $\frac{1}{9}$ of the full circle's 360°, the area of the shaded sector is $\frac{1}{9}$ of the area of the whole circle.

SIMILAR—proportional; of the same shape. *Similar polygons have the same angles.*

Similar triangles

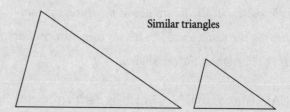

SINE—the ratio of the opposite leg to the hypotenuse.

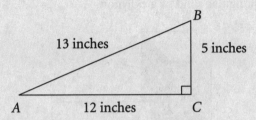

In the figure above, the sine of $\angle A$ *is* $\frac{5}{13}$.

SLOPE—a description of the "steepness" of a line in the coordinate plane, defined as

$\frac{\text{Change in } y}{\text{Change in } x}$. *Lines that go "uphill" (left to right) have positive slopes, and lines that go "downhill" have negative slopes. A horizontal line—that is, a line parallel to the x-axis—is "flat" and has a slope of 0.*

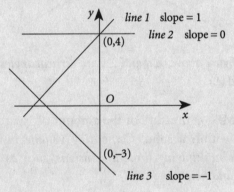

SLOPE-INTERCEPT FORM—an equation in the form $y = mx + b$. *In this form, m is the slope and b is the y-intercept. Line 1 in the figure above has a slope of 1 and a y-intercept of 4, so its equation is $y = x + 4$. Line 2's equation is $y = 4$. Line 3's equation is $y = -x - 3$.*

SOLID—a three-dimensional figure.

Cubes, cylinders, cones, and spheres are all solids.

SOLVING—isolating the given variable.

SPHERE—the set of all points in space a particular distance from a central point. *Visualize a sphere as a ball.*

SQUARE—a quadrilateral with four equal sides and four right angles. *A square can be thought of as a rectangular rhombus.*

SQUARE ROOT—a number that when squared yields the given quantity. *Positive numbers each have two square roots, but negative numbers have no real square roots.*

SUM—the result of addition. *The sum of 3 and 4 is 7.*

SUPPLEMENTARY ANGLES—two angles whose measures add up to 180°.

SURFACE AREA—the sum of the areas of the surfaces of a solid. *Surface area is measured in square units.*

SYSTEM OF EQUATIONS—two or more equations in which each variable represents the same quantity in one equation as in another.

TANGENT (of a circle)—a line that intersects a circle at exactly one point. *Visualize a tangent as a line that just barely "touches" the circle.*

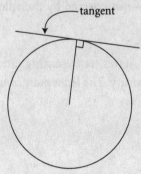

TANGENT—the ratio of the opposite leg to the adjacent leg.

TERM—a part of an algebraic expression that either stands by itself or is connected to other terms with plus and minus signs. *A term has three parts: the coefficient, the variable(s), and the exponent(s).*

TRANSVERSAL—a line that intersects two parallel lines.

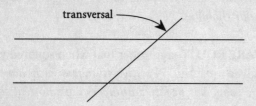

A transversal across parallel lines creates two sets of four equal angles.

TRAPEZOID—a quadrilateral with one pair of parallel sides.

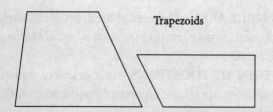

Trapezoids

TRIANGLE—a three-sided polygon. *The three angles of a triangle add up to 180°.*

UNDEFINED—not covered by the rules. *Division by 0 is undefined.*

VARIABLE—a letter representing an unknown or unspecified quantity. *The letter most commonly used for a variable is x.*

VERTEX—a point of intersection, such as a corner of a rectangular solid or a polygon.

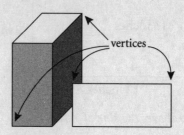

vertices

VERTICAL ANGLES—angles across the vertex of intersecting lines. *Vertical angles are equal.*

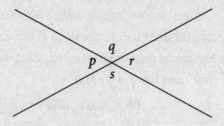

In the figure above, ∠q and ∠s are vertical angles, as are ∠p and ∠r.

VOLUME—a measure of the amount of "space" contained within a solid. *Computing volume invariably involves multiplying three dimensions, such as length, width, and height.*

100 Key Math Concepts for the ACT

NUMBER PROPERTIES

1. UNDEFINED

On the ACT, *undefined* almost always means **division by zero**. The expression $\frac{a}{bc}$ is undefined if either b or c equals 0.

2. REAL/IMAGINARY

A real number is a number that has a **location on the number line.** On the ACT, imaginary numbers are numbers that involve the square root of a negative number. $\sqrt{-4}$ is an imaginary number.

3. INTEGER/NONINTEGER

Integers are **whole numbers**; they include negative whole numbers and zero.

4. RATIONAL/IRRATIONAL

A **rational number** is a number that can be expressed as a **ratio of two integers. Irrational numbers** are real numbers—they have locations on the number line—they just **can't be expressed precisely as a fraction or decimal.** For the purposes of the ACT, the most important **irrational numbers** are $\sqrt{2}$, $\sqrt{3}$, and π.

5. ADDING and SUBTRACTING SIGNED NUMBERS

To **add a positive and a negative**, first ignore the signs and find the positive difference between the number parts. Then attach the sign of the original number with the larger number part. For example, to add 23 and –34, first we ignore the minus sign and find the positive difference between 23 and 34—that's 11. Then we attach the sign of the number with the larger number part—in this case it's the minus sign from the –34. So, 23 + (–34) = –11.

Make **subtraction** situations simpler by turning them into addition. For example, think of –17 – (–21) as –17 + (+21).

To **add or subtract a string of positives and negatives**, first turn everything into addition. Then collect the positives and negatives and reduce the string to the sum of a positive and a negative.

6. MULTIPLYING and DIVIDING SIGNED NUMBERS

To multiply and/or divide positives and negatives, treat the number parts as usual and **attach a minus sign if there were originally an odd number of negatives.** For example, to multiply –2, –3, and –5, first multiply the number parts: $2 \times 3 \times 5 = 30$.

Then go back and note that there were *three*—an *odd* number—negatives, so the product is negative: $(-2) \times (-3) \times (-5) = -30$.

7. PEMDAS

When performing multiple operations, remember **PEMDAS**, which means **Parentheses** first, then **Exponents**, then **Multiplication/Division** (left to right), then **Addition/Subtraction** (left to right).

In the expression $9 - 2 \times (5-3)^2 + 6 \div 3$, begin with the parentheses: $(5 - 3) = 2$. Then do the exponent: $2^2 = 4$. Now the expression is: $9 - 2 \times 4 + 6 \div 3$. Next do the multiplication and division to get $9 - 8 + 2$, which equals 3.

8. ABSOLUTE VALUE

Treat absolute value signs a lot like **parentheses**. Do what's inside them first and then take the absolute value of the result. Don't try to take the absolute value of each piece between the bars before calculating. For example, in order to calculate $|(-12) + 5 - (-4)| - |5 + (-10)|$, first do what's inside the bars to get: $|-3| - |-5|$, which is $3 - 5$, or -2.

9. COUNTING CONSECUTIVE INTEGERS

To count consecutive integers, **subtract the smallest from the largest and add 1.** To count the integers from 13 through 31, subtract: $31 - 13 = 18$. Then add 1: $18 + 1 = 19$.

DIVISIBILITY

10. FACTOR/MULTIPLE

The **factors** of integer n are the positive integers that divide into n with no remainder. The **multiples** of n are the integers that n divides into with no remainder. For example, 6 is a factor of 12, and 24 is a multiple of 12. 12 is both a factor and a multiple of itself.

11. PRIME FACTORIZATION

To find the prime factorization of an integer, just keep breaking it up into factors until **all the factors are prime.** To find the prime factorization of 36, for example, you could begin by breaking it into 4×9:

$$36 = 4 \times 9 = 2 \times 2 \times 3 \times 3$$

12. RELATIVE PRIMES

To determine whether two integers are relative primes, break them both down to their prime factorizations. For example: $35 = 5 \times 7$, and $54 = 2 \times 3 \times 3 \times 3$. They have **no prime factors in common**, so 35 and 54 are relative primes.

13. COMMON MULTIPLE

You can always get a common multiple of two numbers by **multiplying** them, but, unless the two numbers are relative primes, the product will not be the *least* common multiple. For example, to find a common multiple for 12 and 15, you could just multiply: $12 \times 15 = 180$.

14. LEAST COMMON MULTIPLE

To find the least common multiple, check out the **multiples of the larger number** until you find one that's **also a multiple of the smaller.** To find the LCM of 12 and 15, begin by taking the multiples of 15: 15 is not divisible by 12; 30's not; nor is 45. But the next multiple of 15, 60, *is* divisible by 12, so it's the LCM.

15. GREATEST COMMON FACTOR

To find the greatest common factor, break down both numbers into their prime factorizations and take **all the prime factors they have in common.** $36 = 2 \times 2 \times 3 \times 3$, and $48 = 2 \times 2 \times 2 \times 2 \times 3$. What they have in common is two 2s and one 3, so the GCF is $= 2 \times 2 \times 3 = 12$.

16. EVEN/ODD

To predict whether a sum, difference, or product will be even or odd, just **take simple numbers like 1 and 2 and see what happens**. There are rules—"odd times even is even," for example—but there's no need to memorize them. What happens with one set of numbers generally happens with all similar sets.

17. MULTIPLES OF 2 AND 4

An integer is divisible by 2 (even) if the **last digit is even**. An integer is divisible by 4 if the **last two digits make a multiple of 4**. The last digit of 562 is 2, which is even, so 562 is a multiple of 2. The last two digits make 62, which is *not* divisible by 4, so 562 is not a multiple of 4.

18. MULTIPLES OF 3 AND 9

An integer is divisible by 3 if the **sum of its digits is divisible by 3**. An integer is divisible by 9 if the **sum of its digits is divisible by 9**. The sum of the digits in 957 is 21, which is divisible by 3 but not by 9, so 957 is divisible by 3 but not 9.

19. MULTIPLES OF 5 AND 10

An integer is divisible by 5 if the **last digit is 5 or 0**. An integer is divisible by 10 if the **last digit is 0**. The last digit of 665 is 5, so 665 is a multiple 5 but *not* a multiple of 10.

20. REMAINDERS

The remainder is the **whole number left over after division**. 487 is 2 more than 485, which is a multiple of 5, so when 487 is divided by 5, the remainder will be 2.

FRACTIONS AND DECIMALS

21. REDUCING FRACTIONS

To reduce a fraction to lowest terms, **factor out and cancel** all factors the numerator and denominator have in common.

$$\frac{28}{36} = \frac{4 \times 7}{4 \times 9} = \frac{7}{9}$$

22. ADDING/SUBTRACTING FRACTIONS

To add or subtract fractions, first find a **common denominator**, and then add or subtract the numerators.

$$\frac{2}{15} + \frac{3}{10} = \frac{4}{30} + \frac{9}{30} = \frac{4+9}{30} = \frac{13}{30}$$

23. MULTIPLYING FRACTIONS

To multiply fractions, **multiply** the numerators and **multiply** the denominators.

$$\frac{5}{7} \cdot \frac{3}{4} = \frac{5 \cdot 3}{7 \cdot 4} = \frac{15}{28}$$

24. DIVIDING FRACTIONS

To divide fractions, **invert** the second one and **multiply**.

$$\frac{1}{2} \div \frac{3}{5} = \frac{1}{2} \cdot \frac{5}{3} = \frac{1 \cdot 5}{2 \cdot 3} = \frac{5}{6}$$

25. CONVERTING A MIXED NUMBER TO AN IMPROPER FRACTION

To convert a mixed number to an improper fraction, **multiply** the whole number part by the denominator, then **add** the numerator. The result is the new numerator (over the same denominator). To convert $7\frac{1}{3}$, first multiply 7 by 3, then add 1, to get the new numerator of 22. Put that over the same denominator, 3, to get $\frac{22}{3}$.

26. CONVERTING AN IMPROPER FRACTION TO A MIXED NUMBER

To convert an improper fraction to a mixed number, **divide** the denominator into the numerator to get a **whole number quotient with a remainder**. The quotient becomes the whole number part of the mixed number, and the remainder becomes the new numerator—with the same denominator. For example, to convert $\frac{108}{5}$, first divide 5 into 108, which yields 21 with a remainder of 3. Therefore, $\frac{108}{5} = 21\frac{3}{5}$.

27. RECIPROCAL

To find the reciprocal of a fraction, **switch** the numerator and the denominator. The reciprocal of $\frac{3}{7}$ is $\frac{7}{3}$. The reciprocal of 5 is $\frac{1}{5}$. The product of reciprocals is 1.

28. COMPARING FRACTIONS

One way to compare fractions is to re-express them with a **common denominator**.

$\frac{3}{4} = \frac{21}{28}$ and $\frac{5}{7} = \frac{20}{28}$. $\frac{21}{28}$ is greater than $\frac{20}{28}$, so $\frac{3}{4}$ is greater than $\frac{5}{7}$.

Another way to compare fractions is to convert them both to **decimals**. $\frac{3}{4}$ converts to .75, and $\frac{5}{7}$ converts to approximately .714.

29. CONVERTING FRACTIONS AND DECIMALS

To convert a fraction to a decimal, **divide the bottom into the top**. To convert $\frac{5}{8}$, divide 8 into 5, yielding .625.

30. REPEATING DECIMAL

To find a particular digit in a repeating decimal, note the **number of digits in the cluster that repeats**. If there are 2 digits in that cluster, then every 2nd digit is the same. If there are 3 digits in that cluster, then every 3rd digit is the same. And so on. For example, the decimal equivalent of $\frac{1}{27}$ is .037037037..., which is best written $.\overline{037}$.

There are 3 digits in the repeating cluster, so every 3rd digit is the same: 7. To find the 50th digit, look for the multiple of 3 just less than 50—that's 48. The 48th digit is 7, and with the 49th digit the pattern repeats with 0. The 50th digit is 3.

31. IDENTIFYING THE PARTS AND THE WHOLE

The key to solving most fractions and percents story problems is to identify the part and the whole. Usually you'll find the **part** associated with the verb *is/are* and the **whole** associated with the word *of*. In the sentence, "Half of the boys are blonds," the whole is the boys ("*of* the boys), and the part is the blonds ("*are* blonds").

PERCENTS

32. PERCENT FORMULA

Whether you need to find the part, the whole, or the percent, use the same formula:

Part = Percent × Whole

Example: What is 12% of 25?
Setup: Part = .12 × 25

Example: 15 is 3% of what number?
Setup: 15 = .03 × Whole

Example: 45 is what percent of 9?
Setup: 45 = Percent × 9

33. PERCENT INCREASE AND DECREASE

To increase a number by a percent, **add the percent to 100%**, convert to a decimal, and multiply. To increase 40 by 25%, add 25% to 100%, convert 125% to 1.25, and multiply by 40. \ 1.25 × 40 = 50.

34. FINDING THE ORIGINAL WHOLE

To find the **original whole before a percent increase or decrease**, set up an equation. Think of a 15% increase over x as $1.15x$.

Example: After a 5% increase, the population was 59,346. What was the population *before* the increase?

Setup: $1.05x = 59,346$

35. COMBINED PERCENT INCREASE AND DECREASE

To determine the combined effect of multiple percents increase and/or decrease, **start with 100 and see what happens**.

Example: A price went up 10% one year, and the new price went up 20% the next year. What was the combined percent increase?

Setup: First year: 100 + (10% of 100) = 110. Second year: 110 + (20% of 110) = 132. That's a combined 32% increase.

RATIOS, PROPORTIONS, AND RATES

36. SETTING UP A RATIO

To find a ratio, put the number associated with the word *of* **on top** and the quantity associated with the word *to* **on the bottom** and reduce. The ratio of 20 oranges to 12 apples is $\frac{20}{12}$ which reduces to $\frac{5}{3}$.

37. PART-TO-PART RATIOS AND PART-TO-WHOLE RATIOS

If the parts add up to the whole, a part-to-part ratio can be turned into 2 part-to-whole ratios by putting **each number in the original ratio over the sum of the numbers.** If the ratio of males to females is 1 to 2, then the males-to-people ratio is $\frac{1}{1+2} = \frac{1}{3}$ and the females-to-people ratio is $\frac{2}{1+2} = \frac{2}{3}$. Or, $\frac{2}{3}$ of all the people are female.

38. SOLVING A PROPORTION

To solve a proportion, **cross multiply:**

$$\frac{x}{5} = \frac{3}{4}$$
$$4x = 5 \cdot 3$$
$$x = \frac{15}{4} = 3.75$$

39. RATE

To solve a rates problem, **use the units** to keep things straight.

Example: If snow is falling at the rate of 1 foot every 4 hours, how many inches of snow will fall in 7 hours?

Setup:

$$\frac{1 \text{ foot}}{4 \text{ hours}} = \frac{x \text{ inches}}{7 \text{ hours}}$$

$$\frac{12 \text{ inches}}{4 \text{ hours}} = \frac{x \text{ inches}}{7 \text{ hours}}$$

$$4x = 12 \cdot 7$$

$$x = 21$$

40. AVERAGE RATE

$$\text{Average } A \text{ per } B = \frac{\text{Total } A}{\text{Total } B}$$

$$\text{Average Speed} = \frac{\text{Total distance}}{\text{Total time}}$$

To find the average speed for 120 miles at 40 mph and 120 miles at 60 mph, **don't just average the two speeds.** First figure out the total distance and the total time. The total distance is 120 + 120 = 240 miles. The times are 3 hours for the first leg and 2 hours for the second leg, or 5 hours total. The average speed, then, is $\frac{240}{5} = 48$ miles per hour.

AVERAGES

41. AVERAGE FORMULA

To find the average of a set of numbers, **add them up and divide by the number of numbers.**

$$\text{Average} = \frac{\text{Sum of the terms}}{\text{Number of terms}}$$

To find the average of the 5 numbers 12, 15, 23, 40, and 40, first add them up: 12 + 15 + 23 + 40 + 40 = 130. Then divide the sum by 5: 130 ÷ 5 = 26.

42. AVERAGE OF EVENLY SPACED NUMBERS

To find the average of evenly spaced numbers, just **average the smallest and the largest.** The average of all the integers from 13 through 77 is the same as the average of 13 and 77. $\frac{13+77}{2} = \frac{90}{2} = 45$

43. USING THE AVERAGE TO FIND THE SUM

$$\text{Sum} = (\text{Average}) \times (\text{Number of terms})$$

If the average of 10 numbers is 50, then they add up to 10 × 50, or 500.

44. FINDING THE MISSING NUMBER

To find a missing number when you're given the average, **use the sum.** If the average of 4 numbers is 7, then the sum of those 4 numbers is 4 × 7, or 28. Suppose that 3 of the numbers are 3, 5, and 8. These 3 numbers add up to 16 of that 28, which leaves 12 for the fourth number.

POSSIBILITIES AND PROBABILITY

45. COUNTING THE POSSIBILITIES

The fundamental counting principle: if there are **m ways** one event can happen and **n ways** a second event can happen, then there are $m \times n$ ways for the two events to happen. For example, with 5 shirts and 7 pairs of pants to choose from, you can put together $5 \times 7 = 35$ different outfits.

46. PROBABILITY

$$\text{Probability} = \frac{\text{Favorable outcomes}}{\text{Total possible outcomes}}$$

For example, if you have 12 shirts in a drawer and 9 of them are white, the probability of picking a white shirt at random is $\frac{9}{12} = \frac{3}{4}$. This probability can also be expressed as .75 or 75%.

POWERS AND ROOTS

47. MULTIPLYING AND DIVIDING POWERS

To multiply powers, **add the exponents:** $x^3 \cdot x^4 = x^{3+4} = x^7$. To divide powers, **subtract the exponents:** $y^{13} \div y^8 = y^{13-8} = y^5$.

48. RAISING POWERS TO POWERS

To raise a power to a power, **multiply the exponents.** $(x^3)^4 = x^{3 \times 4} = x^{12}$.

49. SIMPLIFYING SQUARE ROOTS

To simplify a square root, **factor out the perfect squares** under the radical, unsquare them and put the result in front. $\sqrt{12} = \sqrt{4 \times 3} = \sqrt{4} \times \sqrt{3} = 2\sqrt{3}$.

50. ADDING AND SUBTRACTING ROOTS

You can add or subtract radical expressions **only if the part under the radicals is the same.**

51. MULTIPLYING AND DIVIDING ROOTS

The product of square roots is equal to the **square root of the product:** $\sqrt{3} \times \sqrt{5} = \sqrt{3 \times 5} = \sqrt{15}$. The quotient of square roots is equal to the **square**

root of the quotient: $\frac{\sqrt{6}}{\sqrt{3}} = \sqrt{\frac{6}{3}} = \sqrt{2}$.

ALGEBRAIC EXPRESSIONS

52. EVALUATING AN ALGEBRAIC EXPRESSION

To evaluate an algebraic expression, **plug in** the given values for the unknowns and calculate according to PEMDAS. To find the value of $x^2 + 5x - 6$ when $x = -2$, plug in -2 for x: $(-2)^2 + 5(-2) - 6 = 4 - 10 - 6 = -12$.

53. ADDING AND SUBTRACTING MONOMIALS

To combine like terms, **keep the variable part unchanged while adding or subtracting the coefficients.** $2a + 3a = (2 + 3)a = 5a$

54. ADDING AND SUBTRACTING POLYNOMIALS

To add or subtract polynomials, **combine like terms.** $(3x^2 + 5x - 7) - (x^2 + 12) =$

$(3x^2 - x^2) + 5x + (-7 - 12) = +2x^2 + 5x - 19$

55. MULTIPLYING MONOMIALS

To multiply monomials, **multiply the coefficients and the variables separately.** $2a \cdot 3a = (2 \cdot 3)(a \cdot a) = 6a^2$.

56. MULTIPLYING BINOMIALS—FOIL

To multiply binomials, use **FOIL.** To multiply $(x + 3)$ by $(x + 4)$, first multiply the First terms: $x \cdot x = x^2$. Next the Outer terms: $x \cdot 4 = 4x$. Then the Inner terms: $3 \cdot x = 3x$. And finally the Last terms: $3 \cdot 4 = 12$. Then add and combine like terms: $x^2 + 4x + 3x + 12 = x^2 + 7x + 12$.

57. MULTIPLYING OTHER POLYNOMIALS

FOIL works only when you want to multiply two binomials. If you want to multiply polynomials with more than two terms, make sure you **multiply each term in the first polynomial by each term in the second.**

$(x^2 + 3x + 4)(x + 5) =$
$x^2(x + 5) + 3x(x + 5) + 4(x + 5) =$
$x^3 + 5x^2 + 3x^2 + 15x + 4x + 20 =$
$x^3 + 8x^2 + 19x + 20$

FACTORING ALGEBRAIC EXPRESSIONS

58. FACTORING OUT A COMMON DIVISOR

A factor common to all terms of a polynomial can be **factored out**. All three terms in the polynomial $3x^3 + 12x^2 - 6x$ contain a factor of $3x$. Pulling out the common factor yields $3x(x^2 + 4x - 2)$.

59. FACTORING THE DIFFERENCE OF SQUARES

One of the test maker's favorite factorables is the **difference of squares**.

$$a^2 + b^2 = (a - b)(a + b)$$

$x^2 - 9$, for example, factors to $(x - 3)(x + 3)$.

60. FACTORING THE SQUARE OF A BINOMIAL

Learn to recognize polynomials that are squares of binomials:

$$a^2 + 2ab + b^2 = (a + b)^2$$

$$a^2 - 2ab + b^2 = (a - b)^2$$

For example, $4x^2 + 12x + 9$ factors to $(2x + 3)^2$, and $n^2 - 10n + 25$ factors to $(n - 5)^2$.

61. FACTORING OTHER POLYNOMIALS—FOIL IN REVERSE

To factor a quadratic expression, **think about what binomials you could use FOIL on to get that quadratic expression**. To factor $x^2 - 5x + 6$, think about what First terms will produce x^2, what Last terms will produce $+6$, and what Outer and Inner terms will produce $-5x$. Common sense—and trial and error—lead you to $(x - 2)(x - 3)$.

62. SIMPLIFYING AN ALGEBRAIC FRACTION

Simplifying an algebraic fraction is a lot like simplifying a numerical fraction. The general idea is to **find factors common to the numerator and denominator and cancel them**. Thus, simplifying an algebraic fraction begins with factoring.

To simplify $\frac{x^2 - x - 12}{x^2 - 9}$ first factor the numerator and denominator: $\frac{x^2 - x - 12}{x^2} - 9 = \frac{(x - 4)(x + 3)}{(x - 3)(x + 3)}$

Canceling $x + 3$ from the numerator and denominator leaves you with $\frac{x - 4}{x - 3}$.

SOLVING EQUATIONS

63. SOLVING A LINEAR EQUATION

To solve an equation, do whatever necessary to both sides to **isolate the variable**. To solve the equation $5x - 12 = -2x + 9$, first get all the x's on one side by adding $2x$ to both sides: $7x - 12 = 9$. Then add 12 to both sides: $7x = 21$. Then divide both sides by 7 to get: $x = 3$.

64. SOLVING "IN TERMS OF"

To solve an equation for one variable in terms of another means to **isolate the one variable on one side of the equation**, leaving an expression containing the other variable on the other side of the equation. To solve the equation $3x - 10y = -5x + 6y$ for x in terms of y, isolate x:

$$3x - 10y = -5x + 6y$$
$$3x + 5x = 6y + 10y$$
$$8x = 16y$$
$$x = 2y$$

65. TRANSLATING FROM ENGLISH INTO ALGEBRA

To translate from English into algebra, look for the **key words** and systematically turn **phrases into algebraic expressions** and **sentences into equations**. Be careful about order, especially when subtraction is called for.

Example: The charge for a phone call is r cents for the first 3 minutes and s cents for each minute thereafter. What is the cost, in cents, of a phone call lasting exactly t minutes? ($t > 3$)

Setup: The charge begins with r, and then something more is added, depending on the length of the call. The amount added is s times the number of minutes past 3 minutes. If the total number of minutes is t, then the number of minutes past 3 is $t - 3$. So the charge is $r + s(t - 3)$.

INTERMEDIATE ALGEBRA

66. SOLVING A QUADRATIC EQUATION

To solve a quadratic equation, put it in the "$ax^2 + bx + c = 0$" form, **factor** the left side (if you can), and set each factor equal to 0 separately to get the two solutions. To solve $x^2 + 12 = 7x$, first rewrite it as $x^2 - 7x + 12 = 0$. Then factor the left side:

$$(x - 3)(x - 4) = 0$$
$$x - 3 = 0 \text{ or } x - 4 = 0$$
$$x = 3 \text{ or } 4$$

Sometimes the left side might not be obviously factorable. You can always use the **quadratic formula**. Just plug in the coefficients a, b, and c from $ax^2 + bx + c = 0$ into the formula:

$$\frac{-b \pm \sqrt{b^2 - 4ac}}{2a}$$

To solve $x^2 + 4x + 2 = 0$, plug $a = 1$, $b = 4$, and $c = 2$ into the formula:

$$x = \frac{-4 \pm \sqrt{4^2 - 4 \cdot 1 \cdot 2}}{2 \cdot 1}$$

$$= \frac{4 \pm \sqrt{8}}{2} = -2 \pm \sqrt{2}$$

67. SOLVING A SYSTEM OF EQUATIONS

You can solve for 2 variables only if you have 2 distinct equations. **Combine the equations** in such a way that **one of the variables cancels out**. To solve the 2 equations $4x + 3y = 8$ and $x + y = 3$, multiply both sides of the second equation by -3 to get: $-3x - 3y = -9$. Now add the 2 equations; the $3y$ and the $-3y$ cancel out, leaving: $x = -1$. Plug that back into either one of the original equations and you'll find that $y = 4$.

68. SOLVING AN EQUATION THAT INCLUDES ABSOLUTE VALUE SIGNS

To solve an equation that includes absolute value signs, **think about the two different cases**. For example, to solve the equation $|x-12|=3$, think of it as two equations:

$$x - 12 = 3 \text{ or } x - 12 = -3$$
$$x = 15 \text{ or } 9$$

69. SOLVING AN INEQUALITY

To solve an inequality, do whatever is necessary to both sides to **isolate the variable**. Just remember that when you **multiply or divide both sides by a negative number**, you must **reverse the sign**. To solve $-5x + 7 < -3$, subtract 7 from both sides to get: $-5x < -10$. Now divide both sides by -5, remembering to reverse the sign: $x > 2$.

70. GRAPHING INEQUALITIES

To graph a range of values, use a thick, black line over the number line, and at the end(s) of the range, use a **solid circle** if the point *is* included or an **open circle** if the point is *not* included. The figure on the next page shows the graph of $-3 < x \leq 5$.

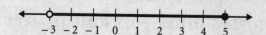

COORDINATE GEOMETRY

71. FINDING THE DISTANCE BETWEEN TWO POINTS

To find the distance between points, **use the Pythagorean Theorem or special right triangles**. The difference between the x's is one leg and the difference between the y's is the other leg.

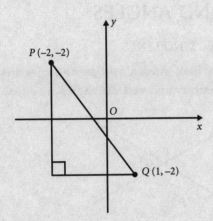

In the figure above, $\overline{PQ}$ is the hypotenuse of a 3-4-5 triangle, so $PQ = 5$.

You can also use the **distance formula**:

$$d = \sqrt{(x_1 - x_2)^2 + (y_1 - y_2)^2}$$

To find the distance between $R(3,6)$ and $S(5,-2)$:

$$d = \sqrt{(3 - 5)^2 + [6 -(-2)]^2}$$
$$= \sqrt{(-2)^2 + (8)^2}$$
$$= \sqrt{68} = 2\sqrt{17}$$

72. USING TWO POINTS TO FIND THE SLOPE

$$\text{Slope} = \frac{\text{Change in } y}{\text{Change in } x} = \frac{\text{Rise}}{\text{Run}}$$

The slope of the line that contains the points $A(2,3)$ and $B(0,-1)$ is:

$$\frac{y_A - y_B}{x_A - x_B} = \frac{3 -(-1)}{2 - 0} = \frac{4}{2} = 2$$

73. USING AN EQUATION TO FIND THE SLOPE

To find the slope of a line from an equation, put the equation into the **slope-intercept** form:

$$y = mx + b$$

The **slope is m**. To find the slope of the equation $3x + 2y = 4$, reexpress it:

$$3x + 2y = 4$$
$$2y = -3x + 4$$
$$y = -\frac{3}{2}x + 2$$

The slope is $-\frac{3}{2}$.

74. USING AN EQUATION TO FIND AN INTERCEPT

To find the y-intercept, you can either put the equation into $y = mx + b$ (**slope-intercept**) form—in which case b **is the y-intercept**—or you can just **plug $x = 0$** into the equation and **solve for y**. To find the x-intercept, **plug $y = 0$** into the equation and **solve for x**.

75. EQUATION FOR A CIRCLE

The equation for a circle of radius r and centered at (h, k) is

$$(x - h)^2 + (y - k)^2 = r^2$$

The figure below shows the graph of the equation $(x-2)^2+(y+1)^2=25$:

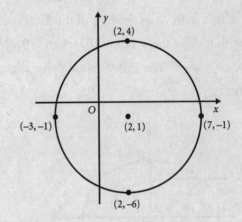

76. EQUATION FOR A PARABOLA

The graph of an equation in the form $y=ax^2+bx+c$ is a parabola. The figure below shows the graph of seven pairs of numbers that satisfy the equation $y = x^2 - 4x +3$:

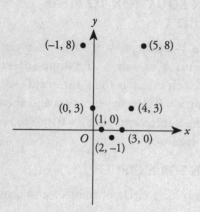

77. EQUATION FOR AN ELLIPSE

The graph of an equation in the form

$$\frac{x^2}{a^2} + \frac{y^2}{b^2} = 1$$

is an ellipse with $2a$ as the sum of the focal radii and with foci on the x-axis at $(0, -c)$ and $(0, c)$, where $c = \sqrt{a^2 - b^2}$. The figure below shows the graph of : $\frac{x^2}{25} + \frac{y^2}{16} = 1$

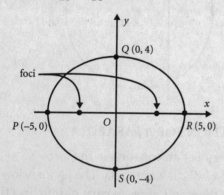

The foci are at $(-3, 0)$ and $(3, 0)$. $\overline{PS}$ is the **major axis**, and $\overline{QS}$ is the **minor axis**. This ellipse is symmetrical about both the x- and y-axes.

LINES AND ANGLES

78. INTERSECTING LINES

When two lines intersect, **adjacent angles are supplementary** and **vertical angles are equal.**

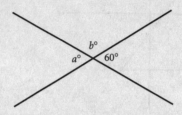

In the figure above, the angles marked $a°$ and $b°$ are adjacent and supplementary, so $a + b = 180$. Furthermore, the angles marked $a°$ and $60°$ are vertical and equal, so $a = 60$.

79. PARALLEL LINES AND TRANSVERSALS

A transversal across parallel lines forms **four equal acute angles and four equal obtuse angles.**

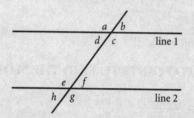

In the figure above, line 1 is parallel to line 2. Angles a, c, e, and g are obtuse, so they are all equal. Angles b, d, f, and h are acute, so they are all equal.

Furthermore, **any of the acute angles is supplementary to any of the obtuse angles.** Angles a and h are supplementary, as are b and e, c and f, and so on.

TRIANGLES

80. INTERIOR ANGLES OF A TRIANGLE

The three angles of any triangle **add up to 180°**.

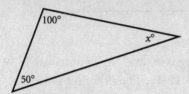

In the figure above, $x + 50 + 100 = 180$, so $x = 30$.

81. EXTERIOR ANGLES OF A TRIANGLE

An exterior angle of a triangle is equal to the **sum of the remote interior angles**.

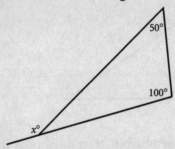

In the figure above, the exterior angle labeled $x°$ is equal to the sum of the remote interior angles: $x = 50 + 100 = 150$.

The three exterior angles of any triangle add up to 360°.

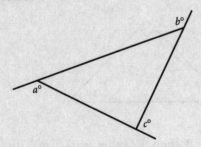

In the figure above, $a + b + c = 360$.

82. SIMILAR TRIANGLES

Similar triangles have the same shape: **corresponding angles are equal and corresponding sides are proportional**.

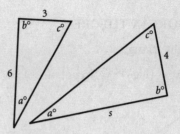

The triangles above are similar because they have the same angles. The 3 corresponds to the 4 and the 6 corresponds to the s.

$$\frac{3}{4} = \frac{6}{s}$$

$$3s = 24$$

$$s = 8$$

83. AREA OF A TRIANGLE

Area of Triangle $= \frac{1}{2}$ (base)(height)

The height is the perpendicular distance between the side that's chosen as the base and the opposite vertex.

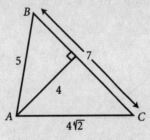

In the triangle above, 4 is the height when the 7 is chosen as the base.

Area $= \frac{1}{2} bh = \frac{1}{2}(7)(4) = 14$

RIGHT TRIANGLES

84. PYTHAGOREAN THEOREM

For all right triangles:

$$(\text{leg}_1)^2 + (\text{leg}_2)^2 = (\text{hypotenuse})^2$$

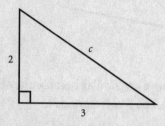

If one leg is 2 and the other leg is 3, then:

$$2^2 + 3^2 = c^2$$
$$c^2 = 4 + 9$$
$$c = \sqrt{13}$$

85. SPECIAL RIGHT TRIANGLES

• 3-4-5

If a right triangle's leg-to-leg ratio is 3:4, or if the leg-to-hypotenuse ratio is 3:5 or 4:5, then it's a 3-4-5 triangle and you don't need to use the Pythagorean theorem to find the third side. Just figure out what multiple of 3-4-5 it is.

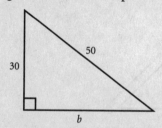

In the right triangle above, one leg is 30 and the hypotenuse is 50. This is 10 times 3-4-5. The other leg is 40.

• 5-12-13

If a right triangle's leg-to-leg ratio is 5:12, or if the leg-to-hypotenuse ratio is 5:13 or 12:13, then it's a 5-12-13 triangle and you don't need to use the Pythagorean theorem to find the third side. Just figure out what multiple of 5-12-13 it is.

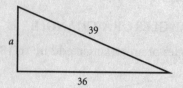

Here one leg is 36 and the hypotenuse is 39. This is 3 times 5-12-13. The other leg is 15.

• 30-60-90

The sides of a 30-60-90 triangle are in a ratio of $1:\sqrt{3}:2$. You don't need to use the Pythagorean theorem.

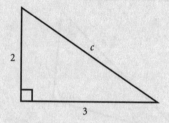

If the hypotenuse is 6, then the shorter leg is half that, or 3; and then the longer leg is equal to the short leg times $\sqrt{3}$, or $3\sqrt{3}$.

• 45-45-90

The sides of a 45-45-90 triangle are in a ratio of $1:1:\sqrt{2}$.

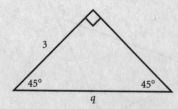

If one leg is 3, then the other leg is also 3, and the hypotenuse is equal to a leg times $\sqrt{2}$, or $3\sqrt{2}$.

OTHER POLYGONS

86. CHARACTERISTICS OF SPECIAL QUADRILATERALS

• Rectangle

A rectangle is a **4-sided figure with 4 right angles**. Opposite sides are equal. Diagonals are equal.

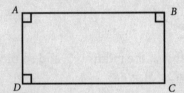

Quadrilateral *ABCD* above is shown to have three right angles. The fourth angle therefore also measures 90°, and *ABCD* is a rectangle.

• Parallelogram

A parallelogram has **two pairs of parallel sides.** Opposite sides are equal. Opposite angles are equal. Consecutive angles add up to 180°.

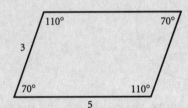

In the figure above, *s* is the length of the side opposite the 3, so *s* = 3.

• Square

A square is a **rectangle with 4 equal sides.**

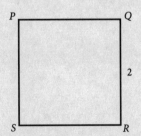

If *PQRS* is a square, all sides are the same length as $\overline{QR}$.

• Trapezoid

A **trapezoid** is a quadrilateral with one pair of parallel sides and one pair of nonparallel sides.

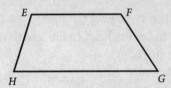

In the quadrilateral above, sides $\overline{EF}$ and $\overline{GH}$ are parallel, while sides $\overline{EF}$ and $\overline{GH}$ are not parallel. *EFGH* is therefore a trapezoid.

87. AREAS OF SPECIAL QUADRILATERALS

Area of Rectangle = Length × Width

The area of a 7-by-3 rectangle is 7 × 3 = 21.

Area of Parallelogram = Base × Height

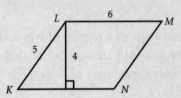

In parallelogram *KLMN* above, 4 is the height when *LM* or *KN* is used as the base. Base × Height = 6 × 4 = 24.

Area of Square = (Side)²

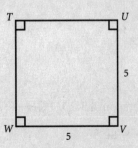

The square above, with sides of length 5, has an area of $5^2 = 25$.

$$\text{Area of Trapezoid} = \left(\frac{\text{base}_1 + \text{base}_2}{2}\right) \times \text{height}$$

Think of it as the average of the bases (the two parallel sides) times the height (the length of the perpendicular altitude).

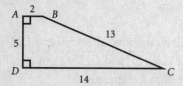

In the trapezoid *ABCD* above, you can use side $\overline{AD}$ for the height. The average of the bases is $\frac{2 + 14}{2}$ = 8, so the area is 5 $\times$ 8, or 40.

88. INTERIOR ANGLES OF A POLYGON

The **sum of the measures of the interior angles of a polygon is $(n - 2) \times 180$**, where *n* is the number of sides.

$$\text{Sum of the angles} = (n - 2) \times 180$$

The eight angles of an octagon, for example, add up to $(8 - 2) \times 180 = 1{,}080$.

To find **one angle of a regular polygon**, divide the sum of the angles by the number of angles (which is the same as the number of sides). The formula, therefore, is:

$$\text{Interior angle} = \frac{(n - 2) \times 180}{n}$$

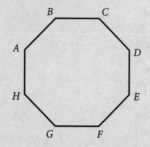

Angle *A* of regular octagon *ABCDEFGH* above measures $\frac{1{,}080}{8}$ degrees.

CIRCLES

89. CIRCUMFERENCE OF A CIRCLE

Circumference of a circle = $2\pi r$

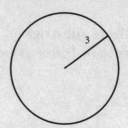

In the circle above, the radius is 3, and so the circumference is $2\pi(3) = 6\pi$.

90. LENGTH OF AN ARC

An **arc** is a piece of the circumference. If *n* is the measure of the arc's central angle, then the formula is:

$$\text{Length of an Arc} = \left(\frac{n}{360}\right)(2\pi r)$$

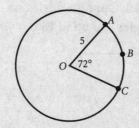

In the figure above, the radius is 5 and the measure of the central angle is 72°. The arc length is $\frac{72}{360}$ or $\frac{1}{5}$ of the circumference:

$$\left(\frac{72}{360}\right) 2\pi \, 5 = \left(\frac{1}{5}\right) 10\pi = 2\pi$$

91. AREA OF A CIRCLE

Area of a circle = πr^2

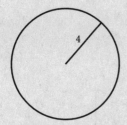

The area of the circle above is $\pi(4)^2 = 16\pi$.

92. AREA OF A SECTOR

A **sector** is a piece of the area of a circle. If n is the measure of the sector's central angle, then the formula is:

$$\text{Area of a Sector} = \left(\frac{n}{360}\right)\left(\pi r^2\right)$$

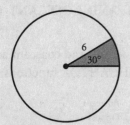

In the figure above, the radius is 6 and the measure of the sector's central angle is 30°. The sector has $\frac{30}{230}$ or $\frac{1}{12}$ of the area of the circle:

$$\left(\frac{30}{360}\right)\left(\pi\right)\left(6^2\right) = \left(\frac{1}{12}\right)\left(36\pi\right) = 3\pi$$

SOLIDS

93. SURFACE AREA OF A RECTANGULAR SOLID

The surface of a rectangular solid consists of 3 pairs of identical faces. To find the surface area, find the area of each face and add them up. If the length is l, the width is w, and the height is h, the formula is:

Surface Area = $2lw + 2wh + 2lh$

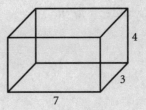

The surface area of the box above is:

$2\cdot7\cdot3 + 2\cdot3\cdot4 + 2\cdot7\cdot4 = 42 + 24 + 56 = 122$

94. VOLUME OF A RECTANGULAR SOLID

Volume of a Rectangular Solid = lwh

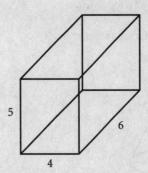

The volume of a 4-by-5-by-6 box is

$4 \times 5 \times 6 = 120$

A cube is a rectangular solid with length, width, and height all equal. If e is the length of an edge of a cube, the volume formula is:

Volume of a Cube = e^3

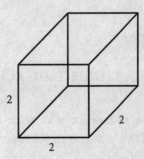

The volume of the cube above is $2^3 = 8$.

95. VOLUME OF OTHER SOLIDS

Volume of a Cylinder = $\pi r^2 h$

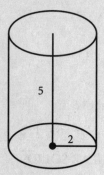

In the cylinder above, $r = 2$, and $h = 5$, so:

Volume = $\pi(2^2)(5) = 20\pi$

Volume of a Cone = $\frac{1}{3}\pi r^2 h$

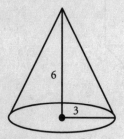

In the cone above, $r = 3$, and $h = 6$. So the volume of the cone is:

Volume = $\frac{1}{3}\pi(3^2)(6) = 18$

Volume of a Sphere = $\frac{4}{3}\pi r^3$

If the radius of a sphere is 3, then:
Volume = $\frac{4}{3}\pi(3^3) = 36\pi$

TRIGONOMETRY

96. SINE, COSINE, AND TANGENT OF ACUTE ANGLES

To find the sine, cosine, or tangent of an acute angle, use **SOHCAHTOA**, which is an abbreviation for the following definitions:

$Sine = \dfrac{\text{Opposite}}{\text{Hypotenuse}}$

$Cosine = \dfrac{\text{Adjacent}}{\text{Hypotenuse}}$

$Tangent = \dfrac{\text{Opposite}}{\text{Adjacent}}$

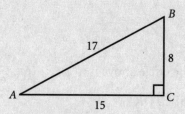

In the figure above:

$\sin A = \dfrac{8}{17}$

$\cos A = \dfrac{15}{17}$

$\tan A = \dfrac{8}{15}$

97. COTANGENT, SECANT, AND COSECANT OF ACUTE ANGLES

Think of the cotangent, secant, and cosecant as the reciprocals of the SOHCAHTOA functions:

$Cotangent = \dfrac{1}{\text{Tangent}} = \dfrac{\text{Adjacent}}{\text{Opposite}}$

$Secant = \dfrac{1}{\text{Cosine}} = \dfrac{\text{Hypotenuse}}{\text{Adjacent}}$

$Cosecant = \dfrac{1}{\text{Sine}} = \dfrac{\text{Hypotenuse}}{\text{Opposite}}$

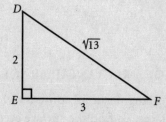

In the figure above:

$\cot D = \dfrac{2}{3}$

$\sec D = \dfrac{\sqrt{13}}{2}$

$\csc D = \dfrac{\sqrt{13}}{3}$

98. TRIGONOMETRIC FUNCTIONS OF OTHER ANGLES

To find a trigonometric function of an angle greater than 90°, sketch a circle of radius 1 and centered at the origin of the coordinate grid. Start from the point $(1, 0)$ and rotate the appropriate number of degrees counterclockwise.

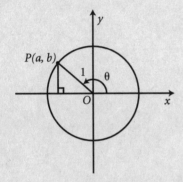

In the "unit circle" setup on the previous page, the basic trigonometric functions are defined in terms of the coordinates a and b :

$$\sin \theta = b$$

$$\cos \theta = a$$

$$\tan \theta = \frac{a}{b}$$

Example: $\sin 210° = ?$

Setup: Sketch a 210° angle in the coordinate plane:

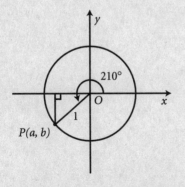

Because the triangle shown in the figure above is a 30-60-90 right triangle, we can determine that the coordinates of point P are $-\frac{\sqrt{3}}{2}, -\frac{1}{2}$. The sine is therefore $-\frac{1}{2}$.

99. SIMPLIFYING TRIGONOMETRIC EXPRESSIONS

To simplify trigonometric expressions, use the inverse function definitions along with the fundamental trigonometric identity:

$$\sin^2 x + \cos^2 x = 1$$

Example: $\frac{\sin^2 \theta + \cos^2 \theta}{\cos \theta} = ?$

Setup: The numerator equals 1, so:

$$\frac{\sin^2 \theta + \cos^2}{\cos \theta} = \frac{1}{\cos \theta} = \sec \theta$$

100. GRAPHING TRIGONOMETRIC FUNCTIONS

To graph trigonometric functions, use the x-axis for the angle and the y-axis for the value of the trigonometric function. Use special angles—0°, 30°, 45°, 60°, 90°, 120°, 135°, 150°, 180°, etc.—to plot key points.

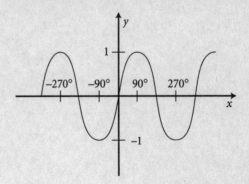

The figure above shows a portion of the graph of $y = \sin x$.

How Did We Do? Grade Us.

Thank you for choosing a Kaplan book. Your comments and suggestions are very useful to us. Please answer the following questions to assist us in our continued development of high-quality resources to meet your needs.

The Kaplan book I read was: _____

My name is: _____

My address is: _____

_____

My e-mail address is: _____

What overall grade would you give this book?　Ⓐ　Ⓑ　Ⓒ　Ⓓ　Ⓕ

How relevant was the information to your goals?　Ⓐ　Ⓑ　Ⓒ　Ⓓ　Ⓕ

How comprehensive was the information in this book?　Ⓐ　Ⓑ　Ⓒ　Ⓓ　Ⓕ

How accurate was the information in this book?　Ⓐ　Ⓑ　Ⓒ　Ⓓ　Ⓕ

How easy was the book to use?　Ⓐ　Ⓑ　Ⓒ　Ⓓ　Ⓕ

How appealing was the book's design?　Ⓐ　Ⓑ　Ⓒ　Ⓓ　Ⓕ

What were the book's strong points? _____

How could this book be improved? _____

Is there anything that we left out that you wanted to know more about?

Would you recommend this book to others?　☐ YES　　☐ NO

Other comments: _____

_____

_____

Do we have permission to quote you?　☐ YES　　☐ NO

Thank you for your help. Please tear out this page and mail it to:

Dave Chipps, Managing Editor
Kaplan Educational Centers
888 Seventh Avenue
New York, NY 10106

Or, you can submit your comments electronically by using Kaplan's online feedback form at http://www.kaptest.com/customer-service/lvl5_comments.jhtml

Thanks!

SIXTY · YEARS · OF · BUILDING · FUTURES

KAPLAN 60

About

Kaplan, Inc. is one of the nation's leading providers of education and career services. Kaplan is a wholly owned subsidiary of The Washington Post Company.

KAPLAN TEST PREPARATION & ADMISSIONS

Kaplan's nationally recognized test prep courses cover more than 20 standardized tests, including secondary school, college and graduate school entrance exams, as well as foreign language and professional licensing exams. In addition, Kaplan offers a college admissions course, private tutoring, and a variety of free information and services for students applying to college and graduate programs. Kaplan also provides information and guidance on the financial aid process. Students can enroll in online test prep courses and admissions consulting services at www.kaptest.com.

Kaplan K12 Learning Services partners with schools, universities, and teachers to help students succeed, providing customized assessment, education, and professional development programs.

SCORE! EDUCATIONAL CENTERS

SCORE! after-school learning centers help K–10 students build confidence along with academic skills in a motivating, sports-oriented environment.

SCORE! Prep provides in-home, one-on-one tutoring for high school academic subjects and standardized tests.

eSCORE.com is the first educational services Web site to offer parents and kids newborn to age 18 personalized child development and educational resources online.

KAPLANCOLLEGE.COM

KaplanCollege.com, Kaplan's distance learning platform, offers an array of online educational programs for working professionals who want to advance their careers. Learners will find nearly 500 professional development, continuing education, certification, and degree courses and programs in Nursing, Education, Criminal Justice, Real Estate, Legal Professions, Law, Management, General Business, and Computing/Information Technology.

KAPLAN PUBLISHING

Kaplan Publishing produces retail books and software. Kaplan Books, published by Simon & Schuster, include titles in test preparation, admissions, education, career development, and life skills; Kaplan and *Newsweek* jointly publish guides on getting into college, finding the right career, and helping children succeed in school.

KAPLAN PROFESSIONAL

Kaplan Professional provides assessment, training, and certification services for corporate clients and individuals seeking to advance their careers. Member units include:

- Dearborn, a leading supplier of licensing training and continuing education for securities, real estate, and insurance professionals

- Perfect Access/CRN, which delivers software education and consultation for law firms and businesses

- Kaplan Professional Call Center Services, a total provider of services for the call center industry

- Self Test Software, a world leader in exam simulation software and preparation for technical certifications

- Schweser's Study Program/AIAF, which provides preparation services for the CFA examination

KAPLAN INTERNATIONAL PROGRAMS

Kaplan assists international students and professionals in the United States through a series of intensive English language and test preparation programs. These programs are offered at campus-based centers across the United States. Specialized services include housing, placement at top American universities, fellowship management, academic monitoring and reporting, and financial administration.

COMMUNITY OUTREACH

Kaplan provides educational career resources to thousands of financially disadvantaged students annually, working closely with educational institutions, not-for-profit groups, government agencies and grass roots organizations on a variety of national and local support programs. These programs help students and professionals from a variety of backgrounds achieve their educational and career goals.

BRASSRING

BrassRing Inc., the premier business-to-business hiring management and recruitment services company, offers employers a vertically integrated suite of online and offline solutions. BrassRing, created in September 1999, combined Kaplan Career Services, Terra-Starr, Crimson & Brown Associates, thepavement.com, and HireSystems. In March 2000, BrassRing acquired Career Service Inc./Westech. Kaplan is a shareholder in BrassRing, along with Tribune Company, Central Newspapers, and Accel Partners.

Want more information about our services, products, or the nearest Kaplan center?

Call our nationwide toll-free numbers:

1-800-KAP-TEST for information on our courses, private tutoring and admissions consulting

1-800-KAP-ITEM for information on our books and software

Connect with us in cyberspace:

On AOL, keyword: "Kaplan"
On the World Wide Web, go to:
1. www.kaplan.com
2. www.kaptest.com
3. www.eSCORE.com
4. www.dearborn.com
5. www.BrassRing.com
6. www.concordlawschool.com
7. www.KaplanCollege.com
Via e-mail: info@kaplan.com

Write to:

Kaplan, Inc.
888 Seventh Avenue
New York, NY 10106

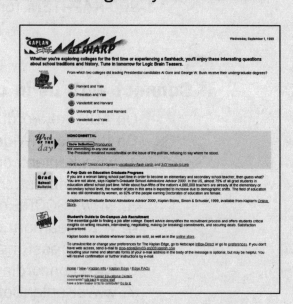

User's Guide to the CD-ROM

CONGRATULATIONS!

You've purchased the best test-prep software on the market, the software that's more fun than an abacus and more educational than an overhead projector. *Higher Score on the ACT* is the most comprehensive, instructive, and entertaining software product in the field of test prep to arrive since . . . well, since the dawn of humankind!

In This Software, You Get:

*   Interactive lessons detailing the famed Kaplan methods for each section of the ACT

*   Full-Length Tests and Practice Tests, so that you can try out your new skills as you move through the sessions

*   A Plan detailing your personalized study plan based on your needs

*   A math reference section, for reviewing mathematical concepts

*   Math, grammar, and vocabulary flashcards

*   Games for reviewing math, grammar, and science for the ACT

*   Invaluable college admissions information, and more

Higher Score on the ACT provides the tools that will help you devise your personal test-taking plan. Each test you take is closely analyzed, with detailed feedback on your strategic perform-ance, including answers to these questions:

*   Do you know when you've found the right answer?

*   If you have second thoughts, should you change your answer?

*   Can you recognize wrong answers?

*   Are you spending too much time on questions?

Naturally, every question comes with a complete explanation. And our detailed scoring charts will track your progress on every type of question. Only *Higher Score on the ACT* offers this range of essential features for successful test performance.

INSTALLATION AND TECH SUPPORT

Windows™ CD-ROM version

1. Start Microsoft Windows™ 95 or later.
2. Insert the Multimedia *Higher Score* CD.
3. Using Windows™ 95 or higher from the Start menu, choose Run and choose d:\setup.exe (where d: is your CD-ROM drive.)
4. When installation is complete, click the Higher Score icon to begin the program.

Macintosh® CD-ROM Version

1. Insert the CD-ROM into the drive.

2. Double-click the *Kaplan Higher Score* Install icon.

3. You will be presented with a dialog box that will let you choose Easy Install or Custom Install. If you choose Easy Install, the program will automatically install *Higher Score on the ACT* and update your files if necessary. If you choose Custom Install, you can choose where to install the different components of the program and whether to overwrite existing versions of files.

4. When installation is complete, click the *Higher Score* icon to begin the program.

Tech Support

If you have any questions or problems that don't seem to be covered in this manual, call our tech support line at (503) 968-4058. You can speak to a tech support rep between the hours of 9 A.M. and 1 A.M. (next day) E.S.T. Monday through Thursday, and 9:00 A.M. to 8:00 P.M. Friday through Sunday.

GETTING STARTED

Double-click on the *Higher Score* icon. The first time you start the program you will be given a Guided Tour to introduce some of the features. (You can skip the tour if you really want to.) You may view the Guided Tour any time by clicking on the tour guide on the main interface, but it will not appear again automatically. The Guided Tour is followed by your Profile in which we ask for your study preferences and other information which we use to develop your customized study plan.

Navigator Help: The first time you see a submenu of the main interface you will view a video featuring one of your guides describing the features of the area you're in. If you would like to replay this video at any time, click on the Help button 🔘 , located on the submenu screen.

The Main Interface

Kaplan Higher Score on the ACT: Main Interface

The main interface has these features:

Lessons: Click on the Lesson icon (the suitcase) on the Main Menu screen to bring up the Lessons submenu; click on the desired submenu.

Reference and Games: Located in the Reference Lounge, the Reference and Games area includes Games, Flashcards, and ACT FAQs (Frequently Asked Questions).

The Test Center: Take Diagnostic, Practice, and Full-Length Tests, get feedback, and see how well you're doing overall.

Next Stop: Clicking in the Next Stop area brings you directly to the next item on your personalized Plan.

Progress Bar: the Progress Bar, located beneath the Next Stop area, lets you know how much of your Plan you've completed.

Admissions: Click on the Admissions icon on the Main Menu screen for info on choosing, getting into, and paying for school, and finding schools that best suit your needs. You can also compare your scores to the average scores at over 1,000 colleges and universities or search for scholarships based on relevant criteria.

Weblink: Click on the "WWW" hood ornament on the car to access the award-winning Kaplan Web site!

The Menus

The File Menu lets you set up your printer and exit the program.

The Options menu lets you set preferences and reset your Profile.

The Goto menu can take you to Lessons, Reference, Tests, Games, the Guided Tour, Admissions, College Search, Compare Scores, and Scholarship Search.

The Help menu will take you to the Help system, or to the Test Tutorial.

YOUR PERSONALIZED PLAN

Your *Higher Score for the ACT* is personalized: Your study plan is customized to your individual needs. Your plan is based on two things:

- Your *Profile*, which you fill out the first time you begin the program.

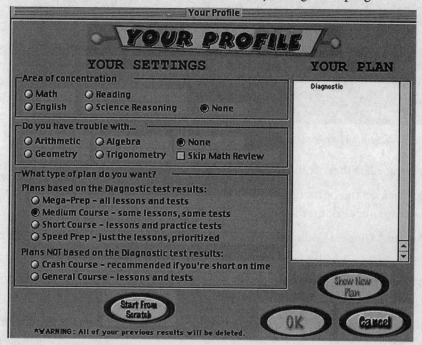

- Your *Diagnostic* results.

We recommend that you take the Diagnostic at the beginning of your preparation, in order to truly personalize your Plan. If you prefer to skip the Diagnostic, choose the Crash Course in the Profile.

Your Plan will cover only the lessons and tests. Admissions, About the Test, and Reference material won't be included in the Plan, but don't forget to check these areas out on your own.

You may move to any item on your Plan by clicking on it. Pieces you have completed are checked (but you can always return to them by clicking again). Redoing your Profile will give you a new Plan (and remember, any previously completed work won't show up on the new Plan).

THE LESSONS

Each scored question type on the exam has its own lesson covering:

- The nuts and bolts of the section (directions, how many questions, timing)
- What you need to know
- The basic Kaplan method
- Strategies, shortcuts, tips on answering questions when you're not sure
- Time management tips

Lesson Navigation

To move to the next page in a Lesson, click the forward arrow button ⬅. To move to the previous page, click the back arrow button ⬅. You can push the replay button 🔄 to replay the section you're in. Clicking on the tabs along the bottom of the screen will take you to the different sections of the lesson, or to Drills within the lesson. To quit the session and return to the Main Menu, click the Main button 🔘.

Sample Questions

Sample questions appear throughout the Lessons. Questions with answer bubbles are exercises for you to answer. Clicking directly on the bubble will show the explanation to that particular choice. When you answer questions in drills, you'll have the option of clicking the "Hint" button for some help.

REFERENCE

Reference resources are located in the Reference Lounge. Be sure to drop by for a visit.

The Lessons emphasize the strategic part of test taking: How to approach the questions, shortcuts for finding the right answer, how to save time. To score well in math, however, you've also got to know basic arithmetic, algebra and geometry concepts. The ACT also requires grammar knowledge. The interactive flashcards in the reference area are a great way to brush up your math and grammar skills.

To move between the different areas of the Reference Lounge, just click on the computers on the screen.

Frequently Asked Questions: Click on the ACT FAQ, then click highlighted links for the answers to lots of questions about the test. If you click on About Kaplan here, you'll also find all kinds of interesting information about Kaplan courses, books, software and other programs!

Flashcards: The flashcards summarize the math and grammar that you need to know for the test.

- You can view the Flashcards directly through the Main Menu (just click on the Reference Lounge and go to the Flashcards area). You can move through the Flashcards by using the left and right arrow buttons, or by clicking the math and grammar topic buttons at the bottom of the screen. These buttons will take you to the first card in that topic.

- The Flip button will flip the card over so you can see the other side. You can choose to see the question, then flip to the answer, or choose to flip from the answer to the question.

- You can select particular cards to be saved for review. When you're viewing a card you wish to select, click the Select button and the card will be added to the Selected group. When you want to look at the cards you've selected, move the Selected/All lever to the Selected position and those cards will be displayed. You can clear the selected cards by clicking Clear Selected. You can go back to the regular view by moving the lever to the All position.

- Links to the Flashcards appear in math and English question explanations. For instance, an example involving Averages would include a link to the Averages flashcard. If you want more information on that topic, click on the highlighted text, and you'll see the flashcard on the topic.

GAMES

You'll find these in the Reference Lounge. The Games are fun and exciting—plus, they reinforce the skills you'll need to succeed on the test!

Each game is played on a 4-by-4 grid of boxes. The object is always the same: match the two boxes that are related in some way. The pieces you pair vary depending on the game you choose (math or verbal). Before each game, you'll receive instructions explaining what you are to match.

To make a match, first click on one box with your mouse. This will highlight the box. Then click on the box which best matches the highlighted box. To unselect a highlighted box, click on it again.

For every correct match, you will receive 20 points. For every incorrect match, you will lose 5 points.

The pieces change position during the game. You can adjust the speed of the changes (slow, medium, fast).

ADMISSIONS

Choose the Admissions icon on the Main Menu screen to get to the Admissions area.

Planner: Click on the Admissions icon on the Main Menu screen to get more information on topics like Early Decision, Essays, Financial Aid, and Recommendations.

Compare Schools/School Search: Find schools best suited to your needs, then compare your scores to the average scores of entering freshman at hundreds of colleges and universities.

Search Screen: Select items by clicking on them. You may select more than one item in a list box by using Ctrl-Click (command-click on the Mac). Use Ctrl-Click (command-click on the Mac) to deselect a choice. Click Search to see your results, or Cancel to resume the lesson.

Results Screen: Click on a school to view its attributes. Click "Search Again" to go back to the Search screen and begin a new search. Click on Compare scores to compare your scores to the schools which resulted from your search or to all schools. Click Done to exit the Search and resume the lesson.

Compare Scores: Compare your current or previous ACT scores to all schools or just the schools which resulted from your search. If you haven't entered your score in the Profile or taken a test in the software, the graph will only show the average scores of the schools you've chosen.

Scholarship Search: Find scholarships best suited to your needs by choosing the Scholarship Search icon. Choose criteria such as Minimum GPA, Activities, Ethnicity, and others.

TESTING

The Test Center is the place to go to start tests or get scoring information. You'll see your Plan there, plus lists of all the tests and scores available to you.

There are three kinds of tests in *Higher Score on the ACT*:

- The Diagnostic is a half-length test that covers all the question types. We use it to develop your Plan, to give you a baseline score, and to analyze your strategic performance.

- The Practice Tests are section-length tests that cover one particular area. Use them to practice using the Lessons and to build up your stamina.

- The Full-Length Tests should be taken near the end of your preparation. Your analysis will tell you how well you're using the Lessons and give you specific advice for test day.

Taking a Test

Before starting, you should have scrap paper and a pencil.

You do not need a clock, as the program will time you.

To begin a test, click on the test you want to take in the Test Center, or click on it in your Plan. If you have already taken the test, you will have a choice of reviewing your results or resetting the test. Resetting a test will erase your previous work and allow you to retake it. You will be offered a short tutorial before beginning your first test. (If you want to see it again later, go to Help.)

The SmartGrid Option: You may choose to view the questions on the screen, or you may follow along in your test booklet. If you wish to use the test booklet, then you may choose the "SmartGrid" option; in this mode, you will view only the answer grid on the screen. The disadvantage of SmartGrid is that the program will not record any question timing information.

Test Mode and Tutor Mode: You may take the Practice Tests (everything other than the Diagnostic and Full-Length Tests) either in Test Mode or in Tutor Mode. In Tutor Mode, you may see hints for the questions while taking the test, and the test is not timed. We recommend that you use Tutor Mode at the beginning of your preparation as you use strategies for the first time. You may set a default for Tutor or Test Mode through the Set Preferences Screen in the Options menu.

The Testing Screen: The Testing Screen contains a Toolbar (Control Bar) on the top, and the Question Screen on the bottom. Use the Toolbar to move from one question to another, to indicate your confidence level (Sure or Unsure), to mark questions, and to indicate when you have finished a section. The Toolbar also displays two clocks, which show the time spent per question and the time remaining in the section.

The window below the Toolbar shows the question. If the question is based on a passage, the passage will appear to the left of the question. If the question or passage is longer than the screen, scroll bars will appear to the right of the passage window.

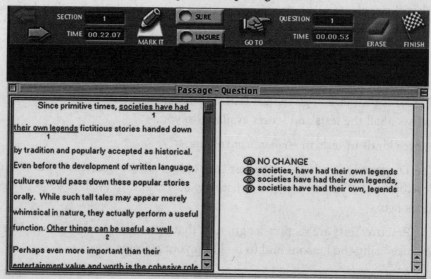

You may view directions or relevant references during the exam through the Windows pull-down menu. Online help is also available through the Help menu. Note that the clock continues to run while you are in Help.

Navigating through the Test

As you begin each section, the first question will be displayed. The question number and the section number are both displayed on the Toolbar.

After selecting your answer choice, use the Right Arrow button to move on to the next question. You can use the Right or Left Arrow buttons to move to the next or previous question in the section. The right arrow button will not operate once you have reached the last question in the section.

At any time you may press the Go To button to see a record of your answer choices within the section. You can then move to any question directly by clicking on the question number and pressing the Enter key.

Selecting an Answer Choice: To select an answer choice, click on the bubble to the left of the answer choice. The bubble will darken. Clicking again will unselect your choice. Selecting a new answer choice will automatically cancel your previous selection. The program will keep track of when you change answers, and whether you change from a wrong to a right answer or vice versa. (Or whether you just change from one wrong answer to another wrong one.)

Eliminating Answer Choices from Consideration: If you know an answer is wrong, you can eliminate it by clicking directly on the text of the choice itself (rather than on the bubble). A line will appear through the choice. Clicking on it again will make the line disappear. The program will track your success in eliminating wrong choices.

Note: You cannot eliminate every answer choice for a given question. To get the most accurate performance analysis, eliminate choices only as you try to identify the correct answer. Once you've chosen your answer, don't eliminate any more choices.

Marking Questions: Mark a question for later review by clicking the "Mark It" button. A check mark will appear to indicate that the question is marked. When you use the "GoTo" button to move to the Answer Grid window, Marked questions will be indicated. To return to a Marked question from the Grid, click on the line corresponding to the question and press Enter.

Confidence: Indicate your level of confidence in your response by clicking the Sure or Unsure button. Use these buttons only when you are very sure or very unsure. If you have only moderate confidence in your choice, do not click on either button.

Timing: Two clocks display the time remaining in the section and elapsed time on the current question. If you find a clock distracting, click on it to hide the time from view. Click again to restore the time. The clock runs when you are viewing questions, indicating answer choices and eliminations, accessing help, browsing through a section, and viewing the "GoTo" screen. If you are interrupted for an extended period while taking the test, you should abort the section by clicking on the erase button and begin the section again.

You will receive a warning when there are five minutes remaining in the section, and another warning when there is one minute remaining. The computer will also tell you when your time has elapsed. (To simulate real test conditions, this isn't possible during the Diagnostic or Full-length Tests.)

Using SmartGrid: If you take a test using SmartGrid, choose your answer by clicking on the answer bubble and note your confidence level by checking the appropriate box. If you want, you may mark questions and return to them later.

To eliminate answer choices:

- For Windows users, click on the bubble with your right mouse button.

- For Macintosh users, hold down the option key while clicking on the bubble.

Grid-in questions appear in SmartGrid as boxes with a triangle next to them. Click on the triangle and a Grid-in window will appear; click on the appropriate bubbles and click on "OK" when finished.

Using Tutor Mode: If you take a Practice Test in Tutor Mode, the highlighted word Hint will appear beneath the question. To view the hint, click on the word

Finishing a Test: Use the Erase and Finished buttons when you are through with a test (or a section of a full-length test). The Erase button will delete the information on the section you are working on. Note that it deletes the information ONLY for that one section in a full-length test. If you choose Erase during a full-length test, resuming the test will bring you back to the beginning of the same section.

Use the Finished button when you are done with a section, and want to keep the record. When you finish a practice test you may see your results and the explanations. When you finish a section in the Diagnostic or Full-length Test, you may continue to the next section.

ANALYSIS AND PRINTING

The Analysis offered at the end of a test is one of the unique features of the *Higher Score on the ACT* software. It allows you to evaluate the success of your test-taking strategies, and can tell you things you may not have suspected about your performance. The information is presented to you in tables, analyzing your performance by question type. For example, you can tell easily whether eliminating choices is helping you more on Reading than on other question types. This allows you to compile your own personalized strategy plan for test day. In addition, bullet points highlight important points and crucial advice for your future performance. Keep in mind, of course, that the analysis is based on a small amount of data. Nevertheless, you should examine the analysis closely.

Once you finish an exam, you can view your results. The Diagnostic and Full-Length Test Analysis includes six separate screens analyzing your performance. (Each practice test has one summary analysis screen).

Diagnostic and Full-Length Test Analysis

For the Diagnostic and Full-Length Tests, the first screen shows the different options available in Analysis Mode. The same buttons appear on each Analysis screen.

- The Main button returns you to the Main interface screen.
- The Scores button provides your raw and scaled test scores, percentile rankings, and a table containing the number of questions correct, incorrect, omitted, and not reached.

Your raw score is calculated from your number correct. It is then converted to a scaled score on the familiar 1–36 scale. On the actual exam, this scaled score is reported to schools. The scaled score is converted to a percentile ranking, which shows how you performed relative to a larger group of test takers. A score in the 65th percentile, for example, indicates that you scored higher than 65 percent of the students in the larger group.

The Scoring Table

The Scoring Table includes information on items Omitted and those Not Reached. A question that you look at but choose not to answer counts as an Omit; a question that you have not seen (or saw for less than five seconds) is considered Not Reached. Neither counts towards your score, but pay attention to the Not Reached: a significant number of Not Reached questions suggests that you have a timing problem.

The Types button gives you a bar graph showing the percentage of questions correct by Question Type. It also provides a table organized by test section, showing the percentage correct, the average time per question, and the number of questions not reached.

Using the Analysis Information

Use the information provided in the Question Type tables to determine your areas of relative strength and weakness and to plan your course of preparation leading up to Test Day. The tables also provide breakdowns of specific question subtypes, so that you can precisely focus your study where it will do the most good. In addition, these subtypes also appear in the Scoring screens, allowing you to track your progress through *Higher Score on the ACT*.

Other Analysis Screens

The other four Analysis screens include a chart showing your strategic performance on the test, listed by question type, as well as short bullet points identifying key points and recommendations.

Sure/Unsure: Sure/Unsure analyzes your performance in terms of the confidence level you assigned to your responses. Organized by question type, it indicates the percentage correct on questions you felt relatively sure of, and the percentage correct on questions that you felt unsure of.

This analysis is particularly useful because you assign the confidence rating at the moment of truth, as you are answering each question. If there is a mismatch between your expressed confidence and your performance, you will be notified by bullet-point messages. Be on the lookout not only for misplaced confidence (which can prevent you from giving a question the careful consideration it deserves) but also for a tendency to underrate your knowledge, which can lead to hesitation or even skipping questions that you might have gotten right.

Answer Changing: This screen lets you know how good you are at second-guessing your answers. A table organized by question type shows the number of times you switched from an incorrect answer to a correct one, and the number of times you switched away from the correct response.

Too much answer changing is not helpful—even if you're switching to the correct response, choosing it directly saves time. But sometimes you'll have to decide whether to go with your first instinct or with your second (or third) opinion. This analysis tracks your success at switching. If there is a trend in either direction, you'll be notified by a bullet-point message. Then you'll have a better idea whether to trust that impulse to switch on the next test you face.

Elimination: Elimination provides several types of information. On the most basic level, a table organized by question type shows the number of questions you got correct using the elimination strategy, and the number of times you eliminated the correct answer. Messages will tell you whether you generally keep the correct answer in contention when you eliminate choices, and whether you tend to select the correct choice from the remaining contenders.

Using the Elimination Strategy well is one of the most powerful ways to improve your score. Remember, indicate only those answer choices you are able to eliminate before you settle on your final choice. That way, the program can give you an accurate analysis of whether you recognize wrong choices when you see them, and whether, having successfully narrowed the field of contenders, you then go on to score points. After all, identifying wrong choices is only useful if you get the question right!

Timing: This screen gives you a table organized by question type, showing the average time you spent before settling on correct responses and on incorrect responses. It provides a listing of the five correct items and five incorrect items on which you spent the greatest amount of time. (Note that this list does not include questions with passages; those naturally take longer since you need to read the passage.) It also gives the average amount of time you spent on questions of low, moderate, and high difficulty.

Using your time wisely is essential to scoring well. Too much time spent on a difficult question can hurt your score if you don't have time to reach an easier question—and you still might not get that difficult question right! The Timing screen will tell you whether your perseverance pays off or penalizes you.

PRACTICE TEST ANALYSIS

The Practice Test Analysis screen shows your performance on the test, and highlights your use of elimination techniques, your answer changing, your confidence, and your performance on the five longest questions. Compare your strategic performance on different tests as you proceed through them.

Printing

You can print any of the Analysis screens by moving to the screen you want to print, then clicking the Print button. To select or set up your printer, choose Printer Setup from the File menu.

EXPLANATIONS

To view explanations to a test, choose the Explain Answers button from the Analysis screen. For a multisection test, entering the explanations will enable the Explanations pull-down menu; use this menu to navigate from one section to another. Within a section, you can use the GoTo button to move quickly from one question to another. The GoTo screen in Explanations Mode has two options: the Summary view (the default) shows you the question number and whether you answered the question correctly. You can easily move to your next incorrect response by just double-clicking on the question number. Clicking the Details button in the GoTo screen shows your response, the correct response, your confidence level, the question timing, and the category of the question. You will not always need this level of detail, but it will prove handy when (for instance) you want to review all your "Unsure" questions or all questions on a particular topic.

The Explanation Window

Each Explanation Window shows the question and its explanation, as well as your answer, confidence level, eliminations, and other strategic approaches. To view passages accompanying questions or the passage explanation, use the pull-down menu. Each explanation is followed by highlighted links to the Reference area.

You may quit Explanations Mode by clicking on the Main Menu button at any point. To return to the explanations of a test you took previously, select the test from the Tests menu, and choose "Results."

Scoring

The Scoring Screens offer invaluable tools for tracking your performance through the Higher Score on the SAT. The first screen shows your overall scores on the Diagnostic and Full-Length Tests; each question type gets its own screen, showing your performance by category for all tests. For instance, you can track your progress on each type of reading question throughout *Higher Score on the ACT*, and use this information to fine-tune your study plans.

Score Reports

Your performances on the Diagnostic, Practice Tests, and Full-Length Tests are charted on bar graphs. This is a visual representation of your progress through the tests. To reach the Scoring area, either click on the Scoring icon on the dashboard, or choose Scoring from the Test Center. The Scoring Overview screen compares your performance on the Full-Length Tests.

If you wish to see your improvement in a particular question type, select from the buttons on the right of the screen. Each Question Type screen displays your overall progress for that question type, and further breaks down your performance by category, again using easy-to-read bar graphs.

HELP AND PREFERENCES

Help

To enter the Help system, use the "Help" pulldown menu (Windows) or the "Balloon Help" menu (Macintosh). The pulldown menu also offers the Test Tutorial.

Setting Preferences

Choosing "Set Preferences" gives you a screen with several options.

- *Smart Grid or On-Screen Questions.* For Diagnostic and Full-Length Tests.

- *Tutor or Test Mode.* Choose whether you want to access explanations during a Practice Test.

- *Distracting Sounds in Tests.* One of the hard parts of taking a standardized test is concentrating on the test itself and tuning out other noises. To simulate a test environment, turn on the distracting sounds.

- *College Bit.* Upon completing a lesson or test, you'll be shown a fun fact about college. To stop these from appearing, choose this option.

- *Skip Intro.* Choose whether to skip the intro movies when starting Higher Score.

- *Browser.* Allows you to choose a Web browser.

KAPLAN

ACKNOWLEDGMENTS

Reading passages in these tests, as on the actual ACT, are condensed and adapted from published material. The ideas contained in them do not necessarily represent the opinions of Kaplan Educational Centers. To make the text suitable for testing purposes, we may in some cases have altered the style or emphasis of the original.

Kaplan Educational Centers wishes to thank the following for permission to reprint excerpts from published material used with test questions appearing herein:

"Artificial Organs: Learning to Live with Risk," by Pierre M. Galletti. Reprinted with permission from *Technology Review,* copyright © 1988.

"Bound for Deep Water," by Scott A. Eckert. Reprinted with permission from *Natural History,* March, 1992. Copyright © the American Museum of Natural History, 1992.

"Drowning Dogs and the Dawn of Art," by Jared Diamond. Reprinted with permission from *Natural History,* March, 1993. Copyright © the American Museum of Natural History, 1993.

"Made of Muscle or Bone," by Karen Sandrick. Reprinted with permission from *Technology Review,* copyright © 1991.

From *Making It,* by Norman Podhoretz. Copyright © 1967 by Norman Podhoretz. Reprinted by permission of Random House, Inc.

"Proxemics in the Arab World," from *The Hidden Dimension,* by Edward T. Hall. Copyright © 1966, 1982 by Edward T. Hall. Used by permission of Doubleday, a division of Bantam Doubleday Dell Publishing Group, Inc.

From *Waiting for the Weekend,* by Witold Rybczynski. Copyright © 1991 by Witold Rybczynski. Used by permission of Viking Penguin, a division of Penguin Books USA Inc.

David V. Edwards, *The American Political Experience: An Introduction to Government,* 1988, p. 471. Prentice-Hall, Inc. Englewood Cliffs, NJ 07632

From "Architects and Power, the Natural Market for Architecture," by Prof. Robert Gutman, *Progressive Architecture,* December 1992.

From "Earth's Ozone Shield Under Threat," by France Bequette, the *UNESCO Courier,* June 1990.

From *Fifth Business,* by Robertson Davies, condensed from pp. 25–29 ©1970 by Robertson Davies. Viking Penguin, Penguin USA Inc.

From *From Slavery to Freedom,* by John Hope Franklin. Copyright © 1947, 1956, 1967, 1974, 1980 by Alfred A. Knopf, Inc. Reprinted by permission of the publisher.

From *A History of Women Artists,* by Hugo Munsterberg. Copyright © 1975 by Hugo Munsterberg. Reprinted by permission of Clarkson N. Potter, Inc., a division of Crown Publishers, Inc.

Photo Credits:

© Archive Photos/Edwin Levick/PNI

© Hulton Deutsch/PNI

© Culver Pictures/PNI

© Magnum/Chris Steele-Perkins/PNI

Minimum System Requirements*

	Windows™	Macintosh®
Operating System:	Windows 95 or higher	System 7.5.5 or higher
CPU Type and Speed:	Pentium	Power PC
Hard Drive Space:	15 MB hard disk space	18 MB hard disk space
RAM:	16 MB RAM	24 MB RAM (more required to run w/Internet browser or Virtual Memory must be enabled)
Graphics:	640x 480/256 colors (thousands/millions recommended)	640 x 480/256 colors
CD-ROM Speed:	2x CD-ROM	2x CD-ROM
Audio:	16-bit audio	16-bit audio
Other:	Mouse	Mouse
	Modem	Modem

*The configuration above will allow you to run all the applications included on the *Higher Score on the ACT* CD-ROM. Only AT&T Worldnet Service™ requires a modem.

Installation instructions are in the User's Guide.

SOFTWARE LICENSE/DISCLAIMER OF WARRANTIES

1. ACCEPTANCE. By using this compact disc you hereby accept the terms and provisions of this license and agree to be bound hereby.

2. OWNERSHIP. The software contained on these compact discs, all content, related documentation and fonts (collectively, the "Software") are all proprietary copyrighted materials owned by Kaplan Educational Centers, Inc. ("Kaplan") or its licensors.

3. LICENSE. You are granted a limited license to use the Software. This License allows you to use the Software on a single computer only. You may not copy, distribute, modify, network, rent, lease, loan, or create derivative works based upon the Software in whole or in part. The Software is intended for personal usage only. Your rights to use the Software shall terminate immediately without notice upon your failure to comply with any of the terms hereof.

4. RESTRICTIONS. The Software contains copyrighted material, trade secrets and other proprietary material. In order to protect them, and except as permitted by applicable legislation, you may not decompile, reverse engineer, disassemble or otherwise reduce the Software to human-perceivable form.

5. LIMITED WARRANTY; DISCLAIMER. Kaplan warrants the compact discs on which the Software is recorded to be free from defects in materials and workmanship under normal use for a period of ninety (90) days from the date of purchase as evidenced by a copy of the receipt. Kaplan's entire liability and your exclusive remedy will be replacement of the compact discs not meeting this warranty. The Software is provided "AS IS" and without warranty of any kind and Kaplan and Kaplan's licensors EXPRESSLY DISCLAIM ALL WARRANTIES, EXPRESS OR IMPLIED, INCLUDING THE IMPLIED WARRANTIES OF MERCHANTABILITY OR FITNESS FOR A PARTICULAR PURPOSE. FURTHERMORE, KAPLAN DOES NOT WARRANT THAT THE FUNCTIONS CONTAINED IN THE SOFTWARE WILL MEET YOUR REQUIREMENTS, OR THAT THE OPERATION OF THE SOFTWARE WILL BE UNINTERRUPTED OR ERROR-FREE, OR THAT DEFECTS IN THE SOFTWARE WILL BE CORRECTED. KAPLAN DOES NOT WARRANT OR MAKE ANY REPRESENTATIONS REGARDING THE USE OR THE RESULTS OF THE USE OF THE SOFTWARE IN TERMS OF THEIR CORRECTNESS, ACCURACY, RELIABILITY OR OTHERWISE. UNDER NO CIRCUMSTANCES, INCLUDING NEGLIGENCE, SHALL KAPLAN BE LIABLE FOR ANY DIRECT, INDIRECT, PUNITIVE, INCIDENTAL, SPECIAL OR CONSEQUENTIAL DAMAGES, INCLUDING, BUT NOT LIMITED TO, LOST PROFITS OR WAGES, IN CONNECTION WITH THE SOFTWARE EVEN

IF KAPLAN HAS BEEN ADVISED OF THE POSSIBILITY OF SUCH DAMAGES. CERTAIN OF THE LIMITATIONS HEREIN PROVIDED MAY BE PRECLUDED BY LAW.

6. EXPORT LAW ASSURANCES. You agree and certify that you will not export the Software outside of the United States except as authorized and as permitted by the laws and regulations of the United States. If the Software has been rightfully obtained by you outside of the United States, you agree that you will not re-export the Software except as permitted by the laws and regulations of the United States and the laws and regulations of the jurisdiction in which you obtained the Software.

7. MISCELLANEOUS. This license represents the entire understanding of the parties, may only be modified in writing and shall be governed by the laws of the State of New York.

ACT, PSAT, and SAT are registered trademarks of their respective owners, who do not endorse or sponsor this product. *Kaplan Higher Score on the ACT*, Copyright 2000, by Kaplan, Inc. All rights reserved. Macintosh, QuickTime and the QuickTime logo are registered trademarks of Apple Computer, Inc. and are used under license. Windows is a registered trademark of Microsoft Corporation, AT&T Worldnet Service is a service mark of AT&T.

If you need assistance with installation, need to request a replacement disk, or have any other software questions, call
Kaplan at (503) 968-4058, Monday–Thursday, 9 A.M. to 1 A.M. (next day)
Friday–Sunday, 9 A.M. to 8 P.M.
(All hours are E.S.T)